55 *Victorian Prose Writers Before 1867*, edited by William B. Thesing (1987)

56 *German Fiction Writers, 1914-1945*, edited by James Hardin (1987)

57 *Victorian Prose Writers After 1867*, edited by William B. Thesing (1987)

58 *Jacobean and Caroline Dramatists*, edited by Fredson Bowers (1987)

59 *American Literary Critics and Scholars, 1800-1850*, edited by John W. Rathbun and Monica M. Grecu (1987)

60 *Canadian Writers Since 1960, Second Series*, edited by W. H. New (1987)

61 *American Writers for Children Since 1960: Poets, Illustrators, and Nonfiction Authors*, edited by Glenn E. Estes (1987)

62 *Elizabethan Dramatists*, edited by Fredson Bowers (1987)

63 *Modern American Critics, 1920-1955*, edited by Gregory S. Jay (1988)

64 *American Literary Critics and Scholars, 1850-1880*, edited by John W. Rathbun and Monica M. Grecu (1988)

65 *French Novelists, 1900-1930*, edited by Catharine Savage Brosman (1988)

66 *German Fiction Writers, 1885-1913*, 2 parts, edited by James Hardin (1988)

67 *Modern American Critics Since 1955*, edited by Gregory S. Jay (1988)

68 *Canadian Writers, 1920-1959, First Series*, edited by W. H. New (1988)

69 *Contemporary German Fiction Writers, First Series*, edited by Wolfgang D. Elfe and James Hardin (1988)

70 *British Mystery Writers, 1860-1919*, edited by Bernard Benstock and Thomas F. Staley (1988)

71 *American Literary Critics and Scholars, 1880-1900*, edited by John W. Rathbun and Monica M. Grecu (1988)

72 *French Novelists, 1930-1960*, edited by Catharine Savage Brosman (1988)

73 *American Magazine Journalists, 1741-1850*, edited by Sam G. Riley (1988)

74 *American Short-Story Writers Before 1880*, edited by Bobby Ellen Kimbel, with the assistance of William E. Grant (1988)

75 *Contemporary German Fiction Writers, Second Series*, edited by Wolfgang D. Elfe and James Hardin (1988)

76 *Afro-American Writers, 1940-1955*, edited by Trudier Harris (1988)

77 *British Mystery Writers, 1920-1939*, edited by Bernard Benstock and Thomas F. Staley (1988)

78 *American Short-Story Writers, 1880-1910*, edited by Bobby Ellen Kimbel, with the assistance of William E. Grant (1988)

79 *American Magazine Journalists, 1850-1900*, edited by Sam G. Riley (1988)

80 *Restoration and Eighteenth-Century Dramatists, First Series*, edited by Paula R. Backscheider (1989)

81 *Austrian Fiction Writers, 1875-1913*, edited by James Hardin and Donald G. Daviau (1989)

82 *Chicano Writers, First Series*, edited by Francisco A. Lomelí and Carl R. Shirley (1989)

83 *French Novelists Since 1960*, edited by Catharine Savage Brosman (1989)

84 *Restoration and Eighteenth-Century Dramatists, Second Series*, edited by Paula R. Backscheider (1989)

85 *Austrian Fiction Writers After 1914*, edited by James Hardin and Donald G. Daviau (1989)

86 *American Short-Story Writers, 1910-1945, First Series*, edited by Bobby Ellen Kimbel (1989)

87 *British Mystery and Thriller Writers Since 1940, First Series*, edited by Bernard Benstock and Thomas F. Staley (1989)

88 *Canadian Writers, 1920-1959, Second Series*, edited by W. H. New (1989)

89 *Restoration and Eighteenth-Century Dramatists, Third Series*, edited by Paula R. Backscheider (1989)

90 *German Writers in the Age of Goethe, 1789-1832*, edited by James Hardin and Christoph E. Schweitzer (1989)

91 *American Magazine Journalists, 1900-1960, First Series*, edited by Sam G. Riley (1990)

92 *Canadian Writers, 1890-1920*, edited by W. H. New (1990)

93 *British Romantic Poets, 1789-1832, First Series*, edited by John R. Greenfield (1990)

94 *German Writers in the Age of Goethe: Sturm und Drang to Classicism*, edited by James Hardin and Christoph E. Schweitzer (1990)

95 *Eighteenth-Century British Poets, First Series*, edited by John Sitter (1990)

96 (1990)

97 *German Writers from the Enlightenment to Sturm und Drang, 1720-1764*, edited by James Hardin and Christoph E. Schweitzer (1990)

98 *Modern British Essayists, First Series*, edited by Robert Beum (1990)

99 *Canadian Writers Before 1890*, edited by W. H. New (1990)

100 *Modern British Essayists, Second Series*, edited by Robert Beum (1990)

101 *British Prose Writers, 1660-1800, First Series*, edited by Donald T. Siebert (1991)

102 *American Short-Story Writers, 1910-1945, Second Series*, edited by Bobby Ellen Kimbel (1991)

103 *American Literary Biographers, First Series*, edited by Steven Serafin (1991)

104 *British Prose Writers, 1660-1800, Second Series*, edited by Donald T. Siebert (1991)

105 *American Poets Since World War II, Second Series*, edited by R. S. Gwynn (1991)

106 *British Literary Publishing Houses, 1820-1880*, edited by Patricia J. Anderson and Jonathan Rose (1991)

107 *British Romantic Prose Writers, 1789-1832, First Series*, edited by John R. Greenfield (1991)

108 *Twentieth-Century Spanish Poets, First Series*, edited by Michael L. Perna (1991)

109 *Eighteenth-Century British Poets, Second Series*, edited by John Sitter (1991)

110 *British Romantic Prose Writers, 1789-1832, Second Series*, edited by John R. Greenfield (1991)

111 *American Literary Biographers, Second Series*, edited by Steven Serafin (1991)

112 *British Literary Publishing Houses, 1881-1965*, edited by Jonathan Rose and Patricia J. Anderson (1991)

113 *Modern Latin-American Fiction Writers, First Series*, edited by William Luis (1992)

114 *Twentieth-Century Italian Poets, First Series*, edited by Giovanna Wedel De Stasio, Glauco Cambon, and Antonio Illiano (1992)

115 *Medieval Philosophers*, edited by Jeremiah Hackett (1992)

116 *British Romantic Novelists, 1789-1832*, edited by Bradford K. Mudge (1992)

(Continued on back endsheets)

DICTIONARY OF LITERARY BIOGRAPHY

DOCUMENTARY SERIES

AN ILLUSTRATED CHRONICLE

VOLUME THIRTEEN

DICTIONARY OF LITERARY BIOGRAPHY

DOCUMENTARY SERIES

VOL.  THIRTEEN

AN ILLUSTRATED CHRONICLE

THE HOUSE OF SCRIBNER
1846–1904

EDITED BY
JOHN DELANEY

A BRUCCOLI CLARK LAYMAN BOOK
GALE RESEARCH INC.
DETROIT, WASHINGTON, D.C., LONDON

The paper used in this publication meets the minimum requirements
of American National Standard for Information Sciences–Permanence
Paper for Printed Library Materials, ANSI Z39.48-1984. ∞™

Library of Congress Catalog Card Number 95-081422
ISBN 0-8103-5706-2

I(T)P Gale Research Inc., an International Thomson Publishing Company.
       ITP logo is a trademark under license.

10 9 8 7 6 5 4 3 2 1

Contents

To Future Publishers, May Their Histories Be As Glorious

Preface

This is an inside story — told from the company's own documents. Housed at Princeton University Library, the archives of Charles Scribner's Sons have been the major source, and raison d'être, for this volume. Perhaps the most extensive of any American publisher, these company records cover the complete 150 years (1846–1996) of the firm's history, including author files, publishing contracts, photographs, business ledgers, copyright files, and manufacturing records. The early years are scantily represented, but correspondence, which I believe best reflects the senses and sensibilities of the organization, is prodigious, from the 1880s on. Credit for the coherence and completeness of the archives must go to the Scribner family, five generations of which have tended to their care, both in New York and here at Princeton. Because of the continuity of this family business, the publishing history is often inseparable from the family history.

How best to document the whole range of activities of this large organization was a decision I reached only gradually as I became more familiar with what was available. Some of the series of records are still not processed; old documents are continually turning up. It soon became clear, however, that one volume would not suffice to cover the history of the House of Scribner: there were subsidiary companies, magazines, bookstores and buildings, and many significant authors. I decided to make 1846–1904 the scope of the first volume to focus on the years during which the company was evolving into a family-owned and run business. While it is true that all of the "outside" partners were gone by 1885 and all subsidiaries were subsumed under the one name "Charles Scribner's Sons" by 1891, the year 1904 provided an organizational turning point, for in January of that year the firm was incorporated and issued stock. A second volume, covering the years from 1905 to 1984 (the year of Scribners' merger with the Macmillan Company), will follow.

The succinct company history of Charles Scribner III presents the overview the volume needed. An illustrated chronology, providing a year-by-year account of major organizational and publishing events, was a requirement for those wanting a context for Scribner authors. The parallel development of the various Scribner magazines also demanded attention, for they all played very significant roles in American literary and publishing history.

Certainly the most interesting aspect of a publisher is its authors. I have chosen three dozen to characterize this early period of the House of Scribner. Though some of the names may not be familiar to readers today, they were important to the firm *at the time* and were major reasons for its success, whether Scribners was their first, only, temporary, or last publisher. I believe their books best represent the core of the company's publications for the period. Even though the volume's cutoff date is 1904, I have not chosen only authors whose books appeared before 1904, nor have I arbitrarily ended an author's publishing record on that date; instead, I have limited my selection to authors who joined the Scribner list before 1905. The authors appear in the volume in the order of the date of their first Scribner book.

To the extent possible, I have relied on archival documents for the "story line," supplementing where necessary — with photographs of books drawn from the Library's Rare Books Division (and elsewhere) and with transcriptions of contemporary newspaper articles. In order to save space and avoid inordinate repetition, *I have identified only non-Princeton items.* All Princeton documents have been taken from the Archives of Charles Scribner's Sons, with two notable exceptions: 1) The *St. Nicholas* correspondence of Mary Mapes Dodge (in the magazine section of this volume) comes from three significant Dodge collections housed at Princeton: the "Donald and Robert M. Dodge Collection of Mary Mapes Dodge," the "Wilkinson Collection of Mary Mapes Dodge," and "*St. Nicholas* Correspondence of Mary Mapes Dodge." 2) I have borrowed many of the author photographs from the Laurence Hutton collection of photograph albums, also here at Princeton.

To simplify the identification of the respective Charles Scribners, I have adopted a dynastic approach:

Charles Scribner, 1821–1871 = CS I
Charles Scribner, 1854–1930 = CS II
Charles Scribner, 1890–1952 = CS III

Charles Scribner, 1921– (who uses the form
"Charles Scribner Jr.") = CS IV
Charles Scribner, 1951– (who uses the form
"Charles Scribner III") = CS V

In all references to the publishing firm of Charles Scribner's Sons I use the word *Scribners*. As an adjective (as in "W. C. Brownell was a Scribner editor"), the word takes its singular form.

Acknowledgments

This book was produced by Bruccoli Clark Layman, Inc. Karen L. Rood is senior editor for the *Dictionary of Literary Biography* series.

Production coordinator is James W. Hipp. Photography editor is Bruce Andrew Bowlin. Layout and graphics supervisor is Penney L. Haughton. Copyediting supervisor is Laurel M. Gladden. Typesetting supervisor is Kathleen M. Flanagan. Systems manager is George F. Dodge. Julie E. Frick is editorial associate. The production staff includes Phyllis A. Avant, Charles D. Brower, Ann M. Cheschi, Patricia Coate, Joyce Fowler, Stephanie C. Hatchell, Margaret Meriwether, Kathy Lawler Merlette, Jeff Miller, Pamela D. Norton, Laura Pleicones, Emily R. Sharpe, William L. Thomas Jr., and Allison Trussell.

Walter W. Ross and Robert S. McConnell did library research. They were assisted by the following librarians at the Thomas Cooper Library of the University of South Carolina: Linda Holderfield and the interlibrary-loan staff; reference-department head Virginia Weathers; reference librarians Marilee Birchfield, Stefanie Buck, Cathy Eckman, Rebecca Feind, Jill Holman, Karen Joseph, Jean Rhyne, Kwamine Washington, and Connie Widney; circulation-department head Caroline Taylor; and acquisitions-searching supervisor David Haggard.

All photographs for this volume were taken by John Blazejewski of Princeton University's Index of Christian Art office. The editor commends him for a job well done — for the care and efficiency with which he undertook and completed this large enterprise. The editor further thanks Alice Clark, of Princeton's Department of Rare Books and Special Collections, for her helpful role in organizing and facilitating this photography work.

Charles Scribner III was very supportive throughout the project and provided useful answers to questions about the Scribner family and Scribner publishing history.

The Department of Rare Books and Special Collections of Princeton University Library made all of its resources available to the editor — many after its normal hours — and the library's Interlibrary Services office conscientiously located the few Scribner volumes needed for this work that Princeton does not already own.

The editor deeply appreciates the acceptance and understanding of his wife and son, Evelyn and Andrew, for what essentially amounted to an extended "family leave."

Permissions

The Manuscript Division of the Department of Rare Books and Special Collections, Princeton University Libraries, granted permission for the use of materials in the following collections: Archives of Charles Scribner's Sons, Donald and Robert M. Dodge Collection of Mary Mapes Dodge, Wilkinson Collection of Mary Mapes Dodge, *St. Nicholas* Correspondence of Mary Mapes Dodge, Laurence Hutton Photograph Albums, Cameron Family Papers, George Palmer Putnam Collection, and Frank N. and Nelson Doubleday Collection. Permissions to print other letters were obtained from these institutions: Tulane University Library (H. H. Boyesen to G. W. Cable, 8 January 1878 and 26 August 1879; Cable Collection); Beinecke Library, Yale University and Ms. Teddy Osbourne Schieferle (Robert Louis Stevenson to Scribners, 3 May 1887); Houghton Library, Harvard University and the James Family (Henry James to Henry James Sr., 11 October 1879). Charles Scribner III granted permission to quote from Scribner family documents.

DICTIONARY OF LITERARY BIOGRAPHY

DOCUMENTARY SERIES

AN ILLUSTRATED CHRONICLE

VOLUME THIRTEEN

Introduction

When Charles Scribner and Isaac D. Baker began their publishing business in the back chapel rooms of the old Brick Church in New York City on 1 January 1846, the phrase "Manifest Destiny" was six months old, and Texas had just been admitted (29 December) into the Union as the twenty-eighth state. The United States was on the brink of the Mexican War.

The timing could not have been better: within months Baker & Scribner had its first best-seller, J. T. Headley's *Napoleon and His Marshals* (2 volumes). This work proved to be the best-selling book of 1846 — no doubt aided by the war climate of the nation — beating out for that honor two publications by Wiley & Putnam authors: Nathaniel Hawthorne's *Mosses from an Old Manse* and Herman Melville's *Typee*. By 1861 Headley's work had gone into its fiftieth edition and had sold hundreds of thousands of copies. More than any other, it is the publication that could be given the honor of "carrying" the House of Scribner to the Civil War.

Having access to deep pockets also helped the firm's chances of survival. Of those publishing firms launched before the Civil War — there were 385 firms publishing in 1856 — less than one-sixth survived into the twentieth century. Business killers included the Civil War and the "Panics" — of 1857, of 1873, and of 1893. When Charles Scribner married Emma Elizabeth Blair, daughter of John Insley Blair (1802–1899), in 1848, he also obtained a kind of business-failure insurance. Blair was at the center of the tremendous railroad expansion of the last century, beginning with the organization in 1852 of the Delaware, Lackawanna & Western Railroad. He joined with Oakes Ames and others to get the charter of the Union Pacific Railroad, successfully lobbied for the route west from Omaha, and built the first one hundred miles. At one time he was president of sixteen different railroads and is said to have owned more miles of railroad property than any other man in the world.

A man of tremendous energy, he was often at his desk at 5:30 A.M. at the age of ninety-seven. Blair was devoted to his daughter, her husband, and their five children, and it is natural that young Charles Scribner turned to him for business advice and timely loans. The two had a close relationship and addressed each other as "father" and "son."

The firm's first three copyrighted works established the general publishing themes of the company for the rest of the century — and, indeed, the rest of its history. The first title was *The Puritans and Their Principles* by Edwin Hall, appearing in February; the second, also in February, was *The Artists of America: A Series of Biographical Sketches of American Artists, with Portraits and Designs on Steel* by C. Edwards Lester; and in March came Charles Burdett's novel *Lilla Hart: A Story of New York*. Religious works and books with a strong moral tone continued to define the fundamental character of the early business; but reference books, including large undertakings supported by subscription, and literary works eventually established its trade reputation.

Developments at Scribners during the nineteenth century paralleled, and sometimes preceded, developments in the trade at large. Several are worth noting: 1) the rise of the house periodical that promoted the name of the publisher and introduced the works of its authors to a wider audience; 2) the increase in the quantity and quality of illustrations as significant aspects of a publication; 3) the gradual recognition that a publisher, in addition to publishing completed manuscripts, could originate ideas for authors to develop; 4) the expansion of "rights" for both author and publisher, demanding a professionalization of the business, that included the achievement of international copyright protection, serial rights, rights to reprints and cheap editions, and foreign rights. Before the end of the century, no publisher was more diversified than Scribners: besides its general publishing business, it ran a bookstore, had a separate company for the importation of foreign books, published textbooks by its educational department, sold special books through its subscription department, and published commercial magazines.

The latter half of the nineteenth century was also a period in publishing that emphasized a personal author/publisher relationship. Charles Scribner enjoyed swapping stories with his authors in his bookstore office; and his son Charles (CS II) joined his authors for rounds of bridge and golf, and occasionally vacationed with them at their

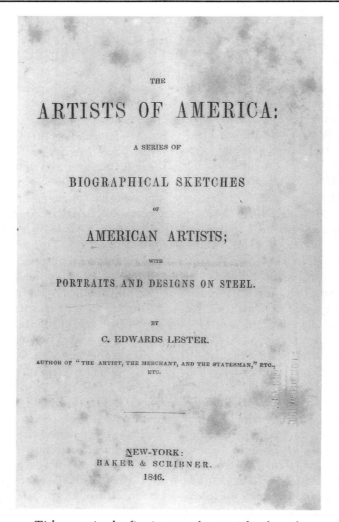

THE

ARTISTS OF AMERICA:

A SERIES OF

BIOGRAPHICAL SKETCHES

OF

AMERICAN ARTISTS;

WITH

PORTRAITS AND DESIGNS ON STEEL.

BY

C. EDWARDS LESTER.

AUTHOR OF "THE ARTIST, THE MERCHANT, AND THE STATESMAN," ETC.,
ETC.

NEW-YORK:
BAKER & SCRIBNER.
1846.

Title page in the firm's second copyrighted work

summer homes. Publishing was a gentleman's profession as practiced by the Scribners, and professional courtesy among publishers was expected.

Beyond the facts of history documented in this volume, however, remains the cultural legacy of the firm, for Scribners became an American cultural entity through the enterprise of the books it published and promoted. And, to the extent that a publisher participates in the development of a national literature, Scribners became a dominant force in the nineteenth century — with its internationally known novelists, storywriters, illustrators, and children's book authors, with its religious books and reference works, with its magazine, with its Fifth Avenue bookstore.

As for the founder's contribution to publishing history, beyond what he published, perhaps his contemporary, George Derby, defined it best when he remarked of Charles Scribner, for whom he had great respect, that he seemed to know intuitively the merits of a good book. That, of course, is the essence of the kind of personal publishing that characterized the great publishing houses in the latter half of the nineteenth century and well into this one. The individual giants of publishing all possessed that kind of intuition and exercised it as their own prerogative for the most part before the decisions were made by editorial boards. While the other publishers of Scribner's early days had the same quality, in greater or lesser degree, it seems most often to have been the product of printing and bookselling — especially bookselling — experience. The first Charles Scribner, without such experience, seemed to have been born with it, and thus was perhaps the first of the truly literary publishers. (John Tebbel, *A History of Book Publishing in the United States,* volume 1 [New York: Bowker, 1972], p. 318)

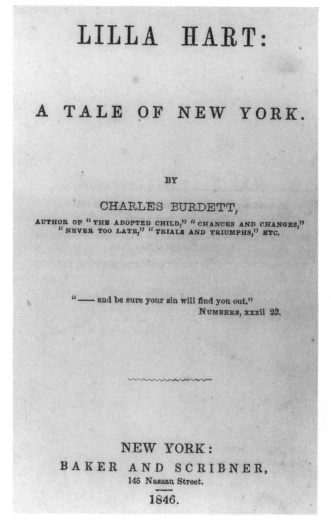

*Title page in the firm's third copyrighted work, its
first book of fiction*

Born 21 February 1821, in New York City, Charles Scribner was a member of an old New York family that traced its line back to 1680 and the arrival in Norwalk, Connecticut, of Benjamin Scrivener. Though the family name was changed to "Scribner" sometime after 1742, the original surname (meaning, literally, "a professional or public copyist or writer") could not have been a more appropriate one for a family that was to become synonymous with publishing. CS was the son of a prosperous merchant, Uriah Rogers Scribner, and his second wife, Betsey Hawley — one of their nine surviving children: the middle child, with two older and two younger brothers and two older and two younger sisters. Uriah's father, a 1775 graduate from Yale, had been a

noted Presbyterian minister, the Reverend D. Matthew Scribner.

For his early schooling, CS was sent to the Lawrenceville School, a boarding school in Lawrenceville, New Jersey, just down the road from the borough of Princeton. In the fall of 1837, he went to New York University as a sophomore, then entered the College of New Jersey (now Princeton University) with the junior class the next fall with his brother William. He graduated from Princeton in September 1840. Two telling records remain from those early academic years at Princeton. The first concerns *The Tattler*, which was a handwritten literary magazine compiled by Princeton undergraduates, 1839–1840. (Volume 1 survives in the Princeton University Archives.) It was the task of the editor to copy out in longhand

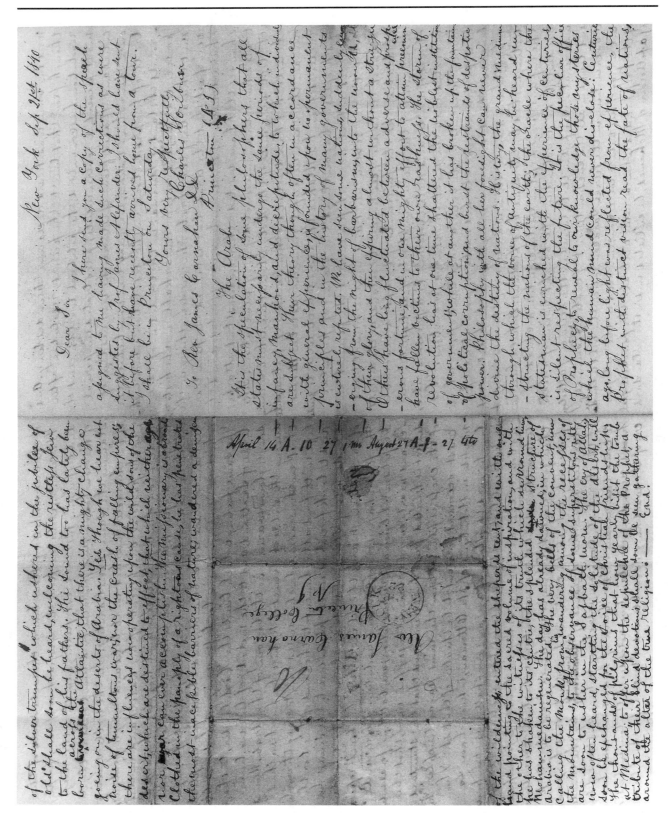

Manuscript of "The Arab," a speech written by Charles Scribner to complete final course requirements before graduation from the College of New Jersey (now Princeton University) in September 1840

the week's contributions and to offer commentary on them at the end in an "Editor's Table." Typical entries were translations of classical poetry, original poems and stories, and discourses on political liberty and feminine beauty. CS edited two issues, those for 24 June and 1 July 1840. This is his "Editor's Table" for the 1 July issue (Vol. 1, No. 25):

> We regret to say that there seems to be a very censurable delinquincy among our correspondents — communication having been received from only a little more than half of our regular contributors. With the communications which have been given in we are glad to express ourselves highly gratified. Their general character as to style is creditable, though the sentiments of some may be objected to. The ladies will do well to attend to Albert's suggestions. They might learn from them a useful and important rule of life. Bunkum's contribution has many merits. His style is vigorous, though bordering on the diffuse, and he would seldom fail to convince did he build his arguments on true principles. In the present instance we think he has failed in this respect. The principle of "no disinterested friendship" which he attempts to prove is one which we imagine the convictions of every man's heart will reject. It is one of those questions which is best determined by an appeal to consciousness. He has however displayed much ingenuity in the treatment of his subject and although some of his arguments appear to us strained all are well presented. N.C. breathes a didactic tone. His remarks are good both in style and matter and applicable to the "times." The Spectator is appropriate — his sentiments are noble and patriotic. Leander's continuation of the "Adventure" is heartily welcome. Our interest in the tale increases as it proceeds. We are both anxious and curious to learn its conclusion.

This evidence suggests that CS had developed a literary interest before he graduated and actually enjoyed an editorial role that allowed him to express his opinions and judgments of the material.

A speech CS wrote for a class assignment is the only other Princeton item that survives. The Reverend James Carnahan, to whom the speech is addressed, was president of Princeton (1823-1854) at the time and also delivered lectures on moral philosophy to the senior class. In his speech, which is simply titled "The Arab," CS writes that neither philosophy nor history can devine the destiny of nations — only the "peculiar office of Prophecy" and, in particular, the "Prophet" can read their fate; that the Arab has attracted an unusual degree of veneration because he has been able to retain the "peculiar character of his ancestors" despite great changes that have

visited other nations; but that the present age is one of "constant revolution" and "nearly every day brings the joyful news, that the despot is hurled from his throne, and that the standard of the cross is planted upon the ruins of the pagan temples." CS prophesies that missionaries have already "shaken, to its centre, the splendid structure of Mohammedanism" and that the thousands of pilgrims that yearly visit Mohammed's tomb at Medina will soon be gathering around "the altar of the true religion." The speech is significant in that it articulates CS's strong Christian faith, which was always to be his dominant characteristic.

Immediately after graduating, he entered the law offices of Charles King in New York. Apparently, health problems interrupted his studies during the next several years. A letter to his brother William, dated 18 February 1843, describes his current situation:

> Though seated in Mr. King's office & professedly ferreting out from the first volume of Chancellor Kent's work the principles of international law, I feel that it would be a far more agreeable task to indulge in a short epistolary interview with you. And now what have I to write you? A thousand things I would say if you were present — the light of the countenance of a dear friend is far more effectual in giving a flow to our ideas than the best pen & ink that can be procured. . . . Uncle Samuel Scribner has been here & spent two weeks with us. He tried to pursuade me to return to Baltimore with him to spend the winter there. I could not however see of what real advantage it would be to my health & thought that I would derive more benefit from remaining home as I am able to study a little & also to superintend our brother Walter's studies who is now going to the University Grammar School. I am able to attend to my reading two or three hours a day & upon the whole enjoy myself much more than when you were here. I have connected myself with a class of Benjamin F. Butler's who is now lecturing on the Evidence of Christianity. He prefers Bishop Wilson's lectures as a text book as they treat principally of the internal evidences & are therefore more appropriate to the Sabbath. I shall be able at some future time to tell you what I think of him. I have also connected myself with a small association of Rodman Pierson myself & two others who meet together to read essays & improve ourselves. Our plan is to choose such questions as are of a practical nature & which will require such investigation as may at some future day be of service to us. . . .

There is a fifteen-month gap in William's notes because, he says, of lost letters. In a letter dated 12 February 1845, CS explains that he has had a "very severe attack of my old complaint" since his last communication but feels "that these severe relapses are necessary for my growth in grace . . ." In an April letter he writes:

> Since I last wrote you my health has considerably improved. I was then suffering from a very severe relapse occasioned by confinement to my studies. I do not think I ever suffered so much from an extreme morbid sensitiveness of the nervous system. I am not yet in as good health as I had the former part of the Winter & I have much apprehension as to the effect of the coming debilitating weather. At present study is suicidal & I have only to wait patiently submissive to the will of God whatever it may be. As I have every reason to believe that this severe attack was occasioned by study & that had I been employed in some active occupation I should have been comparatively well. I can hardly think it advisable to make another experiment. What I shall do, of course, I cannot say & I must wait for some indication of God's providence to direct. I need not tell you that I often have much anxiety & distress as to my future course. While you pray for my spiritual welfare do not forget to ask God that he will if consistent with his holy will so restore me to health as to enable me to be employed in some useful pursuit & that he will guide me by his Holy Spirit in determining what is duty. . . .

In May CS went abroad for health reasons with friends who had planned a tour of Europe. The trip had the intended effect, for, arriving home in October, CS found himself much improved and anxious to settle down to some employment. He had by then relinquished all idea of resuming the study of law. In a letter dated 31 October 1845, he writes to his brother William:

> It is the opinion of physicians & friends & their opinion is confirmed by what I have experienced, that it would be improvident & contrary to duty to hazard my comfortable health by application to study [law]. I am confident that a few months of such application would reduce me as low as ever. But more of this when I see you. You will see my dear Brother that if I ever needed your prayers I certainly need them now. Thrown out of my profession in the Providence of God & uncertain in which way to employ myself how much do I need the guidance of the Holy Spirit. May I be enabled to discover what is God's will, & with a comfortable disposition & divine assistance may I be enabled to perform it. I am anticipating much pleasure in seeing you in your own house. When with the vividness of yesterday I recall our happy College days & the delightful times we have often had together I cannot persuade myself that you are a married man settled in your own house & the pastor of a church.

The "guidance of the Holy Spirit" must have come quickly. For, within two months, CS formed a publishing partnership with a New York City dry-goods merchant, Isaac D. Baker, signed a lease for space in the chapel at the back of the Brick Church, and purchased the stock of a local bookseller named John S. Taylor, previous tenant of the chapel rooms. On 1 January 1846, he was two months short of his twenty-fifth birthday.

John Delaney
June 26, 1995
Princeton, N.J.

Overview

by

Charles Scribner III

When I was first told that the subject I should speak on was the history of Scribners, I gulped — since I obviously wasn't around for most of our history. But my father said to me, "Don't feel shy about telling our story; just remember that a wise philosopher — who happened also to be an editor at Scribners — once said, 'While everyone has been young, not everyone has been old.' " I hardly see how that qualifies *me* for the job, but at least it may justify my subject.

Since I don't believe in delivering footnotes — I leave that to future historians — I feel obligated to preface the following history of Scribners with a blanket disclaimer and equally all-encompassing acknowledgment: my narrative is no more original than my name — I have done hardly more than revise and update my father Charles Scribner Jr.'s original 1957 article, "A Family Tradition," which he subsequently amplified in several delightful conversations. If plagiarism is the sincerest compliment one can pay, then never was it more richly deserved.

The history of Charles Scribner's Sons begins in 1846 with the publishing partnership of Isaac Baker and Charles Scribner. The younger partner, Scribner, was a New Yorker of twenty-five, who had graduated from Princeton in the class of 1840. He had first planned a career in the law, but because of his frail health he was told to give that up for something less strenuous; he turned to publishing as a more congenial profession. I wonder if the relative hardship of the two occupations would still be appraised in quite the same way. Would any doctor dare prescribe a career in publishing today?

The location selected for the new firm was an unused chapel in the old Brick Church (then called the Brick Meeting House) on the corner of Nassau Street and Park Row in downtown Manhattan. In those days the area was a kind of headquarters of the book trade; no doubt it was also comforting to set up shop within such hallowed walls. At that time, to start an independent publishing company — that is, a company devoted solely to book *publishing* — was something of an innovation. Most of the established houses had ei-

Charles Scribner (1821–1871, Princeton Class of 1840), founder of the firm: CS I

ther grown out of printing plants, following the noble tradition of the sixteenth-century Plantin Press in Antwerp, or were offshoots of retail bookshops. On the one hand, a printer might venture into publishing to provide work for his presses; on the other, a bookseller might become a part-time publisher to supply extra books to sell in his store.

There were, however, practical advantages to Baker and Scribner's decision to be more specialized. Since the firm was able to start business without having to worry about the costs of keeping a manufacturing plant busy it was possible to focus on the work of new authors, particularly American authors, without having to compete with others in publishing reprints of the best-selling writers from England — Sir Walter Scott, Macaulay, and the Victorian poets. In short, the firm set out to originate works, to discover fresh talent. It's still a good policy. I might add that in the nineteenth century the more usual occupation

9

*The building in New York City where Charles Scribner and
Isaac D. Baker began their publishing business in 1846*

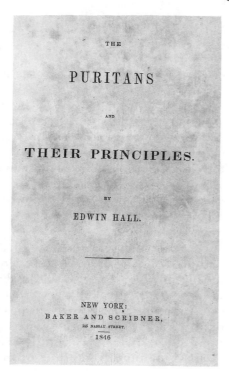

*The first book of the new firm. Edwin Hall
(1802–1877) was pastor of the First Congregational
Society in Norwalk, Connecticut, and based his book
on lectures he had delivered there in 1843–1844.*

*Title page in the first issue (May 1865) of the firm's first
popular magazine,* Hours at Home

of American publishers, publishing reprints of English authors, was not unlike present-day "publishing" in Taiwan: that is to say, American publishers were viewed by their English counterparts as just slightly worse than pirates on the high seas. (In those days there was no such thing as international copyright protection.)

According to modern tastes not all of the first titles of Baker and Scribner would be candidates for the best-seller list. There were lots of theological treatises, most of them almost impenetrable today. I believe that the first work we published was an austere tome entitled *The Puritans and Their Principles* by Edwin Hall. How uncomfortably that book would stand on a shelf today nestled between some of the current best-sellers. Whatever it was, it was no *Joy of Sex*. Of course, nothing does more for a fledgling publishing house than its first best-seller, and I might not be here today were it not for the big sale, at the very beginning of our history, of a book entitled *Napoleon and His Marshals* by the Reverend J. T. Headley. By all accounts it was far from being a model of historical accuracy — but then how many best-sellers are?

There were also the familiar and more-trying cases where the first book or books of an author were disappointments. For instance, there was Donald G. Mitchell, who wrote under the pen name "Ik. Marvel" and who came to the firm after one decidedly non-best-seller at another house. Scribner decided to invest in Mitchell's future but the second book, *Battle Summer*, about the author's travels in Europe during the revolutions of 1848, was equally disappointing. His next book, however, *Reveries of a Bachelor,* published the following year (a book I want to read someday), caught on immediately and the hoped-for success was won in spades. I think the title might have helped. From then on Ik. Marvel was, as we say, a name author — if a name we've since forgotten. A hundred years later, you might be interested to know, while my father was clearing out our printing plant in New York City, he came upon an antique box containing the original printing plates of *Reveries of a Bachelor*. It is difficult to explain why for so many decades these had escaped melting: perhaps through a series of oversights, but perhaps equally as a result of the irrational respect publishers have for a best-seller, even last century's.

Isaac Baker died in 1850 and that left Charles Scribner alone. It was a period of growth, and there were several new projects that did a lot

John Blair Scribner (1850–1879, Princeton Class of 1870)

to put the new firm on the map. Over the years Scribner had been building up a fine list of books on religion. This program reached a high point around the time of the Civil War when he set out to publish an American version of the mammoth work of German biblical scholarship, Lange's *Biblical Commentary*. Eventually completed in twenty-five large volumes — financed at enormous cost — the set was both a commercial and critical success. It was copublished in Britain by Clark of Edinburgh — something of a feather in the cap of the American firm for Clark had already begun his own translation of Lange, which he then dropped in favor of the Scribner edition. Publishing ties are often very old, and here we have a good case in point since Scribners and T. and T. Clark of Edinburgh again collaborated on a revision of Hastings's *Dictionary of the Bible* almost a hundred years later.

In 1865 Charles Scribner and Company took its first step into popular magazine publishing with the somewhat staid (that's an understatement) *Hours at Home*. It was presented as a quasi-religious magazine, one that would bring into every home the virtues by which Americans were supposed to live. The first issue included two short biographies of Early Christian saints, an article on the rivers of Palestine and, in a similar

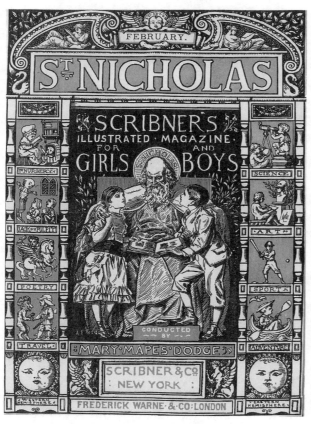

Cover of the February 1881 issue of the firm's popular children's magazine, St. Nicholas

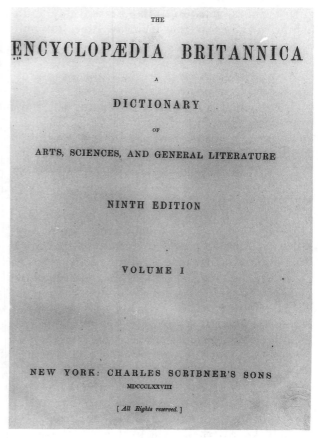

Title page in Volume I of The Encyclopaedia Britannica *(ninth edition). Scribners published the first American edition of this 25-volume set, beginning with the first volume in 1878 and concluding with the index volume in 1889.*

vein, an article about the unsuccessful attempt by missionaries to get the king of the Hawaiis to give up drinking. The magazine, unlike the missionaries, was successful, and plans were soon made to transform it into something far more ambitious.

In 1870 a new company, Scribner & Company, was formed to publish a successor magazine entitled *Scribner's Monthly,* "an illustrated magazine for the people." (The first twelve issues were collected and reprinted a few years ago to mark our one hundred and twenty-fifth anniversary, so you may actually find some copies of *Scribner's Monthly* still around.) The magazine thrived and was soon strong enough to attract young American writers. But the founder did not live to see its success, for Charles Scribner died of typhoid the next year on a trip abroad. Behind him in the firm he left his eldest son, John Blair, and on this young man — he was only twenty-one at the time — fell the whole job of carrying on the family interests in the business.

It was, however, hardly a period of marking time. In two years (that is, in 1873) Scribner &

Company — now this is confusing: Scribner & Company is the magazine company; Charles Scribner's Sons is the book firm — launched a famous children's periodical, *St. Nicholas,* under the editorship of Mary Mapes Dodge, with the prolific Frank R. Stockton as assistant editor. Stockton is perhaps best remembered today for his short story "The Lady or the Tiger?" The magazine brought many now-classic books to the publishing firm and established it permanently in the field of children's literature. Mary Mapes Dodge's own novel, *Hans Brinker, or the Silver Skates,* first published in 1866 and still enjoyed by new generations of readers, is an example of one such offspring of *St. Nicholas* magazine. In a somewhat different vein was the *American Boy's Handy Book,* published in 1882 by the truly immortal Dan Beard. I say "truly immortal" because we still get letters addressed to him. In this connection I have to tell a story on myself: when I first took over our Scribner paperback program in 1976, we had a "new" paperback on the list entitled *Shelters, Shacks, and Shanties* by D. C. Beard, and I tried (very hard) to locate its countercultural, "back-to-nature" author before discovering that he was long since dead and that the book had originally been published in 1910!

A second important development at that time was the coming of age of the subscription book department, which began to undertake some very big things. In association with Messrs. Black of Edinburgh, Scribners brought out the first American edition of the *Encyclopaedia Britannica* (ninth edition); it sold some seventy thousand sets, *four times* as many as were sold in Britain. In those days publishers liked to play up the size of sales figures by various imaginary calculations and thus Scribners advertised that if all those volumes of the encyclopedia were laid end to end they would reach "from New York to beyond Omaha" — an inspiring thought. Perhaps this explains "Scribner, Nebraska" (look it up on the map).

In later years the subscription department published library sets of the works of such well-known authors as Kipling, Stevenson, Henry James, and J. M. Barrie, to name just a few. Its successor, the reference book department, is today, a hundred years later, the foremost American publisher of reference works such as the *Dictionary of American Biography,* the *Dictionary of American History,* and several other series which we'll get to later. It is no exaggeration to say it's our crown jewel.

But let's return to the 1870s, for that was a critical decade. In 1875, Charles Scribner II had graduated from Princeton and at once joined his brother John Blair in the firm. There were two other partners at the time, Edward Seymour and Andrew Armstrong. But Seymour died in 1877 and the next year Armstrong sold the Scribners his share, intending to start up his own concern (foolish man). That left the book publishing company wholly owned and controlled by the Scribner family. The name was now changed to Charles Scribner's Sons, which the firm has retained ever since. The very next year, in 1879, John Blair died, leaving Charles II (this sounds awfully monarchical, or at least reminiscent of *Jaws* or *Rocky*), who was then only twenty-five, to manage the business alone. At first he was to have his hands full. For one thing, there were rumblings in the magazine subsidiary, Scribner & Company:

Charles Scribner (1854–1930, Princeton Class of 1875): CS II

the other owners, it seemed, chafed at being in any way beholden to Charles Scribner's Sons (perhaps they chafed at being beholden to a twenty-five-year-old). In any event, they talked of publishing books themselves; each side soon regarded the other as the tail trying to wag the dog. When in 1881 one of the outside partners, Roswell Smith, bought up enough stock to acquire individual control the equilibrium was disturbed, to put it mildly. Since CS II refused to retain a minority interest in his business he sold to Smith all of his shares in the magazine company. Thus, *Scribner's Monthly* and the children's magazine *St. Nicholas* passed entirely out of the hands of the Scribner family. The remaining owners were reincorporated as the Century Company; *Scribner's Monthly* was by agreement renamed the *Century Magazine,* and the rest, as they say, is history. Under the terms of the sale, Charles Scribner's Sons agreed to stay out of the magazine business for five years. To judge from what happened later, it seems that Scribner kept his eyes on the clock.

Arthur Hawley Scribner (1859–1932, Princeton Class of 1881)

The next decisive step taken by CS II had to do with the textbook business. Beginning in the 1850s the firm had built up a solid and celebrated list of schoolbooks but this area of publishing was becoming increasingly specialized, perhaps too much so for what was then primarily a trade house. In any case, in 1883 Scribner announced the sale of his entire list of schoolbooks to Ivison, Blakeman, Taylor & Company, one of the largest educational houses in the United States.

Within four years of taking over, Charles II had pruned the firm down drastically. But he was by nature a builder, and we can be sure that while part of the business was being dismantled he'd already begun to think of something much bigger and better to set up in its place. The new educational department that he started ten years after the sale of the old one is a good case in point. In 1884, his younger brother, Arthur Hawley Scribner, having graduated from Princeton, came into the firm to help him. (This is an admittedly familiar refrain, one that recurs at regular intervals throughout our family history.) The two brothers

formed a partnership that lasted almost fifty years. The firm soon benefited from Scribner's initial pruning for the remaining branches flowered as never before. Many of the American authors it introduced are still famous. There was H. C. Bunner, whose first book of poems, *Airs from Arcady and Elsewhere,* came out in 1884 in an edition of fifteen hundred copies. Even a century ago the market for new poets was rather special — now, regrettably, it is virtually nonexistent. George Washington Cable first appeared in print in *Scribner's Monthly* with a short story, "'Sieur George," in 1873. Six years later several of his stories were collected and published as the beloved *Old Creole Days.* Another cherished Southern connection was Thomas Nelson Page, whose book *In Ole Virginia* was the first of his many about the South.

Now, lest it be thought that the firm was the literary heir of the Confederacy alone, I hasten to add some names from other parts of the country. There was Henry Adams, whose *History of the United States* was published in 1889 in nine vol-

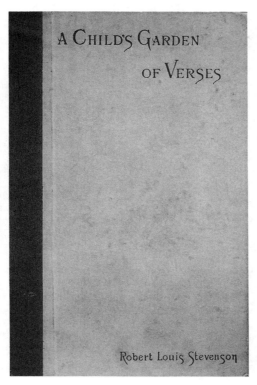

A first edition of A Child's Garden of Verses *(1885), the first Robert Louis Stevenson book published by Scribners*

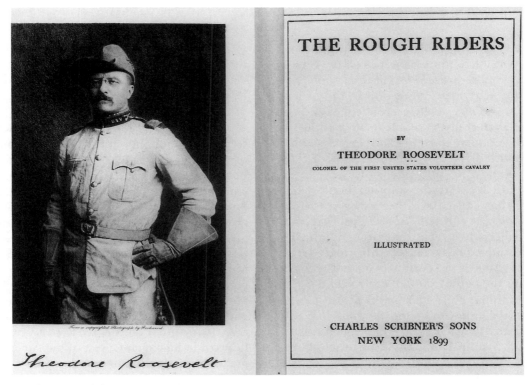

Title page and frontispiece in the first edition of Theodore Roosevelt's The Rough Riders *(1899), the first of his many works published by Scribners*

The home of Charles Scribner's Sons, 1894–1913, at 153–157 Fifth Avenue in New York City, designed by Ernest Flagg, American Beaux-Art architect and brother-in-law of CS II

The 597 Fifth Avenue building occupied by Charles Scribner's Sons from 1913 to 1984, again designed by Ernest Flagg. The first floor was the site of the New York City "landmark" Scribner Bookstore.

umes and whose ironical letters to the firm offer a model for any difficult author to follow. Henry van Dyke, "poet, preacher, author, university teacher, diplomat" (to quote our *Dictionary of American Biography*; a Princeton colleague described him as the only man able to strut while sitting down), contributed to the Scribner list with a pamphlet entitled *The National Sin of Literary Piracy* in 1888; how his publisher must have loved that one. Van Dyke wrote another book a few years later that caused a rather awkward situation: the book was entitled *Fisherman's Luck* and, to its publisher's bad luck, that title contained a prominent and equally regrettable single-letter misprint that almost put Scribners instantly out of business and the author into an early grave.

Three famous children's books of that period were Edward Eggleston's *Hoosier Schoolboy* in 1883; Howard Pyle's *The Merry Adventures of Robin Hood,* also in 1883, and Frances Hodgson Burnett's *Little Lord Fauntleroy* in 1886. Robert Louis Stevenson first appeared on the list in 1895 with *A Child's Garden of Verses.* A later edition of this book, with pictures by Jessie Willcox Smith, was one of the original titles in the "Scribner Illustrated Classics," still in print today. These classics later became famous for their illustrations by Howard Pyle, N. C. Wyeth, and other members of the Brandywine school.

During the 1880s ideas for a new magazine were being thought out as Charles Scribner waited out the five-year moratorium on magazine publishing. It was virtually inconceivable that he could have been content without a magazine. As a boy of fifteen he had started up a little comic monthly called *Merry Moments* and soon had to give it up, not because it proved unsuccessful but because to his father's way of thinking it was far *too* successful for a full-time schoolboy. Few could have been surprised, then, in December 1886 when the clock struck twelve, so to speak, and the firm announced the new *Scribner's Magazine.* Its original editor, from 1887 to 1914, was Edward L. Burlingame, son of the American diplomat Anson Burlingame and literary advisor to Scribners since 1879. Under him the magazine grew into something finer and more successful than the most hopeful would have dared to foresee. But to tell the story of the magazine, to cover its contribution to American literature and American life for more than half a century, is beyond the scope of this brief review. Yet its history would include the very writers whose books helped to build the reputation of the publishing firm, for the magazine was really a double asset to Charles Scribner's Sons: not only in itself, as a profitable magazine, but also as a net for new talent, authors like Edith Wharton who would follow their magazine debuts with many successful books.

In 1894 the firm capped the climax of fifteen years under CS II by moving into a stately, six-story building on Fifth Avenue and Twenty-first Street designed by the renowned American Beaux-Arts architect Ernest Flagg. Flagg happened to be Scribner's brother-in-law — nepotism was also a family tradition. On the ground floor was a magnificent bookstore, the prototype for the more famous store on Forty-eighth Street and Fifth Avenue. (Incidentally, the Scribner building and bookstore on Twenty-first Street later was sold and became a toy warehouse; I hope that's not in some way prophetic.) Scribners was to remain at Twenty-first and Fifth for nineteen years, until 1913, during which time a cornucopia of new authors was added to the house. This was truly a "golden age" of American book publishing, and I don't think there can be any doubt that at the turn of the century Scribners had virtually cornered the market in American literature.

Among our native authors was Theodore Roosevelt, whose *Rough Riders* in 1899 was the first of many successful books for Scribners. The editors tended to get a little carried overboard after the author moved to the White House. On the jacket of one of his books the copywriter hailed him as the "American Homer," which provoked a spate of scornful letters from readers protesting the hyperbole. The embarrassed president asked his editor, "Why at least couldn't you have said *Herodotus?*" Another lasting association was begun in 1896 with the publication of a book on aesthetics, *The Sense of Beauty,* by a young philosophy teacher at Harvard, George Santayana. Almost forty years later Santayana produced a best-selling novel, *The Last Puritan,* published in 1935. It would be hard to think of another philosopher equally versatile in letters. Edith Wharton's first book for Scribners, written in collaboration with Ogden Codman Jr., *The Decoration of Houses,* started a now-famous career (though not in decorating); the book was recently reissued in

Charles Scribner (1890–1952, Princeton Class of 1913): CS III

paperback, which says something about the cycles of taste.

Not long after, two other distinguished authors made their debut, Ernest Seton-Thompson (who later, to the confusion of librarians and card cataloguers, reversed his surnames), with *Wild Animals I Have Known,* published in 1898 and James Huneker, whose *Mezzotints in Modern Music* followed a year later. The turn of the century brought another cluster of famous first editions. John Fox Jr.'s *Blue Grass and Rhododendron* appeared in 1901; two years later Scribners published his novel *The Little Shepherd of Kingdom Come,* which is probably the best seller the house has ever had. A different sort of novelist, Henry James appeared on the list with *The Sacred Fount* in 1901. Sadly, his greatest fame was to come long after his death, but James did live to see the great New York Edition of his novels and stories, which was published from 1907 to 1909 and was reissued in its entirety in the 1950s.

The year 1913 marked a new chapter in the history of the firm. In that year another move was made up Fifth Avenue to the new and even larger Ernest Flagg building at Forty-eighth Street.

DICTIONARY OF AMERICAN BIOGRAPHY

UNDER THE AUSPICES OF THE
AMERICAN COUNCIL OF LEARNED SOCIETIES

EDITED BY
ALLEN JOHNSON

Abbe — Barrymore
VOLUME I

CHARLES SCRIBNER'S SONS
NEW YORK
1928

Title page in Volume I of the Dictionary of American Biography, *the monumental reference work that Scribners published from 1928 through 1937, comprising twenty volumes and an index volume*

(Charles Scribner believed in keeping his brother-in-law busy.) This was the third headquarters since Charles II's presidency and the scene of the last of the almost equal periods in his fifty years with the firm. Scribner had been fielding a whole new team of young editors, the most famous of whom was Maxwell Perkins, about whom a major biography has recently been published and whose volume of extraordinary letters to his authors during his whole career will soon be republished by us. I think it's probably one of the clearest windows into the world of editor-author relations. Lest I sound too worshipful of Perkins, let me tell you two stories that you won't find in Scott Berg's monumental biography. On one occasion Thomas Wolfe was not too happy with the extensive editing (really major surgery) that Perkins did on his manuscripts, which had arrived — literally — in crates. His ego bruised, Wolfe came into Perkins's office and saw on the desk an ashtray given to the editor by the Western writer Will James and fashioned in the shape of a coiled rattlesnake. Wolfe pointed to it and ceremoniously announced: "Portrait of an editor."

Another story, about a best-selling (and still living) novelist, reveals the "passive" side of Perkins's editorial technique. One day this writer came in with her manuscript. She was agonizing and going through the torments of the damned: how was she ever going to get the book written and how was she going to develop her characters and so forth? Perkins sat attentively "taking notes" — doodling pictures of Napoleon, as was his habit. With his hearing aid turned off he was almost stone deaf; he heard nothing of the author's impassioned monologue. He just sat there the whole time nodding and making appropriate social noises and doodling until finally, after about an hour, his troubled author stood up, heaved a great sigh of relief, and said: "Max, I can't tell you how helpful you've been: your advice is infallible." The legend endures.

Another well-known Scribner editor, and a distinguished poet in his own right, was John Hall Wheelock, who died recently. These two men, Perkins and Wheelock, were both young Harvard graduates who invaded a then-predominantly Princeton company and brought it great new success by their editorial intuition and skill.

In 1913 Charles Scribner's only son, another Charles (III), graduated from Princeton and began his own career in publishing. He was a contemporary of Perkins and Wheelock and his age gave him a ready grasp of the importance of the new writers who were beginning to appear on the scene. Another era in American literature was dawning and the firm's enthusiasm for the new authors was to yield it a rich harvest. There was Alan Seeger, whose *Poems* came out in 1916, best remembered for his "rendezvous with death." Four years later, F. Scott Fitzgerald heralded the jazz age with his first novel, *This Side of Paradise*. Stark Young's *The Flower in Drama* appeared in 1923 and, in the following years, Ring Lardner's *How to Write Short Stories* (1924), James Boyd's *Drums* (1925, a year best remembered for *The Great Gatsby*), and John W. Thomason Jr.'s *Fix Bayonets* (also in 1925). In 1926 Ernest Hemingway's *The Torrents of Spring* and *The Sun Also Rises* were both published. In view of Hemingway's later achievements and his equally enduring loyalty to the firm, we shall always think of that as a year set apart. Thomas Wolfe, at the end of this glorious decade, made his debut with *Look Homeward, Angel* in 1929 — a year otherwise remembered less favorably on Wall Street.

Around this time the long career of Charles Scribner II was drawing to a close; "Old C.S.," they now called him, sotto voce. In 1928 he turned over the presidency to his younger brother, Arthur, and continued on only as chairman of the board. (Well, "only" is perhaps not quite the right word; I gather he interfered in everything: older brothers never change their spots.) Happily, he lived to see the first published volumes of the *Dictionary of American Biography,* a project which extended from 1928 to 1937 and a work to which he had given his utmost support; it was probably the most important project the firm had ever undertaken and was developed with the American Council of Learned Societies, which has subsequently collaborated with Scribners on other reference projects. In 1930 Charles II died and was followed two years later by the loyal and patient Arthur, leaving Charles III (my grandfather) to preside alone. He was only forty-one at the time.

It would be hard to think of a more difficult time in which to take over the management of a large publishing house. The Great Depression was in its worst stage and the future must have appeared most uncertain for books. Yet the firm continued to look for fresh talent and take chances on new authors in a way that marks this as one of the most enterprising periods in all our history — an achievement that testifies to the aims and courage of CS III and to the devoted support that his associates, Max Perkins in particular, gave him. In the following years many important new works appeared, not only by already established authors such as Fitzgerald, Hemingway, and Wolfe, but also the first books of many then relatively unknown writers who were later to become famous. Among these firsts by new authors were Marcia Davenport's great biography of Mozart, published in 1932 and still in print; Nancy Hale's *The Young Die Good* (a title I always get wrong), also in 1932; Marjorie Kinnan Rawlings's *South Moon Under,* in 1933 — followed by her most famous novel, *The Yearling,* five years later; Hamilton Basso's *Beauregard,* in 1933; Taylor Caldwell's *Dynasty of Death,* in 1938, and Christine Weston's *Be Thou the Bride,* in 1940. An extraordinary decade of debuts.

The years preceding World War II also saw the growth of a new children's book department under the gifted editorial direction of Alice Dalgliesh. Up until this time there was no formal dis-

Charles Scribner Jr. (1921–1995, Princeton Class of 1943): CS IV

tinction at Scribners between children's books and adult books: children's books were simply considered part of general adult book publishing, a potentially dangerous situation when it came to making publishing decisions. When *The Wind in the Willows,* still one of our juvenile best-sellers, was originally submitted to my great-grandfather there was no way he was going to publish it; he thought is was just a lot of nonsense and foolishness, "something only a child would want to read." Fortunately, President Theodore Roosevelt, on whose recommendation the book had been submitted, persuaded him otherwise. So in the 1930s a separate children's department was finally established; it's now one of the most important branches of the firm. It was founded by Dalgliesh, who in 1934 was already an experienced editor and, indeed, author in her own right. She proceeded to build one of the most distinguished lists of children's books in American publishing. I might note that, having joined the firm as the first female editor, she had been there already three or four days before she went to see my grandfather, who liked her very much and wanted to know how she was getting on. "Oh, just fine, Mr. Scribner, but there is one thing I'd like." "Of course," he said, "What is it?" "Do you think I might have a desk?" And he replied, "Well, yes, I don't see why not, of course you can. It just never occurred to us you'd need one." And so with Miss Dalgliesh the women's movement dawned on 597 Fifth Avenue.

At the same time the 1930s also saw some sad losses. Thomas Wolfe was the most visible, a loss due primarily to his own self-proclaimed dependence on his editor, Max Perkins, which not surprisingly led to his feeling compelled to sever that editorial umbilical cord. Then, in 1937, *Scribner's Magazine* folded after fifty glorious years of publication, a casualty of newer and slicker magazines and, I suppose, of the radio.

Right after the war, yet another Charles Scribner (IV or Jr.: my father, out of Princeton and back from military service) joined the firm. It was to be the last year of Max Perkins's life, but he left behind two budding novelists, James Jones and Alan Paton. Now the manner of Paton's arrival at Scribners is an unusual one. His manuscript came in "over the transom," as we say; in fact, it wasn't even over the transom, for it hadn't got farther than the post office when its box broke open and the manuscript fell into complete disarray. Somebody was called from Scribners and actually went and pieced it together. Fortunately, he also brought it back to Scribners and gave it to Perkins to read. And so *Cry, the Beloved Country* came to be published in 1948. It had a first printing of five thousand copies and within a year after publication there were one hundred and twenty-five thousand copies in print, a fitting debut for that courageous South African writer who is currently at work on his autobiography.

In 1952 Charles III died very suddenly; he had just finished reading the manuscript of Hemingway's short classic, *The Old Man and the Sea,* which was dedicated to him and Perkins, Papa's two closest friends and mentors at Scribners. Although Perkins had always been Hemingway's official editor and had corresponded with him extensively (the letters make wonderful reading), the only "editor" from whom Hemingway ever accepted suggestions was my grandfather. Nobody else could get Hemingway to change a word. I'd love to tell you some of the more colorful ones that were changed —

After his father's death, Charles Scribner Jr. moved back from Washington, where he'd been sent as a cryptanalyst during the Korean War, and took the helm at the ripe age of thirty-one. Now you'll recall his grandfather had had to do the

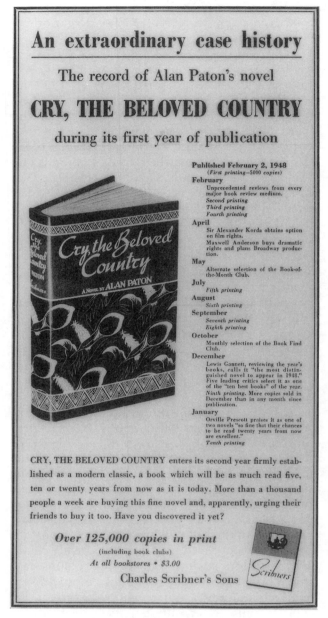

Scribner promotional broadside for Alan Paton's Cry, the Beloved Country

same at twenty-five, one tradition we can live without. One of his first moves was to close the Scribner printing and warehousing plant, which had operated since 1908. It was a few blocks down the street and had been designed (again by Ernest Flagg) as a complete manufacturing unit. But new economic realities indicated that even a relatively large firm could not reasonably support its own printing plant. The only prominent surviving exception is Doubleday; and despite all their book clubs even they face a tough editorial burden feeding the voracious mouths of those presses to keep them running twenty-four hours a day.

Publishing in general had entered a new era. Shortly after CS Jr. took over, he got a phone call from a Hollywood producer who wanted to know the title of the most recent Philo Vance mystery. (The Philo Vance mysteries — the *Canary Murder Case,* the *Benson,* the *Greene,* the *Bishop,* and so forth — were written by S. S. Van Dine in the 1920s and 1930s, and were very successful; all of them had been made into movies.) Well, Scribner thought a moment and said that the last one was the *Gracie Allen Murder Case.* The producer replied, "Oh, no, no, no, I know the *Gracie Allen;* that's not the one I want; that was written ten years ago. I want the most recent, the last one." Scribner responded, "Well, that *is* the last one." The producer exclaimed, "It can't be; what happened?" "What happened is simple. The author died." To which the producer replied with utter incredulity, "Well, you didn't have to let the *series* die, did you?" Indeed, book publishing had entered a new era.

Now in a different spirit Scribner set out to recapture some of our past, our backlist, you might say our literary capital, most of which had by this time been licensed to paperback and cheap-hardcover reprinters. He wanted to bring these books back under the Scribner imprint. This move was soon to prove invaluable. Admittedly, he had no intention at the time of putting them into paperback himself — in fact, one of the reasons he was taking them back was that he didn't *like* paperbacks. He didn't believe in them and compared having your own in-house paperback line to keeping you own pet cobra in your living room. But he soon changed his mind — albeit reluctantly — and invented the Scribner Library, our own line of quality paperbacks, at which point he now had at his disposal an incredible list of classics to convert into paperback, beginning with *The Great Gatsby, Tender is the Night, The Sun Also Rises, Ethan Frome,* and so on. His industry colleagues credited him with uncanny foresight and patience in reverting all those licenses in preparation for Scribners new paperback line. In publishing it's the result, not the motive, that counts.

I think it's fair to say that by the 1950s the star-studded Perkins years had left an unfortunate legacy. The editors were on the perpetual lookout for the new Hemingway or Wolfe to arrive — like Godot. Their attention was fixed on the fiction front, to the exclusion of other areas of publish-

Scribner Library order form (1960)

ing. To restore some balance to the list — and a balanced list is essential to a publisher's survival — Scribner set out to develop fields of nonfiction, history, biography, how-to books; he hired a most gifted editor, Elinor Parker, who invented a new category in practical arts, the needlepoint book, the first of which was Erica Wilson's *Crewel Embroidery.* But Charles Scribner Jr.'s own true love was for reference works, and these years saw the birth of works that have become the staple of every major school, college, and public library. He completed the *Album of American History* and began the *Dictionary of Scientific Biography,* a fifteen-year project, just now nearing completion; sponsored by the American Council of Learned Societies with a grant from the National Science Foundation, it has since become the model for multivolume reference works of original scholarship. There followed the *Dictionary of the History of Ideas,* then the *Dictionary of Foreign Policy.* Most recently he has begun, again with the American Council of Learned Societies, the *Dictionary of the Middle Ages.* These series are especially important today when libraries are increasingly

Charles Scribner III (1951– , Princeton Class of 1973): CS V

short of funds for purchasing monographs. The reference department has become the new creative center of publishing at Scribners.

During recent years the sales force was greatly enlarged, insuring national distribution for all Scribner books as well as for other publishers distributed by Scribners. During the 1960s and 1970s Scribners also became far more active in acquiring books from British firms and publishing the works of British authors, both established and new. A recent example is Anthony Burgess's literary biography of Hemingway. And a newly successful English author launched by Scribners, one in whom we take special pride, is the crime novelist P. D. James; now hailed as the successor to Agatha Christie and Dorothy Sayers, she has finally broken into bestsellerdom, after seven books written during the course of two decades.

In the context of my thumbnail history of Scribners very little of recent times is truly new; we were doing much the same a century ago. In effect, the postwar decades may be viewed as a re-

capitulation of earlier themes; that is to say, striking a balanced list, recognizing the importance of nonfiction, maintaining a backlist, bringing out series of books such as reference sets, and copublishing with English firms. Soon after I joined Scribners in 1975, my first editorial project was to revive, edit, and write an introduction to the one, and long-forgotten, play of F. Scott Fitzgerald, *The Vegetable, or from President to Postman*. That was my way of taking a gentle step from the halls of academia to the realities of Fifth Avenue, involving as it did many glorious hours spent within our publishing archives, which had been donated to Princeton a decade earlier. It was also a good introductory lesson that old books can become new books. Since then there have been many exciting developments at the firm. Our list is always expanding and several new talents have been launched, of which P. D. James, whom I just mentioned, is an outstanding example as well as a personal favorite. I think it is fair to say that a very special place in our collective hearts will always belong to the newly launched novelist, and that's as it should be.

One of the most recent prospects for Scribners is our acquisition of the relatively young and promising house of Atheneum, founded in 1959. Out of the envisioned combination of talents and resources will emerge the new Scribner Book Companies, yet another corporate name, and still more new books and publishing ventures.

A few years ago my father expressed his concern about the future of that antiquated object, the book, to General Sarnoff of RCA. They were having lunch together and Scribner got up the courage to ask whether Sarnoff thought the book would survive the present revolution of technology and mass communication: that is to say, films, cassettes, video, and others yet undreamed of. "No need to worry," assured the general. "Just remember there are more candles sold annually in the United States today than a hundred years ago." A consoling thought.

In a very special way, books themselves provide illumination. Once removed from the shelf, the best give off a steady, glowing light — hardly strobe or flash, and certainly not neon; the light they radiate is mellower and warmer. So unless IBM or RCA or Xerox has a surprise in store for us all, I don't imagine you'll see the Scribner lamp imprinted on a box of candles for some time to come.

Afterword

Since the foregoing account was written and delivered several chapters have been completed and new ones begun in our history. In 1980 P. D. James's novel *Innocent Blood* broke several records as a Scribner best-seller and established its author as an important contemporary novelist as well as the foremost English mystery writer. The same year, the sixteen-volume *Dictionary of Scientific Biography* was completed, and *The Dictionary of the Middle Ages* was well under way. In 1981 we published *Ernest Hemingway: Selected Letters,* the richest and most revealing Hemingway work to appear since *The Old Man and the Sea* a generation earlier.

Joining our Scribner and Atheneum trade imprints, Rawson Associates became a division of the Scribner Book Companies in 1982 after having established an impressive track record of nonfiction best-sellers. Finally in 1984 we took the most important step since our founding when we accepted the offer to merge into Macmillan and become part of its thriving and extended publishing family. A better and more permanent home could not have been imagined for our reference, juvenile, college, and trade departments and authors. Macmillan books were originally introduced and distributed in America by Charles Scribner in 1859 so it only seems fitting that, a century later, the roles be reversed.

Postscript

In the fall of 1988 Macmillan, our parent company, was the subject of a hostile takeover by Robert Maxwell. For the next four years it continued to sail under Maxwell's flag until, after that tycoon's mysterious death and the debacle of his debt-ridden empire, it was sold to Simon and Schuster just prior to the latter's acquisition by Viacom. Today the invigorated Scribner imprint — both in adult trade books and library reference works — continues to flourish within Simon and Schuster as it approaches its sesquicentennial in 1996.

Charles Scribner III, A History of Charles Scribner's Sons (Cleveland: Rowfant Club, 1985). This History was originally presented as a lecture at the Rowfant Club on 11 October 1978.

ILLUSTRATED CHRONOLOGY

Significant Scribner Dates

This chronology provides a selected list of important dates and events in the early history of the firm, noting partnerships, organizational changes, and changes in location. Significant publications and publishing series — selected for the importance of the authors, from a literary standpoint and/or from their commercial benefit to the firm, for the subject, or for the publishing achievement itself, such as the number of volumes involved and the quantity of illustrations — are identified for each year. Many of the authors noted by their "first Scribner book" are covered at greater length in the "Selected Authors" section and are not mentioned further here. For some titles, particularly early ones, only the copyright dates are available in the firm's records.

1846–1849

1846

1 Jan.	Charles Scribner (CS I) and Isaac D. Baker, a New York City dry-goods merchant, open their publishing business, Baker & Scribner, in meeting rooms leased from the Brick Church chapel, at the corner of Nassau Street and Park Row in New York City. Address: 145 Nassau Street (site of the old *New York Times* building). Annual rent: $600.
7 Jan.	CS I and Baker sign contract with bookseller John S. Taylor to publish his books (i.e., to use his stereotype plates) at a set price per copy.
3 Feb.	Edwin Hall's 13 January copyright of his book *The Puritans and Their Principles* is transferred to Baker & Scribner, making this the firm's first book.
16 Feb.	Copyright date of C. Edwards Lester's *The Artists of America: A Series of Biographical Sketches of American Artists,* the firm's second book
14 Mar.	Copyright date of Charles Burdett's first Baker & Scribner book, *Lilla Hart: A Tale of New York,* the firm's third book and first work of fiction
18 Apr.	Publication date of the first volume (of two) of *Napoleon and His Marshals* by J. T. Headley, his first Baker & Scribner book and the firm's first best-seller, which reached fifty editions by 1861 (volume 2 was published on 1 June)

1847

28 May	Copyright date of T. S. Arthur's first Baker & Scribner book, *Keeping Up Appearances; or, A Tale for the Rich and Poor*
1 June	Andrew C. Armstrong, who had been associated with James A. Sparks, publisher of *The Churchman,* joins the firm.
19 June	Copyright date of Headley's *Washington and His Generals* (2 volumes)

1848

13 June	CS I marries Emma Elizabeth Blair, daughter of John Insley Blair, one of the country's future leading railroad capitalists.

27 Sept.	Copyright date of Burdett's *The Gambler; or, A Policeman's Story*, possibly the first American detective novel
1849	
6 Apr.	Copyright date of Nathaniel Parker Willis's first Baker & Scribner book, *Rural Letters and Other Records of Thought at Leisure, Written in the Intervals of More Hurried Literary Labor*
16 May	Copyright date of Caroline M. Kirkland's first Baker & Scribner book, *Holidays Abroad; or, Europe from the West* (2 volumes)
21 Dec.	Copyright date of Donald Grant Mitchell's first Baker & Scribner book, *Battle Summer: Being Transcripts from Personal Observation in Paris, During the Year 1848*, published under the pseudonym of "Ik. Marvel"

LETTER:

Letter by Henry Norman Hudson to CS I, 2 October 1849, from Keene, N.H.

Addressed to "Messrs. Baker & Scribner, Booksellers and Publishers, 145 Nassau Street, New York," this is the earliest surviving author letter in the Scribner Archives. Its personal references and casual, friendly tone were common characteristics of the author/publisher relationships CS I established during the early years of his business. Hudson was an Episcopal clergyman and a Shakespearean scholar; his Lectures on Shakespeare *(2 volumes) was his first work, published by Baker & Scribner in 1848. Other references in his letter are to fellow authors Richard Henry Dana (and his forthcoming* Poems and Prose Writings, *1850) and J. T. Headley.*

John Insley Blair (1802-1899), father-in-law of CS I and railroad capitalist

My dear Mr. Scribner:

I have been intending this long time to write to you; but then you know I am always <u>intending</u> more than ten men could do if they would. You have doubtless learned through Mr. Baker where I am spending this summer. I expect to leave here in the course of three or four weeks: where I shall then go, I have not fully settled. I came here merely to hold religious services and preach through the summer, there never having been a church here; but I have done something which I hope will result in one.

I should like hugely to walk into your store again, as I did in days of yore, when I was a young man; and if you were not so far off, I rather think I should do so: but alas, a lass! age, old age, and the distance prevent me. Which being the case, my heart and other bowels yearn to hear from you: in the first place I want to hear from <u>yourself</u>; in the second, that your precious wife and sisters are well; in the third, whether the book is selling at all or not, (I think my preaching has sold a few copies in New Hampshire this summer); in the fourth, when you are expecting to have Mr. Dana's book out, so that I may be prepared to give it a good

LIST OF BOOKS
PUBLISHED BY BAKER & SCRIBNER,
(SUCCESSORS TO JOHN S. TAYLOR.)

BRICK CHURCH CHAPEL, 145 NASSAU STREET.

NEW-YORK, JANUARY 1, 1846.

Charlotte Elizabeth's Works.

" PERSONAL RECOLLECTIONS, 1 vol. 12mo	50
" HELEN FLEETWOOD, " "	50
" JUDAH'S LION, " "	50
" JUDÆA CAPTA, " "	50
" THE SIEGE OF DERRY, " "	50
" LETTERS FROM IRELAND, " "	50
" THE ROCKITE, " "	50
" FLORAL BIOGRAPHY, " "	50
" PRINCIPALITIES AND POWERS, " "	50
" ENGLISH MARTYRS, " "	50
" THE WRONGS OF WOMAN, " "	50
" THE CHURCH VISIBLE IN ALL AGES, 18mo	50
" PASSING THOUGHTS, " "	38
" FALSEHOOD AND TRUTH, " "	38
" CONFORMITY, " "	38
" IZRAM, a Mexican Tale, " "	38
" OSRIC, a Missionary Tale, " "	38
" THE CONVENT BELL, a Tale, " "	38
" GLIMPSES OF THE PAST, or the Museum, "	38
" PHILIP AND HIS GARDEN, " "	38
" THE FLOWER OF INNOCENCE, " "	38
" THE SIMPLE FLOWER, " "	38
" ALICE BENDEN, and other Tales, " "	38
" FEMALE MARTYRS, " "	38
" TALES AND ILLUSTRATIONS, " "	38
" DRESSMAKERS AND MILLINERS, " "	25
" THE FORSAKEN HOME, " "	25
" THE LITTLE PIN-HEADERS, " "	25
" THE LACE RUNNERS, " "	25
" LETTER WRITING, " "	25
" BACK-BITING, " "	25
" PROMISING AND PERFORMING, " "	25

CHARLOTTE ELIZABETH'S WORKS, Uniform Edition, 12 vols. 12mo ... **6 00**

CHARLOTTE ELIZABETH'S JUVENILE WORKS, (not included in the above 12 vols.) 7 vols. 18mo ... **3 00**

THE PEEP OF DAY, or a series of the earliest religious instruction the Infant Mind is capable of receiving, with verses illustrative of the subjects, 1 vol. 18mo. with engravings ... 50

LINE UPON LINE, by the author of "Peep of Day," a second series ... 50

PRECEPT UPON PRECEPT, by the author of "Peep of Day," etc. a third series ... 50

THEOPNEUSTY, or the Plenary Inspiration of the Holy Scriptures, by S. R. L. Gaussen, Professor of Theology in the new Theological School of Geneva, Switzerland. Third American, from the second French edition, revised and enlarged by the author. Translated by the Rev. Edward Norris Kirk, 1 vol. ... 75

AIDS TO PREACHING AND HEARING, by Rev. Thos. H. Skinner, D. D., 1 vol. 12mo ... 1 00

MEMOIR OF THE LATE REV. WM. NEVINS, D. D., 1 vol. 12mo ... 75

LECTURES ON UNIVERSALISM, by Rev. Joel Parker, D.D., President of the New-York Theological Seminary, 12mo ... 75

JACOB WRESTLING WITH THE ANGEL, and SOLOMON THE SHULAMITE, by Krummacher, author of Elijah the Tishbite, 1 vol. 12mo ... 75

CORNELIUS THE CENTURION, by Krummacher, 1 vol. 12mo. ... 75

SERMONS ON REVIVALS, by Rev. Albert Barnes, with an Introduction, by Rev. Joel Parker, D D., 1 vol. 18mo ... 38

D'AUBIGNE'S HISTORY OF THE GREAT REFORMATION, abridged by the Rev. Edward Dalton, 1 vol. 18mo. 447 pages. ... 50

A VOICE FROM ANTIQUITY, to the Men of the Nineteenth Century ; or, Read the Book. By J. H. Merle D'Aubigne, author of the "History of the Reformation in the Sixteenth Century," 1 vol. 18mo ... 25

THE VOICE OF THE CHURCH ONE, Under all the Successive Forms of Christianity ; by J. H. Merle D'Aubigne, D. D., 1 vol. 18mo ... 25

PUSEYISM EXAMINED, by J. H. Merle D'Aubigne, D. D., with an Introductory Notice of the author, by Robert Baird, 1 vol. 18mo ... 25

THE CONFESSION OF CHRIST, by J. H. Merle D'Aubigne, D D, 1 vol. 18mo ... 25

FAITH AND KNOWLEDGE, by J. H. Merle D'Aubigne, D. D., 1 vol. 18mo ... 25

THE CHURCH IN THE WILDERNESS, and other Fragments, from the Study of a Pastor, by Gardiner Spring, Pastor of the Brick Presbyterian Church in the city of New-York, 1 vol. 12mo ... 50

THE BACKSLIDER, by Andrew Fuller, with an Introduction by John Angell James, 18mo ... 31

SERMONS, by Hugh Blair, D. D., to which is prefixed the Life and Character of the author, by James Finlayson, D. D., 1 vol. 8vo ... 2 00

OBLIGATIONS OF THE WORLD TO THE BIBLE, by Gardiner Spring, D. D. 1 vol. 12mo ... 1 00

A VISIT TO NORTHERN EUROPE, Or Sketches, Descriptive, Historical, Political and Moral, of Denmark, Norway, Sweden and Finland, and the Free Cities of Hamburgh and Lubeck ; containing notices of the Manners and Customs, Commerce, Manufactures, Arts and Sciences, Education, Literature and Religion of those Countries and Cities. By the Rev. Robert Baird, with Maps and numerous Engravings, 2 vols. 12mo ... **$2 00**

HEROINES OF SACRED HISTORY, by Mrs. Steele, 1 vol. 18mo. ... 50

A SUMMER JOURNEY IN THE WEST, by Mrs. Steele, author of "Heroines of Sacred History," 1 vol. 12mo ... 50

MEMOIRS OF MRS. SARAH LOUISA TAYLOR, by Rev. Lot Jones, A. M. Fifth edition, 18mo ... 50

EMANUEL ON THE CROSS, AND IN THE GARDEN, by R. P. Buddicom, 1 vol. 12mo ... 63

THE FAMILY OF BETHANY, by L. Bonnet ; with an Introductory Essay, by the Rev. Hugh White, 1 vol. 18mo ... 38

THE SPIRIT OF PRAYER, Or The Soul rising out of Time into the Riches of Eternity, by Wm. Law, A. M., author of "Law's Serious Call," etc. 1 vol. 18mo ... 31

A PROTESTANT MEMORIAL, Comprising a Concise History of the Reformation, by Thomas Hartwell Horne, B. D., author of "Introduction to the Bible," etc. etc. 1 vol. 18mo ... 38

DANGER AND DUTY, Or a Few Words on Popery, Puseyism, etc., by Rev. Richard Marks, author of the "Retrospect," etc. etc. 1 vol. 18mo ... 31

THE ADOPTED CHILD, or the necessity of Early Piety, by the author of "Emma, or the Lost Found," 1 vol. 18mo ... 31

THE STORY OF GRACE, the Little Sufferer, 1 vol. 18mo ... 31

ADOLPHUS AND JAMES, by the Rev. Napoleon Roussel, translated from the French, 1 vol 18mo ... 31

THE LILY OF THE VALLEY, by Mrs. Sherwood ... 31

SHANTY, THE BLACKSMITH, by Mrs. Sherwood ... 50

THE TRAVELLER, Or the Wonders of Art, 1 vol. 18mo ... 38

MEMOIR OF TELLSTORM, the first Swedish Missionary to Lapland ; with an Appendix giving an account of the Stockholm Mission, by the Rev. George Scott, 1 vol. 18mo ... 31

FLOWER FADED, by the Rev. John Angell James, 18mo ... 38

MEMOIR OF MARTHA, by John Angell James, 1 vol. 18mo ... 31

MEMOIR OF CHARLES LATHROP WINSLOW, 1 vol. 18mo

CLOSING SCENES OF THE LIFE OF SAMUEL WISDOM, illustrating the usefulness of Tract Distribution, and Sabbath School Instruction, 1 vol. 18mo ... 25

THE SABBATH SCHOOL TEACHER'S PATTERN, AND A WORD FOR ALL, by John Angell James ... 25

COUNSELS TO THE YOUNG, by Rev. A. Alexander, D. D. ... 25

SELF CULTIVATION, by Tryon Edwards ... 25

EARLY PIETY, by Rev. Jacob Abbott ... 25

THE CHRISTIAN POCKET COMPANION, selected from the works of President Edwards and others. The above four vols. 32mo. in gilt edges, 31 cts. each. ... 25

HISTORY OF THE SANDWICH ISLANDS, by the Rev. Shelden Dibble, Missionary to those Islands, 1 vol. 12mo ... 75

GENEVA AND ROME, by S. R. L. Gaussen, 1 vol. 18mo ... 25

REFLECTIONS ON FLOWERS, by Rev. James Hervey, author of "Meditations Among the Tombs," 1 vol. 18mo ... 31

TRANSPLANTED FLOWERS, Or Memoirs of Mrs. Rumff, and the Duchesse de Broglie, with an appendix, by the Rev. Robert Baird, 1 vol. 18mo ... 38

HINTS FOR MOTHERS, by a Lady, 1 vol. 18mo ... 31

A TALE OF THE HUGUENOTS, or Memoirs of a French Refugee Family ; translated from the Manuscripts of James Fontaine, by a Lady—with an introduction, by Francis L. Hawkes, D. D., 1 vol. 18mo ... 50

ROCKY ISLAND, and other Parables, by Samuel Wilberforce, M. A., 1 vol. 18mo ... 38

THE LITTLE WANDERERS, by Samuel Wilberforce, M. A., 1 vol. 18mo ... 25

THE KING AND HIS SERVANTS, by Samuel Wilberforce, M. A., 1 vol. 18mo ... 25

THE PROPHET'S GUARD, by Samuel Wilberforce, M. A., 1 vol. 18mo ... 25

ADVICE TO A YOUNG CHRISTIAN, by a village Pastor, with an Introduction, by Rev. Dr. Alexander, (new edition,) 1 vol 18mo ... 38

THE WAY OF SAFETY, by the Rev. L. E. Lathrop, D D., 1 vol. 18mo ... 38

BIOGRAPHY OF THE SAVIOUR AND HIS APOSTLES, with Portraits done on steel, 1 vol. 18mo ... 50

POETRY FOR THE YOUNG, in two parts, Moral and Miscellaneous, 1 vol. 18mo ... 38

THE WORLD'S RELIGION, as contrasted with genuine Christianity, by Lady Colquhoun, 1 vol. 18mo ... 50

THE CHRISTIAN CITIZEN, by the Rev. A. D. Eddy, of Newark, 1 vol. 12mo ... 50

THE ELEMENTS OF ASTRONOMY, designed as an Introduction to the Study, 1 vol. 18mo ... 25

MURRAY'S INTRODUCTION TO THE ENGLISH READER. 12mo. large type ... 25

MURRAY'S ENGLISH READER. 12mo. large type ... 50

MURRAY'S SEQUEL TO THE ENGLISH READER. 12mo large type ... 63

THE SHORTER CATECHISM of the Reverend Assembly of Divines, with proofs thereof out of the Scriptures, in words at length, 18mo. $5 per 100

First broadside announcement of books offered by the new publishing firm of Baker & Scribner

A

$150 Personal Recollections
150 Helen Fleetwood
150 Judah's Lion
150 Judea Capta
150 Siege of Derry
150 Letters from Ireland
150 Rockets
150 Floral Biography
150 Principalities & Powers
150 Theopneusty
150 Memoir of Nevins
150 Heroines of Sacred History
    Memoirs of Mrs Taylor
150 Tale of the Huguenots
150 Shanty the Blacksmith

B

    Passing Thoughts
100 Conformity
100 Falsehood & Truth
100 Izram
100 Osric
100 Convent Bell
100 Glimpses of the Past
100 Phillis & his Garden
100 Flower of Innocence
100 Simple Flowers
100 Alice Benden
100 Tales & Illustrations
100 The Traveller
100 Flower Faded
200 Transplanted Flowers
100 Rocky Island
50 Saviour & his Apostles

C

$75 Story of Grace
75 Lily of the Valley
75 Reflections upon Flowers

D

$40 Backbiting
40 Promising & Performing
40 Memoir of Martha
40 Sabbath School Teacher's pattern
40 Early Piety
40 Pocket Companion
40 Self Cultivation
40 Elements of Astronomy

I hereby agree to allow Baker & Scribner to publish any amount of books they may wish from this list of Stereotype Plates for — for the sum of Seven & a half cents per Copy for the list marked **A**. Five cents per copy for the list marked **B**. Two & a half for the list marked **C**, & two cents for the list marked **D**. and they are to have the right to purchase the plates any time within one year at the prices set opposite each on a credit of 6 12 18 & 24 months from this date. Said tariff of payment to be made at an average credit of eight months. Should they purchase the plates, the amount so paid to be deducted from the price of the Plates.

New York January 7 1846

John S. Taylor

I agree not to print or allow anyone to print from the above plates during the time of this agreement. J.S.T.

Charles Scribner and Isaac D. Baker's original contract with the New York bookseller John S. Taylor establishing their publishing venture in 1846. (Taylor had formed the publishing firm Taylor & Dodd with Moses Dodd in 1839, but it had lasted barely a year, each man going his own way: Dodd to form his own firm that later became known, under his son, as Dodd, Mead; Taylor to publish mostly religious works by himself.) The agreement permitted Baker & Scribner to publish from Taylor's stereotype plates any works on this list at set royalty rates; the titles were grouped (A, B, C, D) according to, presumably, Taylor's estimation of their market value. Within the year, the partners had the option to buy the plates outright from Taylor at the price set opposite each title. Baker & Scribner took up the rooms in the Brick Church chapel that had been rented by Taylor.

Engraving of the Brick Church on Beekman Street in New York City showing the chapel in the rear, where on the first floor Baker & Scribner rented two rooms — one fronting on Nassau Street, one on Park Row.

Contemporary silhouettes of founders Charles Scribner and Isaac Baker and their first best-selling author, J. T. Headley, cut by New York artist Charles Wood at the firm's Park Row address in 1846, with their autographs

An 1849 receipt for sale of copyright: the earliest surviving reference to a publishing agreement with an author in the Scribner Archives. James Kirke Paulding (1778–1860) was an early friend and literary collaborator of Washington Irving and served as Secretary of the Navy under Martin Van Buren. The Puritan and His Daughter, a fictional story of Cromwell's England and Virginia, was his last work.

cutting up; in the fifth, whether you have been able to get the balance due me from Colton's estate; and in the sixth, whether New-York is right side up and at home. Moreover, if you have got or can get the aforesaid balance, I wish you would send it to me, provided you can spare it.

I have worked like a dog all summer; haven't been well much of the time; have had the blues occasionally like the deuce; have hungered and thirsted to meet old Headley again in your store and give him a blowing up for getting married before me; and have multiplied my grey hairs through grief, and want of the light of your countenance. Amen.

Please shake Mr. Baker's hand and crack a good joke upon him, for me, and slap your two clerks on the back, and give my regards to your wife, and kiss all your little ones for me, and believe me

Your sincere friend,
H. N. Hudson

LETTER:
Letter by CS I to his father-in-law, John Insley Blair, 29 October 1849.

In this letter CS I expresses concern about his partner's deteriorating health, his interest in buying Baker's share of the firm, and his need for another partner, possibly his brother Edward, to handle the "strictly business part of it." Edward started to work for him in 1851.

Mr. Baker left me some days since in very feeble health. I have heard from him twice since and he thought himself somewhat improved. Still his disease is so deceptive that I have little or no confidence in any material improvement. Indeed I think it a matter of great doubt whether he ever returns. His absence keeps me much engaged and will confine me more than usual this winter. In the event of his death this winter I hardly know what arrangements I could make.

Still I should be very anxious not to have business suffer by it. Unquestionably if I could buy out his interest at a fair valuation the business would suffer less. Still I should then want a partner — for our business is composed of two so totally different departments — the strictly business part of it — and the department which includes the looking out for good publications, examining manuscripts, arranging with authors and similar duties, that one individual would not do justice. I have often thought that it should be thought prudent for me to purchase Mr. Baker's interest &c. I should be glad to have my brother Edward whose business interest I consider unusually good come in and help me. Perhaps you will think me premature in these thoughts, but as my mind in the anticipation of my partner's decease is considerably agitated with anxiety as to what course it would be best for me to pursue I have been frank and expressed to you my feelings. Our business has been good this fall. We sold a little over $8000 cash at the Fall trade sales and our new publications are doing well.

1850–1859

1850

23 Nov.	Death of Isaac D. Baker
25 Nov.	Copyright date of Donald Grant Mitchell's *Reveries of a Bachelor: or A Book of the Heart,* published under the pseudonym "Ik. Marvel," one of the year's best-sellers

1851

1 Jan.	In consequence of the death of Baker, CS I assumes full responsibility for the firm; "Baker & Scribner" becomes "Charles Scribner & Co."
29 Nov.	Copyright date of Mitchell's *Dream Life: A Fable of the Seasons,* published under the pseudonym "Ik. Marvel"

1852

17 Apr.	Copyright date of Charles Loring Brace's *Hungary in 1851, With an Experience of the Austrian Police,* the first book by this American philanthropist who helped established the Children's Aid Society (1853)

1853

16 Nov.	Copyright date of Philip Schaff's first Scribner book, *History of the Apostolic Church, with a General Introduction to Church History*

1854

5 Dec.	Copyright date of *A Cyclopedia of Missions, Containing a Comprehensive View of Missionary Operations Throughout the World, With Geographical Descriptions and Accounts of the Social, Moral, and Religious Condition of the People* (approximately eight hundred pages, with maps) by Congregational clergyman Harvey Newcomb

1855

3 Dec.   Publication date of the first volume (of two) of Evert A. and George L. Duyckinck's *Cyclopædia of American Literature* (volume 2 was ready on 15 December)

1856

Feb.   Publication of *The Three Gardens: Eden, Gethsemane, and Paradise; or, Man's Ruin, Redemption, and Restoration* by Presbyterian clergyman William Adams, a founder and, later, president of Union Theological Seminary

Mar.   Impending sale of the Brick Church property forces Charles Scribner & Co. to relocate; the firm moves to 377-379 Broadway.

1857

12 Feb.   Copyright date of *Scampavias from Gibel Tarek to Stamboul* by the American naval officer and author Henry Augustus Wise, published under his pseudonym "Harry Gringo"

19 Dec.   CS I takes Charles Welford, son of a London bookseller, as a partner (their respective shares are 2/3 and 1/3) to establish a separate company, Scribner & Welford, for the importing of foreign books. Located in the Scribner bookstore in New York City, the company also established a presence in London when Welford moved there in 1864.

1858

24 Apr.   Publication date of Horace Bushnell's first Scribner book, *Sermons for the New Life*

May   Charles Scribner & Co. moves to the Brooks Building at 124 Grand Street (the corner of Broadway and Grand Street).

1 July   Copyright date of J. G. Holland's first Scribner book, *Titcomb's Letter's to Young People, Single and Married,* published under the pseudonym "Timothy Titcomb"

1 Oct.   Copyright date of Holland's *Bitter-Sweet: A Poem*

1859

Jan.   First issue of the first Scribner periodical, *The American Theological Review*

15 Oct.   Copyright date of Holland's *Gold-Foil, Hammered from Popular Proverbs,* published under the pseudonym of "Timothy Titcomb"

LETTER:
Letter by CS I to his father-in-law, John Insley Blair, 25 November 1850.

In this letter CS I announces the death of his business partner, Isaac D. Baker, and expresses hope to buy out Baker's interest in the firm. He also mentions, at the end, the recent baptism of his first child, John Blair Scribner, who, born the previous spring, was named for his grandfather.

Dear Father
You will not be surprised to hear of the death of Mr. Baker my Partner. He died on Saturday 23rd and was buried yesterday afternoon. During the last six weeks he was confined to his

room and most of the time to his bed and gradually failed, so that for the three or four days previous to his death we were constantly expecting it. He suffered I think much more than persons with his disease generally do. Indeed for more than two years previous to his death he was a great sufferer. He had full possession of his mind to the last and left his afflicted family satisfactory evidence that he died a Christian and has exchanged a state of much trial and daily suffering for one of eternal rest. This event leaves me alone in my business. During his lifetime his relations to the firm were not changed as his feeble health prevented him from personal attention to the matter and his friends naturally felt indisposed to act in the matter while he was living. His executor I presume is Mr. Miles, who furnished him with his capital and has always been a sincere and generous friend to him. He is a very conscientious and straight forward man and while he will properly look well for the interests of the estate, he will I am confident be disposed to act fairly. I have not seen him since Mr. Baker's death but shall probably see him this evening. As it would be very inconvenient for us just now to take an Inventory I presume it will be thought advisable to allow his interests to remain the same until the 1st Jan when we can close the concern without injury to the business. My idea is to purchase the stock in trade if I can do so to advantage and to let the other matters be wound up as fast as practicable. However I will write to you more fully about this matter again and shall wish to take your advice before acting. In the mean time you will be kind enough to give me the benefit of any suggestions you can make which would aid me in coming to a wise conclusion in the premises. Our business is in a prosperous and healthy condition and I am anxious that it should not suffer by the change. It is profitable now and properly managed can be made much more so. From the nature of it it will continue to expand and if under good control is capable of an increase both healthy and lucrative. If I can manage this matter so as not to be crippled by the withdrawal of Mr. Baker's interests, but can bear this without trespassing on our usual facilities I have no fear of the result.

We are all well at home. John was baptised yesterday and behaved like a man. You will be pleased to see how much he has improved. We hope to see you again soon. Kind regards to all

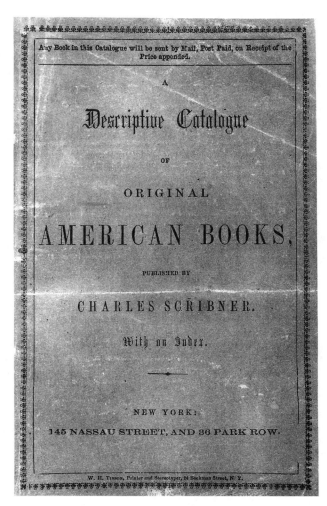

Cover of the 1855 book catalogue of Charles Scribner & Co.

friends. I have written in great haste and in the dark.

Yours affectionately
Charles Scribner

NOTICE:
Notice on front page of the *New-York Daily Tribune,* 1 January 1851.

THE CO-PARTNERSHIP heretofore existing under the firm of BAKER & SCRIBNER is this day dissolved, in consequence of the death of Mr. Isaac D. Baker. The Publishing and Bookselling business will hereafter be conducted by the subscriber, who will settle the business of the late firm.

Charles Scribner

LETTER:
Letter by CS I to Nathaniel West, 16 February 1853.

CS I confirms his publishing agreement with West (1794–1864), an Episcopal clergyman and author, for a work entitled A Complete Analysis of the Holy Bible, Containing the Whole of the New and Old Testaments. *His letter reveals the typical financial arrangements Scribner made with his authors, which were probably also typical of the publishing industry at the time. The major expense is the stereotyping of the work: the production costs must be recovered before any royalty can be paid. Published in a single volume of almost one thousand pages in October 1853, the book went through multiple editions.*

My Dear Sir

I will agree to publish the work you have submitted to me (The Analysis of the Bible) on the following terms. I will publish the work on my own responsibility and agree to stereotype it in the style you propose — and to advertise it thoroughly &c. &c., and will agree to give you ten per cent on the retail price of all copies sold or 50^{cts} per copy — but this copyright is not to be paid until I have reimbursed myself for the expenses of production (that is the money invested in the enterprise), and I will further agree to give you one dollar per copy on all copies which you may be able to dispose of at the retail price of $5 — that is you are to retain the one dollar and to hand over to me $4 and after the expenses are paid for say $1.20 per copy. 2nd If you will furnish to me the stereotype plates free of cost I will then agree to incur the other expenses of publication and will give you one dollar per copy on all copies sold, and two dollars per copy on all copies which you may be able to dispose of at retail price.

3^d If you furnish one half the cost of stereotype plates, I will give you 75^c per copy on all copies sold after deducting the cost of my half of stereotype plates. This you will perceive is equitable, as I would in addition be at the whole expense of manufacturing the Book, advertising &c.

Yours truly
C. Scribner

ADVERTISEMENT:
CS I's front-page ad in the *New-York Daily Tribune* for 16 January 1856.

This was the first such national work published in the United States. By April, six thousand sets had been sold.

AN IMPORTANT NATIONAL WORK. — SOLD ONLY BY SUBSCRIPTION. AGENTS WANTED to canvass New-York City and State.

CYCLOPÆDIA OF AMERICAN LITERATURE.

Embracing Personal and Critical Notices of Authors and Selections from their Writings, from the earliest period to the present day. By E. A. Duyckinck and G. L. Duyckinck, 2 vols., 8vo. With 225 portraits, 425 autographs and 75 views of Colleges, Libraries, and Residences of Authors, and elegant Steel Engravings of J. FENIMORE COOPER and BENJAMIN FRANKLIN. 2 vols., royal 8vo. Bound in fine English cloth. Price $7; half calf, neat library style, $10; full morocco extra and half extra, $16.

It includes Illustrations of the Pulpit, the Bar and other Professional Writers of the Political Oratory, the Educational Institutions and

THE GENERAL LITERATURE OF THE COUNTRY.

The Personal Biography is full and minute, and the Selections comprehend a large portion of the best Literature of America. The latter are made particularly with reference to their completeness and their permanent historical interest, and display every variety of talent from every portion of the country. In this respect the work (the contents of which will equal six ordinary octavo volumes) may be regarded as no inconsiderable

AMERICAN LIBRARY IN ITSELF.

CHARLES SCRIBNER, No. 145 Nassau-st., New-York.

LETTER:
Letter from Washington Irving to CS I, 22 January 1856, written from "Sunnyside," his home near Tarrytown, on the Hudson River.

Praise from the first American man of letters for his complimentary copy of the Cyclopædia of American Literature *(not "of History" as he mistakenly calls it). The work's entry for Irving runs more than twelve pages.*

To Charles Scribner Esq.
Dear Sir

I should have thanked you earlier for the copy of the Cyclopedia of American History which you have had the kindness to send here, but it has remained in town in the hands of my nephew, so that I have but recently received it.

It would be difficult to speak too highly of the value to the student of American Literature of a work which brings together in two ample volumes so much rare and scattered information concerning the authors of our country, and makes him, in one comprehensive glance to grasp the degree and forms of her mental progress and development.

The work is executed with marked ability, and evinces the fine culture, critical insight and amiable spirit for which the Messrs. Duyckincks are so favorably known. I commend it most heartily to the reading public for I consider it, not merely a desideratum, but in some sort a <u>necessity</u>, to every well furnished American library.

> Very respectfully
> Your obliged & Hb Serv
> Washington Irving

LETTER:
Letter by CS I to his father-in-law, John Insley Blair, 7 November 1857.

In this important letter, demonstrating CS I's business acumen, he asks Blair for help in order to join Charles Welford in acquiring the imported stock of Bangs & Co., which was primarily a New York book auction house. Most of the British publishers consigned their books to Bangs; but in this year of the Panic, Bangs wanted to get out of the importing business and concentrate on its auctioneering. Welford ran the importing part of the firm and shared in its profits.

Dear Father

I find this morning that the <u>English business</u> of which I have spoken to you has assumed such a shape that it is necessary that I should know my ability before I make a further move. I regret that I have not an opportunity now of talking with you on the subject but will briefly in this letter lay the matter before you.

The business of which I speak is entirely a <u>commission business</u>. The leading English Publishers have consigned to Messrs. Bangs & Co. their publications for sale — Messrs. B & Co. paying simply the duties and making no advances but settling semi annually for the amt of the sales — giving themselves time to be placed in funds by receipts from their sales here — which have been in the regular course of trade and not by auction. The business began in a small way 3 or 4 years since and has increased rapidly, last year's sale amounting to 97000 and the profits net about $10000, leaving a good margin for expenses, losses &c. The business here has been conducted by Mr. Welford who is an expert in such matters — Messrs. Bangs simply lending the responsibility of their house. Now Messrs. Bangs & Co. have failed and though desirous of holding on to the business are not able to retain it. Mr. Welford therefore who received a share of the profits is seeking a responsible house to take hold of it in connection with himself. Some time since he made application to me and I have <u>carefully looked into the matter</u>. I consider it <u>very desirable</u> if I can meet the terms. It could be added to my present business with very little increase of expense so that the expenses being less than under the former connection the profits would be proportionately increased. Mr. Welford would manage it as heretofore except the financial part — the addition of a Porter would be all that I would need. It would I think greatly help my business in various ways. I would come in contact with the very same parties with whom I am now dealing and of whose responsibility I am acquainted so that in that respect it would be no experiment. No advances would be required to the English consignors. The books are <u>very</u> saleable and their sale I think could be materially increased as the business would do better in my hands than with Messrs. Bangs & Co. who were unpopular and not in constant intercourse with the trade as I am. The risk of doing the business is less than that of my present business — as there is no risk of publishing — the stock being held on commission and settled for only as sold. I have advised with two or three of my friends of judgement in the trade and they regard it as an unusually promising opening — one which in ordinary times would not occur. I am frank to say that I have never since I have been in business seen so good an opportunity of increasing my business legitimately with so little risk. Now I do not feel very ambitious to do a large business and if I was doing well I would not strain myself for the sake of making money — but the fact is the publishing business for the last two years has been poor and is not promising now — and as our expenses are heavy I feel the importance of increasing my business if I can do so legitimately, without too great risk. The opportunity now offered seems to be just what I want if I can avail myself of it and therefore I am very anxious to do so. So much in general.

Now for the terms. <u>1</u>. Messrs. Bangs & Co. have advanced about $8000 for duties insurance &c. on the stock which they now hold amounting to about $80,000. The amt advanced is a <u>lien</u> on the stock and must therefore be paid to them if a new party takes the business. It would however be a perfectly safe investment as under any circumstances stock for many times the amt would be held as security for it. Though Messrs. Bangs & Co. are unwilling to give up the business still their necessities are such that I have no doubt they would relinquish it if they could get soon the monies advanced.

<u>2</u>. An arrangement would be made with Mr. Welford to conduct the business as heretofore receiving a per centage of the profits.

<u>3</u>. An arrangement would have to be made with reference to the sales made since 1st July last — settlement having been made with the English houses up to that time. I would not propose to assume these debts but to turn over the proceeds of the sales until the amt due was paid. I would therefore propose to take no risk in the premises but take the business clean 1st Nov.

4th. I would make such an arrangement for future sales as would give me ample time to be placed in funds by receipts from the sales before settling with English houses.

5th. Mr. Low is now in town with full authority from the parties interested to make all the necessary arrangements. He came over in the Persia and is anxious to return as soon as he can place the business on a firm footing.

6th. To do the business comfortably it would be necessary to raise $10000 — including the amt to be paid to Bangs & Co. Now I do not propose that you loan me the amt. I am already indebted to you for too many favours but it has occurred to me that I can raise it in this way. I have reason to believe that I can get the money from the Park Bank — who will loan the amt for one year. We hold your note for $12000 in favour of Mother. If instead of the present shape you could with Mother's consent give me notes to the amt of $10000 at 90 days at different dates (the whole would not be needed now) and I can arrange with the Bank to renew them so as to loan the money for one year I should be able in that time to dispose of some matters to replace the amt — which I could not do now without heavy sacrifice. Of course I would not entertain the idea of your taking up the notes at maturity or even at the ex-

piration of the year. If you were not giving out your paper for any additional amt and were secured against the liability of taking the notes up at maturity it has occurred to me that under the circumstances you would consent to the arrangement. Of course everything would depend on the arrangement I could make with the Bank. The understanding <u>would be explicit</u> — the necessary facts being stated.

I have had this matter under consideration for some days and it is necessary now to come to a decision. I run the risk every day of losing the opportunity. If I can make the arrangements and terms proposed my mind is clear as to the whole matter. I feel the necessity of doing something to increase my business and I do not see how I can do better. I should say that I owe very little besides what I owe you and the Belvidere Bank and besides the securities which I hold Rail Road Bonds &c my stock of the stereotype plates books &c I think at a low valuation which is less than one half cost are worth $50000 — not including bills receivable & book accounts.

Please give this immediate consideration and advise me if possible by Tuesday's mail as I must come to a decision without delay.

Yours affectionately
Charles Scribner

I should add that the drawbacks which are allowed the consignors pay the freights on the other side so that there is no money to be paid out here for freights — and that the cash sales have always more than paid the duties and expenses.

Under worse times the business would more than pay the expenses & interest on the advance now made.

CS I got the help he needed and took control of the imported stock of Bangs & Co. With Charles Welford as partner, Scribner formed his own importation firm, Scribner & Welford, one month later, and it soon developed into one of the largest of its kind in the country.

ARTICLE:
"Scribner & Welford," *The American Bookseller*, 21, no. 7 (1 April 1887): 214–215 — Number 35 in its Contributions to Trade History series.

Scribner & Welford was subsumed under the name of "Charles Scribner's Sons" on 31 January

1891. Thereafter, all publishing and importing business was conducted under the one name.

The firm of Scribner & Welford was organized in the year 1857 as exclusively an importing house. Mr. Welford, who died May 18, 1885, was the son of a London bookseller, and came to this city with his parents when he was eighteen years of age. He commenced his business career as a clerk in D. Appleton & Co.'s publishing house; remained in that position for three years, and then went into business on his own account as junior member of the firm of Bartlett & Welford, importers of books. In 1852 this firm was dissolved, and Mr. Welford established a connection with Bangs, Brothers & Co., the auctioneers, visiting England periodically during the year and purchasing large invoices of books, which the firm put on the New York market. This arrangement continued until 1857, when the commercial crisis of that year obliged Bangs Brothers & Co. to suspend payment. Mr. Welford found himself with a large stock of books on hand, upon which advances had been made, and his situation was a perilous one. In this exigency he went to Mr. Charles Scribner, with whom he was on intimate friendly terms, and a business arrangement was made between them. Mr. Scribner furnished the necessary amount for repaying the advances made upon the stock, a considerable sum for those days, and the new firm of Scribner & Welford continued the business of importing books on their own account, which they disposed of at wholesale and retail in the usual way, Mr. Scribner still carrying on his business as a publisher in his own name.

The firm did a prosperous business for seven years, and at the end of that time its operation had increased to such dimensions that Mr. Welford removed to London to superintend the purchasing and resided in England till his death, although he made frequent visits to this country. Upon the death of Mr. Charles Scribner, in 1871, his partner in the publishing business, Andrew C. Armstrong, entered the firm, which became Scribner, Welford & Armstrong. Seven years afterward, J. Blair Scribner bought out Mr. Armstrong's interest, and the firm again became Scribner & Welford, as it has since remained, the partners being, since Mr. Welford's death, Mr. Charles and Mr. Arthur H. Scribner.

Apart from his commercial knowledge of books, Mr. Welford was a man of pronounced literary tastes, and was familiar not merely with titles and volumes, but with their contents. He pos-

Charles Welford (d. 1885), English partner in Scribner & Welford, the early importing branch of Scribners

sessed a rare knowledge of old books, and his judgment as a bibliographer, or rather bibliophile, was supplemented by his knowledge of money values in the American and English markets. He was also a writer; and readers of *Scribner's Monthly* will remember sketches from his pen that were published some years ago.

Since Mr. Welford's death the house has been represented in London by Mr. L. W. Bangs, who for some time previous was associated with Mr. Welford there, and who had been with the firm from his boyhood. Mr. Bangs has an office with Messrs. Sampson, Low, Marston & Co. He is thoroughly acquainted with the wants of the New York market, and is constantly on the lookout for rarities in the different departments of literature, and his facilities for obtaining them are excellent.

Important changes have been made in the conduct of the business since the formation of the firm of Scribner & Welford. At first a large proportion of the books they placed on the New York market were received on consignment, while at present the stock they handle is purchased outright. By their early enterprises they created an American market for productions of many English firms, such as Macmillan, Ward, Locke & Co., F. Warne & Co., and others, and the success they had in disposing of their various lines bore no small share in the inducement which led these English houses to establish branches here. They made the market for the extensive and valuable series of *Bohn's Libraries,* of which 100,000 volumes are annually sold in the United States and the United Kingdom. They have always maintained most intimate and cordial relations with all the leading English houses, so that the choicest productions of the London and Edinburgh publishers find their way as fast as they leave the press to the New York head-quarters of the firm. Among their importations are always many novelties — indeed, in most cases, as in that of the quaint issues of Field & Tuer. Their imprint is at once put on the book, and it is issued in New York simultaneously with the publication in England. As regards the classes of books that Scribner & Welford have handled, changes likewise have occurred. In the beginning they did a large business in cheap juveniles, red-line poets, and the like, which they have now abandoned to other houses which make a specialty of these lines. The same may be said of the medical and scientific works they used to import. These they now leave to the firms who deal in these, not in general literature. They have always imported books of the best standard character, such as Rawlinson's *Monarchies,* Wilkinson's *Egypt,* Thiers' *French Revolution,* Ferguson's *Architecture,* and art books such as Ruskin's, the magnificently illustrated *Florence,* and others. At present the tendency of the American purchaser is for biography, belles-lettres, history, and theology. In the former class, they import the valuable series of memoirs by the Duchess d'Abrantes and Bourrienne, of the Napoleon era; the memoirs of Wraxall, Selwyn, and Beau Brummell, Miss Pardoe's *Court of Louis XIV,* Lady Jackson's volumes on the court life of France in the old regime; and, in English history of the seventeenth century, the memoirs of *Lord Herbert, Colonel Hutchinson,* and Cavendish *Duke of Newcastle.* In fact, every new English book of real value is placed on the market here by them almost contemporaneously with the foreign publication. A large part of their business is that of taking editions for this country, which bear their imprint as publishers, and in this line they have done more in the last year than ever before. They can make no use of the cheap editions; they must have fine standard editions, all in fine bindings — in fact, only the best editions and the best bindings. They have thus imported editions of Macaulay, Grote, Lamb, Mrs. Jameson, Dickens, Thackeray, De Quincey, and all leading authors. If, however, we were to select any special line by

which to characterize this branch of their business, it would be that of political and social memoirs, French and English. The catalogue of these importations has grown to a thick pamphlet of nearly a hundred pages, in which can be found the title of nearly every desirable edition of almost every popular or standard English work published within the last hundred years.

LETTER:
Letter by CS I to his father-in-law, John Insley Blair, 7 May 1858.

While writing to mention the move of his retail bookstore and publishing business to 124 Grand Street, CS I takes the opportunity to give Blair a lengthy lecture (here, greatly excerpted) on becoming a Christian.

Dear Father

The Eggs and Butter have come safely to hand and we thank you for them. You will be pleased to hear that we finish moving to-day the entire English Stock of Messrs. Bangs. We have had three men there for nearly three weeks constantly packing and then in the new store unpacking and arranging. I thought I had a pretty accurate idea of the amt of the stock but it far exceeds the estimates of all of us — filling nearly seven hundred boxes. It looks well in the new store and we can certainly increase the sales by being able to display it to advantage. We shall commence moving our own stock on Monday & in two or three days get all in. . . .

I cannot close Father without thanking you for your kindness to me and expressing my earnest solicitude for your spiritual welfare. I have long desired and prayed that you might be a Christian. It is with great diffidence and respect that I address one to whom I am accustomed to look up for counsel and aid and yet I cannot withhold any longer expressing my anxiety for the salvation of your soul. God has greatly blessed you but oh what will it profit a man though he were to gain the whole world and lose his own Soul? . . .

Yours affectionately
Charles Scribner

NOTICE:
"Notice," *The American Theological Review,* 1, no.1 (January 1859), unnumbered first page.

In this inaugural announcement the scope and purpose of the quarterly journal are outlined: to promote unity between Congregationalism and Presbyterianism; to devote itself to theology in its "broad acceptation," which includes philosophy, science, and literature "as these bear upon the interests of Christianity"; and to "counteract" the bad influences of "a subtle infidelity" that is infiltrating current literature and philosophy both at home and abroad.

The present number of this Review was prepared by a Committee of the Company that owns it, and before the appointment of the Editors who are to conduct it in future. In connection with the choice of its editors, a change was made in the proposed title, — from "Puritan Review" to "American Theological Review." Its object remains the same; but its scope and sphere have been enlarged by a union between Boston and New York. Neither in New York or Boston is there a quarterly journal, meeting the wants of those Churches that stand on the common doctrinal basis of Congregationalism and Presbyterianism contained in the Westminster Assembly's Shorter Catechism. So far as relates to doctrine, the Westminster Confession, and the kindred Savoy Confession, were early received by New England Synods (1648 and 1680). Ecclesiastical controversies between Presbyterians and Congregationalists do not come within the province of this Review. Its aim will rather be to revive and promote unity in the faith, and union in all practicable matters.

By such union and co-operation we are placed in a condition to issue a Review of the highest character, with an ample pecuniary basis. It will be devoted to Theology in its broad acceptation; though philosophy, science, and general literature will be included, so far as these bear upon the interests of Christianity. One of our leading objects will be to counteract the influence of a subtle infidelity, which has penetrated so much of the philosophy and literature of our own country and England, as well as Germany. Yet, in doing this, we shall ever strive to show the harmony of true philosophy with a vital faith. Another object will be to discuss and expose erroneous theological views, especially such as make natural ethics the test of revealed truth. The history of theology in our own country will receive particular attention; for it is one of cherished desires to rescue the memory of our fathers from forgetfulness and misrepresentation.

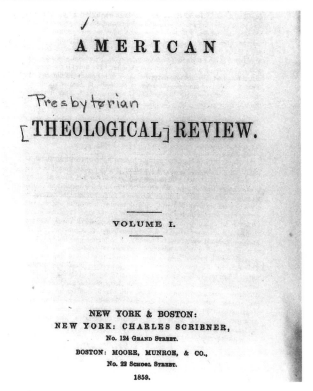

Title page in the first volume of The American Theological Review, *the first periodical published by Scribners (courtesy of the Library of the Princeton Theological Seminary)*

In every number of the Review it is our design to have at least one article in each of the four main departments of theology, — the exegetical, doctrinal, historical, and practical. Each number will also contain a summary of the current history of the church, and a classified list of the most recent publications, at home and abroad. By insisting upon short articles, we hope to secure a sufficient variety to meet the wants, not only of ministers, but also of laymen interested in the great religious questions of the times, and desirous of promoting a sound scriptural faith.

Some of these aims were pursued more directly in the two Scribner periodicals born in the 1860s: The Book Buyer which reviewed "recent publications, at home and abroad" and Hours at Home, subtitled "A Popular Monthly Devoted to Religious and Useful Literature." The American Theological Review underwent a number of transformations in its first decade. It merged with the Presbyterian Quarterly Review in 1863 and became The American Presbyterian and Theological Review, edited by J. M. Sherwood at 5 Beekman

Street; in 1869 it became The American Presbyterian Review, *still edited by Sherwood but published at 654 Broadway — as the title page stated, "at the Book Store of Messrs. Charles Scribner & Co." After 1871 it merged with the* Princeton Review *to form the* Presbyterian Quarterly and Princeton Review, *and was located on Nassau Street. By then, Scribners had abandoned its association and had begun its own major periodical,* Scribner's Monthly.

1860–1869

1860

12 Apr. Copyright date of *Poems, Lyrical and Idyllic* by Edward Clarence Stedman, the first book by this American poet, essayist, and literary critic

1861 Publication of *Tropical Fibres: Their Production and Economic Extraction* by E. G. Squier, American archaeologist and diplomat, considered the leading authority on Central America at the time

1862 Publication of S. A. Felter's *The Analysis of Written Arithmetic. Book First, Being an Elementary Manual Designed for Public Schools, and Containing Mental, Slate, and Blackboard Exercises,* the beginning of his popular textbooks

15 Oct. Copyright date of E. A. Sheldon's *A Manual of Elementary Instruction for the Use of Public and Private Schools and Normal Classes, Containing a Graduated Course of Object Lessons for Training the Senses and Developing the Faculties of Children,* the beginning of his popular textbooks

1863

Feb. Publication of *Political Fallacies: An Examination of the False Assumptions, and Refutation of the Sophistical Reasonings, Which Have Brought on This Civil War* by George Junkin, first president of Lafayette College

1864 Andrew C. Armstrong becomes a partner of the firm.

Charles Welford moves to London to superintend Scribner & Welford's purchases of foreign books.

25 Nov. Copyright date of volume one (*The Gospel According to Matthew*) of the colossal translating and publishing project, edited by Philip Schaff, of Johann Peter Lange's *A Commentary of the Holy Scriptures: Critical, Doctrinal, and Homiletical* — ultimately to reach twenty-five volumes by 1880

1865 Arthur J. Peabody, nephew of philanthropist George Peabody, joins the firm.

May First issue of the Scribner periodical *Hours at Home: A Popular Magazine of Religious and Useful Literature,* edited by J. M. Sherwood

Sept. Publication of Sanborn Tenney's *Natural History: A Manual of Zoology for Schools, Colleges, and the General Reader* (with more than five hundred illustrations), the beginning of his popular textbooks

1866

4 Apr.   CS I and Andrew C. Armstrong sign a lease for the first floor and basement of 654 Broadway, which will be their location for nine years (through 1 May 1875).

12 June   Publication date of Arnold Guyot's first Scribner book, *Primary; or, Introduction to the Study of Geography* (his maps had already been published by Scribners for several years), the beginning of his popular textbooks

1867

27 Apr.   Copyright date of *Public Debt of the United States: Its Organization, Its Liquidation, Administration of the Treasury, The Financial System* by American abolitionist and banker James Sloan Gibbons, author of the famous Civil War song, "We Are Coming, Father Abraham"

1 Aug.   Edward Seymour, a *New York Times* editor and journalist, joins the firm.

15 Oct.   First issue of the Scribner periodical *The Book Buyer: A Summary of American & Foreign Literature*

1868

13 July   CS I, Armstrong, and Peabody sign a lease for the second, third, fourth, and fifth stories (i.e., the rest of the building) of 654 Broadway (through 1 May 1875).

12 Sept.   Copyright date of J. G. Holland's *Kathrina: Her Life and Mine in a Poem*

20 Sept.   Publication date of Le Roy C. Cooley's first Scribner book, *A Text Book of Natural Philosophy: An Accurate, Modern, and Systematic Explanation of the Elementary Principles of the Science,* the beginning of his popular textbooks

1869

Mar.   J. Blair Scribner, oldest son of CS I, begins work in the publishing firm.

6 Mar.   Publication date of the first volumes in the "Illustrated Library of Wonders" series: F. Marion's *The Wonders of Optics,* translated from the French and edited by Charles W. Quin, and W. de Fonvielle's *Thunder and Lightning,* translated from the French and edited by T. L. Phipson

3 Apr.   CS I, Armstrong, and Peabody sublet the third story of 654 Broadway to be used as a "Velocipede Hall" — for the exhibition, exercise, and sale of velocipedes — for a term of one year. These early bicycles were probably models that had iron-rimmed wooden wheels and the front wheel larger than the rear.

RELATED LETTERS:
Letter by CS I to his father-in-law, John Insley Blair, 21 August 1861.

CS I asks for financial help to carry the business through the difficult times brought on by the Civil War.

Dear Father

    We shall have to raise some money to carry us through these times and I do not know that I can go elsewhere than to you unless we make ruinous sacrifices. I have been looking over the matters and find that after allowing for available receipts we shall need $12000 to carry us through

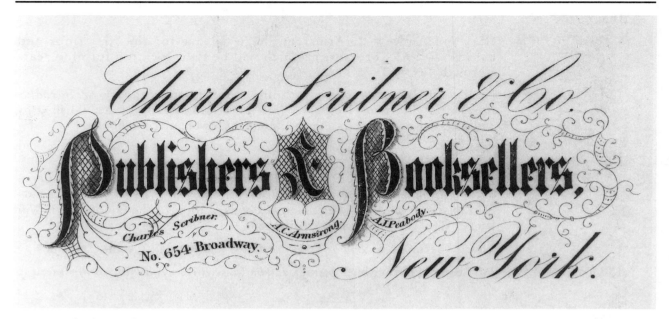

Charles Scribner & Co's 1860s logo giving the new address and the names of the current partners

the next 6 ms. . . . Many of the leading houses in the trade have gone overboard and those who live through this crisis will have all the business to be done. Of course I feel very anxious to get through, as it would take years and considerable money to recover my position if I lose it now. Our English business in good times ought to be worth $5000 per year after deducting expenses, and Mr. Welford's share, and our publishing business certainly more. Our connections with authors and the literary world and our position in the trade are such, that I see nothing in the way of our doing well if we can get through. Our business will I think amt to little until we have peace, but I think we have reason to hope that in 6 ms our troubles will be settled. . . .

> Yours truly
> Charles Scribner

P.S. There are some things which I want to say to you which I cannot in this letter as Edward would see it — but I will write to you confidentially to-morrow. . . .

This is the confidential letter to his father-in-law, dated 23 August 1861, that CS I promised in his last. He complains of his brother Edward, who has been working with him for almost ten years. CS I would rather work for Blair and reduce his debts than to continue to borrow from him with no prospect of repayment, but he believes the publishing firm has a real future.

Dear Father

I wrote to you yesterday as to our financial necessities. I do not know that I have any thing more to say on that point as I advised you fully. It was with extreme reluctance that I made another application to you, and nothing but absolute necessity compelled me to do so. The almost total suspension of our business for nearly a year — ever since the election of Lincoln and the secession of South Carolina — our heavy losses — and the necessity of taking up accommodative paper in consequence of the failure of others — all coming at this time, when it is impossible to realise from securities without heavy losses are matters which we could hardly have foreseen, and provided for. If business had continued as usual we should have had no trouble, though as I have before advised I have been dissatisfied with our way of doing business. I refer to our exchanging notes for mutual accommodation — one of the principal causes of our present embarrassment — also to our holding on to securities which if sold would have cancelled outside indebtedness. The result is that when a crisis like this comes, our own notes are out and must be paid in full — our securities are depreciated, and cannot be sold without serious loss, and we are exposed to the double risk of having to take up as it regards accommodation paper both sides of the Bill book — that is paper which we have borrowed and used for our own benefit, and our own paper which we have loaned and which has been discounted for the benefit of others as in the case of Mr. Orvis. This is all wrong. I determined long since to put a stop to it — and would have done so before this but you know the times have been such ever since 1857 that it has been impossible to sell the securities we held without considerable sacrifice. Were it not therefore that I am obliged again to apply to you for assistance I would not so much regret our present troubles, for they may be the means of getting my business in better shape. And it is as to this matter I wish to advise with you confidentially. If you are willing to aid us I wish you would do it on the conditions, that we keep out of all outside speculations or investments, either as individuals or as a firm, & that we abandon the policy of borrowing or lending notes. This you have already enforced in your letter of some time since, and what you said was of great service, and put a stop to such proceedings. I wish you would also insist on our having all our business matters kept in proper shape, and every thing done on correct business principles. Let me suggest to you to say somewhat as follows. That you do not know precisely what relatives Edward and myself sustain, but the concern is owing you so much money, that you must insist on matters as between us being kept properly — duly recorded in our books, and not left at loose ends as is too often the case when brothers are in business together — that you fear that I am too much disposed to lean on Edward but that I ought to attend to these things myself — that in all your transactions with relatives you have observed always this rule, and that it is the only correct way of doing business. I wish you would be explicit and yet guarded in what you say on this point, for I have been urging on Edward that he must keep our books in better shape, and have them balanced regularly every year, and our individual accounts properly adjusted, and I would not have him suspect that I have advised with you about the matter. I wish you would also urge our adopting the policy of rendering the account of our indebtedness to you and your Bank. You might say that ever since you commenced helping me the amt has been constantly increasing, and that now it had reached such a sum that rather than increase it permanently, you would prefer that I would wind up my business, as you could give me a situation where I could get a salary, or help me in some other way without incurring so much risk as at present. I must however frankly say, that I fear it will be difficult for us to adopt such a course, for the nature of our business is to

absorb capital in stock, which though valuable in the ordinary way of business, is not available as active capital or such as we can realise on in such times as these — so that we really need more bank accommodation than an ordinary business would. And yet our true policy is by economy in expenses, to endeavour gradually to cut down our accommodation with you. If we reduce it 20 per ct per year it could enable us in 5 years to cancel the whole — 5 per ct on each renewal of 3 ms could do it — and in ordinary times we ought to be able to do this comfortably. I would be a thousand times happier to live in the most horrible circumstances, and be gradually liquidating the amt we owe you, than to be situated as I am, and I want Edward to feel so too. These things which I wish you to say for Edward's ear are all right, and I have frequently urged them on him. Our relations with you are such now that you have the power and the right to insist on them. I think I told you that Edward has some property and matters outside of the business. I have just had a plain talk with him on this subject, and have insisted on his closing up all his outside business, and hereafter breaking out of such transactions which he has promised to do. His wife had a little property, and Edward's interest in my Father's estate, on account of his old business not being settled, was left to his wife. This amt I feel unwilling he should jeopardise in our business, as he has a large family and is liable at any moment to be taken away and with the amt of his life insurance ($5000) it would keep them from suffering. But whatever else he has, I have told him he ought to put in the concern which he seems quite willing to do. The $3500 Warren RR Bonds, and the $3000 Lackawanna & Bloomington Bonds belong to him, and have never before been used in our business. As soon as he can sell the real estate which he has, (amt about $6000) which he can readily do when times improve, he proposes to redeem these Bonds which would not realise their par value, and are a good investment for his family, and to give you what would be necessary, with the proceeeds of the D L & W RR Stock to cancel the amt called for ($12000).

As regards Edward's habits you know enough. Of course this is a constant cause of anxiety to me, but he is my own brother, — he has a large and interesting family. Providence has placed him in business connection with me. I believe that my influence with him is good, and I feel it to be my duty to do all I can to save him even though at much personal sacrifice. He is often for

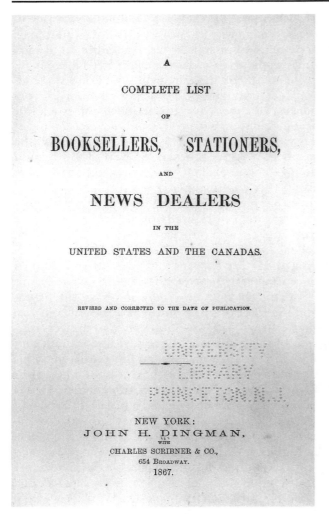

A

COMPLETE LIST

OF

BOOKSELLERS, STATIONERS,

AND

NEWS DEALERS

IN THE

UNITED STATES AND THE CANADAS.

REVISED AND CORRECTED TO THE DATE OF PUBLICATION.

UNIVERSITY
LIBRARY
PRINCETON,N.J.

NEW YORK:
JOHN H. DINGMAN,
WITH
CHARLES SCRIBNER & CO.,
654 BROADWAY.
1867.

Title page in the first booksellers directory (1867) published in the United States. John H. Dingman, a longtime Scribners employee, compiled several more editions.

up our business. I think I am in many respects better qualified for it than any other. I have acquired experience which ought to be of service to me hereafter and if we can get through this war without being used up the prospect for us is I think certainly good.

Yours affectionately
Charles Scribner

Blair once again helped out, and the financial crisis was averted even though the war lasted more than six months. This was a turning point in the history of the publishing firm, for CS I's predictions came true: having survived the Civil War, his business enjoyed much greater opportunity in the years following it. His concern for his brother's health was also justified. Edward died at the age of fifty on 7 January 1864, leaving behind a widow and seven children.

ARTICLE:
Philip Schaff, "Lange's Theological and Homiletical Commentary of the New Testament," *The Evangelical Review*, 15 (1864): 298–300.

Schaff outlines the scope, intent, and plan of his American edition of Lange's Commentary, *which is to be published by Scribners over several years.*

It is proposed to issue an American Edition of the *Biblework, or Theological and Homiletical Commentary, on the Bible,* now in course of preparation by the Rev. Prof. John P. Lange, D.D., of the University of Bonn, in connection with a number of distinguished divines and pulpit orators of Europe. The New Testament is nearly complete with the exception of the Romans and Revelation, and the Old Testament will follow in due time. But the proposed English edition will for the present only embrace the New Testament.

The work of Dr. Lange and his co-laborers was hailed at the appearance of the first volume as a great desideratum, no commentary of this kind having been attempted since Dr. Starke's voluminous *Synopsis Bibliothecæ Exegeticæ,* of 1740, and has already met with unusual success, both in Europe and America. The plan is admirable, and the execution exhibits not only a high order of talent, but in some parts even rare genius and an overflowing wealth of ideas. The work embraces a new and accurate version of the text with an ample introduction and analysis, and a three-fold

months perfectly correct in his habits, and I have hopes that he will yet come out right. I told him a day or two since that you had noticed that his appearance indicated bad habits, and unless there was a change you would lose confidence in his management, and I think this will be a check on him. At any rate he has arrived at such an age that he must reform soon or he cannot live long as I have often warned him — so that there is nothing for me to do but to get along the best I can with him. I believe he is perfectly honest — he has considerable business experience and his judgment is generally good. Besides my health is such that I must have some one in his department to relieve me.

I will only add that I hope you will see your way clear to help us. I have laboured hard to build

commentary under three distinct heads, as follows:

I. *Exegetical and Critical Notes,* which present the most valuable results of ancient and modern investigations of Biblical scholars;

II. *Dogmatical and Ethical Ideas;* or the leading theological and religious thoughts and reflections contained in, or suggested by, the text.

III. *Homiletical and Practical Suggestions;* with a rich variety of themes and parts for sermons, and useful practical hints, well calculated, not by any means to supersede, but to stimulate the labor of preparation for the pulpit, and to open the inexhaustible wealth of the Bible for edification.

The work, though mainly designed for ministers, is free from the pedantry of learning and accessible to educated laymen. Its tone and spirit is sound, truly Christian, evangelical and catholic. We have heard but one voice of commendation in its favor, from eminent divines of various denominations, who are acquainted with it. Of all larger commentaries, it bids fair to become, if it is not already the most useful and popular among ministers, theological students and such laymen who have taste and leisure for a more extended study of the word of God. It is more particularly the *Pastor's Commentary;* it forms almost an exegetical library in itself and must take rank among those books which are constantly consulted as safe guides and intimate friends.

The English translation will aim to be a faithful and free re-production of the German original in its integrity, with such occasional addition in brackets, as might be of special use to the American reader. The Edinburgh translation embraces only the first three Gospels and will not be carried on any further. It will be used as a basis, but subjected to a thorough revision, word for word, according to the latest edition of the original. The typographical arrangement will be altogether different, far more convenient and economical and adapted, as much as possible, to the original.

The American Editor, an intimate personal friend of Dr. Lange, has on consultation with him and with his full approbation, consented to superintend the preparation and publication of the American edition. He has already prospectively secured the co-operation of a number of distinguished divines of the leading evangelical denominations of the land, each of whom will be responsible for the particular portion of the work assigned to him. It is in no sense a sectarian, but a

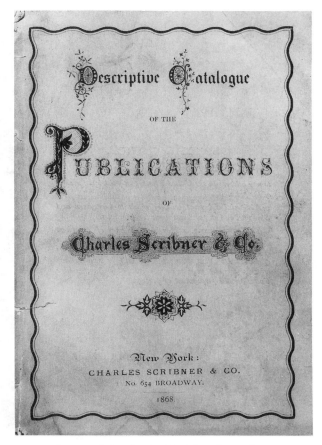

Cover of the firm's 1868 book catalogue

truly evangelical catholic commentary, and in this spirit and aim, will be prepared for the benefit of the American public.

The several books of the New Testament will be issued and sold separately. The first volume, containing the general introduction to the Bible, and the Commentary on the Gospel of Matthew, prepared by the Editor, will appear early this year. The whole New Testament, will embrace from eight to ten volumes and will be furnished in three or four years. Subscribers for the complete work will receive the several parts as they appear, by mail or express, free of expense. But each volume will also be sold separately.

The Evangelical Lutheran Church of America will be well represented in this noble and eminently useful literary enterprise, by the Rev. Prof. Dr. Charles F. Schaeffer, and the Rev. Dr. Charles P. Krauth, Jr., who have already an established reputation, as thorough Biblical and Anglo-German scholars and successful translators. Dr. Schaeffer is busily at work on Lechler and Gerok's

A

COMMENTARY

ON THE

HOLY SCRIPTURES:

CRITICAL, DOCTRINAL, AND HOMILETICAL,

WITH SPECIAL REFERENCE TO MINISTERS AND STUDENTS.

BY

JOHN PETER LANGE, D.D.

IN CONNECTION WITH A NUMBER OF EMINENT EUROPEAN DIVINES.

TRANSLATED FROM THE GERMAN, AND EDITED, WITH ADDITIONS ORIGINAL
AND SELECTED,

By PHILIP SCHAFF, D.D.

IN CONNECTION WITH AMERICAN DIVINES OF VARIOUS EVANGELICAL DENOMINATIONS.

VOL. I. OF THE NEW TESTAMENT: CONTAINING A GENERAL INTRODUCTION,
AND THE GOSPEL ACCORDING TO MATTHEW.

NEW YORK:
CHARLES SCRIBNER, 124 GRAND STREET.
1865.

THE

GOSPEL

ACCORDING TO

MATTHEW,

TOGETHER WITH A GENERAL THEOLOGICAL, AND HOMILETICAL
INTRODUCTION TO THE NEW TESTAMENT.

BY

JOHN PETER LANGE, D.D.

PROFESSOR OF THEOLOGY AT THE UNIVERSITY OF BONN.

TRANSLATED FROM THE THIRD GERMAN EDITION, WITH ADDITIONS
ORIGINAL AND SELECTED,

By PHILIP SCHAFF, D.D.

NEW YORK:
CHARLES SCRIBNER, 124 GRAND STREET.
1865.

Series title page and title page for volume one of the firm's first mammoth publishing project, referred to as Lange's Commentary. Probably the largest undertaking entered upon up to that time by an American publisher, the series totaled twenty-five volumes, containing 15,000 closely-printed pages of two columns, by its conclusion in 1880. In his preface to this volume, dated 31 October 1864, the series editor, Philip Schaff, provides a brief background to the project:

A work of such sterling value cannot be long confined to the land of its birth. America, as it is made up of descendants from all countries, nations, and churches of Europe (e pluribus unum), is set upon appropriating all important literary treasures of the old world, especially those which promise to promote the moral and religious welfare of the race.

Soon after the appearance of the first volume of Dr. Lange's Commentary, I formed, at the solicitation of a few esteemed friends, and with the full consent of Dr. Lange himself, an association for an American edition, and in September, 1860, I made the necessary arrangements with my friend, Mr. Charles Scribner, as publisher. The secession of the slave States, and the consequent outbreak of the civil war in 1861, paralyzed the book trade, and indefinitely suspended the enterprise. But in 1863 it was resumed at the suggestion of the publisher, and with the consent of Mr. T. Clark, of Edinburgh, who in the mean time (since 1861) had commenced to publish translations of parts of Lange's Commentary in his "Foreign Theological Library." I moved to New York for the purpose of devoting myself more fully to this work amid the literary facilities of the city, completed the first volume, and made arrangements with leading Biblical and German scholars of different evangelical denominations for the translation of the other volumes.

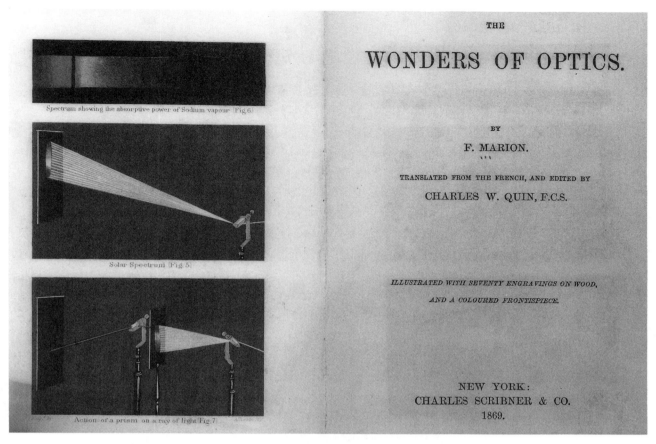

Spectrum showing the absorptive power of Sodium vapour [Fig.6]

Solar Spectrum [Fig.5]

Action of a prism on a ray of light [Fig.7]

THE

WONDERS OF OPTICS.

BY

F. MARION.

TRANSLATED FROM THE FRENCH, AND EDITED BY

CHARLES W. QUIN, F.C.S.

ILLUSTRATED WITH SEVENTY ENGRAVINGS ON WOOD,

AND A COLOURED FRONTISPIECE.

NEW YORK:
CHARLES SCRIBNER & CO.
1869.

Frontispiece and title page for the first volume in the Scribner Illustrated Library of Wonders series, The Wonders of Optics

Commentary on the Acts of the Apostles, which is one of the best parts of Lange's *Bibelwerk,* and expects to have it ready for the press, during the course of the year 1864.

As this Commentary embodies the best fruits of the modern Biblical scholarship and pulpit eloquence of evangelical Germany, and will be especially adapted to the use of American readers by the various translators, it may be certain of a hearty welcome, especially among the ministers of the Anglo-German churches of America.

The publisher, Mr. Charles Scribner, of New York, will spare no pains and expense to get the work out, in a style worthy of its character and of his own reputation as a publisher of good, useful and substantial books.

REVIEW:

Review of the first volume of *Lange's Commentary,* from *The American Presbyterian and*

Theological Review, new series 3 (1865): 155–156.

A Commentary on the Holy Scriptures, Critical, Doctrinal and Homiletical. By JOHN PETER LANGE, D.D. Vol. I of the New Testament. Matthew, by Lange. Translated with additions. By PHILIP SCHAFF, D.D. New York: Scribner. 1865. Royal 8 vo., double columns. pp. xxii, 568. We have often spoken of the value of this new and admirable commentary, and of its general plan. The American edition is not only much superior to the Edinburgh, but it also surpasses the German in several particulars. In the Gospel of Matthew, Dr. Schaff has added about one-fourth to the original, chiefly criticism of the text, and exegetical materials. We know that he has worked hard at it, and all his work bears solid fruit. The Edinburgh version has been revised; its omissions supplied; its mistranslations corrected. A good deal of material has been added from English and American works, not noticed in the original. The textual

This Agreement, made the *sixteenth* day of *November* 1869, Between *C. Scribner & Co.* of the first part, and The Board of Education of the City of Brooklyn, of the second part, WITNESSETH, that the parti*es* of the first part ha*ve* and by these presents, do — agree to sell to the party of the second part, and deliver at the various depots for the Schools of the City of Brooklyn, and in such quantities from time to time as may be needed by the party of the second part and ordered by the Committee on *Libraries* of said Board, during the term of one year from the date of these presents, the following School Books, at the prices herein named, to wit:

Mrs Harpers Practical Compositions at Thirty three cents each

Guyots Elementary Geographies at Twenty eight cents each

do Intermediate do at Fifty nine cents each

do Common School do at Eighty five cents each

And the parti*es* of the first part do — further agree that the books to be furnished as aforesaid, shall be similar to the sample deposited in the Office of the Clerk of said Board, signed by the parti*es* of the first part, and equal thereto in all respects.

And the party of the second part, in consideration of the premises, doth hereby agree to purchase and take from the parti*es* of the first part, for the term of one year from this date, the school books above named, at the price aforesaid, and to pay therefor within sixty days after delivery.

IN WITNESS WHEREOF, the parti*es* of the first part ha*ve* hereunto subscribed *their* name*s*, and the party of the second part hath caused its Corporate Seal to be hereto affixed, the day and year above written.

E. P. Whitlock
Vice President

Attest
Secretary

Charles Scribner & Co.

Purchasing agreement between Charles Scribner & Co. and the Brooklyn Board of Education for Scribner schoolbooks at a reduced cost

criticism, wholly left out in the Edinburgh edition, has been restored and largely supplemented. Thus, *e.g.* the Codex Sinaiticus has been compared throughout. On many difficult passages Dr. Schaff has also supplied a full commentary of his own; especially in cases of peculiar interest to the English student and controversialist. He has likewise enlarged the scope of the "Literature," and introduced references to the chief English and American books and treatises.

We welcome this commentary as, upon the whole, the best single exposition that can be found, comprising all that is essential to a thorough, popular and useful work. Its spirit is evangelical. It treats the Bible as an inspired book; yet it is also critical, meeting and not giving the slip to difficult questions. For textual criticism it affords ample means. Its exegesis is concise and pertinent. The doctrinal and homiletical parts are handled effectively. It is not sectarian, but adapted for use in all denominations. Those who may, here and there, differ from it, will not complain that it is wanting in either candor or learning.

Mr. Scribner deserves the thanks of all our students and ministers for embarking in such times in so costly an enterprise. But we have no doubt he will find it a profitable as well as costly venture. Other portions of the work are in the course of preparation by such scholars as Shedd, Yeomans, Schäffer, Kendrick, Poor, Starbuck, Lillie and Mombert. The volume on Genesis will also soon be translated. . . .

ANNOUNCEMENT:
"Illustrated Library of Wonders," *The Book Buyer,* 2, no. 5 (15 February 1869): 128–129.

With this announcement Scribners launched a successful series of books on aspects of nature, science, and art, the individual volumes of which were English translations of French works issued by Hachette & Co., a Paris publisher. The first series consisted of twenty volumes, classified in four groups: Wonders of Nature, Wonders of Art, Wonders of Science, and Wonderful Adventures and Exploits. A second series of ten volumes followed, edited, usually with additions, by American authors.

During the last few years extraordinary advances have been made in every department of the sciences and the arts, as well as in the discovery of the laws governing the varius phenomena of nature. While these developments have been carefully chronicled in scientific journals, and in special treatises of recognized value, there has been no systematic effort, either in this country or in England, to bring within popular comprehension these discoveries and inventions. In France, however, special attention has been paid to this department of literature. Figuier's works upon Natural History, all of which have been translated into English, have had a large sale in this country and in Great Britain, notwithstanding their high price, giving emphatic proof of the extraordinary and growing interest in these studies; and under the taking title of Library of Wonders (*Bibliothèque des Merveilles*), Messrs. Hachette & Co., of Paris, some months ago commenced the issue of a series of works prepared by the first French scientists, and profusely and expensively illustrated, but produced at so low a price as to bring them within the reach of readers of all classes. Translations of two or three of these works have already been published in London, and Messrs. CHARLES SCRIBNER & CO. have just completed arrangements for reproducing in this country selections from this very valuable library. Three of the volumes, *Wonders of Optics, Thunder and Lightning,* and *Wonders of Heat,* are already through the press, and the dates upon which they will respectively be published are elsewhere announced.

1870–1879

1870

19 July	CS I, Andrew C. Armstrong, Edward Seymour, Arthur J. Peabody, Josiah Gilbert Holland, and Roswell C. Smith form Scribner & Co. to publish the periodical *Scribner's Monthly.*
Nov.	First issue of the Scribner periodical *Scribner's Monthly,* edited by Holland
8 Dec.	Publication date of *Books and Reading; or, What Books Shall I Read? and How Shall I Read Them?* by Noah Porter, editor of Webster's *American Dictionary,* later president of Yale

1871

27 May	Publication date of *Common Sense in the Household: A Manual of Practical Housewifery,* the first Scribner book by "Marion Harland," the pseudonym of Mary Virginia Terhune
26 Aug.	Death of Charles Scribner (CS I)
13 Nov.	Copyright date of Frank R. Stockton's first Scribner book, *Round-About Rambles in Lands of Fact and Fancy*
2 Dec.	Publication date of the first volume in the "Illustrated Library of Travel" series, *Japan in Our Day,* compiled and arranged by Bayard Taylor, the series editor

1872

Feb.	Peabody sells his interest in Charles Scribner & Co.
10 Feb.	Armstrong, John Blair Scribner, and Seymour form a publishing partnership to be known as "Scribner, Armstrong & Co." (the respective shares are 40 percent, 40 percent, and 20 percent).
	Charles Welford, Armstrong, and John Blair Scribner form partnership to be known as "Scribner, Welford & Armstrong" to continue the importation of books for a period of six years from 1 Feb. 1872 (their respective shares are 1/3, 1/3, and 1/3).
	Armstrong and John Blair Scribner sign agreement with Edward Seymour, paying him a salary equal to one-eighth of their share of the profits in Scribner, Welford & Armstrong for services he renders to the company.
14 Sept.	Copyright date of Henry M. Stanley's first Scribner book, *How I Found Livingstone: Travels, Adventures, and Discoveries in Central Africa, Including an Account of Four Months' Residence with Dr. Livingstone,* which was sold by subscription (the first copies were ready in November)
Oct.	The firm organizes a subscription department.

1873

7 Apr.	Mary Mapes Dodge begins at Scribner & Co. as editor of its new children's magazine, *St. Nicholas.*
10 Apr.	John Blair Scribner purchases his grandfather's (i.e., John Insley Blair's) interest in Charles Scribner & Co. and Scribner, Welford & Co.
Nov.	First issue of the Scribner periodical *St. Nicholas: Scribner's Illustrated Magazine for Girls and Boys*
22 Nov.	Publication date of Mary Mapes Dodge's *Hans Brinker; or, The Silver Skates,* her first Scribner book

1874

2 May	Publication date of *Journey to the Center of the Earth,* the first Scribner book by Jules Verne
9 May	Publication date of *Personal Reminiscences of Chorley, Planché, and Young,* inaugurating the Bric-a-Brac series edited by Richard Henry Stoddard
26 Aug.	Publication date of *The Era of the Protestant Revolution* by Frederic Seebohm and *The Crusades* by G. W. Cox, the first two titles in the Epochs of History series, which grew to twenty-nine works by 1889, divided into two groups: "Epochs of Modern History" and "Epochs of Ancient History"
1 Dec.	Armstrong, John Blair Scribner, and Seymour sign lease for first floor and basement of 743–745 Broadway (they take possession on 10 January 1875 though lease begins on May 1 and runs through 1 May 1880), which will be their location for nineteen years (through 1 May 1894).

1875

22 Jan.	Publication date of *Assyrian Discoveries: An Account of Exploration and Discoveries on the Site of Nineveh, During 1873 and 1874* (with illustrations) by George Smith of the British Museum
June	Charles Scribner (CS II) graduates from Princeton and joins his brother John Blair in the firm.
16 Oct.	Copyright date of *The New Day: A Poem in Songs and Sonnets,* the first book by Richard Watson Gilder, assistant editor of *Scribner's Monthly*

1876

27 Apr.	Copyright date of the first volume of *A Popular History of the United States* by William Cullen Bryant and Sydney Howard Gay
17 May	Publication date of *The Life, Letters and Table Talk of Benjamin Robert Haydon,* inaugurating the "Sans Souci" series edited by Richard Henry Stoddard
11 Nov.	Publication date of Noah Brooks's first Scribner book, *The Boy Emigrants*

1877

7 Apr.	Publication date of Frances Hodgson Burnett's first Scribner book, *That Lass o'Lowrie's*
30 Apr.	Death of Edward Seymour

Dec.	Frank Nelson Doubleday, at the age of fifteen, is hired before Christmas to work carrying books from the bindery to the packing-room and leaves nineteen years later as business manager of *Scribner's Magazine*.
1878	Scribners begins publication of the "authorized" American edition of the *Encyclopædia Britannica* (ninth edition). The concluding index volume (volume 25) comes in 1889.
21 Feb.	Armstrong and John Blair Scribner purchase Seymour's interest in Scribner, Armstrong & Co. and Scribner & Co. from his estate.
11 June	Armstrong resigns to head his own publishing firm, A. C. Armstrong & Son. He sells his share of Scribner, Armstrong & Co. to J. Blair Scribner and sells his share of Scribner, Welford & Armstrong to J. Blair Scribner and Welford. Firm names change: Scribner, Armstrong & Co. becomes "Charles Scribner's Sons"; Scribner, Welford & Armstrong becomes "Scribner & Welford."
18 July	The first title to bear the "Charles Scribner's Sons" imprint is published: *Saxe Holm's Stories* (Second Series) by Helen Hunt Jackson.
1879	
20 Jan.	Death of John Blair Scribner
6 Feb.	Publication date of Hjalmar Hjorth Boyesen's first Scribner book, *Goëthe and Schiller: Their Lives and Works*
Mar.	Edward L. Burlingame, a journalist and editor, son of a U.S. minister to China, joins the firm as a literary adviser.
11 Apr.	CS II signs a renegotiated lease (less costly) for the first floor and basement of building at 743–745 Broadway for period from 1 May 1880 through 1 May 1883.
25 Apr.	Welford and CS II form copartnership under the firm name of "Scribner & Welford" to continue the business of importing books for a period of seven years from May 1.
17 May	Publication date of George Washington Cable's first Scribner book, *Old Creole Days*
13 Nov.	Publication date of Sidney Lanier's first Scribner book, *The Boy's Froissart: Being Sir John Froissart's Chronicles of Adventure, Battle and Custom in England, France, Spain, etc.*
20 Nov.	Publication date of the first two volumes of *The Letters of Charles Dickens*, edited by his sister-in-law and eldest daughter

LETTER:
Letter by CS I to his father-in-law, John Insley Blair, 3 May 1871.

The tone and expression of the letter suggests that Scribner knew he would not return from his health-seeking trip to Europe. He died in Lucerne, Switzerland, on 26 August 1871, from an attack of typhoid fever.

Dear Father

I received your very kind letter yesterday. I notice what you say as to paying my passage and also that of my brother William's to England and thank you for it. Indeed I cannot refrain from taking this opportunity to thank you with all my heart for your kindness to me ever since I have known you. You have never refused any request I have made and have very often anticipated my wants. I love you with the affection of a son and shall think of you and pray for you much during our separation. May our knowing Father take care of you — give you health and strength to prosecute your useful plans and above all give you grace to become his child and to consecrate your gift to his service. You have many Christian friends who are constantly praying for you. I cannot tell you how much I am disappointed in not being able to see you again before leaving. We intended to go to the City to day but after receiving your letter I made up my mind to go up to Blairstown this morning and remain there until Saturday. But as William feels quite unwell to day we have concluded to stay until to morrow when we expect to go to Plainfield. There are some things I would like to say to you about the dear children — as regards their future — in case I should not be permitted to return — particularly as to Blair — his impatience to push Emma forward into gay society etc. I feel that there is great necessity of caution on this point. But I will give them all good advice and write them often if my health permits. As regards my future course I shall endeavor to follow the teachings of Providence forming no definite plan but endeavoring to do that which seems at the time to be best. I have more confidence in a sea voyage from past experience than in any thing else and should I improve on the voyage to England and find myself not as well on land I shall either take a sailing packet home and if necessary then take a longer voyage or go from Liverpool to some distant port. The great point now is to use the best means for the recovery of my health and I am encouraged to hope that an entire change will greatly benefit me. I feel that it will probably take considerable time but our business now is in a good condition and I can be better spared than any time from years past. If our heavenly Father will just give me sufficient strength to have the oversight of my business in which I feel that I can be useful and above all as the only surviving Parent will spare me to the children a few years I shall be truly thankful — but he knows and will do what is best and I commit myself and them to his loving care desiring I trust that his Holy will may be done. On the whole I think I have gained some since I have been here though I have not been quite as well this week. As I may think best to remain abroad for some time and to have my brother William stay with me you may be willing to help pay this additional expense as I would be reluctant to draw so heavily on the business which will probably need all its financial resources — and my family expenses are necessarily large. You will excuse me if I have made an improper suggestion. I have always gone to you as freely as to my own Father for help as you have always treated me as a son and encouraged me to do so. I wish most affectionately to be remembered to Mother and all friends and shall always remember you and them with great love.

Yours most affectionately
Charles Scribner

LETTER:
Letter by J. Blair Scribner to his brother Charles, [August 1871], on the death of their father, CS I.

Blair is barely twenty-one, and CS II is sixteen, about to enter Princeton.

My Dear Dear Brother
Sister Emma will tell you everything in regard to our dear honored and beloved father's death. She has copies of all the telegrams and the original letter of Aug. 14th; also papers etc. I do not feel able to write you much. I have attended to all the important details [and] will write some one again to-morrow in case any more news comes to hand. Have a carriage down to Portland Station Thursday evening to meet me. I have ordered of Mr. Kal [name unclear] for you a suit of black clothing. I will spend at least a week with you all in Blairstown. And now my dear brother we must be truly brothers and bear with one another. What has passed between us is entirely forgotten.

Next to me you are the oldest male in our family and a portion of the burden will naturally fall upon you. You and I must unite and work in harmony together doing everything as we know father would have us do were he here with us below. Now my poor fellow good bye

Your affectne. brother
Blair

OBITUARY:
"Charles Scribner," *New York Times*, 28 August 1871, p. 4, cols. 6–7.

The sad news was received on Saturday evening of the death from typhoid fever on that day at Lucerne, Switzerland, of Mr. CHARLES SCRIBNER, head of the eminent publishing house of

CHARLES SCRIBNER & CO., of this City. The intelligence will be received with surprise and pain by the members of the profession of which Mr. SCRIBNER was so distinguished an ornament, and with great grief by an unusually large circle of warmly-attached personal friends.

Mr. SCRIBNER's health has for the last two years been so feeble that he has been able to give but little attention to business, and in May last, in the hope that entire relief from care and change of scene might be beneficial, took passage by sailing-vessel for Liverpool. A brief tour through Ireland, and a stay of two or three weeks at St. Moritz, Switzerland, had greatly benefitted him, and the last letters received from him showed that his mind was turning with all its activity to business. His return in the course of the Fall in renewed health was anticipated, when on Saturday morning a telegram from Lucerne came to hand, announcing his serious illness from an attack of typhoid fever. This message was followed by one a few hours later, bearing the sad news of his death. His brother, Rev. WM. SCRIBNER, who had been his traveling companion, and his brother-in-law, CLARENCE MITCHELL, Esq., of this City, were with him during his sickness, and at the time of his death, and secured for him every possible care and attention. The remains, which were embalmed, will be brought immediately home for interment.

Mr. SCRIBNER was a native of this City, and at the time of his death was in the fifty-first year of his age. He graduated at Princeton College, and at once turned his attention to the study of law, but after three years' application had fully fitted him for admission to the bar, he became satisfied that his health would not endure the laborious confinement of professional life, and he therefore turned his attention to the business of book-publishing, in 1846 forming a copartnership with Mr. ISAAC D. BAKER, under the firm name of BAKER & SCRIBNER, and commencing business in the old Brick Church. Mr. BAKER died in 1850, and the business was prosecuted by Mr. SCRIBNER alone until 1857. He then purchased the large English importing business of Messrs. BANGS, MERWIN & CO., taking as a partner in that branch CHARLES WELFORD, Esq. Under Mr. SCRIBNER'S vigorous and enlightened management, this part of the business has been more than quadrupled since it was first commenced, while his original business of publishing has been so extended that the house, which now includes as partners A. C. ARMSTRONG, A. J. PEABODY and EDWARD SEYMOUR, ranks among the largest and most enterprising in the United States.

As a publisher Mr. SCRIBNER was noted for the sagacity, accuracy, quickness and soundness of his judgment. The breadth, liberality and catholicity of his views, as well as the ripeness of his culture, were admirably represented by the character and high standing of the publications which he issued. While he was quick to appreciate works of excellence produced abroad he was even more prompt in the recognition of American authors, to whom he was always ready to give advice and practical encouragement, and several of the most popular of whom it was his good fortune to introduce to the reading public.

Of Mr. SCRIBNER as a man it is almost impossible to speak in terms which shall not seem exaggerated to all but those who had the privilege of his personal acquaintance. A gentle, sincere and earnest Christianity pervaded his whole life, making him one of the most tender-hearted and sympathetic of men. This characteristic manifested itself constantly in his business as well as in his social life, and made all with whom he came in contact his devoted friends. To every one of them the news of his death will bring the sense of a personal bereavement, all the keener from its suddenness. To the publishing house which he founded, and of which he was for a quarter of a century the honored head, his loss is a most severe one. His associates, however, have been so long connected with him, and are so thoroughly familiar with his views and projects, that it is safe to assume they will fully maintain its old reputation.

TRIBUTE:
"The Late Charles Scribner. Meeting of the Publishers and Book-Sellers — Impressive Tribute," *New York Times*, 23 September 1871, p. 5, col. 2.

An impressive and eloquent tribute to the memory of the late CHARLES SCRIBNER, head of the publishing-house of CHARLES SCRIBNER & CO., was rendered yesterday afternoon, by a meeting of publishers and book-sellers, at the store of SHELDON & CO. Representatives of all the leading houses in the City were present, and the trade-sale was adjourned to allow those in attendance to join in this tribute of respect to their late associate.

Mr. SMITH SHELDON called the meeting to order, and upon his nomination, Rev. Dr. CARLTON, of CARLTON & LANAHAN, was unanimously chosen Chairman. GEO. P. PUTNAM was elected

Secretary, and upon motion, the Chairman named the following as a Committee to draft resolutions expressive of the sense of the meeting: Messrs. GEO. P. APPLETON, J. W. HARPER, SMITH SHELDON, J. C. BARNES and E. P. DUTTON. As representatives of the trade in other cities, J. R. OSGOOD, of Boston, and Mr. INGRAM, of Cleveland, were added to the Committee, which, after a brief absence, reported the following resolutions:

Whereas, By the death of Mr. CHARLES SCRIBNER, one for so long a time and so prominently associated with us as a member of the publishing fraternity, has been removed from us, as well as from a large circle of literary and personal friends, it seems fit and proper that we especially should express our sense of his loss, and render a suitable tribute to his memory; therefore, be it

Resolved, That Mr. CHARLES SCRIBNER, by his rare literary judgment, his ripe scholarship and his generous culture, was eminently well fitted for the high and commanding position which for a quarter of a century he has occupied as a leading American publisher — a position which has reflectd honor upon himself and upon the world of letters, and in which, by his cordial relations with other publishers, with his business associates, and with eminent authors at home and abroad, he surrounded himself with a large circle of friends, who regarded him with profound esteem and fraternal affection, and who will ever tenderly cherish his memory.

Resolved, That the business sagacity, the discriminating literary taste, the industry and unsullied integrity which enabled our friend, Mr. SCRIBNER, to build up one of the most useful and important publishing-houses in America, are qualities which, however remarkable in themselves and in so rare a combination, still appear to us not more estimable than those characteristic traits of mind and heart by which, to all who knew him, he stood forth as the signal representative of the noblest manliness, of every gentlemanly attribute, and of the highest Christian virtues.

Resolved, That to the family of the deceased, whom a few months ago since he left in comparative health and vigor, but to whom from beyond the sea only his material form can be returned, we tender our sincere and heartfelt sympathies, hoping that the remembrance of the esteem in which he was held by all who knew him may in some degree alleviate the sense of irreparable loss occasioned by his death.

Early logo of Scribner & Co., the separate company formed in July 1870 by CS I (and his partners Andrew C. Armstrong, Edward Seymour, and Arthur J. Peabody), J. G. Holland, and Roswell Smith to publish the periodical Scribner's Monthly *and "from time to time such other books, pamphlets and periodicals as may be deemed expedient by the trustees or stockholders of said company"*

Resolved, That upon the occasion of Mr. SCRIBNER'S funeral we will, by our presence at and participation in the ceremonies, render to his memory those tributes of respect and affection which his eminent position and worthiness, as well as our own feelings, must inevitably suggest.

Geo. P. Putnam, Esq., moved the adoption of the resolutions in a feeling and appropriate address. He alluded to the pure tendency and high importance of the works which had gained for the house, of which Mr. SCRIBNER was so long the head, its wide reputation. He also spoke of his personal character, the kindness and natural courtesy of his disposition, and his sensitive integrity, qualities which made his loss a personal affliction to every member of the trade who had the privilege of his acquaintance. He suggested, in conclusion, whether the occasion might not be useful to all present, and whether the character and career of their eminent friend, who had gone to a better world, might not serve for the encouragement and example of those who were left.

Mr. PUTNAM'S remarks were attentively listened to; at their close the resolutions which had been read were unanimously adopted, and on motion, the Secretary was requested to send a copy of them to the family of the late Mr. SCRIBNER, and also to have them printed in the daily papers.

FUNERAL NOTICE:
"Funeral of Charles Scribner. Large Attendance — Address by the Rev. Dr. Murray," *Commercial Advertiser,* 29 September 1871.

The funeral of Charles Scribner, the well-known publisher, who died at Lucerne, Switzerland, on the 26th of August, in the fiftieth year of his age, took place this morning from the Brick Church, at the corner of Thirty-seventh street and Fifth avenue. A large number of relatives and personal and business friends of Mr. Scribner were present; among others Messrs. George Jones, of the *Times*; Fletcher Harper, W. H. Appleton, Ives, Blakeman, Tilly & Co., Oakley, Mason & Co., A. D. F. Randolph & Co., Gerge Putnam and Sons, Osgood & Co., and many other prominent publishers and booksellers.

The funeral services were commenced at ten o'clock by Rev. James O. Murray, D.D., assisted by Rev. W. G. T. Shedd, D.D., Rev. Philip Schaff, D.D., and Rev. J. McDonald, D.D.

Rev. Dr. Murray made an impressive discourse, in the course of which he said that the event for which they had gathered together was sad in the extreme. He (the speaker) had the great pleasure of being acquainted with Mr. Charles Scribner for the past twenty-five years, and during that period had been brought into intimate business and personal relations with him. He had seen him in the sunshine of prosperity, and again when he was bowed down by grief resulting from sad bereavement, and he felt free to confess that under all circumstances it would be almost impossible to find a man more pure in principle, more consistent in conduct, more upright, more charitable, than Charles Scribner. He was a dutiful son, an excellent father, and eminently a good Christian. Mr. Scribner, if alive, would be the last to accept such commendations, so great was his modesty and humility, but the truth should be spoken now that he had passed away. His only trust had been in Christ, he was a truly good and useful man, and

among the many works which he had published there was not one which could work an evil influence or bring a blush to the cheek of innocence. His sudden taking off in a foreign land was a stunning blow, but even here there was room for consolation. There was a silver lining to this dark cloud of sorrow. He died in peace, buoyed up by religious hope, and surrounded by sympathizing friends. His death was a relief from great suffering, and life had ceased to be dear to him since the death of his beloved wife [1869]. He truly went to heaven to join his pious consort. In justice might the words of Holy Writ be applied to him, "Blessed are the dead who die in the Lord."

The speaker concluded with an appeal to his hearers to lead a virtuous life so as to be prepared for death.

After a few remarks from Rev. Dr. Shedd, extolling the many eminent qualities of the deceased the mournful procession filed from the church, and the funeral *cortege* wended its way to the Marble Cemetery in Second street, where the remains were interred. The pall-bearers were Mr. A. C. Armstrong, Mr. Edward Seymour (partners in the house of Scribner & Co.), Dr. J. G. Holland, Donald G. Mitchell, A. D. F. Randolph, B. F. Dunning, W. S. Gillman, and Geo. P. Putnam.

All the book firms in the City suspended business, and closed their establishments this morning in respect to the memory of Mr. Scribner.

ANNOUNCEMENT:
"A Library of Travel and Adventure," edited by Bayard Taylor, *The Book Buyer,* 5, no. 1 (15 October 1871): 16–17.

This series, later called simply the "Illustrated Library of Travel," consisted of eight volumes, published from 1871 to 1874. Five of the titles were edited by Taylor, an American world traveler who had published travel books in the 1850s, had written novels and poetry, and would later become, after translating Goethe's Faust, *a professor at Cornell and the U.S. Minister to Germany.*

Encouraged by the great success of the LIBRARY OF WONDERS, MESSRS. CHAS. SCRIBNER & CO. have undertaken the publication of a work of an equally instructive and popular character, namely, a LIBRARY OF TRAVEL, EXPLORATION, AND ADVENTURE, which will be edited by BAYARD TAYLOR, and profusely and elegantly illustrated.

At this moment, when the various hitherto unknown and mysterious regions of the earth are looming into light, and our knowledge concerning them is gradually changing from the mythical to the real, the presentation of the proposed series — which will not only chronicle the wanderings of the earlier adventurer, but keep pace with the rapid advance of the modern explorer — is exceedingly timely.

The design is to furnish picturesque, practical, and full accounts of the most interesting lands and races, gathered from the narratives of the most reliable travellers and explorers; each volume to be devoted to a special country or region, and to be complete in itself. Every volume, therefore, will give, first, a preliminary sketch of the country to which it is devoted; next, an outline of early explorations sufficient to explain what has been achieved by later travellers; and finally, a condensation of one or more of the most important narratives of recent travel, accompanied by illustrations of the scenery, architecture, and the life of the races. Certain volumes of the Library, however, will be devoted entirely to such stories of individual daring and adventure as may be likely to arrest public attention.

It will be the constant care of the editor — than whom no living writer can be better fitted by experience for this enterprise — to separate what is doubtful or exaggerated in the literature of travel from what is true. The successive books will not only present a fund of sound and practical information for the people, but in every household they will prove an inexhaustible source of entertainment and amusement; especially will they be found useful in satisfying the demand, on the part of the younger members of the family, for really interesting reading — a demand which, if not thus met, will inevitably seek supply in works of an equally exciting but less wholesome character.

The new series will, we are sure, meet with welcome in every quarter of the country. He who begins with the initial volume will gradually, and at no perceptible expense, build up a complete and valuable library, such as will prove an ornament to his shelves, and a perpetual means of education and entertainment. The first volume will appear before the middle of November, and will give the latest and fullest information concerning that ancient and most curious people, the Japanese — a people who just now are attracting the attention of the world by

Series frontispiece for volumes in the Illustrated Library of Travel, Exploration, and Adventure

their rapid advances from the domain of ignorance, isolation, and prejudice, into the light of civilization. The forthcoming book will include a sketch of the history of the Empire, and the successive steps by which it has entered into relations with the other nations of the world.

ANNOUNCEMENT:
"Scribner, Armstrong & Co.'s Subscription Department," *The Book Buyer,* 6 (15 October 1872): 12.

Launched in 1872 with Stanley's How I Found Livingstone, *the subscription department became one of the firm's most successful experiments. By the end of the decade it was publishing the authorized American edition of the* Encyclopædia Britannica *and later added limited editions of illustrated nature works and handsomely pro-*

duced standard editions of authors' complete works.

MESSRS. SCRIBNER, ARMSTRONG & CO. have the gratification of announcing the organization of a department, in connection with their general business, for the publication of books by subscription. They need only say that they shall make it their steady aim to publish works of a higher order of merit than those usually issued by this method, and they hope to call out a class of cultivated efficient men and women as canvassers who will reflect credit on themselves, and be an honor to the house they shall represent. As the best possible indication of the fact that they intend to bring out works only of the highest character, and which shall at the same time be sure of the largest and most ready sale, — just the books, in short, which command the services of the most capable agents, — MESSRS. SCRIBNER, ARMSTRONG & CO. call attention to the following works:

I.

How I Found Livingstone. By Henry M. Stanley.

This is by far the most exciting book of travel to be published for years. The wide interest felt in Dr. Livingstone, and the anxiety regarding his fate until Mr. Stanley discovered the great explorer, have combined to throw an air of romance around this story of "How I found Livingstone," and to secure a lively interest in it on the part of every man, woman, and child who knows how to read. The book is sure to sell more readily than any which has appeared for a long time.

II.

The Universe; or, The Infinitely Great and the Infinitely Little.

This superb work by Pouchet, one of the greatest living naturalists, with its exquisitely executed and numerous woodcuts, has already had a limited circulation in its expensive form. This edition has been produced with special reference to its sale through agents. An eloquent introduction by Prof. Guyot ably summarizes the points of excellence in the work. The letterpress is identical with that of the expensive edition, and not one of the superb woodcuts is omitted; yet in its present form the volume is

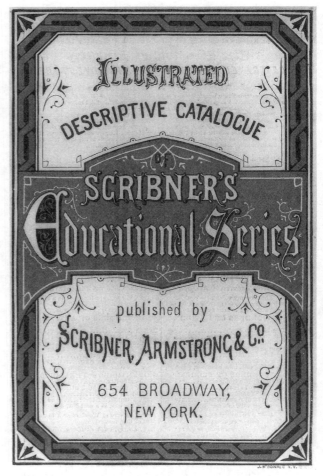

Cover of the 1872 Scribner catalogue for its educational series

supplied at one-third less than before. It is a library in itself, and a book which will last for all time.

III.

Wonderful Escapes and Daring Adventures.

The title of this work sufficiently describes its general character. It contains numerous authentic narratives of marvellous escapes, daring adventures, and perils, and hazards braved by intrepid explorers and travellers in the remotest parts of the earth. The volume contains upwards of *eleven hundred pages,* is illustrated with seventy full-page engravings, and yet is furnished at the exceedingly moderate price of $3.00.

These works are sure of having a large sale. Experienced agents must do better with them than

1875 advertisement in The Book Buyer *for Sheldon's Readers, a graded series of books first published by Scribners in the 1870s. In addition to Arnold Guyot's Geographies and E. A. Sheldon's Readers, Scribners published several other very successful textbook series: Le Roy C. Cooley's Physical Sciences, S. A. Felter's Arithmetics, and Sanborn Tenney's Natural Histories.*

SHELDON'S PRIMER.

Adapted to the Phonic, Alphabet, and Word Methods.

18   *Sheldon's Primer.*

LESSON XII.

map sap gap ram map ran

Sixty Pages. — Each Page Handsomely Illustrated.

The lad has a bad map.

The lad is at the sap.

A ram is at the gap.

The sap ran.

The ram ran.

The lad ran.

SPECIMEN OF TYPE AND ILLUSTRATION FROM

SHELDON'S PRIMER.

609

Specimen page from Sheldon's Primer

is possible with any others now in the market; and those who have never before been in the field will find them the very best works on which to begin canvassing.

ARTICLE:

"Messrs. Scribner & Co.," *New York Times*, 22 December 1874, p. 5.

Anticipating the move of the firm up Broadway in the next month, this article focuses on the last Christmas-at-Scribners experience that book-loving New Yorkers had come to love at this address.

We understand that the well-known house of Scribner, Welford & Co., No. 654 Broadway — a favorite haunt of every booklover in the City —

will shortly remove to new and more commodious premises in Broadway, opposite Astor Place. For a long time past the famous establishment has been hard pressed for room. Every *habitué* of the "old stand" knows that at least one-half of the precious collection of books contained in it are stowed away in cupboards or drawers — always accessible to those who are familiar with the place, but not generally available to the chance customer. The new premises will give an opportunity for the display of the literary wealth collected by that judicious bibliopolist, Mr. Welford, in London, and by the other active members of the firm. But it must not be supposed that even now it is difficult to find any book of which the Christmas purchaser may be in search. On the contrary, Mr. Seymour, or Mr. Bangs, or Mr. Scribner, or any of the well-informed and courteous assistants of the firm, will produce at a moment's notice, almost any work which the experienced bookhunter may desire to add to his library, or to send as a present to some discerning friend. The old frequenter of the store will miss, this Christmas, the face of a true and worthy gentleman, Mr. Kernot, whose sudden death we recorded not long ago. He belonged, by birth, nature, training, and instinct to the good old fraternity of booklovers. To be buried up to his chin in books, to handle them, to dip into them, to show them to discriminating friends, to pat and stroke them as if he loved them and they could return his love — this was to him the greatest happiness the world had to offer. A true and faithful man, a man worthy to live among books, an honorable representative of the house which he served, a devout and humble Christian, he has gone to his rest — let us hope to enjoy that better Christmas which awaits those who are followers of the Son of Man, whose first appearance the Christian world will shortly celebrate.

It is impossible to go to Scribner's at Christmas without thinking of Mr. Kernot, who was as happy when all the good books were out for display as a child is when he wakes up on Christmas morning, and finds that Santa Claus has filled the stocking to the very top. But our places are soon filled up when we are gone — it is the necessity of life — and Mr. Kernot's chair is now occupied by a good scholar and a devoted worshipper of books, those priceless and unfailing pleasures of existence. As for the store itself, seen as it may be this week by night as well as by day, it never was so weighed down with so rich a cargo. There are wonderful editions of great authors with "inserted plates" — those editions which collectors value more even than money, for they usually pay large sums to become possessed of them. Clarendon's *History of the Rebellion,* Garrick's *Memoirs,* "poor Goldsmith's" works, La Fontaine's *Fables,* and many other good books have been bedecked in this luxurious manner, and may easily be found on Scribner's shelves. Every standard author may be obtained, in binding worthy of him — Scott, Dickens, Thackeray, Froude, Tennyson, Macaulay, and a score more, in any dress you please. The beautiful new French book on India — by means of which every old Indian may repeat his travels without the inconvenience of tough chicken and perpetual mosquitoes and jungle fever — is among the latest additions to the collection. We have recently enumerated some of these new books, and need not go over them again. Suffice it to say that there is scarcely any work worth having which may not be found at Scribner's. And there is a wonderful variety of children's books, all carefully selected, and all adapted for Christmas and New-Year's presents. Whether one is able to buy or not, a visit to Scribner's during the last two weeks of December is one of the pleasures of City life which no New-Yorker ought to deny himself.

743–745 Broadway in New York City, home of Scribners from 1875 until 1894

ARTICLE:

"A Bookstore of the Period. The New Establishment of Messrs. Scribner on Broadway — Description of the Interior — Improved Facilities for Examining Books — Convenient Arrangement of the Departments," *New York Tribune,* 8 April 1875, p. 5.

Providing a detailed and obliging description of the rooms and floors of the new Scribner business quarters, this article asserts that the location is deemed "for the book trade, the site of the city."

It seems fitting that the book trade, with its close relations to culture, should enjoy the more tasteful and elegant of business houses. The new quarters of the three firms which constitute the Scribner house, at Nos. 743–5 Broadway, into which they have now removed, and whose furnishment is nearly completed, reach the highest standard of the bookstore, and compare to advantage with the finest that any other business in the city can boast. The building fronts Astor-place, "Booksellers' Row," and extends, in its full width of 52 feet, 200 feet back to Mercer-st. Its location is, for the book trade, the site of the city. The book trade has followed the usual law of the cen-

tering of trades, and this neighborhood seems destined to be its headquarters for many years, several of the half dozen or more houses that remove thither this month having taken leases for a considerable time. The two great libraries, the Bible House, and Cooper Institute, the Trade Salesrooms, and 20 bookdealers are in the immediate vicinity of the Messrs. Scribners' new location. The entire building, with the exception of the second floor, is occupied by them — the basement for the storage and packing of books, and the ground floor for the store and offices of Scribner, Armstrong & Co., publishers and retailers, and Scribner, Welford & Armstrong, importers; the third story for the editorial and counting-rooms of Scribner & Co., the publishers of the magazines, *Scribner's Monthly* and *St. Nicholas,* and the fourth for the art department and mailing rooms of the latter. The last-named firm is composed of Messrs. J. Blair Scribner, Andrew C. Armstrong, and Edward Seymour; the second of this firm and Mr. Welford, the resident London partner, who is one of the best buyers abroad, and whose pleasant letters in *The Bookbuyer,* the monthly circular published by the firm, give an admirable resumé of the new and curious books; and the third of the first-named house again, Dr. J. G. Holland, the

Interior view of the ground-floor bookstore at 743–745 Broadway

Office of CS II, showing portraits of J. Blair Scribner (left) and CS I (right) on the wall

editor, and Mr. Roswell Smith, the publisher, of *The Monthly.*

The capricious store, splendidly lighted at front, back, and from the center skylights, and with its handsome show-windows, gives the visitor free range of one of the finest stocks of books in town. The right entrance brings one directly into the foreign, the left into the domestic book department. Between the two, a space is railed off to make a pleasant reception-room, elegantly furnished, with library table and comfortable chairs, where bookbuyers may examine the treasures of the house at leisure in bibliomaniac bliss. Right by this is the counter for American books in general, of which a stock will be kept. At the left-hand front corner of the store is a series of glass cases, in which will be kept the peculiar treasures, old and rare and otherwise, especially valuable books — a stock that of itself would require the full capital of an ordinary bookstore. Along the left hand wall are in succession a stand for subscriptions to and purchases of the magazines, a stationery department and a department where a full stock of the fine Oxford Bibles and prayer-books is kept on hand. Beyond are the rooms of the educational department, where are accommodations for the reception of teachers and others. On the other side of the left passage, the table-racks display sample copies of Scribner, Armstrong & Co.'s entire line of publications, in alphabetical order. The center of the store is occupied by the clerks of the two firms, and the stairway to the basement floor. On the other side, Mr. Bangs, the manager of the foreign department, reigns supreme. At the left hand of the passage, starting again from the front, the visitor finds a capacious table-rack, on which folios and other extra large works may be conveniently referred to, the rack lifting at any desired angle, while at this and the other tables a hand-rail in nickel-plate finishes them handsomely and protects the books, while making it more convenient for the buyer to examine them. These petty details, often overlooked, but which make so practical a difference in comfort, have been carefully attended to throughout. Next the folio table is that for art works, and on the right another on which will be found English "bargains." The right-hand wall is shelved from floor to ceiling; here are 75 shelves devoted to popular works, novelists, historians, etc., many in fine bindings. The clergyman will find a remarkable stock of imported theological works; and midway back is "the Poet's Corner," as it is called by happy inspiration, where are col-

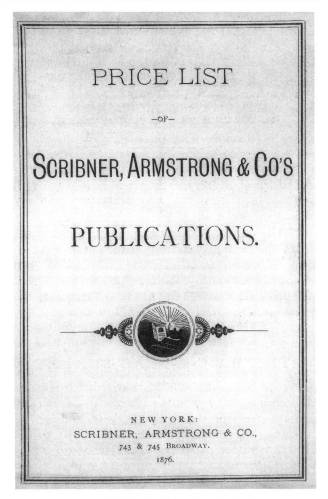

Cover of 1876 Scribner book catalogue

lected the works of all the great poets of our own and other tongues, in exquisite bindings, and where one may buy a Shakespeare at 75 cents or $475. The whole stock is carefully grouped by subjects, so that the visitor can reach what he will, and in each department the books are arranged alphabetically. But the store is so large and the stock is so varied that a little map or guide book is almost a necessity; it should be added to the catalogue of publications at once. One table is devoted exclusively to Bohn's libraries; on another is what is left of the famous "Bibliotheca Diabolica," the attraction which the late Henry Kernot made his hobby. The back part of the store is occupied by platforms, on which editions of new books are piled in quantities, while at the extreme end, on the Mercer-st. front, are the beautifully-fitted business offices and private rooms of the members of the firm.

The spacious store is undivided by full partitions, so that the eye has full scope from one end to the other, The fittings are throughout in ash, with black walnut moldings, a combination of which while elegant gives a light and cheerful appearance to the whole interior. The chandeliers, which were made for this store, are very happy in design. Each arm bears a Roman lamp, which is the emblem of the firm, and appears on the title pages of their books, from whose mouth the gas-jet issues. All the wall space is economized for shelving by the use of a light gallery, accessible to customers by stairways midway back.

The pair of stairs at the side bring us to the magazine floor, where the visitor enters a reception hall with wood-carpeting, furnished with comfortable waiting chairs, and adorned with a reception of Kass's "The Amazon," made by the artist himself. On the left is a charming room, the office of Mr. Roswell Smith, the energetic publisher, to whose vim and push is due much of the success of *Scribner's* and *St. Nicholas* — that devouring ogre of its juvenile contemporaries. The walls are hung with William Morris's papers, and the room is an admirable example of the rich and artistic effect produced by his system of decoration. At the front, to the left, is the office of Dr. Holland, whose experienced judgment guides the editorial conduct of *The Monthly,* and next the room of Mr. Gilder, the assistant editor, and the poetic writer of "the Old Cabinet," and of Mr. Johnston; to the right is *St. Nicholas,* Mrs. Dodge's editorial room and that of the assistant editor, Mr. Stockton. The business offices occupy the intermediate space, under the direct management of Mr. Scott, Mr. Roswell Smith's assistant. Up-stairs again, Mr. A. W. Drake, the managing artist, finds abundance of light, and beauty and the remainder of this floor is occupied by the mailing department.

The Scribner house occupied its former quarters at No. 654 Broadway for nine years, but outgrew its gloomy precincts long ago. In that time many changes have taken place; the honored founder of the house, Mr. Charles Scribner, has been succeeded by a second generation in the person of Mr. J. Blair Scribner, and the new story misses the pleasant face of dear old "Uncle Harry," as Mr. Kernot, that genial enthusiast, was always called. The change would have seemed a strange one to him, the veteran of a by-gone day, when bookstores were not what they are now; but the Scribners are so

Prepublication advertisement for Bryant's Popular History of the United States, *sold by subscription*

well treated in this new house that it would seem that an "Uncle Harry" might grow up and grow old before they should have cause to leave this place for another.

STATEMENT:

"The Illustrated History of the United States," dated October 1875, Roslyn, Long Island.

Presumably issued to the press to clear up a misunderstanding regarding Bryant's role in the historical work, William Cullen Bryant's statement seems, in retrospect, to reflect more of a wish than a fact, for Bryant died halfway through the project. According to J. C. Derby in his Fifty Years Among Authors, Books and Publishers *(1884), Bryant's part of the work was confined to writing the introduction and reading proof. Bryant lent his marketable name and reputation as poet and*

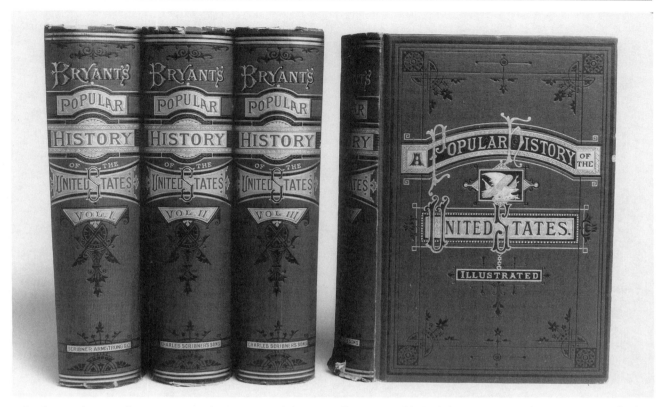

The four volumes of Bryant's Popular History of the United States, *published from 1876 until 1880. Bryant died in 1878, and his co-author, Sydney Howard Gay, completed the set. It was the first "fully" illustrated standard history, including more than twelve hundred engravings. A fifth volume by Noah Brooks, continuing the history from the Civil War to 1894, was published in 1896.*

editor of the New York Evening Post, *and Sidney Howard Gay, listed as co-author, did the work.*

A western periodical having, through misinformation doubtless, affirmed that I have nothing to do with the composition of the Illustrated History of the United States now in press, and about to be published by Scribner Armstrong & Company, it has been thought proper by them that I should set the public right on this point. When the plan of this work was proposed to me by the publishers, I said that, at my time of life I would not undertake the principal labor of it myself, nor would I undertake the work at all, unless I could have an associate whom I should name. They assented, and I named Mr. S. H. Gay, of Staten Island, who has devoted himself to the task with great zeal and diligence, and, as far as he has proceeded, with, as appears to me, uncommon ability. Every thing in regard to the composition is done on consultation with me; every sentence that goes to press has undergone, and will undergo my

rigid revision, and the whole will be published under my responsibility.

W. C. Bryant

MEMOIR:
Frank Nelson Doubleday, "Eighteen Years with Scribner's" [excerpt], first chapter of "Secret Memoirs of a Publisher" (typescript dated December 1926), pp. 3–4. [Doubleday Collection, Princeton University Library]

Doubleday, founder of the publishing firm bearing his name, got his start in the business at Scribners. He was fifteen when he began in December 1877.

When I was fourteen my old father failed. I had not had more than two or three years of schooling altogether and had to go to work. But I was bound to be a publisher, and I went to New York and walked all over town to find out which

Acknowledgment of Scribners' application for space at the Universal Exposition in Paris in 1878. Scribners won several medals, including a gold medal for Arnold Guyot in the class of education and a bronze medal for Scribner & Co.'s magazines, Scribner's Monthly *and* St. Nicholas, *in the books and printing class.*

publisher I would go to, for I did not want to waste myself on a firm which would never amount to anything. I can perfectly well remember the awful cheek that I possessed. It seemed to me quite proper that I should take some trouble to find out who was the best publisher, instead of taking the first job I could get and finding, perhaps, that my opportunities were limited.

I finally decided on Scribner's as most worthy of my situation. They had a store fifty feet on Broadway and two hundred feet deep, which I concluded was just the thing for me and I would get a job there.

So I worked up a letter of introduction from A. S. Barnes & Company, educational publishers, to Mr. J. Blair Scribner, which I presented and asked if he did not want to hire a boy. He said he did not — that he did not hire boys anyhow — that was Mr. Armstrong's business.

So I tackled Mr. Armstrong, whose desk was next to Mr. Scribner's, and asked him if he did not want to hire a boy. He said he did not need any.

"This is the fifteenth of December," I argued, "and you will need help over Christmas. I think you had better take me. It will cost you only three dollars a week."

COPARTNERSHIP NOTICES.

NEW YORK, *June 11th*, 1878.

The copartnership of Scribner, Armstrong & Co. has been dissolved by the death of Edward Seymour, and by its own limitation.

Mr. Andrew C. Armstrong, desiring to retire from the firm, has sold his entire interest in the property and good will of the copartnership to Mr. John Blair Scribner, who is solely authorized to settle the affairs of the late firm.

ANDREW C. ARMSTRONG, } *Surviving*
JOHN BLAIR SCRIBNER, } *Partners.*

NEW YORK, *June 11th*, 1878.

The publishing and book-selling business carried on for many years by Charles Scribner & Co., and afterward by Scribner, Armstrong & Co., will be continued in all its departments, at the old stand (Nos. 743 and 745 Broadway), under the firm name of

CHARLES SCRIBNER'S SONS.

JOHN BLAIR SCRIBNER.
CHARLES SCRIBNER.

NEW YORK, *June 11th*, 1878.

The copartnership heretofore existing between the subscribers, under the name of Scribner, Welford & Armstrong, is this day by mutual consent dissolved.

Charles Welford and John Blair Scribner are authorized to settle the affairs of the late firm.

CHARLES WELFORD.
ANDREW C. ARMSTRONG.
JOHN BLAIR SCRIBNER.

NEW YORK, *June 11th*, 1878.

The undersigned having purchased the entire interest of Mr. Andrew C. Armstrong in the firm of Scribner, Welford & Armstrong, have this day formed a copartnership under the name of

SCRIBNER AND WELFORD,

And will continue the importing and book-selling business at the old premises, Nos. 743 and 745 Broadway.

CHARLES WELFORD.
JOHN BLAIR SCRIBNER.

Announcement of the firm's new name, "Charles Scribner's Sons." The death of partner Edward Seymour in 1877 and the retirement of his other partner, Andrew C. Armstrong, in June 1878 provided J. Blair Scribner the opportunity to consolidate his ownership of the firm. The exporting business, however, continued to be shared with Charles Welford but under the new name of "Scribner and Welford."

He still resisted my blandishments and insisted that he did not need me; but I told him: "You will make a great mistake if you don't take me on. If you hire me, you will get a good boy."

"You seem to have a high opinion of yourself," he remarked.

"Yes," I replied, "I have. I only ask the chance to see if I can't get you to think as favorably of me as I do myself."

"Well," said he, "you are so cheeky that I'll give you a job for a week."

I was there eighteen years.

LETTER:

Letter by J. Blair Scribner to his grandfather, John Insley Blair, 20 March 1878, written from his Scribner office at 745 Broadway.

*This letter notes the beginning of strife within Scribner & Co. that will culminate three years later in the sale of the company, with its two magazines (*Scribner's Monthly *and* St. Nicholas*), to J. G. Holland and Roswell Smith, the editor and the business manager of* Scribner's Monthly.

My Dear Grandfather:-

Yesterday afternoon we to our surprise received letters from Dr. Holland and Mr. Roswell Smith desiring to purchase our 200 shares of magazine stock and that they would name a price which they would be willing to give provided we would sell. They claim that the success of the magazines is due to their efforts mainly and insomuch as important changes are likely to take place in the publishing house they feel that they would prefer to have the entire control of the magazine interests.

I have not yet had one word with Mr. Armstrong on this subject. It is quite possible however that he has had a hand in some way in this movement — and intends, presuming that we are anxious to keep the stock in our family that at any rate we must pay a big price to secure it. This affair quite knocked me at first, and interfered with my rest last night — this morning however I am in better trim and ready for a fight all armed if necessary. My impression is that the magazine people will offer $500 per share or $10000 for the lot of 200 shares.[x] We cannot afford however to part with the stock at any price if we go on in the book business. When will you be down?

Your affectne. grandson
J. Blair Scribner

[x] Please consider this opinion as confidential.

NOTICE:
Untitled notice, *New-York Daily Tribune*, 14 June 1878, p. 4.

Explanation of the partnership changes behind the birth of the name "Charles Scribner's Sons."

A change has just taken place in one of our leading book-selling and publishing houses — that of Scribner, Armstrong & Co. — which under various firm names, as the partnership has been altered from time to time by accessions or by death, has filled for thirty-two years an honorable position in the development of American literature. The firm was founded in 1846 by Charles Scribner and Isaac D. Baker. Mr. Baker died in 1850; Mr. Scribner died in 1871; the partnership consisted after that of Mr. John Blair Scribner (son of the founder of the house), Mr. Andrew C. Armstrong, and Mr. Edward Seymour. Mr. Seymour recently died, and Mr. Armstrong has now sold his interest to the only remaining member of the concern, J. B. Scribner, who has formed a new partnership with his brother, Charles Scribner. The business will henceforth be carried on by "Charles Scribner's Sons," a designation which will pleasantly recall one of the best known and most generally respected of New-York booksellers. Both partners in the firm are gentlemen of culture, literary tastes, and literary knowledge, and they have ample pecuniary resources. There is no doubt that the house which has been identified with the labors of so many American authors, the republication of so many valuable foreign works, and the preparation of so many popular school-books, will be well sustained by the young and enterprising men who have now assumed the full control of its affairs. The change affects the copartnership of Scribner, Welford & Armstrong, in the importation and sale of English books, and this important branch of the business will hereafter be conducted by Mr. J. B. Scribner and Mr. Charles Welford, under the appellation of Scribner & Welford. Mr. Welford, who has been associated with the Scribners in the importing business for more than twenty years, is noted for a marvellously extensive and minute knowledge of books. *Scribner's Monthly* and the *St. Nicholas* are published by "Scribner & Co.," a joint-stock company composed of Charles Scribner's Sons, Dr. J. G. Holland, and Mr. Roswell Smith. Dr. Holland and Mr. Smith retain their stock and continue the management as heretofore.

RELATED LETTERS:
Letters of congratulation to J. Blair Scribner on the occasion of the firm's change in name to "Charles Scribner's Sons."

• *Letter from J. T. Headley (1813-1897), author of the firm's first best-seller,* Napoleon and His Marshals, *published its first year (1846), and thus, arguably, the one most responsible for the successful start of the venture.*

Newburgh Saturday

My Dear Scribner

Nothing has occurred for a long time that has given me so much pleasure as to receive your

The Latest and Incomparably the Best Encyclopædia in the English Language.

THE ONLY AUTHORIZED SUBSCRIPTION EDITION.

ENCYCLOPÆDIA BRITANNICA.

EDINBURGH SUBSCRIPTION EDITION (NINTH).

PRINTED FROM THE ORIGINAL PLATES

WITH OVER TEN THOUSAND ILLUSTRATIONS.

Steel Engravings, Colored Plates, Wood-cuts, Maps and Plans.

THE BEST HOUSEHOLD LIBRARY.

THE WORK OF OVER FIFTEEN HUNDRED DISTINGUISHED WRITERS.

CAUTION.—All alleged "Reprints" of "The Encyclopædia Britannica" issued in this country are to a large extent incomplete, inaccurate, and, by reason of serious mutilations of the text, unreliable for purposes of reference.

Beware of Mutilated and Spurious " Reprints."

Comparison of the ample page, large clear type, superior steel engravings, copper-plate maps and fine wood engravings of the genuine work, with the reduced page, poor print, cheap "process" cuts and "photo-engravings" of so-called reprints, will show that IT WILL PAY TO BUY THE BEST, the authorized and only complete Subscription Edition.

To be completed in twenty-four volumes, averaging 850 pages each. The first twenty-three volumes are now ready, and the twenty-fourth volume will be issued shortly. Sold only by subscription. For further particulars, address

CHARLES SCRIBNER'S SONS, Importers,
743 and 745 Broadway, New York.

Promotional circular for the Scribner edition, "the only authorized edition," of the Encyclopaedia Britannica *(ninth edition). This vast publishing project, begun with its first volume in 1878, concluded with the twenty-fifth volume (the index) in 1889. Over seventy thousand sets were sold at a minimum price of $125. The notice makes reference to alleged "reprints" by other publishers, which were the cause of lawsuits initiated by Scribners to defend its copyright.*

circular & see that Armstrong's name was no longer in the firm. For more than two years his management in it has troubled me much. You may think it strange that I, having no pecuniary interest at stake should have been worried about its management. But you must remember that the house & I grew up together — that I had much to do with its growth & what literary fame I enjoy is connected with it. Besides I liked your father better than any other man on earth, & I could not bear to see a house he had built up with so much painstaking & on such high principles of honor & integrity dragged down by this man, till it seemed to me there was nothing left [of] all he gave to it but its credit. While your father was alive Armstrong was a valuable man in the house, but since

he assumed chief controll, he has used it for his own personal interests entirely. I knew it must come to this in time. I told a man a year ago, that when you thoroughly understood all the workings of the business you would very quickly take the bit in your teeth. I have long since ceased to have any respect for Armstrong's religious principles or any confidence in his truthfulness. Of course I do not know any thing of his course financially, but if he has not robbed the firm as far as he could, his character as I understood it is not complete. Thank God it is over now & the house of Scribner will ever more occupy the high position to which its noble founder lifted it. I shall die easier now.

Very sincerely yours
J. T. Headley

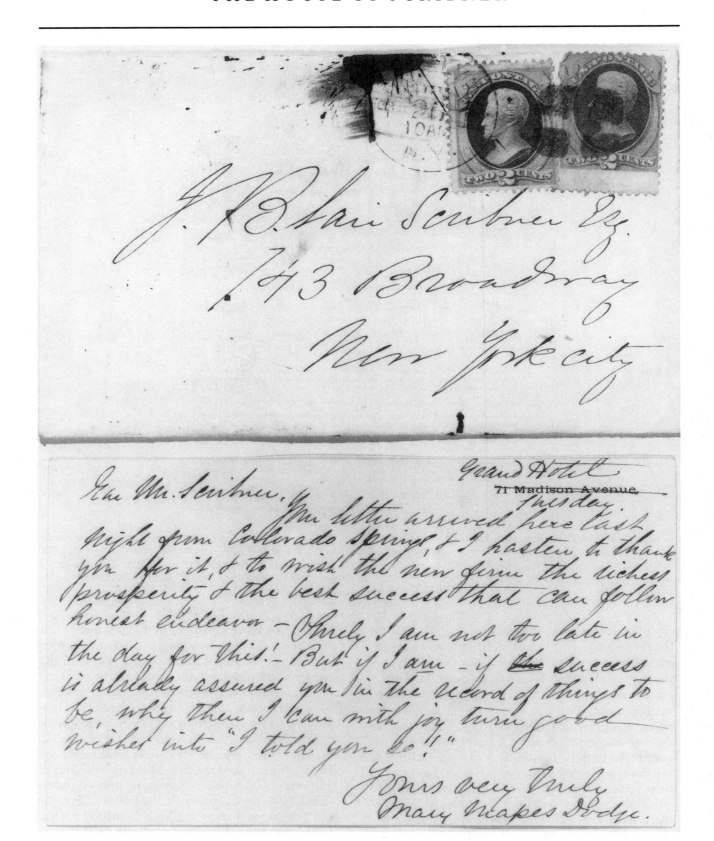

Letters of congratulation to J. Blair Scribner from Mary Mapes Dodge, editor of the firm's children's periodical, St. Nicholas, *and George Harrison Mifflin, partner in the Boston publishing firm of Houghton, Mifflin & Co.*

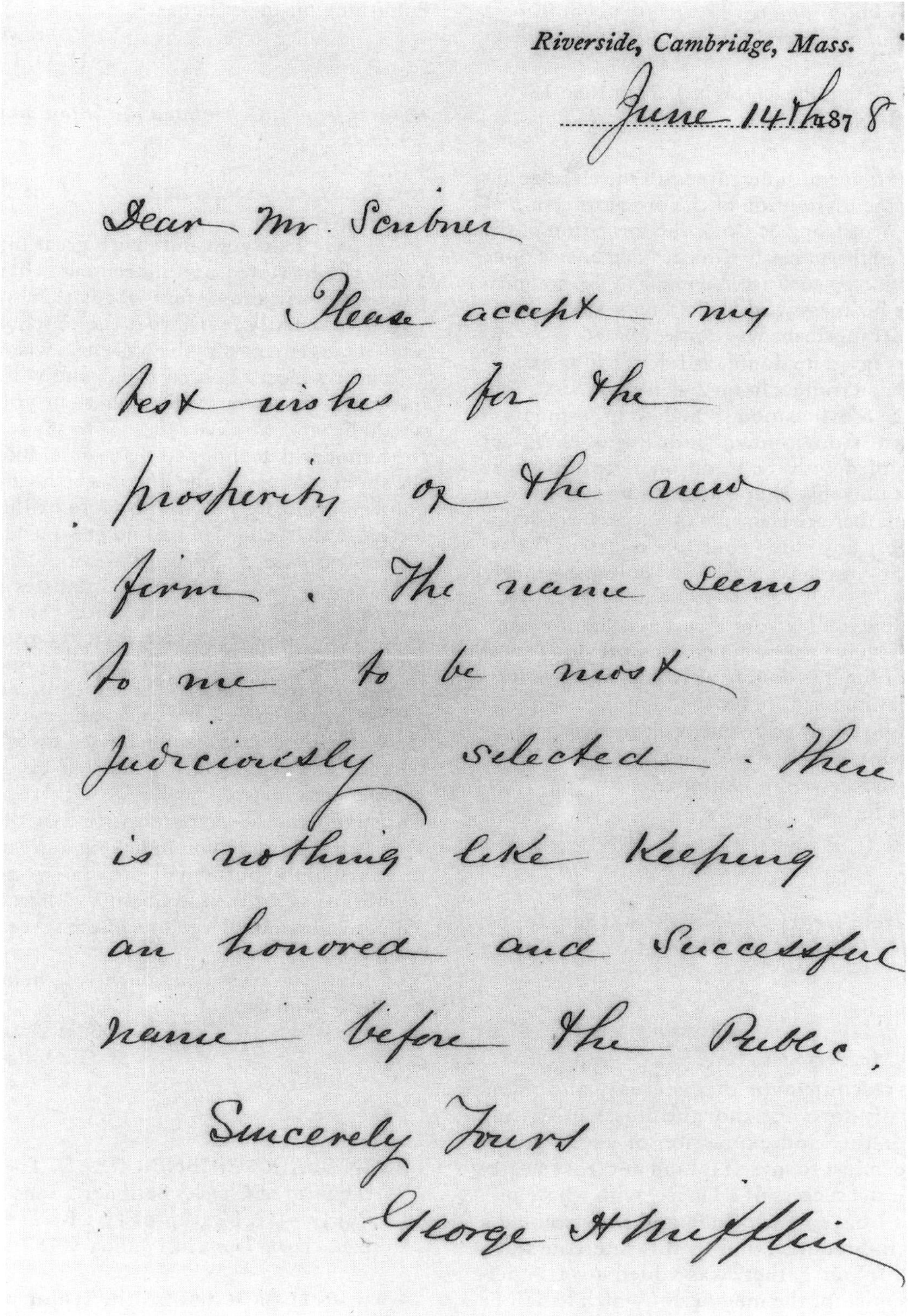

Riverside, Cambridge, Mass.

June 14th 1878

Dear Mr. Scribner

Please accept my best wishes for the prosperity of the new firm. The name seems to me to be most judiciously selected. There is nothing like keeping an honored and successful name before the Public.

Sincerely Yours

George H. Mifflin

• *Letter from Arnold Guyot (1807–1884), whose geography books and wall maps for schools were mainstays of Scribners' Educational Department.*

Princeton N.J. 24th June 1878.
Messrs. Charles Scribner's Sons,
Gentlemen,

Your favor of June 14th with the circular announcing the dissolution of the old partnership of Scribner, Armstrong & Co & the formation of the new, under the name of Charles Scribner's Sons has taken me by surprise. Living, as I do, so much out of the business world, I had no suspicion that this new arrangement was contemplated.

You regret, no doubt, as I do the long experience of a man trained in the business by your honored father & who stood so high in his estimation as Mr. Armstrong; but the industry & energy of youth coupled with the traditional caution of the Firm so admirably shaped & conducted by your lamented father are elements of Success which justify the best hopes for your future career. Be assured that you have my best & most sincere wishes.

I thank you for your assurance that my interests will receive the same care as previously. At my time of life it is doubly welcome, as it is a matter of great importance for me.

I shall shortly pay you a visit to confer about the new edition of Earth & Man.

Please receive the assurance of my sincere regard & believe me

Very truly yours
A. Guyot

• *Letter from Henry O. Houghton (1823-1895), partner in Houghton, Mifflin & Co., the Boston publisher.*

Boston, June 14, 1878
My Dear Mr. Scribner,

I have your favor of yesterday, and thank you heartily for your thoughtfulness in writing me, & for the kind expression of your letter. I should be unjust to myself if I did not feel a hearty interest in the success of a House, with whose predecessors I have had so long and so agreeable a business intercourse, and to this intercourse, in the case of your Father, was added a warm personal friendship, the memory of which I shall be happy to keep alive by transferring it to his sons. I am glad the dead-lock in your arrangements has at last been relieved, and I wish for the new firm all

the prosperity that can be attained in the Book-Publishing business. I am

Yours very truly
H. O. Houghton

• *Letter from J. G. Holland to J. Blair and Charles Scribner.*

June 15, 1878
My Dear friends:

I have read your note with great interest, as well as the printed announcements that accompany it. I wish there were words that would tell you how heartily I wish that the outcome of this new arrangement may be a great, sweet success. You bear a most honored name, and will you permit me — for I am even older than your father would be were he alive today — to say to you that the honor which clings to that name, like odor to the shattered vase, is the honor which Christianity confers? Your father was no more brilliant intellectually than you. He had no great attainments, but he was wise, and true, and good; and he won his best and most memorable qualities by direct sympathy and communion with the Savior of Men. You can never, under any circumstances, be his equals or his thoroughly worthy successors, except you are subject to the same influences, and guided by the same principles, and moved by the same affections to which he bowed his whole gentle nature. To leave such a name as his — won in worthy enterprises, managed with the strictest Christian honor — is quite worth living for.

I congratulate you in having a great concern in your hands, but it will prove — you must remember — just the kind of stuff you are made of. You are now to undergo one of the several tests of manhood.

May God bless you, guide you, help you and keep you from evil!

Yours always truly
J. G. Holland

DEATH NOTICE:
"JOHN BLAIR SCRIBNER DEAD. The Head of the Firm of Charles Scribner's Sons Dies Suddenly — A Sketch of His Brief Career," *New-York Times,* 21 January 1879, p. 5.

JOHN BLAIR SCRIBNER, the senior partner of the publishing house of Charles Scribner's Sons, died at his residence, No. 21 East Forty-eighth-street, at 5 o'clock last evening of pneumonia. Mr.

At a meeting of the employés of Charles Scribner's Sons, and Scribner & Welford, held January 23. 1879. at the Park Avenue Hotel, John H. Dingman, Chairman, resolutions of respect and esteem for the late head of the house, <u>John Blair Scribner.</u> were adopted, and a Committee appointed to prepare a copy of the same for publication :

<u>Resolved</u>, That in the Mysterious Providence which has so suddenly removed from us the beloved head of the house with which we are associated we who have experienced his constant kindness and thoughtfulness, desire to express our heartfelt sorrow and personal loss.

He commanded our willing service by his own example of promptness, energy, and conscientious performance of duty. Following the noble ambition and pure aims which governed Mr Scribner we would indicate by our increased loyalty and devotion to the interests of the house, our appreciation of the work he has left us, and our desire that all his plans and purposes should be attained

We would offer our sincere sympathy to the members of his family, whose bereavement can be measured by no words of ours.

Resolution adopted by employees of Charles Scribner's Sons and Scribner & Welford on the death of J. Blair Scribner, head of the publishing firm

Scribner contracted the disease a short time before the holidays, but recovered from the attack after a few days' illness and was at his place of business up to Thursday of last week. He was then again seized with an attack, but it appeared not to be serious, and no fears whatever were entertained that his life was in danger. After the close of business yesterday Mr. Charles Scribner, the brother and partner of Mr. John Scribner, called to see him, and the brothers conversed on the topics of the day. Mr. Charles Scribner could not refrain from expressing his fears that the illness of his brother might be dangerous, when the elder brother arose in his bed and playfully said: "Cheer up, old fellow; you always look on the dark side; I shall soon be all right again." Then, throwing up his arms, he gave one long sigh, and expired. The only persons present at the time were Mr. Scribner's wife, Mr. Charles Scribner, and two physicians, and to all the death was most sudden and entirely unexpected. Mr. Scribner was educated at Princeton College, but was not graduated. He left college to relieve and assist his father in the cares of the publishing business. Mr. Scribner was a grandson of Hon. John I. Blair, of New Jersey, after whom he was named. He married Miss Lucy Skidmore, daughter of the late Jeremiah Skidmore, of this City. He leaves no family save his wife.

Mr. Scribner was trained to the business in which his father was so eminently successful. With an aptitude for mastering commercial details, he seemed well qualified for the proper discharge of the duties which were early thrust upon him. When Mr. Charles Scribner, the head of the large publishing house, died, seven or eight years ago, the two sons, John Blair and Charles, became the heirs of the name and property, and the firm was continued with but a slight change in style. The American house was known as Scribner, Armstrong & Co., the English importing business being conducted by the firm of Scribner, Welford & Armstrong. The magazine-publishing business was and is in the hands of Scribner & Co., being a firm distinct from that of the bookselling and publishing concern. Latterly, owing to changes in the partnership, the name of the house has been "Charles Scribner's Sons," and this pleasant title is now sadly marred by the death of the elder of the two brothers. Mr. Scribner was an affable, intelligent, and liberal young gentleman. He was respected and popular among his associates, and his death will be felt as a personal grief to many people.

SKETCH:
Untitled sketch, *New-York Times,* 24 January 1879, p. 4.

The late J. BLAIR SCRIBNER was so much admired and loved by his maternal grandfather, Hon. John I. Blair, after whom he had been named, that the latter had determined, it is said, to leave him a large amount of property. He was so desirous that his elder grandson should be the senior partner of the publishing house that he bought, it is said, MR. ARMSTRONG out of the firm in order that its style might be changed from SCRIBNER, ARMSTRONG & CO. to CHARLES SCRIBNER'S SONS. By this change the entire financial responsibility and management of the house devolved upon BLAIR SCRIBNER, who was very capable and ambitious, though not strong enough to endure the strain. He had been ailing for some time, and his physician had urged him last Autumn to go South for rest and recreation. But he was unwilling to leave his post, and by rigidly adhering to it he really died from overwork. Had MR. ARMSTRONG remained in the firm, it is not unlikely that BLAIR SCRIBNER would still have been alive. Thus his grandfather's generosity defeated the very purpose he had so fondly cherished. The uncertainty of life and death is shown in the fact that BLAIR SCRIBNER, less than 30, is dead, while his grandfather, JOHN I. BLAIR, is yet vigorous at over three score and ten. Few young men had brighter prospects or more to live for than BLAIR SCRIBNER, and his early death illustrates the bitter sarcasm of fortune.

INTERVIEW:
"Improvement in the Book Trade. A Talk with Charles Scribner — Effect of Cheap Publications — Relations with English Authors," *New York Tribune,* 25 November 1879, p. 8.

In his discussion of the contemporary book trade, CS II identifies an important issue that will continue to affect Scribners as well as other major American publishers trying to maintain "friendly relations" with foreign authors: the lack of an international copyright.

"The book trade feels the effect of general improvement in the business," said Charles Scribner, of the well-known publishing house, in a talk with a representative of THE TRIBUNE. "Particularly in the West has the demand for books increased. Our agents in that section report an encouraging condition of things. Publishers begin to feel more like taking risks and extending their operations than they have felt for a long time. The business of the last year has been very prudently conducted, however, a good deal of it having been in the way of working off material on hand, and getting out new editions of old works. Some branches of the trade have been damaged by the so-called 'Library' publications retailed at 10, 15 and 20 cents. New American novels and reprints of English novels at the old regular prices have naturally suffered from these cheap issues. People who can get a good novel for 10 cents are not likely to pay a $1 for one no better."

"Is the business of pirating English books on the increase?"

"I think not, except so far as these cheap editions are concerned. The best class of English ancient literature is usually brought out in this country under some arrangement between the author and the American publishers. In the case of such authors as Froude, we pay a regular copyright rate — not large, it is true, and not as large as it would be if there were an international copyright law, and we were assured of protection against the competition of other publishers; but a sum which ensures friendly relations with the foreign authors and gives us a claim to the best sheets of any new work. I believe this plan is followed by other American houses. As many of our books are republished in England as we bring out here of English publications. I think the tendency is, on the whole, toward more and more cordiality and recognition of mutual rights and interests between British and American authors and publishers."

"Has the cost of manufacturing books touched bottom?"

"To all appearances. Paper is now higher and other expenses show an upward tendency. We shall certainly not be able to make books any cheaper than we have been doing, and the selling price will probably advance somewhat. There has been a notable improvement within a few years in the mechanical branches of book-making. Books are now better printed and better bound in this country than ever before."

"Has the tendency toward novel and startling bindings exhausted itself?"

Scribners' announcement in The Book Buyer *of its newly organized Subscription Department. The department was publishing the authorized American edition of the* Encyclopedia Britannica *and later added standard editions of authors' complete works.*

"Yes, except in juvenile publications. Substantial works are now brought out in plain and tasteful dress."

Speaking of the recent publications of his house, Mr. Scribner referred to the volume of Charles Dickens's correspondence just issued, which, he said, was having a remarkably large sale — an evidence of the lively interest still felt by the public in everything concerning the great novelist. Referring to the increasing success of *Scribner's Monthly,* he said that the edition for December — 103,000 copies — was the largest in the history of the periodical.

1880–1889

1880

20 Mar.   Publication date of Brander Matthews's first Scribner book, *The Theatres of Paris*

1881

Apr.   CS II sells his share of Scribner & Co. to Roswell G. Smith et al. As part of the agreement, the name of the corporation and magazine will be changed, dropping the word *Scribner* or *Scribner's,* and CS II will not publish a competing periodical for a period of five years. (*Scribner's Monthly* becomes *The Century Magazine* and Scribner & Co. becomes the Century Company.)

12 Oct.   Death of J. G. Holland

22 Oct.   Publication date of the first two volumes (of thirteen) in the Campaigns of the Civil War series: John G. Nicolay's *The Outbreak of Rebellion* and M. F. Force's *From Fort Henry to Corinth*

1882

4 Oct.   Publication date of *The American Boys' Handy Book: What to Do and How to Do It* by Dan Beard, the first book by this American naturalist and illustrator, who helped establish the Boy Scouts of America

12 Oct.   Publication of *Criteria of Diverse Kinds of Truth as Opposed to Agnosticism, Being a Treatise on Applied Logic* by James McCosh, president of Princeton, the first number (of eight) in his Philosophic Series

1 Dec.   CS II signs lease for the whole building at 743–745 Broadway for the period from 1 May 1883 through 1 May 1886, allowing him to sublet any unused space.

1883

24 Mar.   Publication date of James Russell Soley's *The Blockade and the Cruisers,* the first volume (of three) in the Navy in the Civil War series

1 June   Charles Scribner's Sons sells its school textbook list (Sheldon's readers, Guyot's geographies, Cooley's physical sciences, Tenney's natural histories, Felter's arithmetics, etc.) to Ivison, Blakeman, Taylor & Co.

23 Oct.   Publication date of Howard Pyle's first Scribner book, *The Merry Adventures of Robin Hood of Great Reknown, in Nottinghamshire*

1884

5 Apr.   Publication date of the first two volumes (of ten) of *Stories by American Authors*

June   Arthur Hawley Scribner graduates from Princeton and joins his brother Charles in the family publishing firm.

18 Oct.	Publication date of A. B. Frost's first Scribner book, *Stuff & Nonsense*
Nov.	Publication of *Scribner's Statistical Atlas of the United States, Showing by Graphic Methods Their Present Condition and Their Political, Social and Industrial Development* by Fletcher W. Hewes and Henry Gannett, chief geographer of the United States Geological Survey
25 Nov	Publication date of Henry van Dyke's first Scribner book, *The Reality of Religion*

1885

16 Apr.	Publication date of Robert Louis Stevenson's first Scribner book, *A Child's Garden of Verses*
18 May	Death of Charles Welford, who is succeeded by his assistant, Lemuel W. Bangs, as head of Scribner & Welford, the importing company of Scribners
21 Oct.	CS II purchases Welford's share of Scribner & Welford from his estate.

1886

5 Jan.	Publication date of Robert Louis Stevenson's *Strange Case of Dr. Jekyll and Mr. Hyde*
13 Apr.	CS II and Arthur H. Scribner obtain a certificate allowing them to continue to use the "Scribner & Welford" name.
27 May	Publication date of the first volume (of four) of *Cyclopedia of Painters and Paintings,* edited by John Denison Champlin, containing more than two thousand illustrations
14 July	Publication date of Robert Louis Stevenson's *Kidnapped,* one of the year's bestsellers
7 Oct.	Publication date of Frances Hodgson Burnett's *Little Lord Fauntleroy,* one of the year's bestsellers
15 Dec.	First *Scribner's Magazine* dinner held at the residence of CS II at 12 East 38th Street in New York City

1887

Jan.	First issue of the Scribner periodical *Scribner's Magazine,* edited by Edward L. Burlingame
21 May	Publication date of Thomas Nelson Page's first Scribner book, *In Ole Virginia; or, Marse Chan and Other Stories*
July	Edwin Wilson Morse, music critic and journalist, joins the firm as editor of *The Book Buyer.* From 1894 to 1904 he works as an editor in the trade department; from 1904 to 1910 he serves as secretary and a director of Charles Scribner's Sons, Inc.
26 Oct.	Publication date of Harold Frederic's first Scribner book, *Seth's Brother's Wife: A Study of Life in the Greater New York*

1888

Jan.   W. C. Brownell, a journalist and critic who had worked for the *New York World*, *The Nation*, and the *Philadelphia Press*, joins the firm as a literary adviser and book editor.

16 Feb.   Publication date of *The Tailor Made Girl, Her Friends, Her Fashions and Her Follies* by the American humorist Philip H. Welch

1889

22 Oct.   Publicaton date of the first two volumes (of nine) of *The History of the United States*, the landmark study by American historian Henry Adams

---

LETTER:
Letter by CS II to Charles Welford, 30 March 1881.

In this unburdening to his friend and business partner of what must have been stressful events, CS II details the reasons why he sold his share in Scribner & Co., the publisher of the very profitable and popular magazines, Scribner's Monthly *and* St. Nicholas, *to Roswell Smith, president of the separate company. "A.C.A" is Andrew C. Armstrong, one of the original partners of CS I, whose share in the publishing firm J. Blair Scribner had purchased in 1878, clearing the way for him to name the firm "Charles Scribner's Sons."*

Dear Mr. Welford,

I hoped to find time to write again last week but could not. I have most important news and startling news to communicate concerning Scribner & Co. and "Scribner's Monthly." After next November they will cease to exist. In other words I have just completed (and expect to sign papers tomorrow) a sale of all my stock to Roswell Smith on condition that he takes the name of <u>Scribner</u> off of everything connected with the company and its publications. The price paid to me is $200000 or $1000 a share and the amount is secured by the stock as collateral.

The name is (as I have written) to be dropped altogether before next <u>November</u>; but the Company has the right to use the name as a <u>subtitle</u> for <u>one</u> year longer. It will probably be entitled

"The <u>American</u> (or The Continent — or some such title)
Scribner's Illustrated Monthly

Published by Roswell Smith & Co. (or the <u>American</u> Publishing Co.)

On the other side, I am bound not to issue a competitive magazine for <u>five</u> years. This, I believe, covers all the important points of the sale.

Now; why did I sell? 1st Because I did not control the company but was a minority stockholder. Dr. Holland (as I wrote a long time ago) took Mr. Smith's side on all questions of difference and ended up by selling his stock to Smith after refusing it to me unless I would purchase Smith's at the same time. He has acted very selfishly and rather meaner than anyone else in the whole matter.

<u>2nd</u> If I had not sold out I would have been obliged to oppose the company in many things & the opposition would probably before long have made a lawsuit necessary and that would have injured the magazine stock, my business, and taken too much of my time & strength. You will understand that not only are Holland & Smith now stockholders but they have admitted <u>eight</u> of the young men in the office. These are of course under their influence. They all want to (1st) change the name of the company but retain the magazine name (2nd) move into a different building from C.S's Sons (3rd) increase salaries all around (4th) increase board of trustees from three to five (5th) <u>publish books</u> without any restriction. You can easily see that I would have been forced to oppose all these movements.

<u>3rd</u> If I had succeeded in my opposition (which would have been doubtful) it would have injured the Co. and, in the end, I would have been forced to purchase, or sell at much lower price. I have been able to hold them just where they are since last Oct. but it is injuring the stock every day.

SCRIBNER'S MONTHLY.

ST. NICHOLAS.

SCRIBNER & CO., PUBLISHERS,

743 & 745 Broadway,

J. G. HOLLAND,
ROSWELL SMITH,
CHARLES SCRIBNER'S SONS.

New York, *Nov 13a 1880*

Charles Scribner Esqr
    Dear Sir.

        The object of the interview
to which I asked you to day, at Dr Hol-
lands request—was simply to present
three questions—

1st. Will you sell your interest in "Scribner & Co.

2nd. Will you buy out Dr Holland & myself—

or 3rd. if you do not wish to do either will
you consent to such changes & arrangements, as will make "Scribner & Co." in fact
and name, entirely independent of
your house,—and give the control and
management into the hands of the majority of the stock, where it properly belongs.

        I regret that we wandered from the issue
& indulged in personal recrimination—I
scarcely know who is to blame for that—but since
and I do not know that it is of any consequence to determine—Yours truly
                        Roswell Smith

Letter by Roswell Smith, publisher of Scribner & Co., to CS II, offering him three options regarding the future of Scribner & Co.

<u>4th</u> Mr. Smith, so long as he can do so, will use his connection with this House and its connections to build up a rival business. You are entirely right in thinking it was a mistake to have let him issue the Song books. It not only established a precedent for him but put him in communication with the Trade and thus he stepped right into the relations of established confidence which it has taken this House years to build up.

<u>5th & finally</u> — There was no logical or practical position short of purchase or sale and, <u>at the price and getting the name off,</u> I would rather have sold than purchased. In selling I not only make a good profit (which is <u>just what we paid A.C.A.</u>, as in that purchase the stock of S.A. & Co. was valued at only $100000) but release myself from a false and anomalous position and leave myself free to give all my time to our business and C.S's Sons which I fully understand and have under my eye & control. The trade and many others know well enough (for Smith took pains they should know) that I had little or no voice in the management of S. & Co. and the knowledge has been an injury to me, as it tended to carry with it the further impression that I was little more than a figurehead downstairs also. I got tired of it.

Now; suppose I had purchased. I would have had to expell Smith and most others upstairs and secured new and inexperienced hands and taken for a time at least the management of that immense concern in addition to what I now have on my hands — including the nasty Song book business. Even if I had done this at such tremendous financial risk, the business would not have dovetailed with the regular business downstairs. It has for years developed <u>independently</u> and could not have been made to fit at once into the proper relations with my other interests.

I have given you some of the reasons for doing as I have done because I know the news will be a shock to you and very naturally you will at once think of the loss of prestige it involves and its bad effects in other and more direct ways. I will add here however that I believe I shall secure more good books from the magazines than if I had stayed in. Witness Mrs. Burnett's "Fair Barbarian" which Osgood has just issued.

Of many evils I believe I have chosen the least. I am satisfied. I well could fill pages on

this subject but will leave you to think the question out with the hints I have given you. . . .

Yours sincerely
Charles Scribner

LETTER:
Letter by J. G. Holland to CS II, 6 May 1881, accompanying a printed copy of his June 1881 column in *Scribner's Monthly*.

Dear Mr. Scribner:

Everybody has had his say about the recent changes in this concern but me, and without consultation I have written and we are printing the inclosed which I send to you, hoping that you will either like it, or find it unobjectionable. I suppose it would be quite impossible for us to agree on any statement of these matters, but I have tried to be true on all points, and I certainly have written it with the friendliest feeling toward you personally and toward the house that publishes my works.

Yours very truly
J. G. Holland

COLUMN EXCERPT:
J. G. Holland, "'Scribner's Monthly.'-Historical" from his "Topics of the Time" column, *Scribner's Monthly*, 22, no. 2 (June 1881): 302–303.

Holland died four months later, in October. Richard Watson Gilder assumed the editorship of the magazine, which, in its November 1881 issue, bore the new name The Century Magazine.

So many stories have been told by the newspaper press, recently, about this magazine, — and its internal relations and its history, — and so much public interest has been manifested in regard to the subject, that it has seemed to me to be worth while to tell the story from the beginning, authoritatively.

Thirteen years ago, Mr. Charles Scribner, the founder of what is known as "the Scribner book-house," applied to me to take the editorship of "Hours at Home," a magazine he had started some years before. At that time I had just closed up business in Massachusetts, preparatory to a somewhat extended sojourn in Europe, and I peremptorily declined the invitation. Mr. Scribner insisted, however, that the offer should remain open until my return. The European journey was

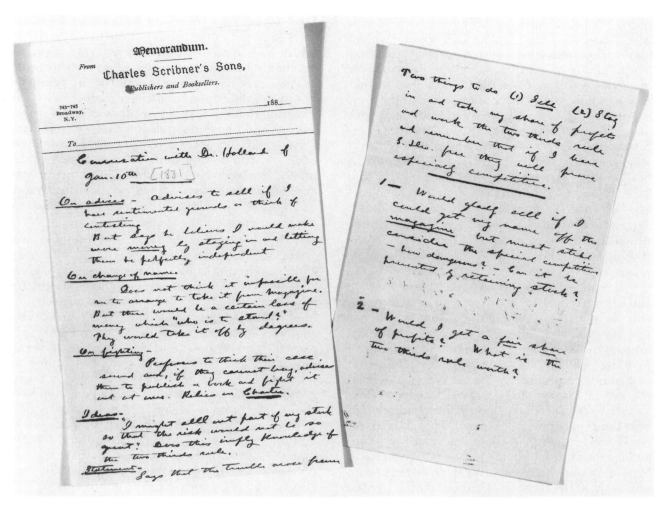

CS II's notes on a conversation with J. G. Holland, editor of Scribner's Monthly, *regarding the future of* Scribner & Co.

entered upon, and I had advanced sufficiently far in it to begin to look beyond it. It was then that this offer recurred to me, and that I began earnestly to consider it. My conclusions were that the place was not a desirable one; that there was no such thing as a great success for that magazine; that I did not myself like it, and that I would not identify myself with it, or tie myself to its traditions; besides, I believed it to be moribund, as a subsequent examination proved it to be.

At about this time I met Mr. Roswell Smith in Geneva, Switzerland, when the matter of the old magazine came up in conversation. I had met and known something of the gentleman before; indeed, we had planned to go abroad together, originally, though something had interfered with our calculations. His home was then in Indiana, and for health's sake, and other reasons, he desired to move East; so that when I said that instead of entering upon the editorship of an old magazine I should like to start a new one, he announced himself ready to undertake, as business manager, an enterprise of that kind with me. The result of the conversation, which was terminated, as I happen to remember, upon one of the bridges in Geneva, was a verbal agreement that we should unite our forces, on our return to America, for the effecting of this project. It was on this bridge, and exactly under those circumstances, that SCRIBNER'S MONTHLY was planned.

Mr. Smith returned to America before I did, and when he came he brought a letter of introduction from me to Mr. Charles Scribner, commending him in such terms to the publisher's consideration and confidence as have been a thousand times justified by his subsequent business history.

As the investors would say: "I claim the discovery of Mr. Roswell Smith, and the combination with Mr. Charles Scribner and myself, which resulted in the production of SCRIBNER'S MONTHLY." It was naturally Mr. Scribner's wish to have the new magazine emanate from the book-house, so that he was not primarily disposed to listen to the project of starting a new and independent house, with magazine publishing as its special business. I refused, however, to have anything to do with a magazine that should be floated as the flag of a book-house, or as tributary or subordinate to a book-house. I did not believe there would be success in such an enterprise, and the plan was at last determined upon that, when I should return to America, a new concern should be formed, for the special undertaking and execution of this enterprise.

I returned from abroad in the spring of 1870, and all our plans for the issue of the new magazine were matured during the following summer and autumn. Mr. Smith had no knowledge whatever of the publishing business, and I had none save that which I had acquired in the publication of a country newspaper, with the details of which, however, I had had little to do. It was deemed desirable by Mr. Scribner that the magazine should bear the name of the book-house. He and his associates served their purpose in that, and Mr. Smith and I were glad to have the prestige of the name in beginning our enterprise. It was, in one aspect, a selfish thing for all of us. The book-house wanted the advertising which the new magazine would give it; and the magazine-house, of which Mr. Smith and I represented the predominate interest, wanted the name for what there might be of popular value in it. In another aspect it was not a selfish matter at all. Through long years of the most brotherly intercourse, I had come into very affectionate relations with Mr. Scribner, and Mr. Smith came very quickly into similar relations, — charmed by his kindly nature and character. It was a pleasure to both of us to attach his name to the new publication, hoping that no circumstances would ever occur to change it. I have said all this simply to explain the "true inwardness" of all the differences which have occurred between Mr. Smith and myself on one side and the representatives of the Scribner book-house on the other. We — the two parties — regarded the enterprise and operations of the magazine-house from radically different standpoints. We who held the majority interest regarded the Scribner connection as something that should inure solely to the benefit of the magazine-house, in which the book-house was interested to the amount of its stock, and not to the benefit of the book-house, in which we had no interest whatever. We felt that if we should desire to publish a book, — which our charter gave us the right to publish, — we ought not to be called upon to consider whether we were affecting the business of any other concern whatsoever; and I have no question that we were perfectly right. We were organized to do our own business, and neither to do or to mind any other man's. We were opposed in this, and this difference lay at the basis, and was the inspiring cause, of all the recent changes that have taken place in the proprietorship of the concern.

Very soon after the first number of SCRIBNER'S MONTHLY was issued, Mr. Putnam came to us with the offer of his magazine. We acceded to his conditions, though I have forgotten what they were, and it was soon quietly left behind with the "Hours at Home." It is remarkable, in reviewing the career of the MONTHLY, that, although it started without a subscriber, it never printed or sold less than forty thousand copies a month. The highest task we set ourselves in those early days was to reach an edition of one hundred thousand copies, — a number now largely surpassed; and now we are looking forward to an edition of one hundred and fifty thousand copies, and the consequent production of two sets of plates and double sets of machinery. That this success has been a surprise to the publishing fraternity is undoubtedly true; that two men, utterly unused to the business, should succeed from the first, in so difficult a field, is, in the retrospect, a surprise to themselves. Of the editorial management of SCRIBNER, I have nothing to say, except that it has been conscientiously and industriously performed, and that I have had a corps of able and enthusiastic assistants, who have given themselves to the work as if the magazine, indeed, were all their own.

I suppose that if any one were asked what, more than anything else, had contributed to the success of the magazine, he would answer: Its superb engravings, and the era it introduced of improved illustrative art. This feature of our work is attributed to Mr. R. W. Gilder and to Mr. A. W. Drake, — the former the office editor, and the latter the superintendent of the illustrative department. Mr. Smith and I, any further than we have stood behind these men with encouragement and money, deserve no credit for the marvelous development that has been made in illustration. Per-

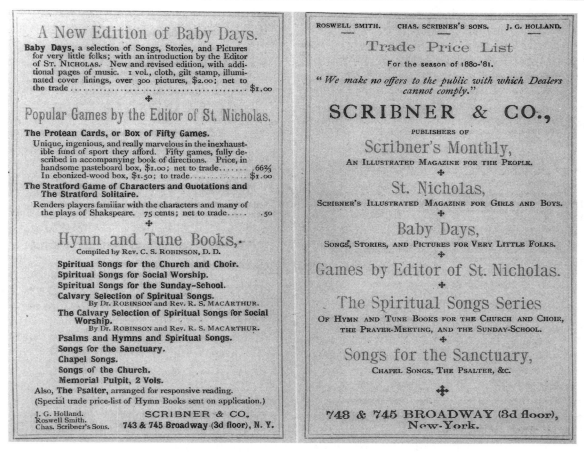

Trade price list (1880–1881) of Scribner & Co. publications

haps this is not quite true, for Mr. Smith was the first to insist on the experiment of printing the illustrated forms on dry paper. This has had much to do with the success of our cuts, and SCRIBNER'S MONTHLY enjoyed a practical monopoly of this mode of cut-printing for years. The effects achieved in this way excited great curiosity, both in this country and in England. Mr. Smith may, therefore, legitimately claim to have revolutionized the cut-printing of the world; and it is another illustration of the fact that reforms are rarely made in their own art by routine men. It takes a mechanic to invent an agricultural machine; a lawyer, turned man of business, to discover that damp paper is not the best for printing cuts on.

The present Mr. Charles Scribner and I have now ceased to be proprietors, and Mr. Roswell Smith has acquired about nine-tenths of the stock. The remainder has been divided among the young men who have done so much and worked so faithfully to make the magazine what it has been and what it is. I am glad that they own it, and that it is Mr. Smith's design that they shall have more as they

win the ability to purchase it. I have no cooperation theories or predilections to gratify, but I owe so much to these men that I shall greatly rejoice in any substantial reward they may reap for their long and faithful service in building up the interests of the concern, and for their attempts to spare me all unnecessary toil.

It is a great satisfaction to me to feel that both SCRIBNER'S MONTHLY and ST. NICHOLAS — the latter of which is peculiarly the child of Mr. Roswell Smith's enterprise — are in the same hands they have always been in, and that the readers of both have lost nothing in the changes that have been made in the proprietorship. Some changes are still to be made in names, for the necessity for which I am sorry; but they involve nothing more than sentiment, and we shall all very soon adapt ourselves to them and forget them.

With the burden of business responsibilities lifted from my shoulders, I hope to find my hand more easily at work with my pen, and trust that for many years I may hold the relation to the great reading world which this editorial position gives me. I risked in this business all the reputation and all the money I had made, and it is a great satisfaction that I did not miscalculate the resources of my business associates or my own.

REVIEW:
"Campaigns of the Civil War," *New-York Times*, 29 October 1881, p. 6.

Scribners' major contribution to the history of the Civil War was a thirteen-volume series called the Campaigns of the Civil War, *which it published between 1881 and 1883. The books sold for $1 each; the boxed set cost $12.50. A three-volume companion series, entitled* The Navy in the Civil War, *appeared in 1883.*

The scheme of publishing a complete history of the Rebellion in the form of a series of independent yet connected volumes, each devoted to a separate campaign, each written by a person with especial qualifications for that particular part of the task, and all together covering the whole field of the great war, was devised by the Scribners several years ago. It was an ingenious, we may say a brilliant, plan; and now that the details are laid before us the wonder is that a work so obviously desirable was not undertaken long before. The subject is so large, the military operations were so diversified in character and spread over so vast an area, that most readers prefer to study the war by campaigns — a preference which may be indulged with the more profit since it was not until near the end of the Rebellion that the armies moved in unison toward a common objective point. A high degree of editorial tact and intelligence characterizes the execution of Messrs. Scribners' excellent undertaking. The division of the work is judicious; the allotment of topics to the various writers is happy; and cordial cooperation has been secured from recognized authorities, from the Government, from distinguished military officers, and from the custodians of public and private records. To all this we may add that the volumes are convenient in size, beautifully printed, and furnished with many clear and simple maps which without being elaborate are sufficient to illustrate the narrative. . . .

LETTER:
CS II wrote this letter to his English partner, Charles Welford, 8 June 1883, regarding the sale of the Scribner textbook business to Ivison, Blakeman, Taylor & Co.

My dear Mr. Welford:

. . .

In his absence [Burlingame's] I have been kept very busy and yet I have managed to carry out a plan which has long been in my mind. I have negotiated a sale of our entire school book department to Messrs. Ivison, Blakeman & Taylor. You will probably hardly appreciate how relieved I feel now that the question is settled and the transfer almost completed. It has been done very successfully & pleasantly — so much so that not even one of our authors (and you know what a sensitive lot they are) finds any fault with the [missing section] indeed it more than I expected. They pay me (confidentially) $45,000 for the plates and take all stock at cost . . . If you take the entire sum invested in the department the sale represents a loss but if you take the price at which Blair & I purchased from Armstrong there is no loss. But I do not like the business, my ambition is not in that direction. I have all that I want to do for the present, and I would have disposed of the business if necessary at a considerable sacrifice. The methods employed in the School book business are even more objectionable than before and the whole business has grown apart from the other departments of the publishing business and is carried on by Educational houses which confine their attention to it. Of these Ivisons is the largest & best. The others are Appletons, Bragg (Cincinnati), and Barnes. These houses have formed a syndicate and work to some extent in common, at least they have made a formal agreement not to displace one another's books without paying an equivalent in money. They also have begun to publish certain books in common. The Harpers are left way behind and it is reported that they also think of selling out.

I could write very much more on this subject but this will probably be enough for I believe you will agree with me that the decision to go out of that business was a wise one. It leaves me free to conduct with greater vigor the really profitable portions of the business. . . .

Yours faithfully
Charles Scribner

This was not the end of textbook publishing for Scribners. A decade later, in 1893, CS II hired Edward Thomas Lord away from D. C. Heath &

Company in Boston to start an educational department again. The result was one of the most successful and enduring textbook departments within a general publishing business.

PERSONAL SKETCH:
Roger Burlingame, *Of Making Many Books* (New York: Charles Scribner's Sons, 1946), pp. 164–165.

This sketch of Lemuel W. Bangs was published in Burlingame's centennial history of the firm; Bangs was in charge of the London office until 1916.

Welford died in 1885 from the first illness of his life. He was succeeded by his assistant — one of the most picturesque characters in the history of publishing.

Lemuel W. Bangs was thoroughly American by birth and taste. At Scribner's he was known as "Bangsy"; the British called him "The Senator" and loved him. He had large mustaches which, as he faced you, seemed to stand out several inches from the sides of his thin face. As far as anyone can remember, they were always gray.

"He wore," wrote Gerald Duckworth, "a peculiar frock-coat made to his own design by Poole, the celebrated tailor of Savile Row, and he had never had the cut altered since he first arrived in London. He had a pretty taste in ties and wore some choice flower in his buttonhole. 'The Senator' had many good stories to tell his friends, and used to present them with cigarettes the size of a cigar."

Duckworth, one of Bangsy's most intimate publisher friends, did not, however, give a complete account of his wardrobe. As "The Senator" died alone in the world, his clothing was sold at auction and the auctioneer's catalog is in the Scribner archives. There were, among hundreds of other items: 16 coats (11 morning, 5 frock), 25 pairs of trousers, 26 lined fancy waistcoats, 17 other suits, 188 ties, 18 pairs of spats, 20 pairs of boots and shoes, 80 silk and cotton handkerchiefs; 9 soft felt, 2 Panama, 1 opera, 1 bowler, hats and 2 caps, 14 overcoats and 31 dozen collars, all in excellent condition.

Every night at the Garrick Club he could be seen at his special table with a pint of champagne. He never varied the vintage until it gave out; then,

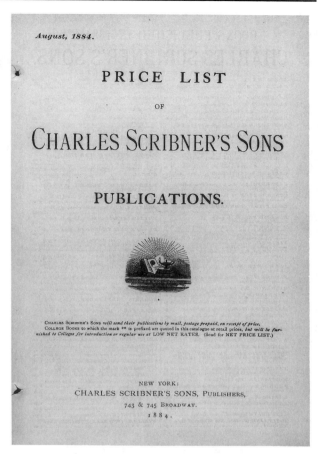

Cover of 1884 Scribner book catalogue

with infinite care, he would pick another and the club laid in a special stock for him. It was served at an exact temperature.

By Bangs's time, London was full of literary agents. Bangs knew them all and got along with them better than C.S. did. He wrote C.S. soothing letters about them. When the Magazine came along, it was Bangs who interested Frederick Warne in publishing its English edition and it was Bangs, too, who calmed Warne when the Magazine printed in its very first issue an article on American coast defense against a hypothetical war with England.

Bangs's work was prodigious. His letters fill ten box files in the archives and through them one can trace a quarter century of British politics, social history, and literature.

LETTER:
Robert Louis Stevenson, "American Rights and Wrongs," *The Academy*, no. 724 (20 March 1886): 203.

In his public letter in this English publication, Stevenson enters the international copyright fray while praising the good faith and generosity he has received as an English author from his American publisher, Charles Scribner's Sons.

Will you allow me to say a word or two on the question of American rights and wrongs?

1. Authors should be careful to understand the bargains into which they enter with English publishers, and either strictly reserve American rights or see that they receive an equivalent. It is a mistake to suppose that, in the worst of cases, America brings nothing. There is always a little money to be got for advance sheets. I have known it to be near a third of what the author could raise (in money down) at home; and this is too great a consideration to be let slip.

2. In most cases, the author will do best to sell the advance sheets to some American publisher, and then forget that such a book existed.

3. There is, in the States, as at home, a difference in publishers. At a time when so many scalded authors rush into print with their complaints, I think it no more a pleasure than a duty to name Messrs. Charles Scribner's Sons. I have had but one year's dealings with this firm; but it would be hard to express my sense of their good faith and generosity.

4. A word to English publishers. I have known them to dispose of advance sheets (without accounting) when the book was burthened with a royalty to the author. I am no lawyer, but I make bold to say this practice is indefensible; and if brought before a judge, would lead to white faces.

5. The proposal (made by an American) of a system of stamp is one of those radiantly simple things that offend such as live in darkness. It will not be accepted yet awhile; but there is no colourable reason against it. It could not hurt the publisher in any fair business; and if he dislike the proposal, it is either from blind conservatism, or —

6. In the meantime, let us try to get our own copyright law amended, and wait, with such civility as we can muster, for the States to follow in our wake. We lie bare to robbery, and we do well to be annoyed; but our American brethren are but imperfectly protected, and a little generous ardour to improve their case will do ours no harm.

Robert Louis Stevenson

INTERVIEW:

"Author and Publisher. Discussion of Their Relations. A Few Words from Mr. Stedman and a Frank Talk with Charles Scribner," *New York Tribune*, 27 March 1887, p. 10.

Describing the basic difference between the financial arrangement between author and publisher in England versus the United States, CS II argues that American authors are treated fairly by the royalty system. The real issue affecting author and publisher is the lack of an international copyright, and Scribner uses as an example his firm's publication of Robert Louis Stevenson.

The lively discussion of the relations between authors and publishers which has carried on of late in England has stirred up a good deal of interest here and led to some inquiries by TRIBUNE reporters. E. C. Stedman was asked his opinion on this controversy and he replied that to state his views with any completeness would require more time than he could now spare. He would say, however, that if what is generally understood of the relations between British authors and the publishers is correct, American authors have far less cause to complain. He believed that our leading publishers were in the main an honorable and even generous class of men, quite above falsifying an author's accounts. As to the division of profits between authors and publishers, the present system was in some respects open to amendment.

Charles Scribner expressed his views in this way:

"I have read with interest what has appeared on this subject in THE TRIBUNE. I suppose that what you refer to particularly is what Mr. Besant has to say on the phase of secret profits made by British publishers. The possibility of such profits comes from the system of division of profits, which American publishers do not adopt. Where, as in England, publisher and author divide profits, the publisher seeking to be dishonest, or desiring to make more profit, I will say, than the author is aware of, has it or may have it in his power to purchase his material or have his binding done, or both, at less rates than those represented to the author. By collusion, or otherwise, he may thus make the expense of a book greater than the open account shows and thus he may secure an additional profit over that which is made apparent to the author, and thus the author may be defrauded of his dues.

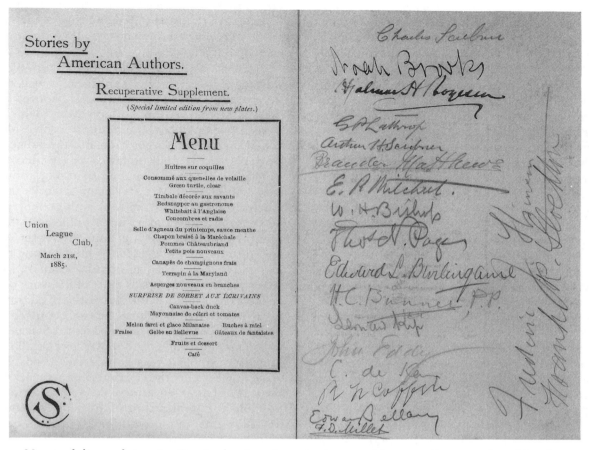

Menu of dinner honoring Stories by American Authors *and its contributors, signed by those attending it. Published in ten small volumes from 1884 to 1885, the set represented a broad range of American writers. In the Scribner tradition of multiple-volume series,* Stories by English Authors *was published in 1896, also in ten volumes; this was followed in 1898 to 1902 with* Stories by Foreign Authors, *another ten-volume set.*

"In this country, however, and certainly in our case, this phase of the matter is removed from controversy through the fact that the royalty system is used, the sharing of profits between publisher and author not being practised. The publisher simply agrees to give the author a certain per cent of the retail price of the work. Of course this system does not remove the opportunity or possibility of 'cooking the accounts' of the number of books sold. A firm may enter a less number of books sold than is actually the case, if it desires to defraud. But so far as I am aware there has been no complaint of this kind, no charge even pointing in that direction as regards the publishing houses here well known in the trade. However, it is, perhaps, but just and fair that an author should have every proper opportunity to satisfy himself fully that he is receiving his royalty upon the number of books to which he is actually entitled by sale.

That he may do this he must needs have opportunity to ascertain through inspection of books or by actual count the number of books received from the bindery by the publisher and the number the publisher actually sells. We ourselves, irrespective of the present discussion of this matter, have been arranging to afford an opportunity of this kind to the authors whose works we sell. They will have the chance, if they so desire, to inspect the 'returns' for themselves, and satisfy themselves of the precise sale of their works. To be sure, even this opportunity would not prevent, necessarily, the possibility of an understatement to the author. Our action is not the result of any complaint from any author or of any expressed desire on the part of anyone for this arrangement, but we have made it in order to indicate our desire that the author should feel that at all times he is at liberty to inspect the books for himself and thus have all possible assurance that he is receiving what is due him. In the case of foreign authors any representative they may choose here may examine the books and secure all information desired which will throw light on his particular account.

"In this country there has been no complaint, so far as I have learned, that the author does not receive his royalty on the full number of books sold. The only bone of contention is, on the part of the author, that he does not receive a sufficiently high per cent on the retail price. Well, the market is an open one, and the author is at liberty to choose his own publisher. If, then, the publisher were making more than a fair profit, some other publisher could afford to give the author a larger royalty, and he would do so. Competition rules among publishers as well as with other people. Publishers have found that fifteen per cent on the retail price is all that they can afford to pay. Now, supposing that a book retails at a dollar, many an author will look at the bare sum and say that for him to toil and agitate his brain and his imagination in producing a work which sells at one hundred cents, while the author gets only fifteen of them, is unjust and that he does not get a proper remuneration.

"Let us look at it, taking the $1 book as a basis. The retail dealer has to have a discount of 40 per cent at least. The publisher therefore receives 60 cents. The cost to him of the manufacture of the book is on the average 25 cents. Adding the author's 15 cents and 20 cents is left for the publisher. But that is not profit. He has to pay for his plant out of that, which consists in the plates, and probably a thousand copies have to be sold first to enable him to make that up. Then there is the advertising in one paper, we will say; if his profits are 10 cents a volume, he must sell 100 copies to make that amount good. Then there is his rent, his salaries to pay, the whole expense of his business. Taking all this into consideration, you can readily perceive how it is that publishers come to the conclusion that a royalty of 15 per cent is about all they can afford to pay. But there is another important feature of this matter. There was a time when a $1 book was considered a cheap affair. But nowadays the tendency is to paper-bound volumes, at 50, 25, 20, and even 10 cents. These paper-covered volumes are handled by the news companies largely, and neither the American, the Union (which supplies trains extensively), the Manhattan, the New-England, nor any other of these companies will handle these volumes except on a discount of 50 per cent and on

sale at that. Being received on sale, many of these volumes are returned soiled and thus rendered almost valueless. You perceive what a reduction of profits all this makes.

"The want of an international copyright is working a great injury to publishers as well as authors in the matter of foreign works. For instance, there is Mr. Stevenson's 'Merry Men,' which we were selling at 50 cents, and for each copy sold allowed the author 15 per cent. But the sale of the work is virtually dead, so far as we are concerned. You have observed that one firm of publishers now sells four of Mr. Stevenson's works in one volume for 20 cents. Any firm in this country can do the same thing and no other publisher can reasonably find fault that it is done, under the existing statutes. Mr. Stevenson is now getting nothing, and this is particularly hard upon him, for he is not a rich man and pens most of his work on his coach as he is an invalid. But with six editions of his works in the field here, he can get no royalty on the sales, enormous as they are, for Stevenson's works are now the most popular here of all living novelists. And this very popularity is assisted, in large numbers, by the cheapness of his works, for the want of an international copyright law makes possible the publication of four of Stevenson's novels in one volume, all for 20 cents. You can readily perceive that a sale thus rendered large enough through the want of statutory protection tends to shut out home products through the very cheapness of the article, thus not only depriving the British author of his dues but interfering with the sale of American novels.

"If authors would look carefully into all these points, bearing in mind, also, the risks which publishers assume in launching a work, as well as the other points to which I have called attention, they cannot but see that they are being pretty well treated here. I see only one way to afford them larger profits; and that is for the retail dealer to demand a smaller discount. But these dealers declare that this is impossible. They, too, have privileged classes who demand a discount in turn. Clergymen, school teachers and various other classes of people have to have, say, a $1 book for 80 cents at least; so that if the retail dealer gets only 20 per cent off, his profits are largely eaten up. Certainly the publisher cannot produce the book more cheaply than he has been doing — at least no way to that result has as yet been discovered — and no larger royalty can safely be allowed, at least on the average. There are exceptions, for special reasons, in all matters.

The only way in which the author can, therefore, secure a greater royalty is to effect an increase in retail prices or prevail upon retail dealers to be content with a less discount. I know that authors often think that their works should bring them in a larger royalty, but, as I have already said, the market is an open one and they have the opportunity to deal with competing houses. So far as this firm is concerned, the authors of works published by us will now have full opportunity to look into their accounts with us, and satisfy themselves, if they wish, regarding the extent of the sales of their works; and although there have been no complaints made on this score, I trust that they will not hesitate to assure themselves by personal inspection that they are receiving their royalties according to the number of books sold. They get their royalty whether we secure payment from our sales or not; so that the publisher is also the protector of the author as well as his agent in placing his works before the public." . . .

REMINISCENCE:

Maxwell Evarts Perkins, part II of "A Companionable Colleague," in *W. C. Brownell: Tributes and Appreciations* (New York: Charles Scribner's Sons, 1929), pp. 62–68.

The legendary Scribners editor gives an insider's view of Brownell.

In recent years Mr. Brownell was much older than his colleagues in the editorial offices. One might have expected that this, added to the high quality of his culture and the high level of his intellect, would have removed him from them and set him apart in a kind of isolation. His appearance too might at first have supported this idea of him: his expression was that of calm detachment as of one who lives above the small irritations and excitements that animate the general run of men. A bust of him could have stood quite naturally among those of the Athenian dramatists and statesmen.

But the truth is, he was the very man to respond to anything in a manuscript that was human, homely, or racy, and his younger colleagues delighted to take into his office whatever they found good in order to share it with him; and often, three or four times a day, he would walk out into the general office, to read something from a manuscript or proof, and cap it with a pointed comment. It was he who gave spice to work that

W. C. Brownell (1851–1928), literary adviser and book editor for Scribners from 1888 until his death. His own critical theories were expressed in such works as Criticism *(1914),* Standards *(1917), and* The Genius of Style *(1924), published by Scribners.*

was otherwise at times monotonous. The human quality of his taste, though it did not so plainly show in his own writings, which were so largely concerned with principles, is evident in the fact that he was an instant admirer of George Ade's fables many years ago, and of Sinclair Lewis's "Main Street"; and though he was less active when Scott Fitzgerald and Ernest Hemingway were first under consideration, he read them with appreciation and supported the enthusiasm of those more closely associated with their publication with sympathy. Toward the end of many and many a day, Mr. Brownell, who left early, would pause in the general office with his hat and coat on, to tell a new story, and often, easily beguiled into the fields of general discussion, he would stand for fifteen minutes or more to the delight of his colleagues, talking in the most brilliant, witty way. And when he would finally depart, it was sometimes with the observation, " Well, as I've remarked before, all we need here beyond what we have is a sideboard."

If a young man worked beside him for some years and failed to become a passable editor he simply had no capacity for the work; for Mr. Brownell's comments were full of wisdom. One of his principles was that almost as much could be learned about an author's abilities by an interview as by reading his manuscript; for "water cannot rise above its source." Another, that the worst reason for publishing anything was because it resembled something else, that, however, unconscious, an "imitation is always inferior." Sometimes a second-rate manuscript was marked by some rare characteristics that made it hard for the staff to surrender it; and Mr. Brownell would close the debate by saying, "We can't publish everything. Let someone else make a failure of it."

In the discussion of a manuscript he was able to describe it in full, to convey its actual qualities, and — when others could speak only in vague general terms to the effect that it was good or bad — to formulate the reasons, completely, as to why it was successful or not; — an ability so valuable in reaching a decision, and one so rare and hard to acquire, that his associates felt hopelessly deficient. His intellectual and verbal skill in this way resulted in one disadvantage: when opposed to a manuscript he was able to lay bare its faults so much more tellingly — for his wit could be caustic — than his colleagues could explain its virtues, that he too readily overcame them. Yet he was always completely considerate of them, and of authors, too; whenever some book of promise was to be rejected, he would write the most sympathetic letter in which he would try to give encouragement by telling of the points he found admirable. These letters were works of art, and as such were produced by effort. They must have softened many a refusal, but once one of them was returned by a novelist with these words written on the margin, "Then why the devil don't you publish it?"

. . .

Mr. Brownell brought dignity to his work as editor. He recognized that a man has an obligation to his profession to make it as high and fine as he can, and that if he fail it in any particular he should acknowledge his failure with humility. He seldom failed as a publisher's adviser, but when he did, as every man sometimes must, he acknowledged it openly. His attitude was that which he showed

when, as a young man on the New York *World* and City Editor, he neglected fully to cover a big story. The next morning *The World* stood beaten. He went to his desk and instantly wrote out his resignation — which was of course refused.

ARTICLE:
"Young Men as Publishers," *The Publishers' Weekly,* October 26, 1889, p. 596.

While in charge of advertising for Scribner's Magazine, *Edward Bok (1863–1930) wrote a series of letters called "Bok's Literary Leaves," which were syndicated in many newspapers. A week before this article in* PW, *he had begun his new duties as editor of the* Ladies' Home Journal, *the start of a career that would make him a world figure.*

Bok's literary letter contains a good story of a sedate and elderly Boston gentleman whose business recently brought him to the Scribner publishing house in New York. His errand concerning itself with the advertising department, he asked to be introduced to the responsible head of that branch of the business. He was introduced to young Edward Bok, who is perhaps twenty-five. He looked the youth over, and concluding that he wanted to talk to an older head, asked to be taken to the manager of the educational department. Compliance with this request brought him to Mr. William D. Moffat, who is twenty-four. Again the sedate, elderly man found his yearnings for some one advanced in years unsatisfied, and asked for the business manager of the magazine, whereupon he was taken to Mr. Frank N. Doubleday, himself twenty-six. This wouldn't do, and as it chanced Mr. O. W. Brewey, the general traveller, or representative of the house, who is twenty-seven, was passing, the Boston man was introduced to him. By this time the Eastern man of years grew desperate and asked to see Mr. Scribner. This disclosed to him Mr. Arthur H. Scribner, the junior partner, who owns to twenty-six summers, and was the final blow to the man seeking after age. Mustering courage to faintly ask for Mr. Charles Scribner himself, he [was] finally brought up in that gentleman's office only to meet a man just turned thirty-five! Then was the Boston man perfectly aghast to find that a group of what were almost boys could conduct one of the largest and most profitable publishing houses in the country

1890–1899

1890

25 Mar.   Publication date of *Expiation,* the first Scribner book of "Octave Thanet," the pseudonym of Alice French

28 June   Publication date of Henry M. Stanley's *In Darkest Africa; or, The Quest, Rescue, and Retreat of Emin, Governor of Equatoria* (2 volumes)

26 Sept.   Publication date of Eugene Field's first Scribner books, *A Little Book of Profitable Tales* and *A Little Book of Western Verse*

1891

31 Jan.   Scribner & Welford is subsumed under the name "Charles Scribner's Sons"; hence, all business is now conducted under the one name.

4 Mar.   As a member of the Joint Committee of the American Copyright League and the American Publishers' Copyright League, CS II has an important role in getting the International Copyright Bill passed this day in Washington, D.C.

18 Apr.   Publication date of Richard Harding Davis's first Scribner book, *Gallegher, and Other Stories*

1892

7 May   Publication of the first volume (of seven) in the American History series, George Park Fisher's *The Colonial Era*

2 Nov.   Publication date of F. Hopkinson Smith's first Scribner book, *American Illustrators*

Dec.   The first Scribner Christmas dinner is held at the St. Denis Hotel in New York City.

1893   Edward Thomas Lord, New England agent for D. C. Heath & Co., joins the firm to start up a new educational department.

14 Apr.   Court decision protects the Scribner edition of the *Encyclopaedia Britannica* (ninth edition) against unauthorized reprints.

11 Oct.   Publication date of *The White Conquerors: A Tale of Toltec and Aztec,* the first Scribner book by Kirk Munroe, a prolific American author of adventure stories for boys

21 Oct.   Publication date of the trade edition of *Cyclopedia of Music and Musicians* (3 volumes, with more than one thousand illustrations), edited by John Denison Champlin

1894

May   Charles Scribner's Sons moves to 153–157 Fifth Avenue into a building designed by Ernest Flagg, brother-in-law of CS II.

2 Oct.	Publication date of *The Woman's Book, Dealing Practically with the Modern Conditions of Home-Life, Self-Support, Education, Opportunities, and Every-Day Problems* (2 volumes, with four hundred illustrations) by various authors

1895

18 May	Publication date of *Princeton Stories* by Jesse Lynch Williams, the first book by this American playwright and novelist
25 May	Publication date of Frank R. Stockton's *The Adventures of Captain Horn*, the #3 best-seller of 1895

1896

7 Mar.	Publication date of Frances Hodgson Burnett's *A Lady of Quality*, the #2 best-seller of 1896
3 Oct.	Publication date of George Santayana's first Scribner book, *The Sense of Beauty: Being the Outlines of Aesthetic Theory*
17 Oct.	Publication date of J. M. Barrie's *Sentimental Tommie*, the #9 best-seller of 1896 and #8 of 1897
	Publication date of the first volume (of twelve) in the Thistle Edition of *The Novels, Tales and Sketches of J. M. Barrie,* which was completed in 1911
23 Nov.	Publication date of J. M. Barrie's *Margaret Ogilvy*, the #7 best-seller of 1897
30 Dec.	At their fifth annual Christmas dinner, the employees and staff of Charles Scribner's Sons celebrate the fiftieth anniversary of the firm.

1897

2 Feb.	Publication date of the first volume (of thirty-six) in the Outward Bound Edition of *The Writings in Prose and Verse of Rudyard Kipling,* which was completed in 1937
1 Mar.	Joseph Hawley Chapin, art editor for McClure publications, joins Scribners as art editor, a position he will hold till 1936.
2 Mar.	Frank Nelson Doubleday leaves Scribners to begin his own business, Doubleday & McClure Company.
22 May	Publication date of Richard Harding Davis's *Soldiers of Fortune*, the #3 best-seller of 1897
10 Nov.	Publication date of the first volume (of sixteen) in the Homestead Edition of *The Poems and Prose Sketches of James Whitcomb Riley,* which was completed in 1916
13 Nov.	Publication date of *London as Seen by Charles Dana Gibson*, his first Scribner book
4 Dec.	Publication date of Edith Wharton's first Scribner book, *The Decoration of Houses,* co-authored with Ogden Codman

1898

28 Feb.	Publication date of the first volume (of five) of *A Dictionary of the Bible, Dealing With Its Language, Literature, and Contents, Including the Biblical Theology,* edited by James Hastings
22 Oct.	Publication date of Ernest Thompson Seton's first Scribner book, *Wild Animals I Have Known*

29 Oct.	Publication date of Thomas Nelson Page's *Red Rock,* the #5 best-seller of 1899
5 Nov.	Publication of the first two volumes (of thirty-six) in the Complete Edition of *The Works of Charles Dickens,* which was completed in 1900
17 Dec.	Publication date of the first two volumes (of twenty-two) in the International Edition of *The Works of Lyof N. Tolstoi,* which was completed in 1900

1899

11 Mar.	Publication date of *Mezzotints in Modern Music* by James Huneker, the first book by this American critic
20 May	Publication date of *The Rough Riders,* the first Scribner book by future U.S. president Theodore Roosevelt

Scribner Books of G. A. Henty (1832–1904)

The boys' books of the English writer G. A. Henty, which were primarily based on military history, proved to be extremely popular children's books for Scribners during the 1890s.

1890

In the Reign of Terror: The Adventures of a Westminster Boy

One of the 28th: A Tale of Waterloo

With Clive in India; or, The Beginnings of an Empire

1891

The Dash for Khartoum: A Tale of the Nile Expedition

Held Fast for England: A Tale of the Siege of Gibralter (1779-83)

Redskin and Cow-Boy: A Tale of the Western Plains

1892

Beric the Briton: A Story of the Roman Invasion

Condemned as a Nilhilist: A Story of Escape from Siberia

In Greek Waters: A Story of the Grecian War of Independence (1812-1827)

1893

A Jacobite Exile: Being the Adventures of a Young Englishman in the Service of Charles XII of Sweden

St. Bartholomew's Eve: A Tale of the Huguenot Wars

Through the Sikh War: A Tale of the Conquest of the Punjaub

1894

In the Heart of the Rockies: A Story of Adventure in Colorado

When London Burned: A Story of Restoration Times and the Great Fire

Wulf the Saxon: A Story of the Norman Conquest

1895

A Knight of the White Cross: A Tale of the Seige of Rhodes

The Tiger of Mysore: A Story of the War with Toppoo Saib

Through Russian Snows: A Story of Napoleon's Retreat from Moscow

1896

At Agincourt: A Tale of the White Hoods of Paris

By England's Aid; or, The Freeing of the Netherlands (1581-1604)

By Pike and Dyke: A Tale of the Rise of the Dutch Republic

In Freedom's Cause: A Story of Wallace and Bruce

The Lion of St. Mark: A Story of Venice in the Fourteenth Century

On the Irrawaddy: A Story of the First Burmese War

Under Drake's Flag: A Tale of the Spanish Main

With Cochrane the Dauntless: A Tale of the Exploits of Lord Cochrane in South American Waters

With Lee in Virginia: A Story of the American Civil War

With Wolfe in Canada; or, The Winning of a Continent
1897
A March on London: Being the Story of Wat Tyler's Insurrection
With Frederic the Great: A Story of the Seven Years' War
With Moore at Corunna
1898
At Aboukir and Acre: A Story of Napoleon's Invasion of Egypt
Both Sides of the Border: A Tale of Hotspur and Glendower
Under Wellington's Command: A Tale of the Peninsular War
1899
No Surrender! A Tale of the Rising in La Vendee
A Roving Commission; or, Through the Black Insurrection at Hayti
Won by the Sword: A Tale of the Thirty Years' War
1900
In the Irish Brigade: A Tale of the War in Flanders and Spain
Out with Garibaldi: A Story of the Liberation of Italy
With Buller in Natal; or, A Born Leader
1901
At the Point of the Bayonet: A Tale of the Mahratta War
To Herat and Cabul: A Story of the First Afghan War
With Roberts to Pretoria: A Tale of the South African War
1902
The Treasure of the Incas: A Tale of Adventure in Peru
With Kitchener in the Soudan: A Story of Atbara and Omdurman
With the British Legion: A Story of the Carlist Wars
1903
Through Three Campaigns: A Story of Chitral, Tirah, and Ashanti
With the Allies to Pekin: A Tale of the Relief of the Legations
1904
By Conduct and Courage: A Story of Nelson's Days

Some of these books were published earlier than the date indicated by Blackie & Son, Henty's En-
glish publisher, but these years appear to be the dates of the Scribner copyrighted editions.*

AUTOBIOGRAPHY EXCERPT:
Robert Underwood Johnson, *Remembered Yesterdays* (Boston: Little, Brown, 1923), pp. 257–260.

As a member of the Joint Committee of the American Copyright League and the American Publishers' Copyright League, CS II participated directly in Washington, D.C., in the passage of the International Copyright Bill during the winter of 1890–1891. In his autobiography, Johnson, secretary of the committee, provides a narrative of the committee's role in the last hours of the session leading up to final passage of the bill on 4 March 1891.

It was about two o'clock, A.M. when the bill was reached by the House. Two other members of our committe, who had also been at work, Messrs. William H. Appleton and Charles Scribner, had been present with me in the Senate when the bill was passed and we spent the next hour, a very anxious and weary period, in the gallery of the House. Was the bill going to encounter another snag? We little knew what was to come.

An amusing circumstance was that during the final debate upon the bill in the House, its noisiest opponent, Payson of Illinois, could be seen by us asleep on a bench at the back of the chamber, his face covered by a newspaper which rose and fell with his stentorian breathing. When at last the roll call came we had an unpleasant quarter of an hour for fear he might awake and rush into the fray. But this time nothing happened and the bill was passed by 127 to 77.

Ordinarily there would be nothing more for me to record. But an unexpected and formidable obstacle was yet to be encountered. The bill was of course promptly signed by Speaker Reed. Mr. Lodge, with practical forethought that had so often helped the bill past emergencies, hastened to the engrossing room, which was in a glut of work, to make sure that no time was lost in preparing it for the signature of President Harrison. For a long time, Mr. Appleton, Mr. Scribner and I sat in one of the corridors reviewing the events of the day and night. We were fairly intoxicated by the realization of the fact that after fifty years of intermittent effort, and after eight years of almost continuous appeal to Congress, the disgrace of tolerating literary piracy had been wiped from the statute book! The bill had yet to be reported back to the Senate with the announcement of its passage by the House, so we again trudged over to the galleries of the upper Chamber. What was our astonishment soon afterward to see Senator Pasco "rise to a question of the highest privilege" and hear him inveigh against the precipitate manner in which the Copyright Bill, as he said, had been "railroaded" to the House; and to our dismay, we discovered that he had moved its reconsideration! Thus a curious spectacle was presented, unique in the history of American legislation: a bill that had been passed by both Houses and had been signed by both presiding officers was in such a parliamentary position that it could not be taken from the custody of a house of Congress for the signature of the President! . . . While the motion to reconsider was pending, the Senate at about 5 A.M. took a recess until nine o'clock in the morning, the fourth of March. The cup of trembling was once more at our lips.

A conference of our group was immediately held in Senator Platt's committee room and a plan of campaign was laid out by him. . . . Senator Platt now dictated a "whip" to all the Senators who were known to favor the bill, and it was agreed that these typed notes should be delivered to them at their residences by the three members of the Joint Committee then in Washington. Mr. Appleton undertook to reach the Senators who were living on Capitol Hill; to Mr. Scribner were assigned the notifications to those living at hotels in the other portions of the city, while the remainder were entrusted to me. This whip announced the parliamentary position of the bill, and urgently requested the presence at nine o'clock of those to whom it was addressed, so that on the reassembling of the Senate the motion to reconsider might be promptly defeated, which would be equivalent to the passage of the bill.

No one of us will ever forget the experience of that sleepless night. Outside was raging one of the bitterest storms I have ever known. Rain was falling and blowing in gales and freezing as it fell. It was about half-past six o'clock and no conveyances were to be had, and even if we had been able to secure cabs, the horses would not have been able to keep their feet upon the frozen and sleety streets. Nevertheless, every message entrusted to us was delivered, and I believe every friend of the Copyright Bill in the Senate

> Announcement.
>
> Messrs. Charles Scribner's Sons and Scribner & Welford wish to announce that the branch of their business heretofore conducted under the name of Scribner & Welford will, after the 31st instant, be carried on under the name of Charles Scribner's Sons, which title will thus include all departments of their business.
>
> This will involve no change in their business of importing books, and is made solely to simplify their methods of work and for the convenience of customers.
>
> 743 & 745 Broadway, New York,
> January 1st, 1891.

Public announcement of the assemblage of all of the firm's business under the one name of "Charles Scribner's Sons"

was present at the reassembling at nine o'clock. We of the committee were in the galleries holding our breath for fear of another contretemps as a malevolent climax to those I have recounted. Every minute was precious to us. After what seemed an interminable prayer and a useless reading of voluminous minutes, the motion to reconsider was voted down at about ten o'clock, by 29 to 21, and the situation was saved! Less than two hours of the session remained.

One thing was still necessary — the signature of President Harrison, who as usual had come to the Capitol so that he might affix his signature quickly to legislation passed in the last hours. . . . the bill was signed at about ten forty-five — the session closing at twelve. The President gave me back the pen and I rushed to the telegraph office to announce the good news. . . .

The exhausted members of the Joint Committee rushed for the first train for New York and slept all the way back. And then from England and France and from all over America, by telegram and letter, began to come the happy messages of congratulation.

CS II DIARY ENTRY:
Friday 14 April 1893

Britannica decision by Judge Townsend in our favor.

SONG:
"From Astor Place to Fifth Avenue, And Other Stories (six and a basement). By E. W. Morse. Bound in stone and brick, zinc top, 59 x 85 feet, $450,000 *net.*"

These lyrics, written by Scribner employee Edwin W. Morse, were sung at the annual Christmas dinner held Wednesday, 27 December 1893, at the St. Denis Hotel in New York City. They celebrate the impending move of the firm from 743–745 Broadway to 153–157 Fifth Avenue.

> While I was strolling through Madison
>   Square,
> One December day that was cold and bleak,
> I met a girl in a tailor-made gown,
> With tears on her velvety cheek.
> "Why are you crying," I said to her,
> "With a face like a sorrowful nun's?"
> "I'm crying because it's so far," said she,
> "Way down to Charles Scribner's Sons."
>
> CHORUS:
> We are all glad we are soon going up-town;
> All the buyers of books are mad,
> The store is so far down.
> And when we get there we'll hustle,
> And rustle, and bustle, and tussle,
> To show, by our looks and by selling more
>   books,
> Our loyalty to the firm.
>
> Leaving the girl, I wandered down,
> To number a hundred and fifty-three;
> There stood a man with the longest hair
> 'Twas ever my fortune to see.
> "I am a poet, good sir," said he;
> "My soul with genius o'erruns.
> I've magazine verse in my pocket for sale;
> Oh, where is Charles Scribner's Sons?"

> *Chorus.*
>
> When I had given him Bridge's address,
> In a den that looks out upon Astor Place,
> I ran plump into a man with a grip,
> And an uneasy look on his face.
> "I am from Kalamazoo," said he,
> "Chased from the town by duns.
> I've a sequel to 'Little Lord Fauntleroy';
> Then take me to Charles Scribner's Sons."
>
> *Chorus.*
>
> When I had shaken the man from the West,
> A girl with a dollar attracted my eye.
> "I want to subscribe to the Book Buyer
>   quick!
> Can't you take me there in a fly?"
> Ent'ring a hansom in joyful haste,
> I entertained her with puns,
> But Bloomingdale keepers arrested her
> Before we reached Charles Scribner's Sons!
>
> *Chorus.*

CS II DIARY ENTRY:
Thursday 24 May 1894

<u>Moved to 153 5th Ave</u>

ARTICLE:
"Charles Scribner's Sons' Removal. Not One of at Least 300,000 Books Injured — Old Building Almost Deserted," *New York Times,* 25 May 1894, p. 8.

Charles Scribner's Sons have almost finished their removal from 743 and 745 Broadway to their new building, built of white limestone and graceful with classic simplicity, on the east side of Fifth Avenue, between Twenty-first and Twenty-second Streets.

There were 300,000 books, at least, to be packed in trays and boxes, besides the manuscripts, letters, and accounts of a business of fifty years. The wholesale department was reduced in the old building to the estimated proportion of books which it might be necessary to deliver for two or three weeks, the old manuscripts were placed in separate safes, and gradually the retail department was limited to the demands of a day, until the old building was like a desert and the new one was as well furnished as if it had been gradually furnised for a decade.

The removal lasted a month, and was executed with so much order, with such method, that the mistakes which were made were insignificant, and that of all the delicately beautiful volumes which were transferred from the old building to the new — missals, books of hours, incunabula, bindings of the old masters, and of Cobden-Sanderson, new editions in covers fresh as the lilacs of May — not one was even imperceptibly damaged.

Not one! The book lovers, who keep their treasures in eiderdown and dread a removal more than the other enemies of books enumerated by Blades, will be interested in the fact that the most extraordinary books of Scribner's were packed in open boxes — but they were packed by the young men who know them, and they were under constant surveillance in the fifteen blocks of their voyage.

There were no accidents. The six floors of the new building are in their appointed order. The packing department is in the basement, the retail on the first floor, the offices occupy the second floor, above them are the Magazine, the subscription-book, surplus stock, and mailing departments. The shelves are made of glass, rounded at the edge, because glass is less than wood amenable to dust and not as implacable a wearer of binding edges.

The heart that there is in inanimate things is no longer impressive in the old building, now that the books have quitted it. It beats in the new building. But it was in the old that Hours at Home, Scribner's Monthly, (now The Century,) and Scribner's Magazine were founded, and that founders of American literature met.

The house of Scribner was removed there in January, 1875, following the march of the city up town, from 654 Broadway, from Grand Street, from 377 Broadway, at the corner of White Street, and from 145 Nassau Street, where it was founded in 1846.

In 1846 the annual rent paid by the house was $400. Its annual rent now must be figured by the taxes and interest on a property the cost of which is more than $500,000.

Charles Scribner's personal attention to the innumerable details of the removal, and the charm of his active interest in the graces of the new building, must remain an agreeable incident of the event, which he has led, in the memory of those who saw him yesterday.

The event is an important one for New-York. The removal of Charles Scribner's Sons takes from Broadway and pays to Fifth Avenue the homage of an enchanting literary atmosphere.

ARTICLE:
"The History of a Publishing House: 1846–1894" [excerpt], Scribner's Magazine, 16, no. 6 (December 1894): 802, 804.

A contemporary description of the new Scribner building at 153–157 Fifth Avenue, noting that it is probably the first in the United States to be designed from the bottom up for the purposes of a publishing house.

In the new building, which was built for the firm by Mr. Ernest Flagg, the architect of the new St. Luke's Hospital and many other public buildings, and of which the dignified and striking facade is already familiar to passers on Fifth Avenue, the ground floor is entirely occupied by the bookstore, which differs in many ways from the conception of a bookstore derived from past examples. Instead of a confused and crowded space with counters and low bookcases, the whole room resembles a particularly well-cared for library in some great private house, or in some of the quieter public institutions. The walls, wainscoted to the ceiling in quartered oak, are for the most part covered with bookcases with glass shelves, on which the finer-bound and illustrated books are ranged from floor to ceiling — a gallery midway around the room aiding the access to them and still further heightening the library appearance. On the floor of wood blocks, laid in asphalt — so that a curious feeling of firmness meets the step like that of a sidewalk rather than a floor — stand large oak tables, upon which are ranged books for the inspection of buyers; and stands and chairs for reading are placed conveniently among these larger tables. Supported by four high columns, but otherwise having its great space quite clear, this ground-floor room is altogether free from offices (excepting at the back those necessary for the manager of this department and his immediate assistants); and with its Indian red decoration and the plentiful sunlight which pours in from the high windows at back and front it is a spacious, airy, and pleasant place. From the back a broad flight of stairs of white marble, di-

Telegram sent by CS II from Washington, D.C., to his brother Arthur
announcing the passage of the International Copyright Bill by
Congress, 4 March 1891

viding half-way up to the left and right, leads to the second floor, where are all the offices of the firm, of the Financial and Manufacturing Departments, the Wholesale Department, the Educational Department, the Book Buyer, and many more. The third floor is occupied altogether by the Magazine, with its different departments — the Editorial, Artistic, Publishing, etc. On the fourth floor is the Subscription Department. The fifth floor is given up to the storage of stock, but in an orderly way; — one may walk with almost as much pleasure through the neat aisles between the many groups of bookcases here as below in the main shop itself. The sixth floor is occupied by mailing-rooms, arrangements for the printing of circulars, and the other miscellany of a great business. The whole building is unique in being perhaps the first in America built from ground to top distinctly for the uses of a publishing house; everyone having contributed to the original planning the experience of years as to the needs in his own department, and the consequence being an almost perfect adjustment of means to ends.

So housed and equipped, the firm in a little more than a year will enter upon its second half-century, with opportunities which it means to use fully in the advance of every department of its work.

SONGS:
The following are lyrics for songs that were sung at the Third Annual Scribner Dinner, held Friday, 28 December 1894, at the St. Denis Hotel in New York City:

At Scribners'
One day last month a friend I met.

Quoth he to me, "Seen Scribners' yet?
Folks who are onto the city say
Of books they make a great display.
Better go there if you want to buy;
Their shop will surely please your eye."
I said to him, "Then that I'll try."
I'll never go there any more.

CHORUS:
At Scribners'! At Scribners'!
They say such things and they do such things
At Scribners'! At Scribners'!
I'll never go there any more.

A present I sought for my mother-in-law.
A spectacled clerk was the first I saw;
He rushed me back to a corner dim,
Where he fashioned a pit and I fell in.
He told me jokes until I grew wan;
We argued the question *pro* and *con*;
I went home with the Decameron.
I'll never go there any more.

Chorus.

I saw their "ad." for a cover design;
Said I to myself, "That is just in my line."
I furnished a studio in which to strive;
I spent eighty dollars to win twenty-five.
Three weeks later, when back it came,
These words on the margin were painfully
    plain:
"You idiot! one of your cupids is lame."
I'll never go there anymore.

Chorus.

With a sonnet by Shakespeare once I went —

To dupe their monthly was my intent.
I told the reader the sonnet was mine;
He scanned it carefully line by line.
Then said, in a manner both grave and sage,
"If there is merit upon this page,
It will only be found in a future age."
I'll never go there any more.

Chorus.

He Is a Scribner Man
When I was a lad I oft did stop
Before the windows of Scribner's shop;
I conned each title and author's name
Until a bibliophile I became.

So many catalogues strewed my floor,
That now I'm a salesman in Scribner's store.
QUARTET — *So many catalogues strewed his*
    floor,
That now he's a salesman in Scribner's store.

CHORUS:
He is a Scribner Man;
Behold him!
For he himself hath said it,
And it's greatly to his credit
That he is a Scribner Man.
For he might have been a Putnam,
Or a Harper, Dodd, or Dutton,
Or perhaps an Appleton,
Or perhaps an Appleton;
But in spite of all temptations
To accept such invitations,
He remains a Scribner Man,
He remains a Scribner Man.

I applied to the house one day for work;
They gave me the post of a mailing clerk.
I licked the stamps with a face so glum,
Objectionable there I soon become.
With great eclat I took the floor,
A full-fledged salesman in Scribner's store.
QUARTET — *With great eclat he took the*
    floor,
A full-fledged salesman in Scribner's store.

Chorus.

They assigned me the task of the doors to
    ope;
I drew them in with a gentle mope.
To regular patrons my smile was bland,
And shyly I pressed each young maid's hand;
I flirted with widows of fifty and four,
Till now I'm a salesman in Scribner's store.
QUARTET — *He flirted with widows of fifty*
    and four,
Till now he's a salesman in Scribner's store.

Chorus.

Door-opening feats I performed so well
I was at length accorded permission to sell.
I made Bridges' "Arcady" quite the rage,
And depleted the stock of the "Viking Age."
I broke all records established before,
So now I'm a salesman in Scribner's store.
QUARTET — *He broke all records established*
    before,

Main floor of the new Scribner building at 153–157 Fifth Avenue

So now he's a salesman in Scribner's store.

Chorus.

Now all ye lads who would emulate me,
Flourish your dusters skillfully;
Weave seductive Northonian snares,
Beguiling your patrons while selling 'em
wares;
Perchance you may one day sit near the
door,
A jovial head-salemsan in Scribner's store.
QUARTET — *Perchance you may one day sit
near the door.*
A jovial head-salesman in Scribner's store.

Chorus.

ARTICLE:
"A Unique Undertaking. The Success of the Plan
of Pulling the A.D.T. Lever Five Times and
Having a History Brought for Examination.

What People Who Have Ordered and Read
'Scribner's History of the United States' Say
of the Plan Organized by the Tribune — A
Perfect System Working Perfectly," *New-
York Daily Tribune,* 16 November 1896, p.
3.

The first four volumes of A Popular History of the
United States *by William Cullen Bryant and Sidney
Howard Gay were published from 1876 to 1880.
Volume 5, completed by Noah Brooks, was available late in 1896 and continued the history from the
Civil War to 1894. Like the others, it was sold by
subscription only. In cooperation with a newspaper
that was using the technology of the time, Scribners
experimented with a most unusual method to get
this popular publication distributed quickly.*

When the Tribune secured the first edition of
the newly completed "Scribner's History of the
United States" it undertook at the same time to
put in operation a plan whereby readers could
have the books brought to them simply by ringing

the messenger call-box five times or telephoning their names to 1820 — 38th-st., where an operator was in direct telephonic communication with all the branches of the American District service. The interest taken by readers and the general use of the system indicated that a host of people were glad to avail themselves of an opportunity to look at a book so widely known without the pressing attentions of a canvasser. Perhaps the most remarkable thing about the enterprise has been the fact that of all the hundreds of sets sent out as The Tribune offered to do on approval not a single one has been returned for any reason whatever.

A Tribune reporter visited on Saturday a number of subscribers to the work to get their opinions not only of the history, but the new idea now first tried of showing a book by messenger instead of by book-agents.

H. B. Plant, president of the great Plant Railroad System, whose office is at No. 12 West Twenty-third-st., said: "I ordered three sets of Scribner's history, for I knew The Tribune and I knew Scribner. The scheme of ordering through the American District Telegraph is the best thing I have ever seen. I was ill in bed and saw the notice. I just thought I would push the button five times and see if the boy would come. Well, he came. I looked the books over, saw that it was good clear print, and ordered the three sets. They were delivered at once — one at Darien, Conn., one to my son, who lives uptown, and one at my own house."

Edward G. Gerstle, of No. 431 Broadway, said: "Yes, I have the Scribner history and the encyclopedia as well. The history I like better and better. Looking over the narrative of the Civil War I had occasion to admire the spirit of fairness that pervades the writing. It is absolutely unpartisan. I ordered through the American District service, and it worked like a charm. I just pressed the button five times and the boy did the rest. In less than ten minutes he was here with a copy for examination, and the set was delivered to me the next day."

E. S. Terry, of No. 309 Broadway, said: "I saw the advertisement, and am free to say that the novelty of employing the American District Telegraph service struck me, and I pressed the button more to see if the boy would come than for any other reason. He came in less than ten minutes, I should say, and I ordered the history. It must have taken lots of work to perfect that plan of distribution all over the city, and it must require an im-

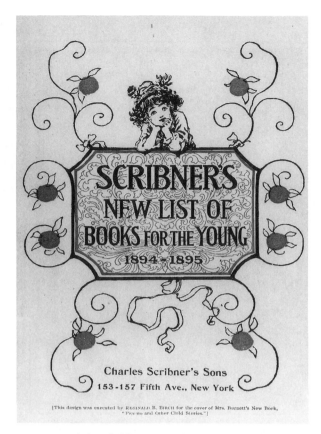

Cover of the children's book catalogue designed by Reginald B. Birch. He was the illustrator for most of Frances Hodgson Burnett's books, including Little Lord Fauntleroy.

mense stock of books." . . . [other similar testimonies follow]

POEM:

Robert Gilbert Welsh, "For the Fifthieth Year of the House of Scribner," in *The House of the Brains* (New York: Privately published, 1896).

This poem, by Scribner employee Welsh, was included in The House of the Brains, *published for those employees attending the fifth annual Christmas dinner which celebrated the firm's golden anniversary.*

I.

Now when the wood is bare, the last bird flown,

Sisters of Song, why sit ye mournful here,

Poster for the fourth Christmas dinner

With tones as sombre as the north wind
    blown
Through ravished branches in the falling
    year?
Ye fain would follow
The vanished swallow.
Up! Up, and seek him in the southern wolds!
And as ye go with lightsome step and fleet,
Crush not the fern belated, which unfolds
Its beauty in the dead leaves at your feet;
Grant as ye pass a benison of song
Unto this homestead nestling by the hill;
Here at the tavern pause, and in the throng
Of merrymakers merrier notes instil.
Pass through the little town, the river cross,
Speed southward still, and still more swiftly
    speed,
For here the city's millions seethe and toss,
And to your gracious gift they give no heed.
Hence then — or stay! Hearken, a weak
    voice dares
Invoke your aid for his presumptuous song.

Within the busy book mart hear his prayers;
Grant him a passing grace, his breath pro-
    long
To sing our House's name and dignity
To its retainers, — bid their pulses stir,
Knowing they follow not unworthy
The ways of Aldus and Elzevir.

II.
How has Time reversed his fateful glass,
And turned the current of how many lives,
Since first our Founder from his Blackstone
    came
Into that calling where he still survives,
Kept by the power of an enduring name!
Five cycles slowly pass, —
Each in appointed order, duly bound,
Measures its length of busy, burdened days,
Fulfils his countless plans in countless ways,
Each big with effort, with achievement
    crowned.

He plans no more, no more through wakeful
    nights
His thoughts are busy with the long day's
    care, —
How sound his sleep who, with his work
    well done,
Trusts younger shoulders, firm and glad to
    bear
The toil by him so long ago begun!
Through storm and changing lights,
Through bitterness of winter, safe he lies,
Unheeding stress or tumult or despair,
And o'er him in the darkness bending there
Sleep in her silence wraps him garmentwise.

He rests, and still his labors grow apace, —
Augmented, and with later life renewed,
Our House has widened borders that were
    wide,
Strengthened her bands that were with
    strength imbued,
And made us proud of her we held in pride.
She with a sober grace
Carries her fifty years, and holds secure
Her place of honor among her peers.
Laud her and wish her well through coming
    years,
Speak her with loyalty, — our House is sure!

III.
Men of the House of Scribner, hear
How in the closing of the year

The gladsome bells of Christmastide
Ring an old message far and wide, —
Peace and good-will, good-will and peace,
Let envy die and love increase!
And we who feel a kindly bond
In seasonable mirth respond, —
Wassail, my fellows, and good cheer,
Our House hath come to fifty year!

As in Mannutio's house of old,
What time a labor manifold
Had reached completion and all eyes
Might read some classic wondrous wise,
The learned Messer Aldo then
Went with a smile among his men;
As they perchance with him were glad,
And spake the kindly thought they had,
So may we speak with right good cheer,
Our House hath come to fifty year!

Now as ye meet give forth your best,
Illume the board with song and jest,
Nor, while the merry mood is on,
Disdain the Motley's coat to don.
Jangle the bells, the bauble toss,
For once set wisdom at a loss;
Laugh as ye can, and laugh full well,
And each to each this greeting tell, —
Wassail, my fellows, and good cheer,
Our House hath come to fifty year!

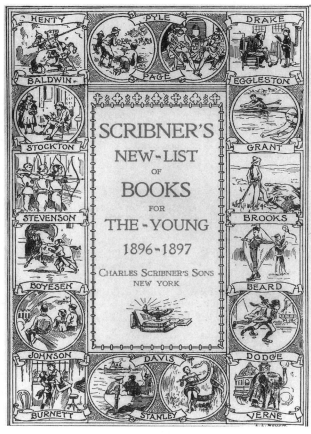

Cover of catalogue featuring the most popular children's authors of the time

ARTICLE:
"Half Century of a Publishing Firm," *New York Tribune,* 1 January 1897, p. 12.

Scribners' fifth annual Christmas dinner, held 30 December 1896, was the occasion for the House's golden anniversary celebration.

At the St. Denis Hotel, the staff of Charles Scribner's Sons, publishers, sat down to the fifth annual Christmas dinner Wednesday night, and also celebrated the fiftieth anniversary of the establishment of the house. John H. Dingman, who enjoys the distinction of having been longest with the firm, presided as toastmaster, and after an elaborate menu had been disposed of, called the guests to order. Under the title, "The Scribner Half Century," he gave a brief history of the house, forty-one years of which he had himself witnessed.

Charles Scribner, the senior member of the firm, was next called upon. He spoke in a happy vein of the pleasure it gave him to be present and congratulated the members of the staff on having established the custom of an annual Christmas dinner. He assured the employees of the firm that the success of the business really depended upon them, and said that no one who could observe the spirit which characterized the present occasion would have any fears for the future of the house. His remarks were received with frequent applause.

The toasts of the evening were then responded to in the following order: "A Merrie Ramble Through Our Catalogue," Rudolph C. Stolle; "Old English Times," Henry L. Smith; "What Book Can We Publish in 1897 that Will Sell 500,000 Copies," E. W. Morse, Charles Walton, Robert Bridges and F. H. Schauffler; "At the End of Fifty Years," Edward T. S. Lord; "By Subscription Only," F. N. Doubleday; "New Ideas in Advertising," W. D. Moffat; "Our Future With a Silver Lining," L. W. Hatch; "For the Fiftieth

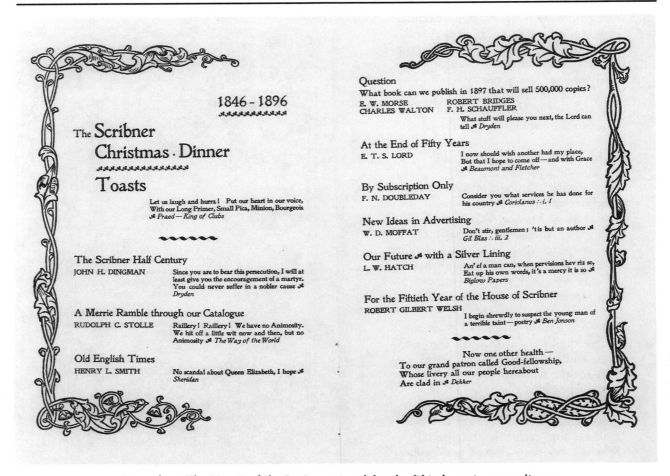

Pages from The House of the Brains, *printed for the fiftieth-anniversary dinner*

Year of the House of Scribner," Robert Gilbert Welsh.

The genuine surprise of the evening was the presentation to each person present of a book entitled "The House of the Brains," which had been prepared expressly for the occasion. It was printed in the characteristic style of the Kelmscott press, each copy being numbered and presented in order, according to the years of service.

CS II DIARY ENTRY:
Wednesday 3 March 1897

Lunched with Doubleday who left for McClures yesterday. Not any too satisfactory interview but retention of friendship.

ARTICLE:
"Books for Christmas. Choice Literature for the Holiday Reader. Charles Scribner's Sons Never Lags in the Publishers' Race to Supply the Season's Demand," *New-York Daily Tribune,* 15 November 1899, p. 10.

This is the time of year when the great publishing houses are redoubling their efforts to bring out a flood of acceptable books and are ransacking the earth for matter that is novel and beautiful for their magazines, in order that they may benefit to the utmost by the increased demand for literature of all kinds, which is one of the unfailing features of the Christmas season. In this perennial struggle Charles Scribner's Sons have never failed to win a gratifying quantity of laurels, and a glance at their newest publications will convince almost any one that this year they are more likely to distance their own record than to fall behind it.

In the forefront of these is "The Letters of Robert Louis Stevenson," in two volumes, edited by Sidney Colvin and illustrated by Guérin and Peixotto. These two volumes will contain upward of four hundred and fifty letters, nearly double the

1897

Philadelphia. November 7th.

My dear Mr. Chapin:

The "Scribner Dinner" cover drawing will go to-morrow — Monday — & thought it would be in your hands long before this, but & made such a pathetic mess of the first conception, that it had to be done over again. Being a "love job" will not, & trust, deter you from asking for any alterations which you think necessary.

Sincerely

Maxfield Parrish

Let us hope this is the pudding's last appearance.

Letter by American illustrator Maxfield Parrish regarding his design for the cover of the 1897 Scribner Christmas dinner menu

number of those which have appeared in "Scribner's Magazine." As these letters came out in serial form, each new instalment aroused in the reader a new delight in and respect for their author's sweet, whimsical and courageous nature, and, collected in book form, they bid fair to become one of those works which are kept close to the armchair, not for a brief time only, but for a generation at least.

New Novel by Mrs. Burnett

This season will be marked by the return of Mrs. Frances Hodgson Burnett to an American field and to American types in a new novel, called "In Connection with the De Willoughby Claim." This is the longest and most important novel Mrs. Burnett has written in several years. It has an original plot, the different scenes being laid in the South, in New-England and in Washington. The De Willoughby claim is fought out in Congress and Mrs. Burnett's intimate knowledge of Washington life in its less familiar phases is fully drawn upon. Interwoven with the legal struggle is the story of a woman deceived by the man of whom the world would have least expected it, his identity being effectually concealed until near the close. This tragedy, intensified by a contrast of fanatical New-England temper with Southern chivalry, is relieved by the love which a romantic child feels for a strong man who is her protector.

For the many Americans who will visit France in 1900 "The Stories of Paris in History and Letters," by Benjamin Ellis Martin and Charlotte M. Martin, is likely to prove highly attractive, as well as useful. It contains sixty illustrations by Fulleylove, Delafontaine and from photographs. The fund of reminiscence, both historic and literary, in which the buildings of Paris are so rich, appears in abundance in these two sympathetic and suggestive volumes. Historic times, from the Merovingian to the modern, live again in these vivid pages, and one can trace the activities of Molière and La Fontaine, of Corneille and Racine, of Balzac and Hugo, as epitomized in their changes of habitations and resorts which still remain to testify as eloquent eye witnesses of these great identities.

Literary Rambles

For persons who enjoy rambling informally along the byways of literature, Donald G.

Maxfield Parrish's cover design

Mitchell has prepared a fine treat in "American Lands and Letters — Leather Stocking to Poe's Raven," in which he treats among others Alcott, Abbott, Bancroft, Bushnell, Channing, Clarke, Emerson, Fields, Garrison, Greeley, Hawthorne, Holmes, Longfellow, Parker, Poe, Thoreau, Whittier and Willis. Though it is nearly half a century since Mr. Mitchell wrote his "Reveries of a Bachelor," his intellect seems to have lost none of its force.

The life of the artist always possesses a large amount of interest for those whose lot is cast in more prosaic fields. Therefore "British Contemporary Artists," by Cosmo Monkhouse, is likely to be widely read. This work contains chapters of high critical and descriptive value upon Burne-Jones, Watts, Alma-Tadema, Millais, Leighton, Orchardson and Poyntor. The illustrations include reproductions of the most celebrated paintings of the British artists of recent year, portraits, studio interiors, etc.

"Santa Claus's Partner," by Thomas Nelson Page, will occupy a place among Christmas stories. It describes how a child transformed the character of a successful business man whose nature had become hard and selfish in the pursuit of wealth. The illustrations, seven of them done in color by W. Glackens, are worth noting.

Blue Sky Philosophy

"Fisherman's Luck and Some Other Uncertain Things," by Henry van Dyke, is a book of stories, woodland sketches and blue sky philosophy in the vein of the author's "Little Rivers." It contains thirteen full page illustrations by Sterner, French, Smedley, Relyea, and from photographs, and is full of personal anecdotes and descriptions of well known people and little known places. It has the out of door flavor of "Little Rivers," and a wider range of human interest.

Emile Michel, well known as the author of a life of Rembrandt, which has taken a first place among the biographies of that great painter, has brought out a new book, "Peter Paul Rubens, His Life and His Work." It is translated by Elizabeth Lee, and contains twenty-nine colored plates, forty photogravures and two hundred text cuts. This illustrative material is unusually varied and rich and the two volumes contain much newly discovered matter relative to the life and work of the great Flemish master.

"The Grandissimes" of George Washington Cable is now published in uniform style with the edition of "Old Creole Days" which was so successful two years ago, and contains twelve full page illustrations and eight head and tail pieces by the same artist, Albert Herter. These are reproduced in photogravure.

Humor and Philosophy

A vein of humor and philosophy runs through Sidney Lanier's book, "The Story of Our Mocking Bird." It is an affectionately intimate tale of the author's feathered pet, Bob, and possesses a literary quality of an unusual kind. The sixteen full page illustrations have been made from photographic studies, and were colored by A. R. Dugmore.

In response to a popular demand Charles Scribner's Sons have issued a uniform edition, in small, tasteful form, of Richard Harding Davis's novels and stories. Each of the six volumes is bound in limp, olive colored leather, and has a frontispiece and a rubricated title page. This set will make a charming holiday gift.

"The Trail of the Lonesome Stag" is another of Ernest Seton-Thompson's famous animal stories. It is a delightful bit of impressionist work, a reproof for the mere bloodthirsty hunter, and a plea for the harmless and gentle creatures of forest and mountain. Eight full page pictures, one in color, and numerous marginal illustrations from drawings by the author illustrate this artistic sermon.

"America To-Day" embodies the views of the English critic, William Archer, upon American traits and American customs as he saw them during his visit here a year ago, together with reflections upon some of the larger political and social problems which are pressing for solution in this country.

"Mrs. John Drew's Reminiscences" is rich in entertaining memories of the American stage. Anecdotes of Macready, the elder Booth, the elder Jefferson, of Fanny Kemble, of the Old Bowery and Park theatres and of forgotten plays and players fill her pages and give them a delightful flavor. The work is profusely illustrated, has an introduction by the author's son, John Drew, and biographical notes by Douglas Taylor, president of the Dunlop Society.

Scribner's Serials

These are only a few of the choice books which Charles Scribner's Sons have ready for the holiday trade. The Christmas number of "Scribner's Magazine" will contain several striking novelties in illustration. Walter Appleton Clark's pictures, which accompany Harrison Morris's "Ballad of Three Kings," are rich in color. The original pictures have been reproduced with fidelity. In the humorous view, W. Glackens has illustrated a farcical story by Arthur Colton. These have also been reproduced in color. A picture story by C. D. Gibson, called "The Seven Ages of American Woman," has been printed on a delicate tint background, after the manner of old engravings. There is also the fourth of Maxfield Parrish's covers, which have been such a feature of the magazine for this year. Other artists represented in the black and white illustrations of the number are F. C. Yohn, Albert Sterner, E. C. Peixotto and Howard Chandler Christy.

Scribner's other serial, "The Book Buyer," will in its Christmas number far surpass its predecessors in literary and artistic value, and the publishers believe it will be generally pronounced the most beautiful and useful guide to Christmas literature yet published. The number will give a full review of the holiday books of 1899. It will include every book of any importance designed by the different publishers for the holiday book buyer. Famous writers will contribute special articles and signed reviews.

1900–1904

1900

5 May	Publication date of *Unleavened Bread,* a novel by the American novelist and poet Robert Grant, which became the #3 best-seller of 1900
25 July	The American Publishers' Association forms with CS II as its first president.
10 Nov.	Publication date of John Fox Jr.'s first Scribners book, *Crittenden*

1901

6 Feb.	Publication date of Henry James's first Scribner book, *The Sacred Fount*
12 Mar.	CS II and Arthur H. Scribner form copartnership (3/4 and 1/4, respectively) to continue the publishing business and determine to carry on all future business under the name and style of "Charles Scribner's Sons."
22 June	Publication date of the first three volumes (of twenty-three) in the Yale Bicentennial series, "issued in connection with the Bicentennial Anniversary, as a partial indication of the character of the studies in which the University teachers are engaged"
17 Aug.	Publication date of Russian revolutionist Maksim Gorky's *Fomá Gordyéeff,* translated by Isabel F. Hapgood

1902

21 Feb.	Publication date of Edith Wharton's *The Valley of Decision* (2 volumes)
31 Mar.	CS II and Arthur H. Scribner modify their articles of copartnership, changing their respective proportions to 3/5 and 2/5.
July	Maxfield Parrish designs the seal for the new Scribner Press.
	The Scribner Press begins operation on Pearl Street in New York City, primarily for the printing of *Scribner's Magazine.*
21 Aug.	Publication date of Henry James's *The Wings of the Dove*
29 Aug.	Publication date of F. Hopkinson Smith's *The Fortunes of Oliver Horn,* the first book to bear the Scribner Press seal
1 Nov.	Publication date of Henry van Dyke's *The Blue Flower,* the #9 best-seller of 1902

1903

29 May	Publication date of Thomas Nelson Page's *Gordon Keith,* the #2 best-seller of 1903

30 Aug.	Publication date of the first six volumes (of thirty) in the Edinburgh Edition of *The Works of Thomas Carlyle,* which was completed in 1904
Sept. 12	Publication date of John Fox Jr.'s *The Little Shepherd of Kingdom Come,* the #10 best-seller of 1903 and #7 of 1904
15 Dec.	Publication date of the first three volumes (of thirty-two) in the Kensington Edition of *The Works of William Makepeace Thackeray,* which was completed in 1904

1904

25 Jan.	CS II, Arthur H. Scribner, Edward L. Burlingame, Henry L. Smith, and Edwin W. Morse form a New Jersey corporation called "Charles Scribner's Sons, Inc.," each receiving shares of stock in the corporation (1198, 799, 1, 1, and 1, respectively).
1 Feb.	CS II and Arthur H. Scribner sell their copartnership in Charles Scribner's Sons to Charles Scribner's Sons, Inc.
30 Apr.	Publication date of *The American Natural History: A Foundation of Useful Knowledge of the Higher Animals of North America* by William T. Hornaday, the American naturalist, conservationist, and first director of the New York Zoological Park
10 Nov.	Publication date of Henry James's *The Golden Bowl* (2 volumes)

ARTICLE:

"Publishers Join Hands. A National Association Formed and Certain Abuses Considered," *New-York Daily Tribune,* 26 July 1900, p. 9.

CS II is elected president of the new American Publishers' Association.

Every large publishing house of importance in the United States was represented at a meeting held yesterday afternoon in the rooms of the Aldine Association, at No. 111 Fifth-ave. The American Publishers' Association was formed, and a plan for correcting certain abuses connected with the sale of books was considered. The call for the meeting was issued on July 2, in the name of the following firms: D. Appleton & Co., The Century Company, Dodd, Mead & Co., Harper & Bros., Houghton, Mifflin & Co., the Macmillan Company, G. P. Putnam's Sons and Charles Scribner's Sons.

A report had been telegraphed from the West that the meeting had been called to form a trust, which, among other economies contemplated, would reduce the royalties paid to popular authors. This, however, is emphatically denied. The real object of the meeting was to compare notes and to see whether something could not be done to prevent the cutting of the prices of books by booksellers. The publishers felt that they needed to be protected against the booksellers, and they also felt that some plan ought to be adopted by which underselling booksellers could be protected against one another. It was reported that the publishers were going to make an attempt to discriminate against the department stores, but this was also denied.

The meeting was called to order by Frank N. Scott, of The Century Company, and Charles Scribner was made chairman, with Frank H. Dodd secretary.

Colonel Harvey Reads Reports

Colonel G. B. M. Harvey then read a report prepared by a committee that had been appointed by the promoters of the association. Besides Colonel Harvey, this committee included Charles Scribner and George P. Brett. The report outlines the purposes and organization of the association. It was unanimously adopted. The report states:

Having been requested to act as a temporary committee for the purpose of outlining suggestions tending to the formation of an association of publishers, we beg to report, as a result of our deliberations, that, in our judgment, such an association, properly organized and conducted, would render a distinct service, not merely to ourselves as publishers, but to authors, booksellers, book purchasers, and, indeed, to every one who is brought into contact, directly or indirectly, with the publishing business.

We regard our interests as identical with those of authors, book manufacturers, booksellers and book buyers, and are convinced that association for mutual advantage can be made far more effective than individual effort to meet such changes in conditions as must necessarily arise in the production and dissemination of good literature. Lack of such co-operation had resulted in the growth of abuses, which, although perhaps minor in importance, have nevertheless reached a point of distinct unfairness to both producer and consumer.

The exact method by which these well known discriminations can be properly corrected or modified has not yet received sufficient consideration to warrant a distinct recommendation, but we see no reason to doubt that such a solution can be reached if all concerned unite upon broad lines and with open minds in an endeavor to work out the problem.

We, nevertheless, recognize the fact that in attempting a task of so much magnitude and involving so many diverse interests it is essential to make haste slowly, for the reason that whatever is done must be necessarily of an experimental nature. Primarily and as a fundamental basis of success of all branches of the business the rights of all, but more especially of book writers and book buyers, must have adequate and satisfactory protection. Moreover, no publisher should, in our judgment, be expected or requested to join an experimental association without retaining full right of withdrawing from any arrangement proposed without prejudice and at will, after having given suitable notice, until the beneficent results of such an association shall have become reasonably manifest.

The Committees and Officers

Colonel Harvey then outlined a method of procedure, which provided for the appointment of a committee of three to draft articles of associa-

Original design for the Scribner Press seal created by Maxfield Parrish in 1902. Charles Scribner III, in an unpublished memo dated 2 June 1994, provides some historical background on its features: "The Scribner logo, with its three key elements of burning antique (Greco-Roman) lamp, book, and laurel wreath, dates back to the Beaux-Arts architect Stanford White's original design for the cover of Scribner's Magazine *(January 1887). The symbol of the book hardly needs to be explained; the laurel crown is a symbol of the highest achievement in poetry or literature, or the arts in general, and it is associated with the classical god Apollo; the lamp is not Aladdin's lamp but rather the lamp of wisdom and knowledge. There is a long tradition in art, going back at least to the time of Petrarch, of a poet being crowned with a wreath of laurel, and such scholars as St. Jerome and St. Thomas Aquinas are traditionally depicted beside such a burning lamp." The adaptation by Parrish appeared on the copyright page of books printed by the Scribner Press; it was not a publisher's colophon but a printer's seal.*

tion. Colonel Harvey, Mr. Dodd and Mr. Brett were appointed to this committee. The following Nomination Committee was appointed: Colonel D. A. Appleton, Frank H. Scott and Frederick A. Stokes. The following Board of Directors was then elected: Charles Scribner, George Mifflin, George P. Brett, Colonel G. B. M. Harvey, General A. C. McClurg, Craig Lippincott, W. W. Appleton and Frank H. Scott.

Officers to serve one year were elected as follows: President, Charles Scribner; vice-presidents,

General A. C. McClurg and George Mifflin; secretary, George P. Brett; treasurer, G. B. M. Harvey.

D. Appleton & Co., Bowen-Merrill Company, of Indianapolis; Century Company, Henry T. Coates & Co., of Philadelphia; Thomas Y. Crowell & Co., Dodd, Mead & Co., Doubleday, Page & Co., Funk & Wagnalls, Harper & Bros., Houghton, Mifflin & Co., John Lane, Lee & Shepard, Boston; The J. B. Lippincott Company, of Philadelphia; Little, Brown & Co., of Boston; Longmans, Green & Co., McClure-Phillips Company, The Macmillan Company, Thomas Nelson & Sons, G. P. Putnam's Sons, James Pott & Co., Fleming H. Revelle Company, F. H. Russell, Charles Scribner's Sons, Silver, Burdett & Co., Small, Maynard & Co., and Frederick A. Stokes Company.

LETTER:
Letter by Scribner editor Edwin W. Morse, 12 April 1901, to Maksim Gorky.

Scribners was the first publisher to introduce the work of Gorky, the Russian writer and revolutionist, to an English audience. He was in a Russian prison when he received this request from Scribners to publish Isabel F. Hapgood's translation of his novel Fomá Gordyéeff. *He cabled his assent, and the translation was published in August carrying a printed copy of his handwritten authorization (in French).*

Dear Sir:

Some time ago Miss Isabel F. Hapgood of this city submitted to us a proposition to translate into English your novel, "Foma Gordyeff." She is an accomplished Russian scholar, having translated several of Count Tolstoy's works from the Russian into English with success. She submitted a translation of a portion of the novel; and we were so impressed by the quality of the work, its power and its truth to universal human nature, that we have determined, with your consent and cooperation, to publish an edition of the book here and so introduce the author to American readers. The popularity of Tolstoy, Turgenief and Gogol in this country leads us to hope for a successful issue for the venture.

We have made a satisfactory arrangement with Miss Hapgood for the translation, contingent upon our obtaining your consent. Several reasons prevent us from making you as advantageous a proposition as we should wish—the cost of the translation, the expense of manufacture and, above all, the risk that we run in publishing a book which cannot be pro-tected by copyright and which may be translated into English and published by any one else, if, as we hope and believe will be the case, the book becomes popular. We shall publish the book at $1.50 per copy in all probability; and our proposition would be to pay you a royalty of 10 per cent on the retail price of all copies sold here after the expenses of publication have been met. If this book is successful we should hope to follow it with others of your works.

We hope that our proposition will be acceptable to you. If it is, will you, in order to save time and to enable us to carry out our plans, kindly send us the following cablegram, HALCANERO being our New York cipher address, viz:

"Halcanero New York Accepted Gorky"

You will send us, please, a memorandum of the cost of this cablegram which we shall be glad to pay.

If our proposal is accepted we wish you would kindly take the trouble to send us by post a few lines in English, or if you prefer in French, stating that by arrangement made with you Messrs. Charles Scribner's Sons are the only authorized publishers in the United States of English translations of your work. This statement it would be our purpose to print in "Foma Gordyeff" as an announcement to the public that ours is the authorized translation, all others being unauthorized.

Trusting that the venture will be mutually profitable, we remain, with best wishes,

Very truly yours,
Charles Scribner's Sons

P.S. We enclose a note from a New York correspondent of yours, Mr. Rosenthal of the Russian Department of the Astor Library.

ARTICLE:
Untitled article, *New-York Daily Tribune,* 20 September 1902, p. 11, about the new Scribner Press colophon.

People who have read "The Fortunes of Oliver Horn" [by F. Hopkinson Smith] and "Captain Macklin" [by Richard Harding Davis] may have noticed on the backs of the title pages a little device showing that the book was printed at "The Scribner Press." Within a month the old house of Scribner has indeed put into operation for the first time a press of its own. It is in Pearl-st., and is intended primarily for the printing of "Scribner's Maga-

ANNOUNCEMENT

MESSRS. CHARLES SCRIBNER'S SONS announce that after February 1, 1904, their business will be carried on as a corporation under the title of CHARLES SCRIBNER'S SONS, Incorporated. There will be no change in the management or methods of the business, which will go on in all its departments as heretofore. Advantage will be taken of the opportunity for associating more closely some of those who for years have been connected with the organization. The officers of the Company are Charles Scribner, President ; Arthur H. Scribner, Vice-President and Treasurer; Edwin W. Morse, Secretary.

New York, January 27, 1904

Public announcement of the firm's incorporation

zine," which has been done by an outside firm ever since it was started. Its equipment is no larger than is needed for this purpose, and it is the intention to use it for book printing only in the short intervals when it is not engaged upon the magazine. No typesetting or electrotyping will be done there, and this part of the manufacture will continue to be done as before by other establishments. It is intended to secure better results if possible in the printing of the magazine by having the work done under the supervision of its proprietors. Only two other New-York publishing houses now have their own presses, the Putnams and the Harpers, at both of which, however, all the mechanical work of manufacture is performed.

NOTE:
Note in *The Publishers' Weekly*, 6 February 1904, pp. 555–556, of Scribners' incorporation.

The change in the name of the Scribner house from a personal firm to that of an incorporated company, does not, as is announced, mark any change in *personnel* or of other significance, but is simply a development in the direction of convenience and continuity of administration.

Mr. Charles Scribner as president of the new company remains the active head of the house, with Mr. Arthur H. Scribner as vice-president, while Mr. E. W. Morse, so long associated with the business in important capacities, becomes secretary of the corporation. We trust, however, that Mr. Charles Scribner, who has declined a re-election as president of the American Pulbishers' Association, will nevertheless find opportunity for larger leisure and more recreative rest than his services to the trade for many years past have enabled him to take. Mr. Scribner has not only been the head of one of our foremost publishing, importing, and retailing houses, but has taken a large part of the responsibility and burden of the reform movement as president of the Association, and has also been treasurer of the American Publishers' Copyright League. There are few men of the present publishing generation who have shown more public spirit and self-sacrifice in keeping the publishing trade up to the highest standards, and setting an example to others among his fellow-craftsmen. It is pleasant to have the opportunity of his retirement from the presidency of the American Publishers' Association to express to him the honor and confidence in which he is held by the trade.

SCRIBNER AUTHORS

J. T. Headley (1813–1897)

Engraved portrait of J. T. Headley (the frontispiece in The Miscellaneous Works of the Rev. J. T. Headley *[New York: John S. Taylor, 1849])*

From a strictly publishing point of view, Headley was a godsend. For the fledgling house of Baker & Scribner, he was the bankroll. The most popular and prolific American historical writer and biographer of the nineteenth century, Headley provided the means by which the firm could develop and expand its list, as best-selling authors have always done for their publishers. Certainly, the tremendous sales of his books carried the firm through the Civil War. His books both reflected and influenced public taste with their patriotic, moral tone and their vivid, "nervous" style. However, his writing often sank to bombast and prolixity, earning him the epithet from Edgar Allan Poe of "Autocrat of the Quacks."

Scribner Books by Headley

1846	*Napoleon and His Marshals* (2 volumes)
1847	*The Sacred Mountains*
	Washington and His Generals (2 volumes)
1848	*Letters from Italy*
	The Life of Oliver Cromwell
1849	*The Adirondack; or, Life in the Woods*
1850	*Sacred Scenes and Characters*
	Miscellanies
	Sketches and Rambles
1851	*The Imperial Guard of Napoleon: From Marengo to Waterloo*
1852	*The Lives of Winfield Scott and Andrew Jackson*
1853	*The Second War with England* (2 volumes)
1856	*Life of George Washington*
	Works (15 volumes)
1859	*The Life of General H. Havelock, K.C.B.*
1861	*The Life of Winfield Scott*

BOOK REVIEW:
W. T. Bacon, "Mr. Headley's New Book," *The New Englander*, 4, no. 3 (July 1846): 364–365, 367.

By defending Napoleon against English historians who had always characterized the French Emperor as a villainous megalomaniac, Headley stirred up controversy for Americans who, themselves, were in the midst of a territorial war with Mexico. The book therefore became an occasion for reviewers to distinquish morally between right and wrong military actions. This review of Napoleon and His Marshals *deals only with the first volume of the two-volume work.*

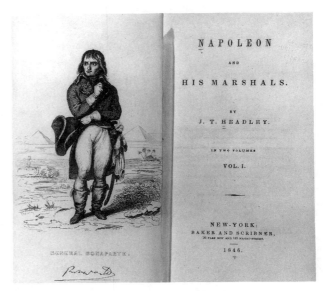

Title page and frontispiece for a first-edition copy of volume one of Napoleon and His Marshals (Olin Library, Cornell University). This historical work, Headley's first Scribner book, was the firm's first best-seller, reaching fifty editions by 1861.

This book is so peculiar in some respects, that, as New Englanders, we cannot pass it over. It comes from a man who we have been accustomed to suppose, took somewhat of a religious view of things, and would not be apt to lay down propositions, or defend men or principles, without at least giving them careful thought. We will suppose Mr. Headley has given the subject of his book careful thought; yet we must differ with him very much in some of his opinions, and we feel called to express that difference.

This volume of Mr. Headley's consists of a series of sketches, containing, or illustrating, the lives of Bonaparte and his Marshals. It is to be published in two volumes — the one before us is the first. This contains the sketch of Napoleon and nine of those who were connected with him, and from this we may obtain some idea of what the whole will be.

As a literary performance, we are disposed to speak with very considerable praise of his ability. Mr. Headley has a lively talent for this species of writing; his style is nervous, and generally correct; and he frequently grasps the whole subject, or scene, with a vividness and power, that evince a high degree of intellectual ability. Much *light* is thrown on one of the most interesting periods of French History, by his sketches. The characters live again, and pass before us. We see the springs at work, that set the different portions of society in motion — the springs that set in motion powers, which upheaved the whole surface of the French nation, rent the land into factions, bound the nation together again in new combination and with tremendous force, and then threw it like a thunderbolt, in fire and fury, on other nations.

As a mere delineator of character, and a sketcher of battle fields, Mr. Headley deserves praise. These characters are conceived with much truth — that is, in their external manifestation; and some of these battle fields are described with a vividness and force, fully equalling in agreeableness some of the pages of Scott. They have not Scott's prolixity; while they have his *life.*

But when we have said this much, we have said all which we care to say, or which we think ought to be said, in praise of the book. Not, indeed, that the author of it did not mean well, and that some of his reflections are not just and calculated to do good; — but we object to the book on the ground, that the conception of the author's mind of Napoleon and his Generals, and of the necessity and use of the whole French war, is — in a moral point of view — wholly and positively erroneous; that his conception of the motive — that is, the *moral* man — in each of these heroes, is not *the* man which in fact existed in the breasts of these individuals, but something which exists rather in the imagination or breasts of those who would admire them, and who would — whether with an evil intention, we will not say — become the apologists for a false spirit and a false age.

Mr. Headley in this volume considers Bonaparte and his Generals, not only heroes in intellectual qualities, but *moral* heroes; and the wars of France in which they engaged, and which they in fact helped to cause, as great *moral* wars. The general opinion of the world thus, based on all which has been esteemed just History, in respect to Napoleon and the wars of France, is boldly assailed, and he, Mr. Headley, would give us the true age and the true man, as they were. For this author's good intention, and for his labor, we have respect; for his conception of what he esteems the moral spirit of the age and men, condemnation. . . .

As to Mr. Headley's fears that he will be censured for inculcating a warlike spirit in this age, we would say we perhaps find less fault with this than aught else in his book. A warlike spirit, in itself, rightly based and rightly kept alive, is only feared by a few modern sentimentalists in religion, in these innovating times. Fourierists, Socialists, and what not, will, of course, find fault with Mr. Headley, as they object to all fighting; — we however belong to the old New England race, who find back in their history, such out of the way and ignoble places as Concord, Lexington, Bunker Hill, &c. &c.; who revere our ancestors for all noble qualities, among which, as not the least best, was their *war* spirit; and we shall not find fault with this or any author, who shows us the intellectual power necessary, or the fame accruing to any and all successful or unsuccessful battles, where a nation's *just* rights are invaded. We are not in favor of cruelty. We go for no aggressive wars. Territory, if we must have it, we would pay for, not with the heart's blood of citizens, but their cash. But we are among the staid and sober — the old blue Connecticut and New England set, who go for such vices as capital punishment, paying for what we buy both as individuals and as states, and who would not (unless like the

Quaker, who threw a man overboard and drowned him though he would not not take his life) at all object to beating back from our coast or soil any foreign enemy who might dare invade us. In other words, we are not for Peace Societies in these days, any farther than these are for cultivating a *just* spirit of peace and forbearance. We are not *non-resistance* people. We believe we should fight, and that with very considerable, if not commendable energy, if any one should seem determined forcibly, to take from us what was our own and we felt we could not well spare. Mr. Headley, then, need not fear any malediction from the New Englander, or we think from any New England man, for giving a warlike spirit to the age. Let him teach a *just* warlike spirit; one that waits for wrongs, and proceeds violently to right them, only when other means fail; and he will — so far — have every right-minded man's approbation.

But for the gigantic and evil Spirit of France he has seen fit to eulogize; for the wars of this giant, by which millions of souls were sent to doom, and thrones in scores were scraped together like so many pebbles, and then piled up for an enormous seat on which himself should be seated; — for attempting to make out that France was just from first to last, Napoleon was just, and all the histories from first to last have slandered both France and her evil Genius; and that the world made a very great mistake when she took this Genius for a devil — for all this we have for Mr. Headley no harsher wish, than that the work may soon pass away from the recollections of our people, as a mistaken act from a mistaken judgment, of one who we doubt not is an amiable, as he certainly is an able and often eloquent man.

In the "Literary Notices" section of the October 1846 issue (vol. 16, pp. 592–594) of The New Englander, *volume two of Headley's work is reviewed in a similar vein, though tempered now by the fact that the work has become a runaway best-seller.*

We had something to say of the first volume of this work in our last No. Our remarks were directed chiefly against the general scope and object of the French wars during Napoleon's career, and the very false aspect in which, as we judged, this author had presented the great war-leader himself. We did not mean to deny the ability of the work. Mr. Headley is a man of undoubted genius, and we very much admire the intellectual spirit of his writings. His travels show a very delicate per-

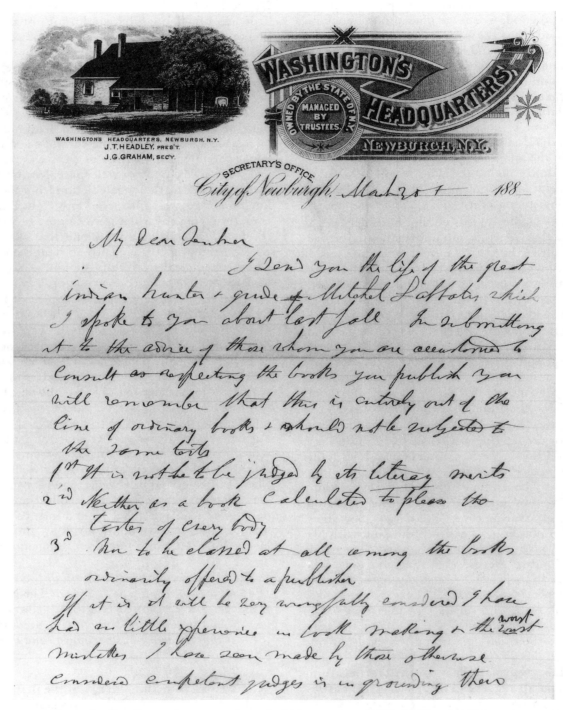

First page of a letter by Headley, written near the end of his career, to CS II, 30 March 1885, accompanying the manuscript of a biography of the Adirondack Indian hunter/guide Mitchell Sabbatis. Appealing to the son of the firm's founder, who had published his earlier books, Headley here puts forth various arguments in favor of his new work. CS II was not convinced, and the book was never published, ending the long, successful relationship between author and publisher.

ception of the beautiful and the picturesque in nature, and a quick eye for the moral traits of men. He has the remarkable faculty of calling back scenes of the past, with the dead actors of those scenes, and of making them stalk before us again, with all their life-like energy, grace and beauty. This work is *the* work of the season. No book has taken a stronger hold of the public mind — whether for good or evil, is not now the question. And there is no book that has been published for a long time, which presents finer passages — both of glowing description and fervid eloquence — than does this. Mr. Headley's conception of individual character also, is noticeable — making allowance for a general bias in favor of every thing connected with Napoleon; and his analyses of the minds of some of those whose characters he has depicted, are equally well done. The work is on the whole one of high intellectual character, and will be read beyond the present day. It is remarkable also, that the author contrives to keep up the interest so continuously through the whole book, dealing as he does with so many characters, and all more or less connected with the same scenes. The same battle fields are sometimes described, more than once, and yet the pictures are as if two separate individuals had surveyed the scene from different points of observation. This shows a fertility of mind, as creditable to the writer as it is of moment in giving interest to his work. We make these remarks, because on a former occasion we had so much to say from another point of the subject — that which was condemnatory; — and because we must still, in honesty, make objections to portions of the work; — and lest it should be supposed that we had not an eye for the intellectual worth, of what, in a moral point of view, we feel bound to condemn.

The great one objection to this whole work by Mr. Headley is, the very favorable bias of his own mind towards any and every thing connected with the wonderful man, whose deeds he here attempts to chronicle anew. . . . From a perusal of the sketch of Napoleon, it is even more obvious than at first, that Mr. Headley has done *injustice* to history, as truly as that history has hitherto done injustice to Napoleon — not indeed by misstating facts, but by not stating *all* that is true. . . . They [the sketches of Napoleon and his marshals] glow as if Scott himself held the pen. Still, there seems to be an insensibility on the part of the painter to the horrible evils these men were causing, and to the selfish ambition which inspired

them; and on this account the book as a whole must be considered radically defective. . . .

We would suggest to Mr. Headley to turn and devote his strong and lively talent, to recovering from the shadows, into which by the inevitable destinies of every thing that is human they are fast falling, the heroes of our own history. Here is a field, not indeed, blazing like the fields of Europe under the tread of Napoleon and his armies, and ringing with the clash of arms; but yet every way worthy of being searched, and capable of illustrating another side of the war-picture. Let him gaze on the full length portrait of Washington, and that of each of his great compeers, as these live in the annals of the country, and in the minds and hearts of a few living men. Let him throw around them the fascination of genius, and cause to live each feature and characteristic of each of these worthies; and we will be bound Mr. Headley will give us another book not a whit less attractive to the mind of his countrymen than those he has written, and far more valuable, because it *must* deal, to be true, with the virtues that dignify and ennoble our race.

The reviewer's advice to Headley to turn his attention homeward to George Washington was followed in, or anticipated, his next work, published by Baker & Scribner in 1847: Washington and His Generals, *another best-seller. According to the* New York Nation, *in 1866* Washington and His Generals *was one of the five secular books to be found on the typical American bookshelf.*

BOOK REVIEW:
Edgar Allan Poe, "Joel T. Headley," *The Southern Literary Messenger,* 16, no. 10 (October 1850): 608–610.

From advance sheets of Poe's The Literati: Some Honest Opinions about Autorial Merits and Demerits, with Occasional Words of Personality, *published later in 1850,* The Southern Literary Messenger *offered Poe's review of Headley's book* The Sacred Mountains, *which Baker & Scribner had published in 1847, the same year as* Washington and His Generals. *Here, Headley falls victim to Poe's "tomahawk-style" of criticism and earns his epithet as a quack.*

The *Reverend* Mr. Headley — (why *will* he not put his full title on his title-pages?) has in his "Sacred Mountains" been reversing the facts of the old fable about the mountains that brought forth the mouse — *parturiunt montes nascitur ridiculus mus* — for in this instance it appears to be the mouse — the little *ridiculus mus* — that has been bringing forth the "Mountains," and a great litter of them, too. The epithet, funny, however, is perhaps the only one which can be considered as thoroughly applicable to the book. We say that a book is a "funny" book, and nothing else, when it spreads over two hundred pages an amount of matter which could be conveniently presented in twenty of a magazine: that a book is a "funny" book — "only this and nothing more" — when it is written in that kind of phraseology, in which John Philpot Curran, when drunk, would have made a speech at a public dinner: and moreover, we do say, emphatically, that a book is a "funny" book, and nothing but a funny book, whenever it happens to be penned by Mr. Headley.

We should like to give some account of "The Sacred Mountains," if the thing were only possible — but we cannot conceive that it is. Mr. Headley belongs to that numerous class of authors, who must be read to be understood, and who, for that reason, very seldom are as thoroughly comprehended as they should be. . . .

The mountains described are Ararat, Moriah, Sinai, Hor, Pisgah, Horeb, Carmel, Lebanon, Zion, Tabor, Olivet, and Calvary. Taking up these, one by one, the author proceeds in his own peculiar way to *elocutionize* about them: we really do not know how else to express what it is that Mr. Headley does with these eminences. Perhaps if we were to say that he stood up before the reader and "made a speech" about them, one after the other, we should come still nearer the truth. By way of carrying out his design, as announced in the preface, that of rendering "more familiar and life-like some of the scenes" and so-forth, he tells not only how each mountain is, and was, but how it might have been and ought to be in his own

opinion. To hear him talk, anybody would suppose that he had been at the laying of the cornerstone of Solomon's Temple . . . [lengthy quotations from the work] . . . Moreover he is a modest man; for he confesses (no doubt with tears in his eyes) that really there is one thing he does not know. "How Heaven regarded this disaster [the crucifixion of Christ], and the Universe felt at the sight, I cannot tell." Only think of that! *I* cannot! — *I*, Headley, really cannot tell how the Universe "felt" once upon a time! This is downright bashfulness on the part of Mr. Headley. He *could* tell if he would only try. Why did he not inquire? Had he demanded of the Universe how it felt, can any one doubt that the answer would have been — "Pretty well, I thank you, my dear Headley; how do you feel yourself?"

"Quack" is a word that sounds well only in the mouth of a duck; and upon our honor we feel a scruple in using it: nevertheless the truth should be told; and the simple fact is, that the author of the "Sacred Mountains" is the Autocrat of the Quacks. . . . the reader will excuse the digression; but talking of one great man is very apt to put us in mind of another. We were saying — were we not? — that Mr. Headley is by no means to be sneered at as a quack. This might be justifiable, indeed, were he only a quack in a small way — a quack doing business by retail. But the wholesale dealer is entitled to some respect. Besides, the Reverend author of "Napoleon and His Marshals" was a quack to some purpose. He knows what he is about. We like perfection wherever we see it. We readily forgive a man for being a fool if he only be a *perfect* fool — and this is a particular in which we cannot put our hands upon our hearts and say that Mr. Headley is deficient. He acts upon the principle that if a thing is worth doing at all it is worth doing well: — and the thing that he "does" especially well is the public.

T. S. Arthur (1809–1885)

Engraved portrait of T. S. Arthur (frontispiece to his Illustrated Temperance Tales, *Philadelphia: J. W. Bradley, 1850)*

Author, editor, publisher, Arthur is best remembered as a temperance crusader. As one of the most prolific, influential American writers of the mid nineteenth century, he offered moral lessons in his fictional writings to adults as well as children. Through his other work he became an authority on marital and family relations, and he was an advocate for women's rights. Scribners was neither his first publisher, nor his major — he was a one-man mill producing fictional cloth for different vendors. Arthur's children's magazine, the *Children's Hour,* was absorbed by Scribners' *St. Nicholas* in 1874. The one title that endures of the more than two hundred novels that he wrote, the temperance classic *Ten Nights in a Bar-Room and What I Saw There* (1854), was published the year after Arthur's last Scribner book.

Scribner Books by Arthur

1847	*Keeping Up Appearances; or, A Tale for the Rich and Poor*
	Riches Have Wings; or, A Tale for the Rich and Poor
1848	*Rising in the World; or, A Tale for the Rich and Poor*
	Making Haste to Be Rich; or The Temptation and Fall
	Debtor and Creditor: A Tale of the Times
	Retiring from Business; or, The Rich Man's Error
1849	*Wreaths of Friendship: A Gift for the Young,* co-authored by F. C. Woodworth
1850	*The Brilliant: A Gift Book for 1850,* edited by Arthur
1853	*Heart-Histories and Life-Pictures*
	The Old Man's Bride
	Sparing to Spend; or, The Loftons and Pinkertons
	Home Lights and Shadows

N. P. Willis (1806–1867)

Nathaniel Parker Willis

Willis traveled widely in Europe for George P. Morris, founder of the *New York Weekly Mirror*, as the first paid American foreign correspondent, sending home character sketches, observations, and columns on fashion and high society. He was the first American to make a comfortable living as a "magazinist." Considered one of the pioneers of the American popular magazine, Willis edited the *Home Journal* from 1846, the birth year of Scribners, till his death. Scribners published his last books and reprinted earlier ones.

Scribner Books by Willis

1849	*Rural Letters and Other Records of Thought at Leisure, Written in the Intervals of More Hurried Literary Labor*
1850	*People I Have Met; or, Pictures of Society and People of Mark, Drawn Under a Thin Veil of Fiction*
	Life, Here and There; or, Sketches of Society and Adventure at Far-Apart Times and Places
1851	*Hurry-Graphs; or, Sketches of Scenery, Celebrities and Society, Taken from Life*
1852	*Pencillings by the Way: Written During Some Years of Residence and Travel in Europe*
1853	*Summer Cruise in the Mediterranean on Board an American Frigate*
	Fun-Jottings; or, Laughs I Have Taken a Pen To
	Health Trip to the Tropics
1854	*Famous Persons and Places*
1855	*Out-Doors at Idlewild; or, The Shaping of a Home on the Banks of the Hudson*
	The Rag Bag, A Collection of Ephemera
1857	*Paul Fane; or, Parts of a Life Else Untold*
1859	*The Convalescent*
1885	*Prose Writings of Nathaniel Parker Willis*, selected by Henry A. Beers

Caroline M. Kirkland (1801–1864)

Engraved portrait of Caroline M. Kirkland (from Evart A. and George L. Duyckinck's Cyclopædia of American Literature, *New York: Charles Scribner, 1855)*

Kirkland was the first American woman author of note that Scribners published, though her literary reputation rests on her early frontier fiction that she published in the decade before she became a Scribner author. Writing from a distinctly female perspective, she focused on her own experiences in the wilderness of Michigan during the 1830s and 1840s — the hard realities, not the tall tales. The work she published with Scribners included gift books, verse miscellanies, and an appeal for the rehabilitation of discharged female convicts.

Scribner Books by Kirkland

1849	*Holidays Abroad; or, Europe from the West* (2 volumes)
1852	*The Evening Book; or, Fireside Talk on Morals and Manners, with Sketches of Western Life*
1853	*A Book for the Home Circle; or, Familiar Thoughts on Various Topics, Literary, Moral and Social*
	The Helping Hand: Comprising an Account of the Home for Discharged Female Convicts and an Appeal in Behalf of That Institution
1854	*Autumn Hours and Fireside Reading*
1864	*The School-Girl's Garland, A Selection of Poetry in Four Parts* (first and second series), edited by Kirkland
1866	*Patriotic Eloquence: Being Selections from One Hundred Years of National Literature, Compiled for the Use of Schools in Reading and Speaking*

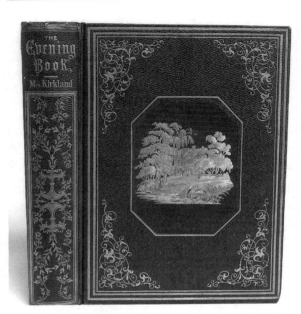

Kirkland's The Evening Book, *a gift book published by Scribners in 1852. A "gift book" was a literary miscellany published in ornamental format for gift purposes.*

LETTER:

Letter by Kirkland to George P. Putnam, 24 January 1849 (George Palmer Putnam Collection, Princeton University Library).

Kirkland explains to her previous publisher why she switched to Baker & Scribner for her new work, Holidays Abroad; or, Europe from the West *(2 volumes). She remained fairly loyal to her "new" publisher — in fact, Scribners proved to be her major publisher — though she was to publish two more books with Putnam (both in 1852).*

My dear Sir — From some causes connected with the departure of my brother for California my note to you was delayed — leaving me to suppose that having made me the best offer you thought prudent, you were not disposed to go any farther — So that I concluded to accept the proposal I mentioned — which though far better than any other I had then received, will as you must perceive afford me but slender remuneration, unless the book should have a far better sale than I can hope for a book of travels. Perhaps it is as well that you escaped what might not have proved profitable while I, on the other hand, have <u>since</u> received what I consider a <u>better</u> offer, which I am not at liberty to accept.

I have omitted to mention that my agreement is with Messrs. Baker & Scribner, who, being in the way of American copyright books, were desirous to secure mine — perhaps without much idea of any great profit from it.

I told them what I will tell you — that I should have much preferred agreeing with a publisher with whom I had already been connected — but as I understood you to say specifically that what you mentioned was the best you could do, I had pretty much given up the idea of your saying any thing further.

Sincerely yours
C. M. Kirkland

Donald Grant Mitchell (1822–1908)
("Ik. Marvel")

Donald Grant Mitchell

With J. T. Headley and J. G. Holland, Mitchell formed the triumvirate of successful authors that carried Scribners through its first decades. A graduate of Yale, where he had been editor of the *Yale Literary Magazine,* Mitchell began a tentative exploration of a literary career by writing about his European travel and on the French Revolution, which he had witnessed firsthand before he found his fame, or it found him, with books of fanciful and subjective reveries that bordered between fiction and essay. Thereafter, he preferred writing about the agricultural aspects and the rural pleasures of his farm, and, in 1868 when Pettingill, Bates & Co. wanted to start an American farm journal, Mitchell was asked to assume its editorship. He gave it the name of *Hearth and Home* and ran it for its first two years, securing both literary and scientific contributions from leading authors and authorities of the time. (Mary Mapes Dodge followed him as editor but left the magazine in 1873 to edit Scribners' children's monthly, *St. Nicholas.*) In later life he confined himself to magazine writing and lecturing, compiling and publishing his talks on English and American literature.

Scribner Books by Mitchell

1850	*The Battle Summer: Being Transcripts from Personal Observation in Paris, During the Year 1848*
	Reveries of a Bachelor; or, A Book of the Heart
1851	*Fresh Gleanings; or, A New Sheaf from the Old Fields of Continental Europe*
	Dream Life: A Fable of the Seasons
1852	*The Lorgnette; or, Studies of the Town* (2 volumes)
1855	*Fudge Doings: Being Tony Fudge's Record of the Same* (2 volumes)
1863	*My Farm of Edgewood: A Country Book*
1864	*Seven Stories, with Basement and Attic*
1865	*Wet Days at Edgewood, With Old Farmers, Old Gardeners, and Old Pastorals*

1866	*Doctor Johns: Being a Narrative of Certain Events in the Life of an Orthodox Minister of Connecticut* (2 volumes)
1867	*Rural Studies, With Hints for Country Places*
1869	*Pictures of Edgewood*
1877	*About Old Story-Tellers, of How and When They Lived, and What Stories They Told*
1884	*Bound Together: A Sheaf of Papers*
	Out-of-Town Places, With Hints for Their Improvement (a reissue of *Rural Studies*)
1889	*English Lands, Letters, and Kings: From Celt to Tudor*
1890	*English Lands, Letters, and Kings: From Elizabeth to Anne*
1895	*English Lands, Letters, and Kings: Queen Anne and the Georges*
1897	*American Lands and Letters: The Mayflower to Rip Van Winkle*
	English Lands, Letters, and Kings: The Later Georges to Victoria
1899	*American Lands and Letters: Leather Stocking to Poe's "Raven"*
1907	*The Works of Donald G. Mitchell* (Edgewood Edition of 15 volumes)

BOOK REVIEW:

"The Battle Summer," *The Southern Literary Messenger*, 16, no. 2 (February 1850): 118–125.

This review of Mitchell's first Scribner book, while laudatory of its subject matter, criticizes its style, which the reviewer compares to the exaggerations of the English historian and critic Thomas Carlyle. Designated as "The Reign of Blouse," the volume was to be followed by a second one called "The Reign of Bourgeois," but, sensitive to public opinion and depressed by the insufficient sales of the first, Mitchell did not continue the narrative. Instead, adding material to his previously published (and praised) article, "The Bachelor's Reverie," he created his next book, Reveries of a Bachelor, *which Baker & Scribner published in the fall of 1850. Within a year it had sold about fourteen thousand copies and established Mitchell's career.*

"Ik. Marvel," our esteemed friend and contributor, has written another book. It lies before us in the clean typography of an excellent publishing house of New York, and we have read it, from the little scrap of Montaigne which is struck by way of motto on the title-page, to the fragment of recondite Latinity which he cites at the conclu-sion. We need scarcely say that the whole book has given us great delight — a sensation which we propose to communicate to our readers by means of that privilege of unlimited quotation accorded to the modern reviewer, who sits like an intellectual Jack Horner at the board of literature, appropriating the plums which garnish the puddings of publishers — *extrahens prunum pollice,* as the "Arundines Cami" has it — with equal ease and satisfaction.

It is a critical moment with the young author who has produced one work of recognized merit, when he comes forward with a second volume for public approval. This second volume is to establish him as an able writer, or to dash to the ground the little reputation he has already built up — and it may fairly be assumed that the author, fully conscious of the issues that wait upon the work itself, has put forth all his powers to ensure a favorable sentence. No allowance is therefore made for haste or inconsideration, and although the Frenchman tells us *Ce n'est que le premier pas qui coute,* we are not sure that the second step is not even more difficult. Considering this fact, we confess to have looked forward with some anxious interest to the appearance of "The Battle Summer," Ik. Marvel's second literary effort. Our apprehensions, such as they were, have been happily quieted as to its merit, and while it is not all we could wish (for we shall have a word or two of gentle complaint to utter by and by) we have no hesitation in declaring that, in our judgment, it fixes the author's position as one of the most graphic and spirited writers of the day.

The gentleman who figures under the domino of "Ik. Marvel" made a tour of Europe, after taking his degree at a Northern College, and upon his return, nearly three years since, like many of his peripatetic predecessors, wrote a book of travels. There was something in the appearance of the volume to attract observation. It did not *look* like the mass of continental diaries and Alpine albums that had been kept by the herd of former tourists in Europe, and what was more — it did not *read* like them. It seemed to be, on the contrary, just such a Sentimental Journey as Laurence Sterne would have written in 1847 — if he had gone flying over the face of Picardy by the rail, instead of travelling in the chaise from Calais with the lady whose "face of about six and twenty — of a clear transparent brown" is so fresh in our recollections. There were passages here and there, scarcely less deeply pathetic than the story of Maria, touches of that peculiar humor that no one else than Sterne ever displayed, and views of life and character indicating an intellect of rare strength and acuteness. The book was generally read. Everybody began to inquire about "Ik. Marvel" and whether that was his real name or not. Meanwhile our pseudonymous author had commenced the study of the law in an office in Wall Street, leaving his literary reputation to take care of itself.

But very soon the news came across the water that strange events had occurred in *la belle ville* — a Republic had been proclaimed for France, and the fat old King had taken flight by a back staircase, without even carrying with him the famous cotton umbrella, the *riffard royal,* to shelter him from the driving rains of the Channel, and altogether without protection against the still more cruel tempest of popular rebuke. — Paris was now to be seen in a new phase, and although it might not wear as gay an air as under the fallen monarchy, though fewer dashing equipages were to be met in the *Bois de Boulogne* and *les Anglaises* had fled, we do not wonder that those Americans who had lived there during the ancient regime, and who still retained delightful recollections of Very's, should desire to see the great metropolis under republican rule. We are not surprised therefore that Ik. Marvel grew weary of my Lord Coke and sighed for a glimpse at *La Liberté*

Engraved title page for Mitchell's first Scribner book. While Mitchell never identified the source of his adopted pseudonym, "Ik. Marvel," saying he had forgotten the circumstances of its selection, his fondness for two seventeenth-century English writers, Izaak Walton, author of The Compleat Angler, *and Andrew Marvell, the poet of "To His Coy Mistress," may have amalgamated their names.*

in the loose flaunting robes of her Babylonian vesture. Our author expresses this desire somewhat differently, in the Dedicatory letter which serves as preface —

"To me, with whom the memories of courts and monarchic splendors were still fresh and green, such sudden news was startling. I tortured my brain with thinking — how the prince of cities was now looking; — and how the shops; — and how the gaiety? I conjured up images of the New Order, and the images dogged me in the street, and at my desk, and made me sleep — a night-

THE HOUSE OF SCRIBNER

mare! They blurred the type of Blackstone, and made the mazes of Chitty ten fold greater. The New Statutes were dull, and a dead letter; and the New Practice worse than new. For a while I struggled manfully with my work, but it was a heavy school-boy task — it was like the knottiest of the Tuscular Questions, with vacation in prospect.

"The office was empty one day: I had been breaking ground in Puffendorf; — one page — two pages — three pages — very dull, but illumined here and there with a magical illustration of King Louis, or stately poet Lamartine; when on a sudden, as one of these illustrations came in, with the old Palais de Justice in the back ground, I slammed together the heavy book-lids, saying to myself; — Is not the time of Puffendorf, and Grotius, and even amiable, aristocratic Blackstone gone by? And are there not new Kingdom-makers, and new law-makers, and new code-makers astir, mustering, with all their souls and voices, such measures of Government as will, by and by, make beacons and maxims? And are not these Newmen, making, and doing, and being, what these old men only wrote of? . . .

"Are they not acting over there in France, in the street, in the court, and in the Assembly, palpably and visibly, with their magnificent Labor Organizations, and Omnibus-built barricades, and oratoric strong-words, and bayonet bloodythrusts, a set of ideas about Constitutional Liberty, and Right to Property, and offences civil, wider, newer, and richer than all preached about, in all the pages of all these fusty Latinists?

" — And I threw Puffendorf, big as he was, into the corner, and said, — I will go and see?" [several additional pages of quotations follow]

The intelligible reader will have been convinced from the foregoing passages that "The Battle Summer" deserves all the praise we have given it. If he should get the volume (as we hope he will) he will be sorry to arrive so soon at the conclusion of the "Reign of Blouse" which terminates on the eve of the sad events of June — finding consolation in the fact, however, (stated in an appended note of the publishers) that the companion volume, "The Reign of Bourgeois" will be issued early in the spring. And now, Mr. Ik. Marvel, sitting in your comfortable study on Fifth Avenue, correcting proof-sheets with the air of an old *litterateur*, we have a word querulous though not angry, for your ear; *ecoutez*.

Why, in the much-abused name of Archbishop Whately, have you so marred a good native style by forced inversions, oddly-compounded words, unnatural forms of expression and all the grotesqueness and *bizarrerie* of Carlyle? There are better models, be assured, if indeed there were need of your imitating any one. You did not learn this in the shady groves of old Yale, for your "Fresh Gleanings" did not so outrage the English of your fathers and you have written of late [September 1849] an article, in our own Messenger — The Bachelor's Reverie — whose simple pathos was expressed in the most beautiful and touching words that ever came out of Dr. Johnson. Why, Sir, the thing out-Herods Herod, and leaves Sartor Resartus very far in the distance. One would think that you had taken the pledge against the definite article and had studied the idiom of Babel amid the confusion of tongues. Oh, reform it altogether. Let us have "The Reign of Bourgeois" undefaced by such conceits — a worthy casket for the gems that you are now rubbing up to be therein enshrined. But *tiens* — we have done.

ARTICLE:
Fitz-James O'Brien, "Mitchell," *Putnam's Monthly Magazine of American Literature, Science, and Art,* 1, no. 1 (January 1853): 74–78.

This article inaugurated the "Our Young Authors" series of Putnam's, *which reviewed promising American writers. In his review of Mitchell, O'Brien, an Irish-born journalist and author, argues that the strengths of the author of* The Reveries of a Bachelor *are his weakness: the graceful, delicate, dreamy style of the sensitive writer becomes cloying to the reader. He begs Mitchell to write no more "dream" lives. Mitchell did not, preferring to write about his gentleman's life on his farm, Edgewood, and its rural pleasures; but he also never again achieved the success of his earlier works.*

The author of the "Reveries" is a natural man, — of course we speak of him as he appears in his books. He does not pad, or stuff, or wear fustian, or a carry a long rapier which is always getting between the legs of its owner. His curls are his own, his color is his own, his breath is sweet, and his smile is pleasant. He is not, to be sure, very grand or forcible. He is no Farnese Hercules, with great huge muscles of thought standing out in bold relief from his form. But he is the Antinous of the Fireside, graceful, delicate and dreamy. He well named his book "Reveries." Dreamland appears to have descended to him by some territorial right, and he wanders with the free step of an

Double frontispiece in Mitchell's 1850 bestseller

owner among his shadowy possessions. Judging from his books, Mitchell is a very impressionable man. His nature is, as it were, iodised, and registers, with the sensitive accuracy of a daguerreotype, every passing light and shade of such characters as come within his sphere. But unlike the daguerreotype, he is not universal. We find in his pictures, no huge granitic masses, such as Hawthorne loves to fling at his canvas, careless where they may stick, or what they deface. He paints only the gentle, the grieving, and the beautiful. A mother weeping over the grave of her son of fifteen summers; a husband stealing with soft step, modulated voice, and imprisoned agony, round the death-bed of his young wife; a love-scene between a youth and maiden, where passion exhales itself into a dreamy mist, enveloping them both and softening their outlines to our vision till they melt away in a cloud of splendor, and leave us pleased, but unsatisfied: these, and such similar subjects, does the author of the "Reveries" depict. How long they are going to last, time only can tell. Like those angelic heads that Sir Joshua Reynolds painted, the delicate colors may fleet,

and leave nothing after them but deathlike memories.

Mr. Mitchell, in his books, has dreams within dreams. He dreams of a hero, who dreams in turn of himself, or some one else in whom he is interested, and so rolls an endless chain of reveries, like the long perspective of receding mirrors, that we see when we place two looking-glasses face to face. This produces, in the end, a most unsatisfactory result. We see no Finis, nor ever will see one. All is vague, sliding and unfinished. A weary panorama, beautifully painted, passes before us, but it has no end, and after a time all features and scenery melt into pretty, unsubstantial clouds. We long to see one good solid rock or tree on which to fasten our attention, but there is none. Like Alciphron we swing in air and darkness, and know not whither the wind blows us.

In his "Lorgnette, or Studies of the Town," Mr. Mitchell has essayed dealing with social realities, more than in his other or later works. Sometimes he succeeds in hitting off a character very fairly, but we see in a little while that analytic humor is not his *forte*. Give him a heart suffocating with tenderness or grief, and he will lay its secrets bare with exquisite gentleness and skill, and have some little anodyne of his own to lay upon the wound afterwards; but the broad, grinning mask of every-day life, is too coarse for him to handle. Farce turns the edge of his delicate scalpel, and we feel instinctively that he had better let it alone altogether. Master Timon, coming home to his boardinghouse, and talking aloud about dandies, and painted, fashionable ladies, does not interest us half as much as the "Bachelor" in his lonely New England farm-house, dreaming sweetly in his arm-chair, and seeing numberless faces, and romances, and recollections, in the white ashes of the pine-logs.

Mr. Mitchell does not bear reading from cover to cover. The want of sustained interest in his books, and the very fragmentary manner in which he arranges them, are indeed unfavorable to a continuous perusal. He is to be taken bit by bit. When you have been all day long slaving at some hard, dry business, that chokes up all kindly sympathies, and parches every secret spring, come home, put on your dressing-gown, place a cup of delicate French chocolate on a table near you, and read the third chapter of the "Reveries of a Bachelor." When you have finished it, be sure your heart will be no longer arid. If nothing else freshens the soil, your tears will at least fall there, and there is no dew so invigorating to our natures as that which we weep ourselves.

But Mr. Mitchell cannot be read entire. There is a sameness about their very perfections that wearies us as we go on. They are the champaign lands of sentiment; beautiful levels over which an hour's gallop or a day's meditation is charming. But to stay there for any length of time induces terrible lassitude, and mental depression. This arises from the almost feminine delicacy of Mr. Mitchell's nature. He takes us captive with those gentle spells for which the sex are famous, and we like to dally for awhile with the sweet thoughts that he whispers to us, and to daintily taste of the rich, ripe fruits that he has spread upon the board. But like Rinaldo in Armida's garden, such pleasures are soon exhausted, and we sigh for the sterner fields of thought that we forsook to join him in his dalliance. Most young American authors of the sentimental school, have one model whom they follow in their first flights. They could scarce have one purer or better than Washington Irving; but it would be better for their originality if they contemplated rather than copied him. There can be no doubt, on looking over Mr. Mitchell's books, of his having been inspired by the author of the Sketch Book. He has much of the rounded gentleness of Irving in his construction, with considerable grandiloquence, which is his own. He has a Bulwerian affection for capital letters and resonant sentences. Though his ideas are seldom forced or conceited, he is exceedingly anxious to present them to you with their best foot foremost. He dresses them up in their shiniest clothes, and groups them after the most approved models. He occasionally, however, draws inspiration from other sources besides the writings of Mr. Irving. In his "Fresh Gleanings" occurs a passage which bears so singular a resemblance to Sterne's famous chapter of "the Monk," that we cannot help thinking that Mr. Mitchell travelled in Styria and Carinthia with the Sentimental Journey in his pocket. . . . [a lengthy quotation]

The book of Mr. Mitchell's, which, in the eyes of the world and ourselves best exemplifies the peculiar beauties of his style, is the "Reveries of a Bachelor." It is, as we said before, desultory and fragmentary in its nature; but in it there are some tender Greuze-like pictures, that it does one good to study. Melancholy is the key-note of the book; but it is subdued and richly toned. No querulous wailing or mad laments; but a sad Æolian harp, over which a Summer wind, laden with the breath of flowers, sweeps, drawing forth a mellow sorrow. The Bachelor mourns like an epicurean, who makes even his melancholy pleasurable; who gazes with a voluptuous grief on the form of the dead. He stands by the bier, cithern in hand, and laments musically; wreaths of violets and lilies lie on the pavement. He picks them up, and twines them around the corpse, and covers the pall with perfume. He mourns as a pastime, and illuminates the book of Death. It is soft, gentle, low, almost effeminate, and one longs every now and then for some fierce, passionate burst of grief, such as tears from the choking throat of Philoctetes, or like what Lear howls forth under the impending shadows of madness and desolation. Witness the following from "The Reveries." A young couple lose their only child; the shock bears the wife down, and she sinks slowly into consumption.

"But the trial comes: — colder and colder were growing the embers.
"That wife, over whom your love broods, is fading. Not beauty fading; — that, now that your heart is wrapped up in her being, would be nothing.

"She sees with quick eye your dawning apprehension, and she tries hard to make that stay of hers elastic.

"Your trials and your loves together have centred your affections. They are not now as when you were a lone man, wide-eyed and superficial. They have caught from domestic attachments a purer tone and touch. They cannot shoot out tendrils into barren world-soil, and suck up thence strengthening nutriment. They have grown under the forcing-glass of home-roof, they will not now bear exposure. . . . [a lengthy quotation]

"Another day of revival, when the spring sun shines, and flowers open out of doors. She leans on your arm, and strolls into the garden where the first birds are singing. Listen to them with her; — what memories are in bird-songs! You need not shudder at her tears — they are tears of thanksgiving. Press the hand that lies light upon your arm, and you, too, thank God, while yet you may!

"You are early home — mid afternoon; your step is not light, it is heavy, terrible.

"They have sent for you.

"She is lying down; her eyes half closed; her breathing long and interrupted.

"She hears you; her eye opens; you put your hand in hers; yours trembles; hers does not. Her lips move, it is your name.

" 'Be strong,' she says, 'God will help you!'

"She presses harder your hand, — 'Adieu!'

"A long breath — another; — you are alone again, no tears now; poor man! you cannot find them! . . . [a lengthy quotation]

"Go into the room where she was sick — softly, lest the prim housekeeper come after.

"They have put new dimity upon her chair, they have hung new curtains over the bed. They have removed from its stand its phials, and silver bell; they have put a little vase of flowers in their place, the perfume will not offend the sick sense now. They have half opened the window, that the room so long closed the air. It will not be too cold.

"She is not there.

"Oh, God! thou who dost temper the wind to the shorn lamb — be kind!"

This is very sweet, pathetic and tender, but there is a want of manly force about it that impresses us with more melancholy than any of the sad details. The author knocks at our hearts with a muffled hand. His grief glimmers like a twilight, soft, lazy, and indistinct. Some of the fine feelings of a heart in sorrow, are disclosed with quiet precision. But we look upon it rather as a curious operation, than the exposition of a terrible interior. Had Hawthorne been painting such a scene, how differently would he have handled it. Analytic as he is when treating of human sentiments, here he would at once have thrown aside the scalpel, and grasped the subject with nervous, quivering hand, and, Milo-like, rent it asunder. We would have had no gently-sorrowing husband, creeping about the house, with slippered grief! no girlish sentiment over gilt-edged saucers of mignonette, no feeble reflections about empty chairs.

The husband would have sat massively, like Marius, amid the shatterd ruins of his love. The sky would have been black above his head; the wind would have shrieked among the fallen pillars, terrible dissonances of sorrow. There would have been no light in the picture, no trustfulness in the Great End, such as Mr. Mitchell paints. All would have been huge, black, mountainous despair, before which we could not help trembling, and which we could not forget.

If Mr. Mitchell could graft some of this rude oak upon his pale rose-bushes, it would make a delicious mixture. His exquisite appreciation of the gentler human sorrows, his tender consideration of all earthly grief, would gain a new soundness and lustre if backed with some solider ground. The diamond, plain, unset, is beautiful, but there is a want of depth in its splendor. It is too pure for effects; one glance goes through it to the other side. Let it be set. Let a solid background be given to it, and it blazes out with surpassing brilliancy. The dark cloud of metal behind is the very cause and origin of its additional splendor. So with Mr. Mitchell. His books are pure to the very core. They are limpid, pellucid streams of thought, flowing in mid-air, with never a bed beneath them. No dark rocks lie at the bottom, no secret channels in the rifled stones whose very mystery invites examination. All is clear, true and transparent, but we find ourselves sighing for some dark unfathomable pool into which we might gaze and wonder, hour upon hour.

Of Mr. Mitchell's "Fresh Gleanings," and "Battle Summer," we would wish to dwell less than on the Reveries. The style in which Mr. Mitchell excels is scarcely suitable to such subjects as the stormy ravings of a mad Parisian mob. Here and there some fine passages strike upon us pleasantly, but the general effect is crude, short-coming and unsatisfactory. He does not deal with Raspail, Blanqui and Rollin, as they should be dealt with. They are too fierce, too headlong, too unsocial, so to speak, for the gentle author of the Reveries to comprehend or sympathize with them. He who painted the wife's death-bed with such

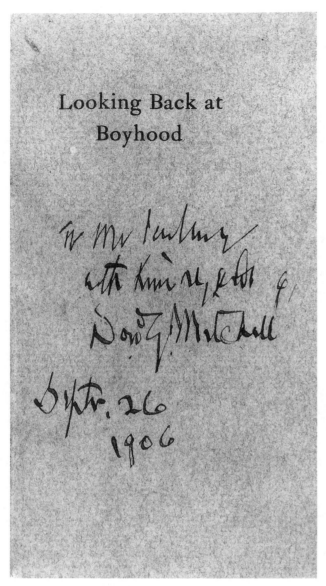

Looking Back at
Boyhood

*Cover of a 1906 booklet containing a reprint of Mitchell's
1892 article in the* Youth's Companion, *inscribed
by Mitchell to CS II*

lost his dreamy secluded nature since then we know not. The style of "the Battle Summer" is not good, inasmuch as it is not Mr. Mitchell's own. It is a very obvious attempt at the Carlylean style of writing, and we confess that we don't like our author in borrowed clothes. He wears his own so gracefully that we would never wish him to change them. All we would alter is the coat. That might be a little more ample and forcible.

Let Mr. Mitchell, as he values his reputation, write no more "Dream Lives." The Reveries were so beautiful and tender, that it was a sad pity to weaken their effect by so pale a reflex. Besides, such a style of writing does not bear repitition. A song in the minor is delicious, and fills us with plaintive pleasure. But who would write a whole opera in such a key? Let him strike another chord. There are plenty around him in the world that will yield full rich tones when struck by such a master-hand.

We understand that Mr. Mitchell is at present engaged on a history of Venice — a noble subject, to which he will doubtless do justice, — but let him remember that Venetian history is a dark, sullen picture, and is not to be treated daintily. Crime and mystery and restless ambition hover over those dark, narrow canals. There lingers the memory of a secret, impenetrable power, unsurpassed in the world's history for undeviating, inevitable vengeance. There treachery has left its signet-ring upon the Lions' Stairs, and the Lions' mouths still gape wide for accusations. There Faliero planned his mighty vengeance; there he was defeated and died. There sleep beneath the bright waters of the Laguna, into which no fisherman dare cast his nets, withering skeletons, victims of unknown assassins.

Mr. Mitchell has a stern task before him. Let him go to it with a stalwart pen.

RELATED LETTERS:
Letter by Mitchell's daughter Susan to Scribners, 6 June 1906, regarding a subscription edition of his complete works.

Dear Sirs.
    Your letter with the proposition regarding the publication of a new subscription edition of my Father, Mr. Donald G. Mitchell's works has been carefully read and my Father is much gratified by the proposal. He will write you himself in a few days in regard to the matter. I wish to suggest you send some one to New Haven to confer with my Father. Some one who is familiar with the

mellow sadness is not at home among the barricades, where blood and powder mingle. He who in the Lorgnette painted with a kind of velvety humor the different phases of cultivated life, the dreamer and the scholar, he cannot sit down in a filthy café, filled with Red Republicans, and foul-mouthed *poissonnières,* and crack jokes with them over bad wine, and submit to be slapped on the back by robbers and called *"camarade."* This is not the Bachelor's element, at least was not, when he wrote the two books of which we are speaking. How far he may have

books & who would accept & then consider any suggestions. And on my own part I wish to say that I know there is on hand the M.S.S. for an additional volume of the English Lands, Letters & Kings — which was delivered in lecture form, embracing Dickens, Browning, Carlyle, Ruskin etc. & which was considered very delightful. It would be a simple matter to put this into shape.

Then I would say also that I think no edition would be quite complete without a re-issue of "Fresh Gleanings" the first book. I happen to own the volume which was given my mother before her marriage which has a venerable fly leaf — a facsimile of which could be made — it looks like a lithograph!

Then I would also suggest a re-issue of "The Lorgnette" — which gives such a remarkable picture of society in N.Y. City over 50 years ago. The fact that these volumes (The Lorgnette) command such a high price would justify, it seems to me a re-issue. And they, together with the "Fresh Gleanings" tell the whole story of my Father's literary career.

He does not know of my writing this — and I would also say that anything I can do to further the matter I will be happy to undertake. I shall probably be in N.Y. for a day or so next week if you would care to have me come in & see you. If, however some one can come & see Papa as soon as possible it would, I am sure be a satisfaction. He had such an affection for Charles Scribner Senior that he would like to feel that a final issuance of his books should bear the name of your house — rather than that a possible arrangement should be made with another house — as has been suggested. In your reply to this please make a full list of the books — would it not be about the same if the number were 14 or 16 or even 18?

Awaiting your reply
I am yours very
Respectfully
Susan Mitchell Hoppin

Edward L. Burlingame, editor of Scribner's Magazine, *was sent to Edgewood, Mitchell's 360-acre farm near New Haven, Connecticut, to talk over the details, and plans for the Edgewood Edition of Mitchell's works went promptly ahead. The idea of adding another volume to his series on* English Lands, Letters, and Kings *was dismissed. Nor was there a reissue of* The Lorgnette, *which had been the little satiric periodical Mitchell had put out anonymously in 1850–1851, the first twelve numbers of which Baker & Scribner had published.* Fresh Gleanings, *Mitchell's first book, published by Harper & Brothers in 1847 and republished by Scribners in 1851, was included, but without the facsimile flyleaf of Ms. Hoppin's copy. The biggest problem was getting Mitchell, who was in his eighties, to write prefatory material for the edition.*

Edgewood 4 Augt. 1907

Dear Mr. Scribner

Your kind letter (of recent date) came duly. I have tried hard to put my mind to the little task you propose — but still (as many a time before) my mind is laggard & won't find fit words for the occasion. I know you've reason to be annoyed — but you haven't made proper allowance for the burden of years.

My daughters try to *put me up* to the work, & say all manner of kind & provocative things; but — the needed words *stay.*

I will try again next week, & shd you fail to receive somewhat by Thursday or Friday, put me down as incorrigible and preface-less.

Very truly yours
Don.^d G. Mitchell

This is Mitchell's last letter to Scribners in the archives. Fortunately, he got the inspiration he needed and, with the help of his solicitous daughters, completed the preface, which ran to seven pages, on 10 August. The publication of the fifteen-volume edition began in September and was completed in December; Mitchell died one year later.

Philip Schaff (1819–1893)

Philip Schaff

Born in Switzerland and educated in Germany, Schaff came to the United States in 1844 as head of the Mercersburg (Pa.) Seminary, where he remained for almost twenty years as a mediator between German theology and American scholarship. *A Commentary on the Holy Scriptures,* the American edition of Johann Peter Lange's much-heralded commentary that Schaff edited for Scribners, became the largest such publishing project of its kind, running to twenty-five volumes. But Schaff was by nature a historian and is considered the father of church history, having written his own ambitious work, *History of the Christian Church* (seven volumes). His presence on the Scribner list ensured a steady stream of important and significant religious and theological works — his own and those of colleagues — for forty years.

Scribner Books by Schaff

1853	*History of the Apostolic Church, with a General Introduction to Church History,* translated from Schaff's German by Edward D. Yeomans
1855	*America: A Sketch of the Political, Social, and Religious Character of the United States of North America, in Two Lectures, Delivered at Berlin, with a Report Read Before the German Church Diet at Frankfort-on-the-Maine, Sept., 1854,* translated from his German
1858, 1867	*History of the Christian Church, from the Birth of Christ to Gregory the Great, 1-600 A.D.* (3 volumes)
1865–1880	*A Commentary on the Holy Scriptures: Critical, Doctrinal, and Homiletical* by Johann Peter Lange and other European divines, edited by Schaff (25 volumes)
1866	*The Person of Christ: The Miracle of History, with a Reply to Strauss and Renan, and a Collection of Testimonies of Unbelievers*
1879–1883	*The International Illustrated Commentary on the New Testament* (also called *A Popular Commentary on the New Testament*), edited by Schaff (4 volumes)
1881	*The Person of Christ: The Perfection of His Humanity Viewed as a Proof of His Divinity*
1882–1910	*History of the Christian Church,* new edition, thoroughly revised and enlarged (7 volumes in eight; Vol. V, Parts I–II, by David S. Schaff)

136

1885	*Christ and Christianity: Studies in Christology, Creeds and Confessions, Protestantism and Romanism, Reformation Principles, Sunday Observance, Religious Freedom, and Christian Union*
1888	*Church and State in the United States; or, the American Idea of Religious Liberty and Its Practical Effects, with Official Documents*
1889	*The Progress of Religious Freedom as Shown in the History of Toleration Acts*
1890	*Creed Revision in the Presbyterian Churches*
	Literature and Poetry: Studies in the English Language; the Poetry of the Bible; the Dies Iræ; *the* Stabat Mater; *the Hymns of St. Bernard; the University, Ancient and Modern; Dante Alighieri; the Divina Commedia*
1893	*Theological Propædeutic: A General Introduction to the Study of Theology*

LETTER:
Letter by Schaff to Edward Armstrong, 17 July 1877, from Edinburgh.

For many of the large religious works undertaken by the firm, Scribners joined with T. & T. Clark of Edinburgh as its English partner. Schaff's multivolume commentaries involved many contributors, both American and English, and thus required him to make trips abroad to visit both contributors and the publisher. The subject of this letter is The International Illustrated Commentary on the New Testament, *which Scribners and Clark finally published between 1879 and 1883 in four volumes. Schaff's reference to "Dr. Riddle" is to the American biblical scholar Matthew Brown Riddle, the major contributor for the first volume.*

My dear Mr. Armstrong:

Mr. Clark seems anxious to anticipate Cassell's Commentary (which is *not* to be illustrated, but otherwise similar to our own and nearly ready). It may be well therefore to push Dr. Riddle & the artist to finish the first half of vol. I., which is to contain the Gospels of Matthew, Mark & Luke. The Mss. for the second half, containing John & Acts, is promised by December & will be set up at Edinburgh.

I heard of Mr. Seymour's death with profound regret. It was a shock to me. I esteemed him highly both for his character & intelligence.

We have safely gone through our great journey, although I was reported to be first massacred and then taken prisoner. Mrs. S. & Mary [wife and daughter] are well and enjoyed the Edinburgh

HISTORY

OF THE

APOSTOLIC CHURCH;

WITH A

GENERAL INTRODUCTION TO CHURCH HISTORY.

BY

PHILIP SCHAFF,

PROFESSOR IN THE THEOLOGICAL SEMINARY, AT MERCERSBURG, PA.

TRANSLATED BY

EDWARD D. YEOMANS.

NEW YORK:
CHARLES SCRIBNER, 145 NASSAU STREET.
1853.

Title page in Schaff's first Scribner book

Council very much. We are sorry that we could see nothing of your son, who was expected there as Mr. Clark thought.

15 East 43rd Street,
New York.

March 31, '88.

My dear Mr Scribner:

I have organized last week an Am. Society of Church History. Will you allow me to enter your name as one of the first members? You are the publisher of many historical works and are entitled to a place in it as much as any body. I should be glad if you would accept before I print the list with the constitution.

Truly yours

P. Schaff.

I have written a notice of Dr. Fisher's Ch. H. for the "Independent" of this week, but had to do it without the bibliograph. Appendix which it seems has been published. I could not get it in your store when I enquired for it.

Letter by Schaff to CS II, asking him to become a charter member of the American Society of Church History, which he has just organized (23 March). Scribner obliged.

The maps for Com. might be done cheapest by Mr. Jones in Edinburgh under Mr. Clark's direction. You better correspond with him about it. We need four for vol. I.

1. Ancient Jerusalem up to date

2. Palestine at the time of Christ (Guyot)

3. Palestine at the present time (for this we have Guyot)

4. The old Roman Empire with the missionary journey of Paul.

We expect to sail in the Steamer Spain of the National Line, Aug. 1, and to reach New York the 10 or 12th. My first business will be to hunt a home for my family which is now very small. Schley has left as a home missionary for Nebraska.

With kind regards to you & your family in which Mrs. S. and Mary cordially join,

I am truly yours
Philip Schaff

Remember me kindly to Mr. Scribner and all your partners & friends in the store.

LETTER:
This idea was gladly supported by CS II, who offered to sell Schaff sets of his church histories at half price and to contribute one set free for each seminary.

February 5, 1887
My dear Mr Scribner:

I wish to distribute about $500 worth of Church Histories among the leading Theol. Seminaries of the country, to be distributed as prizes among the best students of church history.

I shall first address letters like the one inclosed (which please return), to the Professors of Church History in 10 or 12 Seminaries. If they accept the offer, the books will be forwarded by Express (paid).

Will you be so kind as to furnish me with a list of 10 or 12 Seminaries where you think the gift will be most appreciated and do most good, according to your experience as to sales, and to inform me of the price at which you can let me have them within the limits of cost.

You kindly offered to share with me my recent donation to Miss Lange. I declined, because I felt that I ought to shoulder it alone in view of my profits from her father's Commentary. But if you wish to aid me in any way you deem best in this scheme of distribution, I shall gratefully accept it.

Very faithfully yours
Philip Schaff

LETTER:
Responding to a letter from CS II in which he defended his firm's efforts to promote Volume VI of Schaff's revised History of the Christian Church, *including the distribution of nearly one hundred editorial copies, Schaff tries to undo any damage his premature criticism may have done.*

Oct. 11, 1888
My dear Mr. Scribner:

Please dismiss the impression that I had any intention to find fault. Far from it! I never regretted my connection with your house since 1853 and could not wish a better publisher. I am properly satisfied with your part in getting up vol. VI. and have no doubt that you did the best with it. I only wished to divert attention to the fact which just had come to my notice that the Editor of the "Bibli. Sacra," the most important theol. organ had not recd. a copy, & that Dr. Briggs likewise had not recd any for the "Presb. Review." I had presented a copy to my colleagues, but not to him as I took it for granted that he would receive one from the publ. in time for notice in the Oct. no.

I took the liberty of suggesting several papers in Pennsylv. which in this particular volume are likely to be of use as they are specially interested in the German Reformation.

The first notice I saw came from an unexpected quarter last night. It is very good and may be of use to you; here I enclose it. I missed Mr. Burk on my last visit, but shall call again. I expect to hear soon from high authorities in Germany, and will inform you. We are in the same boat & must help each other in every honest & legitimate way.

Your circular of my Hist. is very well done. If you can spare one or two dozen copies I can make good use of them in my ordinary correspondence.

I am reading over vol. VI very carefully & making sundry improvements for a second ed.

Very truly yours,
Philip Schaff

LETTER:
1892 marked the fiftieth year of Schaff's activity as a theological teacher. Many of his friends sent

him testimonies acknowledging their debt, including his publisher. "Dr. Stuckenberg" was the pastor of the American Chapel in Berlin.

Dec. 17th [189]2

My dear Dr. Schaff:

I return Dr. Stuckenberg's letter. It must be very gratifying to receive so many and such exceptional testimonies to the value and usefulness of your work. Let me say for myself and my brother that we regard it as a high honor to act as Publisher for such books and that we feel the responsibility that is upon us to do all in our power to bring them into the widest circulation.

You have been good enough, too, to extend to us the friendship which you had for our father and you must know that we are devoted to your interests.

Yours truly
Charles Scribner

Horace Bushnell (1802–1876)

*Horace Bushnell (portrait from Theodore T. Munger,
Horace Bushnell: Preacher and Theologian, Boston:
Houghton, Mifflin & Company, 1899, p. 346)*

A Congregational minister and theologian, Bushnell resigned his Connecticut pastorate of more than twenty-five years in 1861 for reasons of health. Yet most of his books were published, by Scribners, after he had retired from active service. Called a preacher's preacher because of his poetic mastery of words, Bushnell attempted to restate the truths of religion in terms of human experience. He saw nature and humanity expressive of a divine purpose and filled with a divine presence and accepted intuition as a basis of theological knowledge. His association with Scribners maintained its reputation as a publisher of significant theological works, a reputation it continued to build in the twentieth century.

Scribner Books by Bushnell

1858	*Sermons for the New Life*
	Nature and the Supernatural, as Together Constituting the One System of God
1860	*The Character of Jesus, Forbidding His Possible Classification with Man*
1861	*Christian Nurture*
1864	*Work and Play*

1864	*Christ and His Salvation, in Sermons Variously Related Thereto*
1866	*The Vicarious Sacrifice, Grounded in Principles of Universal Obligation*
1868	*Moral Uses of Dark Things*
1869	*Women's Suffrage: The Reform Against Nature*
1872	*Sermons on Living Subjects*
1874	*Forgiveness and Law, Grounded in Principles Interpreted by Human Analogies*
1877	*The Vicarious Sacrifice, Grounded in Principles Interpreted by Human Analogies* (2 volumes)
	God In Christ: Three Discourses Delivered at New Haven, Cambridge, and Andover, With a Preliminary Dissertation on Language
1881	*Building Eras in Religion*
1903	*The Spirit in Man: Sermons and Selections*

LETTER:

Letter by Bushnell to Scribners, 25 June 1869, from Hartford, Conn.

Though Scribners has just published his work opposing women's suffrage, Bushnell already knows he needs to make some changes. The "Mills" referred to in his letter is the English philosopher John Stuart Mill (1806–1873), who had been advocating women's suffrage and whose latest work, The Subjection of Women, *had recently appeared.*

Gent.

I think it cannot be a great while before your edition will be out and another called for. I want very much to get hold of Mills before that time and add a short chapter. I am also very sick of something in the latter part of the 7th chapt. and of several things in the 8th. What can I do with these — or what will it cost to reproduce the last chapter, and mend in a few places the last but one? These were written as I was going down and represent my pains and discomposures more than my thoughts.

If you have any waste sheets at the binders of the last two chapters, be good enough to send them for cutting up & &.

Send me with Mill 4 more copies having the plain label, not the fancy. I do not like that fancy work at all.

The best label after all would have been "The Reform Against Nature" but that is gone by.

I am glad to find the book well spoken of, but the day of the fury I suppose is to come.

Very truly yours
Horace Bushnell

ARTICLE:

"Dr. Bushnell's Women's Suffrage," *The Book Buyer*, 2 (15 July 1869): 17.

Going to bat for its own publication, Bushnell's book on women's suffrage, this article in a Scribner house organ counterattacks by labeling the critics of the book as radicals.

Dr. Bushnell's treatise upon *Women's Suffrage* has stirred up quite an excitement among those interested in the subject. All thinkers of moderate views endorse Dr. Bushnell's positions in the main, and very cordially; but radicals of all extremes, at least those who have ventured to say anything about the book, unite in condemning it. It is so odd as to be positively amusing to find the *New York Day Book* and the *Boston Commonwealth* — the one the organ of the extreme Democrats, the other the organ of the extreme Republicans — united in opinion even on this subject. The *Day Book*, for instance, declares that Dr. Bushnell "has crammed more ignorance of the principles of government, more misconception of political truth, and more reckless assertion into one small volume than has ever been done by any writer before him." The *Commonwealth* says: "This is the most amusing book we have read for a long time. It would require a volume, instead of a paragraph,

Letter to Scribners from Bushnell, 30 June 1869. His "condition of distress" is obviously the result of the critical reception of his women's suffrage book.

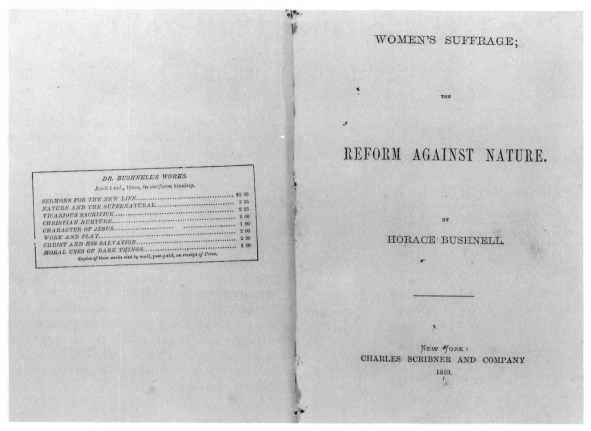

Title page in Bushnell's controversial work opposing women's suffrage

to do justice to this chaotic jumble of assertion and counter-assertion, of elaborate arguments to prove that certain things cannot possibly occur, directly followed by fearful forecastings of the terrible results that will ensue when they do occur," etc., etc. When theorists at both extremes hold such views, it is but natural that the treatise should be endorsed by all others as not only able and conclusive, but eloquent and exceedingly timely.

J. G. Holland (1819–1881)
("Timothy Titcomb")

J. G. Holland

Holland, called "Dr. Holland" because of his medical degree, is remembered most as the editor who helped create one of the most important nineteenth-century literary magazines, *Scribner's Monthly.* Before assuming the editorship of that journal (1870), he had been, after J. T. Headley, the firm's best-selling author for more than a decade, writing from his knowledge of the ordinary problems of ordinary people in moralizing essays, didactic verse, and sentimental novels. It is difficult today to understand the phenomenal popularity and prestige of Holland in his time, but after his death *The New York Times* called him "one of the most celebrated writers which this country has produced." Frank Luther Mott, in *A History of American Magazines,* argues that Holland should be named "in any list of the half-dozen greatest American magazine editors."

Scribner Books by Holland

1858	*Titcomb's Letters to Young People, Single and Married*
	Bitter-Sweet: A Poem
1859	*Gold-Foil, Hammered from Popular Proverbs*
1860	*Miss Gilbert's Career: An American Story*
1861	*Lessons in Life: A Series of Familiar Essays*
1862	*The Bay-Path: A Tale of New England Colonial Life*
1863	*Letters to the Joneses*
1865	*Plain Talks on Familiar Subjects: A Series of Popular Lectures*
1867	*Kathrina: Her Life and Mine, in a Poem*
1868	*J. G. Holland's Select Works* (Brightwood Edition of 6 volumes)
1870–1881	editor of *Scribner's Monthly*
1872	*The Marble Prophecy and Other Poems*

1873	*Garnered Sheaves*
	Arthur Bonnicastle: An American Novel, illustrated by Mary A. Hallock
	Illustrated Library of Favorite Song. Based Upon Folk-Songs, and Comprising Songs of the Heart, Songs of Home, Songs of Life, and Songs of Nature, with an introduction and edited by Holland
1874	*The Mistress of the Manse*
1875	*Sevenoaks: A Story of To-Day*, illustrated by Sol Eytinge
1876	*Every-Day Topics: A Book of Briefs* (first series)
1877	*Nicholas Minturn: A Study in a Story*
	The Puritan's Guest and Other Poems
1879	*The Complete Poetical Writings of J. G. Holland*
1881	*Concerning the Jones Family*
1881–1882	*The Complete Works of J. G. Holland* (16 volumes)
1882	*Every-Day Topics: A Book of Briefs* (second series)

BIOGRAPHY EXCERPT:
Mrs. H. M. Plunkett, *Josiah Gilbert Holland* (New York: Charles Scribner's Sons, 1894), pp. 36–40.

In this excerpt from her biography of Holland, Mrs. Plunkett describes the birth of "Timothy Titcomb," the persona of J. G. Holland's successful early writings, from his work as editor (1849–1857) of the Springfield Republican, *which was owned and published by Samuel Bowles and where the "Timothy Titcomb" letters first appeared. These letters, as she further relates, became the occasion for Holland's long, fruitful relationship with the House of Scribner.*

. . . Mr. Bowles never showed his instinctive knowledge of what the public was hungering for more completely than when he suggested that a series of letters of moral advice would "take"; and certainly his editor, who whatever else was in a man, saw him first and principally as a moral agent whose watchword should be duty, and whose allegiance should be given to the One great invisible Leader, was the man to give the advice. To impart the desired air of venerability he chose the pseudonym of "Timothy Titcomb." They were written for the plain work-a-day people who plough, and sow, and reap, who spin and weave, and forge, and run our engines, and perform the myriad indispensable household tasks that are monotonous and commonplace, and often in such straitened circumstances, or accompanied by such trials and temptations, as to be well-nigh unbearable.

He addressed them on the commonest kinds of omissions and neglects, and as to phases of their lives; had he not seen them all, in the wanderings, and vicissitudes, and deprivations of his own? . . .

It is impossible to reproduce the moral attitude of our country at that time; we look back to it across the mighty chasm of a great civil war which revolutionized modes of thought and methods of living; which did much to dissipate the dreamy speculations of men who fancied themselves thinkers and leaders; it set up new standards in almost every department of life, but neither then nor now, was there ever a time when the true child of New England was indifferent to the questions What *is* Truth? and What ought *I* to do? Dr. Holland aimed to answer these questions for him. . . .

The "Letters" were in three series — to young men, to young women, and to young married people — and were a great and immediate success, and their popularity soon began to tell in the subscription list of the paper. These were over and above the editorial work which was carried unremittingly forward. Nothing was more natural than that they should be gathered into a book and carried to a publisher. Two prominent firms "looked" at them and declined, and another declined them without looking. Armed with a letter of introduction from George Ripley, Dr. Holland went to the late Charles Scribner and begged the privilege of reading three of the letters. Mr. Scribner turned the key of his private office and bade the author proceed. At the end of the third letter he said, "I will take the book." A most sagacious decision, for at the time of Holland's death, in 1881, half a million copies of this and his succeeding works had been sold, and their popularity continues practically unimpaired. Mr. Scribner recognized that there are different strata of readers, and that in the evolution of a man, he sometimes belongs to one and sometimes to another. This was the first in a series of fifteen books, that followed in fifteen years.

BOOK REVIEW:
James Russell Lowell, "*Bitter-Sweet. A Poem.* by J. G. Holland," *The Atlantic Monthly,* 3, no. 19 (May 1859): 651–652.

Only one important periodical bothered to review Bitter-Sweet *when it first appeared: the two-year-old* Atlantic Monthly. *As the magazine's editor and a respected poet in his own right, Lowell wielded a great deal of influence in literary matters, and his high praise in this review of Holland's first book-length poem may have helped propel it to great popular success.*

Unexpectedness is an essential element of wit, — perhaps, also, of pleasure; and it is the ill-fortune of professional reviewers, not only that surprise is necessarily something as rare with them as a June frost, but that loyalty to their extemporized omniscience should forbid them to acknowledge, even if they felt, so fallible an emotion.

Unexpectedness is also one of the prime components of that singular product called Poetry; and, accordingly, the much-enduring man whose finger-ends have skimmed many volumes and many manners of verse may be pardoned the involuntary bull of not greatly expecting to stumble upon it in any such quarter. Shall we, then, be so untrue to our craft, — shall we, in short, be so unguardedly natural, as to confess that "Bitter-Sweet" has surprised us? It is truly an original poem, — as genuine a product of our soil as a golden-rod or an aster. It is as purely American, — nay, more than that, — as purely New-English, — as the poems of Burns are Scotch. We read ourselves gradually back to our boyhood in it, and

were aware of a flavor in it deliciously local and familiar, — a kind of sour-sweet, as in a *frozen-thaw* apple. From the title to the last line, it is delightfully characteristic. The family-party met for Thanksgiving can hit on no better way to be jolly than in a discussion of the Origin of Evil, — and the Yankee husband (a shooting-star in the quiet heaven of village morals) about to run away from his wife can be content with no less comet-like vehicle than a balloon. The poem is Yankee, even to the questionable extent of substituting "locality" for "scene" in the stage-directions; and we feel sure that none of the characters ever went to bed in their lives, but always sidled through the more decorous subterfuge of "retiring."

We could easily show that "Bitter-Sweet" was not this and that and t'other, but, after all said and done, it would remain an obstinately charming little book. It is not free from faults of taste, nor from a certain commonplaceness of metre; but Mr. Holland always saves himself in some expression so simply poetical, some image so fresh and natural, the harvest of his own heart and eye, that we are ready to forgive him all faults, in our thankfulness at finding the soul of Theocritus transmigrated into the body of a Yankee.

It would seem the simplest thing in the world to be able to help yourself to what lies all around you ready to your hand; but writers of verse commonly find it a difficult, if not impossible, thing to do. Conscious that a certain remoteness from ordinary life is essential in poetry, they aim at it by laying their scenes far away in time, and taking their images from far away in space, — thus contriving to be foreign at once to their century and their country. Such self-made exiles and aliens are never repatriated by posterity. It is only here and there that a man is found, like Hawthorne, Judd, and Mr. Holland, who discovers or instinctively feels that this remoteness is attained, and attainable only, by lifting up and transfiguring the ordinary and familiar with the *mirage* of the ideal. We mean it as very high praise, when we say that "Bitter-Sweet" is one of the few books that have found the secret of drawing up and assimilating the juices of this New World of ours.

ARTICLE:
R. T. S. Lowell, "The Better American Opinion: Dr. Holland," *The North American Review,* 95, no. 196 (July 1862): 81–104.

This lengthy article by the older brother of James Russell Lowell considers Holland's seven works

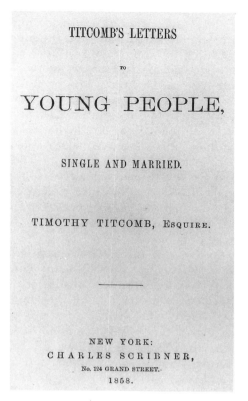

First edition of his first Scribner book

Title pages from three of Holland's bestsellers:

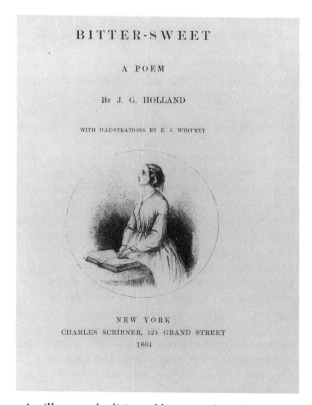

An illustrated edition of his second Scribner book

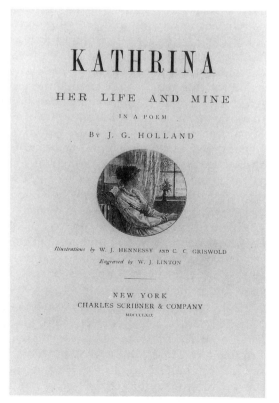

First illustrated edition of his tenth Scribner book. Sales of this title exceeded that of any other American long poem of the time except for Henry Wadsworth Longfellow's The Song of Hiawatha (1855).

to date (the last five published by Charles Scribner) in a discussion of the American theme of reform and the reformer. The following are excerpts:

. . . The general feeling has been (at least while our land was whole) that this country is to show the way and to teach reform, wherever, in governing or achieving, reform is needed, or a way is to be shown. Some one, and an American, is to find out and proclaim; and therefore all must be up and doing. Americans must always be hitting somewhere, and hacking at something. . . .

Happily, for a people of such born and taught reformers, it is a matter of necessity that they should bear with one another, after some sort, and make mutual room for the escaping idea; and so they do, sometimes very wonderfully. . . .

Such as our American people is, it is of the utmost importance that those who lead any large and influential part of them should be such men as can and will lead them well and wisely; for, well led, Americans will follow well. We have written, already, of that large number among us who honestly believe in going on and growing better. Of their accepted writers is Dr. Holland. It is a little difficult to estimate rightly and fairly the author whose books and moral influence have given us occasion for this article. Like a true American, he has tried a good many departments of authorship. We may say of him what Johnson wrote of one of his own, and the world's friends, *Nullum, fere, scribendi genus non tetigit*; and if he has not done all things equally well, he has done many things excellently. Being a journalist, he began, it would seem, with historical sketches in his own journal, and afterward made them into an "outline history"; from history he went over into the adjoining field of romance; next climbed the tempting hill of poesy; and latterly has been gathering — upon this hill elsewhere — and discoursing upon samples and principles of morals. . . .

"Timothy Titcomb's Letters to Young People, Single and Married," is intended to teach the youth of both sexes how to be honest and sensible, and to live like Christians; and "Gold-Foil, hammered from Popular Maxims," is for the teaching of the world at large in general morals and religion. These are good books, both. "Bitter-Sweet" is a poem, whose chief moral object is to work out the thought that evil is part of God's plan, and answers a good purpose in it. Of this book and its subject, we shall have more to say.

Dr. Holland takes openly, but without the least rudeness, the office of reformer and leader of the better opinion among us. This the subjects and objects and general character of his writings, as well as abundant special passages, show. The title-pages tell us that his books have been issued in a great many thousand copies; and after having read them, we cannot wonder that they have been widely read, and cannot doubt that they exert a large influence. His use of American phrases, his choice of utilitarian illustrations, his speaking in the first person to the second person, and his bringing up a second or third time, or oftener, after the manner of a public speaker, a thing or a phrase, — these are all of his part as a leader of American opinion.

That Dr. Holland has imagination in a high degree is shown, not only by many passages in which objects, persons, and scenes are wonderfully well thrown out, but by the whole book, "Bitter-Sweet." That he has good power of reasoning, and a very good command of language and sense of the strength of words, he evinces abundantly. That he has an honest and good purpose, and is in earnest about it, he everywhere proves to us thoroughly. He writes honestly and purely, and he does not write in general, but in the plainest and strongest way rebukes particular vices; and that not like one who willingly meddles with forbidden subjects, but like one who honestly feels that men and women ought to be rebuked for wickedness known to be too common, and ought to be shamed out of it, even at the risk of shocking some false delicacy. . . .

While we write, another of Dr. Holland's books — "Lessons in Life" — comes from the press, and we bring it to our scale. Although it seems to us not equal in merit to Gold-Foil, yet it is very similar in kind. It shows much the same sort of good, and much the same sort of bad, — in some instances not only of the same *sort,* but the same, for the author, as he could hardly fail of doing in the fast getting-out of his books, sometimes writes over again the same things; but, perhaps better than any other of his books, it shows the writer as an American, as a leader of the better public opinion, and as Dr. Holland. The I-and-you style, the honest morality, the plain speaking, the slang, the American use of un-English words, — the want of fineness of appreciation, together with an appreciation of what is good, and a fondness for distinguishing and contrasting, — the happy thoughts, well worded, — the unconscious, yet often strongly-marked irreverence, — are all here. . . .

Arnold Guyot (1807–1884)

Arnold Guyot

Urged in 1848 to come to America by his friend and fellow-Swiss colleague Louis Agassiz, who had preceded him, Guyot lectured on geography and methods of teaching it for six years under the auspices of the Massachusetts Board of Education in institutes and normal schools. In 1854 he accepted the chair of physical geography and geology at Princeton, where he remained until his death. His plan of teaching geography was incorporated in the series of geographies that Scribners published between 1866 and 1875, which constituted the first scientific presentation of geography in American schools. These geographies became models for school textbooks, and their success accounted for much of the growth of the Scribner Educational Department in the 1860s and 1870s. Emphasizing topography in his geography, Guyot created many of his own maps. These, too, were issued by Scribners in both wall atlases and series of map cards.

Scribner Publications by Guyot

The list of maps identified here is, admittedly, incomplete.

1862	*South America,* wall atlas, constructed and drawn under the direction of Guyot
	Guyot's Slated Map Drawing Cards (also published as *Map Drawing Cards* in 1865), drawn by E. Sandoz under the direction of Guyot
1863	*The World in Hemispheres,* wall atlas
	North America, wall atlas
1864	*Central Europe,* wall atlas, scale 1:1,500,000
	Africa, wall atlas
1865	*South America,* wall atlas, card series (2′ x 3′), scale 200 geographic miles equal 1 inch
	The World, wall atlas, scale 1:14,500,000
	Asia, wall atlas, scale 1:10,000,000
	Europe, map drawn by Sandoz under the direction of Guyot, scale 1:3,400,000
	North America, wall atlas, card series (2′ x 3′), scale 150 geographic miles equal 1 inch

Africa, wall atlas, card series (2' x 3'), scale 250 geographic miles equal 1 inch

Italia, wall map of ancient Italy by Guyot and H. C. Cameron

United States, wall atlas

1866   *Guyot's Physical and Political Wall Maps*

United States, wall atlas, small series (42" x 56")

Primary; or, Introduction to the Study of Geography

Geographical Teaching: Being a Complete Guide to the Use of Guyot's Wall Maps for Schools, Containing Six Maps and Diagrams, with Full Instructions for Drawing the Maps in Accordance with Guyot's System of Constructive Map Drawing

Key to Guyot's Wall Maps (also published as *Key to Guyot's Wall Maps: A Series of Constructive Lessons* in 1874)

The Earth and Its Inhabitants: Common-School Geography, prepared with the cooperation of Mary Howe Smith

Descriptive Circular of Physical and Political Wall Maps

Asia, wall atlas, scale 1:25,000,000

Europe, wall atlas, scale 150 English miles equal 1 inch

Graecia, wall map of ancient Greece by Guyot and Cameron

Central Europe, wall atlas, scale 50 miles equal 1 inch

The World, Mercator's Projection, wall atlas

The World, Hemispheres, wall atlas

Australia, wall atlas

1867   *The Earth and Its Inhabitants: Intermediate Geography,* prepared with the cooperation of Smith

Imperium Romanum, wall map of the Roman Empire by Guyot and Cameron

1868   *Elementary Geography for Primary Classes,* prepared with the cooperation of Smith

1869   *Introduction to the Study of Geography*

Asia, wall atlas, scale 1:6,000,000

1870   *North America,* map drawn by Sandoz under the direction of Guyot, scale 500 English miles equal 1 inch

Manual of Geographical Teaching

1873   *Physical Geography* (also published in raised type)

1874   *Guyot's Geographies: Where They Are Used*

Guyot's Grammar-School Geography (also published simply as *Grammar-School Geography*)

The Earth and Man: Lectures on Comparative Physical Geography in Its Relation to the History of Mankind, translated from the French by C. C. Felton (originally published in Boston in 1849)

1875   *Guyot's New Intermediate Geography*

1876	*Geography of Massachusetts*
	Maka-Oyakapi: Guyot's Elementary Geography in the Dakota Language
1877	*Geography of Indiana*
	Geography of Illinois
	Geography of Michigan
	Geography of New York
	Geography of Ohio
1879	*Map of the Catskill Mountains*
	Geography of Vermont
1882	*The Geographical Reader and Primer* (also published as *Scribner's Geographical Reader and Primer*)
1884	*Creation; or, The Biblical Cosmogony in the Light of Modern Science*
	New England States
1885	*East Central States*

LEGISLATIVE ACT:
Act passed by the State of New Jersey to purchase a map published by Charles Scribner & Co. *Acts of the Eighty-Eighth Legislature of the State of New Jersey, and Twentieth Under the New Constitution* (Newark, N.J.: E. N. Fuller, Daily Journal Office, 1864), p. 753.

An act to authorize the purchase of Guyot's Physical and Descriptive Map of the United States for the public schools of this State.

WHEREAS, The public schools of this state are nearly all destitute of correct and well delineated maps of the United States, and the usefulness of said schools would be materially promoted by being furnished therewith; and whereas, the physical and descriptive map of the United States, compiled by Professor A. Guyot, is reported by the committees on education to be such as to answer the necessity for such a work,

1. BE IT ENACTED *by the Senate and General Assembly of the State of New Jersey,* That the state treasurer and state superintendent of public schools shall contract with the publisher of the said map, for a sufficient number of the same, to supply one to each public school in the state at a price not exceeding eight dollars per map.

2. *And be it enacted,* That the said maps shall be delivered by the publisher at his expense and risk to the county clerk of each county, (in the numbers prescribed by the state superintendent of public schools) not to exceed one to each school, in each county, and upon receipt thereof, the county clerk shall give his receipt therefor, which receipt shall be a voucher to the state treasurer of the delivery of said maps.

3. *And be it enacted,* That when the said maps shall be delivered as foresaid, the state treasurer shall be and is hereby authorized to pay for the same at the price agreed upon, out of any money in his hands not otherwise appropriated, but the sum total of such payments shall not exceed twelve thousand dollars.

4. *And be it enacted,* That it shall be the duty of the county clerk to cause the said maps to be distributed among the public schools of their respective counties, in such manner as they deem most convenient.

5. *And be it enacted,* That this act shall take effect immediately.
Approved April 14, 1864.

LETTERS:
CS I's zeal for Guyot's books and the implications in their methodology for improving education almost becomes a religious mission in these letters

151

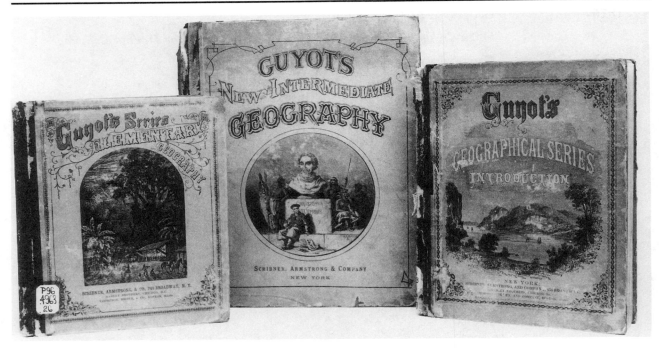

Copies of Guyot's popular school geographies

to his New England bookselling agent, Gilman H. Tucker. "Mrs. Smith" is Mary Howe Smith, who assisted Guyot in the preparation of his geographies.

May 17th 1867

My dear Mr. Tucker

. . . I am not surprised and yet not less rejoiced to hear of Mrs. Smith's success and that you have such a high opinion of her. It has always seemed to me that she was raised up specially by Providence for the work in which she is engaged. Aside from its commercial aspects, it is truly a great work, one in which we all can enter upon with <u>pride</u> and though attended with very great difficulties from its very nature, because it is a revolutionary educational movement, still one feels <u>stimulated</u> and <u>nerved up</u> to it by its very greatness & importance. Whether we realise ourselves the pecuniary advantages or not we may be conscious and thankful that we are the means of starting a great reform which <u>must tell</u> on the educational interests of the country <u>for years</u>. If our lives are spared a few years, we shall both see the day when the present text books on geog will be <u>discarded</u>, and our opponents will <u>come over on our ground</u> or be <u>left out in the cold</u>. I have been expecting what you tell me, a combination of the old style of geographical interests, <u>against Guyot.</u>

<u>They stand or fall together</u> and we are their mortal enemy, from the <u>very nature</u> of our books, not of course from any other considerations. <u>It is the old story. Pilate & Herod</u> have become friends to defeat us. Well I hope you are <u>not</u> intimidated. You <u>don't</u> write as though you were. . . . By the way have you a memorandum of all the public schools & academies in N E using Guyot? We should put them in our circulars. . . .

Yours truly

Charles Scribner

May 22nd 1867

My dear Mr. Tucker

. . . I was glad to notice your remarks as to the importance of having our books <u>started right</u> after they are introduced. This is generally true but in the case of Guyot's books it is <u>specially so</u>. They should <u>be watched some time after their introduction</u>. The teachers will require a little looking after at first as the method is new &&&c. The only argument our opponents can use against us is <u>impracticability</u>. We hear it everywhere. But our books are constantly making their way into the leading schools of the country and if they give satisfaction (and we have yet to hear to the contrary) we shall soon accumulate <u>an irresistible amt of proof as to their practicability</u>. . . . And let me assure you that your remarks with reference to the

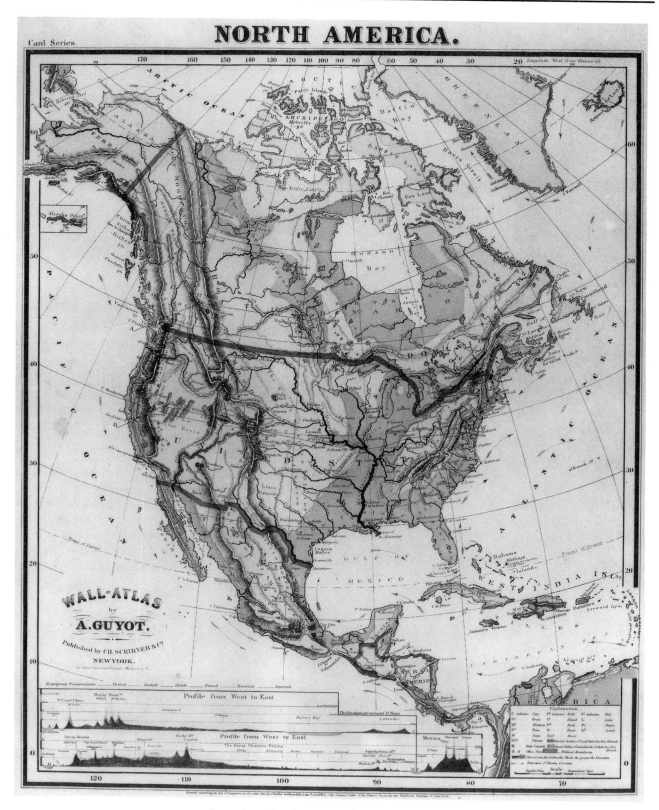

Guyot's wall atlas (1865) for North America

GUYOT'S GEOGRAPHIES.

CARL RITTER,
(From a Portrait in possession of Prof. Guyot.)

" HUMBOLDT is the founder of Comparative Geography, that all-embracing science of our Globe, unfolded with a master-hand by CARL RITTER, and which has now its ablest representative in our own GUYOT."
—PROF. AGASSIZ'S BOSTON ORATION ON HUMBOLDT, SEPT. 14, 1869.

SCRIBNER, ARMSTRONG & CO.,
BROADWAY, NEW YORK.

Cover of the 1875 Scribner catalogue devoted to Guyot's geographies. Included in it are lists of locations where the geographies were being used and recommendations and praise from leading men of science, and school principals and administrators.

magnitude and importance of the enterprise in which we are employed and the enthusiasm and energy with which you have entered it were appreciated and gratefully received & renew my confidence in it and nerve me in <u>my arduous work</u>. There is such a vicious state of things in the School book business, and so much that is discouraging that nothing but <u>a sense of duty</u> could keep me in it. But <u>it is real</u> satisfaction to be conscious that whether or not we realize commercially the reward of our labours we are doing <u>a good work</u> — and as you say there is every reason to expect <u>a commercial success</u>. . . .

Yours truly
Charles Scribner

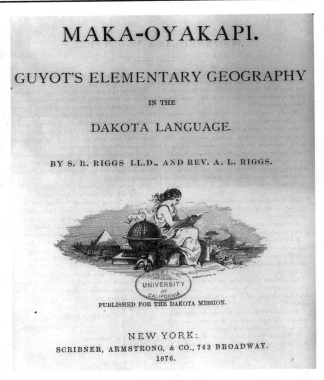

MAKA-OYAKAPI.

GUYOT'S ELEMENTARY GEOGRAPHY

IN THE

DAKOTA LANGUAGE.

BY S. R. RIGGS LL.D., AND REV. A. L. RIGGS.

PUBLISHED FOR THE DAKOTA MISSION.

NEW YORK:
SCRIBNER, ARMSTRONG, & CO., 743 BROADWAY.
1876.

Title page in the special Dakota language edition of Guyot's Elementary Geography *commissioned for the Dakota Mission, a Protestant missionary effort in Minnesota that began in the 1830s (Bancroft Library, University of California, Berkeley)*

Though CS I did live to realize great commercial success in his publication of Guyot's geographies, the "vicious state of things in the School book business" which he recognized in 1867 — the cutthroat nature of it, the bribing of school boards, etc. — ultimately forced CS II in 1883 to sell most of his textbooks, including Guyot's, to a competitor.

LETTER:
Letter by Guyot to Scribners, 5 June 1883, from Princeton, N.J.

In this, one of his last letters to Scribners, Guyot acknowledges with gratitude the support he received years ago from CS I for his geographies in the "cause of public education." A few days prior to this letter, Scribners had sold most of its textbook list, including Guyot's works, to Ivison, Blakeman & Taylor, a firm specializing in schoolbooks.

Gentlemen,
I have duly received your favor of the 31st of May announcing to me that you have decided to

transfer to the house of Ivison, Blakeman & Taylor all your Educational Department including my Series of Geographies & Wall Maps, and that the transaction was to be consummated on the 1st of June.

I believe, as you do, that, owing to circumstances, this change will be for the best interests of both parties; and though regretting to part with your firm for this important business, it is a matter of sincere congratulation that our relations have been characterized, at all time, by uniform mutual courtesy.

Mr. Tucker has informed me that you wish to retain the possession of Earth & Man. Had I not been very ill during the last two months, I would have made much progress toward the contemplated new edition. I am glad that the services of Mr. Tucker continue to be secured for the Geographies.

Allow me to take this opportunity to express my admiration and my affectionate regard for your noble hearted father, who began so manfully an almost unequal struggle against powerful, and often unscrupulous, houses in favor of the Geographies, and continued it, regardless of his own interest, simply because he knew that in doing so he was helping the cause of public education. I was deeply touched by such a course, which is as rare as it is honorable. I shall always hold his memory in high estimation, as will all men who believe in the powers of Christian principle to elevate the motives which guide our actions above the ordinary rules of the world.

Believe me, Gentlemen, very
sincerely your friend
A. Guyot

Mary Virginia Terhune (1830–1922)
("Marion Harland")

Mary Virginia Terhune ("Marion Harland")

A Virginian, Terhune wrote many romantic, moral novels about the South as it was before or during the Civil War. Widely known by the time she became a Scribner author, her pseudonym, "Marion Harland," affixed to the title of a new book would guarantee it a large sale. Her series of household management books that she published with Scribners were the first to treat the subject of "home economics" from a practical and respectful point of view, and they gained a wide, appreciative audience.

Scribner Books by Terhune

1871	*Common Sense in the Household: A Manual of Practical Housewifery**
1875	*Breakfast, Luncheon and Tea***
1878	*The Dinner Year-Book***
1880	*Loiterings in Pleasant Paths*
1881	*Handicapped*
1883	*The Cottage Kitchen: A Collection of Practical and Inexpensive Receipts***
1884	*The Common Sense Household Calendar* (for 1885)
1885	*Eve's Daughters; or, Common Sense for Maid, Wife, and Mother*
	Common Sense in the Nursery**
1887	*Judith: A Chronicle of Old Virginia*
1890	*With the Best Intentions: A Midsummer Episode*
1896	*The National Cook Book*, co-authored by Christine Terhune Herrick (her daughter)
1897	*An Old-Field School-Girl*
1906	*The Distractions of Martha*, illustrated by R. Emmett Owen
1914	*Looking Westward*
1919	*The Carringtons of High Hill: An Old Virginia Chronicle*

* The success of this first work encouraged a "Common Sense in the House-hold" series. Other titles in this series are marked with **.

ANNOUNCEMENT:

"A New Work in a New Vein, by Marion Harland, *The Book Buyer*, 4, no. 7 (15 April 1871): 17.

With this, her first Scribner book, Terhune, an already-popular writer of fiction, unexpectedly achieved popularity in a different field. As a result of its success, Scribners asked her to continue the series, called "Common Sense in the Household."

MESSRS. CHARLES SCRIBNER & CO. have in press for early publication a work by that popular author, MARION HARLAND, which is sure to find even a larger circle, not only of readers but of interested students, than have any of her previous productions; and this, too, notwithstanding the fact that it is a venture in a different field from that in which she has achieved such a wide reputation. The work deals with solid matter of fact, as is indicated by its title, *Common Sense in the Household, a Manual of Practical Housewifery.*

The work is dedicated, to "My Fellow-Housekeepers, North, East, South, and West," and the author states that the "volume embodies the gleanings of many years." From the "familiar talk" which forms the first chapter — "a talk of woman with woman," — we make the following extract, striking the key upon which the work is written: "This" — referring to a serio-comic accident in her early life as a housekeeper — "was the beginning of the hoard of practical receipts I now offer for your inspection. For fifteen years I have steadily pursued this work, gleaning here and sifting there, and levying such remorseless contributions upon my friends, to whom, I fear, the sight of my paper and pencil has long since become a bugbear. * * * My book is designed to help you. I believe it will, if for no other reason, because it has been a faithful guide to myself — a reference beyond value in seasons of doubt and need. I have brought every receipt to the test of common sense and experience. Those which I have not tried myself were obtained from reliable housewives, the best I know. I have enjoyed the work heartily, and, from the first to last, the persuasion has never left me that I was engaged in a good cause. Throughout I have had you, my dear sister, present before me, with the little plait between your

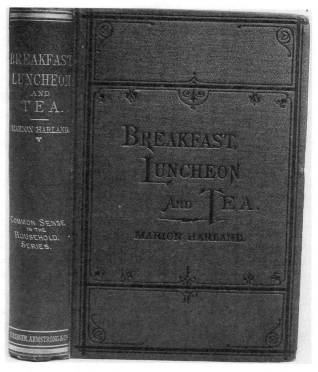

Terhune's second book in her popular Common Sense in the Household series

brows, the wistful look about eye and mouth that reveal to me as words could not — your desire to do your best."

The book is written, from the first page to the last, in the same strain. Even the receipts are not dry details of weights and measures, but told as one housekeeper would instruct her friend how to prepare the dish the latter had just praised. And scattered through the volume are gossipy chapters upon "Company," "Servants," "The Sick-Room," "The Nursery," etc. The author so heartily enjoys her subject — has so succeeded in placing herself *en rapport* with her reader that one forgets he is reading a work which is largely a "Receipt Book." Marion Harland's mission is to the *home*; her unceasing endeavor to show the dignity of needful labor, the beauty, grace, and sacredness of what is called common life. To quote again from her "familiar talk": "You are not ambitious," you say; "you only want to help John, and to make him and the children happy and comfortable." * *

Heaven bless your honest, loyal endeavors! * * * My dear, John and the children and the humble home make your sphere, you say. Be sure you fill it *full*, before you seek one wider and higher. There is no better receipt between the covers than that. Leave the rest to GOD."

In extent and variety, in clearness of expression, in *practicalness* — the quality so earnestly sought in cookery-books and so seldom found, this collection of receipts has never been surpassed by any work of a similar character presented to the public. On every-page is seen the hand of one thoroughly conversant with her subject, of a writer to whom long practice has given ease and force. The book is at once a novelty and a non-pareil of its kind, combining, as it does, a vast fund of useful information with a series of pleasant, spicy essays that are of themselves worth the price of the volume.

LETTER:
Letter by Mary Virginia Terhune to CS II, 15 November 1893, from Paris, France, asking advice about her son, Albert Payson Terhune.

Personal and confidential

Dear Mr. Scribner:

Do you recollect that two years ago, I invaded your sanctum to ask your friendly advice about my son? I said then, "If Charles III were nineteen years of age, with literary tastes and business ambitions, and no hereditary business at his back, what would you do with him?"

You recommended that my son, from this stand-point, make a specialty of English literature, and master, at least, one foreign language. "Then," you were good enough to add, in closing the interview, "when he has finished his college-course, send him to me, and if I can do anything for him, I will."

He has been graduated, and creditably, having made a specialty of English literature and the French dramatists. Mr. Brander Matthews, in whose Literature Class he was, wrote to me; — "I have not a son, but I wish I had one like yours. I consider him one of the brightest and best-equipped young men in any of my classes."

He writes well and strongly; he is steady in habits, pleasing in manner, in perfect physical health, and eager to be at work. His ambition is to get some position in the office of a leading Magazine where there would be a reasonable opportunity of rising.

He is now traveling with me, as a sort of post-graduate course, and it is our purpose, upon our return from the East, to remain in Paris for some weeks to enable him to perfect himself in colloquial French. He reads it with as much facility as he reads English, and speaks it with tolerable fluency.

Will you tell me, with the candor warranted by our old friendhip, it there is any opening — or likely to be — for him in any department of your Magazine, within a few months? I know there is capital stuff in the young fellow, and I feel that he will do well if he can get into the right socket. The few articles he has written and published have been most cordially received, and quite widely copied, such publications as <u>Public Opinion</u> and <u>Current Literature</u> having reproduced several of them without knowledge of the author. He understands, however, that literature, as usually comprehended under that title, is to be used as a staff — not as a crutch.

May I trespass further upon your kindness for a little counsel relative to my own plans? Before leaving America I finished a serial, for a religious weekly, which I shall bring out in book form next autumn, or earlier. It is a thoughtful, practical story of the same school as <u>Stepping Heavenward</u>, and I am anxious to obtain for it a wide reading. With what publisher of religious books would you recommend me to place it? Mr. Randolph — also E. P. Dutton & Co. — have, before this, applied to me for a volume of this general character. I know the book to be good, and I wish it to <u>do</u> good. Who would treat it — and me — most generously? Your house would hardly be interested in a work of this description; else, my application for advice would be put in a very different form.

Up to date, as you will. be glad to know, our journey has been most pleasant throughout. We sail from Marseilles on Saturday Nov. 18 for Port Said, and expect to remain in the East for two months and more.

With kind regards to Mrs. Scribner, I am
Always faithfully yours,
Mary Virginia Terhune

There was no opening, and CS II did not hire him. Albert Payson Terhune, however, did find work on the staff of the New York World *(1894–1916). His books about his collies at "Sunnybank," beginning with* Lad, a Dog *(1919), were internationally popular — but they were not published by Scribners.*

Frank R. Stockton (1834–1902)

Frank R. Stockton in 1895

Assistant editor (1873-1877) of Scribners' children's magazine, *St. Nicholas,* Stockton was already a frequent contributor of stories to *Scribner's Monthly* and other magazines when the success of his first adult novel, *Rudder Grange* (1879), allowed him to live from his writing. His whimsically fantastic, absurdly inventive, and/or cheerfully impossible tales and stories found a large, adoring public. William Dean Howells considered him, after Mark Twain, America's finest humorist; his *Adventures of Captain Horn* was the best-selling American novel of 1895; an 1899 poll by *Literature* magazine placed him fifth among current American authors, ahead of Henry James and Bret Harte. And Stockton may have been the first American science-fiction novelist. Today "The Lady, or the Tiger?" is probably the only Stockton story that is read or remembered.

Scribner Books by Stockton

1872	*Round-About Rambles in Lands of Fact and Fancy*
1875	*Tales Out of School*
1879	*Rudder Grange*
1880	*A Jolly Fellowship*
1881	*The Floating Prince, and Other Fairy Tales*
1882	*Ting-a-ling,* illustrated by E. B. Bensell
1884	*The Lady, or the Tiger? and Other Stories*
	The Story of Viteau
1885	*Rudder Grange,* illustrated by A. B. Frost
1886	*The Late Mrs. Null*
	Stockton's Stories (2 volumes)
1887	*The Bee-Man of Orn, and Other Fanciful Tales*
1888	*Amos Kilbright: His Adscititious Experiences, With Other Stories*
1889	*Personally Conducted,* illustrated by Joseph Pennell, Alfred Parsons, and others
1891	*The Rudder Grangers Abroad, and Other Stories*

1892	*The Clocks of Rondaine, and Other Stories,* illustrated by E. H. Blashfied, W. A. Rogers, D. C. Beard, and others
1893	*The Watchmaker's Wife, and Other Stories*
1894	*Ardis Claverden*
	Fanciful Tales, edited with notes for use in schools by Julia Elizabeth Langworthy, with an introduction by Mary E. Burt
	Pomona's Travels, illustrated by Frost
1895	*The Adventures of Captain Horn*
	A Chosen Few: Short Stories
1896	*Mrs. Cliff's Yacht,* illustrated by A. Forestier
1897	*A Story-Teller's Pack,* illustrated by Peter Newell, W. T. Smedley, Frank O. Small, Alice Barber Stephens, and E. W. Kemble
1898	*The Girl at Cobhurst*
1899	*The House of Martha*
1899–1904	*The Novels and Stories of Frank R. Stockton* (Shenandoah Edition of 23 volumes)
1900	*Afield and Afloat*
1902	*John Gayther's Garden and the Stories Told Therein*
1906	*The Queen's Museum, and Other Fanciful Tales,* illustrated by Frederick Richardson
1908	*The Magic Egg, and Other Stories*

LETTERS:

These letters, ranging over a decade, follow the ups and downs of Stockton's relationship with Scribners, particularly as his growing reputation affected its financial aspects.

July 18, 1878

Dear Mr. Scribner:

I have a little proposition to make to you. When I wrote, for S.A. & Co., the book "Tales Out of School," it was agreed to pay me $500.00, as follows: $300.00 on completion of my work, $100.00 when four thousand copies should be sold, and $100.00 more, when five thousand should be sold. Of this, I have received three hundred dollars, and have had no statement of how the book has sold. If it suits you, I will take one hundred dollars for my remaining interest in the book and thus settle up the matter.

Yours very truly
Frank R. Stockton

J. Blair Scribner replied that the firm could not favorably entertain his proposition because the book's sales had failed to reach the next mark.

July 21/85

My Dear Mr. Scribner:

In considering the subject of the "novelette" which you have proposed to publish for me, I will, first, make some remarks in regard to the price ($1200) which you offer for the book, for the first year. The story will, I think, make a book about the size of "A Jolly Friendship," which, although it ran for a year in "St. Nicholas," was published in very short instalments, not more than half the length of the instalments of a serial story in "The Century." For the manuscript of this story I received $1500, and this, added to the royalty for the first year of the book, made up the total amount to something over $1800. For another serial story for young people, shorter than "A Jolly Fellowhsip" and written for a newspaper, I received $1500.

These stories were written for children and at a period when my reputation as an author was not worth as much as it is now, and I had, therefore, expected that the novelette under consideration would pay me much better.

But there is another point, which, just now, seems to claim precedence of any other, and that is that the story is not yet finished, and I cannot with certainty, say when it will be. I was working very hard upon it, in the Spring, and it was about half completed, when I was interrupted by a series of illnesses, which put an entire stop to the work. Since I have recovered, and have been able to set myself again to writing, I have been obliged to confine myself to work as would produce an immediate income, and have not been able to touch the novelette, which, of course, would bring me in nothing, during the time I was engaged upon it. I am not yet able to devote my time to it, but expect to begin work upon it next month, and hope to finish it some time in the Autumn.

We shall, therefore, each of us, have time to think over the matter, before coming to a final conclusion, and I will keep you advised of the progress of the story.

I am of the opinion, however, that $1200 would not be nearly so much as I would receive for the novelette, if first published in a magazine, and afterward in book-form. But, the remuneration being equal, I should prefer the story to appear first, and only, as a book. It would please me much to have your house publish my first "novel," for such I suppose it might be called, and hope that we may be able to make an arrangement concerning it. In the meantime, I shall go to work on it as soon as I can.

Yours very truly
Frank R. Stockton

When he had the completed manuscript of The Late Mrs. Null *in his hands, CS II raised his offer to $2,000 and agreed to pay a 15 percent royalty after the first year. Stockton accepted. Published on 23 March 1886, the first edition of five thousand copies sold out on the first day.*

Jan 9/89

My dear Mr. Scribner:

I wish now to write you on a subject of much more importance than "The Great War Syndicate" [a book he had arranged to publish first in England]. This concerns a novel, recently finished,

First edition of Stockton's first adult novel (1879)

on which I have worked for a long time. It is, in my opinion, the most important work of my literary career.

It is a long novel of about 170,000 words and contains a great many varied characters, much incident and adventure, and the action is straight-forward and continuous.

It is too long for a magazine but is suitable for publication in a weekly paper or in book-form. I prefer the book, and should be very glad to have you publish it, should you see fit to do so.

My terms for the novel in book-form (without previous publication) are these: I should want, on acceptance of the manuscript, seven thousand, five hundred dollars ($7500). This sum would be counted as advanced royalties and would take the place of payment for the previous publication of the novel in a periodical.

This sum in advance would not be considered as a lump payment of royalties for any specified time, but as soon as royalties on the sale of the book had amounted to the sum named, the calculation of ordinary royalties would begin.

Thus, if the price of the book were two dollars, a sale of 25,000 copies at 15 percent would square the account for the advance payment, and royalties would then accrue, in the usual way, on subsequent sales.

I trust that I have expressed myself plainly, and if this proposition suits you, I shall be glad to submit to you the manuscript, which is now finished and ready for the printer.

Sincerely yours
Frank R. Stockton

The advance demanded was too large, and Scribners declined to meet it. Instead, Dodd, Mead published the novel, Ardis Claverden, *in 1890.*

CS II DIARY ENTRY:
Saturday 9 January 1892

Bought Stockton's story for $5000

Scribner is eager to buy this new story (novel), The Girl at Cobhurst, *having lost out to other publishers recently for Stockton's works.*

RELATED LETTERS:
Letter by CS II to Stockton, 20 March 1893; letter by CS II to Stockton, 26 January 1898.

My dear Mr. Stockton:

It would certainly give us a great pleasure to issue a new collection of short stories this Fall. There would be no objection on our part to your making an independent arrangement for the English edition and we are willing to make an advance on royalty account of say $500.

There will be no cause for delay on account of "Cobhurst." I thought I had placed it with the "Atlantic" for we agreed upon terms but Mr. Scudder insisted upon reading the story and unfortunately he did not like it so well as the "House of Martha." Truly these editors are a hard lot to please. This is my first experience in the position of an author and it is illuminating.

As for the Dodd Mead plates, it would depend upon the price. If they are ready to part with them and only want a fair price we are ready to buy them. But they have never been so popular as your other

Scribner editions of Stockton's works

books and have been put upon the market in a way likely to injure them for some time to come.

Yours sincerely
Charles Scribner

Of the manufacturing plates of Dodd, Mead titles of Stockton offered it, Scribners purchased Ardis Claverden *and published its edition the following year. Meanwhile, Stockton's new collection of stories,* The Watchmaker's Wife, and Other Stories, *appeared in October.*

My dear Mr. Stockton:

We have determined if agreeable to you to publish "Cobhurst" in book form this Spring without waiting for serial publication. It is now so long since we secured the book that I am almost ashamed to write to you about it. We have tried a few times to sell its serial rights but without success and have decided to bring the book out without waiting longer. I hope that this will not interfere with any arrangement of yours and that it will be equally satisfactory to you to give up the serial publication. Could you read proofs at once? And could you give us the choice of some other title? We have never thought "Cobhurst" a particularly attractive title and should be glad to have one that would excite some curiosity.

Yours sincerely
Charles Scribner

Renamed The Girl at Cobhurst, *Stockton's novel was finally published on April 23, 1898, over six years after Scribners had eagerly purchased it.*

LETTER:
Stockton's last letter in the Scribner Archives, written to Edward L. Burlingame, 21 October 1901.

My dear Mr. Burlingame,

It is very pleasant to be asked to write stories, and especially pleasant when the request comes from the Editor of Scribner's Magazine. This remark is not a mere idle pleasantry, but has a sound basis of reason. Which is, that when said Editor asks for a story, he does not stipulate that it shall be exactly so long, or exactly so short; that is shall be particularly funny, or slightly humorous; that it shall conform with the character of several other stories mentioned; or, that it shall not be like any of them, but he simply suggests to an author to put some of the best ideas he has into a story and send it along.

This, my dear Mr. Burlingame, I shall be happy to do as soon as I get a chance. Just now, I am at work on a long story and must finish it before I begin anything new. I hope it may not be very long before it is finished.

This is rather a vague answer to your note, but it indicates my state of feeling in the matter.

Hoping to see you this winter, I am,

Yours very truly,
Frank R. Stockton

Henry M. Stanley (1841–1904)

*Henry M. Stanley, in pose with
African boy*

Brought up in an English poorhouse, Stanley was adopted by an American merchant in 1859. After the Civil War he became a traveling correspondent. His fame as an explorer began with his assignment in 1871 by the *New York Herald* to find the Scottish missionary David Livingstone in the unexplored heart of Africa. On further expeditions he explored the headwaters of the Nile and surveyed Lake Tanganika; putting in stations for steamers along the Congo River and building roads, he helped found the Congo Free State. His geographical studies and discoveries were of the greatest importance for the region, and his writings about his travels drew international attention to himself and Scribners, his major publisher.

Scribner Books by Stanley

1872	*How I Found Livingstone: Travels, Adventures and Discoveries in Central Africa, Including an Account of Four Months' Residence with Dr. Livingstone*
1874	*My Kalulu, Prince, King, and Slave: A Story of Central Africa*
1890	*In Darkest Africa; or, The Quest, Rescue, and Retreat of Emin, Governor of Equatoria* (2 volumes)
1893	*My Dark Companions and Their Strange Stories*
1895	*My Early Travels and Adventures in America and Asia* (2 volumes)
1898	*Through South Africa: Being an Account of His Recent Visit to Rhodesia, the Transvaal, Cape Colony, and Natal*

LETTER:
Letter by J. Blair Scribner to James Gordon Bennett, 26 July 1872.

Bennett was the publisher of the New York Herald *and sponsor of Henry M. Stanley's expedition (1871–1872) in search of Dr. Livingstone, the Scottish missionary. More than twenty American and English publishers wanted to secure Stanley's story. As a result of the efforts of J. Blair Scribner and*

Charles Welford, his English partner, Stanley signed a contract with Scribners on 8 August; the resulting work, How I Found Dr. Livingstone, *appeared later that year, published by subscription only.*

Dear Sir,

Is it possible, with your permission and cooperation to obtain a work from Stanley on <u>The Finding of Livingstone</u>. It would place on permanent record the enterprise of the Herald & the

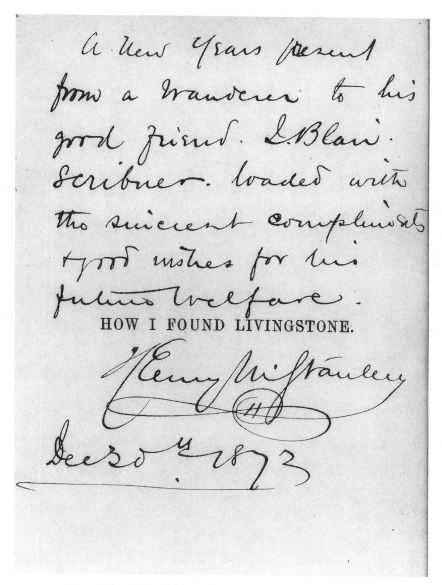

Inscription by Stanley to his publisher, J. Blair Scribner

pluck of its representative, and would, we doubt not, be of mutual benefit.

Please let us have a reply at your earliest convenience and believe us

Yours truly
Scribner, Armstrong & Co.

P.S. We have the pleasure of sending you our last Monthly which contains a Yachting article which may interest you. An illustrated article by Stanley in the Monthly we should be glad to get.

LETTER:

Letter by J. Blair Scribner to Charles Welford, head of the London branch of the importing business, Scribner & Welford, 27 January 1874.

On hearing of Livingstone's death, Stanley undertook another expedition to equatorial Africa under a joint commission from the New York Herald *and the* London Daily Telegraph, *leaving from Zanzibar on 12 November 1874.*

Dear Mr. Welford —

Last evenings papers announced the death of Dr. Livingstone. Undoubtedly a volume will be issued before long either by his relatives or under the auspices of the Geographical Society giving all

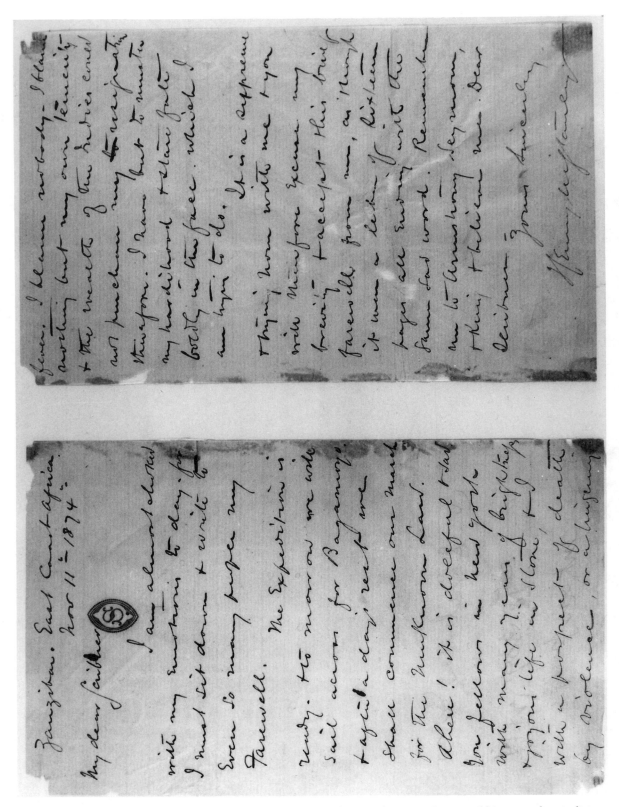

Emotional letter written from Zanzibar by Stanley to J. Blair Scribner on the eve of his second expedition
"Through the Dark Continent"

the information gleaned from the papers, Diary etc etc of the great African Explorer. Now I hope that mention will be made in the book of Mr. Stanley for to tell the truth not one person in a hundred in the United States at present believe that Mr. Stanley ever saw Dr. Livingstone at all. This is I know a hard Statement to make but it is nevertheless true. . . .

Very truly yours
J. Blair Scribner

LETTER:
Letter by Henry M. Stanley to Charles Scribner's Sons, 6 March 1890, from Cairo, Egypt.

With a hefty payment plus a royalty agreement, Scribners was able to secure Stanley's book about his fourth African expedition. More than eighty thousand sets of the two-volume work were sold.

Sirs

    I am happy to inform you that I am so far advanced with the writing of my book "In Darkest Africa, and the Quest, Rescue, & Retreat of Emin the Governor of Equatoria," that more than half the mss. has been already mailed for England. By the 1st April next I hope to have finished with the whole of it. When that is done not Vanderbilt's wealth would induce me to write upon the subject at any length again. Therefore you will be justified, nay, authorized, in stating that the book bearing the above title is the only authentic & complete account of the work performed by the Emin Pasha Relief Expedition which I have written, or shall at any time write.

Yours faithfully
Henry M. Stanley

Stanley's first royalty payment for In Darkest Africa, *sent through Scribners' London office, was directed by Lemuel W. Bangs.*

HOW I FOUND

LIVINGSTONE:

TRAVELS, ADVENTURES AND DISCOVERIES
IN

CENTRAL AFRICA:

INCLUDING AN ACCOUNT OF

FOUR MONTHS' RESIDENCE WITH DR. LIVINGSTONE.

BY

HENRY M. STANLEY,

TRAVELLING CORRESPONDENT OF THE "NEW YORK HERALD."

With Maps and Illustrations after Drawings by the Author.

PUBLISHED ONLY BY SUBSCRIPTION.

New York:
SCRIBNER, ARMSTRONG & CO.
1872.

BOSTON: GEO. M. SMITH & CO.	PORTLAND: H. A. McKENNY & CO.
SYRACUSE: WATSON GILL.	DETROIT: BOOTHROYD & GIBBS.
CHICAGO: HADLEY BROS.	NEW ORLEANS: KAIN & CO.
SAN FRANCISCO: A. L. BANCROFT & CO.	

Title page of Stanley's famous work. This was the first work published by Scribners' new Subscription Department.

CS II DIARY ENTRY:
Tuesday 2 June 1891

Sent Stanley $40,829.87 per Bangs

Mary Mapes Dodge (1830–1905)

Mary Mapes Dodge

Dodge's name was synonymous with children's literature of the highest order during the last decades of the nineteenth century, both as the author of an enduring classic, *Hans Brinker; or, The Silver Skates,* and as first editor and principal force behind *St. Nicholas,* Scribners' landmark children's magazine. Whole generations of young readers were raised on her philosophy that their magazine should be "stronger, truer, bolder, more uncompromising than the [adult's]," without sermonizing and the "wearisome spinning out of facts," and that it must be beautifully illustrated ("Children's Magazines," *Scribner's Monthly,* July 1873). Unequaled in her influence on children's literature in her lifetime, Dodge managed to publish just about every children's writer and poet of note, many of whom are still read today.

Scribner Books by Dodge

1873	*Hans Brinker; or, The Silver Skates: A Story of Life in Holland,* illustrated by F. O. C. Darley, Thomas Nast, and others
1873–1881	editor of *St. Nicholas: Scribner's Illustrated Magazine for Girls and Boys* (she continued to edit this for the Century Company till 1905)
1874	*Rhymes and Jingles*
1876	*Theophilus and Others*
1879	*Hans Brinker; or, The Silver Skates: A Story of Life in Holland* (new edition, with twelve plates)
	Along the Way
1886	*Hans Brinker; or, The Silver Skates: A Story of Life in Holland* (new edition, with sixty original illustrations)
1896	*Hans Brinker; or, The Silver Skates: A Story of Life in Holland* (New Amsterdam Edition), illustrated by Allen B. Doggett
1904	*Rhymes and Jingles,* illustrated by Sarah S. Stilwell

| 1915 | *Hans Brinker; or, The Silver Skates*, illustrated by George Wharton Edwards |
| 1958 | *Hans Brinker; or, The Silver Skates*, illustrated by Peter Spier |

LETTER:

Letter by J. Blair Scribner to Dodge, 1 May 1873, making his publishing proposal for the Scribner edition of *Hans Brinker*.

While the first edition of Hans Brinker; or, The Silver Skates *was published by James O'Kane in 1866, it was under the Scribner imprint that its remarkable popularity developed. The Scribner edition appeared in November 1873, coinciding with the first issue of* St. Nicholas, *the new Scribner children's magazine edited by Dodge.*

Dear Madam

We have at last thanks to the kindness of Mr. Mapes secured the plates and illustrations complete of "Hans Brinker" and partially so of "The Irvington Stories." In regard to the latter we propose to do nothing at present for we understand that it is your intention some time in the future to add to and thoroughly revise the book. <u>Now as to "Hans Brinker."</u>

We intend bringing out early next Fall (say September) an entirely new Edition, getting it up in good shape and advertising it to a considerable extent. We say next Fall because we do not think it would be well to print the book before that time — the Summer is generally an unfortunate season for publishing.

Of course it is necessary that there should be an agreement drawn up in regard to copyright and we should only have <u>this</u> contract apply to "Hans Brinker" as that is <u>the one</u> book <u>now</u> entirely ready for the press. We propose that the contract should be made out on the basis of 10 per cent copyright on the <u>retail</u> price which if the book sells for $1.50 as it probably will would net you 15 cts. on every copy sold.

This is the usual rate of copyright (the greater part of our Contracts are on the same plan) and in this case it is we think exceedingly liberal to you as we have been obliged to invest in a set of plates <u>after the benefits derived from first sales and numerous editions are over</u>. We trust that our proposition will meet with your full approval when the papers will be at once made out and signed before you sail for Europe and we will

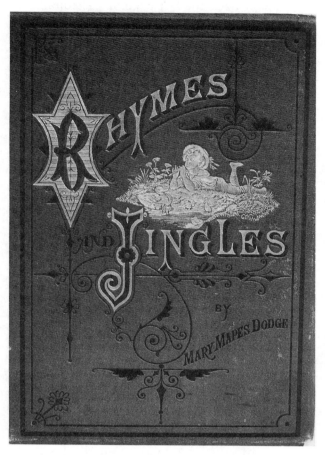

Dodge's second Scribner book, bearing on the cover an illustration (boy with ducks) that had been used as a frontispiece to the first volume of St. Nicholas

thus become your publishers. Awaiting your reply we remain

> very truly yours
> Scribner, Armstrong & Co.

RELATED LETTERS:

Letters by Dodge to Scribner partner Edward Seymour, 14 May and 19 May 1876.

Regarding copy to be used for promoting her new book, Theophilus and Other Stories, *which will be published in June, Dodge's letters reveal her sense of humor, which is also the trait in her work that she most wants her audience to perceive. The "Treasure Trove" refers to a series of books*

(1875) for young people edited by Richard Henry Stoddard. Of ten projected volumes, only three were published; volume 1 consisted of burlesques.

Dear Mr. Seymour —

I sent back the last page of "Theophilus & Others" on Saturday & also forwarded title page, preface etc. so the book is now finished as far as I am concerned.

You asked me to give you a few "hints" about it, and I have tried to do so, on the enclosed sheet, though under the difficulties of a strange combination of great modesty and intense conceit. In fact you may think that my black ink has blushed itself red in writing the dreadful screed, but that's not so. I'm writing with red ink because it flows easily — that's all.

Some where, I have a huge envelope full of notices, letters and all sorts of vain-glorious-nesseseses about my rare and delightful books, my over-whelming genius and stupendous faculties in general, but I don't know just where to lay my hands upon it at the moment. Maybe the accompanying envelopes may afford you a hint or two in getting up the ads. of "Hans B." & "Rhymes & J" that Mr. Marvin says are to be put at the end of Theophilus. Whether they do or not, will you please return them to me, so that I may put them with the aforesaid budget when it turns up?

Do tear up the page of "hints" — it is a disgusting document & I only send it because I'd like to help you. Perhaps you won't want an idea that's in it.

Yours ever
Mary Mapes Dodge

Dear Mr Seymour —

"Mistress Molony and the Chinese Question" (see "Book Buyer" page 6) should read: Miss Malony on the Chinese Question.

Will you allow me to blushingly suggest that the criticism generally made of the various sketches in this collection is that they possess the quality of humor, and many of the old notices spoke of the immortal Mrs. D. as, distinctively, that very rare thing — a female humorist. In support of this, the "Treasure Trove" I suppose may be cited (not by Scribner & Co. of course, but entre nous) as Mrs. D. is the only woman given among the authors of the first vol. [Please eat this note & swallow it, so mortal eyes may never behold it again.] I merely throw out this hint of "humor" as a business suggestion that may or may not be of consequence.

"Dobbs's Horse" is the opening story of the book and is drawn from actual experiences — in our own family. "What a Little Song Can Do" — and "Sunshine," also are true stories. The former is told, word for word, just as it happened.

Is it of any business value to be able to say in your notices that the author has a reputation outside of this country? I get letters from England, Germany, France and Holland (a good many of them) that sometimes make me feel as if I had more warm literary friends there than here. If this is of no business importance please forget it. & don't forget to thoroughly masticate & swallow this letter!!

Yours truly
M. M. D.

RELATED LETTERS:
Letter by CS II to Dodge, 17 March 1883.

Dodge's novel, Donald and Dorothy, *was serialized in* St. Nicholas *from December 1881 through October 1882. The book version should have appeared before Christmas, but Dodge's contractual demands prevented Scribners from publishing it.*

Dear Mrs. Dodge:

Your note of yesterday is at hand and enclosed you will please find our check for the amount due. I regret that the note was forgotten.

Since my call upon you I have had an opportunity to more carefully consider the contract which you proposed and this examination has suggested some obligations which did not occur to me at our interview.

The contracts which we now have are such as are customary between author and publisher and have, so far as I know, proved satisfactory in the past. The contract which you propose is exceptional and one of which Dr. Holland's is the only example in the experience of this business.

I can understand how an author might wish to control the publication of his works and yet I doubt whether it would be nice for a publisher to have upon his list many books which could be withdrawn by the author or representatives without cause or without the consent of the publisher. I think you will see that the position of a publisher is a peculiar one. He not only invests in the plates and other material parts of books, but should also build up through them an interest of another kind — i.e., a valuable list and business, and the clause which you propose might put him in the position

CHARLES SCRIBNER'S SONS,
PUBLISHERS.
743-745 BROADWAY.

NEW-YORK, *Feb. 15th* 1883

Dear Mrs. Dodge;

Enclosed you will please find the usual statement of the sale of your books. You will see that "Hans Brinker" still leads the list. It has been the most successful juvenile that we ever published. I wish that you could see your way clear to giving us "Donald & Dorothy" next Fall.

Yours very truly
Charles Scribner

Letter by CS II to Dodge about the best-selling status of Hans Brinker

of building up this interest only to see it pass into other hands.

These are some of the reasons for hesitating over the change which you propose. Have you found the need of such a clause in the past?

The publication of "Donald & Dorothea" is of course a matter entirely apart from your proposal of a new contract for the books already published. I think that a new contract might be formed for this book which would be satisfactory to both of us and yet not open to the objections argued.

If you desire it, I will devise some form for such an agreement and submit it to you.

I am having copies made of your old contracts and will send them to you in a few days.

Yours faithfully
Charles Scribner

Writing a month later, 19 April 1883, CS II continues his argument:

. . . If I make such a change as you desire in your contracts, I do not see on what grounds I could refuse the same change to such authors as Cable, Mrs. Burnett, Eggleston, or even, Pres. Porter, Dr. Hodge and all others. This would amount to almost a revolution in the business and would make my business life nothing less than one of constant uncertainty and trial. I could not make arrangements for the future with any certainty, for I never could tell when an author would avail himself of the right of taking his books away. . . . in short, I do not see how business could be carried on with any comfort.

. . . I would be unwilling to have you seek another publisher for your new book without letting you know the grounds on which I refuse to accept the conditions on which the new book is offered to me. . . .

The result of this contract dispute was that Dodge offered Donald and Dorothy *to Roberts Bros., the Boston publisher of her friend Louisa May Alcott, who issued the book in November. Except for titles it already owned, Scribners was her publisher no longer.*

Richard Henry Stoddard (1825–1903)

Richard Henry Stoddard

Reared fatherless and in poverty, Stoddard supported himself on the streets of New York with odd jobs and educated himself while serving an apprenticeship as an iron molder. Nathaniel Hawthorne found him an inspector's job in the New York Custom House (1853–1870), where he met Melville. Later, he was literary editor of the New York *Mail and Express* (1880–1903). Stoddard and his novelist wife held a salon that was a center of New York literary life for a time. His work as a literary journalist and poet is not remembered today, but he was greatly admired in the Gilded Age. The two series he edited for Scribners were very popular.

Scribner Books by Stoddard

1874–1876   Bric-a-Brac series — "personal reminiscences of famous poets, novelists, wits, humorists, artists, actors, musicians, and the like" (1877 Scribner catalogue description), edited by Stoddard:

> Vol. 1 *Personal Reminiscences by Chorley, Planché, and Young* (1874)
>
> Vol. 2 *Anecdote Biographies of Thackeray and Dickens* (1874)
>
> Vol. 3 *Prosper Mérimée's Letters to an Incognita, with Recollections by Lamartine and George Sand* (1874)
>
> Vol. 4 *Personal Reminiscences by Barham, Harness, and Hodder* (1875)
>
> Vol. 5 *The Greville Memoirs* (1875)
>
> Vol. 6 *Personal Reminiscences by Moore and Jerdan* (1875)
>
> Vol. 7 *Personal Reminiscences by Cornelia Knight and Thomas Raikes* (1875)
>
> Vol. 8 *Personal Reminiscences by O'Keeffe, Kelly, and Taylor* (1875)
>
> Vol. 9 *Personal Recollections of Lamb, Hazlitt, and Others* (1875)
>
> Vol. 10 *Personal Reminiscences by Constable and Gillies* (1876)

1876   Sans-Souci series — "a library of anecdote biographies" (1877 Scribner catalogue description), edited by Stoddard:

> Vol. 1 *The Life, Letters and Table Talk of Benjamin Robert Haydon*

Vol. 2 *Men and Manners in America 100 Years Ago*, edited by H. E. Scudder

Vol. 3 *Anecdote Biography of Percy Bysshe Shelley*

1880   *The Poems of Richard Henry Stoddard* (complete edition)

1883   *English Verse*, edited by W. J. Linton and Stoddard

1890   *The Lion's Cub, With Other Verse*

1892   *Under the Evening Lamp*

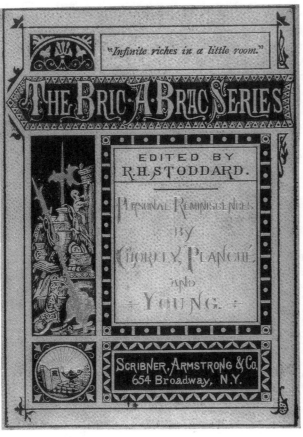

Cover of the first volume (1874) in the Scribner *Bric-a-Brac* series, edited by Stoddard

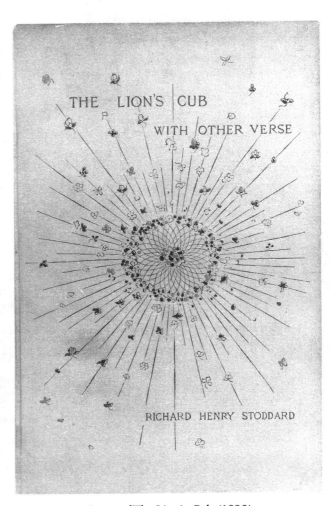

Cover of The Lion's Cub *(1890)*

LETTER:

Letter by CS II to Richard Henry Stoddard, 13 September 1879, requesting the privilege of publishing his poems.

The Poems of Richard Henry Stoddard (complete edition) *was published eight months later on 13 May 1880. Though he had already edited more than a dozen titles for the firm in their Bric-a-Brac* and Sans-Souci *series, this was the first volume of his own work that Stoddard gave to Scribners.*

Dear Mr. Stoddard:

I hear that Houghton, Osgood & Co. have requested you to collect your poems for them to publish.

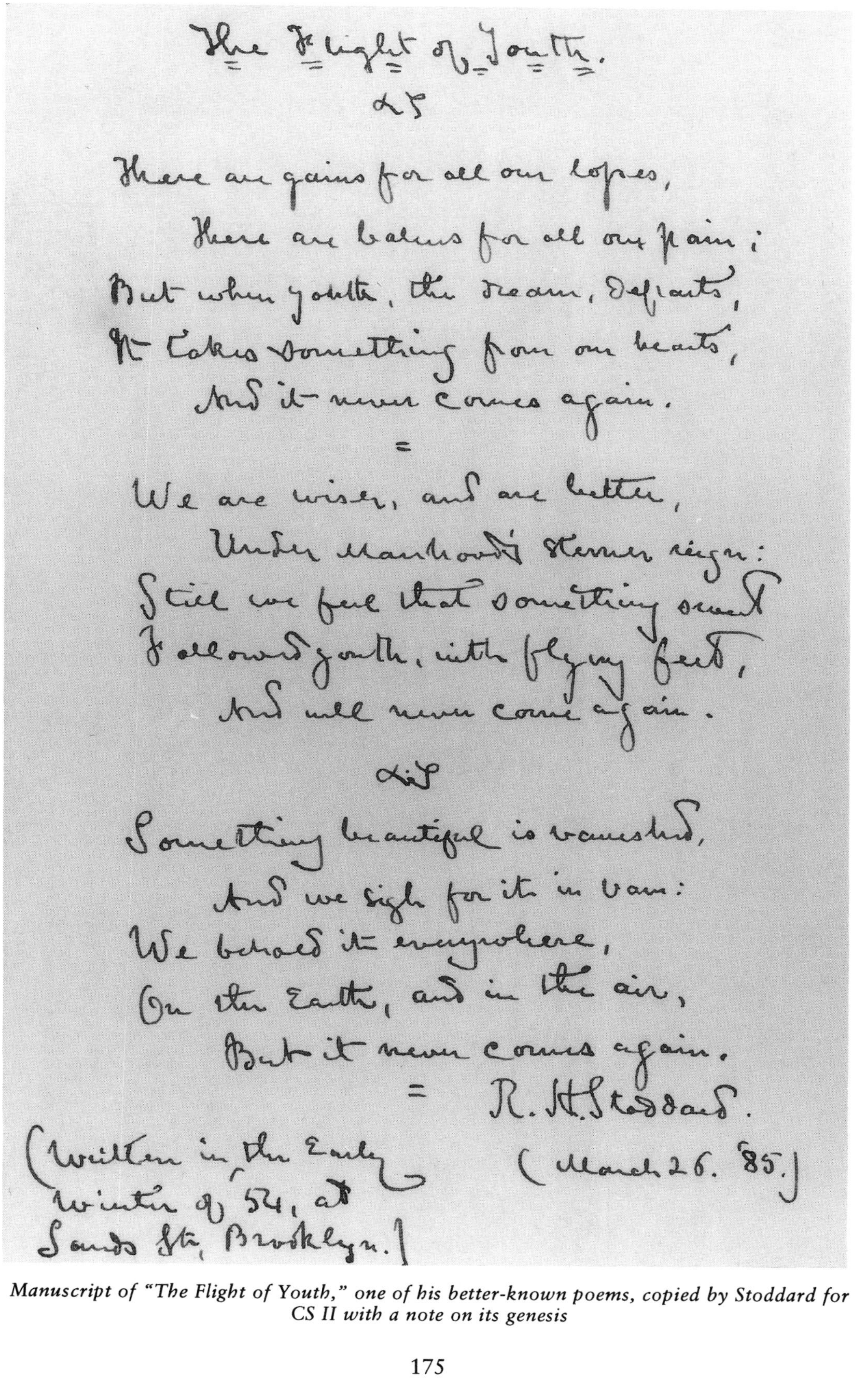

The Flight of Youth.

I

There are gains for all our losses,
    There are balms for all our pain;
But when youth, the dream, departs,
It takes something from our hearts,
    And it never comes again.

We are wiser, and are better,
    Under Manhood's sterner reign:
Still we feel that something sweet
Followed youth, with flying feet,
    And will never come again.

Something beautiful is vanished,
    And we sigh for it in vain:
We behold it everywhere,
On the Earth, and in the air,
    But it never comes again.

R. H. Stoddard.

(March 26. '85.)

(Written in the Early
winter of 54, at
Sands St, Brooklyn.)

Manuscript of "The Flight of Youth," one of his better-known poems, copied by Stoddard for
CS II with a note on its genesis

175

329 E. 15th Street
New York May 19 '90

My dear Mr Scribner:

The title of the new volume will be.

The Lion's Cub.
with? Other Pieces

by R.H.S.

(Motto)

"Devouring Time, blunt thou the lion's paws"
Shakespeare

I enclose the poem from which the collection takes its name. It is the most famous episode in Kalidás' "Magic Ring" a play about 200 years B.C.

I offer it to Scribners Magazine, declined by that I shall offer it to the Century. I have (I think) done no better work for some years

Yours truly
R.H.S.

Mr Charles Scribner,
New York.

Letter by Stoddard to CS II proposing The Lion's Cub *as the title for his new book of poems*

Before you consent to do so I hope you will give us a chance.

It was long Blair's wish, and it is mine, that we should publish your collected poems, and it seems hardly fair for you to run off to Boston with them.

In any event I want to place before you a definite offer to issue them whenever you are ready and pay you the usual copyright of ten per cent.

Please consider that you have such an offer.

Yours very truly
Charles Scribner

LETTER:
Letter by Richard Henry Stoddard to CS II, 25 March 1885.

Stoddard mentions having sat for Julian Alden Weir (1852–1919), the American portrait painter.

(A.M. 12.–55.)

Carolus Mio,

I have bettered (as you see) my careless promise this afternoon (the clock was 5 minutes too slow).

— If Julian Weir makes a success with me, he shall paint you, or Mrs. Scribner, not as in my case, for nothing: but, in your cases, for the honorarium. I stood, and sat, nearly 4 hours yesterday.

Carolus, I have never forgotten Joannius Blairium Scribnerarum. Nor, your good, kind Father, who was grace and goodness itself.

Yours, to the task,
R. H. Stoddard

CS II DIARY ENTRY:
Thursday 14 May 1903

Pallbearer at funeral of R. H. Stoddard

177

Noah Brooks (1830–1903)

Noah Brooks

Brooks had a dual career as a journalist and author. In California, he was assistant editor of Bret Harte's literary magazine, the *Overland Monthly*; in Washington, D.C., he was a correspondent of the *Sacramento Union*; in New York, he became an editor at *The New York Times*. He was a close friend of President Lincoln, and only a severe cold kept him out of the presidential box at Ford's Theater the night of the assassination. Throughout his career he authored popular historical fiction and was invited to contribute to Scribners' inaugural issue of its children's magazine, *St. Nicholas*. His boys' stories and books, written with a realistic treatment of characters and setting, are little known today, but they placed him among the country's best of his time.

Scribner Books by Brooks

1876	*The Boy Emigrants*, illustrated by Thomas Moran and W. L. Sheppard
1880	*The Fairport Nine*
1891	*The Boy Settlers: A Story of Early Times in Kansas*, illustrated by W. A. Rogers
1893	*Statesmen*
1894	*Tales of the Maine Coast*
1895	*Short Studies in Party Politics*
	How the Republic Is Governed
	The Mediterranean Trip: A Short Guide to the Principal Points on the Shores of the Western Mediterranean and the Levant
1896	*Scribner's Popular History of the United States* by William Cullen Bryant and Sidney Howard Gay, revised with fifth volume by Brooks
1898	*The Boys of Fairport*
1901	*Lem, A New England Village Boy: His Adventures and His Mishaps*, illustrated by H. C. Edwards
	First Across the Continent: The Story of the Exploring Expedition of Lewis and Clark

RELATED LETTERS:
Letter by Brooks to CS II, 2 December 1902, and
reply by CS II, 17 December 1902.

*In his early seventies, Brooks and his publisher are
still "bouncing" ideas for boys' books back and
forth. Answering Scribner's letter Brooks wrote
that he was reluctant to pursue his suggestion because Zebulon Pike left behind no journal and
there were few other source materials, but perhaps
John Charles Fremont, "The Pathfinder," would
be a good subject. The discussion never progressed because Brooks became ill, went to California to restore his health, and died in August.*

Dear Mr Scribner:

I should like to write a book for boys which
might be entitled "The Boys' Book of American
Privateering." I have several incidents in that
field which have never been printed, this region
being, as you know, actively engaged in
privateering at the breaking out of the American
Revolution. I have in my possession a Letter of
Marque issued to a Castine skipper, in three languages, and signed in each fold by John Han-
cock, President of the Continental Congress,
and by the Secretary, by way of illustrating how
privateers were commissioned. Such a book,
well illustrated, it seems to me, would be very
popular with boys, as well as with their elders.

As the privateers of 1775 and 6 were the
genesis of the Navy, a Boys' History of the U.S.
Navy would be a good book to follow the afore-
mentioned. I should show how the evolution of
the man-of-war from the privateer came about;
then the evolution of the steamer from the sailing ship and the rifled gun from the smooth
bore; then the screw from the paddle-wheel;
then the iron-clad from the wooden vessel, and
lastly the battle-ship from the seagoing steel-
clad cruiser.

Incidentally, of course, the actions of the
navy (passing lightly over the war of the rebellion), would come in for spirited narration, ending with the Spanish-American war. The Naval
Academy, War College, Apprentice system and
how they are managed and equipped, would
need explanation; also the names, titles and
badges and pay of each, their rations, etc, would
come in for description and illustration. I am
promised a chapter on the evolution of the modern gun by one of my nephews, Lieut. F. Brooks
Upham, who is an ordnance officer on the battle-ship "Oregon." From other officers I can

*Brooks's first book (1876), based on his own
experiences crossing the plains with ox teams
on a trip from Illinois to California before the
Civil War*

have all the inside information I need to make a
clear and understandable story of the U.S. Navy
and its growth.

There is no such book in existence. The
only thing of that sort is B. J. Lossing's "The
Story of the U.S. Navy," which ends with the
battle of the "Monitor" and the "Merrimac"
and is largely taken up with the naval battles of
the Civil War. It is still used as a text-book in
the apprentice-schools, for want of anything
better. An up-to-date book would be useful and
popular, it seems to me.

At present, I am at work upon a short biography of Sir William Pepperrell, for the
Appleton's. It is a small book and will be done
in a few weeks, if I have a fair share of health. I

The Ark.
Castine Maine.
November 27,1899.

Dear Mr Scribner:

When I was in New York, last October, you will remember
that we discussed the project of making a book out of the report of
the Lewis & Clake Expedition of 1803, but came to no definite conclusion. I have now secured a copy of the second edition of the report,
printed by the Harpers in their "School District Library", in 1847. It
is in two volumes, of 370 pages, each, running about 400 words to the page
page, with maps and plates. It is an exceedingly interesting work, I
find, on reading it again after many years. There is no edition now in
print, and your folks had some trouble in procuring this copy.

If you want me to make the book, please let me know about what
amount of letter-press you want, and what you propose in the way of illustration. The plates in the book are not numerous, but the map of the
route is good, and it might be reproduced with lines of the modern map
printed over it in lines of a lighter and different color. Let me
know, also, on what terms you desire the work to be done; for, if you publish by subscription, as you suggested you might, I suppose the terms
would be different than those of copyright.

I shall not be in New York, on my way to Bermuda, until after the
holidays, and I would like to have the matter settled before I leave
here for the winter.

Yours faithfully,

Noah Brooks

Letter by Brooks to CS II about his proposed book on the Lewis and Clark expedition, which was accepted. Published in 1901, the book, as Brooks explained in his preface, told the story "as fully as possible in the language of the explorers themselves."

should like to hear from you on the above-mentioned projects.

Faithfully yours,
Noah Brooks

Dear Mr. Brooks:

As you know we are always interested in any proposal from you and the suggested books on privateering and on the American Navy have much to recommend them. But it does seem to us that the Navy has been worked rather hard during the last few years, particularly for boys. We are much more interested in your old suggestion for a boys' book to be made from the Pike Memoirs. It would require more work, as I understand it, than the Lewis & Clark book but I believe it could be successfully done and the book would have the advantage of following up the other in the same field. Will you not think of the idea and write me.

Yours sincerely
Charles Scribner

Frances Hodgson Burnett (1849–1924)

Frances Hodgson Burnett (engraving made for the February 1886 issue of The Book Buyer*)*

Born in England, Burnett came to the United States in 1865. Though she wrote adult fiction as well, Burnett is recognized today as the author of children's classics, notably *Little Lord Fauntleroy* (1886), *A Little Princess* (1905), and, perhaps her masterpiece, *The Secret Garden* (1911) — the first two books were published by Scribners. These "fairy tales of real life" with their happy endings brought Burnett the label of a "romantic," but that was also the label of her era, which abounded in idealized, sentimental stories. Scribners identified her talent, and, in linking her narratives with the illustrations of such artists as Reginald B. Birch, helped create her early success.

Scribner Books by Burnett

1877	*That Lass o'Lowrie's,* illustrated by Alfred Fredericks
	Surly Tim and Other Stories
1878	*Kathleen Mavourneen* (paperback)
	Lindsay's Luck (paperback)
	Pretty Polly Pemberton (paperback)
1879	*Miss Crespigny* (paperback)

	Theo (paperback)
	Haworth's
1880	*Louisiana*
1886	*A Fair Barbarian*
	Through One Administration
	Little Lord Fauntleroy, illustrated by Reginald B. Birch
1888	*Sara Crewe or What Happened at Miss Minchin's,* illustrated by Birch
1889	*The Pretty Sister of José,* illustrated by C. S. Reinhart
	Vagabondia: A Love Story
1890	*Little Saint Elizabeth and Other Stories,* illustrated by Birch
1891	*Earlier Stories* (first series)
	Earlier Stories (second series)
1892	*Giovanni and the Other: Children Who Have Made Stories,* illustrated by Birch
1893	*The One I Knew the Best of All: A Memory of the Mind of a Child,* illustrated by Birch
1894	*Piccino and Other Child Stories,* illustrated by Birch
1895	*Two Little Pilgrims' Progress: A Story of the City Beautiful,* illustrated by Birch
1896	*A Lady of Quality: Being a Most Curious, Hitherto Unknown History, as Related to Mr. Isaac Bickerstaff But Not Presented to the World of Fashion Through the Pages of* The Tatler, *and Now for the First Time Written Down*
1897	*His Grace of Osmonde: Being the Portions of That Nobleman's Life Omitted in the Relation of His Lady's Story Presented to the World of Fashion Under the Title* A Lady of Quality
	Sara Crewe, Little Saint Elizabeth, and Other Stories
1899	*In Connection with the De Willoughby Claim*
1905	*A Little Princess: Being the Whole Story of Sara Crewe, Now Told for the First Time,* illustrated by Ethel Franklin Betts
1906	*The Dawn of a To-Morrow,* illustrated by F. C. Yohn

LETTERS:

Letter by J. Blair Scribner to Burnett, 30 October 1876, offering to publish *That Lass o'Lowrie's,* which has been appearing in *Scribner's Monthly.*

Mrs. Fanny Hodgson Burnett,

Dear Madam: We have read with interest that portion of your story "That Lass O'Lowrie's" which has thus far appeared in "Scribner's Monthly" and as a result we are willing to make you the following offer for its publication in bookform by us after its completion as a serial in the Magazine.

We will bring the book out in handsome style and bear all expenses attendent to its appearance as well as the cost of the stereotype plates, advertising, etc. — and will allow you a copyright of ten per cent on the retail price of all copies sold after the sale of the first thousand.

We ask you not to require any copyright on the sale of one thousand copies in order that we may thus be able to reimburse ourselves for the outlay (a considerable sum) in making the stereo-

type plates. This arrangement is one which we frequently make with our authors. Hoping that it will prove satisfactory to you we remain
Yours truly
Scribner, Armstrong, & Co.

After Burnett's acceptance J. Blair Scribner wrote (2 March 1877) to Charles Welford, the English agent of Scribners in London, asking for him to arrange for an English edition:

... I send by post the early sheets (the greater part page and the last two Magazine installments) of a new book by a <u>new</u> novelist — and for which we expect a large sale and a decided success — the book will be published by us early in April. The story has been running as a serial through our Magazine and has attracted a great deal of attention. The enclosed slip will give you an idea of the plot. Now we are anxious to see the book published in England and will sell a duplicate set of stereotype plates of the text and illustrations (4 of them) for ½ the cost ... with the understanding that should the book prove a success in England the author is to receive a fair consideration in the profits. It is our opinion that the author has a brilliant future before her. The story is original and powerful and the scene is laid in the old Country and therefore particularly suited to an English audience. ...

Published on April 7th, Burnett's first book was an immediate success and was in its third edition in three weeks.

RELATED LETTER:
Letter by Macmillan and Co. to Scribners, 24 June 1879.

In the era before international copyright, English law required some unusual procedures of foreign authors in order to guarantee them legal copyrights. And these procedures were only followed for the most popular authors like Burnett whose works might be subject to pirating by others.

Dear Sirs,
We find that in order to secure a legal copyright in England for a foreign author it is necessary (<u>vide</u> Drone "Law of Property in Intellectual Productions" page 232) that the author should be at the time of publication in British dominion. We are therefore writing to Mrs. Burnett to ask if she will arrange to go to Canada and to be there on a

Burnett's first book, That Lass o'Lowrie's (1877)

fixed day during the latter half of August upon which we will manage to publish <u>Haworths</u>. We enclose our letter and shall be much obliged if you will forward it at once.
We find that we have not chapters 49, 50, 51 of <u>Haworths</u> — will you kindly send us proof of them <u>at once</u> & oblige
Yours very truly
Macmillan & Co.

LETTERS:
Letters by CS II to his English partner, Charles Welford, 23 March 1881, and Welford's successor, Lemuel Bangs, 25 June 1886, regarding the loss and the regaining of Burnett as a Scribner author.

The "hostilities" refer to the unpleasant circumstances under which CS II decided to sell his stock

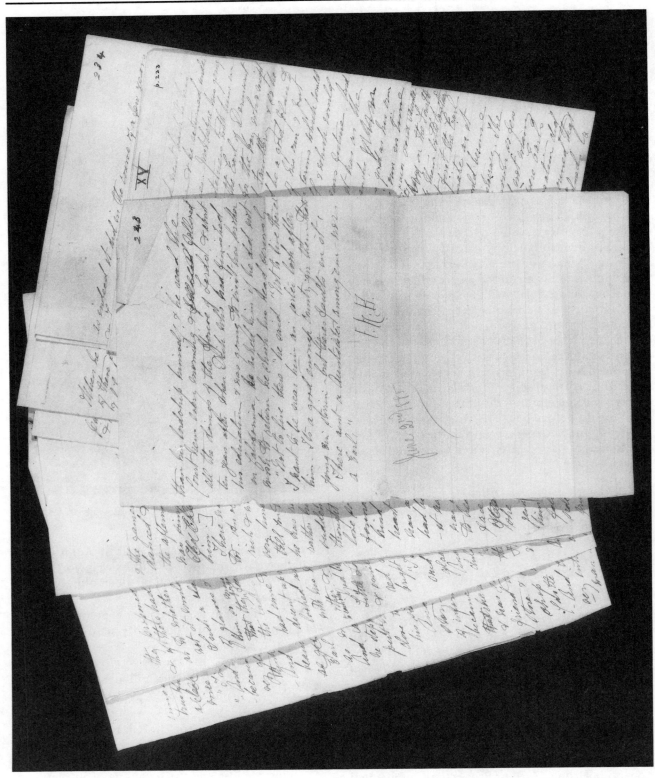

Manuscript pages of the last chapter of Little Lord Fauntleroy. *The book began its serialization in the November 1885 issue of* St. Nicholas, *the Scribner children's magazine.*

in Scribner & Co., the publisher of Scribner's Monthly *and* St. Nicholas *magazines, to Roswell Smith, its president.*

Dear Mr. Welford,

. . .

Mrs. Burnett's books seem to sell fully as well in England as here from what you write. As you know, we have published all her books up to the present but during the hostilities between Mr. Smith & myself he fostered dissatisfaction in that quarter and the result has been an unexpected announcement of the 'Fair Barbarian' by <u>Osgood</u>. It was mean of <u>Smith</u> to negotiate the arrangement (as he did); it was mean of her to leave her former Publisher without any notice; and it was very mean of <u>Osgood</u> to be made a party to such meanness. <u>Smith</u> I expected nothing better of; she did not know any better; but <u>Osgood</u> is much to blame. The truth is he is moving heaven and earth to secure a "list" and is not stopped by the usual rules of courtesy. . . .

My Dear Bangs,

. . .

Mrs. Burnett went off to Osgood at the time of the sale of the magazines but has now returned to the fold and we publish her next book "Lord Fauntleroy" which has been appearing in "St. Nicholas" and secured the plates of the two stories she issued thru Osgood. . . .

Scribners remained Burnett's principal publisher for the next twenty years.

LETTER:
Letter by CS II to Burnett, 29 October 1887.

The success of Little Lord Fauntleroy *even surprised Burnett, who had written Scribners about it from Florence, where she had gone with her family for a lengthy stay on the Continent. The "new" story Scribners wanted and got was* Sara Crewe or What Happened at Miss Minchin's.

Dear Madam,

In response to your letter from Florence I hasten to write that the statement about "Fauntleroy" was altogether true.

It has been one of the most successful books we have ever published: we have printed up to this date 33250 copies and have ordered 10000 more printed. We have accounted to you (up to Aug. last) for the sale of 23244 copies and on Feb. next

A first edition of Little Lord Fauntleroy. *The book was one of the best-sellers of 1886; the 1888 play version ran on Broadway for four years; and several successful movie adaptions have been made.* Little Lord Fauntleroy *has been identified as the first book to spawn an industry of related products: Fauntleroy toys, playing cards, chocolates, and the famous velvet suits with lace collars.*

(the regular date for rendering an account) we shall be able to again make a handsome showing; indeed the sale of the book shows no diminution and we hope for great results next year as well as this. Enclosed I send a rough memorandum of the statement we sent to you to Washington on Aug. last and which perhaps you have forgotten. All your books show an increased sale during the past year. Am I to understand that you wish the next statement sent to you in Florence?

You may be sure that we take the greatest interest in the new story about to appear in St. Nicholas. May we arrange at once for its publication in book form? And have you any different arrangement to suggest than was made for "Lord Fauntleroy"? The new book would undoubtedly start with an immense sale for we have already received many inquiries about it. The fact of it being smaller than "Fauntleroy" will not injure it for

1890

So. Boston, October 16th.
My dear Mrs. Burnett:
I am very happy because you wrote a beautiful story about dear, sweet and gentle little Cedric. I love all small boys and I do love Lord Fauntleroy because he was so kind to Mr. Hobbs and Dick and the poor old woman and Bridget. Some day I shall go to see Lord Fauntleroy in England. I think he will be glad to show me his very ancient castle and the beautiful flowers. We will run with deer and play with rabbits and catch the gray squirrels; and I will ride his gentle pony. I hope Cedric will take me to see his uncle and his very pretty dearest. I shall not be afraid of Dougal because he will not hurt little children. Will you please let Mr. Anagnos have the lovely story about Cedric printed in raised letters for little blind children? Then I shall read it with my fingers.
With much love,
From your little friend,
Helen A Keller.

Letter to Burnett from ten-year-old Helen Keller praising Little Lord Fauntleroy *and asking for a braille edition*

book publication; indeed, as it would be cheaper, it might even be an advantage.

With best wishes I remain
Yours sincerely
Charles Scribner

P.S.

It has occurred to me that perhaps you do not understand that the payment of the royalties (a statement of which was rendered last Aug.) is due on Dec. 1st. Do you want this money sent to you?

RELATED LETTERS:
Letter by Burnett to CS II, 14 April 1895.

Burnett's growing "international" life included extended sojourns in England and on the Continent. In 1893 she again set sail for England and eventually took up residence in a London house next to the Chinese Embassy that contained long, underground passages leading out to the stable alley behind. There was an "atmosphere" about the cellars that caused her to remark to guests she had taken on an excursion downstairs, "What a place to hide the body of a man you had accidentally killed." This was the germ of her next novel, set in the days of the Tatler *and written in the style of Richard Steele (1672–1729), the English author who founded the periodical.*

Dear Mr. Scribner

What will Scribners Magazine give me for a book, a brilliant London critic tells me is the book of my life and the opening of a new career? He is a man of judgements much regarded at present and so I repose myself upon the general belief in him. The book is the Queen Anne Story (A Lady of Quality) which so developed itself that it obliged me to turn back & rewrite the beginning and allow it to be a book. My critic (a jaded man who reads books until I should imagine he would loathe them) said to me last night on hearing some bits of chapters 'Look here, it would be impossible for me to lay that thing down if I once took it up.' He tells me also that no woman has ever written anything so virile. I myself know I never have touched the borders of the world it belongs to. The lady of Quality — a certain Mistress Clorinda Wildairs — afterwards Countess of Dunstanwolde — afterwards Duchess of Osmonde — is the daughter of a roystering, debauched country baronet, of the order Macauley describes. She is a magnificent creature who rides over laws as she leaps fences. Perhaps Scribners Magazine would turn pale at

the sight of her — but to her last word she will be read and fought over & discussed. I am giving two or three people a tentative chance at her — but I confess I should like her to be published in a magazine capable of illustrating her — for she lends herself to it. She is as tall as a man and as beautiful as a goddess, & wears a tower of hair, & brocades, & fardingales [farthingales], & stands by broken sun dials and in old rose gardens — besides being strong enough to carry dead men in her beautiful arms — & break mad horses which kill everyone but herself. I have written now perhaps 80,000 words and the end is coming — but she is so powerful I could not dare to say what she will do or <u>when</u>. Does Scribners shrink shocked before such a Lady — and if not, may I ask the sordid question what does it offer.

Yours sincerely
Frances Hodgson Burnett

Scribner's Magazine editor Burlingame coincidentally was in Europe in April, met Burnett in London, and read her manuscript. Continuing on to Paris he wrote CS II (23 April 1895) his reactions. His reference to "Zangwill" is to Israel Zangwill, novelist, playwright, and friend of Burnett.

. . . The Mrs. Burnett matter has been a difficult one. Some days after I wrote you, she brought me the manuscript of "A Lady of Quality," as far as finished (about 80,000 words — it is to make she thinks about 100,000; but what with the difficulty of making her plot last for 20,000 more when she has virtually reached her denoûment, & her usual tendency on the other hand to overrun, I am quite at sea as to the real length). The arrangement was that I was to read it & talk with her about it on Friday night when she had invited us to dinner.

As far as was in my power I gave weight in my reading to every circumstance in the book's favor; & such changes had been made in the beginning as did away with any impression made by the ten or fifteen pages of MS. I had seen before. But I could only come to the conclusion: — that she had undertaken something quite out of the line of all her best powers, & had done a tawdry & artificial thing, in which the attempt at an archaic style had effectually wiped out the kind of thing generally liked in her writing, & the desire for sensation & aggressive dealing with big elemental violences had wiped out the sentiment. And I can't see that she has shown the power to put anything of equal attraction in their place. To me she is not only an artificial Guy Livingstone,

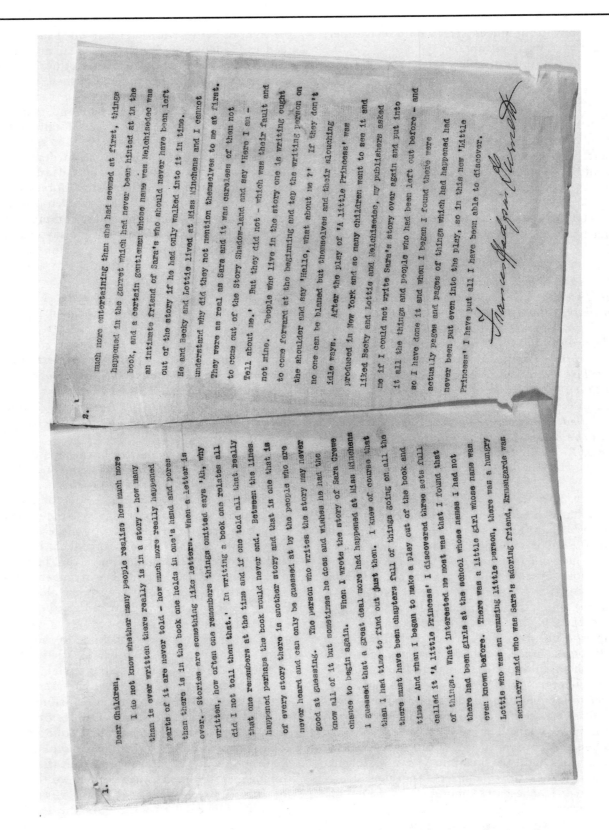

Original typescript of Burnett's foreword to A Little Princess, *her 1905 book sequel to* Sara Crewe

but a dull one. There is a scene where the heroine kills with a loaded riding-whip (commonly used in quelling her horse "Devil" which no one else may ride) her former lover, & her persecutor now that she has found a better life; & hides his body under a divan on which she sits to receive her afternoon guests. It is what would be called the strongest scene in the story perhaps, thus far. I honestly tried to put myself in the place of a reader of sensation, pure & simple; I was sure it would have left him cold. I don't mean that it was contemptible; but it was artificial, imitative, — dull, in short. It seems to me inevitable that people will feel this.

All this is perhaps rather more than I meant to say. I know what experience there is on the side of these widely-read people's instinctively knowing an audience better than we do, & am willing to discount it & prepare for any surprises. There is a sense of course in which this kind of criticism may be all superfluous. Only most of the surprises are not after all downright dull; & what has led me to say so much is that I think this book is.

Naturally I had a hard time of it at the dinner. I knew & felt the importance of our getting the book anyhow, though the Magazine matter had been ruled out, irrespective of merit, by her insistance on serial publication within a year or so, so that she can get out the volume & "make a play of it," which she is most anxious to do. Zangwill, who was at the dinner, & very likely other people, had been telling her "George Eliot couldn't touch it" &c. & c. — I spare you my dif-

ficulties. I can be quite still at times, & I don't think I said anything to pain her; but of course I don't flatter myself that I succeeded in convealing from a shrewd woman that my personal enthusiasm was not at that pitch. I confined myself, in a long talk with her later, to discussion of details in the story, & to showing her the importance of our having the book & arranging for it at once. She strongly insisted on keeping book & serial rights undivided till she heard from New York; apparently her other letter, written simultaneously with that to you, had put the matter in that form. I was going to Paris — she would let me know when I came back. The thing was left in that form; I believing her wise enough to accept no other form, at least, without our knowledge; which against a possible book & serial offer we could hardly pull. . . .

Ultimately, the idea of a magazine serialization was dropped: Burnett accepted Scribners' offer of an advance of $5,000 on 20 percent royalty for the book publication. Published the next spring on 7 March, the novel became the number two best-seller of 1896.

CS II DIARY ENTRY:
Monday 25 January 1897

Went to see "First Gentleman of Europe" with tickets from Mrs. Burnett the author

The opening of the play was at the Lyceum Theater in New York.

Hjalmar Hjorth Boyesen (1848–1895)

Hjalmar Hjorth Boyesen (from Clarence A. Glasrud, Hjalmar Hjorth Boyesen, *Northfield, Minnesota: Norwegian-American Historical Association, 1963)*

Norwegian-born Boyesen immigrated to the United States in 1869, and later became a professor of German at Cornell and Columbia. He was a lifelong friend of William Dean Howells, who serialized his first novel in the *Atlantic,* and George Washington Cable, whose first book Boyesen persuaded Scribners to publish. A versatile author, Boyesen wrote criticism, poetry, boys' fiction, historical accounts, and novels but is probably best remembered for promoting, via his Scribner publications, Norse literature and culture.

Scribner Books by Boyesen

1879	*Goëthe and Schiller: Their Lives and Works*
	Falconberg
1880	*Gunnar: A Tale of Norse Life*
1881	*Ilka on the Hill-Top and Other Stories*
	Tales from Two Hemispheres
	Queen Titania
1882	*Idyls of Norway and Other Poems*
1887	*The Modern Vikings: Stories of Life and Sport in the Norseland*
1890	*Against Heavy Odds: A Tale of Norse Heroism,* illustrated by W. L. Taylor
1892	*Essays on German Literature*
	Boyhood in Norway: Stories of Boy-Life in the Land of the Midnight Sun
1893	*Social Strugglers: A Novel*
1894	*Norseland Tales*
1895	*Essays on Scandinavian Literature*

Two of Boyesen's Scandinavian works, poems (1882) and stories (1887)

LETTER:

Letter by CS II to Hjalmar Hjorth Boyesen, 6 February 1879, about the death of J. Blair Scribner and the publication of Boyesen's first Scribner book, *Goëthe and Schiller.*

Boyesen had gone to Europe to make contacts with the literary men of Germany, Italy, and France. Scribner's reference to "Mr. Taylor" is to Bayard Taylor, the U.S. minister to Germany and the author of a well-received translation of Goethe's Faust. Taylor had died in Berlin on 19 December.

Dear Sir:

Before this letter arrives the sad news of my brother's death will doubtless have reached you. I need not write how great a loss his family and friends have sustained. The blow was so sudden, so entirely unthought of, that we cannot yet realize that he has been taken away. He had been confined to the house only four days, with pneumonia, and at no time until a few hours before his death did we consider him dangerously ill.

I had hoped to write you sooner, but my time has been so overcrowded with the many duties so suddenly fallen to my care that it has been impossible to do so. Our business has of course met with a great loss in my brother's death and one which cannot be altogether replaced, yet I can assure you that no interruption or important change will be necessary and that your interests will remain undisturbed.

We published today your "Goethe and Schiller." We take pleasure in forwarding you at once the three copies as requested and have also sent the various other copies as directed. The appearance of the volume pleases us all very much here & I trust it will prove satisfactory to you. You will see that the idea of an index was given up, though I cannot but think it would have been an improvement. Perhaps you will think it well to prepare one for the second edition. Your corrections, made in view of Mr. Taylor's death, reached us

Original reader's report by Scribner editor W. C. Brownell on Boyesen's novel Social Strugglers, *part of which had already appeared in* Cosmopolitan. *Brownell chose alternative number three when writing to Boyesen directly; Boyesen wrote back (8 February 1893): "I accept your suggestion & will condense the second half of* Social Strugglers. *I had no idea the book was so long as you say. Permit me to thank you, too, for your felicitation, though I was not aware that I was hovering 'on the borderland of romance.' I was flattering myself that I was dealing with very real American people in a very real American milieu. However, if they have also the charm of romance to a romanticist like yourself, I am only the more pleased." The resulting book is considered one of his best novels.*

safely through Mr. Johnson. Those in the preface, as also the date annexed to the poem, have been attended to, but unfortunately the body of the book had been printed when they arrived, so that it was too late to make the other changes for this edition. The plates however have been corrected.

It is needless to write that we shall use every endeavor to push the sale of the book which we hope will not disappoint us. We will freely advertise and send out a good number of editor's copies. This we would do, even if we only considered our own interests, as the cost of the book has been very great and we shall have to look to a large sale. I will send you a lot of notices when enough have accumulated.

In one of my brother's letters to you there is an allusion to a box of glass-ware sent to his care. I can find as yet no trace of the receipt of the invoice but hope soon to come across it. I will of course use every effort to do so & will take good care of the box when found.

Permit me to congratulate you on the honor of having your book translated into the German.

Yours very truly
Charles Scribner

LETTER:
Letter by Boyesen to CS II, 31 March 1891.

My dear Mr. Scribner,

This idea occurs to me & I offer it to you for what it may be worth. Do you not think that a series of histories of literature, of about 100,000 words each (taking up the literature of every important country) would be a profitable enterprise for a publishing house? The Story of the Nations Series has been a great success, & I believe a similar series dealing with the literatures of the nations, i.e., their intellectual & spiritual life rather than their internal achievements would be no less successful. Que dites vous?

Yours faithfully
H. H. Boyesen

P.S. I have submitted this proposition to no one but yourself. H.H.B.

CS II responded "Oui," and Boyesen was able to publish with Scribners his books of essays on German and Scandinavian literature that made his critical reputation.

George Washington Cable (1844–1925)

George Washington Cable

Cable was born in New Orleans, served with Confederate calvary in the Civil War, and worked as a clerk in a cotton factors firm. His first writing was a weekly column for the New Orleans *Picayune* under the heading "Drop Shot," which was so popular that it became a daily feature. Later he began to explore old city records and to fictionalize narratives gleaned from them. In 1872 Edward King, who had been sent by *Scribner's Monthly* on a tour of Southern States for a writing assignment, met Cable, was impressed with his unpublished stories, and induced him to send them to the magazine. Cable was a find; once again, the magazine introduced the publishing firm to new talent. His early stories — " 'Sieur George," "Jean-ah-Poquelin," and "Belles Demoiselles Plantation" — attracted national praise. Like Bret Harte's fiction, Cable's pioneered a new "region" and brought him much critical acclaim. In 1884–1885 he toured with Mark Twain giving readings of his own work. He settled in Northampton, Massachusetts, after 1885, where, in addition to fiction, he wrote books about the South that openly examined issues like slavery and racial discrimination.

Scribner Books by Cable

1879	*Old Creole Days*
1880	*The Grandissimes: A Story of Creole Life*
1881	*Madame Delphine*
1884	*The Creoles of Louisiana*
1885	*The Silent South, Together With the Freedman's Case in Equity and the Convict Lease System*
1887	*Dr. Sevier*
1888	*Bonaventure: A Prose Pastoral of Acadian Louisiana*
1889	*Strange True Stories of Louisiana*
1890	*The Negro Question*
1894	*John March, Southerner*
1899	*Strong Hearts*

The Cable Story Book: Selections for School Reading, edited by Mary E. Burt and Lucy Leffingwell Cable

1901	*The Cavalier,* illustrated by Howard Chandler Christy
1902	*Bylow Hill,* illustrated by F. C. Yohn
1908	*Kincaid's Battery,* illustrated by Alonzo Kimball
1909	*"Posson Jone'" and Père Raphaël,* illustrated by Stanley M. Arthurs
1914	*Gideon's Band: A Tale of the Mississippi,* illustrated by Yohn
	The Amateur Garden
1918	*The Flower of the Chapdelaines*
	Lovers of Louisiana (To-Day)

LETTER:

Cable's first letter to Scribners, 17 October 1871, proposing a book of his fugitive pieces in *The Picayune,* a New Orleans newspaper.

Dear Sirs:

I have a small manuscript ready for publication and desire to arrange for its early issue. It will be about 120 pages 16 mo, mostly prose, but with probably 40 pages of occasional verse. The work takes the form of a story, with scenes laid in and about New Orleans, involving descriptions of scenes & seasons especially characteristic of the places, and portraying three or four personal characters representative of classes peculiar to this community. The verses are component parts of this story, but do not comprise any portion of the narrative.

If you will undertake the publication of this work, please inform me of the cost of issuing one or two or three thousand copies, cloth bound, 16 mo, 120 pages of heavy, sized paper: also the same in flexible cloth covers. Please state what part, if any, of the expense I shall be required to advance, & your lowest terms if undertaken entirely upon my own risk & charge.

In the event of inspecting & rejecting the manuscript, would it be properly returned to the writer, if full postage is previously enclosed to you? Please address G. W. Cable care Mr. A. M. Holbrook, Ed. "Picayune," N. Orleans. I have been an associate editor on the journal mentioned and have Mr. Holbrook's permission to refer you to him for recommendation.

Very Respectfully yours,
G. W. Cable

The proposal was rejected. In 1873, however, his short stories began to find favor in Scribner's Monthly. *Ultimately, they were collected into his first book,* Old Creole Days, *published by Scribners in 1879.*

LETTER:

Letter by Hjalmar Hjorth Boyesen, 8 January 1878, to Cable, with the letterhead of "Editorial Rooms of Scribner's Monthly." (Cable Collection, Tulane University)

An admirer of Cable's magazine stories in Scribner's Monthly, *Boyesen had offered the little-known writer his help to get his book published — even guaranteeing Scribners against loss if they would publish it. Boyesen was assistant professor of European languages at Cornell and, himself, a soon-to-be Scribner author. The two men became good friends.*

My dear Mr. Cable,

Although you never answered my last letter, you have constantly been in my mind. I had the pleasure to-day to induce Mr. Scribner to undertake the publication of your short stories in book form which I understand from Gilder he refused to do last year. I had two interviews with him on the subject & finally succeeded in convincing him that you were a great man.

I think I can sell at least a hundred copies among my students & with the number you have agreed to dispose of in the South, the publishers will be more than safe. I shall rejoice with all my heart to see these delightful stories as a book. It is the first genuinely artistic contribution to our literature which the South has given us & may it be the

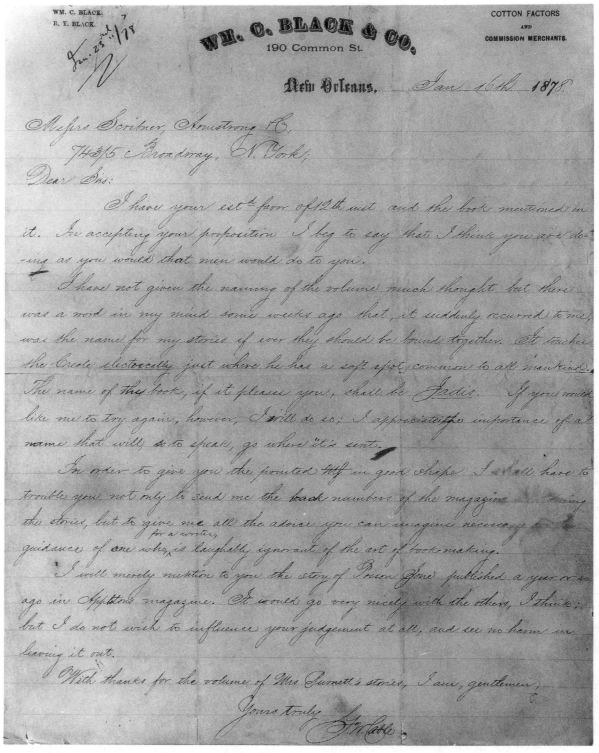

Cable's letter accepting Scribners' offer to publish his first book (Old Creole Days), bearing the letterhead of the New Orleans company where he worked as a bookkeeper. His tentative title for the work, "Jadis," was the first of many stabs, by Cable and others, at finding the right one for his volume of stories.

fore-runner of much more to come. Do let me hear from you soon. I return to Ithaca this week.

Ever cordially yours
Hjalmar H. Boyesen

LETTER:
Letter by Boyesen to J. Blair Scribner, 27 January 1878, regarding Cable's unnamed, soon-to-be-published book.

Dear Mr. Scribner,

I have no doubt that "Jadis" would be a good title for Cable's book, in case it addressed itself only to the New Orleans market; but to the general public, I am afraid it will appear a little too enigmatical. If I comprehend Cable rightly, he means to express something like <u>autrefois</u>, — the times gone by, <u>the good old times</u>. How would that last clause do for a title? It would at all events appeal to a larger public.

As soon as I know approximately the date of publication & the title, I shall send out some newspaper items, calculated to make the public curious about the book & its author. By Jove, we must make this thing a success. No man ever deserved more to be successful.

Very sincerely yours
Hjalmar H. Boyesen

LETTER:
Letter by Edward L. Burlingame to Cable, 14 April 1879.

Burlingame, who had just joined the firm in March as a literary adviser, offers a solution for the title search that is more than a year old. The delay in publishing the book was caused, among other things, by the reorganization of Scribners that took place in 1878 and the death of J. Blair Scribner in January 1879. Old Creole Days *finally appeared in May.*

Dear Sir: —

Won't "Old Creole Days" satisfy you as a title for your volume? We have not of course decided upon it, but it seems to us a step nearer to what the book wants than anything else that has been thought of. — Our objection to the title "Under the Cypress and Orange" applies equally to the suggestion of "Spanish Moss," — it does not, to the reader previously unacquainted with the character of your stories, convey enough idea of them.

Very truly yours
Charles Scribner's Sons

First edition of Cable's first book (1879) and one of the most influential collections of local-color fiction in American literature

LETTER:
Letter by Boyesen to Cable, 26 August 1879, from Cornell. (Cable Collection, Tulane University)

Boyesen became a one-man rooting section for Scribners after his own novel, Falconberg, *was published by the firm in April. "Gilder" is Richard Watson Gilder, the business manager of* Scribner's Monthly *who had persuaded its editor, J. G. Holland, to accept Cable's first story in 1873 and who, since, has also become his good friend.*

My dear Cable,

The terms Scribner's Sons offer you are very good. The usual terms offered to authors who have not already a name are ten per cent <u>after the first thousand</u>; &, as I can see from

Some of Cable's other title suggestions

Several of the Cable works published by Scribners, including an 1897 limited edition of his first book

Chas. Scribner's letter, he proposes ten percent from the start. This is the contract I have at present, but Osgood invariably excluded the first thousand from copyright. The Scribner's are in my opinion the best & fairest firm in the U.S. & their semi-annual statements are absolutely reliable. You know an author has no way of controlling his publisher & if he falls into the hands of sharpers (of which there are several in the publishing business) he is completely at their mercy. It is therefore of the utmost importance to select a reliable firm (or to be selected by one) at the outset, whereby a thousand inconveniences will be spared one. I can assure you that the Scribner's are such a firm.

I rejoice to hear that your first installment is actually in type & I shall look for it with breathless interest (I do not exaggerate). I am laboring with the plot of a new novel which will probably occupy me for a year or more. I have not written

anything yet except notes & scraps; but it must be good, or I shall not write it at all — better than "Falconberg," which I conclude from your silence on the subject you did not like. I know its weaknesses too, but it had also a certain strength. By the way, how did the Univ. of Rome impress you? I expect to finish the Victor Hugo article tomorrow but a year will probably elapse before it will appear.

I foresee already the success of "Old Creole Days," & the bargain I made with Blair Scribner (Gilder tells me he wrote you about it, although it was my intention that you should never know of it) proved happily superfluous. You can safely count on one or two editions more. The better the book is known, the more it will sell.

I wish you would write a little longer letters. You tantalizing little notes always leave me thirsty for more.

We are having an awful time in securing a nurse; something or other is the matter with all of them. Now, my mother-in-law (a most charming woman — not the traditional type) is staying with us, taking care of the boy, who is indeed a splendid specimen of the human species.

With kindest regards from Mrs. Boyesen & myself to you & your family
I remain
Very truly yours
Hjalmar H. Boyesen

Sidney Lanier (1842–1881)

Frontispiece from The Poems of Sidney Lanier *(New York: Charles Scribner's Sons, 1894)*

Consumptive for most of his short life, Lanier, a Southerner and Confederate veteran, kept one foot in the grave while trying to pursue the "two sublime arts" of music and poetry. He believed the laws governing music and verse were the same and attempted to embody the sound patterns of music in his lines. To support himself and his family, he lectured at Johns Hopkins and published prose. His boys' books were fairly popular; the 1917 edition of *The Boy's King Arthur* was illustrated by the well-known artist N. C. Wyeth. Though several of his poems appeared in *Scribner's Monthly,* Scribners rejected a volume of them — only to publish them posthumously.

Scribner Books by Lanier

1879	*The Boy's Froissart: Being Sir John Froissart's Chronicles of Adventure, Battle and Custom in England, France, Spain, etc.,* edited for boys with an introduction by Lanier, illustrated by Alfred Kappes
1880	*The Science of English Verse*
	The Boy's King Arthur: Being Sir Thomas Malory's History of King Arthur and His Knights of the Round Table, edited for boys with an introduction by Lanier, illustrated by Kappes
1881	*The Boy's Mabinogion: Being the Earliest Welsh Tales of King Arthur in the Famous Red Book of Hergest,* edited for boys with an introduction by Lanier, illustrated by Alfred Fredericks
1882	*The Boy's Percy: Being Old Ballads of War, Adventure and Love from Bishop Thomas Percy's Reliques of Ancient English Poetry, Together with an Appen-*

dix Containing Two Ballads from the Original Percy Folio MS., edited for boys with an introduction by Lanier, illustrated by E. B. Bensell

1883   *The English Novel and the Principle of Its Development*

1884   *Poems of Sidney Lanier,* edited by his wife

1891   *Poems of Sidney Lanier* (new edition), edited by his wife

1895   *Select Poems of Sidney Lanier,* edited with an introduction, notes, and bibliography by Morgan Callaway

1897   *The English Novel: A Study in the Development of Personality* (revised edition)

1898   *Music and Poetry: Essays upon Some Aspects and Inter-Relations of the Two Arts*

1899   *Retrospects and Prospects: Descriptive and Historical Essays*

      Letters of Sidney Lanier: Selections from His Correspondence, 1866–1881

      Bob: The Story of Our Mocking-Bird, illustrated from photographs by A. R. Dugmore

1904   *The Lanier Book: Selections in Prose and Verse from the Writings of Sidney Lanier,* edited by Mary E. Burt

1907   *Hymns of the Marshes,* illustrated by Henry Troth

1908   *Poem Outlines,* edited by Henry W. Lanier

1916   *Poems of Sidney Lanier* (new edition), edited by his wife

      Selections from Sidney Lanier, Prose and Verse, with an introduction and notes by Henry W. Lanier

1947   *Selected Poems,* with a preface by Stark Young

LETTER:

First letter by Lanier to Charles Scribner's Sons, 1 September 1878, offering them an edition of Froissart's *Chronicles* which he has edited for boys.

This was the beginning of a series of illustrated books published by Scribners which Lanier, drawing upon classics from the Middle Ages, edited for boys.

Dear Sirs:

I will have soon completed an edition of Froissart's Chronicles of the Middle Ages designed for boys, which I should be glad if you might feel inclined to undertake.

I find that after sifting out such portions of these Chronicles as no boy ought to read, and such others as no boy <u>will</u> read on account of their uninteresting nature, a connected story is left which — as I have found by actual experiment — is in the highest degree fascinating to boys, while at the same time it combines so much solid instruction as to the history of the time treated with so many lively pictures of contemporary manners and customs that there seems fair reason to believe it would constitute a standard boy's book, with permanent sale.

The work will make an octavo of about four hundred pp., and will be called "The Boy's Froissart." It will be prefaced with an Introduction by myself, historical and explanatory, in which the attention of the young reader will be specially called to those persistent remains of Chivalry, and of other features of 14th century civilization, which survive in the constitutions of modern Society.

I could furnish the matter in three weeks from this date, and would be glad if you might see your way clear to print in time for a Christmas book.

Asking a reply at your earliest convenience, I am

Very truly yours,
Sidney Lanier

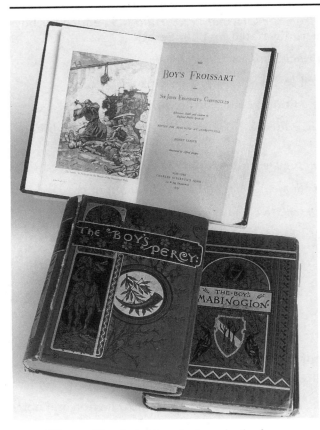

Three of Lanier's historical works for boys

LETTER:

Letter by Lanier to CS II, 22 May 1879, offering him a book of poems.

Scribners did not see any profit in it and did not publish any of his poems till several years after his death — in successive editions edited by his wife.

Dear Mr. Scribner:

I should have an uncomfortable sense of monotony, in sending you another book, but this time it is a volume of my poems and offers some contrast to those which have been offered you before.

I forwarded today by express three envelopes, two containing a collection of my poems written since 1876 — about eighty-four pp. of copy and ms. — and one containing seven pp. of "Subjects for Illustration."

The ms. will make a convenient volume of about one hundred pp., besides the illustrations which I sincerely wish might be copious. My idea would be to print it in smaller type than customary, for the reason that poetry of this sort never

looks wells in large letters: it always stares: and should therefore be in the middle of a page with a wide margin. At least this is an impression so strong with me as to make it seem more than a mere fancy. I ask your attention to the illustrations for the last poem in the book — The Story of Christmas Eve — which might be made extremely taking.

All but two of these poems have appeared in one or other of the Magazines; and I suppose it may be safely said that, as poems, they have quite passed into the region of success. As a commercial venture, I can say nothing to enlighten you, save that I feel sure of personal friends enough to take up an edition of a thousand copies.

Please make me a cash offer for the book, if you see any profit in it. I am absolutely obliged to raise ready money.

Thanks for your check, $200.00. Keep the Malory book [*The Boy's King Arthur*] as long as you like.

Sincerely yours,
Sidney Lanier

LETTER:

Letter by Lanier to CS II, 15 November 1879, written from Baltimore where he was lecturing on English verse at Johns Hopkins University.

Lanier wrote reactions to his first book and suggestions for its promotion, most of which Scribners followed.

My dear Mr. Scribner:

The books came day before yesterday, but I have just found time (I have nine lectures a week from now till December) to get a look at them. We all vote them charming, both outside and in; and my nine-year-old has scarcely found time for his meals since they arrived.

You have certainly made a very attractive volume; and, as the book is a classic, it ought to prove a valuable piece of property.

As to advertisement: I suspect you might find it profitable to announce the book in the Telegraph & Messenger, published at Macon, Georgia — my old home; in the principal paper of Montgomery, Alabama, where I have also lived; in The News, of Savannah; the Chronicle and Sentinel, of Augusta; and The Constitution, of Atlanta. Perhaps, also, an advertisement in The Sun, of Baltimore, and The Evening Bulletin, of Philadelphia, would be well.

Lanier's suggestions for a companion work to his boys' books to be called The Boy's Percy, *with his ideas for the title page*

I will avail myself of your kind offer so far as to ask for <u>three</u> more copies, in the <u>red</u> binding, for my own use.

Besides this: there are a dozen or so people connected in one way or another with the press about the country who would be glad, from friendly motives, to speak of the book in their publications, and who would like a copy from me personally, with my name &c on the fly-leaf; and so, if you think it worth while, you may send a dozen copies, in the red and green bindings, to me for this use. I will forward them to their respective destinations.

I am glad to say, in answer to your kind inquiry, that my health is greatly improved, and that I am very hard at work.

I feel the greatest interest in the Froissart book, and shall be glad to know of its assured success at the earliest moment.

> Sincerely yours,
> Sidney Lanier

LETTER:

Letter by Lanier to CS II, 21 December 1879, regarding his *The Science of English Verse,* which Scribners published the next May in a "popular treatise" form.

My dear Mr. Scribner:

In the course of next week I will send you the <u>ms</u>. of the Science of English Verse complete, for examination, as you desire. I note what you say as to its more probable success if cast into the form of a popular treatise than in that of a text-book; and am so distrustful of my inexperience in such matters, as against your larger outlook, that I hardly dare differ with you in opinion, though I am free to confess that I should think the text-book more likely to command a permanent sale.

It occurs to me, however, that upon reading the <u>ms</u>. you may think — as I do, upon examining it with this special view — that a few slight changes, such as the omission of the section-numbers and a recasting of the opening chapter to a more popular form, might adapt the book to <u>both</u> purposes. At any rate, I shall be very glad to have the opinion of some other reader than myself about the book as it stands: for I have no friend competent to pronounce upon it whom I would be willing to tax so heavily.

Pray make your report as soon as you can: for in the event you should think it convertible into a popular treatise — and should hold to that idea — I would be glad to see it published at the earliest moment.

> Sincerely yours,
> Sidney Lanier

Brander Matthews (1852–1929)

Brander Matthews

Matthews's first two articles in *Scribner's Monthly,* "A Company of Actors" (October 1878) and "Actors and Actresses of New York" (April 1879), began a relationship with the House that would last almost fifty years — and they also identified what would be his lifelong interests: drama and the stage. Matthews went on to become the major literary critic of his generation and the prime American authority on American, French, and British drama. Believing plays were written mainly to be performed, he sought to show how audiences of different times and places demanded different things; hence, plays were not necessarily superior or inferior to what had gone before. His primary goal was to educate the American public about drama and its context. Because of his expertise and reputation, Columbia University created for him the first professorship of dramatic literature in an American university, which he held from 1900 till 1924.

Scribner Books by Matthews

1880	*The Theatres of Paris*
1881	*French Dramatists of the 19th Century* (revised and enlarged, 1891; revised and englarged, 1901)
1882	*Poems of American Patriotism,* edited by Matthews (revised and enlarged, illustrated by N. C. Wyeth, 1922)
1884	*In Partnership: Studies in Story-Telling,* co-authored by H. C. Bunner
1885	*The Last Meeting: A Story*
1886	*A Secret of the Sea*
1901	*The Historical Novel, and Other Essays*
	Parts of Speech: Essays in English
1902	*Pen and Ink: Papers on Subjects of More or Less Importance* (revised and enlarged edition)
	Aspects of Fiction and Other Ventures in Criticism (enlarged edition)
1903	*The Development of the Drama*
1907	*Inquiries and Opinions*

1909	*The American of the Future, and Other Essays*
1910	*Molière, His Life and His Works*
1912	*Gateways to Literature, and Other Essays*
1913	*Shakspere as a Playwright*
1914	*On Acting*
1916	*A Book About the Theater*
1917	*These Many Years: Recollections of a New Yorker*
1919	*The Principles of Playmaking, and Other Discussions of the Drama*
1921	*Essays on English*
	Vignettes of Manhattan: Outlines in Local Color, with an introduction by W. C. Brownell, illustrated by W. T. Smedley
1922	*The Tocsin of Revolt, and Other Essays*
1923	*Playwrights on Playmaking, and Other Studies of the Stage*
1926	*Rip Van Winkle Goes to the Play, and Other Essays on Plays and Players*

RELATED LETTERS:
Letter by Matthews to CS II, 13 February 1889; letter by CS II to Matthews in response, 14 February 1889; letter by Matthews to CS II in response, 15 February 1889.

By 1889 Matthews had already published six books with Scribners. However, irritated by the fact that Scribners would not publish his Pen and Ink *book, which the British publisher Longmans, Green had brought out in 1888, Matthews took the poor royalty statement he received from Scribners in February 1889 as the "last straw": he would break with the House. The following series of letters document that break. From 1889 to 1901, Matthews published several more books with Longmans, Green and more than a dozen with Harper, his new American publisher.*

Dear Mr. Scribner:

I do not understand why you should think that I am "deeply offended."

I hold that the relation between author and publisher is not advantageous to either if the latter does not believe in the former and in his future; and that you do not believe in me thus, is shown by your refusal to publish "Pen and Ink" even at my expense. This being the case, it does not seem to me to be either to my advantage or to yours, that you should continue to publish my books. And this is why I should like to terminate our con-

tracts and to buy from you the plates of the "French Dramatists," the "Last Meeting" and "A Secret of the Sea."

Will you reconsider your intention not to part with the plates? There seems to be an incompatibility of temper between us which affords good ground for a divorce! — you remember Henry Hall's assertion that an author should select his publisher with the same care that he chose his wife?

Yours Truly
Brander Matthews

Dear Mr. Matthews:

I supposed you were deeply offended because of your wish to cancel our contracts. I should be very glad to hear that I am mistaken.

Our decision upon the essays was not intended to carry any such impression as you appear to have received. Nothing was further from my mind. We thought no less of your work than before and the number of books we have brought out is evidence of our appreciation of it.

We are desirous of increasing the popularity of your work and feared the publication of the essays would not tend to this result. It would not be unfair to state that our appreciation of what we had was the principal reason why we did not wish to add a book which we feared would not succeed.

It is quite probable that we were mistaken in our estimate of the book and I have no doubt I was unfortunate in the manner of my declination but this does not change the fact that we meant to convey no such impression as you received.

I hope therefore that you will abandon the inference which you have drawn. It would certainly be very unpleasant to insist upon retaining your books against your wish and yet we do not want to part with them. Please do not force us to such an alternative.

Yours sincerely
Charles Scribner

Dear Mr. Scribner:

I suggested a closing of our contracts, not because I was deeply offended, but because I did not believe that it would be advantageous to either of us for you to continue to publish my books — under the present circumstances. And in spite of the kindly tone of your letter of yesterday, I am of the same opinion still.

As a young writer of great ambitions (and perhaps of as great conceit — the badge of all our tribe) it seems to me best that an author's books should not be in the hands of a publisher who has not faith in that author — the faith that moves mountains. In the past you have lacked this confidence in me; and I doubt if this misunderstanding in regard to 'Pen & Ink' would make it any easier for us to work together in the future.

If you will agree to terminate our contracts, I shall be glad; and I believe that it will be best for both. I have now no desire to issue new editions of any of my books; but I should prefer to own my plates myself and to be ready for contingencies.

Yours Truly
Brander Matthews

LETTER:
Letter by Matthews to CS II, 16 March 1903.

For whatever reason, Matthews was happy to re-join the Scribner stable of authors in 1901 — probably, he learned that Harper could not make his books best-sellers either. And he had never really "broken" with Scribners, for he had been a contributor of articles and "Point of View" essays to Scribner's Magazine during the intervening years. There were new financial conditions, however, in the reestablished relationship: if he paid for the costs of his books' print-

First edition of Matthews's first Scribner book (1880)

ing plates, Scribners would give him a higher royalty.

Dear Scribner:

I have just sent the house a check for the plates of the "Development of the Drama"; and I expect to supply copy for the front matter in two or three weeks. The book will be ready long before the date of publication, next October.

And before it comes out I want to ask two questions. Could you afford to give me 25% on this new book, which is a serious work and not likely to sell largely? And could you not ask more than $1^{25} net for it? — say $1^{50} net.

I think I told you once, a year or two ago, that I was a little disappointed when the price of my series of criticisms and essays was fixed at $1^{25} net. I had been expecting to get my 20% on the long price of $1^{50}. Of course, I recognize that you probably sold a few more copies at $1^{25} net than you would have sold at $1^{50}.

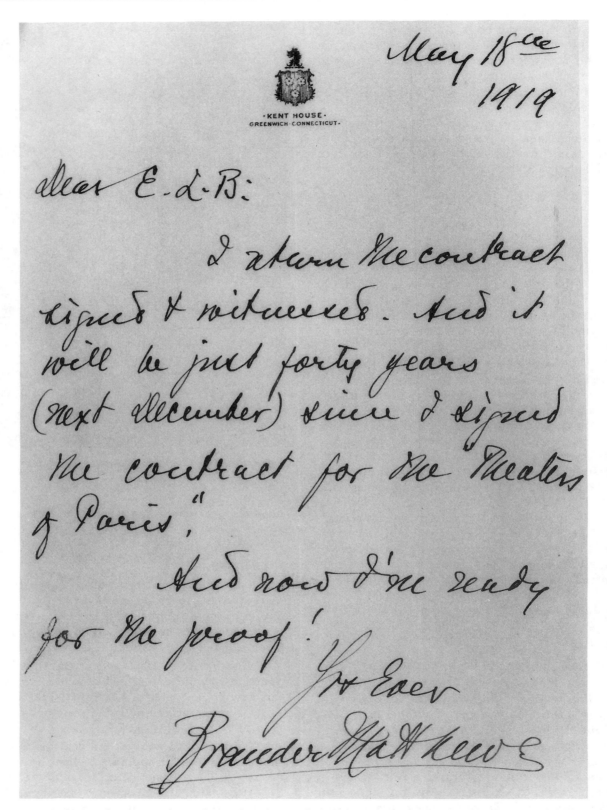

Letter by Matthews to Scribner editor Edward L. Burlingame, returning the contract for The Principles of Playmaking, and Other Discussions of the Drama

You know the conditions of the market so much better than I do, that I do not urge either of these things. But I thought that I might submit then for your consideration.

I think I have already written to you to tell you that it has been a great pleasure to me to have your imprint again on my books.

Yours very truly
Brander Matthews

RELATED LETTERS:
Letter by Matthews to CS II, 18 November 1906; letter by CS II to Matthews in response, 22 November 1906.

From the tenor of these letters, written when both men were ("older, wiser") in their fifties, one would never have guessed of the friends' earlier history. The name references here are to W. C. Brownell, Scribner book editor, and Edward L. Burlingame, editor of Scribner's Magazine.

Dear Scribner:

On Friday I called on you — too late. So I left the MS with Brownell. It is ready for the printer — altho it cannot appear till Burlingame has found room for two of the articles. I suppose it had better go over to next October.

I gave the MS the title of the first article. But I'm hoping to hit on a better name for it. How does this strike you 'Inquiries & Opinions'?

It is nearly twenty-seven years now since I brought you my first book — and that's just half of my years!

Yours Ever
Brander Matthews

My dear Matthews:

Mr. Brownell has handed me the manuscript but I have not yet had an opportunity to look it over. As it cannot be published until the two articles have appeared there is of course no haste necessary but we can make the plates whenever you like. "Inquiries and Opinions" seems to me a good title for such a volume.

It is very pleasant to have you bring me a new volume after so many years of trial. I have myself been making some calculations which rather startle me. It is 31 years since I entered the business and as the business is 60 years old I have been here more than half its life — and 5 years longer than my father was in business, although I have always looked upon him as having had a full business life. You see how dangerous it is to give another man a chance to reminisce.

Yours sincerely
Charles Scribner

LETTER:
Letter by Matthews to Edward L. Burlingame, 26 February 1919.

The short-story book Matthews refers to in this letter was an idea the House had for a volume Matthews would do for its Modern Student's Library: a work on the short story in America. It did not materialize.

Dear E.L.B.:

Now that the war is over might it not be possible to arrange for a London edition of 'These Many Years'?

I've just gone through your catalog & I find that you publish for 13 living members of the American Academy of Arts & Letters: — Blashfield, Brownell, Butler, Cable, Cox, Grant, Dodge, Matthews, Page, Sloane, Van Dyke, Wendell, Woodberry. This is a much longer list than any other publishing house can show.

Yours ever
Brander Matthews

Whenever C.S. decides finally about that Scribner Short-story book, please let me know, as — if I can do it — I'd like to do it before May 1st.

Howard Pyle (1853–1911)

Howard Pyle

Pyle was a one-man movement that greatly raised the standards of illustration in this country. His influence was felt in different ways: as an art teacher at the Drexel Insitute in Philadelphia and in his Brandywine School at Chadds Ford, Pennsylvania, he trained such illustrators as Maxfield Parrish, Violet Oakley, N. C. Wyeth, and Jessie Willcox Smith; as an author, he drew upon legends from the Middle Ages and created classics of children's literature; as an illustrator, he integrated design and mood to create a total book experience. While he is best known for his Scribner books on Robin Hood and the Arthurian legends, and perhaps for his illustrations for Robert Louis Stevenson's pirate stories, all of which remain in print, Pyle's contribution to the development of American illustration is much greater and probably not as well recognized.

Scribner Books by Pyle

1883	*The Merry Adventures of Robin Hood of Great Renown, in Nottinghamshire* (abridged edition, 1902)
1885	*Within the Capes*
1888	*Otto of the Silver Hand*
1895	*The Garden Behind the Moon: A Real Story of the Moon Angel*
1903	*The Story of King Arthur and His Knights*
1905	*The Story of the Champions of the Round Table*
1907	*The Story of Sir Launcelot and His Champions*
1910	*The Story of the Grail and the Passing of Arthur*

Other Scribner Books Illustrated by Pyle
(some contain illustrations by others as well)

1881	*Phaeton Rogers* by Rossiter Johnson
1882	*The Story of Siegfried* by James Baldwin

	The Chronicle of the Drum by William Makepeace Thackeray
1887	*The Story of the Golden Age* by Baldwin
1889	*Recollections of a Minister to France* by E. B. Washburne
1890	*In the Valley* by Harold Frederic
1892	*American Illustrators* by F. Hopkinson Smith
1894	*The Art of the American Wood Engraver* by Philip Gilbert Hamerton
1895	*History of the United States* by E. Benjamin Andrews
	Kidnapped by Robert Louis Stevenson
	The Merry Men and Other Tales and Fables and *The Strange Case of Dr. Jekyll and Mr. Hyde* by Stevenson
	David Balfour by Stevenson
1896	*In Ole Virginia* by Thomas Nelson Page
	The History of the Last Quarter-Century by E. Benjamin Andrews
1897	*The First Christmas Tree* by Henry van Dyke
1898	*The Story of the Revolution* by Henry Cabot Lodge
	Odysseus, the Hero of Ithaca by Mary E. Burt
	Pictures from Scribner's, portfolio of plates selected from *Scribner's Magazine*, containing some plates by Pyle
1902	*The Blue Flower* by van Dyke
1904	*A History of the United States* by Wilbur F. Gordy
1915	*Stories of Later American History* by Gordy

RELATED LETTERS:
Letter by Pyle to CS II, 10 October 1883.

Two weeks before his first book — Robin Hood — is published Pyle wants an advance to help him cover costs associated with a studio he is building in Wilmington, Delaware.

Dear Sir:

Having been lately engaged in building a studio for myself, finding the expenses amounting to somewhat more than I had calculated upon, and not wishing to burden a building like it with a mortgage for such a short time and for such a small amount as I need; I write to inquire whether it will be possible to negotiate a small advance upon the sale of <u>Robin Hood</u> with your <u>House</u>. Five hundred dollars will amply fill all my requirements, and, I presume, my interest from the sale of the work will much more than cover that amount.

I propose that when the first payment of ten per cent of the retail sale of the work matures [his royalty], that the five hundred dollars, with six per cent interest from the time of the loan to that of payment, shall be deducted from it.

I would be very greatly obliged to you if you would favorably consider this matter, as it will save me the annoyance of negotiating and receiving a note of such a small amount.

I am —
Yours respectfully
Howard Pyle

CS II is happy to oblige him if he can wait several weeks. Pyle cannot. In his next response, dated 20 October 1883, CS II becomes an accommodating publisher.

Dear Sir:

Your letter of the 15th duly rec'd.

{Dic.}   WILMINGTON, DEL ————————— December 5th., 18 94.

Messrs Charles Scribners Sons,

New York.

Gentlemen:

I send you herewith the MS. of my story THE GARDEN BEHIND THE MOON.

I send it with a curious feeling of reluctance, for, in correcting

and re-reading it, I have grown very fond of it.

It may be that it will not have the value in your eyes that I

hope but, nevertheless, it embodies some of my ripest thought. I am

glad that you feel inclined to read and consider it, and am

Very truly yours

Howard Pyle

Letter by Pyle to Scribners accompanying his submission of the manuscript for The Garden Behind the
Moon, *which he wrote to help relieve his grief at the unexpected death of his seven-year-old son. The book
is a kind of fairy tale, allegorically dealing with death and the afterlife. Pyle's moon garden is a wonderland
where children play. "In it," the narrator says, "was the little boy whom I loved best of all. He did
not see me, but I saw him. . . . I was glad to see him, for he had gone out along the moon-path,
and he had not come back again."*

It _is_ against our rules to make advance payment of royalty in the way suggested by you but rather than disappoint you we break the rules and send the enclosed note.

The first orders for "Robin Hood" are quite satisfactory and we have renewed confidence in its success.

Yours very truly
Charles Scribner's Sons

P.S. We have sent editorial copies and "ads" to Wilmington papers.

CS II's confidence was repaid: Robin Hood _remained Pyle's best-selling book thirty years later. Most critics consider the book to be the best exemplar of Pyle's ability as a storyteller and artist. It remains an American classic of children's literature._

LETTER:

Letter by Pyle to Edward L. Burlingame, editor of _Scribner's Magazine,_ 1 July 1898, with the heading "Suggestion for an Article upon my Summer School" typed at top.

Pyle's summer classes at Chadds Ford, Pennsylvania, near where the Battle of Brandywine took place in the Revolutionary War, were a great success. His students Maxfield Parrish and N. C. Wyeth became prominent Scribner illustrators. Here, at length, he details the modus operandi of his Brandywine School.

Dear Mr. Burlingame:

I have received your letter of the 28th of June in reply to mine of the 24th, in which I suggested that an article might be written upon my Summer School here at Chadd's Ford.

I do not think that an article on the Summer School need in any way interfere with the more solid and substantial paper upon my Drexel Institute Class, such as I drew up for your approval.

I was moved to form this Summer Class of mine largely with the view to the former proposed article in Scribner's Monthly upon my Drexel Institute Class. I felt that my Class did not do work of sufficient merit to warrant an article upon the School as proposed to you by me. Accordingly I determined to have my students do work out of doors this summer so that there might be no retrogression in their work during the summer holidays and so that they might do sufficiently excellent work this coming winter. To this end I proposed to the Trustees of the Drexel Institute that they

Cover of Pyle's first book (1883). It attracted a great deal of attention in artistic circles, especially in England where the London Academy hailed it as "a new departure in American art."

should found a series of scholarships to be bestowed upon the best ten scholars of the Art Classes of the Institute; that all the expenses of these students should be paid for the ten weeks of the summer. This the Trustees most generously did, voting a fund of a thousand dollars to cover the modest expenses of their boarding in the country. I upon my part promised to give them their instruction free.

My thought was to teach our students the more brilliant and subtle effects of color as one sees it in out of doors nature — that irridescence of tints upon the face of nature which it is almost impossible to introduce into studio instruction.

Besides these ten students there are five others, who, having ample means to support themselves during the summer, have generously waived their right to scholarships. These also I have gathered about me, so that my Summer School comprises fifteen students in all.

My idea of an article upon this Summer Class in a general outline is about as follows: —

I would tell, or rather suggest, in as easy and fluent a manner as possible and I hope in perfectly good taste, how you have desired an article upon my Class teaching at the Drexel Institute. I would then state directly my thought of carrying forward

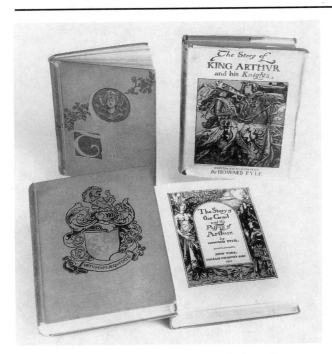

Several of Pyle's Scribner books, including three on Arthurian legends

the work by summer instruction. I would then describe the beautiful surroundings, the free and lovely life which my students live gathered here about me in the lap of Southern Pennsylvania.

I may say in this connection that the house in which I live is a large, square mansion-like place of an older generation which has been unoccupied for some time, and which is all the more natural and luxuriant because of that. Close to me I have established the girls of the Class — nearly all of them living in a quaint little building which was Lafayette's headquarters at the time of the Battle of Brandywine (Of this you have published a picture in Senator Lodge's article on the Revolution, but the house itself is shown rather than the picturesque aspect of it.) It is a beautiful little place perched on the side of a hill, overlooking the stretch of valley to the airy hills beyond, and surrounded by old stone walls with a horse-block and with great buttonwood trees at the sides and sloping fields around.

All of these might be brought into the article, and with it perhaps a picture and a description of the old stone kitchen with a huge fireplace built about 1700.

The boys are a trifle away, settled at the Washington headquarters, equally interesting if not so picturesque as the Lafayette House.

The work of the Class is done in an old mill which I have converted into a studio.

All of this together with the work of the Class during the day, an account of my lectures and instruction, and a suggestive description of the long bicycle rides which the young men and myself take through this beautiful historic country, could be gathered together and built upon around the theme of instruction which my Classs carries through the summer.

The general Class method of instruction follows: — The model is posed in the open air so as to get a brightness of effect and to show the students how the figure really appears out of doors. The students work at the model in the mornings, the afternoons given up to the study and preparation of sketches from nature to be used as possible backgrounds. Every morning I go to the mill-studio where they are working, and criticise their progress. On Friday mornings I give my direct criticisms. On Friday afternoons I go out and criticise their work from nature, and later in the afternoon give them a lecture upon compositions which they make.

The article I would have illustrated by interesting vignette pictures of the beautiful aspects of nature which surround us. I would choose one or two of the best and most dramatic drawings to be published each as a full-page, and the best composition made by the Class and worked up by the individual student making it, I would use as a frontispiece for the article. This would make, say, three full-page illustrations and twelve vignettes scattered through the article so as to amply illustrate it. The twelve vignettes might cover, say, two pages. This would make, perhaps, five pages of illustration and six or seven pages of text — in all about twelve pages. I think it would make a bright, vivacious article, and if it can be illustrated, as I hope it may, I think we shall be able to make something really charming.

Of course the final outcome of all this would be dependent upon the excellence of the work. If my Class should fail to make pictures of sufficient excellence, the whole plan would of course have to be abandoned, but I am in hopes it will be otherwise and that my Class will be able to do beautiful work.

If you do not want the article I would like much to submit it elsewhere. Having proposed the regular School article to you, I would not do anything to interfere with it, but I do not think, even if such an article as this upon my Summer School were published by McClure's or Harper's, that it would interfere with the article upon the Drexel School as proposed to you.

I am going to ask for an immediate reply to this, for, if you do not care for the article upon the Summer School, I shall, if you have no objections, propose it elsewhere at once. For the Class only lasts ten weeks, and its work must be more or less directed toward this aim if such an article be undertaken.

Accordingly, hoping I may hear from you with as little delay as possible,

I am,
Very truly yours
Howard Pyle

Burlingame felt that the first article would detract from the second and that if Pyle wanted to publish the first elsewhere and still wanted both articles, he would relinquish his option on the second. They never reached agreement, and the articles were not written.

CS II DIARY ENTRY:
Wednesday 6 August 1902

Luncheon with Howard Pyle & arranged for his King Arthur

LETTER:
Letter by Pyle to Charles Scribner's Sons, 9 September 1911, written from Florence, Italy, where he had gone with his family in 1910 to study for the first time the work of the masters.

This was his last letter to Scribners: Pyle was stricken by a severe attack of renal colic and died in Florence on November 9th.

Gentlemen —

Mrs. Pyle has this afternoon just received your check for $987.06, and I enclose herewith her acknowledgments and thanks for the same, and my own thanks and acknowledgments and thanks for the check for $91.40.

I am very pleased to see that the royalties go on increasing, and that the young people seem to care for my books as much or more than they ever did. I wish that you had all of them, for while the other publishers are entirely satisfactory, they do not sell so many as you, and I think it is better for one to have the sale of all. But that, I suppose, is not possible now.

I wrote yesterday a letter asking you concerning the check. I was rather anxious as to its coming, and feared perhaps you thought that I had returned to Wilmington. I shall be here until early next summer, and shall ask you to send the February check here to 6 Via Garibaldi, Florence. I look to return home next June, so that after that time the usual address will be Wilmington, as heretofore.

I shall transfer my check of $91.40 to Mrs. Pyle, and I will request you hereafter to include the royalties for "The Story of the Grail" to her account.

Once more thanking you on Mrs. Pyle's account and my own, I am,

Very sincerely yours,
Howard Pyle

A. B. Frost (1851–1928)

A. B. Frost

Frost is best remembered for his visual creations of Joel Chandler Harris's Uncle Remus, Brer Rabbit, Aunt Minervy Ann, and a host of animal characters. An illustrator all his life, he was essentially self-taught, though he had worked as a youth in a wood engraver's shop and the office of a lithographer, and had even studied briefly under Thomas Eakins at the Philadelphia Academy of the Fine Arts. His talent was for dramatic incident, an appreciation of character, and a fine sense of comedy. With these gifts he was probably the most popular illustrator in the country by 1900. Scribners published his first books and portfolios of his hunting drawings, and hired him frequently to illustrate the works of others, books as well as stories in *Scribner's Magazine*. He was also a friend of CS II for more than forty years; the two enjoyed playing golf together and were often guests in each other's home.

Scribner Books by Frost

1884	*Stuff & Nonsense* (enlarged edition, 1888), with jingles by Charles Frost
1892	*The Bull Calf and Other Tales* (republished, 1924)
1895–1896	*Shooting Pictures* (portfolio), with text by Charles D. Lanier
1903	*A Day's Shooting* (portfolio)

Other Scribner Books Illustrated by Frost

1882	*The Chronicle of the Drum* by William Makepeace Thackeray, illustrated by Frost and others
1885	*Rudder Grange* by Frank R. Stockton
1887	*The Story of a New York House* by H. C. Bunner
1889	*Said in Fun* by Philip H. Welch, illustrated by Frost and others
1890	*Expiation* by Octave Thanet
1892	*The Great Streets of the World* by Richard Harding Davis and others, illustrated by Frost and others

	American Illustrators by F. Hopkinson Smith, illustrated by Frost and others
1893	*Stories of the Railway,* stories from *Scribner's Magazine* by various authors, illustrated by Frost and others
	Stories of a Western Town by Thanet
1894	*Pomona's Travels* by Stockton
1896	*Jersey Street and Jersey Lane* by Bunner, illustrated by Frost and others
	That First Affair by John Ames Mitchell, illustrated by Frost and others
	In Ole Virginia by Thomas Nelson Page, illustrated by Frost and others
1897	*Athletic Sports* by various authors (compiled by Scribners), illustrated by Frost and others
1898	*Pastime Stories* by Page
	The Heart of Toil by Thanet
	Pictures from Scribner's, portfolio of plates selected from *Scribner's Magazine,* 11 of 50 plates by Frost
1899	*The Chronicles of Aunt Minervy Ann* by Joel Chandler Harris
1901	*First Across the Continent* by Noah Brooks, illustrated by Frost and others
1904	*Bred in the Bone* by Page, illustrated by Frost and others
	The Soldier in the Valley by Nelson Lloyd

LETTER:
Letter by CS II to Frost, 9 July 1885.

Frank R. Stockton's novel Rudder Grange *was the first complete Scribner book that Frost illustrated besides his own. This letter from his publisher suggests the kind of give-and-take of ideas between all involved parties — publisher, illustrator, and author — that was part of the process of book illustration. Stockton approved of all of Frost's visual interpretations of his work.*

My dear Mr. Frost

Your letter of yesterday and the drawings have been received and I hasten to write how delighted we are with the drawings; they are <u>exactly</u> what we have always had in view for the book.

We have sent them to be reproduced by process and hope to be able to send you proofs in a day or two. We have exactly followed your idea as to size in which they shall be reproduced.

Your drawings reached us just in time for I confess that we were becoming rather discouraged with our luck on this book.

The design for the cover which we hoped [unreadable section] we wanted after the modifications we had in view were made turned out unsatisfactory after all; and we have at last come round again to the conclusion that the canal rudder does not lend itself readily to poetic treatment — it does not afford sufficiently great opportunities for artistic enterprise.

But when we saw your title page our confidence in the possibility of a good cover was renewed; we think that a cover could be made after the design for the title page. You could follow the lettering exactly, take out the picture in the middle and change the top and bottom picture so as to adapt them for the stamp cutter. I think you will understand what I mean — the main thing is the lettering — we discard the idea of a novel design and whatever of that sort is introduced is simply to relieve the lettering. I would make the back of the book on the same principle. The "Rudder Grange" should of course be in gold and the lines

Frank R. Stockton, A. B. Frost & Charles Scribner's Sons.

Please receive this new idea with patience and see if you cannot like it and work it out for us quickly.

I return the title page, as you may have no copy of it; you can send it back as soon as you are through with it. You should also insert an apostrophe in "Scribner's". I also send back the first head piece. You didn't really mean to put three d's in it did you?

Have you written to Stockton? And what was his reply?

Yours very truly
Charles Scribner

CS II DIARY ENTRY:
Tuesday 22 May 1894

Poker at Frost's

Frost lived on a small farm in Convent Station, New Jersey; Scribner lived in nearby Morristown.

CS II DIARY ENTRY:
Saturday 24 October 1903

Golf with Frost in P.M.

LETTER:
Letter by Frost to CS II, December 1906.

In 1906 Frost sold his small farm in Convent Station, New Jersey, and removed his family, after a stop in London, to Paris, where he wanted his two teenage sons, Arthur and John ("Jack"), to receive artistic training. This lengthy, chatty letter, Frost's first written home to his publisher/friend Scribner, draws an interesting portrait of Paris life for the expatriate American artist at the turn of the century. Frost would meet many of the prominent artists of the period during his eight years abroad. References in this letter are to Charles Dana Gibson (1867–1944), the American (and Scribner) illustrator who created the "Gibson Girl"; Frederick William MacMonnies (1863–1937), one of the leading American sculptors of public monuments in his generation, creator of the sensation of the Chicago's World Fair in 1893, the

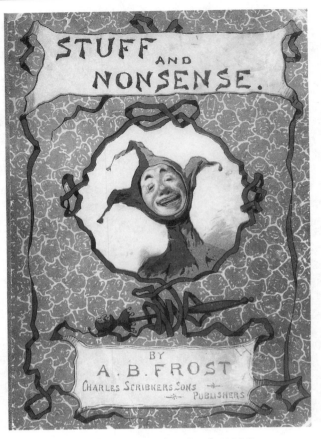

Cover of Frost's first book (1884)

tremendous "MacMonnies Fountain"; Walter McEwen (b. 1860), an American painter; Louis A. Thebaud (1859–1939), an American philanthropist; and F. Hopkinson Smith (1838–1915), American (and Scribner) illustrator and author.

Hotel Dynast, Square de La Tour Moubourg [Maubourg], Paris
Dear Scribner

Well! here we are in Paris. The Frost family, plain hayseeds from the back woods of New Jersey, living here just as naturally as if we had been used to rubbing shoulders with city people for the past 16 years instead of raising daisies and hens, and we like it. We will like it a lot more after we learn the language and can meet the French people without an interpreter. At first I, for one, didn't like it. I was never more disappointed than by my first impressions of Paris. I fairly hated the place and would have liked to have gone back to London at once. But after a week or two things began to look differently and they have gone on changing in my point of view till now I like it very much. There are lots of things I <u>don't</u> like and don't expect to like. But one can get used to things even if they are distasteful.

It is a wonderfully beautiful place and full of things to paint. The life in the streets would keep me in material for a long time, and I am very anxious to do it, too.

We found trouble in getting rooms when we got here. I went to a number of Hotels and found rooms at last in the Rue Daunou close to the Opera. We stayed there a week and then Mrs Dana Gibson told us of this house and we have been here ever since. This is a <u>very</u> comfortable place. Kept by two English women and filled with Americans. It is very clean airy and orderly and the table is excellent, and the price very moderate. We expected to take an apartment but Mrs Frost was, and <u>is,</u> too tired to undertake house keeping yet, and our united French capacity is very small. Jack is the best of the lot, but he can't go very far. I think we will stay here another month or two.

I found Dana Gibson as soon as we came here and I see him very often. He and Mrs Gibson are as nice to us as any two people could be, and Mrs Frost likes Mrs Gibson very much. They have a house at 64 Avenue du Bois du Bologne, and Dana has a studio near. He is doing <u>excellent</u> work, painting from a model every day. The head, or half length and working hard. He has made great progress since he left home and is gaining steadily. His color is very good, and what is most important, he is <u>himself</u>, just as much himself in color as he was in pen and ink.

I have met Fredk MacMonnies, went out to his country place and spent an afternoon there, with Jack. It is a lovely place and he has a very nice home, an old Monastary, with a big barn turned into a studio. Mrs MacMonnies has another studio which I didn't see. MacMonnies was in here two or three times since. I like him very much, a plain straight forward man with no airs whatever. I think I could see more of him, but he is a good way from Paris. I have met McEwen too.

Louis Thebaud was here for a while and I saw him quite often. He has gone to Menton with Mr and Mrs McCurdy. Louis was in much better spirits than when he was at home, really like his old self. He was bright and jolly and full of talk and seemed glad to see us. I saw Hop Smith too for an evening. He was staying at the Montana and I spent an evening with him. He is a wonder, 68 years old, and as active and strong as a boy. His son Berkeley lives here.

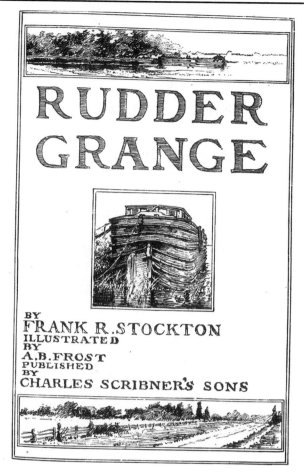

Title page in the first book by another author completely illustrated by Frost (1885)

Jack and I had a great time getting a studio. We began to look for one after we had been here a week and it took over three weeks to find one. We walked the Latin Quarter every day and saw more queer places in more evil smelling streets than I ever expected to see. It was a great experience for it made us acquainted with Paris in a way that would have taken much longer if we had found what we wanted at once. Things are so totally different here from home that you can't get used to them at once. Studios are <u>anywhere,</u> up any old court or back street or in behind any kind of building. We found two very good ones at last at 21 Rue du Vieux Colombier, a big one for Jack and me and a small one in the same building for Arthur. Mine is about as big as the one at home with a very good light, and Arthur's is smaller. They are separated from the street by two courts and are very quiet. The stairs are like most French stairs, very dark and winding. The man who was with me for a year and a half in my studio at home is with us. He sleeps in Arthur's studio and takes care of both, and poses for me once in a while. He is at the Julian School and doing excellent work. Jack is very fond of him, as we all are for that matter, for he is a very good fellow. I can trust him with Jack anywhere.

Jack is going into the Julian School soon. He is working with Mr Noer and doing very well, drawing seriously and making good progress. Arthur is not doing well. He is full of foolish, conceited notions, and his work has fallen off very badly. He was under very bad influence at the Chase School and it has done him a great deal of harm. Emily and I are a good deal worried about it, and very much disappointed. He might as well be in Morristown, for all the good he is getting out of Paris. He is Young and it will all come out right in the end, but he is wasting his time. He is at work, but in the wrong direction.

I am not painting much, for the work I want to do is out of door work, and it rains so much that it is very hard to do much out of doors. I am getting all the Collier work done that I can and will probably do little besides illustrations till the weather grows warmer and I can paint out of doors. There is plenty to paint here. The life in the streets is mightly fine and full of color and character. For instance I saw a workman today with a pair of dirty corduroy trousers on that were the most beautiful violet, and I see lovely faded blues in the blouses and aprons. I want to get them to come to the studio, but my French is too weak to try any experiment. I might get myself into pretty deep water.

I go to the Galleries as often as I can, but the days are so short that I get very little time there. It is too dark at four o'clock to see pictures, but I see what I can and get great satisfaction out of the Old Masters and the Modern Masters too.

... [Regarding London] I hated to leave the fine Museums, Galleries and Parks and the polite decent people. The most polite and decent people I have ever met, and I wish I could go back there to live, but the climate is too bad in Winter and the Art is about as bad as the climate....

We all send our love to you all. We are well and getting along very nicely and the prospects are very good. We see our way to living here very comfortably and economically.

Write care of Morgan, Harjes and Co. please, for we may leave the Hotel at any time.

Affectionately
Frost

Please remember me kindly to Burlingame and Brownell will you?

LETTER:
Letter [excerpt] by Frost to CS II, 25 March 1908, from Paris.

Frost laments the degradation in his oldest son's art and blames it on Henri Matisse, the French painter and leader of the "new impressionists" (the Fauvists), under whom Arthur has been working. Frost's reaction to this new school, where color and form as emotional expression take precedence over naturalistic representation, is, of course, understandable: his whole career as an illustrator has been the exact opposite. He is grateful, however, for receiving illustration requests from Joseph Chapin, Scribner's art editor. The Bal Bullier *to which he refers was the largest dance hall in Paris at the time.*

My dear Scribner

We are all very glad to hear that you are coming to Paris and that we shall see you so soon. I am very sorry that we must give up this apartment on April 15th, but we will have another, possibly one floor higher up in the same house. Our landlord has let our Apartment so we must go. We will have one somewhere, for a month, then we go to the country. . . .

I am just getting over a second attack of Grippe as I write, have been in the house nearly a week, and feel rather slim yet, but "on the way to recovery" as they say in the papers. Emily has been very well excepting the one attack of Grippe.

I am getting to be more reconciled to my confinement. I don't like it, and I never will and would much rather be at home, but I don't fret about it any more and take things more calmly. Arthur is more foolish than ever about his Art, he has reached the limit now, he can't go any farther. He is working under Henri Matisse. The high priest of the Autumn Salon crew. The new impressionists. They have the cheek to call themselves. Arthur has degraded his talent to the very last limit. I can't do anything with him. He acts and talks like an ass and it is impossible to reach him anywhere. I am afraid he will play with all their fads and cranks until he is unfitted for serious work. If he is ever to be a good painter he must learn his trade and that means hard work.

I heard last night that a man had sailed for America with a lot of Matisse's pictures to exhibit them and show America the new, great school. For Heaven's sake take five minutes and see them, if you can. I can't laugh at them. They mean too much to me, but I saw the people, French, Americans, everybody doubled up with laughter at the last Autumn Salon, and my big boy standing there and explaining solemnly to his Mother, who was equally solemn, though for a different reason, how beautiful they were. Well! When I see the other American students, <u>some of them</u>, drunk every night and at the Bal Boullier with a girl every Saturday night, I am thankful the boy is what he is. He is certainly a good chap.

I am sorry I bothered you about the books. I can't do anything with them till next Fall, but I think I would like very much to take one of them up then. We will talk it over when you are here. Chapin sent me a story and it made me feel good all over. I would hate to think I didn't belong to The Magazine anymore. The nice old letter head and the typewritten letter and the galley proofs just hit me exactly in the right spot. I am going to tackle the story as soon as I feel well enough. Maybe I can't do any illustration. I don't know, but I'll make a very serious and determined try at it. . . .

I will be on the lookout for you and we will have some sort of an apartment where we can give you a home dinner and we will all be mighty glad to see you. Emily sends her love to Mrs Scribner, and I my very warmest regards.

Affectionately
Frost

CS II Diary Entry:
Wednesday 22 April 1908

Visit Frost for luncheon at Givency

Scribner was touring in Europe, combining business with pleasure. He had lunched with Edith Wharton in Paris the day before.

Letter:
Letter by Frost to CS II, 22 September 1915.

Frost continued to illustrate stories for Scribner's Magazine, *though with a growing self-reproachment at what he believed was a diminishing talent. In the August and September 1915 issues, he illustrated two Southern "darkey" stories of Una Hunt. In this letter he shows his vicarious pleasure in the developing success of the work of his son John, who had a full-page drawing, illustrating a Lawrence Perry story, in the same September issue. Edith Wharton's book* The Book of the Homeless *(Scribners, 1916) was a fund-raising effort for World War I refugees and homeless children consisting of contributions by literary and*

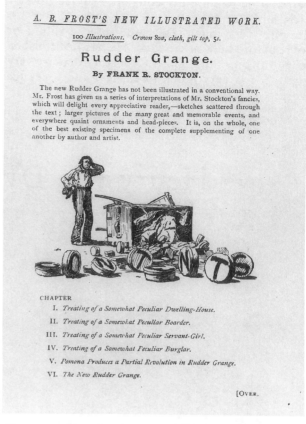

First page of an advertising circular for the English edition of Rudder Grange *(1886)*

artistic "celebrities." Frost damaged his drawing by trying to mount it, and Wharton's book committee rejected his attempt to salvage it.

Dear Scribner

I will send you today a drawing for Mrs Wharton's book.

It is one that I made six or seven years ago but which has not been published. I think it is a characteristic Frost drawing. I hope you will like it, but if you <u>don't</u>, please say no frankly and I will make one.

Thank you sincerely for what you say about my work for the Magazine. I need encouragement just now. I'm horribly blue about my work. I worked very hard over the Una Hunt drawings, making them over and over and they look very badly in the Magazine. Mushy. No snap at all in them. Over dour and old looking, and that's the trouble. I'm getting old and used up my sight is going and I'll soon have to stop.

Jack will take my place soon. I am mighty glad you like his drawing. He would have done better if he had a more congenial subject, pretty girls and out of doors sort of thing. I like his drawing very much. He made three, I think, or four, before he was satisfied. He has just finished four drawings for Colliers for a story that are very good. He is very much in earnest and loves his work.

Thank you. I'll go over to see you some time this Winter and we will have an old time spree.
Faithfully
Frost

Henry van Dyke (1852–1933)

Henry van Dyke

As Presybterian minister, professor of English literature at Princeton (1899–1923), U.S. minister to the Netherlands (1913–1917), and, most of all, as prolific author of popular essays on outdoor life, collections of short stories, poems, volumes of travel sketches and literary criticism, and moralistic essays from sermons, van Dyke had a major influence on the thought of his generation. He was a religious leader who ranged beyond his church, an ardent fisherman who used his joy and appreciation of nature to express his deep religious faith. The two Scribner brothers, CS II and Arthur H., friends of van Dyke and fellow Princetonians, were pleased to publish his works, decade after decade, for almost fifty years. Today, van Dyke is considered a literary representative of the Victorian age and the Genteel Tradition and acknowledged as a master of a lucid style.

Scribner Books by van Dyke

1884	*The Reality of Religion*
1887	*The Story of the Psalms*
1888	*The National Sin of Literary Piracy* (pamphlet)
1889	*The Poetry of Tennyson*
1893	*Straight Sermons to Young Men and Other Human Beings*
1895	*Little Rivers: A Book of Essays in Profitable Idleness*
1897	*The Builders and Other Poems*

The First Christmas Tree, illustrated by Howard Pyle

1898   *Sermons to Young Men* (revised and enlarged from *Straight Sermons . . .*)

The Lost Word: A Christmas Legend of Long Ago

The American Birthright and the Philippine Pottage (pamphlet)

1899   *Fisherman's Luck and Some Other Uncertain Things*

1900   *The Toiling of Felix, and Other Poems*

The Friendly Year, Chosen and Arranged from the Works of Henry Van Dyke by George Sidney Webster

1901   *The Ruling Passion: Tales of Nature and Human Nature*

1902   *The Blue Flower*

1904   *Music, and Other Poems*

1905   *The School of Life*

The Van Dyke Book, selected from the writings of Henry Van Dyke by Edwin Mims, with introduction by editor and biographical sketch by Brooke van Dyke

Essays in Application

The Spirit of Christmas

1907   *Days Off, and Other Digressions*

1908   *The House of Rimmon: A Drama in Four Acts*

Out-of-Doors in the Holy Land: Impressions of Travel in Body and Spirit

1909   *The White Bees, and Other Poems*

1911   *The Sad Shepherd: A Christmas Story*

The Poems of Henry van Dyke (revised and enlarged, 1920)

Who Follow the Flag (pamphlet)

1912   *The Unknown Quantity: A Book of Romance and Some Half-Told Tales*

1914   *The Grand Canyon, and Other Poems*

1917   *Fighting for Peace*

The Red Flower: Poems Written in War Time

1919   *Golden Stars, and Other Verses, Following the "Red Flower"*

The Valley of Vision: A Book of Romance and Some Half-Told Tales

1920   *Studies in Tennyson*

1920–1922   *The Works of Henry van Dyke* (Avalon Edition of 17 volumes; *The Golden Key* added as volume 18 in 1927)

1921   *Camp-Fires and Guide-Posts: A Book of Essays and Excursions*

1922   *Songs out of Doors*

Companionable Books

1924   *Six Days of the Week: A Book of Thoughts About Life and Religion*

1925   *Half-Told Tales*

1926	*The Golden Key: Stories of Deliverance*
1927	*Chosen Poems*
	The Works of Henry van Dyke (Sylvanora Edition of 10 volumes)
1928	*"Even unto Bethlehem": The Story of Christmas*
1929	*The Man Behind the Book: Essays in Understanding*
1932	*A Creelful of Fishing Stories: A Pastime Book*, edited by van Dyke

RELATED LETTERS:

In these excerpts from two letters to Edward L. Burlingame, van Dyke good-naturedly bows to the authority of the Scribner's Magazine *editor regarding cuts to one of his early manuscripts. The shortened version of "Au Large" appeared in the September 1895 issue, but it was returned to its original, expanded form in* Little Rivers, *published later that fall.*

September 27, 1894.

My dear Mr. Burlingame.

I venture to submit to your distinguished consideration the accompanying manuscript, entitled <u>Au Large</u>. If it should appear to you to meet that standard of moral profundity and literary simplicity to which the readers of Scribner's Magazine have been educated, I shall be glad to have it given to the public through that channel, and to receive remuneration, which according to Mr. Howells, the author ought neither to desire nor to refuse. This fragment of composition is one of the meanderings which I hope some day to bring together in a volume of <u>Little Rivers</u>. I have a number of photographs, and if you should want them to stimulate the imagination of the artists who illustrate your pages, you have only to send me word at the Century Club, and I will forward them to you. . . .

October 10, 1894.

. . . You insist, like an editor, that <u>Au Large</u> shall be changed to <u>Au Petit</u>. You ought to supply your contributors with some of that stuff which Alice of Wonderland took when she shrank so fast that her chin bumped her foot. Well, how much do you want to cut out, and where will you thrust in the fatal shears. Specify your pound of flesh! Mark it with a red pencil, symbolic of blood. Take my tender moralizings, take my delicate al-

Price, Five Cents.

The National Sin of Literary Piracy

BY

HENRY VAN DYKE, D.D.

NEW YORK

CHARLES SCRIBNER'S SONS

1888

Pamphlet of van Dyke's sermon that he preached in the Brick Church on 7 January 1888. Attacking the American practice of printing pirated editions of foreign authors' books, the sermon at once became an important reinforcement to the cause of international copyright in the United States. The pamphlet was widely distributed in Europe as well as in America.

Scribner editions of van Dyke's works

lusions, take my fresh quotations, — take all, all for your cruel altar, — but leave me only the little, and pay for it on that scale, and then I'll see whether there is sufficient value in Gilead to enable me to stand the strain on my literary sensibilities.

Yours sincerely,
Henry van Dyke

CS II Diary Entry:
Monday 10 October 1898

Dr. Van Dyke came & we agreed upon the book publication of his stories @ 15% & 20% after 5000 copies.

Agreement about Fisherman's Luck and Some Other Uncertain Things.

Letter:
Letter by van Dyke to Arthur H. Scribner, 19 April 1901.

In explaining his refusal to write promotional copy for his own book, The Ruling Passion: Tales of Nature and Human Nature, *van Dyke offers insight into his philosophy of writing.*

Dear Mr Scribner

A man ought not to write the notice for his new book. If he tells how good he thinks it, (on some days,) he becomes absurd. If he confesses how bad he thinks it, (on other days,) he becomes lugubrious. What he ought to do is tell a friend what he thinks of it when the sun shines, and then let the friend blow the horn and ring the bell. At all events, after our long talk, this is what I'm going to do. The whole thing is to be put in the hands of the House. If it isn't good, and mighty good, the real thing, — why then let's burn it, and save the House and me from a mild respectable fiasco. I think it's good. But how good you've got to say.

One thing is sure. I haven't followed any artificial school or fashion. The book isn't written for dialect, or for costume, for for historical illustration. I've gone straight to nature and the heart of man and told real stories. There is no more moral in them than there is in life, — and no less. They are told for the sake of the story, and because it means something about human nature. The workmanship? — well, I've tried to make it good enough to <u>last</u>.

I send you down the (trial) preface of which you speak. Please keep it for me. I expect to be in town on the 29th and will come to see you.

Faithfully

Henry van Dyke

LETTER:

Letter from Arthur H. Scribner to van Dyke, 1 October 1912.

Approached by a movie company regarding the use of The Story of the Other Wise Man *in a film, van Dyke sought the advice of his friend and publisher, Arthur H. Scribner, even though Harper & Bros. had published the book. "I do not know," he had written to Scribner, "exactly what it means to 'pictureize' a story, and I am much afraid of what I suppose it means, to popularize one." The film industry was very young (movies were still silent), and publishers had not yet realized the financial benefits of film rights.*

Dear Dr. van Dyke:

The moving picture business, as you know, has come up very rapidly and has developed enormously, but I do not know that there is yet any settled method of payment for the material used. We have had no dealings with the Carlton Motion Picture Laboratories, though I see that they are fairly well rated financially. We have had some dealings with the Edison Company and the Katen Company, the payment received not being very large. On several Stevenson novels we gave the right to reproduce for motion pictures at $100 each, and we make a similar offer on Mrs. Andrews's "Perfect Tribute," with a further proviso limiting the time to three years, which proposition has not as yet been accepted. A company also applied for the right to reproduce Mrs. Burnett's "Little Lord Fauntleroy," offering a considerably larger sum, which I do not definitely recall but which was $500 or $1000. She declined this, whether because of the possibility of it conflicting with her play or because she did not think the offer adequate, I do not know.

I have not yet heard of any arrangement on the royalty basis or based on receipts. As I understand it the method of such companies is to have a company of players, appropriately costumed, act for the motion pictures scenes suggested by the story, and in using these pictures there is thrown on the screen every little while a paragraph or two explaining what is to come. I see no objection to your making an arrangement, if you wish, provided you can satisfy yourself that it is adequately done and that you receive reasonable payment. On the other hand, this will be difficult to manage and in any event I would advise your limiting the period. The arrangements so far do not seem to be very satisfactory.

I suppose, by the way, that the Harpers would make no claim to this based on their book publication but if you do go ahead it might be well to have this clear.

Very sincerely yours,

Arthur H. Scribner

LETTER:

Appointed by President Woodrow Wilson as minister to the Netherlands and Luxembourg in June 1913, van Dyke had barely been in The Hague (he arrived in September) nine months when World War I broke out. Trying to juggle his official duties with his writing projects seemed impossible. Edward L. Burlingame had been trying to get him to think of a "long story," i.e., novel, which van Dyke had never attempted (and would never accomplish). This letter to his publisher, Arthur H. Scribner, is dated the day that Germany declared war on France and struck out for France through Belgium and Luxembourg.

August 3, 1914.

My dear Scribner:

Your two letters of July 21st and July 23rd have come to me in the midst of dark and troublous times. The whole sky of Europe is black with the storm-clouds of war. The Hague is full of agitated and distressed Americans who are for the most part destitute of money and desperately anxious to get home. I am working night and day to attend to their necessities, and to do what I can to save the waning hope of peace, or at least to preserve an open door of escape for our citizens under a neutral flag. You can understand that I have not much time to write.

Your suggestion in regard to the title-page of the new volume of poems is entirely in accord with my own intention. Make the title and the whole format of the new book like that of the other small volumes of my verse. Set "<u>The Grand Canyon</u>" as the main title, with "<u>and other</u>

H.v.D.
Avalon,
Princeton, N.J. June, 1925.

Charles Scribner, we are proud to see
Old Princeton tag your name, Litt. D.
For you have been, a long time since,
Proclaimed of Publishers the Prince.
Quick judge of books, lover of Letters,
Your authors are your friends and debtors.

Henry van Dyke.

Manuscript of poem van Dyke wrote on the occasion of CS II's honorary degree from Princeton in 1925

poems" as the sub-title. I am sending you with this the first batch of proof corrected as well as I have been able to do it under the stress which at present rests upon me.

My plan for coming home in September is subject now to serious change. Of course I shall remain at the post of duty as long as there is any danger. My family, I hope, will be able to return as proposed on September 12th.

It is essential at the present moment that the United States should take the proper measures for the protection and the free transit of her citizens, and I sincerely hope that the advices which I have sent to Washington will be regarded. As ever
Affectionately yours,
Henry van Dyke

CS II DIARY ENTRY:
Saturday 26 July 1919

Lunch with Henry van Dyke at Seal Harbor

"Sylvanora," the name of van Dyke's summer home in Seal Harbor, Maine, was used for the ten-volume edition of his works published by Scribners in 1927. The more complete Avalon Edition (1920–1922) was named after his Princeton, New Jersey, home.

LETTER:
Letter by van Dyke to Arthur H. Scribner, 3 December 1920.

A pleasant letter for a publisher to receive from an author — and, no doubt, a rarity — in which requests for rejecting advances and delaying royalties are made. And yet this is typical of the van Dyke/Arthur Scribner correspondence. The Avalon edition van Dyke refers to was the Scribner subscription edition of his complete works, a multivolume publishing pattern the publisher had established with the works of other major writers, such as Robert Louis Stevenson, Rudyard Kipling, J. M. Barrie, and Richard Harding Davis. The "educational friends" mentioned at the end of the letter are members of the Heads of Department Association of the Borough of Brooklyn.

Dear Arthur: —

Yours of the 29th Nov. is gratifying to read in these dull days when a sense of futility hangs around my neck and makes me incapable of any virtue but obstinacy. However, even that poor remnant and last resort has sometimes served as a life-preserver. A man who ought to have been drowned long ago may keep up and go on swimming just because he is too pig-headed to sink. He persuades himself that he is sustained by a sense of duty, but really it is just a habit that he has formed and refuses to break.

You are very kind in what you say about the book-publication of "Campfires and Guideposts." Whether it should be done this spring or next fall is for you to decide. This spring we might count upon the faint interest which the papers have attracted in the magazine, and upon a certain feeble "timeliness" in some of them. By next fall, on the other hand, some of the many reviewers who now especially hate and despise this insignificant author may have forgotten him, or may have passed into the Silence, so that the appearance of his book will cause less offense. But, by the same token, some of his remaining friends, too, may be gone. Spring or fall, — as you will, — but one obstinate request I must make of you. Please send no new book of mine to the newspapers for review. It is wasteful. And it seems to cause pain to the reviewers. Spare them.

What you suggest in regard to terms of royalty, 20%, is more than all right, and your proposal about an advance payment of $5000 is most generous. But please do not do it. We didn't use to have "advances" in the old days of our lusty youth. Why should I have them now in the sere and yellow leaf? No, my dear Arthur, I did not expect, and do not want, any "advance." It is kind of you to propose it; but in these hard times I prefer to share the risk with you, and to wait with you until the book has earned its way, — if it ever does so.

This leads to another thing that I want to say, — about the Avalon edition. You have put a lot of money into it. It is beautifully made. But you can't conceal from me the fact that it goes very slowly. Now, it isn't fair to you to increase the expense. Why sixteen volumes? Why not stop where you are now, — or with volume XIII, the copy for which was sent you yesterday? As in the case of the man who died in Bermuda, there will be no "complaint." The three other volumes are nearly ready: let them stay so. A prospectus is no more to be taken au pied de la lettre than a political platform. It represents a pious wish, subject to the decrees of providence. Please consider this seriously, and be sure that if you decide to stop now, I shall be entirely satisfied and content.

One more "please," — suggested by something general that Charles said the other day. Please don't think that there is any need for paying the August royalty account in December this year. February or March or a later month will suit me just as well. You have a lot of small accounts to settle. You can keep the money for me just as safely as the trust company. So do.

Your educational friends have just sent me in their invitation to make a speech at their luncheon in January, and I have accepted; first, because I think you would like me to do so; and second, because plain working teachers are mighty good people, — and I like to meet them, — though, heaven knows, I have little stomach for any kind of speaking, these days. I want to be spoken to, — kindly, please, and in words of one syllable.

Your obstinate friend,
Henry van Dyke

Despite his "protest," van Dyke received his December royalty payment as usual. But no advance payment was made on his Camp-Fires and Guide-Posts, *which was published in the fall of 1922. The Avalon edition of his works continued to grow, reaching a final total of 18 volumes in 1927 with the addition of* The Golden Key. *However, Arthur Scribner agreed to delay the increase of royalty (from 10 percent to 15 percent) till after two thousand (instead of one thousand) sets of the edition had been sold. Both of the men attended the Brooklyn teachers' annual luncheon on 29 January 1921.*

Robert Louis Stevenson (1850–1894)

Robert Louis Stevenson, about 1887

Best known for his romances, made even more famous later in their N. C. Wyeth–illustrated editions, Stevenson was also a craftsman of the art of writing and included in his literary output poems and ballads, fables, critical essays, travelogues, short stories, political tracts, biographies, and letters. His nonfiction is now attracting greater critical attention and confirms his stature as more than the author of such children's classics as *A Child's Garden of Verses, Kidnapped,* and *Treasure Island* and the psychological novel *Strange Case of Dr. Jekyll and Mr. Hyde.* Scribners was the Scot's "authorized" American publisher, an important issue in the era before international copyright, and it published five multivolume, specially named editions of his works, more than for any of its other authors before or since. Stevenson remains, after more than a hundred years, the most successful foreign author published by the firm.

Scribner Books by Stevenson

1885	*A Child's Garden of Verses*
1886	*Strange Case of Dr. Jekyll and Mr. Hyde*
	Kidnapped: Being Memoirs of the Adventures of David Balfour in the Year 1751
1887	*The Merry Men and Other Tales and Fables*
	Underwoods
	Familiar Studies of Men and Books
	New Arabian Nights
	More New Arabian Nights: The Dynamiter, co-authored by Fanny Van de Grift Stevenson
	Memories and Portraits
	Virginibus Puerisque and Other Papers (second edition)
1888	*Memoir of Fleeming Jenkin*
	The Black Arrow: A Tale of the Two Roses
1889	*The Wrong Box,* co-authored by Lloyd Osbourne

	The Master of Ballantrae: A Winter's Tale, illustrated by William Hole
1890	*Ballads*
1892	*Across the Plains with Other Memories and Essays*
	The Wrecker, co-authored by Osbourne, illustrated by Hole and W. C. Metcalf
	A Footnote to History: Eight Years of Trouble in Samoa
	Three Plays, co-authored by W. E. Henley
1893	*Island Nights' Entertainments*
	David Balfour: Being Memoirs of His Adventures at Home and Abroad
1894–1898	*The Works of Robert Louis Stevenson* (Edinburgh Edition of 28 volumes)
1895	*Prince Otto: A Romance*
	An Inland Voyage
	Travels with a Donkey in the Cévennes
	Treasure Island
	The Silverado Squatters
1895–1912	*The Novels and Tales of Robert Louis Stevenson* [heading changes on the title-pages] (Thistle Edition of 27 volumes)
1896	*The Suicide Club*
	The Ebb Tide: A Trio and a Quartette
	The Amateur Emigrant
	Weir of Hermiston: An Unfinished Romance
	Poems and Ballads
	In the South Seas: Being an Account of Experiences and Observations in the Marquesas, Paumotus and Gilbert Islands in the Course of Two Cruises in the Yacht "Casco" (1888) and the Schooner "Equator" (1889)
	Fables
	Vailima Letters: Being Correspondence Addressed by Robert Louis Stevenson to Sidney Colvin, November 1890–October 1894 (2 volumes)
1897	*St. Ives: Being the Adventures of a French Prisoner in England*
	The Stevenson Song-Book: Verses from a Child's Garden, with music by various composers
1898	*A Lowden Sabbath Morn*, illustrated by A. S. Boyd
1899	*The Letters of Robert Louis Stevenson to His Family and Friends*, selected and edited, with notes and intoduction, by Sidney Colvin (2 volumes)
1900	*A Christmas Sermon*
1901	*Æs Triplex*
1904	*Prayers Written at Vailima*, with an introduction by Mrs. Stevenson
1905–1912	*The Biographical Edition of the Works of Robert Louis Stevenson* (31 volumes)
1906	*The Pocket R.L.S.: Being Favourite Passages from the Works of Stevenson*

Essays of Robert Louis Stevenson, selected and edited with an introduction and notes by William Lyon Phelps

1911   *The Letters of Robert Louis Stevenson* (new edition), edited by Colvin (4 volumes)

Selections from Robert Louis Stevenson, edited by Henry Seidel Canby and Frederick Erastus Pierce

1912   *Edinburgh,* illustrated by James Heron

1913   *The Poems and Ballads of Robert Louis Stevenson: Complete Edition*

1916   *Father Damien: An Open Letter to the Reverend Dr. Hyde of Honolulu*

1920   *Learning to Write: Suggestions and Counsel from Robert Louis Stevenson*

1921   *Moral Emblems & Other Poems Written and Illustrated with Woodcuts*

1921–1923   *The Works of Robert Louis Stevenson* (Vailima Edition of 26 volumes)

1923   *Poems by R.L.S.: A Selection*

The Short Stories of Robert Louis Stevenson

The Complete Poems of Robert Louis Stevenson

1925   *The Works of Robert Louis Stevenson* (South Seas Edition of 32 volumes)

RELATED LETTERS:

Scribners was delighted to become Stevenson's American publisher in 1885 when it was approached by his painter friend Will H. Low and offered sheets for the American publication of A Child's Garden of Verses. *Stevenson had already published ten works, including the highly successful* Treasure Island. *Taking on this popular foreign author, however, created an immediate problem for the firm in the U.S. market where such authors' foreign works were considered fair game for American publishers. What usually counted was the observance of trade courtesy: an American publisher who had first published a foreign author expected other American publishers to respect his claim. Scribners had the backing of the author.*

Messrs. Charles Scribners Sons   6 April 1885
Gent.

We have rec^d yours in explanation of your course in publishing "A Childs Garland of Verse" and we want to say in reply that there is still a little question of courtesy, or the want of it, on your part to be explained.

It is generally known among publishers, and you cannot be ignorant of it, that we have pub-lished several of Mr Stevenson's books & consequently he is considered to be our author.

A long while since we wrote him about this very book & we are sure he would wish us to have it in preference to others, but he is a sick man & entrusts his affairs to others, in fact he has very little business method. Only quite recently an agent of his offered to Harper & Bros. instead of to us the "Dynamite Stories" and they, knowing that Mr Stevenson was our author, with their characteristic courtesy referred the matter to us.

Yours very truly
Roberts Bro$^{s.}$

Dear Sirs: 6 April 1885

We regret to learn by a letter received this morning that you suspect us of a want of courtesy in regard to "A Child's Garden of Verse." It has been our intention to observe all possible obligations of courtesy in this matter, and we sincerely think we have done so. We were, of course, aware that you had published some of Mr. Stevenson's books, and were very careful to assure ourselves before accepting the advance sheets of this one that they were offered to us with the full and deliberate authority of the author. Under the circumstances of their offer it would have been a want of

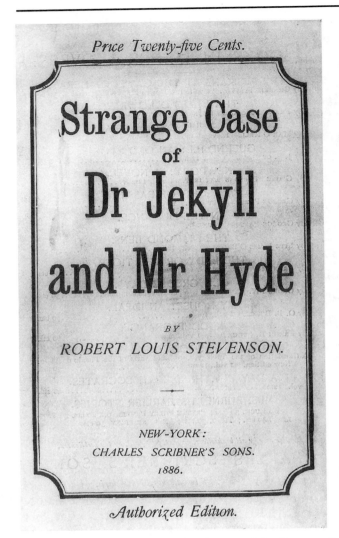

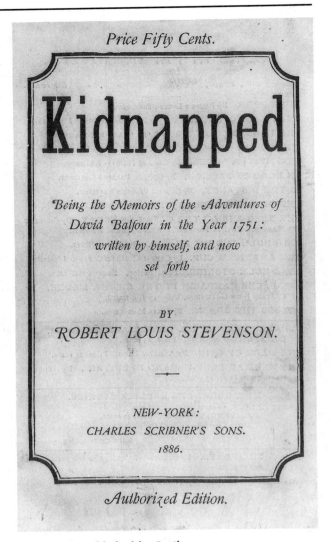

Paperback editions of the first two Stevenson novels published by Scribners

delicacy on our part to have brought the matter to your attention. We do not feel at liberty to quote from Mr. Stevenson's letters, but they are such as to show us that he does not take your view of the relations established between you, and we had a right to suppose that this was well known to you.

We have endeavored to place ourselves in your position in respect to this matter, and we do not see how, under the circumstances, we could have any cause to complain of a want of consideration, and we hope that you will eventually come to the same conclusion. We remain,

Yours Very Truly,
Charles Scribner's Sons

One result of this altercation between the two firms was that Scribners, even after Stevenson had authorized it as his American publisher, was not able to get control of the Stevenson works Roberts had published till after Stevenson's death, though it offered to buy them several times. Writing to Stevenson in October of 1887, CS II was able to report that Scribners now controlled "all your books except those in the hand of Roberts."

RELATED LETTERS:

The absence of an international copyright law to protect Stevenson's work in the United States financially hurt both author and publisher. In March 1887 Stevenson received a letter from Harper and Brothers, the American publisher, stating that they had just published in their Franklin-Square Library series a one-volume edition of his three most popular works, Kidnapped, The

Strange Case of Dr. Jekyll and Mr. Hyde, *and* Treasure Island; *for this right they were sending him a check for £20, having already paid Roberts Bros. for the use of* Treasure Island. *Stevenson was outraged at this callous pirating that would cut off his income at the root and published his reaction together with Harper's letter in the press. He forwarded their check to Scribners, feeling that his American publisher of* Kidnapped *and Dr. Jekyll deserved the money. Scribners suggested that they split the sum. In the following letter, after calculating how he would square his accounts with Scribners' London agent, Lemuel Bangs, Stevenson shows that he and the firm are united in their view of the Harper matter.*

Bournemouth, May 3, 1887
Messrs. Charles Scribner's Sons.
Dear Sirs, I am in receipt of yours and of the returned draft for one hundred and forty seven pound eight and elevenpence sterling

£147. 8. 11
£118. 18. 5
—————
£ 28. 10. 6

and in hopes that my arithmetic is correct shall send a cheque for twenty eight pound ten and six to Mr. Bangs.

This is enough to tell you that I have accepted your view of Messrs Harper's conscience money. I have still to thank you for that, and for the whole tone of your correspondence. Since the fortunate hour when my friend Mr. Low brought me into connection with your house, I have gained a good deal of money; I sometimes think I have gained more in the assured confidence that I now feel in your good taste and honour. The last we shall hope is common, and first is certainly rare, in business correspondence.

I have mailed you — rather late indeed, but you must have seen already how neglectful I am even of important matters — a copy of the Times containing my letter on the Harper business. I have had no reply from these gentlemen, which I regret; I should have enjoyed a longer correspondence, but it seems that they would not. I am, dear Sirs,

Yours very truly
Robert Louis Stevenson
[Beinecke Library, Yale University]

Charles Fairchild (1838–1910), a wealthy banker and businessman, and a friend and patron of the American painter John Singer Sargent, had commissioned in 1887 a portrait of Stevenson for his wife, who greatly admired his writings. The men became good friends, and when the Stevensons came to New York in September 1887, they stayed with the Fairchilds in their hotel and then went to their Newport, Rhode Island, home for several weeks. From October to April of the next year the Stevensons lived in the Adirondacks at Saranac Lake. In the fall Fairchild apparently had acted as an emissary for Harpers, trying to "open communications" with Stevenson who by then had had enough of the "Harper business." If anything, the incident had only proved to strengthen the Stevenson/Scribner relationship, as evident in the following pair of letters.

[Saranac Lake, fall 1887]
My dear Fairchild,
I am very sure you act entirely as my friend, in this matter; and I thank you sincerely for the trouble you have been at, and give my kind expressions. Frankly, nothing would induce me to leave the Scribners; they came forward and used me thoroughly well when no one else did; I believe they find a profit in me; and there is no nameable amount of dollars that would make me pay them back evil for good. Please think (what is the truth) that this sense of loyalty to them, and no spirit of enmity to the Messrs Harpers dictates this return of their communication unopened. And as for yourself, I will do as you say, and keep this step secret. Excuse hurry as I am anxious to get this off, and believe me, my dear Fairchild,

Yours with sincere affection
Robert Louis Stevenson

The Harper incident was only one of many cases of pirating Stevenson suffered at the hands of American publishers. Finally, a week after the International Copyright Act was passed in Congress on 4 March 1891, Scribners was able to accompany its royalty statement to Stevenson, then living in Samoa, with the news:

By the time this letter reaches you you will probably have heard of the passage of our International Copyright Bill. It is perhaps not so liberal a measure as might be desired, but will, we think, be satisfactory to most English authors in that it gives them full copyright here, provided they manufacture their books in America. Such a law in the

First editions of most of the Stevenson books published by the firm in the nineteenth century

past would certainly have very greatly increased your returns from your books.

Yours very truly,
Charles Scribner's Sons

LETTER:

Letter [excerpt] by Edward L. Burlingame, editor of *Scribner's Magazine*, to CS II, 13 February 1888.

While CS II is away on vacation, Burlingame keeps him abreast of developments with Stevenson, quoting from a recent Stevenson letter, written from Saranac Lake (February 6). During this period Stevenson had an arrangement to write a monthly article for the magazine, to which he refers in his letter. His submitted paper on the Irish problem, "Confessions of a Unionist," criticized the American view on the violence in Ireland. Burlingame would not print it, and it was never published during Stevenson's life.

My dear Scribner —

There have been perhaps as many things of interest as usual in these three weeks; but they have nearly all been in some stage of progress hard to write about without many details, & changing from day to day. So I have kept particulars to tell you when you come; & have had little of importance for a letter till just now, when two or three considerable matters are at last in very definite shape. Fortunately, they have gone well.

1. Stevenson. His <u>Master of Ballantrae</u> is a great story; & he has now sent nearly or quite half of it. Really, & with all due allowance for any personal enthusiasm for his work, it is a very great thing; & as a sustained novel far beyond anything he has done. In parts this is true in a literary sense; but in the matter of popularity it is true of the whole beyond a doubt. I will not attempt of course to describe it; but there is one part — where the plot deals with the conflict of two brothers — that is a quite extraordinary piece of work, sure to be followed with the most absorbing interest. You know through your brother of the arrangement which — for the sake of keeping Magazine type free, &c. — seemed best for setting the story up; & it is now going into type very fast at Little's, much in the style of <u>Kidnapped</u>; & galleys have been going to Stevenson for some days past.

Now to the most important thing still pending in regard to this — the business arrangement, which I shall be glad to feel you have before you to consider for the day or two before you come back — when, I suppose, his answer will be needed. — Everything is contained in a passage of one of his recent letters; but I am sorry that before you read it you cannot hear a full account of <u>all</u> our dealings for the last few weeks — which I shall have to reserve until I see you because it would be impossible to write it in enough detail. — Briefly, I have had a somewhat curious time over one of the papers he sent to us — one on the Irish question, "The Confession of a Unionist," which was an ardent plea & appeal to Americans in behalf of the opponents of Home Rule; — and the matter, which has gone on somewhat parallel with the correspondence about <u>Ballantrae</u>, has ended in his most heartily & pleasantly agreeing to withdraw the essay — & somehow or other, I can't describe just how, has resulted in clearing the air greatly; i.e. in making me feel as though I knew S. much better that ever before, & in bringing about a kind of letters between us, quite free on both sides from a kind of imperceptible strain that perhaps existed only in my imagination. — However, I can't describe all this very fully till I can talk of it, & merely mention it to show that what I am going to copy from his letter of a few days ago was written after a good frank correspondence on another matter, & in a pleasanter atmosphere that perhaps prevailed at one time.

"I want to say a word" he writes, "as to the Master. . . . If you like & want it, I leave it to you to make an offer. You may remember I thought the offer you made when I was still in England too small: by which I did not at all mean I thought it less than it was worth, but too little to tempt me to undergo the disagreeables of serial publication. This tale (if you want it) you are to have; for it is the least I can do for you; & you are to observe that the sum you pay me for my articles going far to meet my wants, I am quite open to be satisfied with less than formerly. I tell you I dislike this battle of the dollars; I feel sure you all pay too much here in America; & I beg you not to spoil me any more. For I am getting spoiled: I do not want wealth, & I feel these big sums demoralize me." —

This is straightforward & good. It is only a little enigmatical to me in one respect — does it mean less than we <u>offered</u> before, or less than he would have been willing to take? — But you will know what it will be best to do; & meanwhile I shall write to him that it shall be considered as soon as possible. . . .

The Master of Ballantrae *was not finished till May 1889, when Stevenson was in Honolulu on the first of his South Seas trips; it was serialized in* Scribner's Magazine *from November 1888 through October 1889 and published by Scribners on 21 September 1889.*

Thomas Nelson Page (1853–1922)

Thomas Nelson Page

Born on a Virginia plantation, Page spent his youth among scenes of the Civil War and the postwar Southern Reconstruction, which molded his impressions and his thinking. The bulk of his writing was fiction that dealt with the life of this region and time period, and through his literature he became a spokesman for a generation of Southerners who continued to see only the romance and splendor of the past and not its harsh realities. His books were widely popular for more than thirty years, providing authentic local color qualities of description and dialect that satisfied his audience's nostaglic hunger. In fact, Page is probably the author most responsible for creating and continuing the myth of the Old South. His "period realism," not its vision, is the basis of his literary reputation today. Virtually all of his books were published by Scribners; and Page and CS II were very close. In his condolence letter to Page's brother, Roswell, 23 November 1922, CS II wrote: "I doubt whether you could know how dear Tom was to me. He was one of my two or three most beloved friends."

Scribner Books by Page

1887	*In Ole Virginia; or, Marse Chan and Other Stories*
1888	*Befo' de War: Echoes in Negro Dialect*, co-authored by A. C. Gordon
	Two Little Confederates ·
1891	*On Newfound River*
	Elsket, and Other Stories
	Among the Camps; or, Young People's Stories of the War
1892	*The Old South: Essays Social and Political*
	Marse Chan: A Tale of Old Virginia, illustrated by W. T. Smedley
1893	*Meh Lady: A Story of the War*, illustrated by C. S. Reinhart
1894	*Polly: A Christmas Recollection*, illustrated by A. Castaigne
	The Burial of the Guns
1895	*Unc' Edinburg: A Plantation Echo*, illustrated by B. West Clinedinst

1897	*The Old Gentleman of the Black Stock*
	Social Life in Old Virginia Before the War, illustrated by the Misses Cowles
1898	*Pastime Stories*, illustrated by A. B. Frost
	Red Rock: A Chronicle of Reconstruction, illustrated by Clinedinst
1899	*Santa Claus's Partner*, illustrated by W. Glackens
1902	*A Captured Santa Claus*, illustrated by W. L. Jacobs
1903	*Gordon Keith*, illustrated by George Wright
1904	*Bred in the Bone*
	The Negro: The Southerner's Problem
1906	*The Page Story Book*, edited by Frank E. Spaulding and Catherine T. Bryce
	The Coast of Bohemia
1906–1912	*The Novels, Stories, Sketches and Poems of Thomas Nelson Page* (Plantation Edition of 18 volumes)
1907	*Under the Crust*
1908	*The Old Dominion: Her Making and Her Manners*
	Tommy Trot's Visit to Santa Claus, illustrated by Victor C. Anderson
	Robert E. Lee, The Southerner
1909	*John Marvel, Assistant*, illustrated by James Montgomery Flagg
1911	*Robert E. Lee, Man and Soldier*
1913	*The Land of the Spirit*
1914	*The Stranger's Pew*
1916	*Tommy Trot's Visit to Santa Claus* and *A Captured Santa Claus*
	The Shepherd Who Watched by Night
1920	*Italy and the World War*
1922	*Dante and His Influence: Studies*
1924	*The Red Riders*, completed by Roswell Page

LETTER:
Letter by CS II to Page, 22 October 1885.

Page's first Scribner publication of fiction was his Negro dialect story "Marse Chan," which appeared in volume nine of the firm's Stories by American Authors (1885). Originally published in the Century Magazine (April 1884), the story had caught Scribners' attention as the work of a talented writer. Soon after the publication of Stories the firm inquired about other work and was surprised, as this letter shows, to learn it was almost too late to snag his first book. CS II's references are to Thomas A. Janvier's Color Studies, *which like the planned Page book was a collection of four short stories, and to the A. B. Frost-illustrated edition of Frank R. Stockton's* Rudder Grange. Red Rock *was a novel that Scribners initially rejected and only published after much rewriting on Page's part — thirteen years later.*

My dear Mr. Page:

Your letter reached us yesterday and I hasten to reply.

If we had known earlier of the other short stories which are to be published in the magazines

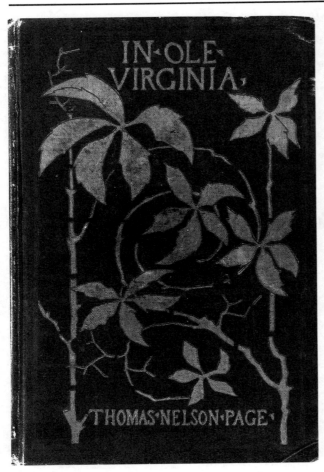

Cover of a first edition of Page's first book, In Ole Virginia *(1887). Writing about it to CS II on 30 December 1886, Page had suggested a way to enhance the "old" quality: "In the Designs it would be well to have this element apparent. I suggest the Virginia Creeper as an emblematic plant for your decorations."*

The question of illustration is an important one and not to be hastily determined. If the stories are illustrated in the magazines the same illustrations could probably be used again to advantage in the book and new ones made for "Marse Chan" or any of the others that had not been illustrated. It would not involve any great expense to make a suitable number of full-page illustrations for the book and there should be little difficulty in finding a good artist.

As to terms of publication — we should want to meet your views or do as well as anyone else. Of course we should bear all expenses of any sort and it would only be a question as to the amount of royalty to be paid and I don't think we should differ much. In a general way I would propose 10% as sufficient if the book were illustrated; if there were no illustrations, the percentage might be increased.

As we wrote in our previous letter we had thought of making you a proposal for the publication of "Marse Chan" by itself for the holidays but we find upon examination that we could hardly make a large enough book and as the season was so far advanced we decided to give it up. I think now that if there is a chance for a volume of your stories in the Spring, or even next Fall, it might be a mistake to issue "Marse Chan" separately now, as this would rob the volume of much of its importance — if so important a feature of it had already been issued in book form.

With much regard I remain
Yours very truly
Charles Scribner

P.S.

You may depend upon our interest in the "Red Rock" in its new form. I hope we shall soon have a chance to see it.

P.S.

I also send a copy of our new illustrated edition of "Rudder Grange" which we think a great success and a good specimen of American illustration.

you may be sure that no one would have anticipated us in applying for their publication in book form. I have hoped that we might have the pleasure of becoming the publishers of your first book and if you have not gone too far with the Harpers, I hope this may yet be possible.

The four stories would be ample for a volume of moderate size, if there are 35000 words. I send with this Janvier's stories which we have recently issued which contains (I am told) 40000.

Of course illustrations would increase the size and importance of the book.

Nothing definite could be done to advantage until all your stories have been published in the magazines but we could agree upon a basis of publication and the questions as to title & illustrations could be determined.

Page had to wait for his stories, already promised to magazines, to appear before book publication could proceed. In the meantime, he added two more stories to the book, which Scribners published on 21 May 1887. Not liking most of the magazine illustrations, Page issued the book without any. However, the main stories were individually published by Scribners later in illustrated editions.

Page's announcement, written on his law office stationery, to CS II of having completed his novel On Newfound River

RELATED LETTERS:
Though he was a published author of several books, Page was still practicing law with his cousin in Richmond, Virginia, at the time of these letters. He took an interest in the public affairs of the city and sought help from CS II, his publisher and friend, in this library project.

Jany 6th 1890

My dear Scribner:

I have organized a Reading Room and Library for boys here in this City and I want you to send me your Magazine for it and help me by a small donation of books of the kind which will interest boys of from ten to eighteen years. My fellows belong to the poorer classes and I am compelled to beg to compliment what I am personally able to do. I hope to do them much good and even dream of opening a new field by this work where literature may grow. I will appreciate any donation of the kind I have mentioned which you may make or get from any other publishers.

Yours faithfully
Thos. N. Page

Jany 12th 1890

My dear Scribner:

The box of books arrived duly yesterday just in time for the first opening and created a sensation. If you could have seen the fellows sitting on the floor in rows with their backs to the wall because there were not chairs enough for them you would have understood what my hope is. Personally I am a thousand times obliged to you. There is not one that I do not thank you especially for. I hope this may become in time the nucleus of a Free Library which to our shame we yet lack in this City.

I have named it "The Rosemary Library and Reading Room for Boys." "Rosemary — that's for Remembrance."

239

Please remember me cordially to Mrs Scribner and thank the House for me.
Your friend
Thos. N. Page

CS II Diary Entry:
Wednesday 19 August 1891

Wrote to Page we would give him $500 "on pub." of Among the Camps

---

Related Letter:
Like that of many authors, Page's interest in seeing his works published did not end with his written words; he took great care in the whole process of creating the physical product, the book. And, like most publishers, CS II had to deal with the suggestions and demands of such authors, regardless of their business sense. In these letters to CS II, Page reveals concerns for both his words and the finished product — in this case, his novel Red Rock: A Chronicle of Reconstruction.

Sept. 2, 1898

My dear Scribner:
I sent you the other day a third install. of MS down to Chap. XXX, incl. I am now mailing you the corrected proof as far as it has reached me: being to Galley 23. Will you kindly inform whoever may be the proper personage, that I wish my Story left as I write it. There is someone in the printing establishment who knows so much that I cant get my Story printed as I wish it. For instance, he insists on always cutting out capitals. (See galley 19.) And I cannot get <u>towards</u> or <u>afterwards</u> printed, to save my life; whilst this word ("whilst") is as completely vanished as though Thackeray and every other good English writer had never used it. Now "toward," "afterward," (sometimes pronounced, I find, afterword), "while," etc. may be the best form today; but as I am writing this Novel, and not the gentleman of the fine pen and fine English whose marks I constantly find on my margins, I prefer my own English to his. So, you will do me a favor to notify him. Wherever I have made a slip or overlooked one his business is to correct it; but I am tired of his undertaking to correct my English, and substitute his own.

Yours faithfully
Thos. Nelson Page

Oct. 26th 1898

My dear Scribner:
Many thanks for the first copy of Red Rock. The misquotation of the verse, "Syria is confederate with Ephraim," is on p 199. I am glad to hear that you have thought it worth while to print another 5000 copies. I hope this means that the demand is already in sight. I think the binding unusually good, and the print comes out clear and strong. The paper, however, does not come up to what I had hoped it would be. It seems to me too thin and light, and this with the immediate juxtaposition of the advertisements of my other books to the text makes the book look cheaper than it should. I know of course that all this was done with an idea that it was for my interest as well as yours, and I feel we are at one as to it; but I feel that it would make the book more dignified if the next edn. should be on a better paper, and the notices of the other books be put on a single page as has been done in the other volumes, or at least divided from the text by a blank page. The vol. can stand being thicker. Nearly all the good novels in my library and many of the poor ones are thicker. So are many other books, and whilst they are perfectly handy they are better looking. Your edn. of "Froude's Caesar" is on paper thicker than is necessary in our case and is 570 pages; "Elsie Venner," in Houghton Mifflin's, Edn. 1888, of Dr Holmes' works, has 586 pp and is on thick paper; yet is not too large. So I have twenty books before me all of about the same no. of pp, and none too large to be handy.

It seems ungracious to be critical where there is so much that is good; but I believe you would rather have my views, in a matter where the error can be corrected, and it seems to me a pity that a book so well printed and bound should be cheapened in appearance by such a small thing. Believe me, my dear Scribner,

Yours sincerely,
Thos. Nelson Page

As a result of Page's complaints, the paper and the placement of the advertisement were changed on subsequent printings.

CS II Diary Entry:
Friday 17 October 1902

Offer Page for his novel on book $10,000 advance on 20% royalty

---

Page accepted this offer for Gordon Keith.

John Marvel

Preface

The most vital fact in our life today, after the never-ceasing play of the passions of Humanity, is the awakening of The People. Like a giant aroused from long slumber, they are beginning to bestir themselves with noise and clamor and tumult enough. But all the time they are advancing, and when they shall have awakened fully, the world will have taken on a new face.

It is in the attempt to show this awakening in our midst that this book has been written and is now dedicated to

To The True John Marvel:
The Worker among the Poor.

T. N. P.

Original manuscript of Page's preface, which was omitted from John Marvel, Assistant *on the recommendation of Scribners.*

RELATED LETTERS:
The opportunity of serializing a novel in Scribner's Magazine *before book publication was a great attraction for Scribner authors. The theory was that the magazine, with its large circulation, would create an immediate, broad recognition and market for the finished book. Financially, the author would benefit twice: from the payment for the serial and from the greater royalties from the increased sales. In 1908, Page was ready to subscribe to that theory again — it had been ten years since one of his novels (*Red Rock*) had been serialized first. (His previous novel,* Gordon Keith, *had skipped the magazine serialization step and still had become the #2 bestseller of 1903.) Beyond detailing some of the logistics involved in serializing* John Marvel, Assistant, *these two letters reveal the mutual feelings of confidence and trust Page had developed with Scribners.*

Sept. 3, 1908

Dear Tom:

It was too bad that I missed you as you passed through the city. I had been in town the night before, but stopped on the way to the office to attend to some personal matters.

My letter about the novel has been delayed until I could talk it over with Mr. Burlingame, who did not return from his vacation until the first of this week. I am glad to be able to write now that we are prepared to engage the serial and, in legal phraseology, I hereby do so. This is the first time since the days of Stevenson that we have committed ourselves to a serial of which we had so little in hand, and I cannot place too much emphasis upon the fact that we do this on your assurance that there will be no failure to supply us with the completed work. It is most desirable, to avoid all danger, that we should have a copy of the entire story in some form early in the winter, and it is, I think, essential that we should always have three parts ahead in completed form for proof correction. Our plan is to begin with the January number, and this means that we should have three completed parts by the close of the first week in November, and a little earlier if possible.

I rather disliked to show the first 130 pages to Burlingame, as they were so far from finished and of course he has not had the benefit of hearing directly from you about what the story will be, but I have tried to pass on to him all the information received. We are returning the manuscript by mail today, and I have asked Burlingame to suggest anything he thought would improve the story, so that you might have the benefit of his ideas in your revision. Please understand that what he does in this respect is directly at my request and in the hope that it will be helpful to you.

As to price, we will pay ten thousand dollars for the serial, which is what we have agreed to pay Mrs. Wharton and more than I should expect to pay almost any one else.

This is a hurried letter, written toward the close of the day, but I have tried to cover the most important points. Unless we hear from you to the contrary, we shall announce the serial almost at once. We must take up with Mr. Chapin the question of illustration.

I hope I need not say how much pleasure it gives me personally to have you so closely connected with the Magazine for next year.

Yours sincerely,
Charles Scribner

Sept 4th 1908

My dear Charles:

I was very much pleased and gratified by your kind letter and as I have already telegraphed you in reply I accept your terms and conditions and D.V. will meet your expectations if it is in my power to do so when I put forth all the powers I possess.

Please say to Burlingame for me that I shall be glad to consider carefully any and all suggestions he may make and I will not only welcome but crave the criticism he may feel proper to give me. The Novel, in a sort, grew out of a criticism he made on the story which I sent him years back and that criticism led me to go deeper than I had dreamed of doing at that time. Acting on a suggestion you made when here I have been laying a broader foundation for the story and have already written some six thousand more words — a way of measuring that I detest; but have to adopt for convenience — and have introduced a negro boy — a follower and hanger-on of my young man — who amuses me and I hope may amuse others — and a bull terrier whom I like and hope to love — also an old lady, as yet vague and sketchy; but still I hope real and alive. The story begins to take on a definite shape and as I am going at it seriously I trust I may satisfy both you and Burlingame. I know I have a good idea and if I am capable of handling the subject artistically I ought to have a good novel. I told Mr. Howells the other day the line I am working on and he appeared to be struck by it. He said he thought it a good idea and one that ought to be worked out. Of course, I know it is all in the handling; but I am not afraid of work and I am not afraid of criticism. So lets have any views that occur to you as the story proceeds and maybe something more than an ephemeral success may be my reward. I am going to do my level best to write a first class novel.

Faithfully yours,
Thos. Nelson Page

CS II DIARY ENTRY:
Friday 20 June 1913

See Page who offers to take Charles as secretary
to Rome

"Charles" is CS III, Scribner's son, who did not go.

LETTER:
Letter by Page to CS II, written from the American embassy in Rome, 16 June 1915.

A strong, prominent supporter of Woodrow Wilson in the presidential election of 1912, Page was appointed U.S. ambassador to Italy in 1913. He sailed for Rome that September to assume his post, the second Scribner author to be an ambassador at the same time (Henry van Dyke was U.S. ambassador to the Netherlands and Luxembourg). In this letter Page talks of F. Hopkinson Smith (1838–1915), friend and fellow Scribner author, who had suddenly died in April.

My dear Charles:

I am sending you by private hand the paper I have written on our old friend Frank Smith, for the Magazine. It has been at once a pleasure and a sorrow to me, for I was sincerely devoted to him, and I miss him very much. Besides this, I am conscious all the time of such an inexpressible sorrow for Mrs. Smith.

You all may find in the paper bits which are rather too intimate, and if so, I give you full permission to cut them out. I shall send you an introductory note for his book. This I have not yet written; but it will be found probably to cover parts of what I have written in this sketch of Hopkinson Smith which I am sending to you, and if so, you can cut out from this sketch what I put in the

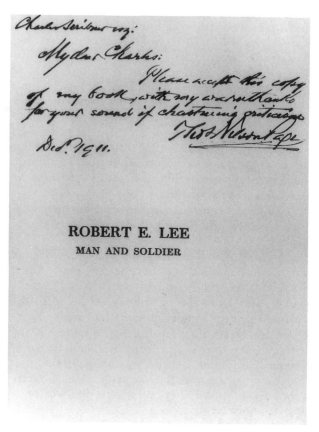

ROBERT E. LEE
MAN AND SOLDIER

The "chastening criticisms" Page refers to in this inscription to CS II are comments Scribner made about the obvious Southern bias in the work: how Page's exaltation of Lee had caused him to deprecate everything Northern.

note. I will sufficiently indicate it for the excising to be readily done.

I have run through many of his volumes since I undertook this sketch and the result has increased greatly my appreciation of him as a writer. It is extraordinary that he should have written so well so much in so short a time, and there are parts in his book which really are as good as the best of them. I knew they were there before; but was rather surprised to find how universal they were.

I hope you may think the sketch sincere and natural enough to make up for any omissions there may be. I have at least felt all the way through that I was discharging an obligation towards one who deserved all the expression of appreciation possible at my hands, for he gave me a very real and deep friendship, as he did you, Charles.

No man in all my wide acquaintance stands out to me more clearly defined and with lines such as one would like to have himself expressed by, than Frank Smith. I trust Berkeley [son of Smith] may now find himself able to swim alone.

Mrs. Page I know wrote Mrs. Scribner a little while ago, urging you and her to come over here for your holiday and pay us a little visit. I wish to Heavens you could do so, and if it be possible I hope you will. We cannot get away from here; but unless some new turn comes, we could readily enough girate around Rome enough to give us some pleasant excursions.

So far as external appearances here are concerned, you would never know that there was war this side of Mars.

Before war was declared we used to have considerable excitement here from time to time; but with the declaration of war, news from the outside and from the in alike, is reduced to the minimum, and Rome is quieter than I ever knew it. We are, so to speak, interned and to get up any flurry, I have to make protests against being prohibited from using English in our telegrams that pass between us and our Consuls. The Government here is, so far, very reasonable and we are on most friendly terms.

If you and Mrs. Scribner come, you will find everything quiet and I believe comfortable, and while you would not be able perhaps to visit Venice or Ravenna, and certainly could not take a run through the Tirol, all of Central and Southern Italy is free for you to do everything in, except take photographs.

Now that your children are married, you and Mrs. Scribner should take advantage of the freedom given you, and come see us. Rome is so far as pleasant as it is peaceful, and it will be an experience for you to meditate on all the rest of your life. Also, you will be able to see how an Ambassador runs an American Embassy in time of war and can add your aid, council and comfort to those of all the rest of Americans in Rome as to how it should be done.

With warmest regards to Mrs. Scribner and to my friends with you as well as to yourself, I am,
Always faithfully yours,
Thos. Nelson Page

Page's remembrance of F. Hopkinson Smith appeared in the September 1915 issue of Scribner's Magazine.

CS II DIARY ENTRY:
Friday 1 August 1919

Leave @ 9.30 and stop for lunch at Page's at York Harbor. First time to see them after return from Rome. All are well and most cordial. Leave @ 3 and night at Boston

---

Page's summer home was at York Harbor, Maine.

Harold Frederic (1856–1898)

Harold Frederic

A journalist all of his life, Frederic never found financial freedom with his own writing. Scribners published his first novel and most of his other fiction; however, the work for which he is best remembered, and his most successful novel (the number five best-seller of 1896), was *The Damnation of Theron Ware*. During his lifetime Frederic was labeled a realist or regionalist and denied enduring importance, but in more recent criticism reevaluating his contributions to American literature he is considered to rank with Stephen Crane (a friend and admirer) and Ambrose Bierce in his unsentimentalized historical fiction about the Civil War and with William Dean Howells and Theodore Dreiser in his perceptive studies of human psychology and social complexities.

Scribner Books by Frederic

1887	*Seth's Brother's Wife: A Study of Life in the Greater New York*
1890	*The Lawton Girl*
	In the Valley, illustrated by Howard Pyle
1893	*The Copperhead*
1894	*Marsena, and Other Stories of the Wartime*
1897	*In the Sixties*

LETTER:
Letter by Frederic to Scribners, [May 1884], accompanying his first submission.

Frederic's story, "Brother Sebastian's Friendship," was accepted and appeared later that year in volume six of Scribners' Stories by American Authors *series. On 11 June 1884 he sailed with his family to London as foreign correspondent for* The New York Times, *a position he held for the rest of his life.*

Dear Sirs:

I enclose for your perusal a story of mine, written in 1879, and first published in the Utica Observer, of which paper I was then the editor. I subsequently became editor of the Albany Evening Journal, and with a perhaps pardonable affection for the thing, reprinted it there. It has been published in a few other papers, reproduced from these sources.

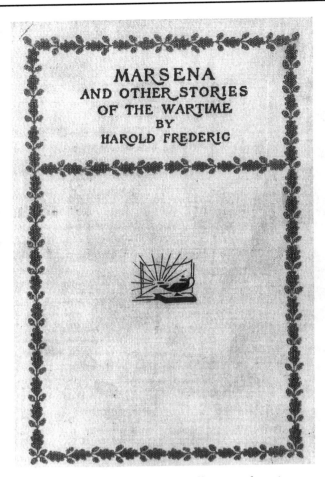

Cover of Frederic's 1894 collection of stories

The incident upon which the tale is built was related to me by Brother Azarias, President of Rocky Hill College, Md., who heard it in France; and it interests me to recall that, at the time, his friends in the communities very strenuously insisted that he was the author of the story — so much were they impressed with the realism of its local color and details.

It may easily be that I overstate its literary and artistic value, but I cannot be blamed for wishing for it a better setting than it has heretofore had in the fugitive form of the daily press. As an enclosed slip indicates, I am to leave the country next month, to serve the New York Times abroad for a term of years. I could expatriate myself with a lighter heart if I knew that my one little ewe-lamb of fiction was to be given a place in your collection of American short stories.

I am to be away from home now, for a week or two, and hope to find an answer awaiting me on my return.

Faithfully Yours,
Harold Frederic

LETTER:
Letter by Frederic to Edward L. Burlingame, editor of *Scribner's Magazine*, 15 April 1887, from London.

Frederic's first novel, Seth's Brother's Wife, *was serialized in* Scribner's Magazine, *beginning with its inaugural number, January 1887.*

Dear Mr. Burlingame:

I thank you sincerely for having so promptly attended to my importunate despatch, and for the gratifying words about the serial in the Magazine. Major Kirkland's letter was a genuine delight to me. I wish you had given me Mr. Bunner's words.

Over here people seem to like it. I have very flattering comments on it from time to time; others not so nice. One Englishman — a journalist too — said to a friend of mine: "Yes, it isn't bad, but I hate so much nigger dialect!"

I have been very nervous, and at times despondent, about "Douw" ever since I sent the first half of it to you. No doubt it was silly, but I could not help construing your silence to mean that it was no good. The result is that I have only done three additional chapters, and these very badly. You seem to say now that you like it — and I shall be encouraged by this to go at it again next week.

All around I have been out of sorts since I last wrote to you. The Times people feel that they want a Sunday letter more in the World-Sun style than mine. It is not in my line; beside, I am tired of newspaper work, and its ceaseless worrying and interruptions. Accordingly, I have today written to Mr. Miller telling him that I have had enough of Europe, and am ready to come home — or shall be by autumn.

What I shall do I don't know. Perhaps I can support myself outside newspaper work; if not, there will be something somewhere for me, I suppose — perhaps in Washington.

I am not worldly-wise, I know, in giving up this berth. But I can't help it. I am giving the best years of my life to work I dislike, in a country I hate, and even if I have to make some sacrifices I feel that I ought to get out.

You will let me know about "Douw" as soon as possible, won't you?

Always faithfully yours
Harold Frederic

Burlingame did like Frederic's second novel, but not his intended title of "Douw Mauverensen," the name of the book's heroine — nor did Howard Pyle who had been hired to illustrate the book. Burlingame finally suggested "In the Valley," under which name the book finally appeared in 1890. The delay was because of serialization conflict in Scribner's Magazine *with Robert Louis Stevenson's novel,* The Master of Ballantrae, *which had been scheduled first. Of Frederic's plans to leave his London position with* The New York Times, *nothing developed. He continued a dual professional life as a journalist and an author, and began a second family with a mistress.*

RELATED LETTERS:
Letter by Frederic to CS II, 1 June 1894, from London; letter by CS II in response, 22 June 1894.

A typical exchange between disappointed author and defensive publisher regarding a perceived lack of promotion (and resulting poor sales) for a book.

Dear Messrs. Scribner:

I am having sent to you, by this post, sheets of the entire volume which is printed here as "The Copperhead," in order to supply you with the three minor stories "The War Widow," "the Eve of the Fourth," & "My Aunt Susan."

These with "Marsena," now just ending in the New York Times, will make a book of about 45,000 words, or at least over 40,000. "Marsena" will be a good enough name for the volume, I fancy.

I should be glad if you would send me an advance on royalties, as in the case of "The Copperhead."

I have just received a great batch of "Copperhead" press notices from America, and am surprised at their almost uniform warmth and even enthusiasm. The book here has had a remarkable critical success, and has done very well in other ways. But you will have had even better opportunities than mine to see how exceptionally the American critics have treated it. You alas also have facilities for knowing how little the American public have bought it.

I don't like to complain, but I _do_ feel keenly that men who do work much inferior to mine get advantage in advertising, and in cognate things, which my books, poor devils, may not hope for. I see your advertisements in a number of different forms, notably The Nation, the magazines & the N.Y. papers. It may be all illusion on my part, but I seem to get less show in these than any other writer whose name is on your books. Even when *The Boston Herald* started a boom for "In the Valley," I heard of it from eight or ten strangers who wrote to me from different parts of New England, but I could not learn that my publishers had lifted a finger to utilize these things.

Doubtless you hear this plaint, or some variation of it, from many people. That will help you to receive this one with the better good nature. But it _is_ a grinding and aggravating thing that books of their character — which you and I don't differ much about — should be left to make their own slow way along, always doing a little I grant you, but doing that little strictly off their own bat, while the whole impetus of organization is put at the disposal of books which, if _they_ were left to

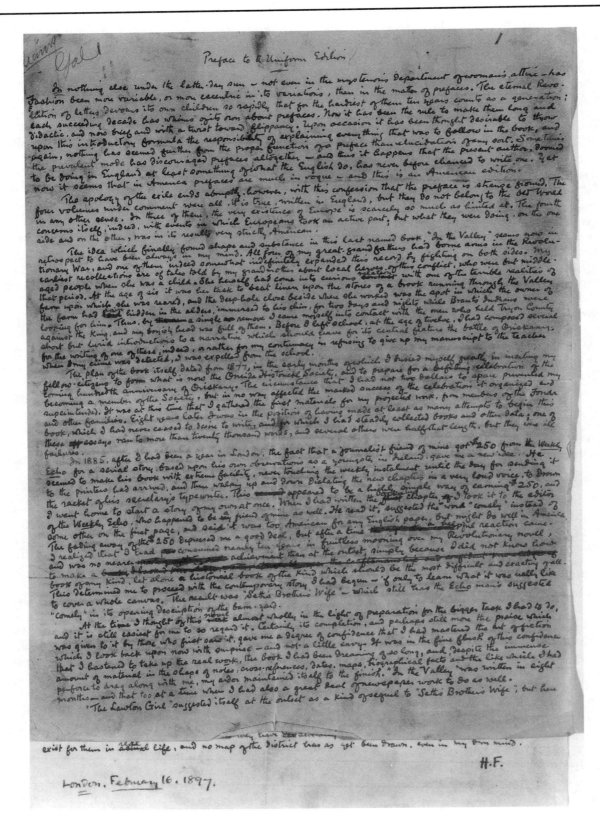

Manuscript of Frederic's preface to the uniform edition of his works published by Scribners in 1897

themselves, would go into the ditch within a twelvemonth.

Don't you agree with me that I have waited a long time, with an excess of patience, and that it is time I had a "look in"?

Always faithfully yours
Harold Frederic

Dear Mr. Frederic:

Your letter of June 1st and the accompanying sheets of "The Copperhead" duly reached me. We shall at once begin work at the printers on the proposed volume sending you galley-proofs which will doubtless be sufficient. By next mail we shall send you contract for the book and the advance as in the case of "The Copperhead"; they could not be ready for this letter.

We can quite appreciate your disappointment that "The Copperhead" has not met with larger sale. It is possible that in these very dull times we have lacked spirit in our publication of it though we have certainly wished to give it our best attention. But after all the complaint is a more general one for we never worked harder over any books than we did over "In the Valley" and "The Lawton Girl" and yet their sale was not proportionate to our efforts.

You of course will recognize that the taste of the public in these matters is altogether capricious and the success of the inferior books which you doubtless have in mind is really due, not to any effort of the publishers, but because they happen to please public fancy. With "Marsena" we shall make an effort to draw attention to all your previous works but we can hardly hope to greatly increase the sale of the old books by such efforts.

We remain
Yours sincerely
Charles Scribner

RELATED LETTERS:
Letter by CS II to Frederic, 21 August 1896.

Dissatisfied with what he perceived as Scribners' poor advertising and the resulting small sales of his books, Frederic offered his next novel, The Damnation of Theron Ware, *to Stone and Kimball, the Chicago publisher. It met with great popular and critical success, both in England, where it was published under the title* Illumination, *and in America. In his letter to Frederic containing a semiannual royalty check, CS II congratulates him.*

My dear Mr. Frederic:

Enclosed you will please find our usual semi-annual report with our check for the amount due. Last time you wished the money deposited in the bank to your credit but as you have sent us no word this time we mail it direct.

I must congratulate you upon the success of your new novel — in London at least and I suppose here too. It was rather hard upon us to take it from our list after we have issued so many from you. You seemed to think that we had not pushed them as much as we should have done, but when you remember that three of them were published first as serials in our Magazine it must be sufficient evidence that they were well advertised. "In the Valley" and "Seth's Brother's Wife" were as a matter of fact unusually thoroughly advertised. And you might remember that Mr. Heinemann [Frederic's English publisher] had just the same experience as ourselves with the earlier books.

But I had not intended to write all this but only to congratulate you and to recall ourselves to your notice if you are disposed to put future books in our way.

Yours very truly
Charles Scribner

Here is Frederic's response, 3 November 1896, from London:

My dear Mr. Scribner:

I ought before this to have answered your letter of August 21, which enclosed $30.42 for the half-year's royalties on what practically are six copyrights. There was so much, however, that suggested itself to be said, that in the result the letter didn't get written at all.

The fact that six books (one of which has been widely discussed, in connection with "Theron Ware," as probably its superior) earn for me an average of ten dollars each in a year, forms a flatly depressing overture to correspondence. I have outworn the anger which it raised in me at the outset, but the pain and puzzlement of the thing do not go so readily. I don't in the least understand it all. It might have been thought that, when "Theron Ware" was being talked of everywhere, it would have occurred to somebody that there were other books of mine. This happens to me in England: it happens to other people in America, I am told — but not to me. The earlier books were more systematically neglected than ever, according at least to the sales reports.

What good is there in discussing an inscrutable situation like this? I would rather thank you cordially for your kind congratulations upon the turn in my affairs, which I feel are entirely sincere, and not talk about the other thing at all. Everything that could be said was said long ago. My pleas, expostulations, tears and curses are all on your letter-files, or vaguely in the memory of somebody on the premises.

What I should like to ask is a question turning upon the terms of our agreement re the older books. It is provided that if, at the expiration of five years, the demand for the book is not in your opinion sufficient to render its publication profitable, the contract shall cease. In such a case, it is open to me to take over the copies and plant at cost. It occurs to me that the three books which you have had more than five years must all come under that category. It cannot be much more profitable to you than it is to me, to be handling books which average, in four forms, a half-yearly sale of 35 volumes each. Are you prepared, therefore, to apply the terms of the contracts, quoted above, to these books, so that I may take them over, at cost, and let them try their fortunes under other conditions?

My friend Mr. Edward Bok, who was good enough to take an interest on the serial prospects of a forthcoming book of mine, wrote a while ago that he had spoken to you on the subject, and that the magazine was full for 1897. I am rejoiced to see that it is filled with two Americans — not that Scribner's has ever been a conspicuous sinner in this matter — but the fact renders it needless to talk about my own book. I have two or three tentative American serial suggestions in hand, but I am not clear that the book won't on the whole do better as a book outright, despite the experience of The Lawton Girl.

Pray read into what I have written that personal liking and respect which would have a chance to express themselves if we were talking instead of writing, and believe me to be always

Most sincerely yours
Harold Frederic

Probably as an effort to show good faith, Scribners offered to publish five of Frederic's books, including his next book, In the Sixties, *in a uniform edition, which they did in 1897.*

Alice French (1850–1934)
("Octave Thanet")

Engraving made for the April 1889 issue of the Book Buyer

French was among the highest-paid American storywriters during the 1880s and 1890s; today her books are out of print. Primarily a Midwest regionalist and local color author, she found success in recording dialect and describing the domestic life of social groups where she lived in Iowa and Arkansas. In her stories she often dealt with marriage, friendship, and relationships between employers and employees, while maintaining a social Darwinian point of view that stressed the superiority of the upper classes. Her pseudonym, "Octave Thanet," a combination of a schoolmate's name and a word she saw chalked on a freight train, contributed a genderless, foreign quality to the public anonymity she sought to maintain. French became a Scribner author through *Scribner's Magazine,* but did not remain one for very long, probably because the firm was more interested in novels and the editors of other leading periodicals and publishers were clamoring for her work.

Scribner Books by French

1890	*Expiation,* illustrated by A. B. Frost
1893	*Stories of a Western Town,* illustrated by Frost
	An Adventure in Photography, "illustrated from photographs by the adventurers"
1898	*The Heart of Toil,* illustrated by Frost

French writes to Edward L. Burlingame, editor of Scribner's Magazine, *who has accepted her multi-part story that will be serialized in the magazine (January–April 1890) and then published as her first Scribner book,* Expiation.

Clover Bend, Arkansas   March 2 [1889]
Dear Mr. Burlingame:

It was very good of you to write me at such length. I don't think any writer even feels aggrieved at an <u>acceptance</u> by telegram.

I am glad you like Sir Guy. It is a very halting and "triflin'" effort to explain a hard problem; but at least it is an honest one; and I think you may have confidence in the "local color."

I shouldn't hesitate to send another story with only one [with?] though I might have felt diffident about overloading you with my wares, had you several in stock. But I have been trying to work through my promises to Mr. Gilder and Mr. Aldrich and several others. And the year has been a very hard one to me, too. My dear father died, last autumn. I saw the death of Mrs. Anson Burlingame in the papers, and my aunt (Mrs. Marcus Morton of Andover, Mass.) wrote us about her own sorrow in losing her old friend. I wondered if she was not your mother. These are losses which no time ever can make up. I wish that my father might have known you; and I had hoped that this summer we might call on you together. Last summer I went to Canada instead of to the seashore with him; we agreed that <u>this</u> summer I should surely go to Massachusetts. But I shall always regret that I didn't go last year. Perhaps you will be in New York in June. I shall hope, in that case, to see you.

I will send the stories as soon as they are copied. Let me say, please, that I feel an unwarranted but almost personal pride and pleasure in the splendid success which you are making of Scribner.

Aren't you going to have something in it sometime about amateur photograph[y]. I am an enthusiastic failure in "the art science" and feel moved sometimes to appeal to the writers on that subject for a little less fine language and more <u>facts</u>. So my friend and I, read almost every advertisement of the future number for something on photography. I must thank you too, for your kindness to my friend, Miss Hill. She is now in New York studying, doing some illustrations for the St. Nicholas for a little thing of mine and acquiring the necessary technical knowledge rapidly.

I hope if you ever come to Arkansas in winter you will let us show you the simple charms of a plantation and an ideal climate.
          Very truly yours,
          Alice French

More than two and a half years later, Burlingame picks up on French's idea of "amateur photography" in the following letter. In fact, his proposals result in her next two Scribner books, An Adventure in Photography *and* Stories of a Western Town.

New York, November 24th, 1891
Dear Miss French: —

I am delighted to have the story, like it heartily (even better than the last "short" short story), and will take it and print it at once with great pleasure.

It came, to tell you the truth, just as I was on the point of writing to you on two things, — the first of which should have been talked of long ago if I had not felt that my last letter about stories might have seemed a trifle importunate, and that I might better wait until I got what had been promised me then before I asked for more.

First, then, I was going to write to say (in general terms) that we were not getting enough good "short fiction," or that somehow or other it did not suit my pallate, and (in specific terms) that it had really been a subject of regret and annoyance to me that in this last year we have had too little of yours. I have wondered if we could have been a little guilty of any <u>laches</u> toward what we had before, but I could not convict myself of anything that would have driven you into other camps and could not imagine that you were importuned so widely that you could not meet everybody's wishes, but met ours as often as you could. I hope this is the case; but how would it be if you could plead a rather more definite engagement in reply, through some proposition of ours which should be satisfactory to you, and perhaps keep your work for a time a little more together and more related? Suppose for instance that we should ask you if you would do for us <u>in a series</u> the sketches of a Western town that you have in mind? or a succession of "short," short stories strung upon some thread of connection as locality or common character from a village group might give them? We should be glad to make such a proposal (say to pay $1,000 for six of them[*]) and afterward ask you to let us have them in a book under a fifteen per cent royalty arrangement.

Clover Bend — Feb. 13 '90

Dear Sirs;

I enclose copy of contract signed and witnessed. Page proofs will be quite suf-ficient.

The contract is very lib-eral (as have been all your dealings with me) and I hope that you will not be disappointed in the book having a modest success

Very truly yours,

Alice French

Chas Scribners Sons.

Letter by French to Scribners accompanying her signed contract for her first novel and first Scribner book, Expiation

A VOICE CRIED, HEARTILY, "COME IN, VI; WHAT ARE YOU WAITING FOR?"

❧❧❧ The Heart of Toil
By Octave Thanet ❧❧❧

Illustrated by A. B. Frost

Charles Scribner's Sons
New York 〰〰〰 1898

Frontispiece and title page in French's last Scribner book

Would you consider such a proposal? It would not necessarily be exclusive, even for a time. We have no wish, even if we had the right, to ask you to "tie yourself up"; but such an arrangement might make it easier for you to let pass some things that you cared less about, — and we are frankly and sincerely anxious to have your work more closely identified with the Magazine, which has had great pleasure in it and I may say depended on it from the beginning.

There is a long "firstly." Here is the second thing about which I have been on the point of writing. You once wrote me (in March 1889) that you should like to write an article on Amateur Photography, its trials, triumphs, etc., with illustrations out of your own experience (like those charming ones I have, I suppose). We were hampered in the Magazine at that time with some other plans, and I could not avail myself of the suggestion. But now comes something which bears upon it strongly. We have an idea that if a little <u>book</u> could be made on just the lines you suggested for an article, — something that should be both a technical guide and a pleasurable companion (a kind of Izaak Walton's Angler of Photography) it would be very successful now, and widely read. Of course it should be written not in the dry old rut, but just as I think you would like to write it; and it seems to me a real opportunity for a good and pleasant, and in no way perfunctory, thing. If you are willing to consider a proposal to do it we should like to make you one, and I am sure something capital and exceptional could be done.

Is this too much for one letter? I am afraid so. So with kind regards from myself, I am
Yours sincerely,
E. L. Burlingame
* I say that on the inferences from your letter that they are quite short — comparatively few pages each?

LETTER:
Letter by French to Arthur H. Scribner, 15 February 1893, about her photography book.

Dear Mr. Scribner: —

Your kind letter and the proof illustration for the photograph book, have both arrived. I am greatly pleased with — well, to be honest, with both!

The illustration has rendered the details remarkably. And the tone is beautiful. I think I asked for two prints of that picture, one to show the figures of the boys — example of mistake in compostion! — the other a vignette, — example how to remedy mistake. To take perhaps a needless precaution I enclose a little note for the illustration, explaining my previous vignetting directions; it is better to be too plain than not plain enough. And I never illustrated a book before, you know!

I have some of the MS ready but have kept it to add some. After the negatives are printed may I have proofs to name them and say where they belong? or is there a better way of doing it?

There are a few more negatives that I shall send next week.

I am trying in a measure to replace some that are broken. Only three more are coming. If I have sent too many, please tell me; and I will select from those already sent.

I hope I shall not disappoint you in the book. It is a pleasure to me to write it.

And may I say here, Mr. Scribner, that I have always appreciated the courtesy, promptness and liberality shown me in all the dealings of your firm with me?

No author could ask more appreciative or generous publishers.

I am always,
Very cordially yours,
Alice French

Eugene Field (1850–1895)

Eugene Field

Labeled as the "poet of childhood," Field was a newspaperman all of his adult life, holding editorial positions on the *St. Joseph Gazette,* the *St. Louis Journal,* the *Kansas City Times,* and the *Denver Tribune.* With his Denver column, "Odds and Ends," he had acquired a large following of readers by the time (1883) he was hired away by the *Chicago Morning News* (renamed the *Record* in 1890) to start another column, called "Sharps and Flats," which he continued till his death. Most of his writings first appeared as newspaper column contributions — satiric essays, imaginary anecdotes, verse parodies, serious poems, stories, literary and bibliographical notes — and they exerted a strong influence on the development of this feature in American journalism. A lover of pranks and practical jokes, possessed of a whimsical nature, Field found his element in sentimental poems about childhood, some of which are still well known today. He chose Scribners as his publisher in 1890, but most of his works were published posthumously.

Scribner Books by Field

1890	*A Little Book of Profitable Tales*
	A Little Book of Western Verse (enlarged)
1892	*With Trumpet and Drum*
1893	*Second Book of Verse*
1894	*Love-Songs of Childhood*
1895	*Echoes from the Sabine Farm,* co-authored by Roswell Martin Field
1896	*The Love Affairs of a Bibliomaniac*
	The House: An Episode in the Lives of Reuben Baker, Astronomer, and of His Wife Alice
	The Holy Cross, and Other Tales (enlarged)
	Second Book of Tales
	Songs, and Other Verse
	Songs of Childhood, verses by Field, music by Reginald De Koven and others

LETTER:
First letter by Field to CS II, 7 May 1890.

Serendipity placed Field's books in the hands of the House of Scribner. Field wrote Scribners from London, where he had taken his family as a respite from Chicago, offering the firm the opportunity of the trade publication of two books he had just published in limited editions. Scribners published the books on 26 September 1890. They were the house's best-sellers of 1890/1891.

Dear Sir: Last October John Wilson & Son printed two books (companion volumes) for me, entitled, respectively, "A Little Book of Western Verse" and a "Little Book of Profitable Tales." I have the plates and am prepared to treat with you if you care to publish these books for the trade.

Two hundred and fifty copies of each volume were printed last October and issued to subscribers at $5 a set (of 2). The sets are now in demand at $25 but are hard to get. It would hardly be in good faith to the original subscribers to issue a reprint of the books. It is my wish to change the titles, the indices and the dedications, and to pad out the book of verse somewhat. The volume of tales contains 200 pages, and that of the verse about 178 pp. It would be wise I think to supplement the latter with perhaps half a dozen of the poems which I have written since coming to Europe.

The plates are held by Mr. Slason Thompson, editor of <u>America,</u> in Chicago and he will forward them to you in case we twain come to an understanding.

It is my wish the books shall be printed <u>handsomely,</u> and I am anxious that they should be pushed in the market. Therefore I give your house an opportunity which I believe you would find fairly profitable.

My address for three months will be 20 Alfred Place, Bedford-square, W., London, and I hope to hear from you. Mr. Stedman has copies of the books; so has Mr. Stoddard; so has Mr. Charles E. Roche, of the New York <u>Herald.</u> I suppose that any of these gentlemen would lend you his copies for a few days in case you have not seen the books.

Very sincerely yours,
Eugene Field

RELATED LETTERS:
Field's reputation as a collector and lover of fine books is illustrated in the details which he suggested for the publication of his own works and in the interest he had in fine printing and limited editions. Francis Wilson, mentioned in this letter, was a well-known comic actor of the period, a close friend of Field, and also a passionate book collector.

Gentlemen: I return herewith the memorandum you require. I am much gratified with the dress you have given the books. I could not have suggested any improvement. You may make any arrangement you choose about selling the books abroad; I certainly shall not make any. I am totally indifferent to the good will and the money of every country that is not bounded on the north by Canada and on the south by Mexico. Pray excuse the exceeding brevity of this note; I am in serious trouble; my oldest boy is sick unto death.

Ever Sincerely yours,

Eugene Field.

3 Montpelier Terrace; Montpelier Square;

South Kensington, London, Oct. 1, 1890.

Letter to Scribners by Field, written from London on receipt of copies of his first Scribner books. The sick son he mentions was Melvin, whose death shortly afterward precipitated the family's return to America.

Chicago, Sept. 16, 1892

Dear Mr. Scribner: Tomorrow night I will send the manuscript for "With Trumpet and Drum," and while I shall defer to you people in every particular, I beg to submit these suggestions:

1. That there be a small etching of the title-page representing a Cupid holding two masks, one <u>T</u>ragedy and the other <u>C</u>omedy.
2. That there be no title to the table of contents, that instead thereof there be a picture of a toy trumpet.
3. That there be a tailpiece (after the last poem) representing a <u>broken</u> drum.
4. That the volume be a 16 mo.; with a preliminary limited edition of 150 numbered copies signed by the publishers; printed upon <u>thin</u> hand-made paper, uncut edges; binding simple, in baby-blue and white; gilt tops.
5. That we share alike on this first edition, after the costs of publishing are charged to me; each take 50 per cent of profits.
7. That you, immediately upon the publication of this limited edition, publish a popular edition.

We must "rob'em" with the limited edition, but a dollar-book (net) ought to follow. I am exceedingly anxious to have a neat, dainty little volume not only <u>for</u> children but <u>about</u> childhood. So now, when you get the copy, whoop things up in your most aesthetic fashion.

By the way, No. 1 of every limited edition of mine must be reserved for Francis Wilson.

I want my daughter, Mary French Field, to have the profits on the copyright of this volume. You had better copyright the work and then we will have a contract drawn up to be signed by you and the "infant's" business representative.

Sincerely yours,
Eugene Field

With Trumpet and Drum was published 3 December 1892, to great success. It included for the first time Field's best-known poems, "Wynken, Blynken, and Nod," "Little Boy Blue," and "The Duel." During the winter of 1892–1893, Field joined with George Washington Cable, another Scribner author, in a tour of readings.

October 20, [189]2

Dear Mr. Field: —

Enclosed you will please find a contract for "With Trumpet and Drum" made out in accordance with what I understand to be your wishes. The contract covers only the regular edition of the book, as the limited edition will we hope soon be a matter of the past. I have thought that the understanding arrived at in our letters would answer as to that.

Will you please send me the full name of your wife, in order that I may have the contract made out for her on "The Second Book of Verse." When do you suppose we shall be able to publish this book? Not until after the holidays I presume; although we could get ready very quickly if we knew your wishes and when we might expect the plates.

We shall have ten copies of "Trumpet and Drum" upon Japan paper as requested and I will sign them. I suppose your idea is that my autograph will bring a high price.

Your intention of going on the platform with Cable was quite new to me. I wish you every success and should be glad to do anything in my power to contribute to it. Cable is rather a lively bird to travel with but I suppose you can take care of yourself.

If the contract is all right please sign and return and we will send you one with our signature.

Yours sincerely,
Charles Scribner

RELATED LETTERS:

The early death of Field precipitated the need to quickly collect his unpublished writings and to deal with the numerous publishing schemes with which others sought to take advantage of Field's popularity. Julia Field, his widow, was also concerned that her husband's literary reputation be maintained; in fact, she felt Field deserved a place among the "standard" writers of poetry, Longfellow, Whittier, Stevenson. She, therefore, strongly objected to Scribners' recommendation of Slason Thompson, Field's friend and newspaper companion on the Chicago Morning News, *as "official" biographer: he would emphasize Field's role as a journalist and — sometimes crude — humorist. Arthur Scribner, brother and partner of CS II, sympathized with Thompson — "a widow being her husband's worst biographer." Looking over Thompson's manuscript at the end of July 1901, he wrote back: "I see nothing in it of such a nature as would complicate our relations with Mrs. Field and we should be very glad to become its publishers." Scribners also felt obligated to Thompson because he had admirably collated for them Field's newspaper columns in the two-volume* Sharps and Flats. *When Thompson's two-volume biography of Field, subtitled* A Study in Heredity and Contradictions, *was published on 7*

December 1902, Arthur was not prepared for Julia's reaction. The objectionable photograph Arthur refers to in his letter shows Field smiling and is captioned "Field the Comedian."

[January 1902?]

Dear Mr. Scribner:

In remembering all your many kindnesses and unfailing courtesies to me and, particularly, at this time, your prompt and generous repsonse in that which was deeply appreciated and will not be forgotten, it comes almost as a blow — the thought that you had to do with the giving to the public this book of Mr. Thompson's. Since the advance sheets appeared in the "Record Herald" more than two weeks ago and since my receipt of the books I have scarcely known what it was to sleep. It has been as a severe illness to me. I have been unable to write you before. Last night I did somewhat better. After I have written you I may have something less to think over when I should be asleep. Mr. Scribner how could you! I trusted you and by no stroke of your pen did you help me. And now I know that I have given the stamp of authority to this publication, in that my publishers issued it, after having sent broadcast the statement that Mr. Thompson had been given the work of writing the "Life" by them and me. If it had been published by another firm there would have been surprise and questions, and so the truth would have been known. Well, I have had a hard, a cruel lesson. I hope I shall have learned to be firm in my convictions in the future. You know how strong they were against Mr. Thompson when you suggested him to me. I knew his inability to rise to an understanding of the man he was to write of — but that he could so wrong him as he has done I never believed. It is beyond comprehension! If he had been Mr. Field's enemy instead of a confessed friend (God saw the mask!) he could have taken no different methods. The books are absolutely vindiction! What the object can be is hard to understand. <u>Colossal conceit</u>, and to ascend into public view on the shoulders of one who had <u>by his own efforts</u> made himself great enough to getting the attention for him, — which he of himself could never hope for. But few I am sure would have paid such a price! You will understand how badly I feel that you Mr. Scribner should have aught to do with it! I know you will regret the day from the bottom of your heart. My confidence in you is gone. I can not but feel that it is the money side you look at. Well, <u>the books will make</u>

First-edition title page of With Trumpet and Drum *bearing the Cupid image Field wanted. His son's death is touched upon in the book's title poem:*

So come; though I see not his dear little face
And hear not his voice in this jubilant place,
I know he were happy to bid me enshrine
His memory deep in my heart with your play —
Ah me! but a love that is sweeter than mine
Holdeth my boy in its keeping to-day!
And my heart it is lonely — so, little folk, come,
March in and make merry with trumpet and drum!

<u>money</u>. I can see already how they are hurting us financially — yet this is my last thought of course. . . . [the rest of the letter is missing.]

Feb. 7, 1902

Dear Mrs. Field:

I have started to write you a dozen or more times, and you must not think that my failing to do so is from my disregard for the pain which Mr. Thompson's book has given you. In fact feeling the matter as keenly as I have has made writing all the more difficult. It is unfair to us that you should hold us accountable for all in the book that pains you, and especially that you should assign to me personally the motive you do, but I do not care to go over the whole matter for the sake merely of justifying myself. Entirely apart from this is a fact that you have been better served by us than if the book had been published by anyone else. The book was to be published and the entire texture could not have been changed by any publisher, but we cut out repeatedly expressions to which we knew that you would take exception, and carried this almost to the breaking point. As Mr. Thompson's publishers our relations with him are confidential, and I ought not perhaps to say as much as I have, but I know that you will respect this — indeed I thought that you would appreciate it without my bringing it up. Our position throughout has been an extremely difficult one, and one in which I fear we are destined to be misunderstood by both parties. I received a day or two ago your second letter and have read the interview with you. It seems to me a perfectly proper statement for you to make, and so far as we are concerned the only wrong impression likely to be derived from it is that Mr. Thompson's book resembles Mr. Field's books in appearance. This is just what we took care to avoid, using different type, different size and entirely different color in binding. The photograph to which

you refer is I presume the one opposite page 254 Vol.2. This was supplied by Mr. Thompson and I am sorry that I did not anticipate your objection to it. I have little doubt that I can persuade Mr. Thompson to omit it after the copies now bound, of which we have unfortunately quite a number, are disposed of. We shall ourselves omit everything of the sort from all advertisements and circulars printed in future. If there is anything we can do for you before you leave Chicago please let me know. I think that I can send you next week a report of the sales of Mr. Field's works in the trade editions and a general idea as to how they have been doing in the Subscription edition, though hardly a detailed report so soon on the latter as we have to wait to hear from our agencies. In case you should wish any advance payment we shall be perfectly willing to make it. As to your literary plans I almost fear that any offer of advice would be misinterpreted but I will, however, venture to say definitely that I think we are both under such obligations to the subscribers of the Sabine Edition that we ought to have the opportunity of offering them, with a view to keeping their sets complete, anything of Mr. Field's that you may have published. If further we can help you in the consideration of material for general publication I hope that you will let me know. I should be sorry to feel that you would not do so.

Very sincerely yours
Arthur H. Scribner

Richard Harding Davis (1864–1916)

Davis, a few weeks before publication of his first book

Davis was born into a literary family: his father was editor of the *Philadelphia Public Ledger* and his mother, Rebecca Harding Davis, was one of the most popular woman novelists of her time (also a Scribner author). After college he pursued a newspaper career that ultimately enabled him to cover six different wars for prominent New York and London papers: the Spanish War in Cuba, the Greco-Turkish War, the Spanish-American War, the Boer War, the Russo-Japanese War, and World War I. This work made him the best-known reporter of his generation. He was equally successful with his fiction, particularly with short stories that were published in the leading periodicals and collected in a dozen volumes; besides a few novels, Davis also wrote twenty-five plays, several of which were produced on Broadway. Gallant, debonair, picturesque, he was the model for Charles Dana Gibson's male counterpart to his famous "Gibson Girl." Called an "American Kipling," Davis was one of the celebrated Scribner authors and one of the first practitioners of the role of author-as-war-correspondent.

Scribner Books by Davis

1891	*Gallegher, and Other Stories*
	Stories for Boys
1892	*The Great Streets of the World* by Davis and others, illustrated by A. B. Frost and others
1896	*Cinderella, and Other Stories*
1897	*Soldiers of Fortune*, illustrated by C. D. Gibson
1898	*The King's Jackal,* illustrated by Gibson
	The Cuban and Porto Rican Campaigns
1899	*The Lion and the Unicorn*, illustrated by Howard Chandler Christy
1900	*With Both Armies in South Africa*
1902	*Ranson's Folly*, illustrated by Frederic Remington and others
	Captain Macklin: His Memoirs, illustrated by Walter Appleton Clark
1903	*The Bar Sinister*, illustrated by E. M. Ashe

1905	*"Miss Civilization": A Comedy in One Act*
1906	*Farces: The Dictator, The Galloper, "Miss Civilization"*
	Real Soldiers of Fortune
1907	*The Scarlet Car,* illustrated by Frederic Dorr Steele
	The Congo and Coasts of Africa
1908	*Vera the Medium,* illustrated by Steele
1909	*The White Mice,* illustrated by George Gibbs
1910	*Once Upon a Time*
	Notes of a War Correspondent
1911	*The Consul*
	The Man Who Could Not Lose
1912	*The Red Cross Girl,* illustrated by Wallace Morgan
1913	*The Lost Road,* illustrated by Morgan
1914	*The Boy Scout*
	With the Allies
1915	*"Somewhere in France"*
1916	*With the French in France and Salonika*
	The Novels and Stories of Richard Harding Davis (Crossroads Edition of 12 volumes)
1917	*The Boy Scout, and Other Stories for Boys*
	The Deserter, with an introduction by John T. McCutcheon
	Adventures and Letters of Richard Harding Davis, edited by Charles Belmont Davis
1927	*From "Gallegher" to "The Deserter": The Best Stories of Richard Harding Davis,* selected with an introduction by Roger Burlingame
1941	*Young Winston Churchill, A Soldier of Fortune*

CS II Diary Entry:
Tuesday 2 January 1900

Agreed to give Davis $1000 bonus in addition to word rate for South African articles.

Davis was about to leave to cover the Boer War. His articles began to appear several months later in Scribner's Magazine.

CS II Diary Entry:
Thursday 24 January 1901

Engaged Davis' next novel "Col. Macklin" for $8000 & 20% royalty with $2000 advance

Letters:
Davis always wanted to write something more important than books suited only, as he used to say,

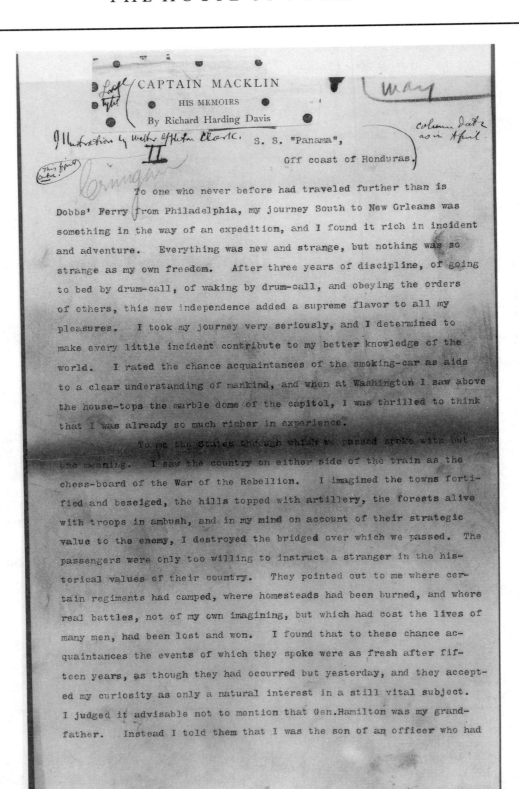

CAPTAIN MACKLIN

HIS MEMOIRS

By Richard Harding Davis

II

S. S. "Panama",

Off coast of Honduras.

To one who never before had traveled further than is
Dobbs' Ferry from Philadelphia, my journey South to New Orleans was
something in the way of an expedition, and I found it rich in incident
and adventure. Everything was new and strange, but nothing was so
strange as my own freedom. After three years of discipline, of going
to bed by drum-call, of waking by drum-call, and obeying the orders
of others, this new independence added a supreme flavor to all my
pleasures. I took my journey very seriously, and I determined to
make every little incident contribute to my better knowledge of the
world. I rated the chance acquaintances of the smoking-car as aids
to a clear understanding of mankind, and when at Washington I saw above
the house-tops the marble dome of the capitol, I was thrilled to think
that I was already so much richer in experience.

To me the States through which we passed spoke with but
one meaning. I saw the country on either side of the train as the
chess-board of the War of the Rebellion. I imagined the towns forti-
fied and beseiged, the hills topped with artillery, the forests alive
with troops in ambush, and in my mind on account of their strategic
value to the enemy, I destroyed the bridges over which we passed. The
passengers were only too willing to instruct a stranger in the his-
terical values of their country. They pointed out to me where certain regiments had camped, where homesteads had been burned, and where
real battles, not of my own imagining, but which had cost the lives of
many men, had been lost and won. I found that to these chance acquaintances the events of which they spoke were as fresh after fifteen years, as though they had occurred but yesterday, and they accepted my curiosity as only a natural interest in a still vital subject.
I judged it advisable not to mention that Gen.Hamilton was my grandfather. Instead I told them that I was the son of an officer who had

Typescript page of Captain Macklin *marked up for serialization in the May 1902 issue of*
Scribner's Magazine

for the "hammock or railroad trains." After Soldiers of Fortune, he deliberately labored slowly on a "serious" novel for several years. Captain Macklin: His Memoirs, as the new novel was called, was first serialized in Scribner's Magazine and then published as a book on 20 September 1902. His editor was ecstatic about his achievement.

Cover of Davis's 1897 novel with drawing by Charles Dana Gibson

May 15, 1901

Dear Davis —

You know I have always expected great things of Macklin, & believed that you were going to do your best work in it. <u>So</u> you must take it as more than an easy-going piece of optimism when I say that I have nothing to do but congratulate you on this first half of it, which more than keeps up with all I had hoped it would be, and is very fresh and vigorous and simple in style, just as I thought you would make your first long story. Don't think I'm a pedant because I mention this matter of style; you had the other things before and I don't say you hadn't a very attractive form of that; but I am impressed by the fact that you have struck a new pace in this particular in Macklin; there is something very refreshing in this straightforward diction and in the successful expression of strong feeling without fireworks. In all your other stories so far you have, from the very nature of the thing, the kind of vividness and go that comes of extreme contemporaneousness, so to speak; all the little momentary touches and fads of speech & thought; — it is rather a fine thing to show that you can do without them, & do even better.

You see, I hope, that I am fully confirmed in my belief that Macklin is going to be your best, in conception, execution and all. It seems to me a capital story, & I am very glad we are to have it.

Yours sincerely
E. L. Burlingame

The book sold well, as did most of Davis's works, but the critics judged it to be an artistic failure. Davis was crushed and vowed he would write no more fiction — even short stories — and asked Scribners not to announce any for him.

Feb. 10, 1903

My dear Davis:

Mr. Burlingame has been warned to include you in no announcement but I earnestly hope that you will not long persist in your determination to write no fiction. In a letter of only a short time ago you expressed satisfaction with the result on the last two books and, so far as I can see, the satisfaction should extend to the way they were received as well as to the number of purchasers found.

It is a fact that all the Olive Green sets have been sold out but if you would like a few, and will let me know how many, I will try to get them for you. I heard last week that there were some for sale in a department store here at $2.50 a set.

Please come to New York soon and get over this attack of fictionphobia.

Yours sincerely
Charles Scribner

The "olive green" sets referred to a six-volume edition of Davis's work that Scribners had published in 1899 as a magazine subscription promotion.

RICHARD HARDING DAVIS

**HOTEL CAMBRIDGE
NEW YORK**

Dear Mr Scribner,
    Many thanks for the royalties. When this cruel war is over, I'll only be too glad to write you a novel, if I can think of one. I'll never desert 155 Fyfth ave anyway. Now, I am just rushing to catch the train to New Haven
            Best wishes always
                Richard Harding Davis

A 1904 letter by Davis to CS II, written just before he left to cover the Russo-Japanese War for Collier's magazine. "155 Fifth Ave" was Scribners' New York address.

[circa February 15, 1903]
My Dear Mr Scribner,

It is not "fictionphobia" that I have. It's because I have so much respect for it, that is keeping me from it. But I always mean to write on travels, and wars (if I can first catch my war), and interesting current public events. So, if you want to announce articles of travel by me for the magazine, I'll try to see something next time I travel that may prove interesting. I expect to go South to the "sheltering palm" in a week or two. I can't stand this snow much longer.

If you really can get me sets of that olive green edition for $2.50 please get me ten sets, as I find them fine for presents and the like.

Sincerely yours
Richard Harding Davis

In November 1903 Burlingame tried to coax a short story out of Davis for Scribner's Magazine. *Apparently, U.S. recognition of the Republic of Panama on November 6th killed his only story idea.*

November 10th [1903]
Dear Mr Burlingame,

I had only one story in mind and the Junta at Panama killed that by creating a republic, and a way out of the canal mix up without waiting for me to tell them how to do it.

I had a beautiful revolution at Panama mapped out with the hero of the "Derelict" story as the prime mover. Now, that that is over, I retire again into the drama and farming. In January I am taking a trip though, and if you care for a sketch of travel or something like the bull fight story or the East Coast of Africa article, I guess I will have some. But fiction still appeals to me as being too serious to write, unless you can do it better than I did it in the brave days of my youth.

Sincerely yours
Richard Harding Davis

Finally, the fiction ice was broken with his story "The Spy," which appeared in the December 1905 issue of Scribner's Magazine.

October 16, 1905
Dear Davis:

The story is here, and read, and in the printer's hands. It is capital, and the end is a great stroke.

It is a great thing to be as certain as I was of this. You always make good; and on your time arrangements I have learned to count as I do on the clock. We are heartily glad to have this in the Christmas number and I really hope it means that you are not going to drop the short story again for so long a time.

Bridges told me that on Saturday when I missed you you spoke to him of a possible two or three part story; I wish that may take shape promptly. I begrudge plays — though I understand their temptation — when they keep you out of these things. Remember I saw you start with "Gallegher," and I cannot help feeling an interest in defending the genre against encroachments.

Always yours sincerely
E. L. Burlingame

Davis resumed his prolific outpouring of articles, short plays, and short fiction, but he only attempted one more novel, The White Mice, *published in 1909. It also was harshly judged by the critics.*

LETTERS:
A remarkable personal relationship between Davis and CS II developed early and remained a constant throughout the years.

[circa February 15, 1905]
Dear Mr Scribner,

I long have suspected that by underhand means you are determined to impose upon me, and make me rich. You cannot make me believe that you honestly owe me all that money! I refuse to believe it! You are a long lost uncle, or something, who in the past robbed the Davis family, and now is trying to make restitution through me. Fortunately, I have no feelings about taking tainted money, so, I say nothing. But, I am sure those books of mine never made all that you have been paying me, and propose to pay me. I now fly to my farm to spend it on golf links, over which some day, I hope you will drive and "put" or "putt" or whatever it is you do. The check came, too, and I am very much obliged. You certainly are a "good provider" and I will at once begin on that story.

My thanks and best wishes to you always.
Richard Harding Davis

Divorced from his first wife, Cecil Clarke, in 1910, Davis married Elizabeth McEvoy ("Bessie McCoy"), an actress, two years later.

["Personal" written on the envelope]

July 6th 1912

My Dear Charles Scribner,

Without your good wishes, it would not have been a real wedding. So, when they came, we were both glad. What you say about our business relations, is a language I do not know. The fact that seeing me always leaves the house bankrupt, may lead you to think that our meeting[s] are business meetings, but, I don't feel that, for, I never leave you, that I am not richer in many ways. You know that no one has been more kind, more gentle, more generously considerate and understanding than you have been to me. Anyway, I know it, and, I am glad your letter gave me the chance to tell you so.

Faithfully yours
Richard Harding Davis

Not realizing CS II had agreed to pay Davis $1,000 for his World War I article on Salonika that was to head the April 1916 issue of Scribner's Magazine, *Robert Bridges, the magazine's editor, offered him $750, based on its length. The extra payment ($250) was the subject of a series of letters.*

March 10th [1916]

My Dear Mr Scribner,

You hurt me when you suggest that any thing could interfere with "our relations." No check yet written could do that. It was like this. Nothing worries me so much as the feeling that the Man Who Pays is not satisfied I am giving him his money's worth.

That was all that worried me. As soon as I learned what sum seemed right to you, that sum seemed right to me and I was at ease and comfortable.

To accept any more would make me so uncomfortable that it is impossible to ask it of me. So destroy the check.

And, please, never again think any thing could disturb the feelings of gratitude and affection I hold for the House of Scribner and for yourself.

Yours faithfully
Richard Harding Davis

P.S. The copy for the book will be marked today, or at least, some of it.

CS II returned the "additional" $250 check for a third time, and Davis at last accepted it. He continued to work on his war book With the French in France and Salonika, *but began to suffer from more frequent bouts of pain caused by angina pectoris and died suddenly a month later, stricken by a massive heart attack.*

F. Hopkinson Smith (1838–1915)

F. Hopkinson Smith in 1900

The great-grandson of a signer of the Declaration of Independence, Smith was an engineer and co-partner of a construction firm for thirty years before he turned to literature at the age of fifty. Among his firm's accomplishments were the Race Rock lighthouse in Block Island Sound and the foundation of the Statue of Liberty. He was also a talented artist with watercolors and charcoal, and his first publications were travel sketches illustrated by his own drawings. His first book of fiction, *Colonel Carter of Cartersville* (1891), grew out of a desire to put into print some of his famous after-dinner stories, which revealed his talent for anecdotal tales and local-color sketches. Thereafter, he wrote best-sellers — both for Houghton, Mifflin, his first publisher, and Scribners, his major one. A versatile and vigorous man, Smith became one of the most popular lecturers of his time and a good friend of his publisher, CS II.

Scribner Books by Smith

1892	*American Illustrators* (portfolio)
1902	*The Fortunes of Oliver Horn*, illustrated by Walter Appleton Clark
1902–1915	*The Novels, Stories and Sketches of F. Hopkinson Smith* (Beacon Edition of 23 volumes)
1903	*The Under Dog*
	Colonel Carter's Christmas, illustrated by F. C. Yohn
1905	*At Close Range*
	The Wood Fire in No. 3, illustrated by Alonzo Kimball
1906	*The Tides of Barnegat*, illustrated by George Wright
1907	*The Veiled Lady, and Other Men and Women*
	The Romance of an Old-Fashioned Gentleman, illustrated by A. I. Keller
1908	*Peter: A Novel of Which He Is Not the Hero*, illustrated by Keller
1909	*Forty Minutes Late, and Other Stories*

1911	*Kennedy Square*, illustrated by Keller
1912	*The Arm-Chair at the Inn*, illustrated by Smith, Keller, and Herbert Ward
1914	*In Dickens's London*, illustrated with charcoal drawings by Smith
1915	*Felix O'Day*, illustrated by Wright
	Outdoor Sketching: Four Talks Given Before the Art Institute of Chicago
1916	*Enoch Crane: A Novel*, planned and begun by Hopkinson and completed by F. Berkeley Smith, illustrated by Kimball

RELATED LETTERS:

It was a case of friends helping friends that brought Smith into the House of Scribner. By 1899 Smith had become a best-selling author with Houghton, Mifflin: his novel Tom Grogan *was the number one book of 1896, as was* Caleb West, Master Diver *in 1898. Apparently Smith was dissatisfied with his royalties and a perceived lack of promotion for his books. He confided in his good friend Thomas Nelson Page, himself a successful author with Scribners. A direct result was the following two letters: acting on Page's suggestion (the first letter), CS II wrote his tactful entreaty to Smith (second letter). And Smith gladly became a Scribner author after his next book,* The Other Fellow, *which was already committed to Houghton, Mifflin.*

June 10, 1899

My dear Scribner:

When Frank Smith was here the other day he was talking about placing his next book with some other publisher than H. Mifflin & Co. who, he thinks, have not the facilities for pushing works of fiction possessed by some other firms. He says he has had a number of applications from other firms for the book. I told him of a firm I know in New York that possessed some ability to bring a good novel up to its legitimate top-notch, and I write now to say that I think if that firm feels that it cares to undertake the next book of F.H.S. it will find him ready to talk. I don't know just what the etiquette of the matter may be under the circumstances; but you can settle that between you. I have done what I hope may prove a good turn to both of you. . . .

Yours faithfully
Thomas Nelson Page

June 13, 1899

Dear Mr. Smith:

A letter has just reached me from an intimate friend of yours stating that you are not altogether satisfied with your present publishers and may go to another house for your next book. If this is so I hope you will consider us. We would make a fair contract with you and I think we could satisfy you in the way we published the book. My relations with Messrs. Houghton, Mifflin & Co. are most friendly and I would not take any step which might lead you to leave them; and indeed I think they have done well with your last book and are well equipped for the publication of the next, though it is only natural I should think our own house the greatest on earth. But if you are "beginning to take notice" we should be glad to have you look in our direction.

Yours sincerely
Charles Scribner

CS II DIARY ENTRY:
Thursday 15 June 1899

F. H. Smith calls about his next novel "Adventures of Oliver Thorne" which he will confer with us about.

LETTERS:

That Smith was happy with Scribners was continually affirmed in his letters to CS II and Edward L. Burlingame, his editor who serialized his novels in Scribner's Magazine. *In this first letter he makes reference to his first Scribner novel,* The Fortunes of Oliver Horn, *which had been published on 29 August 1902. Scribners had also begun that year publishing volumes of Smith's complete works in a subscription edition they called the Beacon Edition. The contract arrangements described in the second letter concern* The Tides of Barnegat, *which Smith tentatively calls "Jane." Serialized in* Scribner's Magazine *in 1905*

For Scribners

CHAPTER XXII (Synopsis).

Chapter opens with a man on horseback entering
grounds of Moorlands in late afternoon. He is
dressed like a sailor, but rides like a Cherokee
Indian.   Has a bundle tied to his saddle behind:
They are the silks he bought of a sailor at Sailors
House—the man had tramped all day trying to sell
them—(a common practice in those days)— and in the
goodness of his heart Harry buys them.   It also occurs
to him to take them to Moorlands and try to sell
them to some one near by and thus find out what was
going on.

Inasmuch as Pawson did not know him,- perhaps
no one will at Moorlands until he finds out how the
land lies.

Grounds – Mental attitude – recollections of
three years before.

Here follows scene of his finding his father in
the business office— (same room in which he had
helped dress Wallis's wounds three years before).
It is nearly dark, and Colonel Rutter is sitting
alone by a lamp on his desk overlooking the accounts
of his estate.   His eyes still trouble him.

**Describe the
way he sat his
horse.**

*Enters same
Gate he and
Kate Entered
3 years before*

Describe.

Typescript page of Smith's synopsis for Kennedy Square *(1911)*

and 1906, the novel was published on 18 August 1906.

24 March [1903]

My Dear Mr Scribner

Many thanks for your kind letter. I am <u>entirely</u> satisfied with the sales of "Oliver" and I can only repeat here what I have so often said to you how grateful I am to you for the liberal way in which you have handled all my work. Under your guidance & assistance I begin to feel as if some day I may be a <u>real author</u>.

I only hope the Beacon may not disappoint you & that it may repay you for all you have expended upon it. The ck will be heartily welcomed & will only be another proof of your generosity.

From your friend
F. Hopkinson Smith

24 April 1903

My Dear Burlingame.

Your letter of 23rd received and your agreement is entirely satisfactory to me and is herebly accepted. viz. $10,000 Serial rights 15% royalty. Payments as stated. Mss delivered July 1904. Time fall 1905 or Jan 1906. You to have the right to publish the story as a serial in some other publication if you cannot possibly use it in Scribners.

This last proviso I propose to leave to you & to Mr Scribner. I do not of course want it printed outside Scribners & I feel sure you do not — nor do I want its publication put off too long for the book royalties can only follow the serial.

When I say I leave it to you I mean that literally & mean that too that I will be entirely satisfied with what you do. My idea is that an author and his publisher are one concern & that the highest good to both can only come through loyalty each to the other's interest. I have steadily maintained that position since I had the good fortune to throw my lot into C S, Sons, hands, although many sirens have beckoned to me. I have had no cause to regret it & I know I never shall.

I shall now go to work on "Jane" & do my level best to make it the best thing I have written. My kindest & best to you both & my renewed thanks for all your courtesies.

Faithfully your friend
F. Hopkinson Smith

LETTER:
This letter to Smith from Edwin Wilson Morse (1855–1924), who worked at Scribners from 1887 till 1910, attempts to alert him to a problem of time period in Peter: A Novel of Which He Is Not the Hero.

May 4, 1908

My dear Mr. Smith:

We have put in type and I have on my desk the galley proofs of all the "copy" which you have sent to us of "Peter" — eleven chapters in all. We shall be glad to receive some more at your earliest convenience.

The only question, aside from minor details of comparatively slight consequence, which has presented itself to me in reading the first few chapters of the book has been the question of time. You have laid the scene of this story twenty years ago, but many of the conditions against which you or your characters inveigh have existed only within the last eight or ten years perhaps. Our period of extravagance in all directions, showing itself in the height of our buildings as well as in our financial irregularities and in our lack of reverence for everything, followed, did it not, our war with Spain, which was, as you remember, only ten years ago. Twenty years ago life was comparatively simple and not, as I remember it, as you have pictured it in parts of these opening chapters. In other words, it seems to me that in order to get the old-time flavor of Peter, with his high stock and his old-fashioned bank, and with his old-fashioned ideas, you have gone further back in point of time than you perhaps realize and have pictured him in your mind's eye in a set of conditions, financial, social, moral, etc., which really have for the most part grown up within the last ten years or, at all events, which have come to a head, so to speak, within the last ten years. I may be wrong about it but I should be willing to lay a small wager, for example, that there were no buildings in New York thirty stories high twenty years ago. Of course if you set the period of your story ahead so as to bring it within the scope, so to speak, of present-day or recent conditions, it may be difficult to preserve the connection with the old-fashioned times, typified by the bank and its receiving teller. I am sure, however, that the situation is one which you can remedy without much difficulty, and possibly I have magnified the apparent inconsistency. I am now free from jury duty and shall be glad to talk the matter over with you if you can drop in on your way up-town or downtown.

Smith's charcoal drawing of Gad's Hill, where Dickens lived and died, for In Dickens's London *(1914)*

I enclose, as a matter of routine, the statement of the sales of "The Romance of an Old-Fashioned Gentleman" to April 27. Allowing for the effect of the panic on trade in general, the showing seems to us to be a very good one.

I remain, with best wishes,
Very truly yours,
Edwin W. Morse

The problem was apparently corrected by Smith or ignored by his adoring public. Published on 29 August 1908, the novel sold more than 100,000 copies in its first six months and was on the bestseller lists for 1908 and 1909.

RELATED LETTERS AND PREFACE:
In this, one of his last letters to Scribners, writing to former Scribner's Magazine *editor Edward L. Burlingame, Smith outlines his plans for a new novel, for which he wants to reserve space in the magazine. Robert Bridges ("Bob") is actually the editor now, Burlingame having just retired. The*

tentative title "we do not want to talk about" is "The Curmudgeon." Smith died several months later after a short illness.

January 22, 1915.
My dear Burlingame: —
This letter is an almanac letter. It is also to have you punch a hole in the year 1917.

I have swept the deck clean, and have turned over my last corrections on "Felix O'Day." The firm have it in the printers' hands. I am now going to begin on another novel, and want you to keep the gate open for me for 1917, provided there is nothing better offered to you. Bob tells me this year and next year are already tied up. That suits me exactly, for I could not have the new novel ready in time to publish it before the last months of 1916, in other words to deliver to you, I should say, July 1916. I shall start in at once, and by the first of the coming July shall have the entire plan sketched out and several of the chapters written, so that you can get an idea about it; as you and I have often talked over our plans together, so we can talk over this.

I gave Bob an outline of what I propose to do, told him the title, which, of course, we do not want to talk about, and some idea of my purpose. The story will be of New York life, — one principal character will dominate the whole book. I want, if possible, to make it as humorous as I can, as everybody is supping on horrors, and will continue to do so for a year at least. It will be in a new field of anything I have ever touched, and will, as far as I see now, draw its material from our finest Club Life, the kind you and I know so well, with the grotesque figure of this principal character puncturing all their shams and winning out at last, of course, by his good heart and hard common sense.

It has been some years since I had the Magazine. "Kennedy Square" was the last. I have given up the writing of short stories, and hope you will agree with me that my turn will come around again about the time this novel is finished.

And now let me again repeat that this is only for the purpose that you should stick a pin into your almanac, preventing you from doing anything precipitate until you get a look at what I am going to do, which will take sufficient shape for you to form an opinion by the first of the coming July.

With all good wishes.

> Always your sincere friend,
> F. Hopkinson Smith

The task of completing the novel was left to Smith's son Berkeley, an author of travel books and fiction. Working on the book while living on the coast of Normandy in France in the midst of World War I, he describes his progress to CS II in this letter excerpt.

23d August 1915

Dear Mr. Scribner.

Just a line to tell you I have been daily at work on "The Curmudgeon" since I last saw you, and finished the 9th chapter yesterday. I have stuck rigidly to the synopsis, & the story, & now that I have gotten into the swing of the book, am turning out a chapter about every ten days. But as I told you, I write & rewrite, & polish, and there are scenes in every novel which take time & cannot be hurried. Writing this book has taught me a lot — one thing especially, the admirable logical way father <u>constructed</u> everything so that when he came to build, he had his timber measured, cut &

ready, & nothing left but the joining planing & chiselling to do. So many young writers cut their shipload of inspiration loose from her moorings, not knowing exactly where they are going, or how they are going to land their passengers — and I have been one of them.

. . . You would never believe there was war, save that there are none but old men & boys & the women left in the village, & now and then a glimpse of a convalescent wounded soldier flashing by in an auto for an airing. Mrs. Smith has been working hard over her colony of poor little French boys & girls who have lost their fathers at the front. They are all happier & brown & rosey in two comfortable villas close beside us by the sea.

With kindest regards to all & thanking you again for your generous encouragment believe me

> Faithfully yours
> F. Berkeley Smith

The book was published on 16 September 1916, with the title Enoch Crane, *which Berkeley had suggested. In his published preface, dated "New York, 1916," Berkeley describes the gestation of the novel.*

It was my father's practise, in planning a novel, first to prepare a most complete synopsis from beginning to end — never proceeding with the actual writing of the book until he had laid out the characters and action of the story — chapter by chapter.

This synopsis, which closely resembled the scenario of a play, he kept constantly enriching with little side-notes as they occurred to him — new ideas and points of detail.

So spirited were these synopses, and so clearly did they reflect the process of his mind, that by the few who saw them in the course of publishing consultations, or friendly confidence, they were remembered often after the finished novel had obliterated its contructive lines.

A scheme like this he had prepared for "Enoch Crane" — a story which, like "Felix O'Day," he had very much at heart. Once he had begun a novel it occupied his whole mind. He lived — as it were — with the characters he was developing, to the exclusion of all other work. He would talk to me constantly of their welfare or vicissitudes, and was often in grand humor when any of them had proved themselves worthy by their wit, their courage, or their good breeding.

They all seemed to be old personal friends of his, whom by some chance I had never met.

My father had written three chapters of "Enoch Crane" when his brief illness came. Thus there has remained to me as a legacy of his unquenchably youthful spirit an unfinished novel, which to reach his readers needed to be wrought out on the lines he had so carefully laid down with that untiring enthusiasm with which he undertook everything; and this — his last story — it has been my privileged task to complete.

> **CS II DIARY ENTRY:**
> Sunday 11 April 1915
>
> Attend funeral of Hopkinson
> Smith as pallbearer and go
> to Woodlawn

Woodlawn is a cemetery in New York City.

George Santayana (1863–1952)

George Santayana (frontispiece to his The Middle Span, *New York: Charles Scribner's Sons, 1945)*

Born in Spain, raised and educated in the United States, and a resident of Italy for almost forty years, Santayana was a citizen of the world as his final autobiographical volume (*My Host the World*) proclaimed. He is known as one of America's foremost philosophers and also as a man of letters, having written philosophical works that are highly literary, and poetry, a novel, and other literary works that are highly philosophical. The Santayana/Scribners author/publisher relationship holds the House record for duration for a living author: more than fifty years. Santayana went abroad to live in 1912 and never returned, so that the majority of his works were edited by a man, John Hall Wheelock, he never met, or so he thought. Actually, Wheelock had been a student at Harvard when Santayana was teaching there (1889–1912) and had taken some of his courses.

Scribner Books by Santayana

1896	*The Sense of Beauty: Being the Outlines of Aesthetic Theory*
1900	*Interpretations of Poetry and Religion*
1901	*A Hermit of Carmel, and Other Poems*

1905	*The Life of Reason; or, The Phases of Human Progress: Introduction and Reason in Common Sense*
	The Life of Reason; or, The Phases of Human Progress: Reason in Society
	The Life of Reason; or, The Phases of Human Progress: Reason in Religion
	The Life of Reason; or, The Phases of Human Progress: Reason in Art
1906	*The Life of Reason; or, The Phases of Human Progress: Reason in Science*
1913	*Winds of Doctrine: Studies in Contemporary Opinion*
1916	*Egotism in German Philosophy*
1920	*Little Essays Drawn from the Writings of George Santayana*, by Logan Pearsall Smith, with the collaboration of the author
	Character & Opinion in the United States: With Reminiscences of William James and Josiah Royce and Academic Life in America
1922	*Soliloquies in England and Later Soliloquies*
1923	*Poems, Selected by the Author and Revised*
	Scepticism and Animal Faith: Introduction to a System of Philosophy
1925	*Dialogues in Limbo* (enlarged edition, 1948)
1927	*Platonism and the Spiritual Life*
	The Realm of Essence: Book First of the Realms of Being
1930	*The Realm of Matter: Book Second of Realms of Being*
1931	*The Genteel Tradition at Bay*
1933	*Some Turns of Thought in Modern Philosophy: Five Essays*
1936	*The Last Puritan: A Memoir in the Form of a Novel*
	Orbiter Scripta: Lectures, Essays and Reviews, edited by Justus Buchler and Benjamin Schwartz
	The Philosophy of Santayana: Selections from the Works of George Santayana, edited, with an introductory essay, by Irwin Edman (enlarged edition, 1953)
1936–1940	*The Works of George Santayana* (Triton Edition of 15 volumes)
1938	*The Realm of Truth: Book Third of Realms of Being*
1940	*The Realm of Spirit: Book Fourth of Realms of Being*
1942	*The Realms of Being* (one-volume edition)
1944	*Persons and Places: The Background of My Life*
1945	*The Middle Span: Vol. II, Persons and Places*
1946	*The Idea of Christ in the Gospels; or, God in Man, A Critical Essay*
1951	*Dominations and Powers: Reflections on Liberty, Society, and Government*
1953	*My Host the World: Vol. III, Persons and Places*
	The Poet's Testament: Poems and Two Plays, edited by John Hall Wheelock and Daniel Cory

| 1954 | *The Life of Reason; or, The Phases of Human Progress* (one-volume edition), revised by the author in collaboration with Cory |
| 1955 | *The Letters of George Santayana*, edited, with an introduction and commentary, by Cory |

MEMOIR:

Extract from volume two of Santayana's autobiography, *The Middle Span* (New York: Charles Scribner's Sons, 1945), pp. 156–157.

In a chapter about his teaching career at Harvard University, Santayana describes the circumstances by which his first book was written and published, beginning a half-century relationship with the House of Scribner. Barrett Wendell was a Harvard colleague of Santayana.

I was a kind of poet, I was alive to architecture and the other arts, I was at home in several languages: "aesthetics" might be regarded as my specialty. Very well: although I didn't have, and haven't now, a clear notion of what "aesthetics" may be, I undertook to give a course in that subject. It would help to define my status. I gave it for one or two years and then I wrote out the substance of it in a little book: *The Sense of Beauty.* The manuscript of this book went from local publisher to publisher, and was rejected. I had given up all expectation of getting it published when Barrett Wendell, always friendly to me and the humanities, sent me word that he thought Scribner's would accept it. I sent it to Scribner's; it was printed and did not prove a financial loss to the publisher, although it had neither a large sale nor a warm reception from the critics. However, it was a book, *a fact;* and it established pleasant relations between me and Scribner's which have lasted for fifty years.

LETTER:

Letter by W. C. Brownell, Scribner editor, to Santayana, 2 May 1896.

Brownell's comments on Santayana's first book typifies what would be the House's position on most of his subsequent philosophical works: he knows a good thing when he sees it, though he is also aware of the limited financial reward to be gained by publishing it. Some authors' work is too

Dust jacket of The Last Puritan. *Published on 1 February 1936, the novel became an immediate best-seller. Writing to Santayana several days later (4 February 1936), CS III proclaimed: "No novel published in the twenty odd years that I have been in the business has had such an enthusiastic reception from the press, which has showered it with praise without a dissenting note.... I cannot tell you how pleased and proud we are to cap our association with you of so many years with the publication of this novel, which promises to be a national success." In fact, the novel proved to be second only to Margaret Mitchell's* Gone With the Wind *in 1936 sales.*

important in terms of content to ignore — and Scribners believed Santayana's was one of them.

Dear Sir:

We should apologize for the delay which we have imposed upon your patience in the examina-

Rome, Oct. 6, 1946
Via S. Stefano Rotondo, 6,

Please send a copy of my book,
The Idea of Christ in the Gospels,
to the address below, and charge
it to my account.
Santayana

Mr. Ezra Pound
Saint Elizabeth's Hospital,
Washington,
D. C.

In his letter to John Hall Wheelock (6 October 1946) accompanying this request, Santayana had written: "It happens that I had recently had an enigmatic letter from him from Washington, D.C., and in answering it I mentioned that I had been reading his poem on Christ as Gangster, and had been amused to think how he would despise my Idea of Christ, *while his delightfully amused me. Now I get a reply from which I gather (it is partly in Chinese characters) that he wants my book." Judged to be of unsound mind, Pound had been committed to a sanitarium (at St. Elizabeth's Hospital) instead of being tried for his treasonous radio broadcasts in Italy during World War II.*

tion of your essay on "The Sense of Beauty." Our excuse must be the merits of the work combined with the difficulty of estimating precisely what appeal a book on such an abstruse subject could hope to make to the general public. We have been unwilling to neglect the opportunity of adding to our list so thoughtful, original, and pleasing a work, and on the other hand we have found it difficult to rid ourselves of some misgivings as to the practical commercial outcome of undertaking it. We are, however, at present prepared to publish it, assuming all the expenses connected with its publication, and trust that our efforts to make it a success will be rewarded in such measure as we have a right to expect. We should be prepared to pay you what is called "the regular royalty" of 10

per cent on the retail of all copies sold, and of course to issue it in appropriately attractive style. If this proposal seems to you, as it does to us, a fitting one in the circumstances, we shall be very glad to hear from you at your convenience and to put the manuscript in hand ere long with a view to issuing it in the Autumn.

Very truly yours,
Charles Scribner's Sons

LETTER:
Letter by Santayana to Charles Scribner's Sons, 25 May 1904, from Cambridge, Mass.

Santayana's plan for publishing his magnum opus, The Life of Reason, *in five separate, slender vol-*

umes, as outlined in this letter, seemed most reasonable to Scribners. W. C. Brownell, on the firm's behalf, readily offered him a 10 percent royalty and suggested publishing the volumes serially to avoid overwhelming the public. Contrary to Santayana's belief (and a pleasant surprise to Scribners), it did not take years for the editions to sell out: the one thousand copies constituting the first printings of each volume were sold within a year of publication, and the books continued to sell, albeit slowly, for decades.

Gentlemen:

I am sending you a first installment of my <u>magnum opus</u> "The Life of Reason." There are four more Books, which will follow in a few weeks if you are favourably disposed towards the idea of publishing them. I send this part ahead, as I am anxious to have all arrangements for publication made before I leave this country, as I am to be away for fifteen months.

This book is not like my former ones, a mere incidental performance. It practically represents all I have to say of any consequence, so that I feel a special interest in having it done in a way that shall express its own character and suggest the spirit in which I would have it read. My ideas may seem to you wrong, and of course I shall not insist on them if they prove to be really unreasonable; but if objections to them rest only on financial considerations, I should be inclined to run the risk and insure you against loss in any way that seems to you suitable, provided the liability is not beyond my means.

What I desire is chiefly this: that the five books be bound separately, making five small volumes, so that they may be easily held and carried about, and may also, at least eventually, be sold separately as well as in sets. The remaining parts are on Society, Religion, Art, and Science respectively, and might well be independent books. A system runs through them all, but there is no formal continuity, or only such as might well exist between three plays in a trilogy.

The page might well be like that in the "Sense of Beauty" (better than in The Interpretations) or even smaller and more closely set: I don't think large print really attractive: I hate a sprawling page. A compact page with a rather generous margin would be my ideal; and in this margin might be the running summary I have provided. This might be instead, if you thought it better, at the upper corner of each page, or in an indentation (as in The Sense of Beauty). But in whatever

form it appears it is a very important feature, because it is meant not merely to help the eye and carry along the thought over the details, but often to be a commentary as well as a summary and throw a side light on the subject.

The binding might be in more than one form: I should be glad to have the book as cheap as possible so that students might buy it. Why are hardly any books sold in paper covers in this country? Boards surely are a respectable garment, and seem to suggest that the body is more than the raiment. I confess, however, that I don't know what difference in prices would be involved in different sorts of binding, and I should be much interested if you would tell me.

Proof would have to be sent to me abroad; but there is no need of sending the MS with it, and the delay, once the operation has begun, is insignificant.

I shall probably not sail until the middle of July and shall be once or twice in New York in the interval, when I could easily call upon you.

Yours very truly
G. Santayana

LETTER:
Letter by Santayana to Scribner editor John Hall Wheelock, 27 July 1935, from Cortina, Italy.

Santayana explains at length his concerns about libel regarding his "memoir in the form of a novel," The Last Puritan. His English publisher, Constable & Company, had again raised the issue and was serious about making some changes in the work. Scribners was not. In his reply, Wheelock reassured Santayana, "You may set your mind at rest on this score."

Dear Mr. Wheelock

In looking over the proofs of <u>The Last Puritan</u>, Mr. Kyllmann of Constable & Company has reopened a question which had been on my mind, and which I had proposed to him, at the beginning: namely, whether the mixture of fact and fiction, and in particular the references to places, landlords, landladies, and incumbents of churches, might not give offence and cause people to bring suits for libel. We are making a few alterations, and Mr. Kyllmann is thinking of taking legal advice on the subject: but the book is really what I call it, "A Memoir in the Form of a Novel" and, although not an autobiography, it is rooted throughout in my personal recollections. It would be impossible to remove the setting in the places I know and have frequented, or the use of episodes that have actually occurred in my life-time or in my familiar circle. Is there any danger of this being resented, in regard to the American part? All the leading characters are fictitious; but the house in Beacon Street is real, Mr. Nathaniel Alden is a recognizable caricature of two real persons, long since dead, & both old bachelors; Montana must have senators; would any of them think himself libelled in my Senator Lunt? Something like the homicide in the Harvard College Chapel was said to have been perpetrated, before my time, by a well-known person of excellent family, dead too; but his children are living. The Secret Society, I believe, has now changed its character or ceased to exist; but it was notorious all through my thirty years at Harvard. There must have been a head-coach of the Harvard crew in the years covered by my account of Oliver's appearance there: I don't know, or have forgotten, who he was; would he regard my description of Dr. Wilcox's manners as a libel? These and other such points might be raised if people don't sympathize with my reconstruction of the past. It is a fanciful reconstruction, and generally entirely fictitious. As you know, for instance, there is no Great Falls, Connecticut; but I invented that town because I don't know any New England town, except Boston and Cambridge, well enough to put my story in it. I believe — I have asked about it — that there are no Van de Weyers in New York: anyhow, the family I describe is wholly imaginary. Yet a lot of flotsam from my experience & observation comes up throughout: if I didn't use it, I should have no materials: and therefore it is a question of leaving the book practically as it stands, or suspending publication altogether.

What do you think?

Yours sincerely

G. Santayana

LETTER:

Letter by Santayana to his Scribner editor, John Hall Wheelock, 29 October 1941, from Rome.

Santayana's lines of communication with Scribners, already deteriorating because of the war in Europe, were severed completely in the fall of 1941. Blocked from mailing his publisher the finished, first volume of his autobiography, Persons and Places, he settled into a room at a nursing home in Rome run by nuns, as he describes in this letter, which proved to be his last to his editor for the next three years. Daniel Cory, his secretary and literary executor, was living in New York at the time. Fortunately for Santayana, his nephew, George Sturgis, was able to pay for his uncle's lodging by sending money to a Chicago house run by the same order of nuns.

Dear Mr. Wheelock: Unless you have heard it from Cory, I have a bad piece of news to give you in regard to Persons & Places. The MS was returned to me from the Post Office with the information that no manuscript or printed matter was accepted any longer for the mails, but letters only. This seems to preclude all possibility of publishing the book, or anything else of mine, until after the war. I am very sorry to disappoint you and Cory in this matter, and possibly, if I went later to Switzerland or to Spain, I might be able to despatch the MS (which I have kept unopened and ready for the post); but the journey to Spain is beyond my strength and courage under present conditions, and the Swiss government refuses permits of residence to foreigners. If you are annoyed at this delay and can exert influence on the Swiss authorities to give me a special licence to live say, at the Hôtel des Trois Couronnes at Vevey, I might be able to go there in the Spring: in fact, I should be glad to go there (or to Glion, just above), if communication of all sorts were interrupted between the U.S. and Italy, since this would leave me penniless and cut off from most of my remaining friends.

However, the financial problem for me seems to be solved, in essentials, by living in this Nursing Home. The Order, called the "Little Company of Mary," has a house in Chicago; and the Superior or "Mother General," who lives here, has agreed to let me pay my bills in Chicago, which George Sturgis can easily do by cheque, so that I am provided with food, lodging, and attendance, including nursing, apparently gratis. The few hundred dollars that I have on hand will suffice for my personal expenses for the winter, but not for ever; so that if I receive nothing from America and the war lasts, I shall be reduced to begging. However, I am confident that through some channels, like this of the Irish Sisters, I shall be able to obtain enough to get the daily paper and pay postage on my letters.

This establishment is rather complete: there is even a library with English books, and the prospect is quite rural towards the south, over the valley of the Tiber; and I write this by a

Tra Santo Stefano Rotondo, 6
Rome. Dec. 30, 1949

Dear Mr Wheelock

I write today to ask you to repeat the favour you have done me several times and to send a wedding present of $500,= in my name to

> Mr. Robert Lowell
> 29 W. 104½ St.
> New York City.

I assume that there is sufficient credit to my account, and also that you know of the curious telepathic friendship that has arisen between Robert Lowell and me in the last two or three years. Lately our correspondence ceased, because he had fallen under a cloud, a compound over-excitement and profound depression. Yesterday I received a very calm letter, in the old manner, telling me of his marriage (I had heard of it from his friend Robert Fitzgerald, who had visited me here with his wife, and had afterwards written to me about our friend's troubles and illness; also, recently, of his recovery. But the direct renewal of communications with Lowell direct has been a real satisfaction to me, and I want to do something to express it.

I am writing to him separately, so that he will understand your missive when it arrives.

Cory and I continue our work merrily.

Yours sincerely
G Santayana

JAN. 9

DEAR MR. WHEELOCK:
I WANT TO ACKNOWLEDGE AND THANK YOU FOR THE CHECK FROM MR. SANTAYANA, WHICH I HAVE RECEIVED AND CASHED.

YOURS SINCERELY,
Robert Lowell

Santayana's request to his Scribner editor, John Hall Wheelock, to send American poet Robert Lowell a wedding gift of $500 from his royalty account, with Lowell's acknowledgment. Two years later (30 January 1951) Santayana would write Wheelock about Lowell: "I am, and have been for some years, particularly interested in Robert Lowell's mind and work. He is now in Italy, and spent a week or more in Rome in the autumn, when I saw him almost every day. I think that he is a good deal like Rimbaud, or like what Rimbaud might have become if he had remained devoted to his poetic genius. There are dark and troubled depths in them both, with the same gift for lurid and mysterious images: but Lowell has had more tragic experiences and a more realistic background, strongly characterised. In these London articles [Times Literary Supplement articles on contemporary American poetry] he is highly spoken of, and although he is not a person about whose future we can be entirely confident, it may well turn out brilliant."

wide-open French window, with a balcony. If there were no war I should be quite happy — but if there were no war, I shouldn't be living in a convent of nuns. Such are the contradictions of hope!

Yours sincerely
G. Santayana

Scribners was able to get Santayana's manuscript out of Italy — one year later — only after securing the aid of the Papal Secretary of State, the Cardinal Maglione, and the Papal Nuncio in Madrid. From there the manuscript was forwarded via diplomatic pouch by Carlton J. H. Hayes, the American ambassador in Madrid, to Washington, D.C. It finally reached Wheelock's hands by the end of October 1942. Though the book was quickly chosen by the Book-of-the-Month Club in December, the club did not schedule it until January 1944; hence, Scribners had to wait till then to publish its edition.

LETTER:
Letter by Daniel Cory, Santayana's literary executor, to John Hall Wheelock, 18 September 1952, from Rome.

After the war Santayana continued to live in the Rome nursing home run by the Blue Nuns and received monthly packages, arranged by Wheelock, of tea, coffee, cocoa, and biscuits. The third and last volume of his autobiography remained, in the meantime, in the Scribner safe in New York, according to his instructions that it be published posthumously. The time for that decision, as Cory explains in this letter, was fast approaching.

Dear Wheelock:

Thank you so much for your two letters — and the enclosed remittance. I will do my best to read to him this afternoon your brief but very touching little personal letter.

The last few days The Master has been getting regular injections of — I believe — morphine. At any rate he has been sleeping a good deal and is not complaining of pain. I saw his doctor personally and said quite firmly that unless something was done immediately to relieve him I was going to get another doctor and if necessary have him removed on a stretcher to a more "human establishment." This threat of mine, which I had every intention of putting into effect, did the trick and curbed the strange supernatural economy of the Blue Sisters.

I don't think he can possibly last much longer — it is a question of days. He spoke so beautifully to me yesterday about the most profound questions in philosophy that I broke down completely and cried like a child. Then he dropped off to sleep and I hoped he was dying, as I know he longs for the "peace that passeth all understanding." But he woke up in about an hour and said to me with a smile, "Cory, I thought that we had just had our last interview."

It is all very tragic — but I am here with him to the end. He said to me "I like to think that the last volume of my autobiography will soon be published." And there is no reason why it should not be. I am his literary executor, and can exercise my discretion in the matter. There is nothing in his Will to prevent it. Well, my friend, I will keep you informed of everything, and let you know at once by cable when "that which drew from out the boundless deep, turns again home."

Yours most sincerely,
Cory

Santayana died about ten days later, and his last autobiographical volume, My Host the World, *was published on 9 March 1953.*

Charles Dana Gibson (1867–1944)

Charles Dana Gibson

In the years between 1886, when Gibson sold his first drawing to *Life* magazine, and 1920, when he became the owner and editor in chief of the magazine, Gibson achieved an immense influence on the society of his time. His pen-and-ink sketches and illustrations of square-jawed, manly heroes and, particularly, of queenly, elegant women captured for mass readership the life, manners, and attitudes of smart society. The "Gibson Girl," inspiring costumes and hairdos and promoting the image of the athletic girl who played tennis and golf, rode horseback, swam, and bicycled, became the symbol of the Gay Nineties. Apprenticed briefly with the sculptor Augustus Saint-Gaudens, encouraged by the illustrator Dan Beard to study at the Art Students League (New York) with Thomas Eakins, Kenyon Cox, and William M. Chase, Gibson developed his own personal style of drawing; with fine lines, cross-hatching, and subtle shading he evoked a distinctive type of American woman that was the dominant model till it was replaced by the "flapper" in the 1920s. His collaborations with friend and fellow Scribner author Richard Harding Davis resulted in some of their best work.

Scribner Books by Gibson

1897	*London as Seen by Charles Dana Gibson*
1903	*Eighty Drawings, Including The Weaker Sex, The Story of a Susceptible Bachelor*
1904	*Everyday People*
1905	*Our Neighbors*
1906	*The Gibson Book: A Collection of the Published Works of Charles Dana Gibson* (2 volumes)
1911	*Other People*
1916	*Gibson New Cartoons: A Book of Charles Dana Gibson's Latest Drawings*

Other Scribner Books Illustrated by Gibson

1895	*College Girls* by Abbe Carter Goodloe
	The Art of Living by Robert Grant, illustrated by Gibson and others
	The Bachelor's Christmas, and Other Stories by Grant, illustrated by Gibson and others
1896	*That First Affair and Other Sketches* by John Ames Mitchell, illustrated by Gibson and others
1897	*The Soldiers of Fortune* by Richard Harding Davis
1898	*The King's Jackal* by Davis
1903	*Gallegher, and Other Stories* by Davis

CS II DIARY ENTRY:
Wednesday 25 March 1903

Offered Gibson 25% with guarantee of $20,000

Royalty terms for Eighty Drawings, Including The Weaker Sex, The Story of a Susceptible Bachelor, *which was published in October.*

LETTER:
Letter by Arthur H. Scribner to Gibson, 18 May 1906, about the completion of *The Gibson Book,* Scribners' two-volume compendium of Gibson's previous eleven books.

My dear Gibson:

Your book is at last completed and the first indications are most encouraging. I may say that we have never had a Magazine proposition which promised better at this stage. I say this with hesitation as this is an uncertain business and one cannot tell when the fortune will change, but I think we may all feel very much encouraged. It has been an almost endless job to get together the plates, arrange the captions and turn out the completed copies; the printing alone has taken a long time. Various questions have come up from time to time and we have made such decisions as were necessary only after the most careful and thorough consideration, actually consulting with the managers of our branches and in some cases with the canvassers themselves. The result is that we have put the work in two volumes and that we have made the price, with the Magazine, $12.00. I enclose a

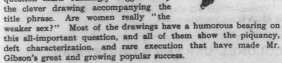

CHARLES SCRIBNER'S SONS
FALL PUBLICATIONS, 1903

FINELY ILLUSTRATED BOOKS

THE GIBSON BOOK FOR 1903
THE WEAKER SEX
BY CHARLES DANA GIBSON

Uniform in size with previous volumes.
$4.20 *net* (Postage additional)

Mr. Gibson's 1903 book, made up, as heretofore, of selections from his most popular drawings, will be especially attractive this year, not only because of the larger number of cartoons than usual, but, in particular, of the greatly increased popularity and the telling character of his latest work. The keynote is found in the question mark cunningly suggested by the clever drawing accompanying the title phrase. Are women really "the weaker sex?" Most of the drawings have a humorous bearing on this all-important question, and all of them show the piquancy, deft characterization, and rare execution that have made Mr. Gibson's great and growing popular success.

De luxe edition of 250 copies, numbered and signed by the author, with signed artist's proof in photogravure for framing.

$10.00 *net*

CHARLES SCRIBNER'S SONS, PUBLISHERS
153-157 Fifth Avenue, New York

Gibson's books were also published in limited editions for collectors.

sample of our circular and subscription blank. Making the work in two volumes of course somewhat increases the cost of manufacture but I am

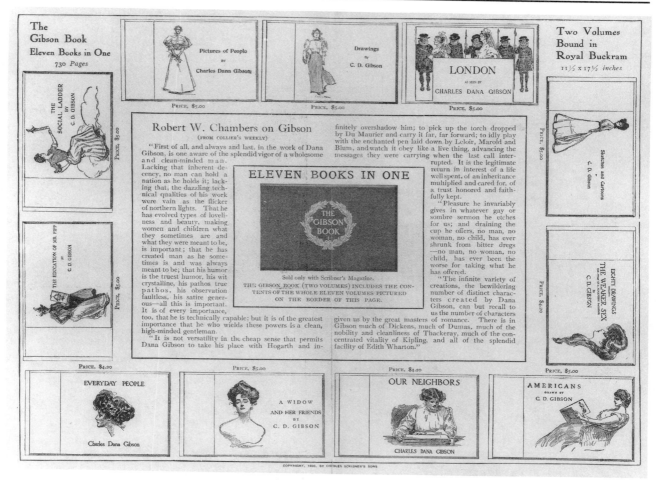

Promotional circular for the two-volume collection of Gibson's works issued by Scribners in 1906

sure that it also greatly increases the chance of large success. My understanding is that your royalty increases with the increase of price and will be 60¢ instead of 50¢. I am sending over two sets as requested by express prepaid and hope that you will be satisfied with their appearance. Some of the cuts do not come up quite as well as we should like, but we will try to "do better next time," and I am sure that there will be another printing very soon.

I presume that you have been working hard and gaining confidence in your new work. Do not expect too quick results from the new book and I hope we will not ultimately disappoint you.

Please remember me to Mrs. Gibson and believe me

Very sincerely yours
[Arthur H. Scribner]

P.S. I have just seen Chapin [head of the Art Department] and found him making notes of matter to be improved next printing.

LETTER:
Arthur H. Scribner suggests that Gibson change the name of his new book, tentatively titled "The Gibson Book for 1912."

July 18, 1911

My dear Gibson:

Early in the month we sent to our London representative the dummy of your new book, with additional proofs and other particulars, for offer of the English publication to John Lane, who, you will remember, purchased your previous books over there. I have now received a telegram from my brother, who sailed for London a couple of weeks ago, in which he states that "Lane will order Gibson if title changed. Any reasonable title without date sufficient. Strongly advised." My brother and I felt from the first that the title selected was unfortunate but we hesitated to urge our opinion. This has now been reinforced, as you see, by Mr. Lane and it is also borne in on us by

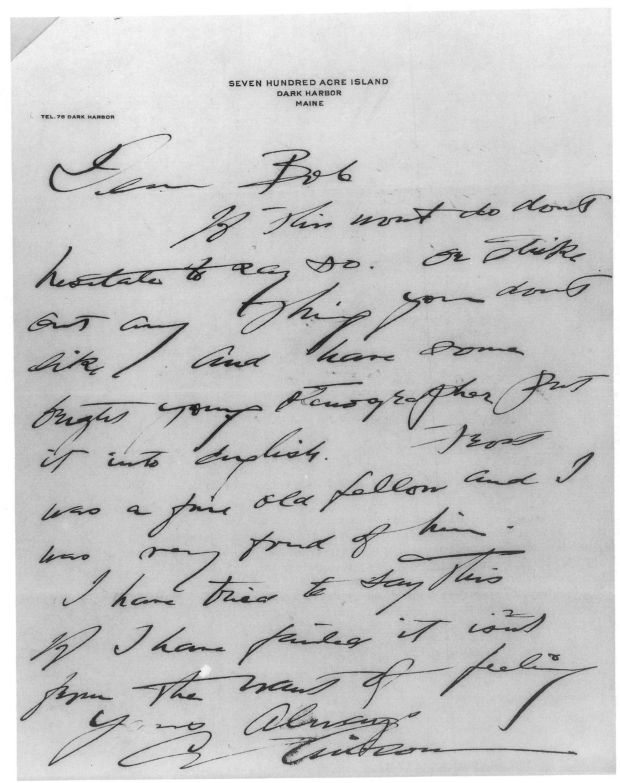

SEVEN HUNDRED ACRE ISLAND
DARK HARBOR
MAINE

TEL. 75 DARK HARBOR

A 1928 letter by Gibson to Robert Bridges, editor of Scribner's Magazine, *regarding his tribute to fellow artist A. B. Frost, who died in June. Gibson's article, "A. B. Frost — A Personal Tribute," appeared in the November issue of the magazine.*

the results of the orders so far taken by our travelling salesmen. The title seems a perfunctory one and it would be impossible to get the best results without a change. I appreciate your position, that you hope to have a number of books in succession and that it will be difficult to find a distinctive title for each. However I think we must try, and as a somewhat lame contribution to the subject I enumerate some that have occurred to us:

Other People, by C. D. Gibson
The Life around Us, by C. D. Gibson
Men and Women, by C. D. Gibson
Characters, by C. D. Gibson
Stories in Pictures, by C. D. Gibson
Stories Told in Pictures, by C. D. Gibson
The Human Comedy, by C. D. Gibson

The first seems to me the best, but perhaps these will suggest something better to you, and I am sure you will appreciate that we are urging this in your best interests as well as our own.

You have been fortunate in escaping the last few weeks of extreme weather here, as I presume you must have been reasonably comfortable, and I now am glad to say the weather here has changed for the better.

Let me hear from you as soon as you can.

Very sincerely yours,
Arthur H. Scribner

Gibson had no objection and agreed that the first suggested title was best. Other People *was published on 21 October 1911.*

Edith Wharton (1862–1937)

Edith Wharton at her desk, 1905

Wharton is the most significant woman writer published by Scribners, and, though she essentially abandoned the firm after 1923, her most important and permanent works — *The House of Mirth, The Custom of the Country, Ethan Frome* — appeared under the Scribner imprint. Born into a distinguished New York family, she never attended school or college, but, educated by governesses and tutors and by long residences abroad, she acquired a wide knowledge of society and a deep understanding of people, which she successfully translated into American literature of the first rank. Her talent found form primarily in the novel and short story, where her common themes included the contrast of domestic and foreign manners, the conflict of morals and social conventions, the frustration of the individual trapped and isolated from acceptable avenues of escape. She was the first woman to receive an honorary degree from Yale and the first woman to be honored with a gold medal from the National Institute of Arts and Letters. Besides her literary efforts, Wharton was heavily involved in volunteer relief, particularly during World War I, for which work she was made a chevalier of the French Legion of Honor. One hundred years after the publication of her first book, Wharton's work is studied ever more widely.

Scribner Books by Wharton

1897	*The Decoration of Houses,* co-authored by Ogden Codman
1899	*The Greater Inclination*
1900	*The Touchstone*
1901	*Crucial Instances*
1902	*The Valley of Decision* (2 volumes)
	The Joy of Living: A Play in Five Acts by Hermann Sudermann, translated from the German by Wharton
1903	*Sanctuary,* illustrated by Walter Appleton Clark
1904	*The Descent of Man, and Other Stories*
1905	*Italian Backgrounds,* illustrated by E. C. Peixotto

LETTER:

More than five years passed between the time (November 1893) Edward L. Burlingame, editor of Scribner's Magazine, *suggested a volume of short stories to Wharton and the date it actually appeared (March 1899): an important period of apprenticeship and confidence-building in her creative development. As the editor who had published her first story (July 1891), Burlingame exerted a strong influence over her, as this letter reveals. When the volume did appear, it included only Wharton's most recent fictional efforts. "Something Exquisite," revised, was renamed "Friends" and appeared in the* Youth's Companion *in 1900; no Wharton story with the title "Judged" was ever published. The "Carducci Sonnet" she mentions was a poem written in the style of Giosuè Carducci, a nineteenth-century Italian poet.*

Florence, March 26th [1894]

Dear Mr. Burlingame,

I have just received your letter of March 13th, in which you tell me that you don't like the story which I called "Something Exquisite." Pray, by the way, have no tender hearted compunctions about criticizing my stories — your criticism is most helpful to me & I always recognize its justice. While I think that an inactive dilettantism produces just such maudlin over-sensibility as my poor heroine is afflicted with, I see perfectly that the contrast is too violent between her "schwärmerei" [rapture] in pink satin & the ensuing squalor.

I did not suppose that you would care at present for any more stories for the magazine — , & I sent "Something Exquisite" & the other story called "Judged" only to see if you approved of them for the volume. I am therefore going to suggest detaching the squalid part of "Something Exquisite" from the prelude & epilogue, which have nothing to do with the story & including it in the volume in that shape. I should like to do this, unless you distinctly disapprove, for it seems to me that the sketch of the two schoolteachers, if it stands by itself, will no longer appear exaggeredly squalid, & may perhaps do fairly well among the other stories.

I should like to bring out the book without adding many more stories, for I seem to have fallen into a period of groping, & perhaps, after publishing the volume, I might see better what direction I ought to take and acquire more assurance (the quality I feel I most lack). You were kind enough to give me so much encouragement when I saw you, & I feel myself so much complimented by the Messrs. Scribner's request that I should publish a volume of stories, that I am very ambitious to do better, & perhaps I could get a better view of what I have done & ought to do after the stories have been published. I have lost confidence in myself at present, & if you think "Judged" a failure I shall feel I have made entirely "fausse route." Pray don't regard this as the wail of the rejected authoress — it is only a cry for help & counsel to you who have been so kind in giving me both.

I didn't intend to withdraw the Carducci Sonnet, but merely to ask you to publish it after the others — but if you have too many pray don't hesitate to return it.

When you next write will you tell me in all how any stories will be needed for the volume? You spoke of ten, but perhaps a smaller number would do.

Yours sincerely
Edith Wharton

LETTERS:
Brownell did not directly respond to this letter in which Wharton harshly criticizes Scribners' promotional effort for her first volume — nor did CS II, who was traveling at the time. By September, however, when the first sales report was due, the book had gone into a second printing, and Brownell's praise was able to gloss over any perceived failing on the firm's part — in fact, he almost suggests that quality and popularity are inversely related. Within a week of receiving his letter, Wharton offered Scribners her next work, The Touchstone. *John Lane was the English Publisher of* The Greater Inclination.

Washington April 25th, [18]99

Dear Mr. Brownell,

I have been unwell or I should have replied sooner to your letter of April 18th. I am much obliged to you for allowing me ½ royalty on the first 500 of Mr. Lane's edition of my book.

At the same time, you will pardon my saying that I do not think I have been fairly treated as regards the advertising of "The Greater Inclination." The book has now been out about six weeks, & I do not think I exaggerate in saying that it has met with an unusually favourable reception for a first volume by a writer virtually unknown. The press-notices have been, almost uniformly, not only approving but very flattering; & such papers as the Springfield Republican, the N.Y. Times, Literature, &c, have given a column of commendation; while I hear the Bookman is to publish an article in the coming number. In addi-

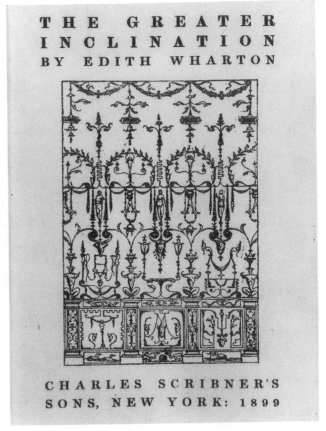

THE GREATER INCLINATION
BY EDITH WHARTON

CHARLES SCRIBNER'S SONS, NEW YORK: 1899

Title page of Wharton's first book of fiction, designed by one of the best-known designer/printers of the time, D. B. Updike at the Merrymount Press. "I venture to suggest," Wharton had written to W. C. Brownell (18 September 1898), "that I should be very glad if Mr. Scribner were disposed to give the printing of the book to Mr. Updike. I say this from no desire to drum up business for Mr. Updike, who, as it happens, stands in no need of such assistance, but simply because I like his work so much better than any one else's."

tion to this, the book was taken by an English publisher within a fortnight of its appearance here.

So much for <u>my</u> part in the transaction: now as to Mr. Scribner's. I have naturally watched with interest the advertising of the book, & have compared it with the notices given by other prominent publishers of books appearing under the same conditions. I find that Messrs. McMillan, Dodd & Mead, McClure, Harper, &c., advertise almost continuously in the daily papers every new book they publish, for the first few weeks after publication, giving large space to favourable press-notices; in addition to which, they of course advertise largely in the monthlies. So far, I have seen once, in a Sunday paper, I think, an advertisement of the Greater Inclination, with a line or two from the "Sun" review, which appeared among the first. Even that notice I have not found since, till it reappeared in the same shape in the new "Scribner" for May, without the addition of any of the many notices that have come out.

In calling your attention to these facts I don't of course, flatter myself that there is any hope of modifying the business methods of the firm; but I think myself justified in protesting against them in my own case.

If a book is unnoticed, or unfavourably received, it is natural that the publisher should not take much trouble about advertising it; but to pursue the same course towards a volume that has been generally commended, seems to me essentially unjust. Certainly in these days of energetic & emphatic advertising, Mr. Scribner's methods do not tempt one to offer him one's wares a second time.

Sincerely Yours
Edith Wharton

September 22, 1899

My dear Mrs. Wharton,

. . . Certainly "The Greater Inclination" has done very well for a volume of stories, as one may professionally say. If it had done very much better one might have wondered if it was really as good as it seemed, I suppose a believer in the "remnant" theory would add. But it has been appreciated so much in many directions that I have heard of that you can assuredly plume yourself on having joined the "note" of universality to that of distinction. I am glad I guessed right myself in thinking that the succès d'estime sale of 600 at the outset indicated an aftermath of genuine popularity. Of course you may think 2500 or 3000 not so impressive a figure as I am presuming; but I speak from a mixed literary & publishing viewpoint in accordance with my functions, and am really only trying to say that we hope you will agree with us that the book has done well, considering its delicate quality. No doubt, too, it is still going on. . . .

Sincerely yours
W. C. Brownell

LETTERS AND MEMORIAL:
Wharton's two editors at Scribners, Edward L. Burlingame (magazine) and W. C. Brownell (book), react to her novel The House of Mirth. *Se-*

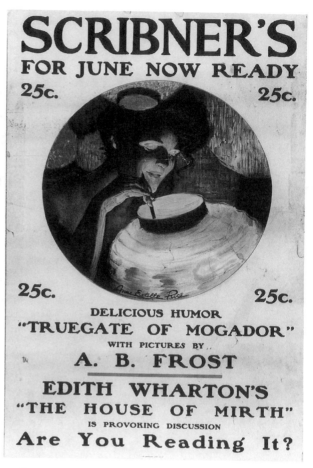

Poster announcing the June 1905 issue of Scribner's Magazine. Wharton's novel *The House of Mirth* was midway through its serialization.

rialized in Scribner's Magazine *from January to November 1905, the book was published on 14 October with Brownell's suggested frontispiece. It became an immediate best-seller — one of the top ten works of fiction for both 1905 and 1906.*

September 21, 1904

Dear Mrs. Wharton:

I have had two unexpected interruptions on successive days, so that it is only to-day I can tell you about my reading. I abound with things I want to say about it in detail; but the sum of them all is that for me the story is fulfilling all its promise — and I say it soberly and critically, and not a bit as an easy general statement. I can see, I think, what revision may do for parts of the last fifty pages, but I can honestly say that I nowhere see the <u>need</u> of it even in the matter of finish. The <u>vitality</u> of the story is extraordinary; and this time

53 rue de Varenne, Paris,

May 3rd, 1912.

of so

Dear Mr. Scribner,

Your letter of April 10th was duly received, and I
was glad to know that we had at last been able to agree on a date
for the serial publication of the "Custom of the Country".---- I
hope you will find it has been worth waiting for!----

I should say it would be about the length of "The
House of Mirth". With regard to the date of delivery of the manuscript, I can certainly give you a large part of it by September
first, which would give you five or six months for the consideration of practical questions. The whole thing I hope to put in
your hands two months before publication, and possibly much sooner.

Since I last wrote you I have received from the
Messrs. Appleton a very high offer for a novel. As I was just
finishing the short novel I have been working on during the last
year, and as the terms they offered are so advantageous, I have
decided to give them the tale in question, which they are to publish in September or early October.

I believe this will be to your advantage as well as
mine, as it will perhaps be the means of reaching a somewhat different public, and if the story is a success will in some
sort act as a preparation for "The Custom of the Country".

I have just accepted the offer, and wish you to
hear of it at once.

Yours very sincerely

Edith Wharton

Letter by Wharton to CS II signaling a move to a different publisher for her next work. CS II responded on 12 June 1913: "It has taken me a month to recover from the shock caused by your announcement that you had arranged with Appletons for the publication of your next book . . . . Of course I am very sorry to lose the honor of exclusive publication for you and it will be a little difficult for me to explain to others why you made a change. But I try to be broad minded about it . . . ." While relations between Wharton and CS II remained cordial, after the publication of The Custom of the Country *(1913) D. Appleton increasingly became the publisher of her fiction.*

The break with Scribners — never more directly explained than in this letter — was probably more a reflection of Wharton's developing independence and need for wider recognition than a mere response to greater money. She had complained before of Scribners' less-than-expected promotion of her works; she no longer needed or wanted to rely on the editorial guidance of Burlingame and Brownell; and, like a belle with many suitors, she could not resist the temptation to play the field.

so outruns the sense of technical skill which sometimes puts an element of consciousness into my enjoyment of your characterization, that I take a new kind of pleasure in it (in addition nota bene to the old). If I were going into the critical epigram business, I should be tempted to say that you make these people so perfectly because they are so alive, rather than that they are alive because you make them so perfectly — and that, I mean, is sincerely the way they present themselves to me this time. One may discuss all day as to which way of putting it implies the greater praise to the writer's art, qua art, but there is no kind of question as to which is more likely to bring the novel into the Great Succession.

I am not without small criticisms, — the largest of which is that I am a little disappointed at a certain monotony of motive in the types; but I am prepared to admit that it is perhaps a necessity of what you are doing. I do not suppose there was any variety of motives in Teufelsdröckh's "jarful of Egyptian vipers each struggling to get to the top"; and after all this is criticism of the general topic and point of view that one could discuss endlessly. Perhaps I do not mean monotony of motives after all so much as monotony of the kind of motive. I shouldn't expect any more touches of largeness in these particular dramatis personae, but I think I should expect a little more obvious self-deception — some of them thinking of themselves differently.

This, though, is the kind of thing one talks, not writes; and I repeat with the utmost sincerity that I think the story comes on with wonderful strength and interest. Execution and the capital things said by the way, I have grown to take for granted with you, but I assure you that these too have never seemed to me better.

I have sent pages 102–176 (i.e. up to the beginning of the carbon copy) to Miss Thayer today. Pages 1–102 I understand to be duplicate, which we can keep here and show to the artist if necessary. Pages 177–197 I also keep, and understand that Miss Thayer will fill the interval as soon as she has time.

"The House of Mirth" captures us all. I think it is the inspirational title we have been hoping for. I was satisfied with and even liked "The Year of the Rose," as you know, but this is very much better, crisper, more vigorous, without a suggestion of preciosity, and telling its own story to perfection. We all adopt it without a dissenting vote, and it shall at once go into the paragraph of the prospectus which you returned. I am glad the substance of the paragraph satisfied you; I did not read over the Swinburne lines on the proof, taking for granted the printers had copied them straight — so I did not notice what a mess they made. Dropping them and substituting the new title shall be the only changes in the paragraph.

I did not write about "The Cost" because a letter of mine crossed yours suggesting it, in which I supposed you would see my preference plainly for "The Year of the Rose"; but I have since learned that "The Cost" has just been used as the title of a novel by David Graham Phillips, so it would be out of the question anyhow.

Yours sincerely
E. L. Burlingame

At the top of the letter, Brownell has written: "For a frontispiece my choice is Lily on the Landing or 'She lingered on the broad stairway, looking down into the hall below' — from, I think, the February no. Do you approve?"

Aug. 3, 1905

Dear Mrs. Wharton,

When your letter about the proof came, the mfg. dept. informed me the pages accompanied by the galleys you wished were already on the way to you. So I assumed they would constitute a substantial reply — and deferred writing till I should be able to think of some proper expression of the pleasure what you said about my distinguished self gave me, though perhaps you will not have expected it fully to change my previous notion that possibly "there are others." Mais, il s'agit bien de moi! Since then I have read The House of Mirth, comprenez-vous? I got the back numbers of and the advance proofs from Mr. Burlingame and read it all at one sitting with a couple of brief stops for (other) refreshments. And since then I have been too full for any adequate utterance about it. There can't be two opinions. The way in which the study of moeurs melt into the novel of character — ah, well it is the whole shooting-match. It must seem nice & cosey to have done an incontestably big thing. That is the way to write a novel — make it a human document and an imaginative poem at the same time. Just paint like Titian, so to speak. At first I was mainly interested in Lily's activities, but I developed a great fondness for her — & I suspect her author did. She got through a particularly indurated carapace (I fear) and to an extent I hesitate to confess, at my age. I mean just at the last, especially, and I do not think it was my nerves either. Joh! When you wish to be affecting

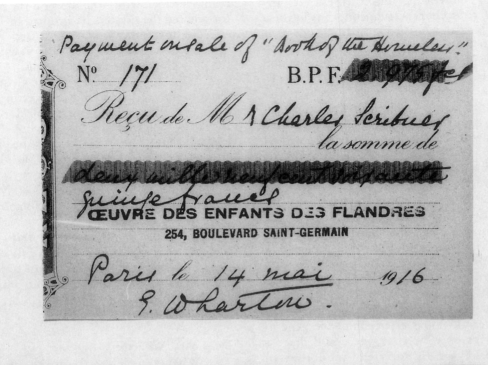

Receipts for the first profits from The Book of the Homeless, *signed by Wharton on behalf of the two benefiting charities: The American Hostels for Refugees and The Children of Flanders Rescue Committee. Ultimately, about $3,000 was realized after costs of producing the book were deducted; a separate auction of the original artwork and manuscripts netted close to an additional $7,000.*

you can excel in that, too. I feel like devoting my ingenuity to trying to think how you are going to "develop" now. Would it not have been cannier to postpone perfection till you could use it as the cap-sheaf of your oeuvre? There is one thing the "reviews" may not point out and so it may escape your notice. But if you will glance over the book I think you will be struck by the extreme <u>beauty</u> of much of it — an effect quite apart from, or rather interpenetrating, the sapient grand construction and the polish of the (always) contributing details. Enfin, it's the first book <u>I</u> have read in many years that I propose to read again and read all of again. Perhaps then I shall be able to find out why or in what it isn't — no, I don't believe I shall. I am all tired out thank you, & bound for Moosehead ere long — where I ought to have gone last year & didn't. I hope you are both in enviable shape —

Sincerely yours
W. C. Brownell

In this excerpt from her memorial to Brownell ["William C. Brownell" from W. C. Brownell: Tributes and Appreciations *(New York: Charles Scribner's Sons, 1929), pp. 14–15], Wharton salutes both of her editors.*

. . .

How can I end without one personal word of the friend who was even wiser than the critic? I wonder to how many beginners it happens to be met on the threshold by two such guides as Brownell and Edward Burlingame, his colleague in the house of Scribner? I do not think I have ever forgotten one word of the counsels they gave me. Edward Burlingame's were often lapidary; as when, in the attempt to stem the first outrush of my fiction, he said to me one day, with his exquisite gentleness: "And now, wait awhile. You mustn't run the risk of becoming a magazine bore."

Mr. Brownell would not have needed to say that; he made me feel it. As in criticism he achieved the difficult feat of setting up a standard which was classical without being academic, so in his spoken counsels the eagerest open-mindedness was combined with an unwavering perception of final values. Rarely as I saw him — alas, too rarely! — the sense of his wisdom and sympathy was always with me, like a guiding touch on my shoulder. Even now that light hand remains, to stimulate and restrain — surely the two chief offices of friendship. In thinking of him to-day I again give thanks for them.

CS II DIARY ENTRY:
Monday 22 October 1906

Night in City. Attended first night with Louise of "House of Mirth" with tickets given by Mrs. Wharton. Fay Davis as Lily Bart. I think the play a failure.

Scribner's estimate was universal: this stage version of Wharton's The House of Mirth, *co-authored by Clyde Fitch, promptly closed.*

LETTER:
To raise money for her refugee work in France during World War I, Wharton proposed the idea of publishing an attractive volume of original and unpublished poetry, prose, and artwork donated by well-known authors and artists. Though she sought out Scribners to publish it, she wanted D. B. Updike (of Boston) to do the printing and design and Robert Grant, a friend and fellow writer, to centralize the gathering of contributions; she also hoped that the well-known illustrator Maxfield Parrish would be able to provide art for the cover. CS II was enthusiastically supportive and, as he answered in this letter, offered the services of his house gratis. However, he had strong doubts about the selection of Updike, given the conditions of the book's publication, the difficulty of distance, and the lack of time. And he tried, here, to make a logical case for taking the volume on his own.

August 3, 1915

Dear Mrs. Wharton:
     Your letter of the 19th arrived Friday just as I was leaving for Dublin, New Hampshire and on my return this morning I have the one of the 22nd and the corrected circular. Let me say at once that we shall cooperate with enthusiasm in the preparation and publication of the book and I have cabled "Glad to publish refugee book, all profits to be paid societies after deducting actual expenditure. Forwarding Parrish Letter. Approve Updike if he will take full responsibility for preparation. Writing." I hope this will be fairly clear and give you promptly the information immediately required. I do not know what plan for publication you have in mind but my proposal is to place the services of

Hotel de Crillon
Place de la Condorde
   Paris.

                          November 7th 1922

Dear Mr.Scribner,

    Many thanks for your letter of October 25th.

      I am glad you do not think that the technical mistake in the first chapters of "A Son at the Front" will make much difference. As you say, nationalities are so confused at present that it may pass unperceived, and at any rate the correction can easily be made for the book. It is really not my fault that the mistake was made, for I applied for information to a good authority.

      With regard to the moving-picture rights of "A Son at the Front", I should much prefer that you should deal with the matter for me. I prefer a sale outright to the cinema Company rather than any royalty contract. In the case of "The Glimpses of the Moon", which I asked Messrs. Appleton to dispose of for me, I received $15.000 for the sale of the rights. I do not know who their agent is, but it might be worth while to find out.

      In this connection I want to tell you that I had a letter from Mr.Jewett the other day expressing the warmest wishes for the success of "A Son at the Front", and mentioning the cordial relations between your two firms.

      Many thanks for sending me the copies of the new Ethan Frome. I am sorry the book is not satisfactory to you in appearance, but I hope it will be as regards its sale.

            Believe me, dear Mr. Scribner,

                  Yours very sincerely

                   E. Wharton

Letter by Wharton to CS II chiefly about her novel A Son at the Front. *Her "technical mistake" was in assuming French military service was obligatory for an American boy born in France who had one French parent. Technically, the father had to be French for this to obtain, while in Wharton's novel the mother was French. No change was possible at the time because the novel had already begun its serialization in Scribner's Magazine. Rutger Bleecker Jewett was Wharton's editor at Appleton. The "new Ethan Frome" is the limited edition of the work, designed by Bruce Rogers, which Scribners published in November 1922 with an introduction Wharton had written for the edition.*

this house fully at your disposal to get the best results on the book, charging only for money actually expended — I mean making no charge for the personal services of anyone here, for commissions or anything of that kind; we should make no charge either for advertising in our own Magazine or catalogue. This seemed to me the best arrangement. Until we know more clearly the amount of literary material and illustration and the format of the book, the price must be very uncertain but I am in favor of as high a price as can reasonably be charged, particularly if Mr. Updike makes the book. I think we would do better in trying to sell a smaller number at a higher price than in reaching out for a tremendously large sale. The question of time is a very important one; there are always so many unexpected delays and of course the book cannot be printed until the last contribution is received.

With your letter to Mr. Parrish I have written a personal note. I hope he is at home and will do the cover for us. We can give him the exact dimensions a little later but my idea would be something like the King Albert and Princess Mary books. We have copies of the Book of France in the Custom House and mail but have not yet seen it.

Your suggestion that Mr. Updike should print and prepare the book seemed to me at first troublesome. Naturally his charges are higher than those of the ordinary printer and it takes a little longer to have work done in Boston, but what I feared most was the difficulty of cooperating on the details of the work, if there was a division of responsibility. If he will take entire charge of the preparation of the book, deciding upon the type, headlines, captions et cetera, placing of illustrations, method of reproduction, paper and binding, I have no doubt but that we should get something of real bibliographical value. Of course we have a good deal of experience of our own in book making, and the Magazine is a miscellaneous collection of prose and poetry and illustration not unlike the proposed book, but we have not always found it easy to cooperate with Mr. Updike, as he has his own strong preferences. We shall be very glad to give him all the assistance desired but one or the other of us must have a free hand or at least the right to finally decide. I am writing in some haste and I fear I may not have made the situation clear. It is more of less a practical one. We can make the book here in our way and might

make use of Updike as printer, but if he is to take any part on the editorial side, I think it would be easier and better to let him take full charge. Probably in a full concordance with him we could come to a satisfactory understanding as to all the questions involved — certainly I would try to do so.

Robert Grant has been away salmon fishing but I think he is back now and no doubt we shall both hear from him promptly. I wish he was in New York, for we are so accustomed to exercise some personal supervision of manuscript before it goes into the printer's hands, but if Mr. Updike has charge it will be less important. So many writers and artists are now on their vacation that it may be very difficult to get in "copy" quickly, and in some cases it will be necessary to decide whether to hold the book back for a particular contribution.

I will write to you again about other questions.

Yours sincerely
Charles Scribner

Wharton prevailed with her choice of Updike. But, as CS II had imagined, the production was complicated and took too much time, and as a result the book missed the important Christmas book-selling season. (Published on 22 January 1916, the book had a printing of thirty-three hundred copies and cost five dollars; in addition, a deluxe, limited edition of 175 copies was printed, 125 on Van Gelder paper at twenty-five dollars each and 50 on French handmade paper at fifty dollars each.) Moreover, in the delay of getting the books to France, Wharton asked Macmillan, the English publisher, to supply the French contributors with its copies, which bore its imprint. This greatly disappointed CS II, whose firm had worked so hard with Updike and borne much of the associated expenses.

RELATED LETTERS:
CS II's efforts to secure another novel from Wharton after The Custom of the Country *continued for many years, starting with an informal agreement in 1913. World War I took the major blame for their lack of success — for the obvious emotional and psychological reasons and because of the practical demands brought on by Wharton's refugee work. As Scribner observed to Wharton (29 September 1919), "We did not expect the war to last so long or to bring such terrible changes." One of the changes was the enor-*

WHARTON, EDITH   A SON AT THE FRONT

1923 Sept.	Atlantic Monthly	12.00
~~Aug~~ Sept.11	Publishers' Weekly	17.00
	1923 Catalog Amer. News Co.	100.00 129.00
Oct.	Yale Review	6.00
Sept.1	Amer. News Trade Journal	60.00
Sept.	Books of the Month	70.00
Oct.	No. American Review	20.00
Oct.	Atlantic Monthly	80.00
Oct.	Bookman	30.00
Oct.	Century	42.00
Autumn No.	Brentano's Book Chat	42.00
Sept.7	Chicago Post	56.10
Sept. 8	Chicago Tribune	153.00
Sept. 8	Boston Herald	89.25
Sept. 8	Boston Transcript	89.25
Sept. 9	N.Y.Herald	102.00
Sept.16	N Y.Times	193.80
Sept. 9	N.Y.Times	459.04
Sept. 1	Publishers' Wkly	26.00
Aug. 25	Publishers' Wkly	23.00
Sept.	Int. Bk. Review	140.00
Aug. 18	Publishers' Wkly	23.00
Sept.	Scribner's Magazine	87.00
Sept. 7	N.Y.Post	7.40
Sept. 4	N. Y. World	12.00
Sept. 7	N. Y. Times	25.00
Sept. 7	N.Y.Tribune	7.60
Sept. 8	Phila. No. American	39.00
Sept. 8	Phila. Public Ledger	127.50
Sept. 8	N. Y. Post	94.35
Sept. 9	N. Y. World	77.35
Sept. 9	N. Y. Tribune	76.50
Sept. 9	Phila. Record	32.50
Sept. 12	Chicago News	122.40
Sept. 8	N.Y.Post	8.00
Sept. 5	N.Y.Sun	8.00
Sept.10,12,14	N.Y.Sun	30.00
Sept. 8,10,12,14	N.Y.Times	135.00
Sept. 8,10,11,12,13,14	N.Y.World	90.00
Sept. 10,12,14	N. Y. Post	27.75
Sept. 7	Boston Herald	7.00
Sept. 11,13.14	Boston Herald	26.85
Sept. 8,11,13,14	N.Y.Tribune	30.00
Sept. 10,12,14	Chicago Post	16.50
Sept. 11,13	Phila. Record	12.50
Sept. 7	Phila. Public Ledger	10.00
Sept. 10,12,14	Phila. Ledger	37.50
Sept. 7	Boston Transcript	7.00
Sept. 10,12,14	Boston Transcript	26.85
Oct.	Harpers	37.00
Sept. 15	N.Y.Post	10.00
Sept. 16	N.Y.Tribune	20.90
Sept. 17,19,21	N.Y.Tribune	28.00
~~Sept. 23 N.Y.Times~~		~~218.00~~
Sept. 17,19,21	N.Y.Times	101.25
Sept. 17,19,21	N.Y.Sun	30.00 to p.2

First of six pages of records for Scribners' advertising of Wharton's novel A Son at the Front, *published 7 September 1923. Expenditures through March 1924 total more than $13,000.*

mous amount of money Wharton was being offered for her work, which was making it difficult for Scribners to compete.

Feb. 23rd, 1914

Dear Mr. Scribner,

As you said you wished me to fix a date early in the spring for the serial publication of my novel, I think I ought to let you know that there is practically no chance of its being finished by next January. Moreover, as it develops, I begin to fear it may be too long for serial publication. It is to be a rather full and leisurely chronicle of a young man's life from his childhood to his end, and I don't see how I can possibly get it into less than forty-five chapters, which make a book of about 170,000 words or more. In the circumstances, would it not be better to give up the idea of serial publication? I should regret it naturally, but every subject carries its own length within itself, and I can't see this as a short book. I want it to be my best and most comprehensive piece of work, and it must move slowly. . . .

Yours sincerely
Edith Wharton

Dec. 29th, 1914

Dear Mr. Scribner,

. . .

And now as regards my next novel: the war, as you know, has temporarily interrupted all my work, & for the present there is too much to do for the unfortunate creatures all about one to think much of literature. I don't mean, however, to abandon my trade for much longer, & I am as eager as ever to get at my novel & finish it. But I cannot fix any date for its completion, & even could I do so, I should not think it right to hold you to the price we agreed on last winter if, when the time comes, circumstances make you feel that it is too high. I think it would be fairer to drop the question of its publication till I can give you more definite news of it. . . .

Yours sincerely
Edith Wharton

March 16th 1919

Dear Mr. Scribner,

. . .

"Literature." I feel that I am gradually approaching the time when it will again be possible to write a novel that is not concerned with the war, and my first idea would be to finish "Literature" if you are still disposed to take it. Will you let me know if this contract still holds, or if you prefer to be released from it? Believe me

Yours very sincerely
E. Wharton

September 12th 1919

Dear Mr. Scribner,

. . .

You remind me that I have not yet replied to your enquiry in a previous letter as to "Literature." The letter in question was, if I remember rightly, in answer to one from me saying that I thought I should be able to take up the book again before long. In the first relief from war anxieties I thought it might be possible to shake off the question which is tormenting all novelists at present: "Did the adventures related in this book happen before the war or did they happen since?" with the resulting difficulty that, if they happened before the war, I seem to have forgotten how people felt and what their point of view was. I should feel ashamed of these hesitations if I did not find that all novelists I know are much in the same predicament. Perhaps it will not last much longer and we shall be able to get back some sort of perspective; but at present, between the objection of the public to so-called war-stories and the difficulty of the author to send his imagination backward, the situation is a bewildering one. As you know, I several times, during the war, offered to replace "Literature" by other novels, which did not involve the study of such complex social conditions and dealt with people less affected by the war. As you preferred to wait for "Literature" these two tales, "Summer" and "The Marne," were given to other magazines, and I continued to hope that I should see my way to going on with "Literature." At present, I can only suggest waiting a few more weeks and then writing to you definitely. . . . Believe me

Yours very sincerely
Edith Wharton

Feb. 9, 1921

Dear Mrs. Wharton:

. . . I should so much prize an opportunity to talk with you about your work, for I have not abandoned the hope of securing future novels. The loss of your books was the greatest blow ever given to my pride as a publisher. All I ask is an opportunity to meet other publishers on a business basis but it is almost impossible to make progress without a personal interview.

Yours sincerely
Charles Scribner

In Europe with his wife, July–September 1921, CS II records this entry in his diary for September 4th:

> See Mrs. Wharton buy serial for
> $15,000 & 20% on book
> Two articles this year on art of fiction
> Very satisfactory

September 17th, 1921

Dear Mr. Scribner,

Many thanks for your letter of Sept. 11th, in answer to mine. I am always glad to have my name associated with that of my first publishers, and I hope my novel may appear serially in Scribner's. . . .

Yours very sincerely
Edith Wharton

Serialized in Scribner's Magazine *from December 1922 through September 1923,* A Son at the Front, *Wharton's last Scribner novel, was published on 7 September 1923.*

Ernest Thompson Seton (1860–1946)

Born Ernest Evan Thompson, he assumed the family's ancient Scottish surname of Seton in 1883. His mother prevailed on him in 1887 to change it back again "as long as I am alive." This Seton did until her death in 1897: he signed his letters Ernest E. Thompson but signed his artwork Ernest Seton-Thompson. His books bore the same name. In 1901, after he had moved to the United States, he legally changed his name to Ernest Thompson Seton. Soon thereafter he requested that Scribners change his name on his reprinted books and, later, on the signed plates in his books.

Author, illustrator, naturalist, Seton is best remembered for his realistic animal stories that appeal to all ages and for his interests in educating and instructing boys in woodcraft and Indian ways. His lengthy publishing career with Scribners began with a best-seller and ended with his autobiography; in between, Seton's books of fiction and fact made him an international figure. Born in England, raised in Canada, he grew up wanting to be recognized as an authentic artist and a scientific observer of nature. He exhibited his art in Paris and at the Chicago World's Fair, and became the official naturalist of the Canadian province of Manitoba. An ardent propagandist for conservation, Seton is also considered to be one of the three founders (with Dan Beard and Robert Baden-Powell) of the Boy Scouts movement. He was chief scout in the United States from 1910 to 1915 and authored the first American Boy Scouts' *Handbook* (1910).

Scribner Books by Seton

1898	*Wild Animals I Have Known, and 200 Drawings*
1899	*Lobo, Rag, and Vixen, and Pictures*
	The Trail of the Sandhill Stag, and 60 Drawings
1901	*Lives of the Hunted: Containing a True Account of the Doings of Five Quadrupeds & Three Birds, and, in Elucidation of the Same, Over 200 Drawings*
	Pictures of Wild Animals (portfolio)
1902	*Krag and Johnny Bear, With Pictures*
1904	*Monarch, The Big Bear of Tallac, With 100 Drawings*
1905	*Animal Heroes: Being the Histories of a Cat, a Dog, a Pigeon, a Lynx, Two Wolves & a Reindeer and in Elucidation of the Same Over 200 Drawings*
1907	*The Natural History of the Ten Commandments*
1909	*Life-Histories of Northern Animals: An Account of the Mammals of Manitoba, with 68 maps and 560 drawings by Seton (2 volumes)*
1911	*The Arctic Prairies: A Canoe Journey of 2,000 Miles in Search of the Caribou*
1922	*Bannertail: The Story of a Gray Squirrel, With 100 Drawings*
1935	*Johnny Bear, Lobo, and Other Stories*
1937	*Great Historic Animals: Mainly About Wolves*
1940	*Trail of an Artist-Naturalist: The Autobiography of Ernest Thompson Seton, with illustrations by Seton*

LETTER:
Letter by W. C. Brownell, Scribner book editor, to Seton, 6 June 1898.

After successfully publishing several of his animal stories in magazines, Seton felt the next step was to seek their collection in book form. Edward L. Burlingame, editor of Scribner's Magazine, *had published some of the stories and shown interest in a book. In this letter Burlingame's Scribner colleague W. C. Brownell shares the interest in the stories but does not see much profit in the illustrations.*

Dear Sir,

We have read the two stories we had not read hitherto and judging from the five now before us we are prepared to say that we should be very glad to undertake the volume you propose, if the remaining material seems to us satisfactorily equivalent in interest to that we have now; and if we can arrange satisfactorily with regard to your proposed illustrations. This, we think, is the chief difficulty to contend with in the matter, as we take it the stories we have are fair "samples" of the rest of the text. But we fear the prospects of the book are not considerable enough to make its illustrations commercially practicable. How much illustrating did you have in mind & what payment should you expect us to make for it? In advance of a clear understanding of these points it is, as you can of course comprehend, somewhat difficult for us to make you a proposition for the book's publication with the requisite definitiveness.

Very truly yours
Charles Scribner's Sons

Page from a company ledger showing the early manufacturing history of Seton's first book, Wild Animals I Have Known, *with title page of the book. In his autobiography Seton claimed that the book "founded the modern school of animal stories, that is, giving in fiction form the actual facts of an animal's life and modes of thought."*

Seton's text proved inseparable from the illustrations with which he adorned the book, and Wild Animals I Have Known *was published with them. All of the books Seton would publish with Scribners were self-illustrated. The illustrations proved to have attractive promotional uses, in exhibitions and advertising, for both author and publisher.*

MEMOIR:
Ernest Thompson Seton, *Trail of an Artist-Naturalist* (New York: Charles Scribner's Sons, 1940), p. 352.

In his autobiography Seton describes how the deal for this first book was finally sealed in a meeting he had with CS II.

Their official readers all approved it. Then I went to Scribner himself for a final discussion.

He began by telling me what a hazardous profession was that of a publisher; how most books were failures, and that that had to be kept ever in mind. So that 10 per cent on the published price of the book, and something extra for illustrations, was the best they could offer.

"How many must you sell to cover your outlay?" I asked. "Not less than 2000," he answered.

Then I sprang my counter-offer, beginning: "Remember, my plan is not simply to throw this into the hopper with a hundred other new books. I am going forth to talk about it, lecture about it, give exhibitions of my illustrations, and sell copies in every town where I lecture. I am so sure of its success that I will forego all royalties on the first 2000 copies, which lets you out, provided you *will double it* ever afterward."

I had completely surrounded him with a fence of his own construction, so there was nothing for him to do but consent.

I had three titles to suggest: *Lobo and Other Tales, Four Kings and a Crow, Wild Animals I Have Known.* Scribner thought the first colorless, the second sounded like a poker hand, so decided on the last.

The contract was signed on July 1, the book copyrighted October 20, 1898. Within three weeks the 2000 of the first edition were sold; and, before Christmas, three more large printings. The book was a best seller. This boom did not die out for several years, so that it left me in easy circumstances.

Gifted with a powerful voice and stage presence, Seton was a popular lecturer who liked to act out

his stories and was thus a natural promoter of his own books. He appealed equally to adults and children.

CS II DIARY ENTRY:
Thursday 22 February 1900

Holiday
Took children to hear
Seton-Thompson

TELEGRAM AND RELATED LETTER:
Cable by Seton to CS II, 3 November 1904; letter by CS II to Seton in response, 4 November 1904.

Lecturing in England, Seton did not receive the first copies of his new book, Monarch, The Big Bear of Tallac, *till 3 November. Scribners had published it on 15 October in an edition of 33,175, and only 13,910 copies remained in the bindery by the time the firm got Seton's cable.*

Chas Scribners & Son
153 Fifth Ave
Serious error Monarch chapters fourteen fifteen transposed stop edition. Seton

My dear Seton:

We have not had time to recover from the shock of your telegram of yesterday notifying us of the transposition of the two chapters in "Monarch." Although some thousands of copies have been distributed for almost a week, no one has detected the mistake. We shall at once reprint those chapters and correct our sheets and also the bound copies on hand, but it does not seem necessary or indeed possible to recall those which have gone out and I suggest that you say as little about the mistake as possible.

I at once rang up Mrs. Seton on the telephone but found that she sailed on Saturday. She will be able to give you information also about the first sales of the book. The accident seems to have been caused by an original mistake in the order of the titles of these two chapters. When passing the page proofs Mrs. Seton called attention to this on the table of contents, giving directions that the titles should be transposed. No directions were given in the body of the book and the printer transposed the <u>chapters</u> themselves as well as the <u>titles</u>. It is most unfortunate but I think you will see how it might

THE WOODCRAFT LEAGUE OF AMERICA

13 WEST 29TH STREET

NEW YORK CITY

OFFICE OF THE PRESIDENT

May 23, 1922

Dear Mr. Scribner:

     Next Saturday is the "Great Day." I am counting on your being present.

     My woods will be populated with Woodcrafters from early morning, but the official feast does not begin until four o'clock. Then we have the barbecue to which all members are invited. In the evening, from seven o'clock until nine, we have the Grand Council.

     Don't fail to be there as there are some important questions of policy on which we want your judgment.

     Sincerely yours,

Ernest Thompson Seton

Chief.

Mr. Charles Scribner,
549 Fifth Avenue,
New York City

L

Invitation by Seton to CS II to join him in a meeting of his Woodcraft League. Founded by Seton in 1902, the Woodcraft League was the first national boys' organization and became the source for Robert Baden-Powell's Boy Scouts.

have happened, but the printer is undoubtedly to blame.

I was delighted to hear that your lectures promised to be so successful but I hope you will not find the English field so inviting that you will abandon God's country.

Yours sincerely
Charles Scribner

LETTER:
Letter by Seton to CS III, 10 August 1939.

This letter bears the letterhead of Seton Institute. In 1930 Seton and his second wife, Julia, moved to a twenty-five-hundred-acre ranch in the heart of Navajo country near Santa Fe, New Mexico, to build a retirement home and a summer college of Indian arts and philosophy. Their "Seton Castle" and "Seton Village" were registered as national historic monuments in July 1966.

Dear Mr. Scribner:

For some years now, I have been writing MY TRAIL THROUGH THE WOODS, i.e., my Autobiography. It is now finished up to 1900. At that time, I was forty years old, I had attained to an established position, and was in easy circumstances. That seemed a logical place to end the first volume.

I am sending it to you now, with about 100 illustrations, hoping you will see your way to publish it.

You were my first and most important publisher, you have most of my books, and I certainly would like to see this come out with your imprint.

It contains about 150,000 words; and the 100 illustrations can be increased to any desired number. Most of them are unpublished drawings by myself.

The text is, for the most part, adventures in the animal world and in the Wild West. It has no lack of thrill, and has been loudly praised by Garland, Bok, Doubleday, Marcosson, Burroughs, and President Roosevelt. I have, however, added, by request, a number of chapters from my journals. These are not particularly thrilling, but are given to show the young readers how I got my information about the animals, how much patient tracking, trailing, measuring and watching was necessary. These can be shortened, or even omitted, if it seems best.

I am lecturing steadily these winters, and with great success. Sometimes I give readings from MY TRAIL, and always have a host of hearers who say: "You can put me down for a copy of that."

I feel confident that I personally can sell 2000 copies a year. As Frank Doubleday said: "The mere fact that it is Seton's Wild Life, will make it desired by a million American boys."

After 1900, I met a great many famous men, and had pleasant experiences with them, — Mark Twain, Kipling, Riley, Burroughs, Theodore Roosevelt, etc. These would be detailed in the second volume, if it is called for.

If the effort appeals to you, terms along your usual lines would be satisfactory.

Yours sincerely,
Ernest Thompson Seton

The reaction of CS III was positive, but he was convinced that two volumes would be too much and that Seton should concentrate on "that which has to do with America and particularly your early life in the West, also what you have written about animal life." If Seton could agree to that, they had a deal. He could, and they did. The task of achieving that one-volume goal was given to Maxwell Perkins, who observed: "Our view is that a biography nowadays of a man, however eminent, is not all-inclusive." In the editorial work Perkins emphasized Seton's artist-naturalist career and, in fact, supplied the title under which the book appeared, Trail of an Artist-Naturalist: The Autobiography of Ernest Thompson Seton.

John Fox Jr. (1863–1919)

John Fox Jr. (frontispiece to his A Mountain Europa, *New York: Harper & Brothers, 1899)*

Fox was born in Kentucky and died in Virginia. Educated at Harvard, he turned to newspaper work in New York, later became a war correspondent for *Harper's Weekly* during the Spanish-American War, and went to Japan in 1904 to cover the Russo-Japanese conflict for *Scribner's Magazine.* His fame rests, however, on the novels, novellas, and stories that he wrote about the Cumberland Mountains, in which he showed a thorough familiarity with his native region's dialect, and with the habits and thinking of its mountain residents. Two of his works, *The Little Shepherd of Kingdom Come* and *The Trail of the Lonesome Pine,* are among the most popular books ever published in American literature, though to current critics they seem mawkishly sentimental period pieces. Fox began as a Harper author in 1895 but switched in 1899 to Scribners, with whom he contentedly stayed for the remaining twenty years of his life; during that period he became a personal friend of CS II.

Scribner Books by Fox

1900	*Crittenden: A Kentucky Story of Love and War*
1901	*Blue-Grass and Rhododendron: Out-Doors in Old Kentucky*
1903	*The Little Shepherd of Kingdom Come,* illustrated by F. C. Yohn
1904	*A Cumberland Vendetta: A Novel*
	"Hell fer Sartain," and Other Stories
	The Kentuckians: A Novel, illustrated by W. T. Smedley
	A Mountain Europa
	Christmas Eve on Lonesome, and Other Stories, illustrated by Yohn and others
1905	*Following the Sun Flag: A Vain Pursuit Through Manchuria*

1906	*A Knight of the Cumberland,* illustrated by Yohn
1908	*The Trail of the Lonesome Pine,* illustrated by Yohn
1909	*Christmas Eve on Lonesome; "Hell-fer-Sartain," and Other Stories,* illustrated by Yohn, and others
	The Kentuckians; A Knight of the Cumberland, illustrated by Smedley and Yohn
	A Mountain Europa; A Cumberland Vendetta; The Last Stetson, illustrated by Yohn and Louis Loeb
1913	*The Heart of the Hills,* illustrated by Yohn
1917	*In Happy Valley,* illustrated by Yohn
1920	*Christmas Eve on Lonesome; "Hell-fer-Sartain"; In Happy Valley*
	Erskine Dale — Pioneer, illustrated by Yohn

RELATED LETTERS:

Instrumental in bringing F. Hopkinson Smith into the Scribner stable, Thomas Nelson Page was similarly successful with John Fox Jr. Both writers were friends who frequented York Harbor, Maine, in the summer. In this first letter the "little invalid" mentioned by Page is his own book, Santa Claus's Partner, *proofs of which he is in the process of correcting. Henry Mills Alden was editor (1869–1919) of* Harper's Magazine, *and Bowen-Merrill was an earlier name of the Bobbs-Merrill publishing company of Indianapolis.*

York Harbor, Maine   July 22d 1899
My dear Scribner:

We are at last up here safe and sound and our little invalid seems to be reaping the benefit of the change day by day.

I wanted to let you know we are here, so you can send anything you have for me here. I am moved as I am writing to speak of another matter.

John Fox is here, just finishing the first draft of a Story he wrote at the request of the Harpers for their Magazine — a (Cuban) war-novel. They now say, through Mr. Alden, that it is so long after the Cuban war that it does not suit for serial pubn in the Magazine. I know nothing of the merits of the Story and suppose the Harpers are right in their view of its non availability for serial pubn

in its present shape; but as they knew the outline of the Story, and Fox laid by a novel he was engaged on, which I think much the best thing he ever did, to write it for them, I think they have treated him in a very cavalier fashion, and I want him to send it to you with a view to having you consider its publication as a volume, and, if it suits you, as a serial as well. He is inclined to do this; but as he had counted on placing the Story serially he had also counted on getting some cash for it this Summer, and I think he believes McClure or someone else would be more likely to have a place for it now than you. I too think this probable; but it occurs to me that the matter might possibly be arranged in some way by an advance on acct of royalty, if you care to undertake the pubn as I sincerely hope you may. He is withheld from writing you by his diffidence about making such a proposal, which, however, is from what I know of his affairs almost necessary. I want him to place his books with you for his own sake, and I feel sure from the part I have seen of his other Novel, "The Little Shepherd of Kingdom Come," that I am doing you a good turn also in trying to arrange it. Besides these two books he has enough hunting sketches and stories finished — or will have in a month — to make another volume, and he will submit them all to you. You may have seen his fox-hunting and hare hunt stories in the <u>Century</u>.

Inscription by Fox to CS II in a copy of A Mountain
Europa *(New York: Harper & Brothers, 1899)*

If you feel inclined to consider the suggestion I have made, you can either write to me or to Fox himself here, and unless I am greatly mistaken it will prove to be to the interests of both of you; for I feel sure that Fox will in the next few years do work that will give him a wide reputation. The Bowen-Merrill people are after him; but I want him to go to you, and he would I know prefer it.

Yours faithfully
Thos. Nelson Page

CS II was very interested but did not want to take the initiative, as he wrote back to Page, because his relations with Harpers were very "pleasant" and he felt obligated to observe "the old courtesy." Instead, he suggested that Fox write directly to him.

York Harbor, Maine   July 26, 1899
Dear Mr. Scribner:

Tom has kindly shown me your letter of the 24th and I am very glad to take the initiative by offering the story at once. To relieve you com-

pletely, I will add that, if you do not see your way to using the novel, it will go elsewhere and anywhere but back to the Harpers for book publication.

I will say, moreover, that with this offer goes as well to you the first refusal of a book of Hunting Stories that can be got together in about a month, and of another novel, "The Little Shepherd of Kingdom Come" which will be finished next year, I hope, and which, I believe, will be the best thing I've done.

The war-novel I offer now is called "Crittenden." It is about 60,000 words in its present unfinished state, was meant to be 70,000 when finished and may be reduced to 40,000 words, particularly if your judgement on the war part of it coincides with Mr. Alden's. To be quite frank I send you my letter to him and his to me — explaining, however, that I never dreamed of getting the novel ready "soon after the termination of the Spanish War" — that is absurd — and that I couldn't get it ready for the spring, because I was ill. And I must explain further, before making you a proposition, that the Cuban fever kept me from steady work until March and that, in order to get the present rough draft of the novel in to Mr. Alden, according to promise, by July first, I put aside the other novel and gave up reading and lecturing — counting upon a part payment from "Crittenden" of at least $1000 on August first. So, my proposition is this: if on "Crittenden", in its present shape — and remember, please, that I propose to revise, alter and rewrite the whole of it — and on the promise of the first refusal of the Hunting Stories and "The Little Shepherd" you can advance that sum, I will complete "Crittenden," as soon as possible, and send it to you for publication as a serial or a book, according to your preference. Though I think the better plan would be to print the two remaining Hunting Stories — four of them have been published, one in Harper's Weekly and three in The Century, with illustrations by Klepper which I can, I am sure, get from the Century Company on very reasonable terms — and bring this book out in November; postponing "Crittenden" until next Spring, Summer or Autumn, as you may prefer, and thus giving me plenty of time to do my best work on it. As for the Hunting Stories "Fox-Hunting in Kentucky" — I forget the titles — Coon-Hunting at night, and Rabbit-Hunting on horseback without Dog or Gun — some of my friends think them my best work and they attracted a good deal of attention in England. The titles of the two unfinished ones are "The Breaks of Sandy," a fishing trip, and "Down the Kentucky on a Raft." One of these at least I should want to submit to Scribner's Magazine.

These stories would go better, of course, after "Crittenden" was published, provided of course the novel proved a success. But I want more time on "Crittenden." Still, if you think it wiser, I will complete the novel at the Earliest Day possible.

With very kind regards, believe me,
Sincerely yours,
John Fox, Jr.

July 28th 1899

Dear Mr. Fox:

Your very cordial letter with proposal that we should become your publishers is greatly appreciated. I certainly want you "on our list" and see no reason why we cannot do as well for you as any other publisher. Leaving to one side the ques-

tion of just what form our first publication should take I send you enclosed our check for $1000 which Bridges says may be looked upon as a retainer. We should prefer to begin our publications for you with the novel "Crittenden" rather than with the hunting stories, though I know that the stories, as they have appeared, have excited unusual interest. This would give us plenty of time to publish one in the Magazine and illustrate it if desirable. Our Fall numbers are already so full that it would be difficult to squeeze in even a single story. But you must not think it necessary to crowd work on the novel; I have no doubt it will do equally well next Winter and it would be a shame to let it leave your hands before you have quite finished with it.

Without reading the manuscript it is never safe to express positive opinion but Mr. Burlingame and I are disposed to think that it will be better now to cut the war part pretty radically. Of course it will serve as the background of the story but I think descriptions of the military operations might best be omitted. There is a tremendous reaction now against all war literature and it is important to prevent a story being so classed. When we see the manuscript we can determine about the serial publication. As I wrote Page, I fear it will be very difficult to get it in next year but the situation may change. It is also possible that we may find suitable publication for it elsewhere even if we could not use it ourselves.

It is awfully good of you to come to us so cordially and I shall do my best for you in all ways. I return the Alden letters.

Yours sincerely
Charles Scribner

York Harbor, Maine   July 31, 1899
My dear Scribner:

. . . That was a mighty nice thing, Scribner, you did for John Fox — and I wish you could have seen him when he got your letter. He was overwhelmed. He has never been treated so in his life — and he can't get over his astonishment. He is at work revising his Story, and I feel sure you will find you have secured a man who will make his mark. He is writing you himself; but I wanted to thank you too. "And may we all live long and prosper."

Yours faithfully,
Thos. Nelson Page

"I hain't nothin' but a boy, but I got to ack like a man now."

The Little Shepherd of Kingdom Come

BY

JOHN FOX, Jr.

Illustrated by F. C. Yohn

CHARLES SCRIBNER'S SONS
NEW YORK ::::::::::::::::::1903

Title page and frontispiece in The Little Shepherd of Kingdom Come *(1903). This novel is believed to be the first to sell one million copies in the United States.*

CS II DIARY ENTRY:
Wednesday 30 July 1902

Fox comes out for golf & night

Offer Fox $5000 & 15% with
1000 or 1500 advance

Scribner enjoyed playing golf with author-friends, including A. B. Frost, Thomas Nelson Page, and Fox. These terms for The Little Shepherd of Kingdom Come *are for serialization in* Scribner's Magazine *and book royalty rate; Fox received a $1,500 advance on publication.*

RELATED LETTERS:
Fox first mentioned "The Trail of the Lonesome Pine" in a letter to Burlingame in the summer of 1903: "the idea being that a 'furriner' should get interested in a mountain girl and send her away to be educated." But the Russo-Japanese War, where he was sent by CS II as a war correspondent for Scribner's Magazine, *and other stories prevented him from beginning work on it. Then, in 1906 and early 1907, when he did dig in, promises to Scribners about meeting the completion date for the serialization of the novel and concerns about the quality of the story and the writing itself began to worry him. He needed encouragement from his editor and his publisher and got just what he needed from both, as these letters show. Burlingame makes reference at the end of his letter to the main characters of Fox's story, June Tolliver and John Hale.*

July 9th, 1907

My dear Fox:

The manuscript came the day before the 4th of July just as I was starting to spend that and the end of the week in the country; this ac-

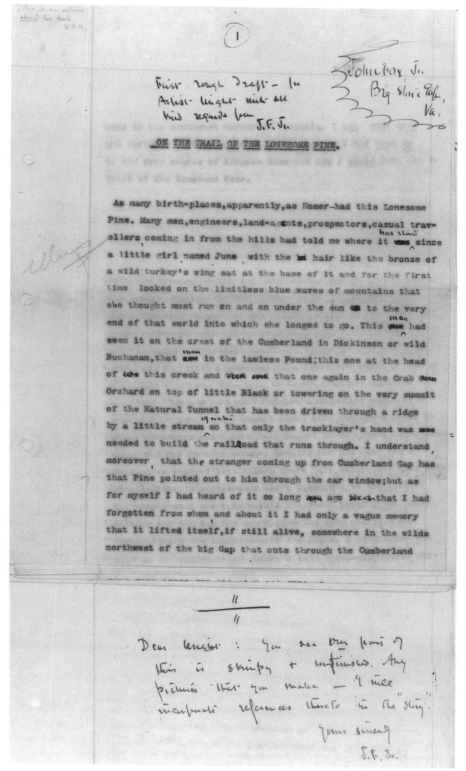

First page of Fox's article (rough draft) about his book The Trail of the Lonesome Pine, *with his note to George Wright, the illustrator, at the end. The illustrated article was published in the October 1910 issue of* Scribner's Magazine.

counts for your not hearing from me till to-day. In the meanwhile I have read it through and parts of it more than once — and let me say directly how much I have enjoyed it and how fine and successful it seems to me to be. I had my expectations keyed up very high. You know I was very fond of the Little Shepherd, and felt very warmly — more so perhaps than I ever quite succeeded in telling you — about both its art and the fine moving human quality in it; so that I have looked forward to the Lonesome Pine with uncommon hopes. I wish I could tell you how well it fulfils them; it seems to me very strongly and beautifully done, and I have finished my reading with that immensely refreshing sense which comes altogether too seldom in these days, of a good, sane, sincere, virile piece of work with a heart in it, in the midst of all the half-done things of various degrees of artificiality. It is a very great satisfaction that we are to have the story for next year, and we shall make a success of it.

What is finished it seems to me couldn't well be better. I see — and think I should have seen without your marking — the places where it seems to you necessary to fill out the color, to account more fully for some things and to write more at length what is now in one or two places rather summarized; this of course not to speak of the big hiatus at page 279 which I can readily understand you want to fill with your eye perfectly fresh from mountain country. At the same time what is here is so much more comprehensive and complete in the sense of plot and motif, than what I had expected it to be from your letter, that I am immensely encouraged as to time. It seems to me that what remains to do even if the quantity is large is so likely in a sense to write itself — that it has so entirely got its impetus and swing — that it will naturally go quickly. Of course we are most anxious, for all sorts of practical reasons, to see it in its quite final shape at the earliest moment possible. We must lay out the installments, plan Yohn's illustrations so as to fall properly in them, and especially be careful not to subject all of us to the anxiety — which nobody knows who hasn't tried it — of beginning before the whole is complete. Of course there will always be the possibility of work on details in the proof but the way the presses eat up time and overtake any essentially unfinished spot is a nightmare. I am hoping from your letter that you feel like that work in the mountains very soon, so that the longest gap will be supplied. Yohn asked me the other day when I thought you would be going, and said he would conform his plans of work entirely to yours. If you think the psychological moment to go is now he will go down and meet you if you like, where and when you like. But if not he will go to work at once on the first two or three pictures for which the early finished part that we have here will give him ample material and will go to the mountains later.

I don't know whether you care for impressions in detail, but once in a while it is interesting to know what strikes a fresh eye when one has been a long time at a thing. The chief — indeed the only — criticism of the psychology of the story seems to me to be that in its present shape June's re-action against Hale needs a little more justification — artistic justification I mean — a little more color, a little more dwelling upon the subtler things that bring it about, and so on. But this is very likely just one of the things you had in mind to give.

I am afraid I have given you very little idea of several different kinds of pleasure I have had in the manuscript; but anyhow I congratulate you most heartily on a capital and fine achievement.

Yours sincerely
E. L. Burlingame

July 11, 1907

Dear Charles:

You know how by repeating any word over and over it ceases to have any meaning whatever? Well, I had got that way about the story and if you had jumped on me with both feet and told me that the work was rotten all through — I'd have believed you and had not a word to say. Your second note was like a temporary stay to a toothache which Mr. Burlingame's letter cured completely to-day. You've no idea of the worry I've had over that story (and with other things) and I've been working in an unbroken nervous fit that has nearly driven me crazy. But the tension has snapped now and I'll worry no more. You see, my first purpose was to get the story in such a shape that any illness or accident couldn't prevent you having it in printable shape — even if it was only a long story & not a novel: to save you from being in a hole. I had understood you were to start it in November and my letter to you was based on that supposition. I supposed your first letter was due to a misunderstanding of mine and whatever hint there was in it that was not pleasant was not taken much to heart and was utterly wiped out by your second. So — shake! I want to go over in the mountains with Yohn — then I'd like ten days at the sea-shore and come back to finish up — or fill up, rather — the hiatus. When that's done — I'd like to have the division you will make of installments so that I can give each the same care and finish that I'd give so many short stories.

I'm afraid I'm going to need some more money meanwhile — for expenses and for my sister's wedding (it occurs the middle of August) but I'll want no more than will actually be necessary. I'm more glad than I can say that Mr. Burlingame likes the story so much and I'm grateful for his letter: but the story has yet to satisfy me.

Good luck & with kind regards to all, believe me

Sincerely & faithfully
John Fox, Jr.

The novel was serialized in Scribner's Magazine *in eleven installments, running from January through November 1908; the book was published on 17 October 1908, and became the number five best-seller of 1909.*

CS II DIARY ENTRY:
Friday 16 April 1915

Down town nearly all day on Fox moving picture case in which I was a witness

Lunch with Fox

Fritzi Scheff was a comic opera star whom Fox had married in 1908. The Plaza Hotel opened in October 1907.

CS II DIARY ENTRY:
Saturday 12 March 1910

Play bridge with John Fox and Fritzi at Plaza

The case involved infringement by a movie company of the dramatic rights to The Trail of the Lonesome Pine *held by Marc Klaw and Abraham L. Erlanger, New York producers. Three different cinema versions of the book were ultimately made, all by Cecil B. De Mille — 1916, 1922, 1936 — the latter featuring Fred MacMurray, Henry Fonda, and Sylvia Sydney.*

Henry James (1843–1916)

Henry James

Born in New York City, James lived mostly in Europe after 1866, permanently after 1875, and became a British citizen in 1915 to signify his allegiance to the Allied cause in World War I. While his fiction was never popular with the masses, James was a pioneer of psychological realism and an architect of literary form. He is considered to be the best novelist of that international triangle protracted between New York, London, and Paris, and his complex prose style has been described as unequaled in English in terms of its subtlety of phrase and idea. Of the three "phases" of James's writing which critics have defined, Scribners was his publisher during most of his "major phase," the last twenty years of his life when he became more interested in examining the "unlived life" and his characters' states of feeling. His formal critical works as well as his own stories and novels have had a weighty and continuing influence on literature in America and Europe.

Scribner Books by James

1901	*The Sacred Fount*
1902	*The Wings of the Dove* (2 volumes)
1903	*The Better Sort*
1904	*The Golden Bowl* (2 volumes)
1907–1909	*The Novels and Tales of Henry James,* selected and revised by James (New York Edition of 24 volumes, 1907–1909; 2 more volumes added in 1917)
1910	*The Finer Grain*
1911	*The Outcry*
1913	*A Small Boy and Others*
1914	*Notes of a Son and Brother*
	Notes on Novelists, With Some Other Notes
1917	*The Ivory Tower,* edited by Percy Lubbock
	The Sense of the Past, edited by Lubbock
	The Middle Years, edited by Lubbock

Lamb House,

Rye,

Sussex.

Sept. 12th, 1902.

Messrs. Charles Scribner's Sons.

Dear Sirs.

I am obliged to you for your letter of Aug.28th, accompanying a copy of the two vols. of "The Wings of the Dove" & mentioning your having sent out for me the other copies.   I shall have to ask you to be so good as to send one more.   Kindly despatch it to Miss Rosina Emmet, 105 Waverley Place New York City.

I greatly appreciate your having brought out the book in two volumes, & such charming ones.   I feel that I have never been so well presented, materially, & that my prose itself very essentially gains thereby.   It is really much in its interest, I think, even commercially, to be materially well presented.   As I compare the London edition dejectedly with yours, I feel yours to be, beyond comparison, the book.   I promise you, however, not to abuse, in future, the privilege of finding such happy antidotes of form to my long-windedness.   Believe me yours very truly

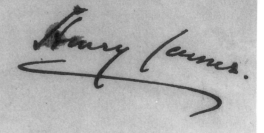

Letter by James thanking Scribners for the attractive two-volume edition of his novel The Wings of the Dove, *published 29 August 1902*

| 1920 | *The Letters of Henry James* (2 volumes), selected and edited by Lubbock |
| 1934 | *The Art of the Novel: Critical Prefaces,* with an introduction by Richard P. Blackmur |

RELATED LETTERS:
Though James had earlier published several stories in Scribner's Monthly, *his novel* Confidence *was his first book-length work to be serialized in the magazine; it appeared in six parts, from August 1879 through January 1880. Scribners was keen to secure it for book publication, but failed — not for lack of trying — as these letters document.*

Letter by Scribner editor Edward L. Burlingame to James, 5 August 1879.

Dear Sir: —
    We take the liberty of asking whether you have in view any arrangement for the publication here, in book form, of your story of "Confidence," now appearing as a serial in our Magazine? — Should you have made no definite plan in regard to it, it would give us much pleasure to submit to you an offer for its issue by our house; and we should be glad to know whether such a propostion on our part would be agreeable to you. — We are

Very truly yours
Charles Scribner's Sons

Postscript of letter by Burlingame to CS II, 29 August 1879

    I enclose a personal letter just received — and a copy of one that has just come from Henry James, & that seems to need immediate attention. Doesn't it seem to you — as it certainly does to me — that it is worth while to make him a decidedly good offer on this opportunity? He is (thus far) almost entirely unattached in the matter of publishing; and his future is certainly valuable enough to make an effort to connect him here. But of course all of this "goes without saying" after all.

Letter (excerpt) by James to his father, 11 October 1879.

. . . It may interest you to know that I am (for my next novel at least,) leaving the unremunerative Macmillans. I received for the first time a fortnight since their statement of accounts, for the six publications they have made for me; and it was so largely to their advantage and so little to mine, that I immediately wrote to Chatto & Windus, to ask them on what terms they would publish Confidence for me next Christmas. They instantly replied in so favourable a sense (offering me a substatial sum down for the copyright for three years) that I have closed with them; and I trust it will operate as a salubrious irritant to Macmillan, who wants my books very much, but doesn't want to pay for them! I did the same six weeks ago to Scribner & Co., who immediately offered me for the volume — Confidence — much better terms than Osgood (a sum down and a royalty, larger than O's); meanwhile I received from Osgood such a plaintive letter, more in sorrow than in anger, that I have given him the book — a weak proceeding, natural to the son of my father. . . .

[Houghton Library, Harvard University]

Twenty years passed before James finally accepted another Scribner offer.

LETTER:
When James did become a Scribner author, his situation was unusual if not unique for an American writer: he was already a well-established literary figure; he lived abroad (in England); and he used a literary agent, James B. Pinker, whom he paid a commission for placing his work. While Burlingame had published some of James's work in Scribner's Magazine, Harper & Bros. *and* Houghton, Mifflin *had been James's American book publishers. The following letter to Scribners changed that.*

July 27th, 1900
Dear Sirs,
    When I had the pleasure of seeing your Mr. Burlingame, earlier in the year, we discussed Mr. Henry James's work, and he told me he thought it would be very agreeable to you, if you had the opportunity of publishing some of his books. Mr.

James has today placed in my hands the MS. of his new novel entitled "The Sacred Fount," and in accordance with my promise I have pleasure in sending it by this mail for your consideration. Mr James thinks that serial publication for it is out of the question, and his idea is that it be issued in book form, either in the Spring or Autumn of next year at his option. He is aware that I am offering it to you, and it will afford him great pleasure if we are able to arrange for it to come out under your care.

The arrangement as to terms which would be most convenient to Mr. Henry James is one providing for an immediate payment for the bookrights, and he suggests the sale of the American bookrights outright for a period of five years for the sum of £400, and I hope this suggestion will commend itself to you as a suitable one. It will be a great convenience to Mr. James if you are to come to a prompt decision in the matter, and if you could cable to me I should be extremely obliged.

In the event of your not liking Mr. James's proposal as to terms, perhaps you would suggest an alternative arrangement, that would meet as far as possible his desire for immediate financial result. . . .

Faithfully yours,
James B. Pinker

Answering for Scribners, book editor W. C. Brownell cabled that the terms were acceptable and followed up with a letter asking for slight modifications. The Sacred Fount was published on 9 February 1901.

RELATED LETTERS AND MEMORANDUM:
James's idea of a collected edition of his works that would be a major monument to his reputation consisted of several parts: the edition would be a selection that grouped together works for a "common effect"; he would "retouch" (revise), particularly earlier pieces, where he saw the need; and he would write prefaces for each volume by which he, for the first time, might reveal "confidential" history and theory about the subject. In addition, James wanted an attractive, dignified publication with some illustrative material. Scribners' Subscription Department had already established a good record in similar large publishing projects. All of his ideas were presented to Scribners in the late summer of 1905, beginning with Pinker's cover letter and James's lengthy memorandum.

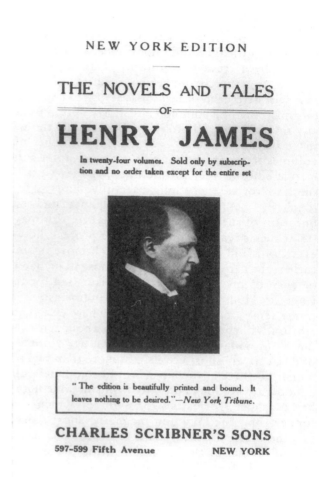

NEW YORK EDITION

THE NOVELS AND TALES OF HENRY JAMES

In twenty-four volumes. Sold only by subscription and no order taken except for the entire set

" The edition is beautifully printed and bound. It leaves nothing to be desired."—*New York Tribune.*

CHARLES SCRIBNER'S SONS
597-599 Fifth Avenue NEW YORK

Cover of the promotional pamphlet for the New York Edition of James's collected works

1st August 1905

Dear Sirs:

Bearing in mind your wish to have as soon as possible the material on which to base your prospectus, I have got Mr. Henry James to dictate to me his views about the edition, and I now enclose a copy of his memorandum. I think you will find this answers all the points you asked me to put before him. . . .

Faithfully yours
James B. Pinker

To Charles Scribner's Sons [30 July 1905]

My idea has been to arrange for a handsome "definitive edition" of the greater number of my novels and tales — I say of the greater number because I prefer to omit several things, especially among the shorter stories. I should wish probably to retain all my principal novels — that is with the exception possibly of one.

My impression is that my shorter things will gain in significance and importance, very considerably, by a fresh grouping or classification, a placing together, from series to series, of those that will help each other, those that will conduce to something of a common effect. My notion is, at any rate, very rigidly to sift and select the things to be included, thereby reducing the number of volumes to an array that will not seem, for a collective edition, very formidable. My idea is, further, to revise everything carefully, and to retouch, as to expression, turn of sentence, and the question of surface generally, wherever this may strike me as really required. Such a process, however, will find its application much more in the earlier, the earliest things than in those of my later or even of my middle period. It is called for in Roderick Hudson and The American for instance, to my sense, much more than anywhere else. The edition will thus divide itself into about ten volumes of regular novel length, into a few volumes of distinctively short novels, not more than two of which, or three at the most, would completely fill a moderate volume; and into a considerable number of short stories, six or eight of which are longer than the common magazine short-story, and the whole list of which is susceptible of an effect of revival by the re-classification that I have mentioned. A good many of these, which have all been collected in volumes, I shall wish, as I say, to drop; but the interest and value of the edition will, I think, rest not a little on the proper association and collocation of the others.

Lastly, I desire to furnish each book, whether consisting of a single fiction, or of several minor ones, with a freely colloquial and even, perhaps, as I may say, confidential preface or introduction, representing, in a manner, the history of the work or the group, representing more particularly, perhaps, a frank critical talk about its subject, its origin, its place in the whole artistic chain, and embodying, in short, whatever of interest there may be to be said about it. I have never committed myself in print in any way, even as much as by three lines to a newspaper, on the subject of anything I have written, and I feel as if I should come to this part of the business with a certain freshness of appetite and effect. My hope would be, at any rate, that it might count as a feature of a certain importance in any such new and more honorable presentation of my writings. I use that term honorable here because I am moved in

the whole matter by something of a conviction that they will gain rather than lose by enjoying for the first time — though a few of the later ones have in some degree already partaken of that advantage — a form of appearance, a dignity and beauty of outward aspect, that may seem to bespeak consideration for them as a matter of course. Their being thus presented, in fine, as fair and shapely will contribute, to my mind, to their coming legitimately into a "chance" that has been hitherto rather withheld from them, and for which they have long and patiently waited.

My preference would be to publish first, one after the other, four of the earlier novels, not absolutely in the order of their original appearance but with no detrimental departure from it; putting The American, that is, first, Roderick Hudson second, The Portrait of a Lady third, and Princess Casamassima fourth. After this would come three or four volumes of the longer of my short stories — to be followed by The Tragic Muse in two volumes, a book which closes, to my mind, what I should call as regards my novels, my earlier period. I think, though as to this I am not positive, that I should then give three or four more volumes to completing the group of such minor productions; and should wind up with my five later novels, The Awkward Age, The Wings of the Dove, The Ambassadors and The Golden Bowl in the order of appearance. And I repeat that I am proposing nothing but my fiction.

If a name be wanted for the edition, for convenience and distinction, I should particularly like to call it the New York Edition if that may pass for a general title of sufficient dignity and distinctness. My feeling about the matter is that it refers the whole enterprise explicitly to my native city — to which I have had no great opportunity of rendering that sort of homage. And — last of all — I should particularly appreciate a single very good plate in each volume, only one, but of thoroughly fine quality. I seem to make out (though I have not been able yet to go into the whole of the question) that there would not be an insuperable difficulty in finding for each book, or rather for each volume, some sufficiently interesting illustrative subject.

There are two or three points more.

Messrs. Scribner's complete edition of Rudyard Kipling offers to my mind the right type of form and appearance, the right type of print and size of page, for our undertaking. I could desire nothing better than this, and should be quite content to have it taken for model. (But

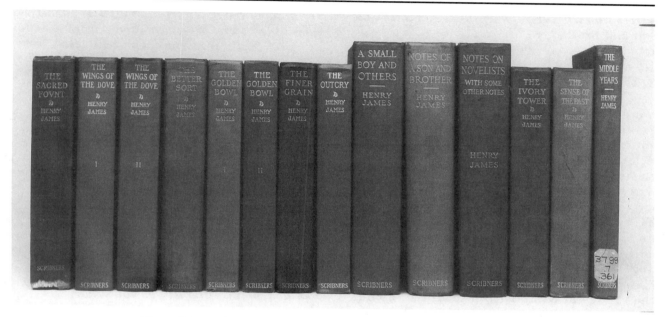

First editions of most of the Henry James titles published by Scribners

I think, also, by the way, that I should like a cover of another colour — to differentiate — than the Kipling.)

As for time of delivery of first copy I should find it convenient to be able to take from the present date to the 25th of September to send the two first books, completely revised (with the very <u>close</u> revision and re-touching that for these cases I have spoken of) and with their respective Prefaces, of from 3000 to 5000 words. The revision, the re-manipulation, as I may call it, of <u>The American</u> and <u>Roderick Hudson</u> is demanding of me, I find, in the extreme (and very interesting) deliberation; which will tend, however, absolutely to improvement (and not to say, perhaps, even to making of the works in question, in their amended state, unique — and admirable, exemplary — curiosities of literature).

I should not omit, finally, to note that in the foregoing I have, inevitably, left the question open of the inclusion or the non-inclusion of my longer novel <u>The Bostonians</u>. I cannot take time, have not the freedom of mind to decide this minor matter just now; but I shall do so later on, and if in the affirmative a convenient place in the whole order will be found for the book.

Henry James

The size of the project was, itself, rather daunting, but, as long as James's other pub-lishers would not make it financially difficult for Scribners by demanding unreasonable terms for permissions, the firm wanted to proceed. Only Houghton, Mifflin, publisher of the American editions of such James novels as Roderick Hudson *and* The Portrait of a Lady, *initially created a problem. But courtesy among the publishing houses, and particularly between the heads of those houses, prevailed.*

RELATED LETTERS:
Concerned about her friend and fellow Scribner author's finances, Edith Wharton hatched a scheme with CS II in 1912 to pay James $8,000 under the guise of an advance against future royalties for his new novel, The Ivory Tower. *Wharton would furnish the money. When he was in Europe on business in September, CS II made a point of visiting Wharton in Paris, primarily to talk about her own new novel,* The Custom of the Country, *which Scribners was planning on publishing the next year — but also to confirm their secret arrangement. CS II's diary entry for 17 September 1912 notes their agreement: "Lunch at Mrs. Wharton & bring away 3 parts of Custom of the Country — also agree about Henry James $8000." The resulting letter that CS II wrote made a "somewhat unusual proposal"; by addressing it directly to James, Scribner hoped to avoid his agent's involvement and commission. The "volume of your brother's*

letters," which CS II refers to, became Notes of a
Son and Brother.

September 27, 1912

Dear Mr. James:

It was very gratifying to be able while in
London to complete arrangements with Mr.
Pinker for the publication of the volume of
your brother's letters and for the magazine articles, and to hear that we may expect the articles before the end of the year. But I do not
write now about that book. What interested
me even more was the information that you
have in contemplation an important American
novel. As the publishers of your definitive
edition we want another great novel to balance the Golden Bowl and round off the series of books in which you have developed
the theory of composition set forth in your
preface. In our opinion such a book would
be of very great advantage to our common
interests and it is most desirable that it
should be produced as soon as possible. We
know that such a work demands much time
and all your time for a considerable period,
and we have thought that under all the circumstances it might be acceptable to you to receive a somewhat unusual proposal. If you can
agree to begin the book soon — say within the
next twelve months — and to give up your
other work for it, we will pay you $8000. for
all rights in the manuscript everywhere. The
payments could be made as most convenient
for you; we would suggest half the amount
when the book was begun and the other half on
the completion of the manuscript. You will see at
once that our proposal is quite different from the
usual royalty and advance, and for America only,
but I have tried to formulate the plan which
would make possible the largest outright payment. If desired, we would agree to offer the book
first to Macmillan of England and in any case that
firm would have it in the collected edition.

I shall be glad to hear from you at your
convenience and would consider willingly any
change in the form of our offer.

It has not seemed to me necessary to make
this proposal through Mr. Pinker, but as I like
him and do not wish him to suspect me of any
indiscretion, I am sending a copy of this to him.
You will know to what extent it is desirable or
necessary to act through him.

Yours sincerely
Charles Scribner

*In January 1913 Wharton and CS II formally
signed their secret agreement, and toward the end
of March Scribner received a grateful letter from
James acknowledging his receipt of half of the
money as specified by their publishing "contract"
("half the amount when the work was begun"). "I
am proceeding," he said.*

April 2nd 1913

Dear Mrs. Wharton:

The enclosed letter just received from Mr.
James shows that our full purpose was successfully accomplished. I feel rather mean and caddish
and must continue so to the end of my days.
Please never give me away.

Yours sincerely
Charles Scribner

Penciled on this letter is Wharton's note:

I gave Mr. Scribner this $8000 from the earnings of
"The House of Mirth," to encourage H. J. to go on
writing, as he was so despondent about his work.
The result was successful, & no one ever knew.

EW
6 Nov. 27
St Brice

[Beinecke Library, Yale University]

LETTER:
Letter by James to CS II, 12 December 1914, from
London.

*This letter, the last letter by James in the Scribner
Archives, written several months after the start of
World War I, is probably his most personal to CS
II. Occasioned by the desire to supply some addresses of friends to which he wants Scribners to
send his latest book,* Notes on Novelists, With
Some Other Notes, *James cannot help but talk
about the war and the effect it is having on him
and his writing. He is glad that his native America
recognizes the moral superiority of the Allies, and
assures Scribner that the spirit of the artist (in
him) will not be beaten by the "entirely objectionable and so far insurmountably destructive
Enemy." In fact, the war has given an intensity to
his life that he would not have wanted to pass
away without knowing (James was seventy-one at
the time). Last, he has three books begun "for
you."*

Dear Mr. Scribner:

I feel covered with shame in learning by your good letter of Nov. 10th that my last letter to you failed to contain its intended list of a few addresses to which I desired my "Notes" to be sent. The appearance of levity in this omission would in fact weigh upon me to the point of plunging me into a still more abashed and prolonged silence, were it not that I have now come to feel how much more likely you are to attribute my accident to grave preoccupations than to frivolous ones. The truth is indeed that one really has one's attention here and at present but too imperfectly at one's command for anything other than the great gravities which surround us. Nine-tenths of one's thought is for them even when one is trying hard to apply, in some decent interest, the whole of it: that interest has mainly to make shift with the single poor remaining tenth. Let me make up, please, for my late blankness by really enclosing herein three or four names of persons to whom I should like the volume to be sent. The two copies meanwhile recently received from you excite my admiration and gratitude: they invest the book, to my sense, with much more outward charm than the London presentation of it — though to this Mr. Dent gave great consideration and care, a zeal that half convinced me for the time, though a good deal against my taste — especially now that I have seen your form.

I think I quite understand what you tell me of American feeling in presence of our prodigious European situation. It is the feeling that I gather without exception from the letters of my relatives and friends on your side of the sea, and I couldn't ask or dream of anything better. I confess that without this impression and expression of it I should be deeply unhappy, so strong and so distinguished, morally speaking, do I find the position of France and England, to say nothing of that of the inestimable Belgium, in face of the most insolent and fatuous arrogance of aggression that a group of self-restricting nations surely ever had to face. It is all very horrible, from this near view of ours — I mean the immeasurable, the unspeakably lamentable sacrifice of splendid young life and manhood is; but War even on the abominable scale on which we are being treated to it has in it this of infernally inspiring and exciting and even sustaining, that after the first horror and sickness, which are indeed unspeakable, Interest rises and rises and spreads enormous wings — resembling perhaps alas too much those of the hovering predatory vulture, and hangs sublime over the scene, as if not to lose a single aspect of its terrible human meaning. It is very dreadful, but after half dying with dismay and repugnance under the first shock of possibilities that I really believed had become extinct, I began little by little to feel them give an intensity to life (even at my time of it) which I wouldn't have passed away without knowing. Such is my monstrous state of mind, of sympathy, of participation, of devotion, let me frankly call it, in its poor way, touching all our tremendous strain and stress. The curse of these things, I admit, from the poor old discomfited artist's point of view, is that such realities play the devil even with his very best imaginations and intentions — so that he has, unless he gives everything up, to contrive some compromise betwen the operation of his genius (call it) and that of his immediate oppression and obsession, in which all sorts of immediate and subversive sympathies and curiousities and other damnable agitations are involved. He can fortunately say to himself that there is nothing of these even that won't be indirectly and eventually fertilising to his blest faculty — which yet for the time may so suffer from them; but he hates to be beaten if only temporarily, and — well, what I think I am saying, let alone feeling, in fine, is that I'm not beaten, not at all, but positively fighting as hard as if all the plans and proposals, all the begun things, in my head, were the arrayed and increasing Allies themselves, and the blight that presumptuously would be, but that steadily and inevitably less and less shall be, were the entirely objectionable and so far insurmountably destructive Enemy. I have no less than three books admirably begun for you, but with one of them, for which present conditions are most favourable (or, more exactly stated, less unfavourable) stretching out his neck furthest in the race, and almost certain, I conceive, to come in first. On him I am now putting my money, and hope to let you know before long that he is within sight of the winning-post. On this assurance believe me, dear Mr. Scribner, all faithfully yours

Henry James

All three books — The Sense of the Past *(the front-running horse),* The Ivory Tower, *and* The Middle Years — *were unfinished at the time of James's death in February 1916.*

SCRIBNER MAGAZINES

Scribner Magazines

Scribners did not originate the practice of a publisher issuing its own magazine to attract readers to its publications and writers to its publishing services. Harper & Brothers had been doing that with *Harper's New Monthly Magazine* since 1850. But Scribners' efforts, beginning with *Hours at Home* (1865–1870) and *The Book Buyer* (1867–1880, 1884–1918, 1935–1938), evolving into *Scribner's Monthly* (1870–1881) and *St. Nicholas* (1873–1881), and culminating with *Scribner's Magazine* (1887–1939), were among the most successful in American literary history. Other publishers tried to develop popular magazines, such as G. P. Putnam with *Putnam's Monthly Magazine* (1853–1857, 1869–1870, 1906–1910), D. Appleton with *Appleton's Journal of Popular Literature, Science and Art* (1869–1881), and J. B. Lippincott with *Lippincott's Magazine of Literature, Science and Education* (1868–1915) but achieved less successful results.

The idea had marvelous circular logic: a general magazine would reach a wider readership, thus promoting house-name recognition; greater house-name recognition would increase magazine circulation; a larger circulation would attract more advertisers and sell more books, adding revenue to the firm; more readers would attract more writers; more revenue would permit better payment to writers; better writers would promote house reputation. House reputation would attract the best writers, the most readers, and the best-paying advertisers: all would benefit. Certainly, from an author's perspective, the opportunity of first serializing a novel in a popular magazine, thereby creating an eager public for the published book, was an attractive advertising and financial dividend. Many of Scribner's late nineteenth- and early-twentieth-century novelists, such as Frances Hodgson Burnett, Robert Louis Stevenson, Thomas Nelson Page, Richard Harding Davis, F. Hopkinson Smith, Edith Wharton, and John Fox Jr., greatly profited from this additional exposure in Scribner magazines. The magazines also provided a ready market for short stories, poems, topical articles and essays, and illustrations — helping to encourage and develop the talents of their practitioners.

Though Scribners started down that publishing road right after the Civil War, finding the right magazine vehicle took some time. The public's verdict on *Hours at Home* was that it seemed too stodgy with its religious tone and evangelical motive. *The Book Buyer,* in its various format permutations, performed more like a house organ for Scribners, for both its own publications and its imports, though *The Book Buyer* later accepted other publishers' ads and reviewed their books as well. In its limited function it worked well and had a long life. But with *Scribner's Monthly,* edited by well-known journalist and respected author J. G. Holland, Scribners had a clear winner. It was also the first high-quality, large-circulation to accept advertising. From its first issue of forty thousand copies in November 1870, the circulation of the magazine passed one hundred thousand by 1880. With its second issue, *Scribner's Monthly* absorbed *Putnam's Monthly* (second series) and a Boston juvenile, the *Riverside Magazine;* in 1875, it also absorbed Edward Everett's *Old and New.*

The main juvenile periodicals of the nineteenth century were *Youth's Companion,* begun in 1827, and Scribners' contribution to the field, *St. Nicholas,* organized and edited by Mary Mapes Dodge in 1873. Though it was launched in a year of national financial panic, *St. Nicholas* earned and maintained a rather steady circulation, upward of seventy thousand. *Youth's Companion* became really popular only after 1857, when it was sold to Daniel Sharp Ford, who became its chief editor. Much of its extraordinary success (circulation of five hundred thousand by 1890s) was because of its extensive use of premiums, ranging from cheap books to sewing machines, which it offered to new subscribers, to old subscribers for renewal, and to "clubs" of subscribers. The two magazines were rivals in their appeal to youth and the cultivation of family interests, but emphasis of *St. Nicholas* was more literary and artistic and is probably better remembered today because of that.

When the first number of *Scribner's Magazine* was issued, in January 1887, it immediately joined the first rank of quality general magazines — the *Atlantic Monthly* (circulation 12,500), *The Century* (the former *Scribner's Monthly*, 222,000), and *Harper's New Monthly Magazine* (185,000) — with a distribution of 100,000 copies. Charging a quarter instead of thirty-five cents (three dollars a year instead of four dollars), provided a distinct advantage. Eventually, by 1900, its circulation surpassed that of the others and reached a high point during 1910 of 215,000 with the serialization of Theodore Roosevelt's *African Game Trails*.

Hours at Home (1865–1870)

HISTORICAL SKETCH:

Roger Burlingame, *Of Making Many Books* (New York: Charles Scribner's Sons, 1946), pp. 191–197.

In his centennial history of the House of Scribner, Burlingame provides a sketch of the firm's first attempt at a commercial magazine, Hours at Home, *and relates how by its death a successor was born: Scribner's Monthly. He is not correct in stating that the firm had scorned magazines for twenty years. In 1859 the first volume of* The American Theological Review *was published with Charles Scribner as the imprint. Succeeding volumes listed J. M. Sherwood as publisher. The title pages of later volumes specifically cite "the Book Store of Charles Scribner & Co." as the place of publication. It is obvious that J. M. Sherwood was chosen as editor of* Hours at Home *because he was known to Charles Scribner — in fact, had worked with him in the same building — on* The American Theological Review. *In 1869, however, he relinquished editorial work on* Hours at Home *to assume the editorship of the* Review, *which had renamed itself* The American Presbyterian Review.

For nearly twenty years, the Scribners scorned magazines. When, as the Civil War ended, they were finally beguiled into one, it made little concession to popular entertainment. As we read it today, we are surprised that it found any audience, for it combined heavy literary material with theological dialectics and was shadowed by a dark moral asceticism; most of it was hard reading with only lyrical relief coming from verses which

sobbed over the death of someone (usually a child). Yet this sedate monthly with its incredible title *Hours at Home* seems, in the six years of its career, to have built up a large and loyal circulation.

To J. M. Sherwood, its editor, *Hours at Home* was only one of a chain of papers he edited. He is a shadowy figure today, but he must have been a busy, vigorous person, hopping from magazine to magazine and interviewing whole coveys of the clergy at the same time. He knew more reverends and doctors of divinity (all Protestants) than you could have shaken a stick at; incidentally, however, he had scraped together some explorers, scientists, and disapproving readers of immoral books from whom he extracted articles. He processed the articles carefully in his chain bath with the result that nothing ever appeared in *Hours at Home* (or, presumably, in the rest of his string) which could not be read, without defilement, even on the Sabbath.

Hours at Home, according to the blurb which covered its launching, was

designed to stand among our monthly magazines as the representative of the religious element of American Literature. Besides articles on purely religious subjects, it will contain Reviews of Books; Biographical and Historical Sketches; Poetry; Notes of Travel; Moral Tales; Papers on Popular Science; and Essays on Miscellaneous Topics. Discarding the Frivolous, the irreligious and corrupting, it will aim to furnish a pure, healthful and instructive literature; it will be animated also by a thoroughly Catholic [not Roman] spirit so that it may belong to the entire American church.

In a paragraph by itself:
"A limited number of unexceptionable Advertisements will be inserted in each number, at a fair price."

Scanning the unexceptionable advertisements in the first number we find a page devoted to "Health Tracts" with, among others, these titles: *Burying Alive; Cancer; Cute Things; Charms; Clergymen; Clothing Changed; Deranged; Dying Easily; Feet; Cold; Growing Beautiful; Hyrdophobia; Insanity; Inverted Toe-Nail; Law of Love; Loose Bowels; Perspiration Checked; Private Things; Urination; Vices of Genius;* and *Women's Beauty.*

The text of the first issue, however, suggests less variety. There is a piece on Saint Elizabeth of Hungary; one on Christ, "The Model Man"; one on German painters (religious); "The Marys; or

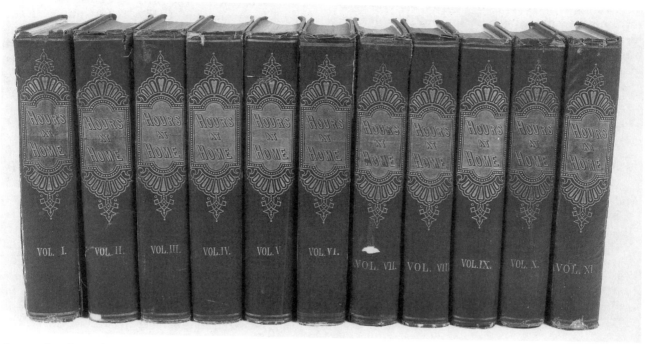

A complete bound set of Hours at Home. *The magazine ran from May 1865 through October 1870 (volumes I–IX, no. 6); its subtitle, "A Popular Monthly of Religious and Useful Literature," was changed to "A Popular Monthly of Instruction and Recreation" starting in the June 1867 issue. The name of its initial editor, J. M. Sherwood, was dropped from the magazine beginning with the May 1869 issue, when Richard Watson Gilder assumed the editorial duties anonymously.*

Silent Faith the Mother of Great Lives"; an astronomical article with religious color, added, perhaps by Mr. Sherwood; a piece contrasting the drunken playwright, Sheridan, with the "Christian Statesman," William Wilberforce; one on the rivers of the Holy Land; one on Lyman Beecher and Martin Luther; an attack on the Mormons; an unsuccessful effort to show that the King of the Sandwich Islands was induced by Protestant missionaries to give up drinking; two stories, one a fictionized argument against atheism and the other a concession to humor but weighted with morals; seven poems, four of which are about death, though in one the dying child turns into an angel.

The modern reader of *Hours at Home,* if he can persuade himself to read much of it, must, however, admit a curious mesmeric effect. The hypnotism derives partly, perhaps, from the long-stride rhythm of the prose in which, indeed, there is too a kind of stately melody like the tune of a funeral march; partly from the insistence of the theme upon the ethereal spirit, the song of the angels, the effulgent light of heaven, the entrancing and sublime melodies of the golden harps, the

soul's flinging off its earthly stain "as the bird from its wing the summer rain." One is suddenly in a dusty room with one fly buzzing; the street outside is silent in the awful Sabbath; not the passing of a single hoop-skirt inflames the flesh, not a whiff of enticing lager drifts over the corner saloon.

Beginning in the spring of 1865, it was natural that this magazine should give space to Lincoln and the generals of the War. These articles try to emphasize the Christian character of the heroes, their modesty and their temperance. Lincoln, it seems, was always on the point of making a public profession of his faith, "but the very tenderness and humility of his nature would not permit the exposure of his inmost convictions, except upon the rarest occasions, and to his most intimate friends." The author of the article on Grant had a still more difficult time with Grant's indulgence in liquor. One article on the American Sabbath states that "the names of Big Bethel, Bull Run, Ball's Bluff, Mill Spring and Pittsburgh Landing confirm the experience that, as a *rule,* Sunday battles turn out disastrously to the aggressive party."

In its later years, *Hours at Home* branched into more secular subjects. In 1869, the department of Books and Reading, reaching out beyond purely religious literature, discovered Walt Whitman.

"A generation cannot be entirely pure," wrote the editor, "which tolerates writers who, like Walt Whitman, commit in writing an offence like that indictable at common law of walking naked through the streets, and excuse it under the pretext that 'Nature is Always Modest.'"

And he went on to warn his readers

"that literary catholicity must be too broad for those who 'afford to keep a conscience,' which excuses or applauds such lecherous priests of Venus as Algernon Swinburne. . . . Let the imagination of such writers be ever so brilliant, and their diction be ever so enchanting, the altar at which they serve is that of harlotry and pollution."

By this time certain members of the Scribner staff became restive under the cool, humid shadow of *Hours at Home*. This was symptomatic of the changing times. Darwin and Spencer, partly interpreted to Americans by John Fiske, along with the new knowledge of science and technology, were making inroads upon the old-time revealed religion. So Edward Seymour, later a partner of Scribner, Armstrong & Co., tried to freshen *Hours at Home* by getting a young newspaperman, Richard Watson Gilder, to edit it. "My editing . . . being anonymous," wrote Gilder, "I naturally was pleased and encouraged to come upon a notice of the magazine in the 'Tribune' expressing surprise at its marked improvement."

But Charles Scribner (senior), though he believed in Gilder, wanted an impressive name attached to the magazine. He thought the immense prestige of Dr. Josiah Gilbert Holland would bring it into new life and success and he invited Holland to take charge.

Holland was on the top shelf of Scribner authors. His *Timothy Titcomb,* a book of fictional letters giving advice to youth, would hardly impress our generation. But its success in the sixties was tremendous. He was the Henry van Dyke of the age: deeply religious but called "tolerant" and by the extreme Jonah-whale diehards "heretical." He was, indeed, so unorthodox, as it turned out, that he refused to salvage *Hours at Home* on the ground (as he later expressed it) that it was "moribund."

Nevertheless the offer sowed a seed in the vigorous promoter field of his mind. As it sprouted, he got a friend — a real, all-out promoter and capitalist to boot — named Roswell Smith to help him work out an idea. They discussed it, according to Holland, on a bridge in Geneva where both men were on vacation. When they had it all wrapped up, they presented it to Charles Scribner, not as a gift but as a subject for his good will and investment.

That is why the celebrated magazine *Scribner's Monthly* (which became the still more famous *Century*) must always be considered a Scribner stepchild. Holland and Smith wanted to start a brand-new magazine. But this was a big venture. If they could have a name like Scribner to attach to it — so that it could compete with "Harper's" or "Lippincott's," "Putnam's" or "Appleton's," in name at least — its start would be secure. So they offered Charles Scribner four-tenths of the stock for his name and favor and what other assistance he cared to give. Yet to avoid identifying it too definitely with the book house of Charles Scribner & Co., why not start a new joint-stock company for the purpose and call it "Scribner & Co.," minus the Charles?

If Mr. Scribner had had the astuteness of his son, he might have seen trouble ahead. He would have understood that Holland's insistence on the new company came from his refusal, as he later expressed it, "to have anything to do with a magazine that should be floated as the flag of a book-house, or as tributary or subordinate to a book-house," and that such a situation was inherently absurd. And he would have understood too that "we [Holland and Smith] who held the majority interest regarded the Scribner connection as something that should inure solely to the benefit of the magazine-house, in which the book-house was interested to the amount of its stock, and not to the benefit of the book-house, in which we have no interest whatever." And finally, C.S. would have realized that Holland and Smith intended, too, if they felt like it, to have Scribner & Co. publish books as well as magazines!

But Charles Scribner, Sr., was much governed by his affections. He loved Holland and Gilder (who was to be part of the new set-up), and he took it for granted that his firm and the magazine were all to play along happily and without friction together.

The only reason to recall all this dusty history is that it led to one of the most important and healthiest divorces in the whole of publishing history in America; that out of it came not one but three of the greatest American magazines and two vigorous book-houses in an era when all of them were urgently needed.

In October, 1870, then, came the requiem of *Hours at Home*:

"With this last number . . . there are no farewell words to say. To be sure, by the old pleasant name Maga will be no longer; but it will be baptized into a new life; it will come to the familiar firesides — where so long and warmly it has been welcomed — and to many others, in cheerier, more attractive form than ever."

The public, presumably, was set agog by this mysterious notice, but its suspense was short-lived, for in November *Scribner's Monthly* came in its glory. "HOURS AT HOME," announced the first issue, "whose unpretending dress and suggestive title had grown familiar to the eyes of many thousands of American families, died in October — died not of disease, not of decay — died simply that SCRIBNER'S MONTHLY might live."

The Book Buyer (1867–1880, 1884–1918, 1935–1938)

HISTORICAL NOTE:
Roger Burlingame, *Of Making Many Books* (New York: Charles Scribner's Sons, 1946), pp. 202–203.

Son of Edward L. Burlingame, first editor of Scribner's Magazine, Roger Burlingame also worked for Scribners — first as a publicity manager (1914–1917), then as a book editor (1919–1926). A novelist, biographer, and freelance writer, he wrote the centennial history of the firm, Of Making Many Books. *Here, in his chapter on the house's magazines, he provides a brief history of* The Book Buyer. *Contrary to what he states, the magazine did not die "on the eve of its fiftieth birthday"; rather, its reincarnation ceased in May 1918 but was revived in the late 1930s. The last issue was one for Christmas 1938. The "flippant young man" he refers to is himself.*

The longest-lived periodical the Scribners published was a little affair called *The Book Buyer*, which began and ended its life as a house organ. It started in 1867, aiming, frankly, as its first issue announced, "to draw the attention of

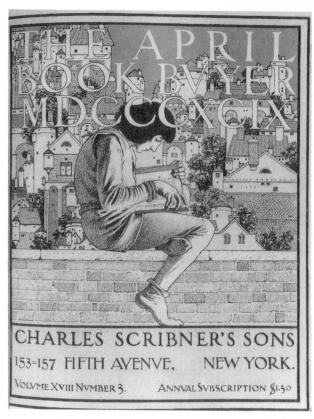

Cover of The Book Buyer *for April 1899, designed by the American illustrator and artist Maxfield Parrish (1870–1966)*

the reading public generally to the works imported by Scribner, Welford & Co., and to those issued by Charles Scribner & Co., and it will do this partly by printing extracts from the books rather than by tedious descriptions of them." The snobbery of putting the importations first was characteristic of the period. In 1918, when *The Book Buyer* had gone back to its original status, the flippant young man then in charge of the House's publicity got so bored with it that he let it die on the eve of its fiftieth birthday.

But in its middle years *The Book Buyer* blossomed out into a literary magazine comparable to the later *Bookman* or today's *Saturday Review of Literature*. It reviewed impartially the books of all publishers, carried their advertising, had a paid subscription list, and was illustrated with magnificence. When it reached the peak of its career, it published signed articles by E. S. Martin, Lawrence Hutton, Bliss Perry, Henri P. du Bois, Royal Cortissoz, Harriet Prescott Spofford, Gerald Stanley Lee, Russell Sturgis, John C. Van Dyke, Hamilton Mabie, and other distinguished writers of the

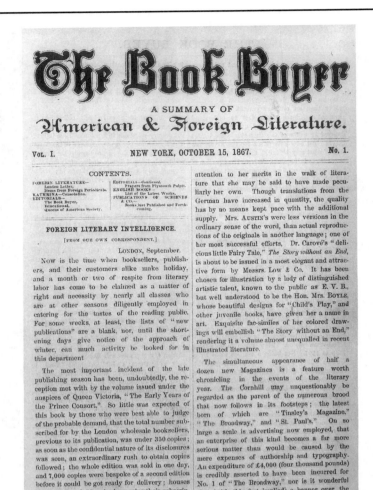

First page of the inaugural issue of The Book Buyer. *Its editorial (p. 4) announces:*

In this manner very many of the best sayings of the best writers, as well as of the ablest and most original thinkers in this country and Europe, will from time to time be made to do duty in its columns. The current number, for instance, contains curious and instructive facts from Professor Whitney's work on Language; eloquent thoughts and interesting points from Froude's Short Studies on Great Subjects; thrilling incidents of the war from Mrs. Hoge's admirable book, the Boys in Blue; *some graceful verses from Dr. Holland's latest and, already, it may almost be said, his most popular poem, Kathrina. Such a combination of attractions as these is seldom found in a single publication — especially one of such modest pretensions as THE BOOK BUYER. In addition to them we have what will be regarded as the most valuable feature of THE BOOK BUYER, — a clear and exceedingly interesting resumé by MR. CHARLES WELFORD, a partner in the firm named, of the latest foreign literary intelligence. MR. WELFORD'S thorough acquaintance with general literature, his long experience in the trade, and his quick and accurate appreciation of the very points upon which book buyers in this country wish to keep informed, taken in connection with the fact that he is permanently residing in London, and that he is in constant communication with literary circles there, all combine to make his letters of the greatest value and interest, and they will doubtless be eagerly anticipated. These statements indicate sufficiently what the readers of THE BOOK BUYER may anticipate in point of literary attractions.*

This series (volumes 1–10) lasted from 15 October 1867 until December 1877.

The Book Buyer

A SUMMARY OF

American and Foreign Literature.

NEW SERIES. }
Vol. I.—No. 1. }
NEW YORK, FEBRUARY, 1884.
{ ANNUAL SUB'N, 50 CENTS.
{ SINGLE NUMBER, 5 CENTS.

CHARLES SCRIBNER'S SONS'
New and Forthcoming Books.

Luther: A Short Biography.

By JAMES ANTHONY FROUDE, M.A., Honorary Fellow of Exeter College, Oxford. 1 volume, 12mo, paper, 30 cents; cloth, 75 cents.

My House: An Ideal.

By OLIVER BELL BUNCE. 1 volume, small 12mo, antique leather, $1; paper, 50 cents. [In Press.]

Newport: A Novel.

By GEORGE PARSONS LATHROP. 1 volume, 12mo, $1.25. Cover designed by Mr. Francis Lathrop. [Immediately.]

Creators of the Age of Steel.

By W. T. JEAMS. 1 volume, 12mo, $1.50. [Immediately.] Short biographies of Sir Henry Bessemer, Sir John Brown, Sir William Siemens, Sir Joseph Whitworth, S. G. Thomas, and G. S. Snelus.

The Question of Ships.

By Lieut. J. D. J. KELLEY, U.S.N. 1 volume, 12mo, $1.25. [Immediately.]

A Day in Athens with Socrates.

By the author of "Socrates." 1 volume, 12mo, paper, 50 cents; cloth, $1.

Creation;

OR, THE BIBLICAL COSMOGONY IN THE LIGHT OF MODERN SCIENCE.

By ARNOLD GUYOT, Blair Professor of Geology and Physical Geography in the College of New Jersey; author of "Earth and Man." 1 volume, 12mo, with full-page wood engravings from the Waterhouse Hawkins paintings at Princeton College, and lithographic plates. $1.50. [Immediately.]

The Works of Arthur Penrhyn Stanley, D.D.,

Late Dean of Westminster. A new and cheap edition. Per volume, 12mo, gilt top, $2.

Lectures on the History of the Eastern Church.

With an Introduction on the Study of Ecclesiastical History. 1 volume.

Lectures on the History of the Jewish Church.

With maps and plans, and a new portrait of Dean Stanley. 3 volumes. [*Nearly ready.*]

Quotations in the New Testament.

By C. H. TOY, D.D., LL.D., Professor of Hebrew in Harvard University. 1 volume, 8vo, $3.50. [Immediately.]

Dr. McCosh's Philosophic Series.

No. V.—LOCKE, WITH A NOTICE OF BERKELEY. 1 volume, paper, 50 cents.

Among the Holy Hills.

By HENRY M. FIELD, D.D., author of "From the Lakes of Killarney to the Golden Horn," etc., etc. 1 volume, crown 8vo, with a map, $1.50.

Kadesh-Barnea.

Its Importance and Probable Site, with a Story of a Hunt for it, including Studies of the Route of the Exodus and the Southern Boundary of the Holy Land. By H. CLAY TRUMBULL, D.D., editor of the *Sunday-School Times.* 1 volume, 8vo, with two maps and four full-page illustrations, $5.

*** *These books are for sale by all booksellers, or will be sent, postpaid, by*

CHARLES SCRIBNER'S SONS, Publishers,
743-745 BROADWAY, NEW YORK.

First page in the first issue of the "new" (second) series of The Book Buyer. *This series (volumes 1–2, no. 6) ran from September 1878 through April 1880.*

[NEW SERIES.]

The Book Buyer

SCRIBNER & WELFORD'S

Literary Letter, & Monthly Record

OF RECENT IMPORTATIONS,
COMPRISING ALL THE MORE IMPORTANT

New English Publications,

Choice Standard and Classical Books, English and Foreign, Ancient and Modern,
adapted for Public and Private Libraries, at Low Prices, in
every department of LITERATURE, SCIENCE and ART,

For Sale at their Store, 743 & 745 Broadway, New-York.

☞ *The number of NEW BOOKS imported being often limited, orders for them are considered open to be filled within FIVE WEEKS FROM RECEIPT, as that time is sufficient to replace them, if previously sold. OLD and SECOND-HAND BOOKS cannot be replaced with equal certainty, but can generally be supplied within a moderate time.*

| Vol. I. | NEW YORK, SEPTEMBER, 1878. | No. 1. |

LONDON, August 20th.

As the absorbing interests of the last few months have been political rather than literary, it is not surprising that comparative quiet has been the rule in the book market. The continued depression in general business has also naturally affected the supply of books, and, as might be expected, the production of any works involving considerable outlay is postponed until a more convenient season. Still, a fair number of books of average merit have been brought out, and, indeed, a stock of new reading-matter has become such a universal necessary of life that nothing short of a social catastrophe can put a stop to its appearance.

It is too early at present to look for the many books that the late war will infallibly be the subject of. At present the duty of the contemporary historian is performed by the able and energetic war correspondents of the English daily press, whose contributions, when collected into volumes, like Mr. Forbes' *Daily News Correspondence of the War*, etc., form a record of current events that can never lose its value. A natural curiosity to become acquainted with the native races of the regions where the armies of the conflicting empires have met, will find ample gratification in a new work: *The Englishwoman in Turkey ; Twenty Years' Residence among the People of Turkey—Bulgarians, Greeks, Albanians, Turks, and Armenians, by a Consul's Wife and Daughter*, 2 vols., crown 8vo. It is edited by a gentleman, Mr. Stanley Lane Poole (nephew of the great Oriental scholar, Edward Lane), whose long experience in the East gives value to his high praise of the authoress's book. Speaking the languages of most of the above-mentioned races, and familiar with them from her childhood, the advantages she enjoyed were quite exceptional for

First page in the first issue of the "new" (third) series of The Book Buyer. *A brief note on its editorial page (p. 8) introduces the series:*

For ten years, beginning October, 1867, THE BOOK BUYER was published by the house which now sends forth this new issue of the periodical. During this time it obtained a large circulation, and made, it is believed, many friends who will be glad to welcome it in its new form. What THE BOOK BUYER is designed to be this initial number, we trust, will sufficiently indicate. The subscription price has been placed at fifty cents a year, that its publishers may place a literary paper containing a concise and interesting summary of American and foreign literature within the reach of every book-lover.

This series (volumes 1–43) ran from February 1884 to May 1918 and experimented with several different subtitles in an apparent attempt to find its audience: "A Summary of American & Foreign Literature," "A Review and Record of Current Literature," "A Monthly Review of American and Foreign Literature," and "A Monthly Guide to the Intelligent Buying of Books." For a few years (February 1903 to January 1905) the series bore the name The Lamp.

nineties. Departments were conducted by Rossiter Johnson and Mark Antony De Wolfe Howe — Howe's column being *Book News* from Boston, whose prestige as the country's literary center was still independent of collaboration by its police department. In its Christmas number, 1896, *The Book Buyer* contained 118 pages of text and carried 91 pages of non-Scribner advertising.

At one point *The Book Buyer* became so highbrow that it changed its name to *The Lamp* — an affectation which may have been adopted to remove from it all commercial taint and one which should have aroused the indignation of authors to whom the frank and open buying of books must always appear as one of the noblest of human exercises.

St. Nicholas (1873–1881)

ARTICLE:

Mary Mapes Dodge, "Children's Magazines," *Scribner's Monthly*, 6, no. 3 (July 1873): 352–354.

Already at work as the editor of St. Nicholas *but four months before its debut, Mary Mapes Dodge describes the basic points of her philosophy on children's magazines in this article: no sermonizing or condescension, "heartily conceived and well executed" illustrations, "pleasant, breezy things" instead of "harsh, cruel facts" — in short, a magazine that is a child's friend. Having gone abroad with relatives in May, she was in Holland when the article appeared, writing a preface to the new Scribner edition of her well-known children's book,* Hans Brinker. *The book was published in November to coincide with the birth of the magazine.*

Sometimes I feel like rushing through the world with two placards — one held aloft in my right hand, BEWARE OF CHILDREN'S MAGAZINES! the other flourished in my left, CHILD'S MAGAZINE WANTED! A good magazine for little ones was never so much needed, and such harm is done by nearly all that are published. In England, especially, the so-called juvenile periodicals are precisely what they ought not to be. In Germany, though better, they too often distract sensitive little souls with grotesquerie. Our magazines timidly approach the proper standard in some respects, but fall far short in others. We edit for the approval of fathers and mothers, and endeavor to make the child's monthly a milk-and-water variety of the adult's periodical. But, in fact, the child's magazine needs to be stronger, truer, bolder, more uncompromising than the other. Its cheer must be the cheer of the bird-song, not of condescending editorial babble. If it *mean* freshness and heartiness, and life and joy, and its words are simply, directly, and musically put together, it will trill its own way. We must not help it overmuch. In all except skillful handling of methods, we must be as little children if we would enter this kingdom.

If now and then the situation have fun in it, if something tumble unexpectedly, if the child-mind is surprised into an electric recognition of comical incongruity, so that there is a reciprocal "ha, ha!" between the printed page and the little reader, well and good. But, for humanity's sake, let there be no editorial grimacing, no tedious vaulting back and forth over the grim railing that incloses halt and lame old jokes long ago turned in there to die.

Let there be no sermonizing either, no wearisome spinning out of facts, no rattling of the dry bones of history. A child's magazine is its pleasure-ground. Grown people go to their periodicals for relaxation, it is true; but they also go for information, for suggestion, and for to-day's fashion in literature. Besides, they begin, now-a-days, to feel that they are behind the age if they fail to know what the April *Jig-jig* says about so and so, or if they have not read B — 's much-talked-of poem in the last *Argosy*. Moreover, it is "the thing" to have the *Jig-jig* and *Argosy* on one's drawing-room table. One must read the leading periodicals or one is nobody. But with children the case is different. They take up their monthly or weekly because they wish to, and if they don't like it they throw it down again. Most children of the present civilization attend school. Their little heads are strained and taxed with the day's lessons. They do not want to be bothered nor amused nor taught nor petted. They just want to have their own way over their own magazine. They want to enter the one place where they may come and go as they please, where they are not obliged to mind, or say "yes ma'am" and "yes, sir," — where, in short, they can have a brand-new, free life of their own for a little while, accepting acquaintances as they choose and turning their backs without ceremony upon what does not concern them. Of course they expect to pick up odd bits and treasures, and to now and then "drop in" familiarly at an air castle, or step over to

ST. NICHOLAS.

VOL. I. NOVEMBER, 1873. NO. 1.

DEAR GIRL AND BOY—No, there are more! Here they come! There they come! Near by, far off, everywhere, we can see them,—coming by dozens, hundreds, thousands, troops upon troops, and all pressing closer and closer.

Why, this is delightful. And how fresh, eager, and hearty you look! Glad to see us? Thank you. The same to you, and many happy returns. Well, well, we might have known it; we *did* know it, but we hardly thought it would be like this. Hurrah for dear St. Nicholas! He has made us friends in a moment.

And no wonder. Is he not the boys' and girls' own Saint, the especial friend of young Americans? That he is. And isn't he the acknowledged patron Saint of New York—one of America's great cities—dear to old hearts as well as young? Didn't his image stand at the prow of the first emigrant ship that ever sailed into New York Bay, and wasn't the very first church the New Yorkers built named after him? Didn't he come over with the Dutch, ever so long ago, and take up his abode here? Certainly. And, what is more, isn't he the kindest, best, and jolliest old dear that ever was known? Certainly, again.

Another thing you know: He is fair and square. He comes when he says he will. At the very outset he decided to visit our boys and girls every Christmas; and doesn't he do it? Yes; and that makes it all the harder when trouble or poverty shuts him out at that time from any of the children.

Dear old St. Nicholas, with his pet names—Santa Claus, Kriss Kringle, St. Nick, and we don't know how many others. What a host of wonderful stories are told about him—you may hear them all some day—and what loving, cheering thoughts follow in his train! He has attended so many heart-warmings in his long, long day that he glows without knowing it, and, coming as he does, at a holy time, casts a light upon the children's faces that lasts from year to year.

Never to dim this light, young friends, by word or token, to make it even brighter, when we can, in good, pleasant, helpful ways, and to clear away clouds that sometimes shut it out, is our aim and prayer.

Frontispiece and first page in the first issue of St. Nicholas

fairy-land. They feel their way, too, very much as we old folk do, toward sweet recognitions of familiar daydreams, secret goodnesses, and all the glorified classics of the soul. We who have strayed farther from these, thrill even to meet a hint of them in poems and essays. But what delights *us* in Milton, Keats and Tennyson, children often find for themselves in stars, daisies, and such joys and troubles as little ones know. That this comparison holds, is the best we can say of our writers. If they make us reach forth our hands to clutch the star or the good-deed candle-blaze, what more can be done?

Literary skill in its highest is but the subtle thinning of the veil that life and time have thickened. Mrs. Browning paid her utmost tribute to Chaucer when she spoke of

" — his infantine
Familiar clasp of things divine."

The *Jig-jig* and *Argosy* may deal with Darwinianism broadly and fairly as they. The upshot of it all will be something like

"Hickory, dickery dock!
The mouse ran up the clock.

The clock struck one
And down she ran —
Hickery, dickery dock!"

And whatever Parton or Arthur Helps may say in that stirring article, "Our Country to-day," its substance is anticipated in

"Little boy blue!
Come, blow your horn!
The cow's in the meadow
Eating the corn."

So we come to the conviction that the perfect magazine for children lies folded at the heart of the ideal best magazine for grown-ups. Yet the coming periodical which is to make the heart of baby-America glad must not be a chip of the old Maga block, but an outgrowth from the old-young heart of Maga itself. Therefore, look to it that it be strong, warm, beautiful, and true. Let the little magazine-readers find what they look for and be able to pick up what they find. Boulders will not go into tiny baskets. If it so happen that the little folks know some one jolly, sympathetic, hand-to-hand personage who is sure to turn up here and there in every number of the magazine or paper, very good: that is, if they happen to like him. If not, beware! It will soon join the ghosts of dead periodicals; or, if it do not, it will live on only in that slow, dragging existence which is worse than death.

A child's periodical must be pictorially illustrated, of course, and the pictures must have the greatest variety consistent with simplicity, beauty and unity. They should be heartily conceived and well executed; and they must be suggestive, attractive and epigrammatic. If it be only the picture of a cat, it must be so like a cat that it will do its own purring, and not sit, a dead, stuffed thing, requiring the editor to purr for it. One of the sins of this age is editorial dribbling over inane pictures. The time to shake up a dull picture is when it is in the hands of the artist and engraver, and not when it lies, a fact accomplished, before the keen eyes of the little folk. Well enough for the editor to stand ready to answer questions that would naturally be put to the flesh-and-blood father, mother, or friend standing by. Well enough, too, for the picture to cause a whole tangle of interrogation-marks in the child's mind. It need not be elaborate, nor exhaust its theme, but what it attempts to do it must do well, and the editor must not over-help nor hinder. He must give just what the child demands, and to do this successfully is a matter of instinct, without which no man should presume to be a child's editor and go unhung.

Doubtless a great deal of instruction and good moral teaching may be inculcated in the pages of a magazine; but it must be by hints dropped incidentally here and there; by a few brisk, hearty statements of the difference between right and wrong; a sharp, clean thrust at falsehood, a sunny recognition of truth, a gracious application of politeness, an unwilling glimpse of the odious doings of the uncharitable and base. In a word, pleasant, breezy things may linger and turn themselves this way and that. Harsh, cruel facts — if they must come, and sometimes it is important that they should — must march forward boldly, say what they have to say, and go. The ideal child's magazine, we must remember, is a pleasure-ground where butterflies flit gayly hither and thither; where flowers quietly spread their bloom; where wind and sunshine play freaks of light and shadow; but where toads hop quickly out of sight and snakes dare not show themselves at all. Wells and fountains there may be in the grounds, but

Mary Mapes Dodge (1830–1905), first editor of St. Nicholas

water must be drawn from the one in right trim, bright little buckets; and there must be no artificial coloring of the other, nor great show-cards about it, saying, "Behold! a fountain." Let its own flow and sparkle proclaim it.

ARTICLE:

Earnest Elmo Calkins, "When St. Nicholas Was Very Young: Our Very First Reader Tells What He Read and How He Enjoyed It," *St. Nicholas*, 58, no. 8 (June 1931): 566–567, 598, 600.

Though St. Nicholas *continued to enjoy its unparalleled success as a children's magazine under the ownership of the Century Company, its birth and formative years were nurtured by Scribner & Co. This nostalgic look by Calkins (1868–1964), an advertising man and author, covers, for the most part, only those early Scribner years.*

In 1873, a boy in a western Illinois town was five and a half years old. One evening in November his father came home from downtown bringing the first number of a new magazine, gay with red-and-black cover. Its full name was "St. Nicholas for boys and girls, conducted by Mary Mapes Dodge." To that boy it was the opening of a door into a new world.

There had been children's magazines before. But nothing so splendid as ST. NICHOLAS had yet come to his print-hungry mind.

No boy or girl in these days of abundant reading-matter can possibly know how eagerly we who were little folks fifty years ago longed for something to read — something of our own kind, about boys and girls, instead of grown-up books. We read everything we could find; the dullest and most unpalatable books you can imagine — great thick volumes printed on poor paper from small type, such as "The Scottish Chiefs," and "Thaddeus of Warsaw"; even "The Conversion of Hester Ann Rogers," and Whiston's "Josephus," because they were on the shelves and there were few others, and almost none for children. There was one, however, undoubtedly for children. "Line Upon Line," the story of the Bible told in simple and somtimes sugary words. It was the first book the boy read. He began to read to himself when he was four, and by the time he was seven he could read each number of ST. NICHOLAS from the frontispiece to THE RIDDLE-BOX.

Having read the magazine through, and even solved some of the puzzles and rebuses at the end, he waited patiently a slow month for the next number. Long before it could possibly arrive he began to haunt Knowles & Lescher's — for his subscription was sent in through the bookseller who had given his father that first sample copy. When so unlucky as to get it at noon, how hard it was to go back to school again, and how long the hours of waiting before he could read the next installment of "The Boy Emigrants," by Noah Brooks, or "Under the Lilacs," by Louisa M. Alcott.

Naturally he liked the stories best, particularly the continued stories, of which there were always two, and sometimes three. They overlapped in November, which was the beginning of a new subscription-year — a coincidence, the boy

thought. He did not know then that it was a device of the editor to make him pester his parents to renew the subscription! Although there were few spare pennies in that little prairie home, somehow we always managed to scrape together the three dollars that insured the monthly visits of ST. NICK for the next twelve months. Nothing that money could buy seemed so desirable as the next installment of "The Tinkham Brothers' Tide-Mill," by J. T. Trowbridge.

What good stories they were! Would that I could find a book to-day that seems half as good to me as those tales were then. "The Cat and the Countess," a translation by Thomas Bailey Aldrich of Bédollierres's famous and time-honored French classic for children, "Mère Michel et son Chat," with silhouette illustrations; "A Jolly Fellowship," and "What Might Have Been Expected," by Frank Stockton; "Dab Kinzer," by W. O. Stoddard; "Jon of Iceland," by Bayard Taylor; "The Story of Windsor Castle," by Mrs. Oliphant; "Rose in Bloom," by Miss Alcott; "Pattikin's House," by Joy Allison; "The Young Surveyor," and "Fast Friends," by J. T. Trowbridge.

Trowbridge's "His Own Master" gave me my first disillusioning intimation of worldly wisdom. Jacob sets out with all his worldly possessions — eighty-seven dollars and forty-five cents — tied up in his handkerchief. He meets Professor Alphonse Pinkey, suave and ingratiating. Alphonse persuades him that it is unsafe to carry money so, and generously offers to keep it in his own money-belt. Jacob thinks that most kind of him — and so did I, but my father did not agree. "That is the last Jacob will ever see of his money," he said. Father was right. Next morning Professor Alphonse disappeared. Would any boy of nine to-day be as trustful and confiding as I was then, I wonder?

"Phaeton Rogers," by Rossiter Johnson, initiated me into the art of printing, for it was the story of a group of boys who set up a press and did "gob printing," as they spelled it until Jack-in-the-Box gave them some advice about proofreading. I could not rest until I had done the same with an old second-hand rickety press in the woodshed. Thus I became a printer, and later worked at that trade (a most fascinating trade it was then, before the advent of the typesetting machine) and finally, by a natural transition, became an advertising man.

A few years ago I had occasion to tell in print how this story had influenced my life, and won-

New York, _____ *1873.*

To Authors.

Messrs. Scribner & Co., New York, will begin early in the fall of the present year, the publication of an **Illustrated Monthly Magazine, for Girls and Boys,** the name of which shall be hereafter announced.

The magazine, which is to be profusely illustrated by the best artists at home and abroad, will be edited by Mrs. Mary Mapes Dodge, author of "Hans Brinker," and for the last four years editor of the children's department of Hearth and Home. While aiming indirectly to instruct its young readers, and to inculcate a true Christian spirit, it will be entirely unsectarian in character, and will avoid anything like formal teaching or preaching. The spirit of mirthfulness shall be invoked from the first, and all good things fresh, true, and child-like, heartily commended, while every way to juvenile priggishness shall be bolted and barred as far as the management can effect.

Mrs. Dodge will spend a portion of the summer in Europe, gleaning materials and securing contributions for the new venture. Meanwhile it is desired to procure from our home writers, the very best reading matter for boys and girls. Brief, bright, entertaining, original stories, sketches, and other articles for young folks, of from five to sixteen years, will be acceptable, if the subjects and treatment be in accordance with the purposes of the magazine, and accepted matter will be liberally paid for without waiting for the day of publication.

As articles for the early numbers should be secured without delay, you will confer a favor by an early response.

Address " Editors of Children's Monthly," care of Scribner & Co., 654 Broadway, New York.

1873 announcement soliciting authors for the as-yet-unnamed children's magazine

dered if it had ever been made into a book. It had, and was still bought and read by new generations of boys. Don Parker, for many years in charge of advertising in ST. NICHOLAS, thoughtfully sent me a copy, and I read the story again after fifty years with some of the old glamour. And just now I learn that the author is still living, and writing his reminiscences!

It was in ST. NICHOLAS I read the "Peterkin Papers," by Lucretia P. Hale, sister of Edward Everett — Agamemnon, Solomon John, Elizabeth Eliza and the "little boys in their India-rubber boots," with the Lady from Philadelphia always at hand to help them out of their preposterous adventures. But of all the never-to-be-forgotten stories read in ST. NICK, "Tom Sawyer" was *not* one, though some estimable people are certain they read it there. Even if there were not my own, in this case, infallible recollection (and the file copies to check up, for that matter), Tom was not the ideal Mrs. Dodge sought to set before her readers. Neither were the heroes of Oliver Optic and Horatio Alger, Jr., with their quick and easy success, though I read them also, as well as Tom Sawyer, surreptitiously in the hay-loft. My mother had much the same scruples as the editor of ST. NICHOLAS.

During those critical years of my life, from five to ten, I remember as more or less regular contributors Elizabeth Stuart Phelps, Laura E. Richards, Rebecca Harding Davis — mother of the more famous Richard, "H.H." who was Helen Hunt Jackson, and Saxe Holm, whose identity I never learned ["Saxe Holm" was Helen Hunt Jackson's other pseudonym]. Two names that caught me by their musical charm, as well as their efforts to give us the proper feeling toward poetry, were Celia Thaxter and Lucy Larcom.

I must not forget the funny pictures and jingles that eked out the unfinished half-pages; no such dull vulgarity as the modern comic-strip, but such true Lewiscarrollisms as:

"The owl, the eel, and the warming-pan,
They went to call on the soap-fat man.
The soap-fat man was not within;
He'd gone for a ride on his rolling-pin.
So they all came back by way of the town,
And turned the meeting-house upside down."

Or;

"They didn't have a penny
And couldn't borrow any
And owed exactly half a dime for coal.

So they said 'We'll run away,'
When a goose came out to say,
'You must pay two cents apiece all round for toll.' "

with pictures by Sol Eytinge or F. Opper or Addie Ledyard.

It is really singular that I remember the names of any artists, for little was made of them for the first few years, and I had only the sometimes indecipherable signature on the cut to go by. On the other hand, I first heard of such men as Rubens or Reynolds because steel engravings of their work were used as frontispieces, with some account of their lives. Reynolds' *Penelope Boothby* and *The Strawberry Girl* were thus used, and are the first great pictures I ever knew.

We learned these jingles, and sang and chanted them. I could quote them by the hour if it would amuse you as much as it does me. I say "we," for the family in the prairie home grew as fast as ST. NICHOLAS, and when the boy was eight he had two brothers and two sisters, who began to read ST. NICHOLAS as soon as they were able. From the time until the youngest was too big to read it any longer, we had it every month, and the contest to see who should read the magazine first never lost its fervor, even after we were big enough to disguise it with a semblance of politeness.

Of special interest were the various things to do with tools, pencil, paint-brush, or wits. I tried them all. I worked for weeks to build Christmas City and Holiday Harbor, cardboard models; fashioned the George Washington Centennial penwiper described so graphically, and solved many of the rebuses. Every story, picture, verse, and useful article (for ST. NICHOLAS was not all stories) is stamped upon my mind more indelibly than the book I read last week. I can almost write the index. Every six months the numbers were bound and added to the row on the lower shelf of my own private three-shelf library. I wish I had them now! In the year of famine in Nebraska, when the grasshoppers ate all the crops, we sent a box to some Western cousins, and I impulsively added my set of ST. NICHOLAS, under the impression that the grasshoppers had devoured printed leaves as well as the other kind.

Mrs. Dodge was rather fond of stories with a moral, and these parables appeared at frequent intervals. Many were written by "H.H." They were nearly all interesting for the story alone. Not long ago I used as a starter for a speech the fable about a man who covered the earth with leather. It was from an early number of the magazine; however, I had forgotten no essential point. These bits of literature have often come in handy as starters for speeches and advertisements. There is a certain old-time quaintness about them that adds to their effectiveness.

In the back of each number were several departments — a story in large type "for very little folks," THE LETTER-BOX, THE RIDDLE-BOX, and sermons by Jack-in-the-Pulpit on current events. To these was added in the early 80's, when I was entering high school, a new department, the purpose of which was to organize readers of ST. NICHOLAS into societies for the study of what was then called natural history. This was the Agassiz Association, and was conducted by Harlan H. Ballard. Soon there was a flourishing chapter at Galesburg composed of boys in our class (1885), of which I was first president. The other day I spent an evening in Boston with Charles Ferris Gettemy — now Assistant Federal Reserve Officer, but fifty years ago secretary of the Agassiz Association, and probably the best secretary that or any other society ever had. We spent the evening looking over the neatly-kept minute-books of our chapter, and the files of the miniature newspaper, hand-written, in which news of the association of a more sensational character was duly chronicled.

Gettemy had produced periodical after periodical with unflagging patience, at first in manuscript, and finally in print, and we had both become members of the National Amateur Press Association which flourished at that time. The members were boys who published miniature newspapers. To-day those members, now in their sixties, have a retrospective alumni association called The Fossils, which celebrates with an annual dinner. Among its members are Cyrus Curtis, still a publisher, Thomas A. Edison, Josephus Daniels, Joe Mitchell Chapple, James M. Beck, John H. Tennant, Howard M. Carter, Minna Irving, John Irving Romer, H. Gordon Selfridge, and others.

I stopped reading ST. NICHOLAS when I left home to seek my fortune, but have always looked at it with interest whenever it came my way. My former affection for it received a fillip on the announcement of its new editor. ST. NICHOLAS had its best days under Mary Mapes Dodge, and now, after many years, a woman is again "conductor," I shall watch it with the liveliest curiosity and sympathy, though I no longer possess the fresh impressionable mind of that boy.

LETTER:
Letter from Edmund Clarence Stedman to Mary Mapes Dodge, 26 October 1873.

This, the first fan letter to Dodge about St. Nicholas, *came from her friend Edmund Clarence Stedman, a poet and successful Wall Street broker. His later anthologies, such as* A Library of American Literature *(11 volumes, 1888–1890), edited with Ellen M. Hutchinson, helped develop a broader appreciation of American literature.*

Dear Mrs. Dodge:

I want to congratulate you upon the first number of your magazine. I have given it a thorough examination, from beginning to end, and like it immensely. So far as I am a judge, it is the best youth's magazine ever yet published, and is sure to be a great success. The Introduction, with its brevity, naturalness, & perfect understanding of the child-nature — added to perfect love of children, is a true work of art, founded upon nature; & such a little "Cameo" as no one save M.M.D. knows how to cut. It is evident that you are going to be very happy in your new & well-deserved position, & I must take a moment's time from unpleasant duties to have the pleasure of telling you how much I rejoice in your success.

Very faithfully
Your friend,
Edmund C. Stedman

LETTER:
Letter from Robert Dale Owen to Mary Mapes Dodge, 2 December 1873.

This is a letter of congratulation from Robert Dale Owen (1801–1877), son of the "father of English socialism," who immigrated to the United States from Scotland in 1825, was active in his father's New Harmony (Indiana) community, served in Congress, and was minister to Italy. He was interested in, and wrote about, spiritualism and was a longtime friend of the Dodge family. His reference to "our young folks" is to Our Young Folks, *the only remaining serious rival to* St. Nicholas, *published in Boston by Ticknor & Fields and purchased in 1873 by Scribner & Co. Its last issue appeared in October, thus providing continuity into* St. Nicholas.

I hope you got my autobiography.

I wonder whether it will do to address Mrs. Mary Mapes Dodge as "Lizzie dear?" She will al-

Louisa May Alcott (1832–1888)

I don't think that you can keep up to the first number of St. Nicholas; nor could it be expected; nor is it necessary. There never <u>was</u> as good a number of a child's magazine issued on this side of the Atlantic, if indeed on the other, as your November Number: from its gravest article to your inimitable "Oh no!"

I subscribed for it & had it addressed to my granddaughters, Grace & Daisy Dale Owen.

Till tomorrow, if the skies permit.

Ever affectionately yours
Robert Dale Owen

LETTER:
Letter from Mary L. Booth to Mary Mapes Dodge, 30 October 1874.

Praise on the first volume (first year) of St. Nicholas *from Mary L. Booth (1831–1889), editor of* Harper's Bazaar.

My dear friend and sister,

Let me thank you, and through you, Messrs. Scribner & Co., for the sumptuously bound volume of the St. Nicholas which welcomed me on my return home last evening.

I should think that such a firstling would delight your heart. You have won a signal triumph in making what is confessedly the brightest and best of American juvenile magazines; and its interest isn't confined to the juveniles either! For my part, I always feel myself defrauded when some evil chance prevents me from reading it each month, as is my custom. I am very proud that a woman has won this success in the journalistic world, and proud above all that thou art the woman! With all my heart do I congratulate you on your triumph. . . .

Yours affectionately,
Mary L. Booth

LETTER:
Letter by Christina Rossetti (1830–1894), the English poetess, to Mary Mapes Dodge, 10 August 1875.

Titled "An Alphabet from England," Rossetti's contribution — with the corrected "G" line — appeared in the November 1875 issue of St. Nicholas.

Dear Mrs. Dodge

Your obliging letter finds me also out holidaying, tho' not I dare say in quite such scenery as

ways be "Lizzie dear" to me, even if she <u>has</u> dropped the E. So I think it had better stand so.

I got your card last evening. Though I have not been well lately, I started this morning for 215, but seeing every one who came into the car, even with an umbrella, ringing wet, I concluded that it would be rather a tempting of Providence; so I got out at the transfer car, 34th St., & fairly turned back.

Unless this unchristian weather lasts over tomorrow, I'll certainly try to find you tomorrow morning.

How <u>very</u> fortunate that Scribners bought out our young folks! You have the game in yr own hands now. I think you wd have succeeded in any event; but this places the matter beyond all possible doubt.

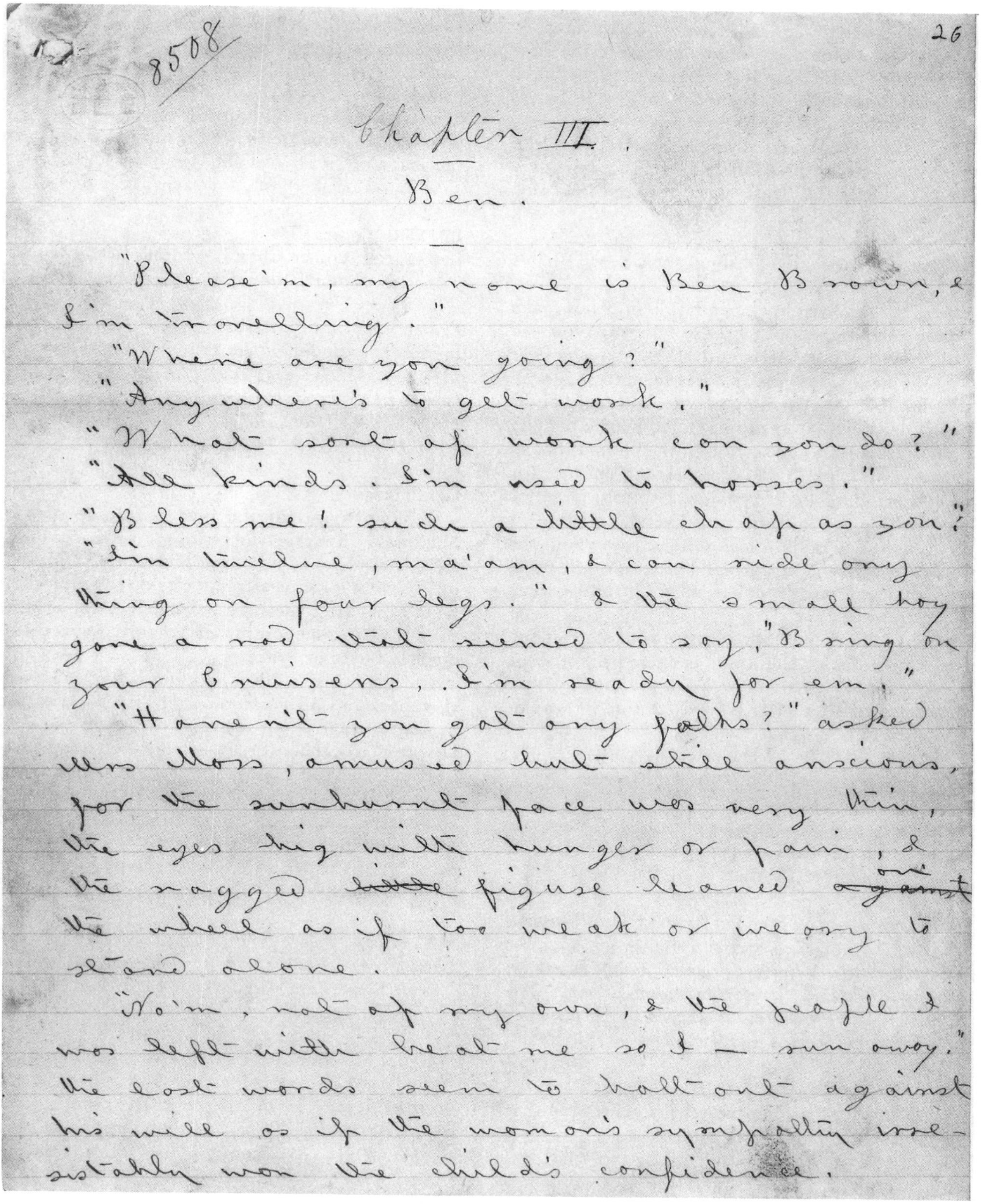

8508

26

Chapter III.

Ben.

"Please'm, my name is Ben Brown, & I'm travelling."

"Where are you going?"

"Anywhere's to get work."

"What sort of work can you do?"

"All kinds. I'm used to horses."

"Bless me! such a little chap as you!"

"I'm twelve, ma'am, & can ride any thing on four legs." & the small boy gave a nod that seemed to say, "Bring on your bruisers, I'm ready for em."

"Haven't you got any folks?" asked Mrs Moss, amused but still anxious, for the sunburnt face was very thin, the eyes big with hunger or pain, & the ragged ~~little~~ figure leaned ~~against~~ on the wheel as if too weak or weary to stand alone.

"No'm, not of my own, & the people I was left with beat me so I — run away." the last words seem to bolt out against his will as if the woman's sympathy irresistably won the child's confidence.

Manuscript page from Louisa May Alcott's Under the Lilacs, *which was first published in* St. Nicholas

surrounds and recruits you. However our green luxuriant Clifton boasts charms of its own & would shew plenty of fine colour were the sunshine more & the rain less. As it is the rains have been so prolonged that one cannot but feel anxious about the harvest.

Your acceptance quite pleases me, & spirits me up to burden you (may I?) with an improvement to letter G. Please make the first "G" line read

"G is the Gander, the Gosling, the Goose" — .

Of course this weighty emendation may not reach you in time, but should it do so I am sure you will oblige an anxious fellow author!

Somehow my possibilities seem to range between babies & grown up people, so I fear youths & maidens of 16 may not be suited by me: happily babies are a standing section of the population, so my next offering to your editorial acceptance (or rejection) shall be unabashed babyish, if better may not be, — & if after all I send, as I think I shall, a second trifle. I feel quite at ease about the purse department; & cordially pleased in the prospect of seeing my alphabet, as you promise me a copy, in print.

As I am not certain whether your stay among the Adirondack Mountains is to be prolonged, I direct once more to New York; supposing that thus most of all a letter is likely to find its way to you correctly.

Very sincerely yours
Christina G. Rossetti

LETTER:
Letter from Bayard Taylor to Mary Mapes Dodge, 9 September 1875.

This is a letter of feigned protest from Bayard Taylor, the American travel writer, poet, lecturer, and translator, in response to a request from Dodge for a story. Taylor's Icelandic story, "The Story of Jon of Iceland," appeared in the January, February, and March 1876 issues of St. Nicholas.

My dear Mrs. Dodge:

I had just read in yesterday's Tribune that you are returned from the Adirondacks in perfect health, and now comes your melancholy letter! I have a poor, beggarly, starveling idea of an Icelandic story, but it has nothing to do with Xmas or the Centennial. I shall probably write it, in a state of desperation, during the coming ten days:

but how can you, or "any other man," expect one author to be literary maid-of-all-work, and turn out Tribune letters, Odes on Goethe, new lectures and children's stories, just as one lays down the broom and takes up the dust-pan? It's not my way of working — but if you force me into it, 'tis you who are responsible for the result. This much in the shape of "a ray of light." In haste, ever truly,
Bayard Taylor

LETTER:
Letter from Louise Chandler Moulton to the publishers of *St. Nicholas*, 30 October 1875.

Praise for St. Nicholas. *Poet, children's author, literary correspondent for the* New York Tribune, *Moulton (1835–1908) held a Friday salon in Boston, which drew such guests as Longfellow, Holmes, Whittier, and Lowell. Her library was given to the Boston Public Library.*

Gentlemen —

Thank you for the bound volume of "St. Nicholas" just received. I should wish I were a child again to read it, except that being "a grown-up" I find it quite as attractive as do the juniors. It would be hard to select a more delightful volume than this, or one combining so varied entertainment in the same space.

Admirable serials, sparkling poems, pleasant sketches, and all arranged and displayed to the best advantage by an editress who knows so well how to marshal her forces — truly the young folks of to-day are to be congratulated on such a treat. Commend me to Mrs. Dodge, as to one who has solved the puzzle of "Woman's Mission," and found her "Sphere."

Yours Cordially —
Louise Chandler Moulton

LETTER:
Letter from the American poet John Greenleaf Whittier to Mary Mapes Dodge, 31 May 1876.

His first St. Nicholas *contribution was the poem "The Pressed Gentian," which had appeared two months before in the March 1876 issue. A year would pass before Whittier's next appearance in the magazine: "Red Riding Hood" in May 1877.*

Dear Mrs. Dodge,

I don't like to say no to anybody, but thee are one of those to whom, what Carlyle calls the "everlasting yea" seems to belong by divine right. I scarcely see what I can say, or how I can say it, on the theme proposed, but I will think about it.

I hope thy editorial duties do not prevent thee wholly from enjoying this beautiful season of bloom and greenness. Spring always seems to me a miracle. The older I grow, the more keen is my enjoyment of nature.

Mrs. Sargent and & her young friend Alice Gibbons spent last Saturday with me at Oak Knoll in Danvers — a delightful day in the woods.

Believe me very heartily thy friend
John G. Whittier

LETTER:

Letter from the English astronomer Richard Anthony Proctor (1837–1888) to Mary Mapes Dodge, 16 June 1876.

Proctor lectured widely in America after his Handbook of the Stars *(1866) made his reputation. His idea of a monthly star map of the sky was tried in the 1877 issues of January through October, the last one including maps for October, November, and December — hence, a full year.*

Dear Mrs. Dodge,

I owe you many apologies, though in reality I tried very hard while in America to get time to write. (I put off apology writing till I could send a paper, hoping that I might be able to do so.) Engagements to lecture were made for me on days I had set aside to write, — on other days I was made to go over institutions, visit localities & so forth, — then over work told on me at times — and lastly, for the first three weeks after my return to England I was simply prostrate. I ought by the way to add that on Thursday in December last when I appointed to call upon you at Scribner's, I had to lecture at New Brighton — & the 'at home' card reached me when I was at Waterville in Maine. During the last nine week days I gave 11 lectures, & though the papers posted me as stopping at the Westminster I was in reality only there for an hour or two on my way through New York, on such journeys, as — from Worcester to Princeton, from Baltimore to Springfield — from Springfield to Philadelphia — & so on. The following little table of lectures will give you some idea of the way in which my time was occupied

Monday April 24   lectured at Springfield Mass

Tuesday — 25   Worcester Mass

Wednesay — 26   Springfield Mass
Thurs — 27   Philadelphia Penn
Fri. — 28   Worcester Mass
Sat — 29   Worcester aft. at Springfield in evening
Sunday — 30
Monday May 1   Philadelphia Penn
Tuesday — 2   Mt. Vernon N.Y.
Wednesday — 3   sailed for Europe

I send the first part of paper on Venus — & will forward the other part next week <u>sure</u>.

The numbers of the St. Nicholas mentioned in your letter have not yet arrived — (a week later) possibly they have been lost, a thing which happens now rather often with book parcels — newspapers &c.

Pray excuse this hasty note & imperfectly worded apology for my manifold delays — and Believe me

Very respectively & sincerely yours
Richd A. Proctor

Mrs. M. Dodge —

P.S. I received the map of August skies. It seemed to me too complicated for young folks — & I thought of suggesting a set of very simple maps of the monthly skies, to come out month by month, but I fear that your experience of my misdoings would make you very unwilling to run the risk of irregularity in the appearance of such maps.

LETTER:

Letter from the American poet Henry Wadsworth Longfellow (1807–1882) to Mary Mapes Dodge, 26 April 1877.

"King Trisanku" and "Haroun Al Raschid," the two poems Longfellow enclosed, appeared in the following August and October issues.

Dear Mrs. Dodge,

It is impossible to resist the "<u>affectuoso grido</u>," — the affectionate appeal of your letter. So powerful is it, that I send you two pieces instead of one.

As they were not written expressly for the St. Nicholas, you may find them not at all suited to that periodical. In that case, be kind enough to send them back to me without hesitation or word of apology.

I should like very much to have the bound volumes you offer. Though not yet "<u>tombè en en-fance</u>," I have "<u>rentré en jeunesse</u>," and like the

A St. Nicholas circular for August 1878

things that belong to youth. They tend to keep us young, and as long as you remain Editor of the St. Nicholas, you will never grow old.

I remember always your pleasant call, and hope that at no distant day I may again have the pleasure of seeing you within these walls. If walls had tongues as well as ears, or could find them as the Alps and Jura do in Byron's verse, what a cheerful sound of friendly voices we should have around us!

With great regard,
Yours faithfully
Henry Wadsworth Longfellow

LETTER:
Letter from the American children's writer Louisa May Alcott, author of *Little Women* (1868), to Mary Mapes Dodge, 3 June 1877.

Alcott's Under the Lilacs, *her novel-in-progress, is the subject of this letter. She is hopeful that the illustrator, Mary Hallock Foote, will not be too distracted by her new baby, as she was unhappy with the illustrations for her first book that was serialized in* St. Nicholas, Eight Cousins. Under the Lilacs, *illustrated by Mrs. Foote, was serialized in* St. Nicholas *in eleven installments, beginning with the December 1877 issue. Another book,* Jack and Jill, *appeared serially in 1879–1880 issues.*

Dear Mrs. Dodge.

The tale goes slowly owing to interruptions, for summer is a busy time & I get few quiet days. Twelve chapters are done, but are short ones & so will make about six or seven numbers in St. Nicholas.

I will leave them divided in this way that you may put in as many as you please each month, for trying to suit the magazine hurts the story in its book form, though this does no harm to the monthly parts I think.

I will send you the first few chapters during the week for Mrs. Foote, & with them the schedule you suggest, so that my infants may not be drawn with whiskers & my big boys and girls in pinafores as in Eight Cousins.

I hope the new baby won't be set aside too soon for my illustrations, but I do feel a natural wish to have one story prettily adorned with good pictures, as hitherto artists have much afflicted me.

I am daily waiting with anxiety for an illumination of some sort as my plot is very vague so far, & though I don't approve of "sensations" in childrens books, one must have a certain thread on which to string the small events which make up the true sort of child life.

I intend to go & simmer an afternoon at Van Amburg's great show, that I may get hints for the further embellishmnet of Ben and his dog. I have also put in a poem by T. B. Sanborn's small son, & that bit will give Mrs. Foote a good scene with the six-year-old poet reciting his verses under the lilacs.

I shall expect the small tots to be unusually good since the artist has a live model to study from. Please present my congratulations to the happy momma and Mr. Foote Jr.

Yours <u>warmly</u>
L.M.A.

LETTER:
Letter from a thirteen-year-old Rudyard Kipling to the editor of *St. Nicholas*, 22 August 1879.

The poem Kipling submitted with this letter was called "The Dusky Crew," and it described how three schoolboys were caught in their off-limits hideout and punished. Mary Mapes Dodge declined it, writing "Poem really too poor to use. Refused as courteously as I could" on the envelope. The verses were subsequently printed, however, in the private publication Schoolboy Lyrics *(1881). Both probably forgot this early rejection, for, in later years, Kipling's stories and poems were a major attraction of* St. Nicholas.

Dear Sir:

I send with this a little poem which I hope you may think suitable for St. Nicholas Magazine.

I am an English schoolboy, thirteen years old and the verses describe an episode in the last term.

I believe American schoolboys are wisely allowed more liberty than we enjoy and may perhaps sympathize with the difficulties of our dusky crew.

Yours truly,
J. R. Kipling

United Services College.
Westward Ho
North Devon
England.

See Catharine Morris Wright, "How 'St. Nicholas' Got Rudyard Kipling," Princeton University Library Chronicle, 35 (1974): 259, 262.

LETTER:
Letter from W. S. Gilbert to Mary Mapes Dodge, 11 February 1880.

This is a polite "no" from the English comic opera duo of W. S. Gilbert (1836–1911) and Arthur Sullivan (1842–1900). Earlier in 1879, Mary Mapes Dodge had suggested they write a children's opera for St. Nicholas. *She tried again in 1880.*

Dear Madam.

I am extremely sorry for the cause of your recent absence from New York. I am well acquainted with the literary & artistic quality of "St. Nicholas" — indeed I believe it is almost as well known in London as in New York. I regret very much, that at present our hands are so very full of work, both for the United States & for England, that it is quite out of our power to undertake the work you propose. At some future time we may, perhaps, be able to see our way to it.

With many thanks for the compliment implied in your letter, I am,

Very truly yours,
W. S. Gilbert

LETTER:
Letter from Frances Hodgson Burnett to Mary Mapes Dodge, [late 1880], from Washington, D.C.

Frances Hodgson Burnett (1849–1924) offers a story idea based on a supposedly true incident in President Garfield's campaign. Burnett had become a close friend of Mary Mapes Dodge, and several of her works had already appeared in St. Nicholas. *Her children's classic* Little Lord Fauntleroy *would be serialized in the magazine (1885–1886) and subsequently published by Scribners (1886).*

Dear Mrs. Dodge

Political feeling has run so high among the juvenile portion of the community during the past Presidential campaign & I have heard so many delicious stories that it has this instant occurred to me that I might write something amusing on the subject if you think it would do.

I have just written to General Garfield enclosing a letter from the Mother of a little girl of seven whose unceasing & wildly enthusiastic efforts are supposed to have carried Connecticut & whose rapture at the result of the Campaign was only destroyed by the harrowing discovery that Garfield did not realize [?] she was 'for him' which point the letter settles. Let me know if you would like such a thing — if it continues to amuse me as much as it does at the present moment it will be great fun. I wrote the first page a few moments ago & called it "How Lottie elected the President."

Yours very sincerely
Frances Hodgson Burnett

Scribner Years of *St. Nicholas*: 1873–1881
A Selected List of Contributors
Alcott, Louisa May (1832–1888)
Aldrich, Thomas Bailey (1836–1907)
Barnard, Charles (1838–1920)
Barrow, Frances Elizabeth Mease (1822–1894)
  "Aunt Fanny"
Beard, Dan (1850–1941)
Boyesen, Hjalmar Hjorth (1848–1895)
Brooks, Noah (1830–1903)
Bryant, William Cullen (1794–1878)
Burnett, Frances Hodgson (1849–1924)

Butterworth, Hezekiah (1839–1905)
Child, Lydia Maria (1802–1880)
Davis, Rebecca Harding (1831–1910)
Dodge, Mary Abigail (1823–1896) "Gail Hamilton"
Dodge, Mary Mapes (1831–1905)
Dodgson, Charles Lutwidge (1832–1898) "Lewis Carroll"
Eastman, Elaine Goodale (1863–1953)
Eggleston, Edward (1837–1902)
English, Thomas Dunn (1819–1902)
Eytinge, Margaret (b. 1833) "Madge Elliot"
Fawcett, Edgar (1847–1904)
Goodale, Dora Read (1866–1953)
Foote, Mary Hallock (1847–1938)
Hale, Lucretia P. (1820–1900)
Harte, Bret (1839–1902)
Hawthorne, Julian (1846–1934)
Hay, John (1838–1905)
Higginson, Thomas Wentworth (1823–1911)
Holland, J. G. (1819–1881) "Timothy Titcomb"
Jackson, Helen Hunt (1830–1885) "H.H." "Saxe Holm"
Jewett, Sarah Orne (1849–1909)
Johnson, Rossiter (1840–1931)
Larcom, Lucy (1824–1893)
Linton, William James (1812–1897)
Longfellow, Henry Wadsworth (1807–1882)
Miller, Harriet Mann (1831–1918) "Olive Thorne Miller"
Mitchell, Donald Grant (1822–1908) "Ik. Marvel"
Oliphant, Mrs. (1828–1897)
Phelps, Elizabeth Stuart (1844–1911)
Proctor, Richard A. (1837–1888)
Pyle, Howard (1853–1911)
Richards, Laura E. (1850–1943)
Rideing, William Henry (1853–1918)
Rossetti, Christina (1830–1894)
Scudder, Horace E. (1838–1902)
Spofford, Harriet Prescott (1835–1921)
Stockton, Frank R. (1834–1902)
Taylor, Bayard (1825–1878)
Tennyson, Alfred (1809–1892)
Terhune, Mary Virginia (1830–1922) "Marion Harland"
Thaxter, Celia (1835–1894)
Townsend, Virginia Frances (1836–1920)
Trowbridge, J. T. (1827–1916)
Warner, Charles Dudley (1829–1900)
Whittier, John Greenleaf (1807–1892)
Whitney, A. D. T., Mrs. (1824–1906)
Woolsey, Sarah Chauncey (1835–1905) "Susan Coolidge"

Volumes I–VIII (Part I): November 1873 – April 1881

Scribner's Monthly (1870–1881)

LETTER:
Letter by J. G. Holland to CS I, 11 May 1869.

This letter is written from Paris. Before Holland left in the spring of 1868, CS I had offered him the editorship of his languishing periodical Hours at Home. *Holland was a natural choice because of the widespread popularity of his Scribner books and his long editorial experience on the* Springfield Republican. *Holland was not very impressed with the Scribner magazine, nor did he think much of its future. But he wanted time to consider the offer while he was abroad. Scribner's wife, Emma, had died in February while giving birth to their daughter Isabelle. After consoling Scribner in his grief, Holland argues that the magazine needs a "first class business man" and that he already knows the perfect person. Though Holland prefers not to name the man now, allowing Scribner time to adjust first to the idea, it becomes clear in subsequent letters that Roswell Smith is the old friend.*

My Very Dear Friend:

I received your long, sad, saddening, but most welcome letter yesterday, and read it through with many tears. I thank you for pouring out your head to me so fully. Such confidence honors worthily my love for you and the hearty sympathy I give you in all your trial. I know I cannot measure your grief. I only know that you are suffering the profoundest grief that can befall a loving heart, and that in my heart there springs the wish to help you, to comfort you, to assure you of my affection, to brace you in your weakening, and to give you companionship. I know you pretty well, and I know how strong a hold the lost one had upon your affections. I can measure that, for the strength of that tie is fully illustrated in the tie that binds my own dear wife to me. Mrs. Scribner was one of the purest, truest, simplest and best of the many Christian women whom it has been my privilege to know. You cannot help lamenting her. You cannot cease to lament her. You can only go to Jesus Christ, your precious Lord and Master, and ask him by special ministry to draw the sting from this great sorrow. And he can do it. You can be happy in this sorrow. I do not undertake to show the mode by which he works, but I

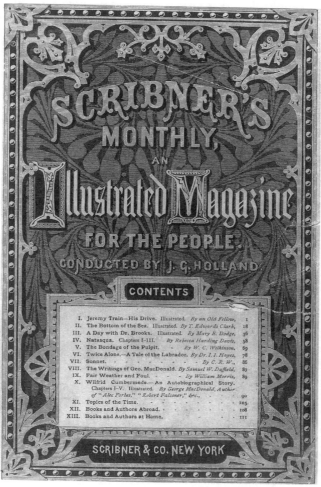

Cover of the first issue (November 1870) of Scribner's Monthly. Scribner & Co. *published the magazine from November 1870 until April 1881 (Volumes I–XXI), when CS II sold his stock in the company to J. G. Holland and Roswell Smith, the magazine's editor and business manager. They renamed the company Century Company and the magazine* The Century Magazine.

believe He can fill your heart with such peace and joy as you have never known, if, in perfect faith, you go to him for help. May you be able to find this help, and may God in his infinite tenderness fold you to His heart.

Remember me most kindly and lovingly to Emma [daughter]. I have great faith in her, and you are to have great comfort in her.

My letters have already informed you sufficiently of my plans, so far as they relate to my stay abroad. As to what I am to do after getting home — if I shall ever be so happy as to reach America again — let us talk. I confess that I am thinking seriously of taking up the "Hours at Home," and now I propose to broach the plan that I have had in mind for some months. My opinion is that the Magazine, to achieve its high-

est success, should have the undivided attention of a first class business man, in the management of its printing and publication — in the large and in detail. There is no man in your concern who can be spared from the other business, and who, at the same time, is adapted to this particular work. He should have money, business training, religious sympathy with ourselves, education, and a good position. He should know how to meet men and deal with men. He should be a first rate correspondent.

I know just this man. I have known him for years, and he is in Paris to-day. He is rich, he is educated, he is a lawyer by profession, and a business man by natural gift and inclination. He is a far-seeing, organizing, determined, efficient, man, and, withal, a Christian gentleman. Without compromising you or myself, or committing either you or myself in any way, I have spoken of this matter to him, and find him ready to go into the enterprise, if I will — indeed, I think he would go into it without me; and, yet, I presume that is a thing he has not considered. I haven't, certainly. I presume that should Mr. Sherwood [current editor] leave, he would help you to make good his place until such time as I should join you. He will return to America in August, and if you favor the idea of his joining us, will call upon you. Would you be willing to have him own a third, me a third, and retain a third yourself?

With this man in New York, to take all the care of publication off your shoulders and mine, I can remain in Springfield, and perform there, with entire efficiency, the editorial work of the Magazine. I shall not be content with a circulation smaller than 50,000 copies, and shall be disappointed if I do not raise it to 75,000 copies. With any such circulation as this — and I certainly would not touch the magazine if I did not expect to reach it — you will recognize the necessity of a distinct Magazine Bureau, presided over by a competent man, who shall find in the administration of this Bureau his whole business. I do not mention my friend's name to you, or give you his references, because I do not wish to compromise or commit him. He is now out of business, measurably, and living on his income; but he is only forty years old, and is conscientious in his desire to fill out a life of usefulness. In this magazine — in making it a great success — he feels that he can not only get such a reward for his time and money as every business man looks for, but be useful as an American Christian citizen. You see how fully I believe in him; and I assure you that I have not only unbounded faith in his business ability and integrity, but in his adaptation to work in perfect harmony with you and me. In short, he is one of our sort. Need I say more?

Now please write me at once on this matter, after consulting with your partners. Get hold of Mr. Sherwood's share at once if you think well of the plan, and hold it for my friend or me. My idea would be to let S. drop out without sayng much about it, and keep things along as well as you can till I come home. I mean to write a volume of poems next winter, and publish them in England and the U.S. simultaneously, in the autumn of 1870, and to go into the Magazine on the tide of that volume. All that we can talk of afterward. What I care for now is to know what you think of my project, so far as it relates to my friend.

My little boy, under Dr. Shelaton's care, is slowly recovering the soundness and the use of his foot. He is very well generally, as are all my precious little flock. Ah! how precious they are to me! And how much they fill for me the satisfaction of life. I rejoice in work; I rejoice in my family and a few friends; I rejoice in prosperity and the favoring care of Providence. I rejoice in the religion of Jesus Christ. What lives outside of these I care very little for. You know that I within possess nor seek for literary society, because in that society I find little or no sympathy in those things that have highest place in my affections and my life. I love you, among my few friends, and propose, with your leave, to hold myself associated with you while I write and you publish.

I was in London last week. They were all busy in canvassing the prospect of a war, and were feeling very very sore over Mr. Sumner's speech. To-day, I have been through the Annual exhibition of pictures at the Palais de l'Industrie; and a magnificent affair it is, with at least ten times the number of pictures ever seen at the Academy's exhibition in New York.

Paris is a lovely city, and we are all enjoying it as much as we can enjoy anything out of America.

Mrs. Holland sends her love to you and to your dear children. Give mine to them, and believe me always yours.

J. G. Holland

LETTER:
Letter from J. G. Holland to CS I, 26 July 1869, from Lucerne, Switzerland.

In another lengthy letter, written while still abroad on his European tour, Holland offers more comfort to CS I, who is still grieving over his wife's death in February, and affirms his abiding affection for him. Then he turns to the business purpose of his letter: a presentation of the specific changes he would want to make in a "new" magazine.

Dear Mr. Scribner: —
Day before yesterday I reached my 50th birthday. I felt pretty soberly about it, but am getting gradually adjusted to the thought that I am growing old. My life has been so sweet a thing to me — so full of loves and friends and successes — that I sometimes grudge the passing hours the treasures which they filch from me.

I received yours of the 23rd ult. on arriving here from a three weeks trip through Holland and

Belgium and through Rhenish Prussia up the Rhine. The men were very busy during those three weeks, and came out of them tired, but generally improved, after having been about worn out by the Paris climate. Mrs. Holland and Kate are very well indeed; Teddy is slowly improving so far his poor foot is concerned. Annie is getting strength and flesh after her Parisian diptheria, and as for myself, I am getting heavy, without a resort to bad habits. On the whole, we have a good and grateful report to render of ourselves as a family. I thank God for his great goodness to me, and to mine.

You speak of the freedom with which you have unveiled your sorrows to me. Mr. Scribner, my family are nearly all passed away. My father and brother and six brothers and sisters have gone to their rest. The only living brother writes me that he has twice bled at the lungs. He is now fighting for life among the Adirondack Wilds and expects to die. I pray God he may be spared to me and to his dear wife and child. You see, then, how my circle gathers in, and how much I think of the friends who stand next to it. I account you among my very best friends, and indeed I have more of brotherly intercourse with you than with my own brother. So I beg you never to feel that I can possibly feel indifferent to any sorrow of yours, and to believe that I feel honored by being made the recipient of your confidences. Rest assured that you have my sympathy in all your sorrows as well as your satisfactions. I love you. Why should you not trust me and pour out your heart to me?

I gave to my friend Mr. Roswell Smith a letter of introduction to you which I presume he has already presented to you. If so, you have talked up the magazine project in detail. You ask me what I propose in regard to changes, supposing I really engage on the magazine. Well,

First. I propose a change of name. There is something of T. S. Arthur and Jacob Abbott [American authors of numerous moral tales and tracts] in the present title which never did please me. My proposition would be to call it

Scribner's Magazine
of
Home Literature.
Edited
by
J. G. Holland

I think that will make a presentable title page — sufficiently elastic, sufficiently suggestive. I take it that your name and mine stand for Christian literature without any programme or any professions.

Second. I propose to publish no sermons unless they should happen to be remarkable ones, such as one might hear once a year — a sermon that marks an epoch in thought or Christian history — never a sermon for padding.

Third. I propose by personal effort to rally around the magazine the best Christian writers of the country, to do this by making my house a social center, by awaking so far as I am able an interest among the productive minds of the country in myself, by paying a good living price for work, and by so making the magazine the delight of the people and the exponent of the best thinking and creating, as to have every writer feel that he or she is honored by being reckoned among its contributors.

Fourth. I propose to drop all that which may be called distinctively religious teaching. I do not propose to drop the discussion of, or allusion to, religious topics, but such discussion and mention shall be upon broad Christian ground, and as coming within the range — the legitimate range — of literature. Specially this — that no man shall write a poem, or a story, or a review, or a disquisition who does not recognize Jesus Christ as the center and sun of our civilization. In short to make a magazine which shall be as true to evangelical Christianity as the Atlantic has always been to Unitarianism and paganism.

Fifth. To print it better, on better paper. While I would make it more popular in its materials, I would make it more elegant in its externals. I would make it as handsome a magazine as America produces, and by the proper business management win the wide patronage that would make it pay.

As for illustrations, I cannot write about the matter. My present impression is that the expense that you would put in to illustrations would, if put into superior paper and typography, and in working out certain details of current interest, bring as good a return with less trouble. I am not well enough informed in regard to expense to speak upon the math, so that will have to be left to be talked up. If we go into engravings, it will be necessary to go into printing, so that we may do our own work. We cannot job out all the details of such an enterprise. They should all be under one roof. But of that I only hint, that you may consider the math in calculating the chances. I expect to be as much troubled in doing up attractively the political, religious, social and literary intelligence as in any department of the magazine. To have these things done as they can be done, I would sacrifice illustrations and all they would bring us. What we want mainly is <u>to give the public a great deal of good, interesting, entertaining and valuable material for a reasonable sum of money, and to give it in good shape</u>. Without professing or pretending to be distinctively religious, we wish to be recognized as the literary agent and representative of the Evangelical Christians of the United States of all sects whatsoever. That is a great point to be aimed at and gained. That will be done not by advertising but by the most considerate and generous treatment toward clergymen of all denominations and by numbering among our writers representatives of all the sects. The businessman of the concern will have this upon his hands quite as much as the editor who will have quite enough to do to keep the magazine in fodder.

I have been intending to sit down here and write an elaborate article for the magazine on a subject on which I feel a good deal stirred, and about which I have something new to say; but I doubt now whether I shall do it. I am subject to too many interruptions, and exposed to too many temptations to stir about among the mountains. Nevertheless, I mean to do it by and by.

If I am to go into the magazine, aim to do nothing, but make it as good as possible and to bring into it all the patronage possible on the present basis; because when the change comes we want to make it an era in everything connected with the periodical.

Always truly yours,
J. G. Holland

LETTER:
Letter from Roswell Smith to CS I, 15 October 1869.

A successful lawyer and real-estate speculator, Smith had become a good friend of J. G. Holland. The two planned for their families to tour part of Europe together; when they met in Geneva, Switzerland, in the summer of 1869, the two men discussed the Scribner offer and agreed instead to propose to CS I a new magazine venture, with Holland as editor and Smith as publisher and business manager. Smith returned to New York to complete the business arrangements. In this lengthy letter, written from his office in Lafayette, Indiana, and which he has marked Private, Smith relays what he has heard from his good friend, J. G. Holland, who is still in Europe, about the planned Scribner's Monthly.

My Dear Mr Scribner.

I have just written to Doct Holland; this is my first moment of leisure, since I wrote you last, and now will tell you the story I promised. The Poem I sent you was my first Poem. I did not know that I had any talent of that sort. I was forty years of age. When I was in Rome last winter I was much interested in the studios of our American Artists — and especially in the Marble group. The Father & Son (Return of the Prodigal Son) by Mosier — I cannot stop to describe it, or tell you how it affected me. Suffice it to say, I think it the finest work in marble I ever saw: but Mr Mosier spoke of it somewhat sadly. It had cost him nearly $10,000 and two years hard work. He now expected to realize its cost, &c. I felt pity for him — & for all artists with chisel or brush. It seems to me their work <u>costs so</u> much & does so little. I said to myself do I envy these men their great gifts? And my heart answered No! A thousand times, no. And I said with great thankfulness to God, I had rather have my poor gift of language, poor & weak as it is, than their great gifts with brush, or pencil, or chisel. And I resolved to cultivate the talent God had given to me, with greater fidelity, and consecrate its use more fully to his service. Time passed on. I went to Paris. Attended the opera. I had never been to opera, except once at Venice & once at Turin. The Play was Faust. Nillson had the part of Marguerite. N. is young, simple in manners, beautiful in person, and sings like an angel. The whole story is a sad one. Mephistopholes who is only the Devil in the disguise of a man tempts Faust to seduce Marguerite. The seduction scene is terrible — I cannot describe it — and the end disgrace — remorse — a prison &c.

Well, it made a deep impression on my mind — and life in Paris seemed to me faithfully rendered by the Play. One morning, I conceived the idea of putting Mephistopoles teachings into verse — and composed the first verse of the Poem. Got up and wrote it down before breakfast, with some half a dozen others of less merit, which were struck out at a white heat — but hastily. The next day, I took them down to H's parlor & asked if I might read them to him. He said yes. I read. At the end of the first verse he covered his face with both his hands as I looked up and said, go on. When I

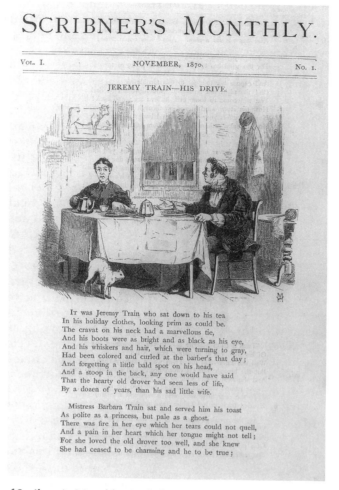

SCRIBNER'S MONTHLY.

Vol. I.   NOVEMBER, 1870.   No. 1.

JEREMY TRAIN—HIS DRIVE.

It was Jeremy Train who sat down to his tea
In his holiday clothes, looking prim as could be.
The cravat on his neck had a marvellous tie,
And his boots were as bright and as black as his eye,
And his whiskers and hair, which were turning to gray,
Had been colored and curled at the barber's that day;
And forgetting a little bald spot on his head,
And a stoop in the back, any one would have said
That the hearty old drover had seen less of life,
By a dozen of years, than his sad little wife.

Mistress Barbara Train sat and served him his toast
As polite as a princess, but pale as a ghost.
There was fire in her eye which her tears could not quell,
And a pain in her heart which her tongue might not tell;
For she loved the old drover too well, and she knew
She had ceased to be charming and he to be true;

First page in the first issue of Scribner's Monthly, *including J. G. Holland's long narrative poem, "Jeremy Train —
His Drive." In the magazine's table of contents, the poem's author is identified as
"an Old Fellow."*

finished with averted face, he held out his hand and said let me have them. He read them over & over again & then he said — Do you know which of these verses is the best. I said I think I do. The first one. He said. Do you know why it is the best? I said, it has had the most work done on it. He replied, I thought so. Do you know how good it is. I said no — that is what I want to know. Well, it is simply perfect. That is all. Now said he, do the best you possibly can, on the whole poem, and let me see it again. I worked upon that Poem a month. It grew to some ten or twelve stanzas. I had undertaken to do the most difficult thing in the world — to put into verse the devils teachings, — not simply impiety, blasphemy, obscenity, infidelity — but all these covered up under a fair disguise, not stated but insinuated — & not simply insinuated, but insinuated with a sneer.

Each alternate verse was addressed to the Young Man — & then to the Maiden. And I attempted to cover a great deal of ground — & to give the Devils Philosophy not only in relation to love, but wealth, wine, knowledge evil &c &c. Of course I failed. And when at last H. put his pencil through all but the four stanzas sent you, and said read these alone — & praised those as making a very effective little Poem by themselves, & gave high praise to the last stanza as he had to the first, I saw that he was right. So far the poem had been written with a pure heart — but when I saw the four stanzas together, I saw the sensuous nature of the whole, as you see it. I had not seen or felt it before. In the play Mephistopoles curses Faust because in the Garden scene he only kissed Marguerite, when he might have seduced her. Faust returns to the Garden & the seduction takes place.

That sentiment I had not rendered at all; but I did then render it into a stanza, which I had better not send you. There were first & last some forty stanzas, of which only four survive. And now you ask me to send you something else equally as good. Well, I can't. I have not got it and probably never could produce it. Certainly it would take a month of hard work & then the vivid first impression on the soul would be wanting. I wrote afterwards a Hymn, but it is not above mediocrity — it cost almost nothing, & is worth just what it cost — no more certainly. And a Ballad. The latter is better. Has sixty stanzas — and I shall read it sometime. I did not read it at the State convention of YMCA as had been suggested because there was no lack of able speakers from abroad.

From all this you will see how intimate have been the relations between H & myself. How many hearty laughs we had over my taking to Poetry after reaching 40 years of age — but we both concluded that Poetry is not my "forte" and that I am to be simply a man of business in the future. Do you remember Artemus Ward's essay on "fortes." Every man has his forte. His Artemus's was so & so. General Washington's forte consisted in not resembling the modern politicians to any remarkable extent.

I hope you have seen my wife, and that you will like her, and that she will like you. She is a very noble woman. I cannot speak too highly in her praise & we are the most ardent of lovers, and the best of friends.

H. has written me a long letter — which he desires me to read to you — but as I cannot do so, I will copy all the material portion of it. He says, "I would have nothing to do with the magazine, unless I should be at liberty to say what I should feel moved to say, on any subject whatever. The Magazine must be an aggressive, free speaking thing with a flavor of vitality about it. I should desire to be perfectly free to discuss the New York Observer, or any other respectable relative of Mrs. Grundy. To preserve the good opinions of the mucker element in religion especially in New York, is to surrender success from the start. To conduct a magazine with the slightest respect to that element is to kill it. I cannot afford to put myself in a position that would bring me into conflict with Mr Scribners feelings & judgments in this matter. I have no sentiments of respect for the New York Grundies in religion, and I could not manifest any. I should expect and intend to offend them. Harper monopolizes the market for harmless & inoffensive literary pap. We have no field

there — but a magazine that would boldly lead in the denunciation of social and political abuses from a Christian standpoint, and from the same stand point discuss all questions relating to partizanship free religion — that would undertake with candor and ability to be a power for good in America, irrespective of the prejudices and opinions of men, would at least stand a chance to live. I am afraid that Mr Scribner does not wish to have his name associated with such a magazine as this, and to trust its conduct to me without the wish to question, or the power to veto. I am afraid he would feel called upon to explain and apologize for me, to those whom I should offend, rather than to defend me & the magazine. As I say, I cannot afford to put myself into these relations with Mr Scribner. We have been like brothers — were more harmonious than most brothers are — and this relation must not be disturbed. I am willing that you should read this over to him, for one cannot afford to have any but plain talk among us" x x x x x x x x x "For myself I wait the development of events. I hope to be in America sometime during the first half of June. You know me well enough to know that I will redeem every pledge I have made to you in regard to the magazine, and abide by every encouraging word I have spoken about it, provided that at that time such fulfillment shall seem desirable to us all."

If I were in New York, I should read H's letter in full. It is a charming letter — written at a white heat, and on receipt of my first letter from N.Y. when I had only just seen you — and before we had progressed a single step in our negotiations. It seems to have been written to cover a point not discussed between us. H. well knew that there would be no conflict of views between us — but he does not seem quite so sure that there may not be between you and himself. I can trust him implicitly as Editor. I know that he is sound in the faith now delivered to the saints — and again I know that he is not such a terrible radical as many think him. Again I have great respect for his prudence & candor and caution. And I have often seen how he studies things that make for peace. At fifty a man is not what he was at thirty — but more conservative. Now the question is can you trust him, thus fully & implicitly. It is not a question now of publishing a book by Doct Holland — but of allowing your name and the value of your house to go to the world as a quasi endorsement of his monthly & daily life and utterances on public questions. It is a question for <u>yourself</u> alone to answer. A personal question. It need not be answered now, or quickly. It may be put off. It is a question between H. & yourself. And I wish it that it had not been presented through me — but still I do not shrink from the duty assigned me of faithfulness to both the old and the <u>new</u> friend. I trust the bond of friendship in either case will endure the strain upon it — and I venture to feel sure that it will.

I am as ever faithfully yours
Roswell Smith

You once spoke to me of the Memorial Church. I wish you could go up there & spend a Sunday, and read its confession of faith, and see its work, and hear how even Doct Ide [George Barton Ide, 1804–1872] once its worst enemy has become its friend. It is not such an iniquity after all, as some regard it. If you do go, may I give you a letter of introduction to Mr Atwater [Lyman H. Atwater, 1813–1883], Doct H's especial friend?

The four stanzas of Smith's poem which Holland thought made an "effective little Poem by themselves" ultimately appeared in Scribner's Monthly *(May 1871) under the title "What the Devil Said to the Young Man":*

O! YOUTH, so brave and strong,
    The maiden's looks belie her;
Though she seem shy, a song —
    A kiss — well, only try her!

Love is the wine of life
    That flows alone for pleasure;
Dull husband and tame wife
    Know not the sparkling measure.

Discovery — that's crime;
    No sin but this, no sorrow;
No punishment in time —
    None in the far to-morow!

Drink off the golden cream
    Of youth, and wealth, and pleasure;
Then spill life's purple stream
    And drop the empty measure!

It was his first and only poetic contribution to the magazine.

LETTER:
Letter from J. G. Holland to CS I, 15 December 1869.

Writing from Stuttgart, Germany, Holland encloses a long narrative poem for CS I to consider as a small book publication. Sideways, at the top of the letter, he instructs: "If you publish be <u>very very very</u> particular about the proof." No such book was published, but Holland's poem appeared under the title "Jeremy Train — His Drive" as the first item in the first number of Scribner's Monthly, *the new magazine he began to edit in November 1870.*

Dear Scribner:
This letter is private strictly. I enclose with it a little poem of 526 lines in regard which I give you this project. It is so unlike my ordinary writing that I wish to try it in a brochure, or rather, a little book, like Whittier's "Snow Bound," Lowell's "Legend of Sir Launfal," "[illegible words]," etc. and <u>anonymously</u>. The lines are long, and will run over, so that it will only take ten lines to make a page. The book with a preface will make about 60 pages, and she will sell, I suppose, for about 75 cents. I should like, if it is practicable, to get about ten (10) cents a copy out of it myself. If the poem is what I think it is — a very interesting and perfect piece of art in its way — and is launched as you and Armstrong and Seymour know how to handle it, it will sell enormously, and will sell all the better if the authorship is kept strictly private among you three, and any mystery about it industriously fostered. I would issue it as early as the middle of January. If it is successful, I will embrace it in the collection to come out next fall. You will see also that it can be illustrated if desirable. There is a man here — a great genius in the way of silhouette pictures who would do it most uniquely. He has illustrated "Midsummer Night's Dream" admirably and is now on the character of Falstaff for an English house. If you would like a duplicate set of plates I can arrange the matter for you. It will be a splendid affair. This however only by the way.
I want you to take the poem home and read it by yourself, first, and before speaking to anybody. Then, if you approve the project, let Armstrong and Seymour into it. If you do not like it, keep it for me, and say nothing about it. <u>I want no living soul in America but you three to know anything of the authorship, under any circumstances</u>. I have felt under the necessity of reading it to two or three ladies here, in order to confirm my own judgment that there is nothing in it that should be offensive to good women. I have tried my best to write it delicately, and to

hold up the character of old Train to the contempt of all, but in order to give his character I was obliged to tread on difficult ground, and ground that is not pleasant to my feet. The whole thing, however, has amused me immensely. If you publish it, I would put the principal edition in paper cover and advertise well. It will pay, I feel very certain, and the time for issue will not be bad.

We are all pretty well and getting impatient about our return to America. We expect to leave here the first of April, and to sail from Liverpool about the fifteenth of May, say about five months from this present writing. Tomorrow, I propose a little run down to Heidelberg where Prof. H. B. Smith and family and Erastus Hopkins and family are spending the winter. I have finished "Laocöon," but I believe I told you that before. I have been very industrious since I came here, and shall be compelled to continue so for the rest of my stay in order to pass away the time. It is a quiet place, and a capital place for writing. I really wish to do something handsome and I shall try very hard to please myself at least.

In regard to the magazine project, I do not propose to write anything more. We are too far apart to handle the matter easily and discreetly. Mr. Smith will probably tell you why I wrote to him as I did, and disturbed you. You and I never had any difficulty in dealing face to face directly, and we are not likely to have.

I suppose I am indebted to you for three numbers of "Hours at Home." It has improved in matter, typographical appearance, paper and proof-reading since I have seen it, and some things that I have written about it to you would not have been written had I known of these improvements. In the meantime I see that the Atlantic does not look as well as formerly. I wonder what the reason can be. I thank you for the magazine for I have none too much reading, and of course had a special interest in the "Hours." That article by George B. Bacon is very clever. Hold on to that man.

To come back for a moment to our friend Jeremy Train. Act in this matter with entire freedom, without the slightest regard to my feelings. You know that I have great confidence in your judgment, discretion and personal friendship. You can regard me as your old father or your son — at least as an affectionate member of your literary family who will do about what you

tell him to do in a matter of this kind, and submit to your wishes without a murmur.
Yours always truly,
J. G. Holland

LETTER:
Letter by J. G. Holland, 1 February 1875, protesting the "new" quarters for Scribner & Co. in space rented by Scribner, Armstrong & Co. at 743 & 745 Broadway.

The Burnett "story" Holland mentions in his letter is That Lass o'Lowrie's, *Burnett's first novel, which was serialized in* Scribner's Monthly *beginning in August 1876. Scribner, Armstrong & Co. published the book version, illustrated by Alfred Fredericks, in April 1877.*

Scribner, Armstrong & Co.
Gentlemen: —
I saw this evening, on my way up town, for the first time, the amount of space allotted to Scribner & Co. for the proposed rent of $500, and was both disgusted and angry. So far as I am personally concerned, I will not consent to occupy any space, on that floor, unless we can have more, and have enough. For myself I prefer decidedly to have all our business done on the third floor. There is where it belongs, and I think it a matter for serious consideration, both with yourselves and us whether the project of having any business of S. & Co. on the ground floor had not better be relinquished. We shall be more peaceable and have a better understanding if we do not mix our business. Certainly if it is not for your interest to give us a fair show it is poor policy for us to be tucked into a corner that you can use for little else.

I write frankly, because it is better to have a fair understanding. The arrangement under the circumstances is simply unjust — not intentionally of course — but unjust in that it ignores the importance of the magazines to your own house and ignores our merits and our rent.

I have written this note because I am to be at the dentists to-morrow and shall not see you.
Yours always truly,
J. G. Holland
P.S. Mr. Smith & I were talking on the way up about Miss Hodgson's story. Don't agree to take it, of course, unless you want it. I carried it to you first, as in friendship's hand, but I would like definitely to arrange with somebody about the illustrations. I can dispose of it without any problem if you prefer not to take it.

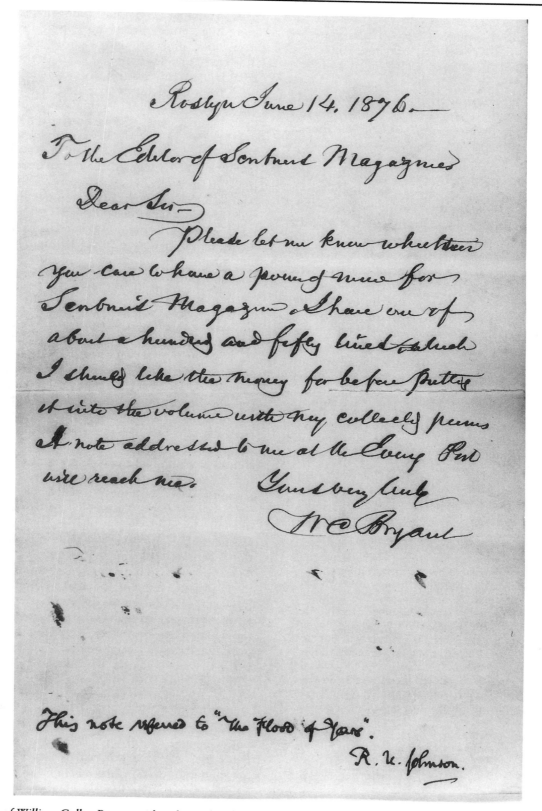

Letter of William Cullen Bryant to the editor of Scribner's Monthly. *His poem, "The Flood of Years," appeared in the August 1876 issue. Robert Underwood Johnson, then an editorial assistant, became editor of the renamed periodical in 1909.*

BOOK EXCERPT:
Harry Houston Peckham, *Gilbert Holland in Relation to His Times* (Philadelphia: University of Pennsylvania Press, 1940), pp. 179-189.

Peckham credits innovations in engraving techniques, new advertising policies, controversial subject matter, and an overall discerning editorial taste for the success of Scribner's Monthly.

The first issues of *Scribner's Monthly* made a widely favorable impression — so widely favorable, we may be sure, as to bring *Harper's* to a speedy realization of the fact that at last it had a real rival in the illustrated magazine field. And it soon became apparent that as rapidly as possible the new monthly intended to introduce attractive innovations.

As a starter, *Scribner's Monthly* was inheriting two small subscription lists: that of the already-mentioned *Hours at Home*, and that of *Putnam's Monthly Magazine*, which, for not quite three years, had struggled along in a none-too-successful effort to revive an earlier *Putnam's*. In this connection, a perusal of Holland's opening editorial makes it clear that Holland and Smith expected to build their subscription list largely upon the wide personal following that Holland had gained as author and as lyceum lecturer. Said the editorial in part:

It is an exceedingly pleasant reflection to the editor that he and those for whom he prepares this magazine are not strangers. In books, newspapers, periodicals, and public addresses, he and they have met many times during the last twenty years. In that period he has experienced much of their kindness, and they have had abundant opportunity to become acquainted with him. To their generous confidence he appeals in presenting to them this new enterprise. He asks them to believe that it is his purpose to obtain for them the best reading that money will buy, to furnish the finest illustrations procurable at home and abroad, and to make a magazine that they will all desire to possess, and will feel the richer for possessing....We shall try to make a magazine that is intelligent on all living questions of morals and society, and to present something in every number that will interest and instruct every member of every family into which it shall have the good fortune to find its way.

The first volume of *Scribner's Monthly* contained parts of lengthy illustrated serials by Hans Christian Andersen and George Macdonald respectively; a three-installment novelette by Rebecca Harding Davis; half a dozen short stories, including "Huldah the Help," by Edward Eggleston; and more than a score of poems. Its illustrated articles included "Life in the Cannibal Islands," a richly informative essay on New Zealand, by J. C. Bates; "Fairmount Park," an interesting account of Philadelphia's huge playground, by Newton Crane; "Strassburg after the Surrender," a timely Franco-Prussian war article, by M. B. Riddle; and "King Gambrinus and His Subjects," a diatribe against Bavarian beer-drinking, by William Wells. This last-named article, which bears all the earmarks of having been solicited if not directly inspired by Editor Holland, comes much nearer to being downright propaganda than any other contribution to the volume. In this article, both the text and the grotesque illustrations undertake to show that beer is inherently and necessarily a most demoralizing beverage. . . .

At the very beginning, *Scribner's Monthly* followed the old American magazine custom of withholding the names of individual contributors. In the earliest issues, for example, the only *Scribner's* authors whose names were attached to their work were such foreign celebrities as Andersen and Macdonald. Not until the appearance of the first table of contents for the entire first volume, in April 1871, were the names of most of the contributors revealed. Apropos of this fact, it should be remarked that the practice of withholding magazine authors' names was one of long standing. In 1859 James Russell Lowell, then editor of the *Atlantic Monthly,* had expressed definite opposition to the publishing of names. And, as one literary historian has truly remarked, up to the seventies the majority of magazine articles were as strictly anonymous as were the majority of newspaper articles. Both Holland and Smith, however, felt that magazine authors were as fully entitled to public recognition as were book authors. They felt, moreover, that the publication of prominent names would be of distinct commercial value to the magazine. Consequently, it was not long until the names of leading *Scribner's* contributors, particularly the writers of serials, were attached regularly to their contributions. That other magazines soon recognized the wisdom of this new policy may be seen from an examination of old *Atlantic* files. *Harper's* was somewhat slower in coming round, but in due time it also followed suit.

Another attractive new feature inaugurated by *Scribner's Monthly* was the improved process of engraving. Illustrations in the old *Harper's,* the old *Putnam's,* and other ante-bellum magazines look rather crude to us, and this crudeness is largely due to clumsy, primitive methods of transferring artists' drawings to engravers' blocks. Prior to the seventies the only known way to make woodcuts was the very slow, laborious backhand copying of the original pictures upon the wooden surfaces. But Alexander Wilson Drake, art editor of the new *Scribner's Monthly,* was mainly instrumental in changing all this. Drake, an enterprising and talented young New Yorker with valuable experience both as a painter and as a wood engraver, quickly recognized the success of experiments in transferring pictures from paper to wood by the photographic process. He saw, as other engravers came to see a little later, that both in speed and in accuracy the photographic process was immeasurably superior to the awkward backhand method of drawing line for line. The result was that *Scribner's Monthly* immediately surpassed all of its competitors in the matter of attractive illustrations. The further result was that British authorities were soon admitting that the best contemporary illustrations were being printed in America, not Europe. Beginning in 1875, Drake had a most able assistant in the person of Timothy Cole, who ultimately surpassed Drake himself as a wood engraver. Cole's beautiful reproductions of famous paintings, which accompanied the late W. C. Brownell's articles on art, made *Scribner's Monthly* easily the most artistic general magazine of the day. Incidentally, another very important contributor to the esthetic excellence of the old *Scribner's* was Theodore Low De Vinne, internationally famous exponent of artistic painting, from whose press issued all but the first volumes of the Holland-Smith magazine.

Another *Scribner's* innovation, probably instituted by Smith, but certainly approved by Holland, was the acceptance of advertising upon a large scale. William W. Ellsworth is not quite accurate in his statement that "up to the beginning of that periodical [*Scribner's Monthly*] magazines did not print advertising at all"; for, as a matter of fact, *Harper's* printed miscellaneous advertising as early as 1864, and the *Atlantic* as early as 1860. Mr. Ellsworth is, however, quite correct in his implication that *Scribner's Monthly* was the first high-grade magazine to solicit advertising — the first high-grade magazine to consider extensive advertising entirely compatible with the tone and dignity of a superior periodical. From the very start, *Harper's* had advertised Harper books; but its miscellaneous advertisements had never exceeded fifteen or twenty to the issue, and all of these had been small and inconspicuous. In fact, at about the time *Scribner's Monthly* was founded, *Harper's* had actually rejected a proposition to advertise the Howe Sewing Machine on its back cover for one year for $18,000. Moreover, as Roswell Smith recognized, *Harper's* advertising rates were so steep as to discourage rather than invite advertisers. *Harper's* charged $500 a page for an ordinary page of each issue; $1,000 a page for space next to reading matter; and $1,000 a page for space on the cover. *Scribner's Monthly* decided to charge $100 a page for an ordinary page; $200 a page for space next to reading matter; and $150 a page for space on the cover. It is, therefore, not to be wondered that the Holland-Smith firm were soon getting all of the advertisements that they could find space to print. Today, as we all know, the price of a good magazine is invariably much lower than cost of publication; and the only commercial value of a large circulation lies in increased value of advertising space. *Scribner's Monthly,* however, was the first magazine really to appreciate this obvious fact.

Closely related to the problem of magazine advertising is the problem of magazine distribution. Up to the time when *Scribner's Monthly* was established, the method of paying magazine postage was one that we should consider indeed peculiar. All postage was paid quarterly at the post-office by the subscriber. Roswell Smith concluded that this was a ridiculous system — a system that tended to drive people away from taking magazines. Why, he asked, should not the publishers pay the postage? The postage bill would be relatively small; and, anyhow, the prepayment of postage would probably result in a noticeably larger subscription list. True, no subscriber ever paid more than fifteen or twenty cents postage a quarter, but these payments were manifestly a nuisance. Holland and Scribner were interested in Smith's suggestion, but they wondered about the feasibility of attaching stamps to thousands of magazines each month. Well, why bother with stamps at all? Why not arrange with the postal authorities to make wholesale payments of magazine postage? To us of today, these questions of Smith's are all so very simple that we wonder how it could ever have been necessary for anyone to ask them. Thanks to Roswell Smith, American magazines were soon being distributed in a new manner — a manner that won the good will of subscribers everywhere.

A Scribner's Monthly *advertising circular for*
August 1878

It takes more, however, than generous advertising and postal prepayment to make a magazine popular. It takes more, even, than attractive illustrations and beautiful printing. And here we come to the big part played by Editor J. G. Holland in the success of *Scribner's Monthly.* *Scribner's,* from the day of its first appearance, bore the subtitle *An Illustrated Magazine for the People.* It was just that — in the best sense of the word. Of course it made no particular appeal to "the people" in the Jacksonian sense; that is, to the illiterate or the vulgar. It did, however, win a much wider clientele than any first-class magazine had ever won before. *Harper's* and the *Atlantic* and the *North American* had gone regularly into the homes of the leading professional men in communities large and small throughout the country. *Scribner's Monthly* reached the families of the more substantial business men as well.

A particularly good reason for the old *Scribner's* winning of this wider clientele lay in the fact that the Holland-Smith magazine was not afraid to tackle controversial subjects, especially those pertaining to politics and religion. Up to 1870, American magazines of general appeal had cautiously avoided such subjects on the ground that whatever interest they might arouse, they would likewise kindle such resentment as to alienate more readers than they could hope to gain. Editor Holland, however, stoutly insisted upon bringing these debatable topics out into the open; he was firm in the conviction that since "the two subjects in which people of this country are most interested are politics and religion," those subjects ought to be discussed most freely, not tabooed. As a result, *Scribner's Monthly* "took a conspicuous stand in the advocacy not merely of civil-service reform and religious liberalism, but of international copyright, kindergarten instruction, tenement-house improvement, and other causes." And thereby, thanks to Josiah Holland's courage and sagacity, this forward-looking magazine "not only lived and prospered . . . but gained enduring distinction."

Turning to more purely literary materials, we find that under J. G. Holland's astute editorship *Scribner's Monthly* published such interesting and memorable fiction as Henry James's *Adina,* William Dean Howells' *A Fearful Responsibility,* Bret Harte's *Gabriel Conroy,* Rebecca Harding Davis' *Natasqua,* George Macdonald's *Wilfrid Cumbermede,* Frances Hodgson Burnett's *Louisiana,* George W. Cable's *The Grandissimes,* and Mrs. Oliphant's *At His Gates,* as well as the Holland novels we considered in our last chapter. Most of the author's names just mentioned are almost as familiar today — at least to the student of literature — as they were threescore years ago. George Macdonald is, perhaps, nearly forgotten; but up to the time of his death at an advanced age in 1905 he remained one of the conspicuously popular British novelists. Macdonald was a Scotch Calvinistic minister, and, as might be supposed, he wrote novels that were as ethical and evangelical in tone as the novels of Holland himself. Cable and "Fanny" Burnett were real *Scribner's* discoveries. In the seventies, both of them were youngsters, and it was through the columns of *Scribner's Monthly* that both of them first attracted nation-wide attention. Among the notable poets whose work appeared in the old *Scribner's* were Richard Watson Gilder, Edmund Clarence Stedman, and Richard Henry Stoddard. It will thus be observed that Josiah Gilbert Holland had rather good editorial taste. . . .

It should, however, be pointed out that Holland had a most able assistant in the person of Richard Watson Gilder. Gilder, although a much younger and less experienced man than Holland, was possessed of a finer discrimination and decidedly more catholic and cosmopolitan outlook. Undoubtedly it was Gilder rather than Holland who first appreciated the talents of that promising young Southerner, George W. Cable. Undoubtedly, too, Gilder's monthly department *The Old Cabinet* is of far more enduring literary value than Holland's *Topics of the Time*.

But Holland's editorial influence must not be minimized. It was Holland more than anyone else who made *Scribner's Monthly* a distinct public educational force. It was at Holland's suggestion that the Southern people were ingratiated and the Northern people enlightened by a series of illustrated articles on the New South — articles from the pen of Edward King. The King articles, by the way, were published in book form in 1875, under the title *The Great South,* and enjoyed a wide sale. The timeliness of these articles may be seen from the fact that not until the inauguration of President Hayes in 1877 did a post-bellum chief executive adopt a sane and at the same time conciliatory attitude toward the South. It was, moreover, Holland who, partly through his own *Topics of the Time* and partly through articles by the Reverend William Cleaver Wilkinson and the Reverend Augustus Blauvelt, first popularized the merits of biblical higher criticism. And this, in the United States of the seventies, was a courageous thing to undertake.

To Editor Holland, I think, even more than to Publisher Smith, we must credit the phenomenal success of *Scribner's Monthly* during the eleven years of its existence. In that period of a trifle over a decade, the old *Scribner's* more than tripled its original circulation of forty thousand; and in the United States of the seventies, with its relatively small, relatively unenlightened population, that was indeed a wonderful feat for a high-toned magazine.

Scribner's Monthly
A Selected List of Author Appearances

Akers, Elizabeth (1832–1911) "Florence Percy"
Andersen, Hans Christian (1805–1875)
Atwater, Lyman H. (1813–1883)
Barnard, Charles (1838–1920) — conducted column "The World's Work" (1875–1884)
Bates, Charlotte Fiske (1838–1916)
Boyesen, Hjalmar Hjorth (1848–1898)
Bradley, Mary E. (1835–1898)
Brooks, Noah (1830–1903)
Brownell, W. C. (1851–1928)
Bryant, William Cullen (1794–1878)
Burroughs, John (1837–1921)
Burnett, Frances Hodgson (1849–1924)
Cable, George Washington (1844–1925)
Cook, Clarence (1828–1900)
Davis, Rebecca Harding (1831–1910)
De Vinne, Theodore Low (1828–1914)
Dodge, Mary Mapes (1830–1905)
Dorr, Julia C. R. (1825–1913)
Duffield, Samuel Willoughby (1843–1887)
Eggleston, Edward (1837–1902)
Foote, Mary Hallock (1847–1938)
Froude, James Anthony (1818–1894)
Hale, Edward Everett (1822–1909)
Harte, Bret (1839–1902)
Hay, John (1838–1905)
Headley, J. T. (1813–1897)
Herrick, Sophie Bledsoe (1837–1919) — joined editorial staff in 1879
Higginson, Thomas Wentworth (1823–1911)
Holland, J. G. (1819–1881)
Howells, William Dean (1837–1920)
Jackson, Helen Hunt (1830–1885) "H.H" and "Saxe Holm"
James, Henry (1843–1916)
Kimball, Harriet McEwen (1834–1917)
King, Edward (1848–1896)
Kinney, Elizabeth C. (1810–1889)
Lathrop, George Parsons (1851–1898)
Lossing, Benson J. (1813–1891)
MacDonald, George (1824–1905)
Matthews, Brander (1852–1929)
McClellan, George Brinton (1826–1885)
Miller, Joaquin (1839–1913)
Moulton, Louise Chandler (1835–1908)
Oliphant, Mrs. (1828–1897)
Osgood, Kate Putnam (1841–c. 1912)
Powell, John Wesley (1834–1902)
Rideing, William H. (1853–1918)
Roe, E. P. (1838–1888)
Rossetti, Christina (1830–1894)
Saxe, John G. (1816–1887)
Schuyler, Eugene (1840–1890)
Spofford, Harriet Prescott (1835–1921)
Stedman, Edmund Clarence (1833–1908)
Stockton, Frank R. (1834–1902)

Volumes I – XXI: November 1870 – April 1881

Scribner's Magazine (1887–1939)

ARTICLE:

Frederick Lewis Allen, "Fifty Years of Scribner's Magazine," *Scribner's Magazine*, 101 (January 1937): 19-24.

Allen's article discusses Scribner's Magazine *in the broader context of journalism and its changes brought about by the demands of the educated classes that were/are its audience. He argues that the magazine — in contents and format — is a reflection of the course of American literature and the changing manners and customs and modes of thought of our time.* Scribner's Magazine *ceased publication in 1939.*

A fiftieth birthday is a solemn occasion: not quite so solemn for a magazine as for a man or a woman, since magazines can be rejuvenated, yet impressive nonetheless. There is something awesome about a half-century. This is the fiftieth birthday of SCRIBNER'S MAGAZINE, and it warrants both a feast of congratulation and also, perhaps, a moment or two of reflection — reflection on what the passage of time has done to this particular institution, to periodical journalism in general, and to the world about us.

At the outset I must pause for a word of historic explanation, lest people with long memories rush to tell me that SCRIBNER'S is certainly more than half a century old and I must have got my dates mixed. There was an earlier *Scribner's* — an elder sister, as it were, who married and moved away and changed her name. As far back as 1870 a Middle-Westerner named Roswell Smith, who had made money in real estate, went on a trip to Europe with Doctor J. G. Holland, a writer of estimable if puritanically pious books. Standing one day on a bridge in Geneva, the two men decided to start a magazine. They returned to New York, interested Charles Scribner, the book publisher and bookseller, and joined with him in launching *Scribner's Monthly*. The publisher fell in with their plans the more eagerly because he had already been publishing a small "family magazine" called *Hours at Home*.

Roswell Smith was a man of energy and imagination, of whom it used to be said that he would come to the office each morning with three new ideas; it would take his associates till eleven o'clock to persuade him that two of them were no good, and the rest of the day to carry out the third. *Scribner's Monthly*, under his guidance, was the first magazine to make a business of soliciting advertising. Other magazine publishers had considered such practice undignified. Smith also employed women clerks in the magazine office — a decided innovation in the seventies, when most families would as soon have cast their daughters into a den of wolves as into a business office. (Incidentally, Roswell Smith's wife had had a memorable part in introducing another innovation. It was she who, as a young girl in 1844, had sent the first message over Professor Morse's telegraph machine: "What hath God wrought?") Doctor Holland was an able editor, if perhaps over-anxious to elevate the moral tone of the community; he enlisted genuine talent, and the magazine prospered, even in the seventies, a dark period for American culture.

But after a while Roswell Smith, who had meanwhile begun book publishing on his own, and had established *St. Nicholas* as a children's magazine, decided that the time had come to set up his own establishment. Charles Scribner the elder had died; and in 1881 Roswell Smith purchased from the Scribner Sons their stock in *Scribner's Monthly*, changed its name to the *Century*, and organized the Century Company. As the *Century* the magazine continued a long and illustrious career.

It had been agreed that to give subscribers a chance to accustom themselves to the new name, the Scribner firm would not publish any competing periodical for five years. The end of that time found Charles Scribner the younger busy with plans for an illustrated magazine of the general nature of the *Century* and *Harper's*. In an office above the Scribner bookstore, up a flight of stairs from Broadway (near Astor

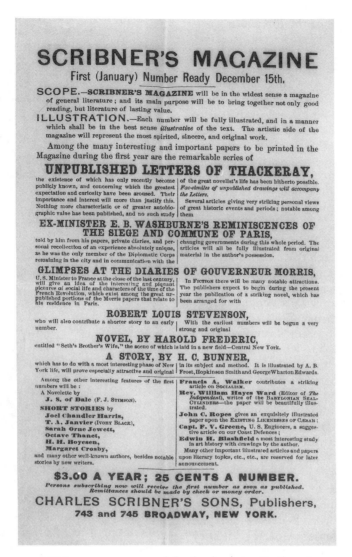

SCRIBNER'S MAGAZINE

First (January) Number Ready December 15th.

SCOPE.—SCRIBNER'S MAGAZINE will be in the widest sense a magazine of general literature; and its main purpose will be to bring together not only good reading, but literature of lasting value.

ILLUSTRATION.—Each number will be fully illustrated, and in a manner which shall be in the best sense *illustrative* of the text. The artistic side of the magazine will represent the most spirited, sincere, and original work.

Among the many interesting and important papers to be printed in the Magazine during the first year are the remarkable series of

UNPUBLISHED LETTERS OF THACKERAY,

the existence of which has only recently become publicly known, and concerning which the greatest expectation and curiosity have been aroused. Their importance and interest will more than justify this. Nothing more characteristic or of greater autobiographic value has been published, and no such study | of the great novelist's life has been hitherto possible. *Fac-similes of unpublished drawings will accompany the Letters.*

Several articles giving very striking personal views of great historic events and periods; notable among them

EX-MINISTER E. B. WASHBURNE'S REMINISCENCES OF THE SIEGE AND COMMUNE OF PARIS,

told by him from his papers, private diaries, and personal recollection of an experience absolutely unique, as he was the only member of the Diplomatic Corps remaining in the city and in communication with the | changing governments during this whole period. The articles will all be fully illustrated from original material in the author's possession.

GLIMPSES AT THE DIARIES OF GOUVERNEUR MORRIS,

U. S. Minister to France at the close of the last century, will give an idea of the interesting and piquant pictures of social life and characters of the time of the French Revolution, which exist among the great unpublished portions of the Morris papers that relate to his residence in Paris. | In FICTION there will be many notable attractions. The publishers expect to begin during the present year the publication of a striking novel, which has been arranged for with

ROBERT LOUIS STEVENSON,

who will also contribute a shorter story to an early number. | With the earliest numbers will be begun a very strong and original

NOVEL, BY HAROLD FREDERIC,

entitled "Seth's Brother's Wife," the scene of which is laid in a new field—Central New York.

A STORY, BY H. C. BUNNER,

which has to do with a most interesting phase of New York life, will prove especially attractive and original | in its subject and method. It is illustrated by A. B. Frost, Hopkinson Smith and George Wharton Edwards.

Among the other interesting features of the first numbers will be:
A Novelette by
J. S. of Dale (F. J. STIMSON).
SHORT STORIES by
Joel Chandler Harris,
T. A. Janvier (IVORY BLACK),
Sarah Orne Jewett,
Octave Thanet,
H. H. Boyesen,
Margaret Crosby,
and many other well-known authors, besides notable stories by new writers. | **Francis A. Walker** contributes a striking article on SOCIALISM.
Rev. William Hayes Ward (Editor of *The Independent*), writes of the BABYLONIAN SEAL-CYLINDERS—the paper will be beautifully illustrated.
John C. Ropes gives an exquisitely illustrated paper upon the EXISTING LIKENESSES OF CÆSAR;
Capt. F. V. Greene, U. S. Engineers, a suggestive article on our Coast Defences;
Edwin H. Blashfield a most interesting study in art history with drawings by the author.
Many other important illustrated articles and papers upon literary topics, etc., etc., are reserved for later announcement.

$3.00 A YEAR; 25 CENTS A NUMBER.

Persons subscribing now will receive the first number as soon as published.
Remittances should be made by check or money order.

CHARLES SCRIBNER'S SONS, Publishers,
743 and 745 BROADWAY, NEW YORK.

1886 announcement of the forthcoming Scribner's
Magazine

Place), E. L. Burlingame of the Scribner book editorial department was established as editor of SCRIBNER'S MAGAZINE, Josiah Millet as art director; and presently the first issue appeared, the issue for January, 1887.

Fifty years ago this month. Grover Cleveland was president of the United States — and at the moment was concerned with a problem which no longer distresses our Federal officials: the problem of an obstinate and embarrassing surplus in the annual accounts of the Treasury! It was a time of furious and undisciplined expansion: the West was still being opened up (indeed, the Indians had not yet been entirely subdued); Hill, Huntington, and the notorious Jay Gould were ruling over their railroad empires; the four big packers in Chicago were making fortunes out of their effective control of the meat market; a lean Clevelander named John D. Rockefeller had devised the Standard Oil Trust — a secret alliance of ostensibly rival companies — with such ingenious legal aid from the astute Samuel Dodd that the Trust was closing the year 1886 with a profit of fifteen million dollars; other magnates by the dozens were adopting the new and remunerative formula, and new trusts were being born every month and gobbling up American opportunity.

Meanwhile the public was becoming restive at the exploits of the business barons: the Interstate Commerce Act (a feeble thing, but at least a gesture toward regulation) was about to pass Congress, and the passage of the Sherman Anti-Trust Act was not far off. Labor was restive, too. The Knights of Labor (led by a "grand Master Workman" with the resounding name of Terrence V. Powderly) were over 700,000 strong; the United Mine Workers had just been organized; the echoes of the Haymarket bomb explosion in Chicago still stirred the air; and in New York City Henry George, the single-taxer, with a huge labor vote behind him, had barely been beaten for Mayor by Abram S. Hewitt in a three-cornered campaign in which the third corner was occupied by a youth named Theodore Roosevelt.

Van Wyck Brooks, in *The Ordeal of Mark Twain,* has crowded three of the chief qualities of those years into a single phrase: "the puritanical commercialism of the Gilded Age." Puritanical and evangelistic it was with a vengeance, as well as commercial: Anthony Comstock's vice crusades and Moody and Sankey's revivals were as characteristic of it as Rockefeller's or Carnegie's or Gould's ruthless acquisition. And the age was gilded, too: new-made millionaires were descending upon New York in droves, buying brownstone houses, engaging English butlers, hoping to marry their daughters to European peers, and penetrating, one by one, the walls of Mrs. Astor's and Ward McAllister's fortress, New York society.

Meanwhile the tide of immigration was pouring past the brand-new Statue of Liberty, which, in Cleveland's words, kept "watch and ward before the open gates of America." (They are closed now, those gates, as is the frontier.) . . . Above Fifty-ninth Street in New York there were great stretches of rocky land, unoccupied save by squatters in their huts. . . . There was no subway, and the elevated trains ran by steam. . . . Travelers from the hinterland gaped at the newest wonder of the world, the Brooklyn Bridge. . . . At Hartford and Springfield, cyclists raced perilously on high-wheeled bicycles. . . . Robert Bonner of Tarrytown was driving Maud S. to new trotting records. . . . John L. Sullivan, the strong boy of Boston, was champion of the ring. . . . Edwin Booth was still seen on the stage, and William Gillette had just appeared in *Held by the Enemy.* . . . There wasn't a golf course in America; lawn tennis, however, was popular at Newport and Saratoga and Long Branch. . . . In hundreds of thousands of high-ceilinged front parlors, gas chandeliers shed their light upon silk-draped marble

Cover designed by Stanford White for the first issue of Scribner's Magazine

mantelpieces, marble-topped tables which supported plush bound photograph albums, betassled plush curtains of prodigious weight, carpets patterned with huge roses; upon whiskered gentlemen encased in somber frock coats, and ladies sitting stiffly upright because they were so corseted and bustled that in perpendicularity alone could they find comfort.

II

Pick up the first issue of SCRIBNER's — Volume I, No. 1, January, 1887. The first thing that strikes your mind, after you have accustomed yourself to the small compact type and the wood-engraved illustrations, will probably be the fact that the subject-matter of the magazine was not primarily devoted to affairs of every-day life.

Two articles of timely import there are: one by a captain of engineers on "Our Defenceless Coasts," with a precise account of the inadequate fortifications of New York; and another on the trend toward socialism, which even then disturbed conservative citizens. But the leading article of the first issue is an account of European events of seventeen years before — "Reminiscences of the Siege and Commune of Paris," by ex-Minister E. B. Washburne; and one is also offered "Glimpses at the Diaries of Gouverneur Morris" (in eighteenth-century Paris) and a sober treatise on "The Babylonian Seals." Turn to the second issue, and you will find that the leading article is a paper by John C. Ropes on "The Likenesses of Julius Caesar" — a comparison of the portraits of Caesar in statues and on coins. There are also articles on the Navy, the rising interest in Russian novels, and the French actor, M. Coquelin. But there are no discussions of President Cleveland's policies, railroad regulation, the new typewriter and telephone, the advent of stenographers, or cowboy life on the plains . . . types of subjects that were to be published later on. Some of the articles in these issues are timely only in a broad sense.

We are struck, too, by the all-enveloping propriety of the early pages. The canons of decorum were strict in those days, readers were virtuously censorious, and any editor who transgressed in the slightest degree risked a flood of venomous letters. One letter in particular is remembered still in the SCRIBNER offices. When, in the nineties, the magazine illustrated an article on French art with a reproduction of a nude, a banker in upper New York State protested that at the sight of the picture a young female member of his household had "uttered a low cry and fled from the room." From that time on, illustrations which might be considered unduly revealing by a puritanical audience were referred to in the SCRIBNER office as "low-cry" pictures.

But we are also impressed by the dignity and graciousness of those early issues of SCRIBNER'S. Burlingame, the editor, son of that Anson Burlingame who had represented both the United States and China in the courts of the world (and father, incidentally, of Roger Burlingame, who wrote one of the best novels of 1936, *Three Bags Full*) was a gentleman of wide erudition and of zeal for excellence. The cover of the new magazine was designed by Stanford White. The contributors included men and women of high ability, not only in letters but in those other fields which a journal addressed to the educated public would cultivate. In the first year of its life, SCRIBNER'S brought out work by Robert Louis Stevenson (then living at Saranac), by Sarah Orne Jewett, Thomas Nelson Page, H. C. Bunner, Andrew Lang, Austin Dobson, Harold Frederic; a series of unpublished Thackeray

Edward L. Burlingame (1848–1922), first editor (1886–1914) of Scribner's Magazine

letters; an article on psychology by William James; and one on geology by N. S. Shaler. Bret Harte and Henry James were presently to join the growing list of contributors. The magazine had a solidity and fineness of content, an untroubled grace of presentation.

Indeed, as we turn over those yellowing pages we become aware that the remoteness from the contemporary American scene which first caught our attention was not the product of a distaste for the immediate reality. It represented a valid ideal: the ideal of the educated man, the philosopher, who is at home not merely in his own land and his own age, but in all lands and ages; from whose point of perspective the Babylonian seal-workers are as interesting as the Pittsburgh steelworkers; who lives not merely in the world of food and drink and shelter and business and politics and everyday commonplace, but in the timeless world of ideas.

III

To compare the best magazines of the eighties with those of the thirties is to realize anew how much water has gone under the bridge in half a century. I am not thinking chiefly of those obvious changes in our environment which all of us can parrot without a second thought: the new inventions and comforts, the increase in speed, the shrinking of the world with rapid transportation

Robert Bridges (1858–1941), assistant editor (1887–1914) and editor (1914–1930) of Scribner's Magazine

and communication: automobiles, six-lane concrete highways, four-day transatlantic liners, airplanes, sky-scrapers, the movies, the radio, and so on. Nor am I thinking particularly of the waning of puritanism, the weakening power of formal religion, the greater freedom in dress and in social intercourse: of the Sunday golf match, the unchaperoned party, the one-piece bathing suit, the bold speech of the girl taking her Martinis at the bar. I am thinking of differences a little less obvious and perhaps as fundamental.

First, the vastly altered economic system in which we live: the coming of the giant impersonal corporations, with their thousands of employees and hundreds of thousands of stockholders; the immensely increased complexity and instability of our machinery for credit and speculation.

Second, the steady growth, in size and power, of our governmental units, and their long struggle — one set of titans against another — to keep the unruly activities of business in check.

Third, the rise of the United States (dramatized in the Spanish War and World War) from a subordinate to a commanding position in world affairs.

Fourth, the increasing interdependence, economic and political, not only of towns and states, but of nations — so that our individual personal fortunes today depend much less upon our own unaided industry than they used to, and much more upon conditions and events far beyond our individual control: upon drought in Kansas, speculators in Wall Street, bureaucrats in Washington, Hitler in Germany, Stalin in Russia. To a far greater extent than in 1887, the civilized world is now a single organism.

These changes have had mighty effects upon the intellectual climate in which journalists and publishers operate. The rise of America to world power has been accompanied by a new national self-awareness. We are less deferential now toward Europe, less colonially uncertain of our own culture, our own arts and letters. We no longer assume that it is permissible for Europeans to write about nakedness and adultery but that it would be improper for one of our own writers to do so — as if our own were promising schoolboys. (Thomas Beer reminds us that in the nineties the editors and the reading public would permit Kipling a license in writing which they would not tolerate in an American. Certain magazines would publish Arthur Morrison's realistic stories of slum life in London, but not Stephen Crane's realistic stories of slum life in New York.) Nor do we any longer look forward to the future appearance of "the great American novel"; we take it for granted that a great novel may appear any day, and why not in Chicago as well as in London or Paris? We are no longer modestly unwilling to regard American life as worthy of the respectful interest of cultivated minds; indeed, some of the intellectuals of the nineteen-thirties are almost too single-heartedly excited about American conditions, problems, morals, and ideas.

So conscious are we, furthermore, of our economic interdependence, that we instinctively regard our economic problems as matters for collective action and therefore for constant public debate. Note this contrast: in the years 1893 and 1894, during the depression of the nineties, SCRIBNER'S printed two timely articles on economic and political conditions; in the year 1932 it printed no less than twenty.

And is there not a striking difference today in our attitude toward international affairs? Not only are we conscious of the interdependence of Montana and Austria, Massachusetts and Japan;

the World War has left with all of us an ominous sense that a match dropped anywhere may ignite the world. At the turn of the century the Boer War was a matter of intellectual excitement to the educated public, and some people even took sides emotionally (somewhat as one would for a Schmeling-Louis fight); but they did not feel that at any moment they might find themselves personally involved. The battle was far away; other people were waging it. Nowadays when we read about Ethiopia or the Spanish civil war, there is always in the back of our minds the thought that we too may be sucked in.

Is it any wonder, then, that there should be today, in the minds of thoughtful men and women, such a sense of crisis that an objective, impersonal journalism like that of the eighties could no longer satisfy us? Perhaps we should like to be able to preserve an Olympian calm, to feel as deeply about the likenesses of Caesar as about the policies of Hitler. But we cannot do so, nor will we let our journalists do so. For we feel that we are searching for a way past chaos, and that we must have their help.

IV

I have been speaking, of course, of the attitude of the educated classes, for whom SCRIBNER'S (along with *Harper's* and the *Atlantic*, and other magazines of what has been called the quality group) was and is edited. And at once I must take note of a concurrent change in the world of journalism itself.

When Burlingame began his editorship in 1887, the quality magazines stood almost alone in the field of monthly journalism. Men and women who were incapable of understanding or caring about the things of the mind either tried to read the quality magazines or went without. But in the nineties there was a revolution: Munsey and McClure invented a new kind of magazine, cheaper, easier, and more familiar. The next twenty years showed the extraordinary possibilities of mass circulation and national advertising (best exemplified in the rise of the Curtis and Hearst magazine groups). There came also the mammoth Sunday paper, the movies, and the radio.

The old intellectual aristocrats of journalism were almost lost among the new democrats. With less money to spend than their young rivals, with circulations measured in scores of thousands instead of in millions, they faced a danger of extinction: not because public taste had deteriorated but

because the new agencies of mass entertainment were so ubiquitous and so persuasive.

Some of the old aristocrats succumbed. Those which did not, survived only by virtue of sheer excellence: by virtue of imaginative editing, a keen eye for quality, and an ability to follow the changing trend of the times. SCRIBNER'S in particular not only survived but maintained its high reputation because Burlingame, and Robert Bridges after Burlingame's retirement, and Alfred Dashiell after Bridge's retirement, were editors who sought distinction, backed by a publishing house which believed in distinction.

I can suggest no more fascinating occupation to anybody who is interested in the course of American literature and in the changing manners and customs and modes of thought of our time than to pull down, one after another, the bound volumes of SCRIBNER'S and to trace the magazine's development: the change in the temper of the fiction from the days of Stevenson and Bunner to the days of Hemingway and Faulkner and Wolfe; the gradually increasing attention paid to social and economic conditions; the trend toward timeliness — gradual before the war, more rapid after it; the changes in illustration and format were brought about by the coming of the half-tone, by the coming of reproduction in full color, by the rise of engraving costs after the war (which forbade lavish illustration), and by the changing exigencies of advertising (which prompted the enlargement of the size of the magazine in 1932). The only difficulty about making such an investigation is that you will find yourself constantly lingering by the wayside — the issues of the magazine are so temptingly readable.

To follow the procession of bound volumes is to be fascinated by the encyclopedic variety of the articles — accounts of travel all over the globe; reports on scientific progress; discussions of everything from French painting to department-store management, from women's rights to skyscraper design, from English usage to municipal reform. There is variety in the SCRIBNER memoirs, too; the autobiographers range from General Sheridan and Henry M. Stanley to Michael Pupin, who landed from Serbia as an immigrant boy with five cents in his pocket, and became one of the chief American inventors. Again and again, in those volumes, you come upon some memorable book appearing modestly in serial form: George Meredith's *The Amazing Marriage*, for example, or Barrie's *Sentimental Tommy,* or

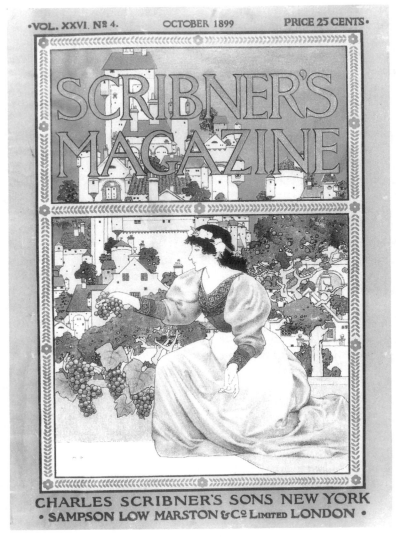

Cover of the October 1899 issue of Scribner's Magazine, *designed by Maxfield Parrish*

Thomas Nelson Page's *Red Rock,* or Edith Wharton's classic *Ethan Frome,* or Galsworthy's tales of the Forsytes. Among the serials are some huge popular successes; here, for instance, is *The Little Shepherd of Kingdom Come,* which in book form had a sale which it will take even *Gone with the Wind* some time to equal — a sale of 1,225,000 copies. In each volume of SCRIBNER'S you find also a profusion of short stories, most of them, of course, long since forgotten, but others almost as familiar now as if they had appeared yesterday: Kipling's ".007," let us say, or Richard Harding Davis' "Gallegher" and "The Bar Sinister."

You will be especially struck — unless your memory is both long and exact — by the richness of the appearance of the magazine during the first fifteen years or so of this century, the heyday of the illustrators, when men as gifted as Howard Pyle, Frederic Remington, Walter Appleton Clark, Maxfield Parrish, and A. B. Frost were at the disposal of Joseph Chapin, SCRIBNER'S art editor. To the reproduction of their work Chapin gave the most scrupulous and unhurried care. As you and I look back on those volumes the typography may seem to us undistinguished, for great strides have subsequently been made in the handling of type; but the illustrations, even if somewhat dated by now, are sumptuous.

There is no room here to tell the full story of fifty years of SCRIBNER'S. But one likes to think of Theodore Roosevelt, just back from the Spanish

SCRIBNER'S MAGAZINE.

VOL. IX.　　　　　JANUARY, 1891.　　　　　No. 1.

THE PIGMIES OF THE GREAT AFRICAN FOREST.

By Henry M. Stanley.

IN my book, "In Darkest Africa," I have slightly hinted at the complacent self-satisfaction that I derived from regarding anything ancient that belonged to man, or to the work of his hands, and of the reverence I felt on first seeing the Pigmy Adam and his female consort in the wild Eden of Avatiko, near the banks of the Ituri River. I feel strongly on this subject, and have done so for many years. It was apparent to me for the first time, when I was in Washington, in 1872, while conversing with a South Carolina senator, who thought fit to go to an opposite extreme on discovering my favorable inclinations to the Dark Man of Inner Africa. The senator's rather warm allusions to abolitionist principles immediately provoked a silent indignation against his narrowness of mind, and I mentally condemned him as a man whose ignorance prevented him from regarding man philosophically. I find it is a common failing with the man of civilized lands, of America or elsewhere. One of the most frequent questions put to me since my return from Africa is: "Is the pigmy a real human being?" Another is: "Is the pigmy capable of reasoning?" And another is: "Do you think he can argue rationally about what he sees; or, in other words, has he any mind at all?" And whenever I hear such questions I mentally say: "Truly, I see no difference between the civilized man and the pigmy! For if the latter could but speak his thoughts in a dialect familiar to me, there is not the slightest

A Pigmy Warrior on the Alert.

doubt that he would have asked me, 'Can the civilized man reason like us men of the forest?'"

For the benefit of such of your readers as take an interest in pigmy humanity, I have taken the trouble to write this article, that they may have a little more considerateness for the undersized creatures inhabiting the Great Forest of Equatorial Africa. They must relieve their minds of the Darwinian theory,

First page of an article on pygmies by Henry M. Stanley, the explorer and author of How I Found Livingstone *and* Through the Dark Continent

War, inviting Robert Bridges to meet him at Sagamore Hill, and after lunch taking him aside on the lawn and assuring him that the story of the Rough Riders would go to SCRIBNER'S, though Hearst had offered much more money for it. . . . Or the same T. R., years later, perching night after night on a campstool in the African jungle, his face draped with mosquito netting, his hands gauntleted against insects, writing in longhand the successive chapters of *African Game Trails,* for the serial rights to which the magazine paid him $50,000. ("President Roosevelt is coming out as a penny-a-liner. It is a great pity," wrote King Edward VII to Spring Rice when he heard of this price — not knowing that once again T. R. had turned down

higher pay to appear in the magazine of his choice.)

One likes to think of Robert Louis Stevenson, far off in Vailima, being supplied with books by Burlingame and supplying him in turn with essays and stories — with *The Wrecker,* for instance, and *The Master of Ballantrae.* . . . Of Burlingame suggesting to Edith Wharton the perfect title for the serial novel which was to turn New York society upside down: *The House of Mirth.* . . . Of Stephen Crane, shipwrecked off the Florida coast, drifting for fifty drenching hours in a dinghy, and thereafter writing for SCRIBNER'S "The Open Boat" — that extraordinary tale which, as Joseph Conrad put it, "by the

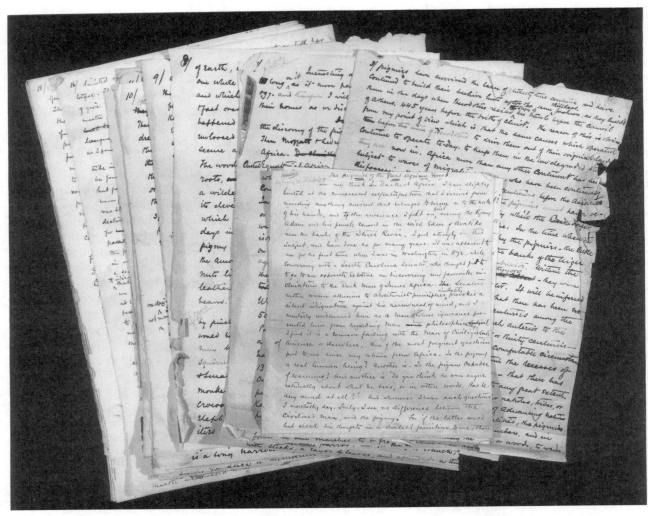

The manuscript that Henry M. Stanley submitted for his Scribner's Magazine *article on pygmies*

deep and single humanity of presentation seems somehow to illustrate the essentials of life itself, like a symbolic tale." . . . Of Charles Scribner deciding to break all precedents and reprint Mary Raymond Shipman Andrews' Lincoln story, "The Perfect Tribute," in book form — because, he said, he had given it to one of the coolest-headed men in the office to read and the man had wept. "If it made Marvin weep, we'd better publish it," said Scribner — never dreaming then that the tiny book would sell a million copies. . . . Of Max Perkins, long years later, handing over to Bridges for serial publication a very different story, Hemingway's *A Farewell to Arms,* which aroused the disapproval of the Boston censors and the enthusiastic approval of the literary critics. . . . Or of Willard Huntington Wright (S. S. Van Dine) working

on his first detective serial to appear in print: *The "Canary" Murder Case.* . . .

Now Harlan Logan and his colleagues have taken over the editorial task at SCRIBNER'S, and as the magazine rounds out its fiftieth year, it is demonstrating once more its ability to renew youth.

There are three reasons, I think, why we should be glad to join in the feast of congratulation and well-wishing. The first is that, today as yesterday, the quality magazines have an opportunity to further the cause of a really vital American literature — an opportunity such as no magazine can have which is dependent for its fortunes upon the conventional-minded millions. The second reason is that they have an opportunity also to throw genuine light upon the terrific problems which beset us today — to search more deeply into the nature of these problems than can any hurriedly edited newspaper, any read-as-you-run digest, any mass-circulation magazine which must be at pains not to tax or unsettle the mass mind. Their influence cannot be gauged by circulation because they reach men and women who play a large part in determining the course of public affairs, people who are in a position to change institutions, ideas, accepted ways of living in the light of progressive thought. If they deal in realities, not in evasions, this influence can be salutary. And the third reason is that, even in an atmosphere of crisis, they have an opportunity to deal, from time to time at least, with those enduring values which are above and beyond time and place and the event, and with which SCRIBNER'S MAGAZINE has dealt from the moment of its founding fifty years ago.

RELATED LETTERS:

Letter from CS II to Stanford White accompanying a check for payment of his cover and contents designs for *Scribner's Magazine*, 15 December 1886.

Architect Stanford White (1853–1906), associated post 1880 with Charles F. McKim and W. R. Mead in their firm McKim, Mead & White, worked with great skill in different styles. His designs included plans for houses, jewelry, furniture, and gravestones. His most enduring achievement is perhaps the Washington Arch in New York City — he also designed the original Madison Square Garden (1889). "Mr. Paton" was William Agnew Paton, first business manager of Scribner's Magazine. His "sudden departure" apparently was occasioned by a drinking problem, and his position was filled by Frank Nelson Doubleday.

My dear Mr. White:

The sudden departure of Mr. Paton has delayed our settlement with you for your work on cover &c.

I am really at a loss to know how to estimate our obligations to you; we recognise that they are great and the cover itself will, I am sure, be a constant joy to us.

I send you our check for $400 (with a copy of the new maga.) and beg of you to let us know frankly if it does not fit the bill; we want you to feel well repaid for your actual labor and care;

your good will and kindness we can only repay in kind.

Yours sincerely
Charles Scribner

My Dear Mr. Scribner

I received your very kind letter this morning. I beg to assure you that you have not only "filled the bill" — but that the "bill" hardly knows what to say.

As I wrote Paton — I felt adverse to sending in any bill at all. A great deal of the time spent on the cover was owing to my having to make so many experiments to arrive at the best result — and I certainly did not like to charge my friends for my lack of experience. My desire — really — was to let the whole matter stand as one of good will & friendship.

You have now reversed the tables upon me. I feel somewhat diffident in accepting your check — but do so with many thanks — and with the understanding that when you need your cover for the Bound Volumes I shall be allowed to wipe off my slate.

I was much distressed to hear about Paton last night — at the Tile Club.

I think the magazine shows up splendidly & feel sure it has a glorious future in store. I hope to see you soon.

Believe me.

Sincerely yours,
Stanford White

RELATED LETTERS:

Letter from Edward L. Burlingame to Bret Harte, 20 October 1892; letter from Harte to Burlingame in response, 12 December 1892.

In the early 1870s, Bret Harte was the best-paid and possibly the most popular American writer, having pioneered the use of California local color in his stories of the mining country, such as in "The Luck of Roaring Camp" and "The Outcasts of Poker Flat." Though Scribners had never been his book publisher, the firm's magazines had printed some of Harte's poems and stories, and had serialized his novel Gabriel Conroy. It is no surprise, then, that Burlingame wanted a contribution from him for his World's Fair issue of "representative" writers of the last twenty-five years.

My dear Harte:

Scribner's Magazine has planned to mark the opening of the World's Fair and International Ex-

Telegraphic Address,
MORRISTOWN, N.J.

Convent Station,
Morris Co., N.J.

May 7/99

My dear Mr Burlingame:
The incident of my story seemed good as it was told to me, but now, on cool consideration, I agree with you, and am much obliged to you for telling me your opinion of it. I don't want anything but my best work to go into Scribner's. But an author, who is interested in his work, is not always a good judge of its merits. He needs the services of a friendly editor.
Sincerely yours
Frank R. Stockton

Rejection and acceptance: the two sides of the editor/author relationship exemplified in these two letters by author Frank R. Stockton to Scribner's Magazine editor Edward L. Burlingame

Charles Town,
Jefferson Co.
West Va.
July 6, 1900

Dear Mr Burlingame:

I am de-
lighted to know that you like
my married girl.

An appreciative editor is
one of the largest of the base-
rocks of literature.

With thanks for your
note, I am

Very sincerely yours
Frank R. Stockton

position at Chicago, next May, by the issue of a number which shall be especially important, and shall form in itself perhaps the most characteristic "exhibit" in its own field of work — showing, as we hope, something like a typical number of a good American Magazine, with all the literary and artistic resources open to it.

We hope to have in this special number something from each of twenty or more writers here and abroad who are in the best sense really representative of the last ten to twenty-five years; and under these circumstances we should feel that the undertaking would be particularly incomplete unless you were represented in it.

Will it not be possible for you to contribute a story to it, not longer perhaps than ten of our pages, letting us have the manuscript by January 15th next? And if so would you kindly let us know upon what terms you would do this?

We have the plan very much at heart, and want to do a good and memorable thing, without any sensational or perfunctory features, but confining the number to things of real literary importance. We are to have a great array of artists too.

I strongly hope that you may be willing to do what we ask for all reasons, — the exceptional occasion, the pleasure of having you with us again, and the wish we have to make the plan really representative, which it would hardly be without you. With kind regards, I am

Yours sincerely,
E. L. Burlingame

My dear Burlingame,

I owe you an apology. During one of my absences from London I mislaid your pleasant invitation to contribute to the Special No. of Scribners, and only yesterday recovered it. But with the progressive fatuity of a blunderer, I had meantime misconceived enough of it to calmly refer it (as is my custom) to my agent, Mr. A. P. Watt, as an application from the Century Magazine! asking him to communicate, (as usual), with them, regarding terms, condition &.&c. which he did!

Now, I do not know if it is too late to remedy the error. He will, however, write to you, telling you what I can do for you and when, and I can only reiterate to you my personal regrets for my own stupidity. Believe me, my dear Burlingame,

Yours always
Bret Harte

It was not too late. Harte's story, "The Reformation of James Reddy," appeared in the World's Fair issue of Scribner's Magazine *(May 1893) in the company of stories by W. D. Howells, Thomas Hardy, Henry James, H. C. Bunner, Sarah Orne Jewett, and George Washington Cable, a continuing serial by Frances Hodgson Burnett, and a poem by Robert Louis Stevenson.*

RELATED LETTERS:
Considered in his later life as the preeminent living American man of letters, William Dean Howells had not published a book with Scribners. (Though Scribner's Magazine *serialized his novel* The Story of a Play *in 1897, Harper had published the book.) But it was not because Howells had never tried: in August of 1900 he offered Burlingame a seventy-five-thousand-word story for the magazine and for subsequent book publication. CS II was on vacation, but Burlingame — who was in the process of starting his own vacation — thought it important enough to write him. The name references in his letter are to J. M. Barrie, the English author who later wrote* Peter Pan; *Kate Douglas Wiggin, future author of* Rebecca of Sunnybrook Farm; *George Washington Cable, author of* Old Creole Days; *W. C. Brownell, Scribner literary adviser; and Ernest Thompson Seton, author of* Wild Animals I Have Known.

Pittsfield, Aug. 18, 1900

My dear Scribner —

This month is certainly a case of "it never rains but it pours." I am afraid it must seem to you worse away than at the office, and I had no intention of adding three letters a week to the budget; but here is another thing of rather an uncommon kind in its larger bearings that I hardly like to act upon without your having it before you.

Just before I came away yesterday this letter came from Howells. As to the serial matter, I am coming to the opinion that having Barrie in prospect for the last months of 1901, and a number of attractive short things — especially if we get the Wiggin — for the opening of the year, we are quite as well off to be without any large serial unless of the very first compelling rank. (This is putting the question of the Cable aside for the moment — if we decide to use that at once the difficulty of taking anything more is still further increased.) Nobody thinks more highly of much of Howells's work than I, or has a greater liking for some of it. But I do not think a 7 or 8-part serial work by him is enough to tip the scales under the present conditions; and I should somewhat regretfully admit that under more favorable ones it was questionable whether at his prices it would be a good business investment; — though Brownell was saying yesterday that because it had "become established literature under our eyes" and had no element of curiosity or sensation about it, he thought we might easily undervalue his work generally & underestimate the real numbers of his constituency.

I should be inclined to say no to his letter therefore, without asking to see the story; on the grounds that being purely practical would be least disagreeable to him. But I realize that the thing has one peculiar & rather epoch-making feature, in its being the first time he has ever offered <u>a book</u> to the house, & that in the present break-up of old lines this may easily mean more than the offering of a single detached book would ever have done before.

I can easily make my being away here an excuse for not answering his letter quite as promptly as usual; & just a line here will tell me whether you think this consideration deserves longer debate. If so I can write putting him off a while.

Seton-Thompson was in late Thursday; very cordial about everything. He promises a Christmas story in good season.

It is delightfully cool here & I am feeling set up already.

Yours sincerely
E. L. Burlingame

Scribners declined on practical grounds. Here is Howell's response.

Annisquam, Aug. 24, 1900
Dear Mr. Burlingame:

I am sorry you cannot see your way to taking my story, but I understand how things are, and I wish to thank you for the very kind terms of your denial: an old fellow likes to have his disappointments padded. I should be glad to try a novel with the public that had not been serialized, but at present I cannot afford to do it, though if I cannot sell my story to some magazine you may find me at your door again with your assurances concerning Messrs. Scribner's Sons in my mouth.

It may seem rather odious to come back at once with another proposition, but I venture this quick return in behalf of a short story which I have just about finished, and which is long enough to make a little book of twenty odd thousand words. It is rather odd, and I am at present much in the humor of it. I call it The Apparition. It is the social and psychological experience of a man who has really seen an apparition, or has had a preternatural vision which he is never able to explain. The phantom drops out of the story almost immediately, and figures thereafter merely in the hero's consciousness as the pivot upon which his love-story turns. The motive is a sort of comedy motive, and yet the characters are serious, and I hope that I keep always audible a certain strain of poetry inherent in the facts.

The question is whether you would like to see this story with a view to publication in the magazine, and then to republication by your house in book form. I think I could send it to you by the middle of next week.

If you like it, I have a fancy of having Messrs. Scribner's Sons offer me a sum outright for its use in the magazine, and for two years' use of the copyright without royalty to me.

Yours sincerely,
W. D. Howells

Burlingame rejected this story for similar reasons, and Howells was able to sell it later to Harper's Monthly. *No other fiction was ever offered by Howells to* Scribner's Magazine, *and Charles Scribner's Sons never published a Howells novel.*

Cumulative Index

Dictionary of Literary Biography, Volumes 1-160
Dictionary of Literary Biography Yearbook, 1980-1994
Dictionary of Literary Biography Documentary Series, Volumes 1-13

Cumulative Index

DLB before number: *Dictionary of Literary Biography*, Volumes 1-160
Y before number: *Dictionary of Literary Biography Yearbook*, 1980-1994
DS before number: *Dictionary of Literary Biography Documentary Series*, Volumes 1-13

B

O

S

Spofford, Harriet Prescott
1835-1921 .... DLB-74

Squibob (see Derby, George Horatio)

Stacpoole, H. de Vere
1863-1951 .... DLB-153

Staël, Germaine de 1766-1817 ...... DLB-119

Staël-Holstein, Anne-Louise Germaine de
(see Staël, Germaine de)

Stafford, Jean 1915-1979 .... DLB-2

Stafford, William 1914- DLB-5

Stage Censorship: "The Rejected Statement"
(1911), by Bernard Shaw
[excerpts] DLB-10

Stallings, Laurence 1894-1968 ..... DLB-7, 44

Stallworthy, Jon 1935- DLB-40

Stampp, Kenneth M. 1912- DLB-17

Stanford, Ann 1916- DLB-5

Stanković, Borisav ("Bora")
1876-1927 .... DLB-147

Stanley, Henry M. 1841-1904 .... DS-13

Stanley, Thomas 1625-1678 .... DLB-131

Stannard, Martin 1947- DLB-155

Stanton, Elizabeth Cady
1815-1902 .... DLB-79

Stanton, Frank L. 1857-1927 .... DLB-25

Stanton, Maura 1946- DLB-120

Stapledon, Olaf 1886-1950 .... DLB-15

Star Spangled Banner Office DLB-49

Starkey, Thomas
circa 1499-1538 .... DLB-132

Starkweather, David 1935- DLB-7

Statements on the Art of Poetry DLB-54

Stead, Robert J. C. 1880-1959 .... DLB-92

Steadman, Mark 1930- DLB-6

The Stealthy School of Criticism (1871), by
Dante Gabriel Rossetti DLB-35

Stearns, Harold E. 1891-1943 .... DLB-4

Stedman, Edmund Clarence
1833-1908 .... DLB-64

Steegmuller, Francis 1906-1994 ..... DLB-111

Steel, Flora Annie
1847-1929 .... DLB-153, 156

Steele, Max 1922- Y-80

Steele, Richard 1672-1729 ..... DLB-84, 101

Steele, Timothy 1948- DLB-120

Steele, Wilbur Daniel 1886-1970 ..... DLB-86

Steere, Richard circa 1643-1721 ..... DLB-24

Stegner, Wallace 1909-1993 .... DLB-9; Y-93

Stehr, Hermann 1864-1940 .... DLB-66

Steig, William 1907- DLB-61

Stein, Gertrude 1874-1946 .... DLB-4, 54, 86

Stein, Leo 1872-1947 .... DLB-4

Stein and Day Publishers DLB-46

Steinbeck, John 1902-1968 ... DLB-7, 9; DS-2

Steiner, George 1929- DLB-67

Stendhal 1783-1842 .... DLB-119

Stephen Crane: A Revaluation Virginia
Tech Conference, 1989 .... Y-89

Stephen, Leslie 1832-1904 ...... DLB-57, 144

Stephens, Alexander H. 1812-1883 .. DLB-47

Stephens, Ann 1810-1886 .... DLB-3, 73

Stephens, Charles Asbury
1844?-1931 .... DLB-42

Stephens, James 1882?-1950 .... DLB-19, 153

Sterling, George 1869-1926 .... DLB-54

Sterling, James 1701-1763 .... DLB-24

Sterling, John 1806-1844 .... DLB-116

Stern, Gerald 1925- DLB-105

Stern, Madeleine B. 1912- ... DLB-111, 140

Stern, Gerald, Living in Ruin DLB-105

Stern, Richard 1928- Y-87

Stern, Stewart 1922- DLB-26

Sterne, Laurence 1713-1768 .... DLB-39

Sternheim, Carl 1878-1942 ..... DLB-56, 118

Sternhold, Thomas ?-1549 and
John Hopkins ?-1570 .... DLB-132

Stevens, Henry 1819-1886 .... DLB-140

Stevens, Wallace 1879-1955 .... DLB-54

Stevenson, Anne 1933- DLB-40

Stevenson, Lionel 1902-1973 ...... DLB-155

Stevenson, Robert Louis
1850-1894 ... DLB-18, 57, 141, 156; DS-13

Stewart, Donald Ogden
1894-1980 .... DLB-4, 11, 26

Stewart, Dugald 1753-1828 .... DLB-31

Stewart, George, Jr. 1848-1906 ...... DLB-99

Stewart, George R. 1895-1980 ...... DLB-8

Stewart and Kidd Company DLB-46

Stewart, Randall 1896-1964 .... DLB-103

Stickney, Trumbull 1874-1904 ..... DLB-54

Stifter, Adalbert 1805-1868 .... DLB-133

Stiles, Ezra 1727-1795 .... DLB-31

Still, James 1906- DLB-9

Stirner, Max 1806-1856 .... DLB-129

Stith, William 1707-1755 .... DLB-31

Stock, Elliot [publishing house] DLB-106

Stockton, Frank R.
1834-1902 .... DLB-42, 74; DS-13

Stoddard, Ashbel
[publishing house] DLB-49

Stoddard, Richard Henry
1825-1903 .... DLB-3, 64; DS-13

Stoddard, Solomon 1643-1729 ...... DLB-24

Stoker, Bram 1847-1912 .... DLB-36, 70

Stokes, Frederick A., Company DLB-49

Stokes, Thomas L. 1898-1958 .... DLB-29

Stokesbury, Leon 1945- DLB-120

Stolberg, Christian Graf zu
1748-1821 .... DLB-94

Stolberg, Friedrich Leopold Graf zu
1750-1819 .... DLB-94

Stone, Herbert S., and Company DLB-49

Stone, Lucy 1818-1893 .... DLB-79

Stone, Melville 1848-1929 .... DLB-25

Stone, Robert 1937- DLB-152

Stone, Ruth 1915- DLB-105

Stone, Samuel 1602-1663 .... DLB-24

Stone and Kimball DLB-49

Stoppard, Tom 1937- DLB-13; Y-85

Storey, Anthony 1928- DLB-14

Storey, David 1933- DLB-13, 14

Storm, Theodor 1817-1888 .... DLB-129

Story, Thomas circa 1670-1742 ..... DLB-31

Story, William Wetmore 1819-1895 ... DLB-1

Storytelling: A Contemporary
Renaissance Y-84

Stoughton, William 1631-1701 ..... DLB-24

Stow, John 1525-1605 .... DLB-132

Stowe, Harriet Beecher
1811-1896 .... DLB-1, 12, 42, 74

Stowe, Leland 1899- DLB-29

Stoyanov, Dimitūr Ivanov (see Elin Pelin)

Strachey, Lytton
1880-1932 .... DLB-149; DS-10

Strachey, Lytton, Preface to Eminent
Victorians DLB-149

Strahan and Company DLB-106

Strahan, William
[publishing house] DLB-154

Strand, Mark 1934- DLB-5

The Strasbourg Oaths 842 .... DLB-148

Stratemeyer, Edward 1862-1930 ..... DLB-42

V